CRITICAL SURVEY
OF
DRAMA

CRITICAL SURVEY
OF
DRAMA

REVISED EDITION
Mor-Sha

5

Edited by
FRANK N. MAGILL

SALEM PRESS
Pasadena, California   Englewood Cliffs, New Jersey

∞ The paper used in these volumes conforms to
the American National Standard for Permanence of
Paper for Printed Library Materials, Z39.48-1984.

**Library of Congress Cataloging-in-Publication
Data**
  Critical survey of drama. English language series/
edited by Frank N. Magill.—Rev. ed.
      p. cm.
  Includes bibliographical references and index.
  1. English drama—Dictionaries. 2. American
drama—Dictionaries. 3. English drama—Bio-
bibliography. 4. American drama—Bio-bibliography.
5. Commonwealth drama (English)—Dictionaries.
6. Dramatists, English—Biography—Dictionaries.
7. Dramatists, American—Biography—Dictionaries. 8. Commonwealth drama (English)—Bio-
bibliography.
I. Magill, Frank Northen, 1907-
PR623.C75   1994
822.009'03—dc20   93-41618
ISBN 0-89356-851-1 (set)   CIP
ISBN 0-89356-856-2 (volume 5)

PRINTED IN THE UNITED STATES OF AMERICA

LIST OF AUTHORS IN VOLUME 5

JOHN MORTIMER

Born: London, England; April 21, 1923

Principal drama

The Dock Brief, pr. 1957 (radio play and televised), pr. 1958 (staged), pb 1958 (one act); *I Spy*, pr. 1957 (radio play), pr. 1958 (televised), pb. 1958, pr. 1959 (staged); *Call Me a Liar*, pr. 1958 (radio play and televised), pb. 1960, pr. 1968 (staged); *What Shall We Tell Caroline?*, pr., pb. 1958 (one act); *Lunch Hour*, pr., pb. 1960 (one act); *The Wrong Side of the Park*, pr., pb. 1960; *Lunch Hour and Other Plays*, pb. 1960 (includes *Collect Your Hand Baggage, David and Broccoli, Call Me a Liar*); *Collect Your Hand Baggage*, pb. 1960, pr. 1963 (one act); *Two Stars for Comfort*, pr., pb. 1962; *A Voyage Round My Father*, pr. 1963 (radio play), pr. 1970 (staged), pb. 1971; *A Flea in Her Ear*, pr. 1966, pb. 1967 (adaptation of Georges Feydeau's play); *The Judge*, pr., pb. 1967; *Cat Among the Pigeons*, pr. 1969, pb. 1970 (adaptation of Feydeau's play); *Come as You Are: Four Short Plays*, pr. 1970, pb. 1971 (includes *Mill Hill, Bermondsey, Gloucester Road, Marble Arch*); *Five Plays*, pb. 1970 (includes *The Dock Brief, What Shall We Tell Caroline?, I Spy, Lunch Hour, Collect Your Hand Baggage*); *The Captain of Köpenick*, pr., pb. 1971 (adaptation of Carl Zuckmayer's play); *I, Claudius*, pr. 1972 (adaptation of the Robert Graves's novels *I, Claudius* and *Claudius the God*); *Collaborators*, pr., pb. 1973; *Heaven and Hell*, pr. 1976, pb. 1978 (2 one-acts: *The Fear of Heaven* and *The Prince of Darkness*); *The Bells of Hell*, pr. 1977, pb. 1978 (revision of *The Prince of Darkness*); *The Lady from Maxim's*, pr., pb. 1977 (adaptation of Feydeau's play); *John Mortimer's Casebook*, pr. 1982 (includes *The Dock Brief, The Prince of Darkness, Interlude*); *Edwin*, pr. 1982 (radio play), pr. 1984 (televised), pb. 1984 (stage version); *When That I Was*, pr. 1982; *Edwin and Other Plays*, pb. 1984; *A Little Hotel on the Side*, pr. 1984 (adaptation of a play by Feydeau and Maurice Desvalliers); *Three Boulevard Farces*, pb. 1985.

Other literary forms

In addition to his stage plays, John Mortimer has written in a variety of other genres. His earliest work was as a novelist (*Charade*, 1947; *Rumming Park*, 1948; *Answer Yes or No*, 1950; *Like Men Betrayed*, 1953; *The Narrowing Stream*, 1954; and *Three Winters*, 1956); in the late 1950's, he wrote the first of many screenplays on which he has worked; he began writing specifically for television in 1960 and has since then written such popular successes as the *Rumpole of the Bailey* series (1975, 1978, 1979) and *Brideshead Revisited* (1981; adaptation of Evelyn Waugh's novel). He also continued to be a regular newspaper critic and interviewer. Mortimer has published an autobiography, *Clinging to the Wreckage: A Part of Life* (1982). His later works include the novels *Titmuss Regained* (1990) and *Dunster* (1992) and the short-story collection *Rumpole on Trial* (1992).

Achievements

In his autobiography, Mortimer says that a novice writer is obsessed by "the panic-stricken search for a voice of his own. His ears are full of noises, a cacaphony of sweet airs from the past and the even more delightful sounds of the present." Early in his career as a dramatist, Mortimer found a proper voice, as a writer of comedies of manners, sex farces, and Chekhovian one-act plays in which he attempted "to chart the tottering course of British middle-class attitudes in decline." He has said that comedy "is the only thing worth writing about in this despairing world," which "is far too serious to be described in terms that give us no opportunity to laugh." His choice of subject matter, he has written, "was dictated by myself, my childhood, and such education as I was able to gather . . . ," for he believes that a writer "can only work within that narrow seam which penetrates to the depths of [his] past." Within such a "narrow seam" he has created memorable moments in the theater. Though his farces, such as *Marble Arch* and *Mill Hill*, are little more than whimsies, other plays have enduring merit, particularly *The Dock Brief*, *The Judge*, and *Collaborators*, and the autobiographical *A Voyage Round My Father* is a major achievement. Mortimer has been a diligent practitioner of the brief play ("In a one-act play the enthusiasm has no time to die") and must be credited with demonstrating not only the commercial but also the artistic viability of the form on the modern stage; concerning the latter, he has written:

> A play, even if it lasts not more than five minutes, should be able to contain at least one life, with a character that can be conceived as stretching backwards and forwards in time, with an existence longer than those moments which actually take place on the stage. A play is a demonstration, in which an audience can recognize something about themselves. As with a picture, this can be achieved by a few lines in the right position.

Mortimer's experience with writing radio plays and his mastery of the dramatic form, as well as his work in the cinema, prepared him for television scriptwriting. He clearly prefers radio plays, which he has described as having many advantages: "They are not subject to the technical mischances and distractions of the theatre and television. They call on the audience to make a great effort of imagination and in them words must be used, as they were in the Elizabethan theatre, to paint scenery or suggest changes of light." On the other hand, "If you're in a theatre where you know everything is unreal and you know it's all an act of the imagination—and you know that all you have are actors standing on a platform—then you can do anything, just because it's entirely imaginary. But if you're in the cinema where you have to try to be literal, then I think it's much harder." His television scripts have developed his largest audiences and gained for him his most widespread critical acclaim, particularly the *Rumpole of the Bailey* series, which began in 1975, and the 1981 adaptation of Evelyn Waugh's novel *Brideshead Revisited*. During the decades in which he has been writing plays—for radio, stage, and television—Mortimer has demonstrated his ability to conceive of clever situations and manage them deftly, to create believable characters even when they are stereotypes, to write dialogue that abounds with witticisms, and to endow even his whimsies with the insight of a perceptive social conscience. He has led theatergoers to a better understanding of themselves while making them laugh.

Biography

John Clifford Mortimer was born on April 21, 1923, in Hampstead, London, to Clifford and Kathleen May Smith Mortimer. His father was a barrister who went blind when Mortimer was still young but continued to practice law. Mortimer studied at Harrow School in Middlesex from 1937 to 1940, and at Brasenose College, Oxford, from 1940 to 1942. Because of his poor eyesight, he was exempted from military service during World War II and worked as an assistant director and scriptwriter with the Crown Film Units. He was called to the bar in 1948, and in the years since has practiced law in London while writing for radio, television, the theater, film, and newspapers. He became Queen's Counsel in 1966 and Master of the Bench, Inner Temple, London, in 1975. As a barrister, he has been a leading figure in freedom of speech and press cases; in part as a result of his efforts, the Lord Chamberlain's censorship authority was abolished with the passage of the Theatre Act of 1968, which—according to Mortimer— raised the status of playwrights "to the most carefully protected of all public performers." Mortimer married Penelope Fletcher (a novelist, known first as Penelope Dimont and then as Penelope Mortimer) in 1949. They were divorced in 1972, and Mortimer remarried in the same year, to Penelope Gollop.

A regular contributor to *The Times* of London, Mortimer enters the intellectual world from four directions at once: As a barrister, he holds forth in essays and letters to the editor on events that have an impact on the world of law; as a television writer, his name is ubiquitous among the credits of dramatic and comic specials; as a stage writer, his plays continue to find audiences in London and the provinces; and as a detective novel writer and inventor of the famous Rumpole character, he has produced a best-selling novel every few years. He was awarded the Cross of the British Empire in 1986 and was named chairman of the Council of the Royal Society of Literature in 1989. In 1991, in a typical gesture of responsible citizenship, Mortimer appeared at one of his old schools in a charity appearance to raise money for school equipment.

Mortimer settled in Chiltern Hills, north of London, with his second wife, Penelope, and the younger of their two daughters, Rosamond, spending considerable time campaigning against overdevelopment near his rural home, Turville Heath, which he immortalized in *A Voyage Round My Father.*

Analysis

John Mortimer won the Italia Prize in 1958 for *The Dock Brief,* which the British Broadcasting Corporation's Third Programme produced in 1957. This radio play and *What Shall We Tell Caroline?* were presented as a double bill in London in 1958.

The Dock Brief features an old barrister whom success has eluded for a half century (and who may be, Mortimer has speculated, "a distant cousin of a far more extrovert creation, 'Rumpole of the Bailey,' whom I wouldn't begin to think about for another fifteen years"). The barrister is randomly selected to defend "an equally unsuccessful criminal" who is accused of murdering his wife. In the man's cell, the two rehearse their courtroom scenario, assuming the roles of judge, witnesses, and jurors. At the actual trial, the barrister becomes befuddled and loses the case, but the judge frees the defendant because the barrister's incompetence has rendered the legal process "ever so null and void." The pair rationalize that the counsel's "dumb tactics" won the day, and they depart whistling and dancing. Funny though it is, *The Dock Brief* also has a message: "I wanted to say something about the lawyer's almost pathetic dependence on the criminal classes, without whom he would be unemployed, and I wanted to find a criminal who would be sorrier for his luckless advocate than he was for himself." The play also exemplifies Mortimer's belief that comedy should be "truly on the side of the lonely, the neglected, the unsuccessful" and "against established rules and . . . the imposing of an arbitrary code of behaviour upon individual and unpredictable human beings." When *The Dock Brief* was revived in London in 1982, it was as part of *John Mortimer's Casebook,* which also includes *The Prince of Darkness* and *Interlude* and is a trilogy that criticizes three pillars of society: the law, the Church, and medicine.

What Shall We Tell Caroline?—Mortimer's first play written expressly for the theater—is a sensitive character study in which a curmudgeonly headmaster who is constantly at odds with his wife convinces an assistant to continue a pretended affair with her, for "If we stopped quarreling over her now . . . think how empty her poor life would be." Caroline, their overprotected eighteen-year-old daughter, silently observes the sparring, but at the close of the one-act play she announces her intention to go to London to live and work. Her escape from the stifling home environment anticipates Mrs. Morgan's desertion of her husband in *I Spy* and Paddy's flight to Paris in *Collect Your Hand Baggage*. The play also foreshadows later works in which variants of the *ménage à trois* motif are present, such as *The Wrong Side of the Park*, *Bermondsey*, *Gloucester Road*, and *Collaborators*. The characters in all of these plays—including *The Dock Brief* and *What Shall We Tell Caroline?*—have a comic vitality touched with pathos. They have trouble communicating with others and coping with life, and they make accommodations that only superficially resolve their problems. Except for *The Dock Brief*, all of these plays are about unhappy marriages.

In 1959, "with a good deal of trepidation," Mortimer wrote his first full-length play, *The Wrong Side of the Park*, which opened in London the following year with Peter Hall directing and starring Margaret Leighton. The central character, according to Mortimer, was his house in the Swiss Cottage section of London, but this *ménage à trois* play also features "an anglicized Blanche Dubois" who is wed to a "dull boy" and lives in squalor with her in-laws. When she is attracted to a lusty boarder who reminds her of her first husband, she fantasizes about her first marriage, but in a somewhat contrived happy ending, she is reconciled with her present husband, who is made to seem better than he actually is. Although reviewers praised Mortimer's original treatment of old-hat subject matter, some said that the play was too long, with neither characters nor plot adequately sustained. It enjoyed a modest popular success, with a run of 173 performances. In 1962, *Two Stars for Comfort*, Mortimer's next full-length play, had an even longer run of 189 performances, with Trevor Howard as a solicitor-turned-publican "who," Mortimer has said, "always told people what he thought they wanted to hear, an extension of the pleasure principle which only works in the extremely short term." A reworking of an early, unpublished novel, the play is the first in which Mortimer presents the law as a repressive force.

The law as repressor is also a theme of *The Judge*, which was criticized for diffuseness when it opened in London in 1967 (it ran for only sixty-seven performances). According to one reviewer: "Conditioned by his naturalistic habits, [Mortimer's] plotting is ill served by his non-naturalistic structure." Writing about the play years later, Mortimer saw as a primary weakness the fact that its "central character remained entirely in the resonant and archetypal stage; it was a play that appeared, I noticed to my embarrassment when I saw it, with its symbols showing." These fundamental flaws notwithstanding, *The Judge* is an intriguing study of obsession and a disturbing look at how the law sometimes functions. In it, Mortimer's nameless high court judge (who has a reputation for severity) returns to his hometown for his last assize before he retires; obsessed with guilt for having abandoned in his youth a local girl he thought he made pregnant, he comes home to be judged instead of to judge. The girl, Serena, who is now middle-aged, is content with her life, running an antique shop that also provides a variety of sexual services. Mortimer skillfully develops a number of character-revealing and tension-building episodes that give a context to the judge's attempts to force a confrontation with Serena, which he manages to achieve in the penultimate scene: refusing to accept her forgiveness, demanding in vain that she "proceed to judgment," and finally trying unsuccessfully to carry out his own sentence upon himself as his last judicial act.

The law also is central in the autobiographical *A Voyage Round My Father*, Mortimer's best and most popular stage play. It was performed at the Haymarket Theatre, London, in 1971 and ran for 501 performances, with Alec Guinness as the father, Leueen MacGrath as the mother, and Jeremy Brett as the son. (Sir Laurence Olivier starred in the 1982 television adaptation.) Spanning more than twenty years, it dramatizes the symbiotic relationship between the playwright and his blind father. According to Ronald Bryden, in a review of a 1970 production at the Greenwich Theatre of the first version of the play, its "style is an expression of the father's. . . . His jokes and stories are the public face of a very private man, whose privacy Mortimer respects, and it is that chosen persona, clownish, dignified, amusing and amused, which Mortimer celebrates lovingly." In his autobiography, Mortimer tells of anxieties he had about the work:

> I had written a play which was about to open; into it I had collected my memories of my father, and written lines for him, so that a man who had filled so much of my life seemed to have left me and become someone for other people to read about and perform. In one way I felt detached from it; but a play is a public exhibition with its own peculiar dangers, another sort of trial. Not for the only time in my life I felt that the theatrical drama in which I was involved was more real than the Old Bailey and the due process of law. Also I was about to tell a wider public a fact which, in our small family, had been the subject of a discreet conspiracy of silence, something, which in our English determination to avoid the slightest embarrassment, we never mentioned. My father had been blind.

Shaping forces other than the father also are in the play—teachers, girls, wartime experiences, friends—and all closely parallel real people and events. Despite the far-reaching concerns of this drama of two lives, however, the play is not at all diffuse. Instead of being divided into separate scenes, the episodes flow into one another, united by the son as the reflective narrator, bridging past and present and providing a clearly defined point of view.

The action begins with the old father recalling wistfully with his son his regular ritual of drowning earwigs that attacked the dahlias in his garden ("a cross between Trooping the Colour and a public execution"), moves to the boy being taught to whistle by a girl who reappears in a later adolescent initiation scene, and then proceeds to the boy's school experiences with a simpleminded headmaster and masters who still suffered the aftereffects of World War I shell shock and battle fatigue. Years later, through the intercession of two lesbians who run a bookshop, the son gets a wartime job as an assistant director with a propaganda film unit. Then, soon after meeting a film writer (whom he marries when she is divorced), he decides to study law. Pervading the play is a series of episodes involving the iconoclastic blind father, whose world is bound by his garden and the courtroom, each of which he strives to dominate: the earwigs that prey upon his flowers and the barristers for the opposition. Though the father pretends not to take much of life very seriously, he has a sense of dignity that proscribes mention of his blindness, and he engages in selfless acts of kindness toward children and animals. Neither a demonstratively affectionate husband nor an openly loving parent, he does occasionally express his feelings, about marriage, for example: "You know, the law of husband and wife might seem idiotic at first sight. But when you get to know it, you'll find it can exercise a vague medieval charm." In the same speech, to his son, he adds: "Learn a little law, won't you? Just to please me. . . . " The son's reaction (as narrator, to the audience) reveals the first of several conjunctions of the views of father and son: "It was my father's way to offer the law to me—the great stone column of authority which has been dragged by an adulterous, careless, negligent and half criminal humanity down the ages—as if it were a small mechanical toy which might occupy half an hour on a rainy afternoon." Despite this statement, the episodes that show the father at work in the courtroom and the son's faltering attempts to emulate him present the law as something more than a mere mechanical toy.

A Voyage Round My Father is a memory play with a son as narrator and *raisonneur*; Tennessee Williams' *The Glass Menagerie* (pr. 1944) inevitably comes to mind. Mortimer's narrator, however, is not haunted by the past as Williams' Tom Wingfield is; he merely retells it. At the end of the play, after his father dies, the son says: "I'd been told of all the things you're meant to feel. Sudden freedom, growing up, the end of dependence, the step into the sunlight when no one is taller than you and you're no one else's shadow. I know what I felt. Lonely."

Collaborators, which had a 1973 London run of 167 performances, similarly has autobiographical connections. In *Clinging to the Wreckage*, Mortimer writes about Henry Winter, a pacifist and conscientious objector who was his closest Oxford friend, through whom Mortimer met his first wife, and who became a physician. Years later, Winter killed a patient's wife, with whom he was having an affair, and then committed suicide. In the play, the main character is also named Henry Winter. Winter is a struggling barrister who also writes radio plays and enjoys cooking (one of Mortimer's own recreations); his wife, Katherine, has been wed once before (which was the case with Penelope Fletcher); and he is on the verge of having an affair with his secretary as a means of escape from the teetering marriage. He meets Sam Brown, an American for whom he starts writing a screenplay about marriage (Mortimer worked as a screenwriter for a time in California), a project that becomes a three-way collaboration, with the American becoming part of the Winter household and alternately wooing husband and wife. Soon, Mortimer's play for his West End audience becomes indistinguishable from the script that the Winters are doing for Brown, just as the reality of their lives becomes intertwined with the fiction of the screenplay they are writing. Midway into *Collaborators*, Katherine suggests to Henry: "I'm not asking you for gimmicks, Henry. . . . Forget the action sequences. Forget the box office even. Suppose we start to examine two people mistaken about each other from the start." By the final curtain, the foreign intruder is gone, the husband's nubile secretary has been scared off, and the married couple is alone—scarred by their domestic sparring and wearied by children grown tall enough "to eat the pornography" (which is moved to a higher shelf). Having collaborated on their screenplay, Katherine and Henry are ready now to collaborate anew on another project, their marriage. It is inevitable that one will want to compare *Collaborators* with Edward Albee's *Who's Afraid of Virginia Woolf?* (pr. 1962)—the situation and pacing are to a degree similar—but Mortimer is wittier than Albee.

In 1982, Mortimer continued to work familiar territory and at the same time to expand his horizons with the productions of *When That I Was* and *Edwin*. *When That I Was* is a one-character play featuring Jack Rice, an old actor at Shakespeare's Globe. *Edwin* began as a radio play for the British Broadcasting Corporation (starring Emlyn Williams, it was broadcast as one of the British Broadcasting Corporation's Sixtieth Anniversary Plays), then was made into a television play with Alec Guinness, and has since been published in a stage version. It is a one-act play featuring a retired judge, Sir Fennimore Truscott; his wife, Margaret; and a neighbor, Tom Marjoriebanks, a potter. Truscott fantasizes that Tom was Margaret's lover in years past and fathered Edwin, the Truscotts' son, but the more the old men talk about Edwin, the less interested each is in claiming the young man as his son, for Edwin's life-style is repellent to both of them. They finally decide to confront Margaret with the matter and ask her to settle the dispute. She responds: "I mean, you may love someone . . . you may love the way they spin a potter's wheel with such outrageous confidence, or go to work at the Law Courts each morning trembling with fear and trying to put a ridiculously brave face on it. And you may love the way someone prunes roses, stooping so easily, or weeds the strawberry bed all day in the hot sunshine . . . with the dark stain of sweat growing on the back of his shirt." Oblique though her answer may be, its import is clear: Neither the senile judge nor the foppish potter sired Edwin. Cattermole, the longtime gardener, is the one. The play concludes with the old men as friends, no longer rivals, and thankful, at least, that the wine being stored as a legacy for Edwin they now can drink, since the young man is not their concern any more. Says Truscott: "Not ours, Tom. Let's thank God for it. Not ours!" Whimsy tempered with a semitragic note is the prevalent tone of this play, as it is of so many of its predecessors. Though the characters may find it hard to cope with their lot—Truscott, for example, once retired and dozing in his basket chair, forever pretends that he still is on the bench—they eventually make accommodations with reality, reconciled to their lot in life.

The Fear of Heaven, a 1976 one-act play, concerns two Englishmen who think they are in heaven because the ceiling of their Italian hospital room has a celestial fresco. One of the men dies, while the other lives; at the play's end, the survivor celebrates his good fortune ("Fletcher dead! And I'm alive. Harmlessly alive") at the same time that he laments his fate ("You know what I have discovered? Everything *interesting* happens to Fletcher!"). This ambivalence, which typifies the lives of so many of Mortimer's characters, mirrors life as he sees it. Near the end of *Clinging to the Wreckage*, he tells this anecdote:

> In the years that were to come, I was to invent a down-at-heel old barrister with a certain low courtroom cunning who was to become the hero of a television series. I sat in the usual embarrassed silence with an East End totter whom I had been defending on a charge of attempted murder. He had been accused of stabbing the man next door with the knife he used to cut up carrots for the pony that drew his cart. The motive suggested was that the son of the next-door neighbour had stolen my client's Victory Medal. As we sat together, the totter and I, in the cells beneath the Old Bailey, waiting for a word from the Jury, and as I thought, as usual, of all the things I might have said, art took its revenge on life.
>
> "Your Mr. Rumpole could've got me out of this," the totter said, "so why the hell can't you?"

Other major works

NOVELS: *Charade*, 1947; *Rumming Park*, 1948; *Answer Yes or No*, 1950; *Like Men Betrayed*, 1953; *The Narrowing Stream*, 1954; *Three Winters*, 1956; *Paradise Postponed*, 1985; *Summer's Lease*, 1988; *Titmuss Regained*, 1990; *Dunster*, 1992.

SHORT FICTION: *Rumpole of the Bailey*, 1978; *The Trials of Rumpole*, 1979; *Regina Rumpole*, 1981; *Rumpole's Return*, 1981; *Rumpole and the Golden Thread*, 1983; *The First Rumpole Omnibus*, 1983; *The Second Rumpole Omnibus*, 1987; *Rumpole on Trial*, 1992.

NONFICTION: *No Moaning at the Bar*, 1957 (as Geoffrey Lincoln); *With Love and Lizards*, 1957 (with Penelope Mortimer); *Clinging to the Wreckage: A Part of Life*, 1982; *In Character*, 1983; *Character Parts*, 1986.

SCREENPLAYS: *Ferry to Hong Kong*, 1959 (with Lewis Gilbert and Vernon Harris); *The Innocents*, 1961 (with Truman Capote and William Archibald);

Guns of Darkness, 1962; *I Thank a Fool*, 1962 (with others); *Lunch Hour*, 1962 (adaptation of his play); *The Running Man*, 1963; *Bunny Lake Is Missing*, 1964 (with Penelope Mortimer); *A Flea in Her Ear*, 1967 (adaptation of his play); *John and Mary*, 1969.

TELEPLAYS: *David and Broccoli*, 1960; *Desmond*, 1968; *Rumpole of the Bailey*, 1975, 1978, 1979; *Rumpole's Return*, 1980; *Brideshead Revisited*, 1981 (adaptation of Evelyn Waugh's novel); *A Voyage Round My Father*, 1982; *Paradise Postponed*, 1986; *Titmuss Regained*, 1991.

Bibliography

Barnes, Clive. "'Little Hotel' on Slight." Review of *A Little Hotel on the Side. Post* (New York), January 27, 1992. A review of the "racily idiomatic adaptation" of a French farce, here in Mortimer's version called *A Little Hotel on the Side.* The Belasco Theater was the site for this second offering of the first season for Tony Randall's National Actors Theater. As in all farce, "the story doesn't matter."

Hayman, Ronald. *British Theatre Since 1955: a Reassessment.* Oxford, England: Oxford University Press, 1979. Mortimer is grouped with Robert Bolt and Peter Shaffer, and all are seen as playwrights who "have repeatedly tried to move away from naturalism, [oscillating] between writing safe plays, catering for the West End audience, and dangerously serious plays, which might have alienated the public they had won." Contains an overview of *The Dock Brief, Two Stars for Comfort,* and *The Judge.*

Honan, William H. "The Funny Side of Social Issues." *The New York Times,* May 12, 1990. p. A13. Honan profiles Mortimer in midtown Manhattan, promoting *Titmuss Regained.* He finds that Mortimer admires Anthony Trollope and Charles Dickens and shares their intent "not only to expose human foible but to elucidate the social issues raised by his story." Provides a good conversational biography, starting with the 1958 radio play *The Dock Brief.*

Stevens, Andrea. "The Smile Button for Tragedy." *The New York Times,* January 26, 1992, p. B47. A brief but informative look at *A Little Hotel on the Side.* Mortimer says, and Stevens quotes, that "[f]arce is tragedy played at about 120 revolutions a minute." Interviewed by telephone, Mortimer remarks that "all these pompous middle-class men and well-upholstered women [in his work]—underneath they are selfish little children."

Taylor, John Russell. *The Angry Theatre: New British Drama.* Rev. ed. New York: Hill & Wang, 1969. A separate chapter provides a good long discussion of Mortimer's traditional influences and place among more experimental peers, but with the same subject, "more often than not the failure of communication, the confinement to and sometimes the liberation from private dream-worlds." Treats *The Dock Brief*, *The Wrong Side of the Park*, *Two Stars for Comfort*, and about a dozen shorter plays.

Gerald H. Strauss
(Updated by *Thomas J. Taylor*)

THOMAS NASHE

Born: Lowestoft, Surrey, England; November, 1567
Died: Yarmouth(?), England; 1601

Principal drama

Dido, Queen of Carthage, pr. c. 1586-1587, pb. 1594 (with Christopher Marlowe); *Summer's Last Will and Testament*, pr. 1592, pb. 1600; *The Isle of Dogs*, pr. 1597 (with Ben Jonson; no longer extant).

Other literary forms

Thomas Nashe was primarily a pamphlet writer, although he also wrote a work of long fiction (*The Unfortunate Traveller: Or, The Life of Jack Wilton*, 1594), a long poem (*The Choise of Valentines*, 1899), and several songs and sonnets, as well as the plays listed above.

Achievements

Nashe was best known during his own day as the writer of pamphlets who used lively rhetorical devices, a ready wit, and outrageous personal attacks to get the better of the pompous scholar Gabriel Harvey. Harvey, who took himself and his ideas seriously, was no match for Nashe, the young university wit who used words as a soldier did a rapier. The attacks that Nashe leveled at the Puritans have none of the romantic niceties of Thomas Lodge, the euphuistic panegyrics of John Lyly, or the literary balance of Thomas Deloney: His language is direct, stark, without pedantry. Nashe offers no pleasant dialogues or polite deviations. When Harvey suggested a truce in the war of words between Nashe and him, Nashe responded that he would make "Uncessant warres with waspes and droons," and he dismissed Harvey simply as a dunce. The magnificent invective found in the speeches of William Shakespeare's Falstaff, Prince Hal, and (especially) Kent was almost certainly derived from the monstrous hyperbole and the extravagant vituperation Nashe hurled at his adversaries.

Among modern students of literature, Nashe is remembered for his most unusual work, the picaresque novel of adventure *The Unfortunate Traveller*. It tells the story of a young page who, after serving in the army of King Henry VIII, travels to Europe to find a means of earning a living. The underworld realism that Nashe presents in his descriptions of Jack Wilton's escapades has earned him a reputation for being more than a mere pamphleteer, a hurler of invective. The book is not a unified work of art; its characters, other than Jack himself, are not particularly memorable. Its descriptions of the harshest elements of human life, such as disease, hunger, torture, rape, and murder, place it in stark contrast to the sweet absurdities of romance; it thus shows the way to the modern novel.

Biography

Thomas Nashe was born in November, 1567, the second son of William Nashe, a minister in Lowestoft, moving in 1573 to West Harling in Norfolk, where his father took up the duties of rector. There Nashe likely remained until he left for Cambridge in 1581 or 1582.

R. B. McKerrow and others have suggested that young Nashe's early education was probably accomplished at home with his father as tutor, a likely suggestion since no suitable school existed in West Harling. Wherever he attained his schooling, it was of such quality as to allow young Nashe to enter St. John's College, Cambridge, where, as Nashe himself later wrote in *Nashe's Lenten Stuffe* (1599), *Have with You to Saffron-Walden* (1596), and the preface to Robert Greene's *Menaphon* (1589), he did well in his studies and enjoyed the academic life. Although he complained that the curriculum at Cambridge was weighted too heavily toward vague theology and too little toward the ancient philosophers, he nevertheless praised St. John's and was proud of his college's reputation for sound scholarship. The Puritan influence at Cambridge, with its emphasis upon utilitarian training rather than upon Humanistic inquiry, did not please the inquisitive Nashe.

Nashe received his bachelor's degree from Cambridge in 1586 and left school in 1588 without taking his master's degree. Whether he ended his education because he lacked funds to continue (his father had died in 1587) or because he did not fit well into the Puritan narrowness at the school is not clear, but it is clear from his comments in *The Anatomie of Absurditie* (1589) that he thought Cambridge had failed him.

Leaving Cambridge with no resources but a ready wit, Nashe followed the lead of fellow University Wits Robert Greene and Christopher Marlowe by moving to London to attempt to support himself as a professional writer. Nashe may have been acquainted with both Greene and Marlowe at Cambridge; it is certain that he knew both in London. Like Nashe, both loved poetry and detested Puritans. In the same year that he left Cambridge, Nashe published *The Anatomie of Absurditie*, a dull, preachy work reflecting his inexperience and brashness. Nashe's intent was to use the satiric pamphlet form against the satiric pamphlets of the Puritans, chiefly against Philip Stubbs's *The Anatomie of Abuses* (1583), but his fervor to condemn the lack of learning and discrimination shown in the narrow Puritan tracts blossomed into a general diatribe against bad books, bad science, bad poetry (generally that produced by the balladmongers), bad actions, bad thinking—bad everything. The result was that in trying to accomplish too much, he succeeded in accomplishing nothing much.

Many of Nashe's early works were dedicated to various personages of noble birth, the hope clearly being that the noble person might like the quality of the work, be flattered, and be moved to reward the young writer. *The Anatomie of Absurditie* was dedicated to Sir Charles Blount, who, perhaps seeing that the work had little intrinsic value, offered Nashe no support. As a young writer struggling to sustain life while he earned his reputation, Nashe needed patrons. He dedicated several of his pamphlets to a variety of people in a position to offer him assistance, but he never found much support for his work from among nobility. Finally, after the dedication of *The Unfortunate Traveller* to Henry Wriothesley, Earl of Southampton, Nashe decided that patrons were more trouble than they were worth. Hating hypocrisy in others and finding himself forced into hypocrisy in order to be paid for his work, Nashe turned to writing only for his middle-class readers and depending upon them to reward his efforts.

What gave Nashe's literary career its largest boost was neither patrons nor the excellence of his ideas. What gave him the chance to display his vigorous style of writing and gained for him public attention was the famous Martin Marprelate controversy. The controversy, which was begun by a Puritan attack against the Anglican Church, centered on whether the Church should be ruled by a hierarchy of bishops or by the preachers. From the beginning, with the publication in 1572 of the Puritan pamphlet *Admonition to Parliament*, the Puritans had had the better of the argument, especially after an unusually gifted writer entered the lists on the side of the Puritans. This author, unfortunately but necessarily anonymous, called himself Martin Marprelate and wrote some eight pamphlets which effectively routed the less lively, less witty apologists for the Anglicans.

Nashe entered the lists against Martin on behalf of (and probably hired by) the prelates, writing *An Almond for a Parrat* (1590). Using the same type of invective, parody, hyperbole, and specious logic used by Martin, Nashe portrayed his adversary as a hypocrite, a heretic, and a traitor, an attack which drew a response from Gabriel Harvey, a friend of Edmund Spenser who, unlike Martin, was not anonymous, not without influence, and not as capable a writer as Nashe. It was in this battle of wits that Nashe found his place as a writer, low though the place was. Here the verbal street-fighter had the great good fortune to be attacked by a man of reputation who was his inferior both in wit and in writing ability. Beginning with a slap at Harvey in his preface to Greene's *A Quip for an Upstart Courtier* (1592) and ending with *Have with You to Saffron-Walden*, Nashe earned a reputation and a fair living from his anti-Harvey prose. Finally, in 1599, Archbishop of Canterbury John Whitgift ordered a halt to future writings by both men and confiscated their existing works.

Nashe's most important work is a picaresque novel published in 1594, *The Unfortunate Traveller*. A kind of pamphlet itself, but longer and more complex, the work was not particularly popular during his lifetime, but today it is his best-known work.

Nashe left London in 1597 when the authorities decided that *The Isle of Dogs*, a play he had begun and which Ben Jonson had finished, was "seditious." Jonson was jailed and Nashe sought, but the famous pamphleteer had fled to Yarmouth, in Norfolk. By 1598 or early 1599, he had returned to London, where *Nashe's Lenten Stuffe* was entered in the Stationers' Register.

After *Nashe's Lenten Stuffe*, Nashe wrote no more, and in 1601 history records a reference to his death.

Analysis

As a young man who chose to make his living as a writer, Thomas Nashe would almost certainly have tried his hand at drama. With the strong traditions of native English drama at his back, classical drama in his brain, and Renaissance hybrid drama daily before his eyes, Nashe could hardly have escaped the temptation to enter the field. His contributions to dramatic literature are not as plentiful as those to prose, nor perhaps as plentiful as he might have wished. Evidence exists which indicates that Nashe participated to a greater or lesser extent in the writing of five plays.

Nashe's first experience with drama probably occurred while he was at Cambridge. A contemporary of his wrote that Nashe "had a hand in a show called *Terminus et non terminus*," but neither the play nor the extent of Nashe's participation in it is known. The next reference which connects Nashe to drama was made by Nashe's friend Robert Greene. In *Greene's Groatsworth of Wit Bought with a Million of Repentance* (1592), Greene draws a comparison between Christopher Marlowe and "yong *Iuvenall*, that byting satyrist, that lastly with mee together writ a comedie." Because Nashe had been closely associated with Greene and because he best fits the description that Greene gives, most scholars believe that Nashe is "yong *Iuvenall*." Which one of Greene's plays it is to which Nashe is supposed to have contributed is not clear, although some scholars offer *A Knack to Know a Knave* (pr. 1592) as a possibility. There is no evidence, however, to lead to any definite conclusion. The third play with which Nashe is connected is *Dido, Queen of Carthage*. Although the title page lists "Christopher Marlowe, and Thomas Nash, Gent." as authors, most scholars believe from internal evidence that Nashe had little if any part in the authorship. A final play, also coauthored, this time with Ben Jonson, was presented in 1597. *The Isle of Dogs*, no text of which is extant, was reported to the Privy Council as being "a lewd plaie ... contanyng very seditious and sclanderous matter." An order was issued to prohibit the play's being acted, and warrants were issued for the arrests of both Nashe and Jonson. Nashe, who later wrote that he had "begun but the induction and first act of it" and was unaware of what was added without his consent later, fled London and escaped prosecution. Jonson, on the other hand, was jailed.

It is Nashe's fourth try at drama that survives in full and from Nashe alone. *A Pleasant Comedy, Called Summer's Last Will and Testament* was published in 1600, but it was almost certainly written and presented in 1592 at the home of Archbishop Whitgift in Croydon. Written not for the public but for a private audience and a special occasion, *Summer's Last Will and Testament* shows little of what Nashe might have accomplished had he attempted a complete drama in the tradition of Thomas Kyd, Marlowe, Shakespeare, Jonson, and others. Nashe himself distinguishes between regular English drama and his work by including in his prologue the assertion "nay, 'tis no play neither, but a show," and truly the work is more in the form of a seasonal pageant than a play. Nashe's pageant is in the form of a debate, or a series of debates, and thus *Summer's Last Will and Testament* is not far removed from the style of his pamphlets.

Written almost certainly to be performed by amateur players as informal entertainment at the home of Archbishop Whitgift, *Summer's Last Will and Testament* treats two themes (with the usual digressions which help to identify Nashe's style): the hot summer just drawing to a close and the plague then devastating London. Will Summers, the famous jester of Henry VIII, is cast as narrator, chorus, and general analyst of the proceedings, serving as Nashe's apologist for the light content of the pageant. In a self-deprecating vein, Nashe has Will reflect on the suitability of having a famous jester as commentator for this particular drama: " . . . one fool presents another; and I, a fool by nature and by art, do speak to you in the person of the idiot our playmaker." In answer to his own question about the significance of the ideas in the work, Will remarks, "Deep-reaching wits, here is no deep stream for you to angle in." After he delivers the "scurvey Prologue" Nashe wrote for him, a speech Will criticizes regularly while delivering it, he decides to stick around to "flout the actors and him [Nashe] at the end of every scene." Almost true to his word (he rarely waits until the end of scene to comment), Will Summers condemns the ideas, language, and acting throughout the work.

Will Summers' denigrating comments are the best part, except for an occasional excellent lyric poem, of an otherwise dull drama. After an overly long speech early in the first scene on the subject of begging, Will swears that it was as boring as a sermon: "So we come here to laugh and be merry, and we hear a filthy beggarly oration in the praise of beggary. It is a beggarly poet that writ it." "This play," he says, "is a gullimaufry," an absurd mixture—and indeed it is.

As the action continues, Will Summers becomes less intrusive, probably because he is bored to sleep, but he still interrupts every scene with his witty comments. The work consists, after the introductory comments and prologue, of ten scenes and an epilogue. The central character, Lord Summer (a personification of the season, not to be confused with Will Summers) appears in each scene, his purpose to interview his "officers" to determine what is left of the wealth he gave to them. With the help of

Vertumnus (god of the changing seasons), Summer questions and argues with Autumn, Winter, Ver (spring), Solstitium (solstice), Sol (sun), Orion, Harvest, Bacchus and his companions, and Christmas and Backwinter (sons of Winter). Various Morris dancers, clowns, and maids round out the *dramatis personae*.

Lord Summer enters, supported by Winter and Autumn. In attendance are satyrs and wood nymphs, who sing the song "Fayre Summer Droops," a conventional lament on the passing of summer which helps to set the elegiac theme of the entire work. Summer reinforces the theme by pronouncing his own impending death and seeking to settle his affairs by calling his "officers" to account for how they have used what Summer gave them.

Ver enters, accompanied by singers and dancers, and announces to old Summer, "What I had I have spent on good fellows, in these sports you have seen, which are proper to the spring, and others of like sort—as giving wenches green gowns, making garlands for fencers, and tricking up children gay. . . ." Summer condemns Ver as a "monstrous unthrift," but Ver fortunately has Nashe to help him defend himself and therefore builds a magnificent argument using appeals to authority and to nature in praise of begging. Considering his servant prodigal, dying Summer announces that Ver shall hereafter always be accompanied by Lent, whose "scarcity may countervail thy waste."

Solstitium enters next, an old hermit carrying a set of balance scales. Representing the summer solstice, the one day when the sun appears balanced before it starts its southward journey, Solstitium is the golden mean, and he gains moralizing Summer's unqualified approval: "I like thy moderation wonderous well," says Summer. "A pattern is to princes and great men." Both Summer and Solstitium give sage advice, but neither is as witty as Ver—or, for that matter, as witty as Sol, Orion, Harvest, or Bacchus, who follow.

Sol is accused by Autumn of wronging Daphne by descending "to Thetis' lap," but Sol defends himself admirably in lyric blank verse. Orion and his huntsmen are called next to be condemned by Autumn for causing unhealthy days: The hunting dogs that Orion leads cause the season's dog days. Orion, Nashe-like, accepts the challenge to debate and presents an excellent defense of dogs, "proving" quite beyond doubt that dogs are the rarest of creatures. Harvest, who enters next, is accused by Summer of hoarding and selfishness. After merely singing several merry songs as a response, Harvest effectively defends his selflessness, his liberality. Bacchus enters extolling the virtues of drink, asking Winter and Summer to drink with him. When they refuse, Bacchus turns to Will Summers, who accepts and is dubbed Sir Robert Toss-pot. Bacchus happily uses Plato and Aristotle to support his praise of wine. Disgusted, Lord Summer says, "no more of this. I hate it to the death," and has Bacchus removed.

Announcing that "worse servants no man hath," Summer is ready to re-sign his crown in favor of Autumn. Winter complains in the classical Nashe fashion of misapplied learning that autumn is the favorite time of useless scholars, poets, and philosophers. Winter/Nashe's use of learning to con-demn learning is, as G. R. Hibbard points out, reminiscent of the king in Shakespeare's *Love's Labour's Lost* (pr. 1594-1595), who comments on Berowne's similar argument by saying, "How well he's read to reason against reasoning." Summer, to quiet Winter, makes him Autumn's guard-ian, but now Autumn complains that Winter's two sons, Christmas and Backwinter, are so horrible that Winter deserves no consideration. Called to appear before Summer, Christmas and Backwinter prove to be at least as bad as Autumn had suggested. Christmas enters with no music, declar-ing that he believes hospitality to be out of date and downright sinful. Backwinter rudely threatens to be worse than Winter. They are both or-dered out by Summer.

Left then to the business of his last will and testament, Summer itemizes his effects: his crown, flowers, long days, short nights, and the like. An-nouncing "here Summer ends," old Summer is carried out by the singing satyrs and woodnymphs who brought him in.

The plot of *Summer's Last Will and Testament* is, as has been shown, slight. Will Summers puts it quite completely in one sentence of the pro-logue: "Summer must come in sick; he must call his officers to account, yield his throne to Autumn, make Winter his executor, with tittle tattle Tom boy." The characters, whom Hibbard sees as individualized rather than "mere allegorical ghosts," are still little more than figures for the witty arguments of Nashe. Summer is facing death, but he has not the stature to be an emblem for man. When Nashe brings his audience to face death, it is by means of his excellent lyric poem "Song: Adieu, farewell earths blisse," not by means of old Summer. Summer is himself moved to aware-ness by the song.

The pageant presented by Nashe as entertainment at Croydon is witty enough, moral enough, and properly debunked by Will Summers. The ar-guments offered in their own defense by the various servants of Summer, because they include topical subjects, personal references to members of the audience, and displays of learning and rhetorical devices, would surely have pleased the audience for whom they were presented. Such characters as Ver, Orion, and Bacchus provide the same kind of diversion as did the holiday Lord of Misrule in their unpragmatic actions and sophistic defenses of those actions. Summer offers the proper social balance with his moral objections to misrule, but, in the hands of the anti-Puritan Nashe, Summer never becomes so dull a moralizer as to become a churl. The play is uni-fied, consistent, and complete—an evening's pleasant entertainment. It would not have been a success on the London stage, but Nashe did not have that audience in mind when he wrote the play.

Some elements of general social interest to a modern audience are included in *Summer's Last Will and Testament*. The representation of Christmas, for example, as an inhospitable churl points to a significant problem in sixteenth century England—the decline of the community-based system with the introduction of free enterprise. A subject addressed most clearly during Nashe's time by Thomas Deloney, the lack of charity shown by man for his neighbor, was a problem addressed by many writers of the day, including Shakespeare and Nashe's friend Greene. Nashe has Christmas enter his pageant unaccompanied by festive music (or music of any kind). Christmas is against tradition, against authority, against enjoyment—in short, he is a Puritan. Like Shakespeare's Malvolio, Christmas, because he is virtuous, expects there to be no cakes and ale. Autumn calls him "a pinchbeck, cutthroat churl,/ That keepes no open house, as he should do,/ Delighteth in no game or fellowship,/ Loves no good deeds, and hateth talk." Harvest, the direct opposite of Christmas in the pageant, represents the discharge of social obligations. Harvest has distributed his crops equitably and with goodwill. He declares that he "keeps good hospitality" and presents good evidence of his claim. Persuaded, Summer praises Harvest above all of his servants.

Analysis of social problems, however, is not a major part of Nashe's pageant. If the social implications are slight, the personal reference narrow, and the arguments usually merely rhetorical, what is there to the pageant to interest someone other than an antiquarian? What pervades the work from beginning to end—sometimes relegated to the background, sometimes brought to the front—is the theme of impending death. The days are hot, the plague threatens each life, and summer is dying. The song which ushers old Summer onstage, "Fayre Summer Droops," raises the specters of tears, sorrow, and the grave. The song that leads Summer out announces the sad news that "short days, sharp days, long nights come on apace." Each of the two stanzas of that song, "Autumn hath all the summer's fruitful treasure," ends with the refrain, "From winter, plague, and pestilence, good Lord deliver us." As Summer dies, so must we all. Human weakness in the face of natural elements, a truth exhibited daily to Nashe and his audience at Croydon, is the theme of *Summer's Last Will and Testament.*

This theme is nowhere more apparent or more poignantly expressed than in what is generally considered to be the best of Nashe's lyrics, "Song: Adieu, farewell earths blisse," sung to the dying Summer by Will Summers. Nashe recognizes in the refrain which follows each of the six stanzas that he is sick, that he must die, and he prays: "Lord have mercy on us." In a logical development, Nashe first introduces the theme of the medieval morality play *Everyman*: "Fond are lifes lustful ioyes." In succeeding stanzas, he develops each of the "lustful ioyes" in turn. "Rich men" are warned not to trust in their wealth, "beauty" is revealed as transitory, "strength" is pictured surrendering to the grave, and "lust" is useless to dissuade Hell's executioner. In a very specific, orderly manner and in spare lines of iambic trimeter, Nashe presents the theme of the pageant: Man's death-lament and prayer for mercy. One stanza will show the strength of the whole poem:

> Beauty is but a flowre,
> Which wrinkles will deuoure,
> Brightnesse falls from the ayre,
> Queenes have died yong and faire,
> Dust hath closed Helen's eye.
> I am sick, I must dye:
> Lord, have mercy on vs.

Other major works

NOVEL: *The Unfortunate Traveller: Or, The Life of Jack Wilton*, 1594 (includes poetry).

POETRY: *The Choise of Valentines*, 1899.

NONFICTION: *Preface to Robert Greene's Menaphon*, 1589; *The Anatomie of Absurditie*, 1589; *An Almond for a Parrat*, 1590; Preface to Sir Philip Sidney's *Astrophel and Stella*, 1591; *Pierce Penniless, His Supplication to the Divell*, 1592 (includes poetry); Preface to Robert Greene's *A Quip for an Upstart Courtier*, 1592; *Strange News of the Intercepting of Certain Letters*, 1592 (includes poetry; also known as *The Four Letters Confuted*); *Christ's Tears over Jerusalem*, 1593; *The Terrors of the Night*, 1594; *Have with You to Saffron-Walden*, 1596; *Nashe's Lenten Stuffe*, 1599.

Bibliography

Crewe, Jonathan V. *Unredeemed Rhetoric: Thomas Nashe and the Scandal of Authorship*. Baltimore: The Johns Hopkins University Press, 1982. A fascinating study of the conflict between orthodox values and a cynical perception of society's injustice and exploitation that cuts across Nashe's career, complicating and adding tension to his work. At all levels of discourse there is a split between the manifest rhetorical purpose and the latent anarchy of the language. To the poststructuralist critic Crewe, Nashe asserts the humanist faith in the power of rhetoric to maintain order yet undercuts it by his own excesses.

Hibbard, G. R. *Thomas Nashe: A Critical Introduction*. Cambridge, Mass.: Harvard University Press, 1962. As a historical critic, Hibbard situates Nashe firmly in the context of the 1590's. Hibbard discusses the causes of the split in Nashe's work between the traditional rural and urban life. Nashe's imaginative response to adversity impelled him to write works that reveal the contradictions of Elizabethan society rather than the idealized myth. Nashe's work encompasses aspects of life excluded by prevalent idealistic literary modes. At their best, his works show the urban life of his time with a clarity and force that surpass their limitations.

Hilliard, Stephen S. *The Singularity of Thomas Nashe.* Lincoln: University of Nebraska Press, 1986. Hilliard discusses the concept of "singularity," or individuality, in Nashe's life and work. In sixteenth century terms, Nashe's controversial standing as an author reflects, according to Hilliard, Elizabethan ambivalence about singularity, a quality both prized and condemned—a difference from, yet also a threat to, the social order. Nashe's singularity was both a literary goal and a condition forced upon him by his estranged status. While his humanistic conception of the exalted social role of the poet justified his own singularity to him, Hilliard points out that his critics saw him as a presumptuous hack writer.

McGinn, Donald J. *Thomas Nashe.* Boston: Twayne, 1981. Contains insightful commentary on Nashe's life and works. Instead of recounting the intrigues of kings, the adventures of knights and ladies, and the agonies and ecstasies of courtly love, McGinn points out that for his literary material Nashe sought the crowded streets, shops, and taverns of his contemporary London. Focuses on Nashe's works as portrayals of the various types of middle-class Londoners—their appearance, their manners, and their customs. Contains bibliography, chronology, and appendix.

Nicholl, Charles. *A Cup of News: The Life of Thomas Nashe.* Boston: Routledge & Kegan Paul, 1984. Nashe's writings, according to Nicholl, offer a vividness of presentation that make them perhaps more representative of Elizabethan England than the works of almost any other writer. He goes on to say that this aspect of his work is partly why Nashe is described as a "pamphleteer" rather than an "author." Nicholl does not, however, find that term pejorative; rather, the topicality and reportage in Nashe's writing even suggest the more modern term "journalist." The study argues that Nashe's work combines the characteristics of journalism, satire, and entertainment. Bibliography, illustrations, documents.

Eugene P. Wright
(Updated by *Genevieve Slomski*)

NGUGI WA THIONG'O

Born: Kamiriithu village, near Limuru, Kenya; January 5, 1938

Principal drama

The Black Hermit, pr. 1962, pb. 1968; *This Time Tomorrow: Three Plays*, pb. 1970 (includes *The Rebels, The Wound in My Heart*, and *This Time Tomorrow*); *The Trial of Dedan Kimathi*, pr. 1974, pb. 1976 (with Micere Githae-Mugo); *Ngaahika Ndeenda*, pr. 1977, pb. 1980 (with Ngugi wa Mirii); *I Will Marry When I Want*, 1982); *Maitu Njugira*, pb. 1982 (with Ngugi wa Mirii; *Mother, Sing for Me*, 1986).

Other literary forms

Ngugi wa Thiong'o is also known as a novelist, having published one of the first English-language novels by an East African, *Weep Not, Child* (1964). This novel, *The River Between* (1965), *A Grain of Wheat* (1967), and *Petals of Blood* (1977) re-create the cultural history of the Gikuyu people and the emergence of modern Kenya. His fifth novel, *Caitaani Mutharaba-Ini* (1980; *Devil on the Cross*, 1982), combines elements of Gikuyu oral tradition with satire on neocolonial exploitation and realism portraying the victims of that exploitation. Writing fiction for the first time in his native Gikuyu, Ngugi completed his own translations into Kiswahili and English. In addition to his novels, Ngugi has also published a collection of early short stories, *Secret Lives and Other Stories* (1975), which gathers his work in this genre from the early 1960's to the mid-1970's.

Ngugi has also written extensively as a social and literary critic. His collection of literary criticism, *Homecoming: Essays on African and Caribbean Literature, Culture, and Politics* (1972), testifies to the maturation of his social vision, including speculations on Mau Mau, nationalism, socialism, and capitalism. A second collection of essays, *Writers in Politics* (1981), asserts that the function of the writer in society is essentially a political one, however explicitly mute or vocal the writer may choose to be on social issues. In *Detained: A Writer's Prison Diary* (1981), Ngugi records his experience during his politically motivated incarceration, openly indicting the corruption of neocolonial Kenya and offering insights into his development as a writer and an activist. In a subsequent collection of essays, *Barrel of a Pen: Resistance to Repression in Neo-Colonial Kenya* (1983), Ngugi employs the ideals of the Mau Mau movement to analyze the role of writing and education in contemporary Kenya. His fourth collection of essays, *Decolonising the Mind: The Politics of Language in African Literature* (1986), addresses the need for awareness of the dominating colonial legacies of British culture and the obligations of a neocolonial writer in Africa to address his compatriots, his cultural and historical milieu, and his global readership. Ngugi has also granted a number of interviews that have been published; in the 1960's, he contributed forty-four columns to the *Daily Nation*, a newspaper in Nairobi, useful for their witness to his humanistic and political growth as a writer and thinker. In 1990, Ngugi expanded his literary canvas still further by publishing two children's books, *Njamba Nene's Pistol* and *Njamba Nene and the Flying Bus*. Because Ngugi's themes and concerns are often interwoven among his various modes of discourse, virtually all of his writings help provide an informative context for the reading of his drama.

Achievements

Ngugi is the foremost writer of modern East Africa. Through his novels, essays, and plays, he has garnered the respect of both Africans and others. His fiction offers the single most impressive record of an African country's precolonial history, its exploitation under colonial rule, its turmoil in gaining independence, and its subsequent struggles to maintain a democratic government in the midst of neocolonial corruption. His essays, often forthrightly polemical, have resulted in the emergence of East African literature as a serious topic of criticism among scholars of world literature; he has also made a significant contribution to curriculum reform in African universities, emphasizing the study of African literature.

Ngugi's plays, like his early fiction, reveal a well-schooled and well-read background in British and European literature, but they evolve, as do his novels, from a humanistic, ethical focus to one of a leftist, radical program for social reform. By adapting *The Trial of Dedan Kimathi* and *I Will Marry When I Want* to experimental forms that include aspects of the Gikuyu oral tradition, and by producing and writing the latter play in Gikuyu, Ngugi succeeded in reaching the masses with his drama and his concerns. His explicit commitment to democratic Socialist reform and the strong popular support of Ngugi's *I Will Marry When I Want* resulted in Ngugi's detention.

While Ngugi, then known as James Ngugi, was recognized early as a promising young writer, his later work—perhaps because of political circumstances and his refusal to desist from polemics and activism—has not been accorded the same official status. His first play, *The Black Hermit*, was selected for performance at the 1962 Ugandan independence celebration, and *Weep Not, Child*, his first published novel, received an award from the East African Literature Bureau in 1965 and first prize in the 1966 Dakar Festival of Negro Arts. In that same year, Ngugi traveled to the United States as an honored guest of the 1966 International PEN Conference. While formal recognition waned over the next two decades, Ngugi's reputation has continued to grow. Perhaps his greatest achievement has been his ability to appeal both to those who concern him most, the working classes of Kenya, and to a diverse international readership.

Biography

Ngugi wa Thiong'o was born James Ngugi in Kamiriithu village, twelve miles northeast of Nairobi, on January 5, 1938. His father, Thiong'o wa Nducu, was a farmer who had been dispossessed of his land in the White Highlands of the Kiambu District and forced to squat as a laborer on what had been his homeland. As a result of the British Imperial Land Act of 1915, many Gikuyu farmers—deprived of legal rights—had been reduced to farming the land of well-to-do British settlers or influential Africans who had been granted parcels in the confiscation of the fertile area by the British governor; Ngugi's father farmed for one of the few Africans who had retained property. His mother was one of four wives, and he was one of twenty-eight children in the extended family.

Until about the age of nine, Ngugi was reared according to a mixture of traditional Gikuyu customs and Christian principles. In 1947, he attended the mission school of Kamaandura in nearby Limuru for two years; subsequently, he completed his primary education in the village of Maanguu at a school established by the Karing'a, the Independence Schools Movement, a cooperative undertaking by Kenya's Africans who viewed education as a vital component in their struggle for freedom from British rule. From his earliest years in school, Ngugi experienced both the colonial and the nationalistic perspectives inherent in the respective curricula.

Ngugi's secondary education was at Alliance High School in Kikuyu. There Ngugi encountered Carey Francis, the principal, a man with rigid missionary views and a strict bias for the values of European civilization, who would become the prototype of the missionary headmaster in Ngugi's fiction. There, too, Ngugi acquired a complex religious sensibility, integrating biblical study and Christian mythology with his own Gikuyu background. His experiences at Alliance High School constitute one of the shaping influences of his adolescent life.

During this period, Ngugi's family was deeply involved in the Mau Mau resistance. His brother, Wallace Mwangi, fought with the clandestine Mau Mau forces in the forests from 1954 to 1956. His parents, as well as other relatives, were detained for the subversion of colonial rule. A stepbrother was killed by government troops, and his home village was relocated. Ngugi himself did not engage in combat, and although his youth provided him with a measure of justification, he suffered considerable guilt. Reflection on the Mau Mau as an ideal model for the fight against social injustices would be a central theme in his work.

After Ngugi's graduation from high school, he entered Makerere University College in Kampala, Uganda, the only school then conferring degrees in English literature in East Africa. An outstanding student, he completed work in the Honors English program in 1963. During this period, Ngugi began his creative writing, editing the student journal *Penpoint*, writing several short stories, drafting his first two novels, and writing his first play, *The Black Hermit*, as well as two one-act plays, *The Rebels* and *The Wound in My Heart*. He also began writing columns for the Nairobi newspaper *Daily Nation*, a task that was to lead to a stint as a junior reporter in Nairobi in the year following his graduation. Also during this period, Ngugi married Nyambura in 1961 and had the first two of his five children.

In 1964, Ngugi continued his education, pursuing a degree in English studies at Leeds University in England. Exposed to the radical views of fellow students and finding himself in a community which encouraged open inquiry into social and political issues, Ngugi began work on Caribbean literature as well as the extensive drafting of *A Grain of Wheat*, projects which helped him to delineate his views into the most systematic line of thought that he had yet achieved. He also traveled to literary conferences in Damascus, New York, and Moscow, meeting a number of writers and widening his access to diverse social and literary perspectives. Although his teachers at Leeds encouraged him to complete his M.A. thesis, Ngugi chose to pursue his writing and returned to Kenya in 1967.

At Nairobi University, Ngugi worked to reform the curriculum, encouraging an emphasis on African Studies, but he resigned in protest in March, 1969, siding with students who confronted the government for their lack of academic freedom. The next year found Ngugi in Makerere again, as a Fellow in creative writing, where he helped conclude curriculum revisions and organized a writers' workshop. In March, 1970, while addressing a church conference in Nairobi, at which he renounced Christianity, James Ngugi was challenged by an old man who pointed out that his name was contrary to his denial; thereafter, the writer used the traditional Gikuyu name. By then, however, he was well-known as simply Ngugi. Later that same year, he went to Northwestern University, where he taught African literature. While in Chicago, Ngugi witnessed the degraded conditions of African-American ghetto life, becoming convinced that American racism was the result of systematic economic and political exploitation. Returning to head, eventually, the Nairobi University English Department in August, 1971, Ngugi completed the curriculum changes which he had helped to initiate two years earlier. While his teaching was to continue until his detention, Ngugi had, by 1977, become the leading proponent of radical East African literature with the publication of *Petals of Blood*, his fourth novel.

After the successful and popular reception of *The Trial of Dedan Kimathi* and the release of *Petals of Blood*, Ngugi's activism provoked the anger of authorities during his staging of *I Will Marry When I Want* at the Kamiriithu Community Educational and Cultural Center in Limuru. While the play had been granted a license for production, a district official revoked permission after only a few performances, fearing that peasants would be moved to challenge the power of the upper class. The government, perhaps fearing Ngugi's outspoken convictions, arrested him on December 31, 1977. Despite international protests, appeals, and special delegations to Nairobi, Ngugi was detained without charges or trial in Kamiti Maximum Security Prison until December 12, 1978. Although the conciliatory climate in the early months of President Arap Moi's government probably facilitated Ngugi's release, he was not reinstated at Nairobi University, which terminated his appointment shortly after his detention, despite Ngugi's repeated attempts to regain his position. Ngugi continued to write, working on three collections of essays, his prison diary, his novel in Gikuyu and his own translation of it, *Devil on the Cross*, and a new play, a musical in Gikuyu written in collaboration with Ngugi wa Mirii. In March, 1982, the authorities dismantled the Kamiriithu center just when the new musical, *Mother, Sing for Me*, was in its final rehearsal. Making his residence in London but returning to Kenya whenever the prevailing government allows, Ngugi remains a powerful free-lance voice, speaking and writing on behalf of the landless, ordinary people and calling for social justice. Identifying strongly with his fictional creation, Matigari, from the novel *Matigari ma Njiruungi* (1986; *Matigari*, 1989), written in the Gikuyu language and banned in Kenya, Ngugi is a committed writer, attacking neocolonialism and advocating reformist possibilities. He is optimistic about the future but militant in his stance against oppression.

Analysis

Ngugi wa Thiong'o's drama explores the issues germane to the transition within Kenya from a colony to an independent nation. Often unabashedly didactic in his plays, Ngugi probes the challenges which young black intellectuals must overcome, if they are to alleviate conflicts of tribe, race, and religion that threaten the unity of nationalism. While his early plays of the 1960's usually revolve around the qualities of leadership, they also initiate themes concerning the tension between traditional, rural life and modern, urban life; the role of African women in developing a strong nationalism; and resistance to the continuation of colonial practices which perpetuate exploitation in the new country. As these themes evolve in the plays of the next decade, Ngugi's drama becomes even more decidedly didactic, using an idealized history of Mau Mau, straightforward calls to action, and realistic portrayals of the exploited that are interspersed with pageantry to evoke the grandeur of African culture and the tragedy of colonial history. From his earliest play *The Black Hermit* to his volatile *I Will Marry When I Want*, Ngugi gradually shifts his attention from the confusion of a central character beset by conflicts among his loyalties to the community's determination to achieve a democratic voice in the political and economic development of the nation.

In *The Black Hermit*, the protagonist, Remi, the only university-educated member of a small tribe, wavers between loyalty to his customs and desires for his own happiness. As the play opens, the villagers await Remi's return from the city. He is, however, returning to a bewildering array of anxious expectations in the village. Before he left for the city, Remi had fallen in love with Thoni, but, by the time he had mustered courage enough to propose, he learned of his brother's marriage to her. Six months later, his brother was killed in a car accident; custom required that Remi marry his dead brother's wife, which he did, hesitantly, believing that Thoni did not love him. Just after the ceremony, he fled to the city. Thoni, however, does love him, and, having remained faithful, she is hopeful of their reconciliation upon his return. His mother, Nyobi, expects him to comfort the abandoned Thoni and to start a family; the village priest wants Remi to reaffirm Christianity in the tribe; and the elders, having been convinced by Remi before his departure to support an African party in elections, hope that his return signals his willingness to lead them to power in the government.

Act 2 finds Remi still in the city and entangled in an affair with a white woman, Jane. While he must end the affair before returning, Remi realizes that Jane does not have similar experiences under colonialism and cannot ever understand him, despite her sincere affection. Remi's belated admission that he has been married to Thoni while carrying on the affair provokes Jane's anger, and she leaves him, calling into question Remi's own sense of ethical standards. Meanwhile, Remi and his friend Omange debate the powers of the new black government. Both oppose tribalism and support the new nation, but Remi refuses to sanction the right of workers to strike, while Omange envisions a state based on black workers rather than foreign aid. Despite Remi's support for the government, he refuses to enter politics when the elders visit the city to plead for his return. When the priest visits him, he sends word of his return, but his motives are confused.

Upon his return to the anxious village, Remi rants against tribalism. Yet he reveals himself as an obsessed, arrogant intellectual whose egotism renders him incapable of recognizing the strengths and appreciating the values in his own people. He renounces Christianity, but he has sacrificed his own spiritual awareness and interpersonal sensitivity to his rigid, nearly desperate, adherence to unquestioned principles of nationalism. When Remi renounces his marriage to Thoni, she flees and kills herself. Having asserted his individuality as more important than the complexities of traditional, communal society, Remi realizes, too late, that he has not thwarted tribalism and custom but profaned the mutual love and respect upon which the traditions are founded. He recognizes, in short, that African traditions must inform the evolution of African nationalism. Although Omange, the priest, Jane, and Remi himself are type characters in *The Black Hermit*, the elders suggest a ceremonial dignity and ritual wisdom, represented by "Africa's anthem" and sung in Kiswahili. The women Nyobi and Thoni provide models of genuine sensitivity in their mutual support to overcome the literal and figurative departure of Remi: Leaders, they assert, cannot take leave of compassion.

The critique of leadership extends from *The Black Hermit* to the three one-act dramas in *This Time Tomorrow*. In *The Rebels*, a young man returns home with a Ugandan fiancée, Mary, only to find that his father has chosen a local girl to be his bride. When he hesitates to accept the arrangement dictated by custom, the humiliated prospective bride kills herself, and he loses Mary as well. Implicitly, the play attacks the lack of black unity among the emerging nations of East Africa; by his use of a Ugandan for the character of Mary, Ngugi focuses on tribal prejudice rather than racial or colonial repression as the source of conflict. *The Wound in My Heart* portrays Ruhiu, a Mau Mau detainee, who eagerly returns to his village after his release only to find his wife with a child from an adulterous affair with a white man. Before she can hear Ruhiu's reaction, his wife kills herself. The fatalism inherent in *The Black Hermit* and these two one-acts, despite their sympathy with the role of African women in the emerging nation, yields to the undeveloped social protest of *This Time Tomorrow*, a later one-act, an attack on the affluent classes for their demolition of a slum in the interests of foreign investment and tourism. This play prefigures the social commitment of Ngugi's next two plays.

In *The Trial of Dedan Kimathi*, Ngugi shifts his concern from confused though well-intentioned leading characters to the strength of group commitment in reforming colonial practices which continue in independent Kenya. The play shapes the historical Dedan Kimathi into a heroic figure who embodies the idealistic principles of Mau Mau resistance. By idealizing a myth of Mau Mau, Ngugi and Micere Githae-Mugo, his collaborator, hoped to create a call to action, extolling Mau Mau glory and criticizing the neocolonial betrayal of the Mau Mau goals for social justice. An appeal to popular audiences, the play eulogizes Kimathi while celebrating his resistance to colonial enemies and staging re-creations of his tribulations, both in the courtroom and in private confrontations in his cell. Using an extremely loose structure—by Western standards—of three "Movements" rather than formally designed acts, each of which includes "Trials" and randomly juxtaposed rather than tightly meshed scenes, Ngugi creates an atmosphere of sad, undefined urgency in which characters, events, time, place, and conflict "flow into one another" until the play feels like and appears to be "a single movement."

As the play opens, the audience views a crowded courtroom and hears the charges against Kimathi for possessing a revolver. Although the date of this trial is 1956, Kimathi's refusal to plead guilty or not guilty gives way to a mimed pageant of "the Black Man's History," showing Kimathi's silence to be a gesture of disdain for repressive colonial law. As "phases" of the pageant progress, gunshots, voices, whiplashes, and drumbeats fade to a mime of mourning that evokes slavery, orphaned children, forced labor on Kenyan plantations, and black betrayals of the Mau Mau resistance, concluding with defiant shouts of "anti-imperialist slogans."

With the unfolding of the First Movement, the audience is witness to a number of rapidly shifting scenes; they see the inhabitants of a village harassed and arrested for supporting Mau Mau fighters, intimidating interrogation of peasants which is abetted by a black informer, and an important discussion between a Woman and a Boy (a Girl later appears) who are symbolic of the birth of freedom and its hope for the future. Implicit in this First Movement is the African urban, colonial city as an archetype of corruption; the Boy is an orphan, who, with the Girl, hustles tourists in Nairobi and who himself eventually seeks to exploit the Girl for small sums of money. Confronting the Boy's sexist behavior toward the Girl, the Woman redefines manhood as possessing a Socialist, ethical awareness of the country's needs and conflicts. When the Boy agrees to deliver a loaf of bread, containing a gun, to the scene of Kimathi's trial, he does so out of a vivid clarity about his choice of political ideals. The threat to the Woman and the Boy in this Movement is not only from the colonial soldiers but also from the black soldiers, informers, and collaborators, the "black masters" who hope to profit by preserving colonial rule. While Ngugi keeps the play set safely in the 1950's, the premise is obvious to the audience: Present neocolonial corruption in land reform and court decisions began in the Mau Mau period and has continued to thrive in postcolonial Kenya. To attack that corruption will require the courage and dedication of the Mau Mau.

In the Second Movement, scenes move rapidly between the street outside the jail where Kimathi is imprisoned, the courtroom, and Kimathi's cell, in which his four Trials take place. (The cell becomes, in a sense the courtroom, and the courtroom, in turn becomes a cell.) Meanwhile, the historical pageant continues to be mimed in the dimly lit background onstage. In costuming, demeanor, and dialogue, the contrast between the peasants and the elite is pronounced. Kimathi, in his trial, repudiates the double standard of colonial law, favoring, in the Judge's words, "Civilization... Investment... Christianity... [and] Order," and condemns colonially inspired individual betrayals and tribalism. He rejects an offer to spare his life in return for naming fellow Mau Mau, and he refuses a banker's offer to make him wealthy. In rejecting colonial claims of progress and paternalistic benevolence, Kimathi, clearly a spokesman for Ngugi, espouses an anticapitalistic, classless society of laborers who draw upon their own customs for values rather than those of Christianity. In the Movement's closing, Kimathi, suffering from torture and beatings, refuses to surrender or to betray his compatriots.

The Third Movement begins with the Woman clarifying the plan to rescue Kimathi with the Boy and the Girl. She tells them stories that contribute to Kimathi's legendary status, honoring the qualities of his leadership. Thus, the Woman links respect for the oral tradition to qualities necessary for the people's support of a revolutionary leader. The major portion of the Movement consists of a flashback to Kimathi's command in a guerrilla camp in the Nyandarua forest. In long, didactic monologues, Kimathi, in the midst of directing the executions of British and African soldiers, justifies the Mau Mau war with minilectures on the pan-African arms supply to revolutionary movements, preaching self-sufficiency in weaponry, production, and education; the study of the lives of heroes as necessary training to comprehend history; and black pride as the basis for African self-determination. Calling for "unity and discipline in struggle," Kimathi touches on a number of issues, calling for the subordination of the individual's desires to the community's needs and calling explicitly for the implementation of an African Socialist philosophy. As the flashback closes, Kimathi, in a demonstrative act of compassion, spares the lives of several collaborators, among them his younger brother. They escape, however, and flee to the British, to betray the Mau Mau again with their testimony against Kimathi in the closing courtroom scene. When the Woman, having failed in the rescue attempt, is detained, Kimathi is sentenced to hang, and the Boy and the Girl fire their gun as darkness falls on the stage. A moment later, the stage erupts with the Boy and the Girl—the potential of the uneducated masses now having attained a vision of their own wisdom and power from the Woman—leading a crowd of workers and peasants in a freedom song in which the audience is encouraged to participate. The ambiguous end of Kimathi's life is thus downplayed, despite the construction of his legend throughout the play. Instead of merely celebrating a heroic revolutionary leader, the play's conclusion emphasizes a revolutionary spirit that remains potent long after Dedan Kimathi and the Mau Mau resistance have passed away.

Like *The Trial of Dedan Kimathi*, Ngugi's Gikuyu *I Will Marry When I Want* rejected the proscriptions for well-made drama in favor of an indigenous combination of mimed dance, historical realism, social vision, and heroic symbolism. While the former play is passionate in rhetoric and plain in diction, it was accessible only to those who comprehend English, and it was written by playwrights for an audience. *I Will Marry When I Want*, on the contrary, grew not only from Ngugi's collaboration with Ngugi wa Mirii but also from the collective contributions of the Kamiriithu community center. Changes by actors and crew were incorporated into the play both in its script and its performance, as there was much opportunity for improvisation. Consequently, the play includes a greater number of Mau Mau songs and Christian hymns, a much more extensive use of ritual and dance, and many more proverbs and striking images than the earlier play of the same period. Unlike *The Trial of Dedan Kimathi*, *I Will Marry When I Want* is set in contemporary neocolonial Kenya. Further, to a greater extent than does the earlier play, it embraces the entire history of the country—from before the coming

of white settlers to a vision of a just, compassionate society of the future—
centering on the village marriage ceremony as the symbol of a united,
classless society. Ironically, Ngugi's dramas in the 1960's often presented marriage as an emblem of conflict and constraint; in *I Will Marry When I Want*,
marriage is transformed from a deceptive scheme to swindle a poor family
out of its land into an ideal that has the capacity to renew the strength of
traditional family life in contemporary times.

The plot of *I Will Marry When I Want* pits the hypocritical piety of a Christian elite against the dignity and desperation of traditional Gikuyu, who are
forced to work factory shifts or as farm laborers. The elite Ahab Kioi wa
Kanoru and his wife Jezebel wa Kanoru conspire with foreign investors and
Kenyan middlemen to swindle the poor Kiguunda and his wife, Wangeci, out
of their last acre of land by coercing him to use his property as collateral for
a loan to cover the costs of a Christian wedding between Kiguunda's daughter Gathoni and Kioi's son John Muhuuni. Kiguunda's land, on which stands
his one-room house, has been selected for the site of an insecticide factory,
thus keeping it at an agreeable distance from the homes of the wealthy and
near the exploited laborers who will work there. Believing that Kioi plans a
union of the two households, Wangeci condones the wedding, only to learn
that John has abandoned the pregnant Gathoni. When Kiguunda insists on
the marriage, Kioi dismisses them with contempt. When Kiguunda cannot
meet the payments on the loan, he loses his furniture and, presumably, will
eventually lose his house and his land as well. The play closes with Kiguunda
drunk, Gathoni working as a prostitute in a local bar, and Wangeci crushed
by hopelessness.

Both of Ngugi's plays of the 1970's call for adherence to traditional values
in an egalitarian society. Those values, however anchored in the past, must
be adaptable to changing conditions and responsive to the needs of the exploited, or they become only faint memories. Kiguunda's mimicry of Kioi's
hollow Christian piety and his aspirations to the elite's ruthless materialism
are as much responsible for his downfall as is Kioi's merciless conspiracy.
Wangeci, for example, blinded by her own materialism, believes against all
reason that Kioi actually wants to unite their two households. Kiguunda
believes in neither a coherent social vision of freedom and justice nor a
committed life-style of traditional values. Like the earlier betrayal of the
Mau Mau, Kiguunda's betrayal of his own origins and values is a failure of
leadership; Gicaamba, a factory worker and neighbor, provides the contrasting model. He opposes Kiguunda's flirtation with the elite Kioi and, throughout the play, portrays a leader who converts struggle and despair into pride
in human dignity and protest against the elite. Echoed in the communal pageantry of song and dance, these attributes of leadership reverberate in
speech rhythms of free verse, permitting easy identification and empathy by
the audience. The audience, then, views a play wherein they themselves are

the heroic force of social change, a dynamic relationship between stage and audience that evokes the drama of communal commitment overcoming the greedy whims of egocentric power brokers.

Entirely African in its design, *I Will Marry When I Want* represents the enactment of Dedan Kimathi's teaching: "unite, drive out the enemy and control your own riches, enjoy the fruit of your sweat." Ngugi's success as a dramatist is exemplified by the enthusiastic but violent reactions of audiences attending the first few performances before the government banned the play and detained Ngugi. *Mother, Sing for Me*, a musical that explores Kenya's past, was also suppressed. Few playwrights in the history of drama have suffered so for their power to move an audience to action.

Other major works

NOVELS: *Weep Not, Child*, 1964; *The River Between*, 1965; *A Grain of Wheat*, 1967; *Petals of Blood*, 1977; *Caitaani Mutharaba-Ini*, 1980 (*Devil on the Cross*, 1982); *Matigari ma Njiruungi*, 1986 (*Matigari*, 1989).

SHORT FICTION: *Secret Lives and Other Stories*, 1975.

NONFICTION: *Homecoming: Essays on African and Caribbean Literature, Culture, and Politics*, 1972; *Writers in Politics*, 1981; *Detained: A Writer's Prison Diary*, 1981; *Barrel of a Pen: Resistance to Repression in Neo-Colonial Kenya*, 1983; *Decolonising the Mind: The Politics of Language in African Literature*, 1986; *Writing Against Neocolonialism*, 1986.

CHILDREN'S LITERATURE: *Njamba Nene's Pistol*, 1990; *Njamba Nene and the Flying Bus*, 1990.

Bibliography

Cook, David. *African Literature: A Critical View*. London: Longman, 1977. In this careful study of some neglected African literature, Cook deals with Ngugi's *A Grain of Wheat*, in a separate chapter entitled "A New Earth." Cook says of Ngugi that he writes "not in tragic terms but in a positive demonstration that some alternative to mutual destruction is possible for human beings."

Gugelberger, Georg M. "'When Evil-Doing Comes Like Falling Rain': Brecht, Alioum Fantoure, Ngugi wa Thiong'o." *Comparative Literature Studies* 24, no. 4 (1987): 370-386. Presenting a valuable tie-in with Brechtian ideas, Gugelberger cites Ngugi's use of a Bertolt Brecht poem in his prison diary and mentions Brecht's *Leben des Galilei* (1943; *Galileo*, 1947) in Ngugi's essay, "Freedom of the Artist." He points out that "both Brecht and Ngugi are facilitators of social change."

Howard, W. J. "Themes and Development in the Novels of Ngugi." In *The Critical Evaluation of African Literature*, edited by Edgar Wright. London: Heinemann, 1973. Touches on Ngugi's plays and essays but concentrates on the novels. Speaks of *The Black Hermit* as "a play . . . best passed over in silence" but cites the "dramatization" in Ngugi's short stories and novels. Contains a generous discussion of Ngugi's general aesthetic, with long quotations from his prose work.

Ross, Robert L., ed. *International Literature in English: Essays on the Major Writers.* New York: Garland, 1991. G. D. Killam gathers this information on Ngugi, pointing out his progress from *The River Between*, Ngugi's second novel, to *Matigari.* Provides some direct discussion of his plays, especially the portrait of Dedan Kimathi and the "simple folk" of *I Will Marry When I Want.* Contains a strong bibliography of articles in African literature sources.

Sharma, Govind Narain. "Socialism and Civilization: The Revolutionary Traditionalism of Ngugi wa Thiong'o." *Ariel* 19 (April, 1988): 21-30. Offers comments on Ngugi's commitment to Marxism, his contempt for the middle class, and his observations on the Mau Mau Uprising, "the epitome of a revolutionary movement by the peasantry." Deals extensively with *I Will Marry When I Want* and *Devil on the Cross*, dividing African history into a pre- and postimperialist era.

Michael Loudon
(Updated by *Thomas J. Taylor*)

PETER NICHOLS

Born: Bristol, England; July 31, 1927

Principal drama

The Hooded Terror, televised 1963, pr. 1964; *A Day in the Death of Joe Egg*, pr., pb. 1967; *The National Health: Or, Nurse Norton's Affair*, pr. 1969, pb. 1970; *Forget-Me-Not Lane*, pr., pb. 1971; *Neither Up nor Down*, pr. 1972, pb. 1987; *Chez Nous*, pr., pb. 1974; *The Freeway*, pr. 1974, pb. 1975; *Harding's Luck*, pr. 1974 (adaptation of E. Nesbitt's novel); *Privates on Parade*, pr., pb. 1977; *Born in the Gardens*, pr. 1979, pb. 1980; *Passion Play*, pr., pb. 1981; *Poppy*, pr., pb. 1982; *A Piece of My Mind*, pr., pb. 1987; *Plays*, pb. 1987, 1991 (2 volumes).

Other literary forms

Peter Nichols is a prolific writer who is the author of dramatic works for motion pictures and television as well as for the stage. Among his many teleplays are *A Walk on the Grass* (1959), *The Continuity Man* (1963), and *Daddy Kiss It Better* (1969); he has adapted for the small screen works by F. Scott Fitzgerald and Evelyn Waugh. His film scripts include *Georgy Girl* (1966; with Margaret Foster; adaptation of her novel) and an adaptation of his stage play, *The National Health* (1972). In 1984, Nichols published his autobiography, *Feeling You're Behind*.

Achievements

Nichols has risen rather slowly through the ranks of his profession, with even *A Day in the Death of Joe Egg* undergoing limited runs in the initial London and New York productions. Nevertheless, he has become internationally recognized as one of Great Britain's leading playwrights, and his work has entered the standard repertory of professional, university, and community playhouses. His first official support came with an Arts Council Bursary, a small stipend, in 1961. With the first stage productions of his work, the awards began to accrue, including the John Whiting Award in 1969, four *Evening Standard* Best Play awards, two Society of West End Theatres Best Musical awards, the Ivor Novello Award for Best Musical Comedy, and the 1985 Tony Award for Best Revival. Though he has received limited critical attention, Nichols provides a rare blend of popular entertainment and intellectual challenge. Drawing on materials as diverse as English pantomime, military vaudeville, and intimate autobiography, Nichols has created plays with unique theatrical structures and intense, unusually extreme emotional effects. His work from the 1970's has been anthologized as representative of the best in contemporary British drama. Because he has so well captured the spirit of the times and done so in such wide-ranging topics and genres, his place in the history of dramatic literature has been secured.

Biography

Peter Richard Nichols was born and grew up in Bristol, in the generation that went through grammar school in the wake of local hero Cary Grant's rise to fame. Nichols has documented his early years in Bristol in two of his stage plays and, most extensively, in his autobiography, *Feeling You're Behind*. Nichols' family home, Palatine Lodge, was a rambling sort of unfashionable house located across the street from a large boys' orphanage that would serve during the war as an American military barracks. The presence of the orphanage, the example of Cary Grant, and the excitement of the American influx combined in Nichols' upbringing to create an environment that was alternatively either daunting or rife with the potential for upward mobility.

Both of Nichols' parents were performers of a sort. His mother, Violet Poole, had certificates in both piano and voice from the London Academy of Music and tutored students at home during the week. After the war broke out, she began to perform occasionally in service reviews but always when husband Richard, a traveling salesman, was away. The interest her performances aroused in the audience almost led to a split in the family during the war, but Nichols' parents eventually reunited. Richard Nichols was a self-styled musical-hall clown and classical music collector. The monologue passages in *Forget-Me-Not Lane* and the autobiography appear to have been lifted almost verbatim from the bitterly comic routines the elder Nichols rehearsed at home and then used in local club performances. When Peter Nichols first tried his hand at performance, as "the Miserable Mirth Maker" in wartime service reviews, his act owed something to his father's precedent. The strong, eccentric style developed by his father later constituted an important obstacle for the younger Nichols (who also had to overcome his father's admonition that motivation for success should come from making a habit of "feeling you're behind"), until Peter managed to master and use the style for his own effects.

While attending Bristol Grammar School, Nichols cultivated a comic self-image, and his exploits with his best friend, Cliff Browne, a gifted cartoonist, centered on the kind of irreverent ironic invention that would later pepper the sentiment of plays such as *A Day in the Death of Joe Egg*. When Nichols joined the military after the war, however, his attitude shifted; he became a dedicated diarist, trying hard to impress the other servicemen with his sophistication. Stationed in a dismal camp near Calcutta during the Indian independence movement, a melancholy Nichols observed with some detachment the effects of political conflict and mantained the discipline of keeping a journal, as he would for the rest of his life. Transferred to the Royal Air Force (RAF) entertainment unit in Singapore, he worked with mostly male performers, among whom were many homosexuals and transvestites, and he colorfully documented the experience in his musical comedy *Pri-*

vates on Parade. The flamboyance of the entertainment unit and its productions left an impression on Nichols that encouraged bold choices in his later use of theatrical technique.

Nichols was eventually "invalided out" of the service because of repeated bouts with dysentery. On his return to Bristol, he enrolled in the Old Vic theater school and attempted a career in acting. Though he was able to gain occasional roles in local repertory companies, Nichols gradually became disillusioned with acting. First leaving on impulse to teach English for the Berlitz school in Florence, Nichols shortly returned to England and entered teacher training at the Trent Park Training College. There, he met Bernie Cooper, the model for Ben Spray, and began the routine of classes and writing that would continue through his teaching years in the late 1950's and early 1960's. His academic years supplied Nichols with material for a number of television plays as well as parts of later stage works such as *Chez Nous.*

The first break came for Nichols through the British Broadcasting Corporation, and he began writing regularly for television until his *A Day in the Death of Joe Egg.* While his second teleplay was in production, Nichols suffered a collapsed lung and was hospitalized. Through his parents, he was reacquainted with Thelma Reed, a childhood friend of his brother whom he had used as a model for a television character. Her hospital visits led to their marriage in 1960. For the next few years, Nichols settled into a routine of television work and family life, though the latter was increasingly clouded by the realization of his eldest daughter's severe mental disability. When some screenplay work provided Nichols with the money to write daughter Abigail's story, she served as the model for Josephine—Joe Egg—in the play that would launch Nichols' career as a professional theater writer.

In 1967, the year *A Day in the Death of Joe Egg* premiered in Glasgow, Nichols began working steadily, producing a number of important plays, as well as some less successful thesis and autobiographical plays. The major plays have been regularly adapted by Nichols for the screen, and he has also continued to write occasional adaptations and scripts for television. His work for the stage has been generally acclaimed since 1967, when he began working with director Michael Blakemore. Later, Nichols would direct some of his own work, such as the Bristol Old Vic production of *Born in the Gardens* and the Guthrie production of *The National Health.* The intensity and theatrical inventiveness of *A Day in the Death of Joe Egg* continued through a series of plays on social issues and family life that peaked with *Passion Play* and his most accomplished musical, *Poppy.*

Nichols announced his retirement from the stage in 1983, at a relatively early point in his career as a playwright. The decision was regrettable—and apparently not final. His plans to work on a trilogy of novels resulted in an adaptation for the stage in 1987 entitled *A Piece of My Mind,* which chronicles a writer's failure to write in narrative form. Nichols "pre-retirement" plays were collected in two volumes for the Methuen World Dramatists series, and the occasion of their republication offered Nichols an opportunity to comment on the biographical circumstances of their composition and to summarize his work. His own conclusion was that he valued the role of the audience in the theater. One example of this is an incident, Nichols recounts, that occurred during the "performance of *The National Health* when someone in the stalls had a cardiac arrest and, from a stage full of actors robed and masked for a surgical operation, one had to ask, 'Is there a doctor in the house?' " This demonstrates Nichols' unique intuition for opportunities to "cast the audience."

Analysis

Critical analyses of Peter Nichols' major works have emphasized correspondences between events and characters in the plays and the playwright's personal experiences. For the most part, Nichols does not, in fact, write unadorned autobiography. When dealing with autobiographical material, Nichols has been able to bring much passion and insight to his work, but this material has been transformed in every instance by the bold use of theatrical devices. The difference in quality between Nichols' television work and his stage plays comes fundamentally from his skill in manipulating the communicative potential of the theatrical medium and not necessarily from his use of highly personal source material. His ability to sustain complex theatrical structures and to use them to exploit his subject matter makes Nichols unique in a generation of British playwrights that has typically written with great personal reflection and political commitment. Nichols might be considered somewhat conservative in comparison with his more radical peers, yet his use of theatrical resources allows the less controversial subject matter of his plays to have a strong emotional impact on his audiences.

The pattern of biographical reception for Nichols began with the international success of *A Day in the Death of Joe Egg*. Many details from the play were drawn from Nichols' personal experience as the father of a spastic child; his decision to represent such a character onstage had such a strong aesthetic impact at the time that biographical revelations only increased the play's potential for sensationalist responses. The central character within the play, however, is not Joe Egg but Bri, the father, a young schoolteacher, and it is the father's thoughts—in opposition to those of his wife—that direct the course of the play's events. The argument between the married couple over their responsibility to the daughter provides a classically simple dramatic plot that has no biographical parallel; other particular events, such as the attempt to kill the child through exposure, are also inventions.

The play's sense of intimacy in performance comes not so much from the audience's knowledge of the writer's biography as from the use of direct address. Nichols has acknowledged that the demands of expressing the couple's thoughts about their child seemed to defy the kinds of representational strategies he had employed as a writer of realistic television plays. The child herself could not realistically speak, and the characters were dealing with such a taboo subject in such a pressurized personal situation that it seemed implausible that they would express their thoughts openly to one another. Thus, Nichols chose to have the stage figures acknowledge the audience as listeners. This decision motivated a kind of ironic semantic split which has since proved to be the most enduring, characteristic aspect of Nichols' style.

A Day in the Death of Joe Egg begins with a "teacher skit" that Nichols wrote for an impromptu salon audience during his own teaching years. In the skit, the teacher speaks directly to the members of the audience, treating them as his class. This device served as a kind of bridge that allowed the audience gradually to be acknowledged at a time when modern realistic plays seldom did so. The teacher skit dissolves fairly quickly, but the apparent realism into which it dissolves remains pervaded with the trappings of theater: gag spiders, mad doctor bits, intentional comic misinterpretations. When Bri finally returns to soliloquy, the theatrical gesture seems more honest, more stable, than the troubled domestic scene.

The device of splitting the situations and characters into multiple semantic perspectives continues through both acts of the play and represents a kind of structural logic in the play's development. Soon after Bri's first monologue, describing the monotony of his daily life and the revulsion he feels, Sheila gets a chance to tell her side of the story in a pair of extended speeches. The final moment of the act is a *coup de théâtre* of the same order, in which the actress playing Joe Egg skips onstage jumping rope, apparently healthy and normal. The audience realizes that she is merely a projection of Sheila's maternal fantasy when the actress calmly undercuts the childish image with an announcement of the intermission. In the first act, Nichols progressively applies the semantic split between confessional monologue and dishonest realistic behavior, between the character's thoughts and actions, to both Bri and Sheila. Then, when the same device is applied to Joe Egg, there is no inner life to reveal, no consciousness, only an actress embodying a role. In act 2 the realistic action of the play gets split twice again. Because of the intimacy the audience acquired with the leading characters in the first act, it is able to see through the lies and delusions that occur in the parts that follow. The principal events in the second part are two visits, the first by married friends Freddy and Pam, the second by Bri's mother, Grace. These visits gradually intensify both the pressures on the couple to justify their decisions and the audience's sympathy for the couple, who must deal with the heartless, trivial behavior of the other adults. The ironic effect of the realistic dialogue continues through to the play's conclusion, when Sheila has returned with Joe Egg from the hospital after Bri's attempts to allow the child to die. Bri has finally abandoned his wife and child when Sheila has a last witless word with Joe about how devoted her Daddy is. The play ends enigmatically, with the handicapped child alone onstage. The multiple meanings encouraged by the other theatrical devices are finally distilled into the emblematic figure of Joe Egg, hopelessly alive.

The splitting of characters and situations in *A Day in the Death of Joe Egg* causes not only pathos but comedy as well. The same strategy of creating bitter comedy through ironic juxtapositon characterizes the form of Nichols' second major play, *The National Health*. The play draws on Nichols' repeated hospital stays during his military service and when suffering a collapsed lung. Nichols has removed this play more completely from autobiography, however, by adding an independent interior play, a send-up of hospital soap opera. This decision to split the play into two parts is again based on the need to manipulate audience response. The first version of *The National Health* was a realistic television play called *The End Beds*. This play, of which Nichols was particularly proud, was roundly rejected by television producers; they preferred conventional, romantic hospital drama to Nichols' grim, mordant chronicle play. Nichols responded by incorporating both attitudes toward hospital experience into the same play and changing to a theatrical venue where television norms could be viewed with more detachment. With the exception of the title character, the interior play has little contact with the unfolding of the more realistic hospital scenes, yet the principle of comparison deepens and informs the whole work.

A progressive principle applies again as well. When the play begins, there are six beds in the hospital ward; when it ends, there is only one. This image of gradual decay finds reinforcement in many other details, such as the gradual amputation of a cheerful, singing patient's limbs or the discharge of a vigorous young motorcyclist who returns from another accident brain-damaged and helpless. These patterns of progression replace what might ordinarily be considered a plot; each patient's background is sketched and his fate is sealed in the course of the action. The nearest approximation of a main character is Ash, a frustrated teacher with a stomach ulcer who worries himself helping the other patients while undergoing a more gradual decline of his own. His pathetic attempts to educate the helpless cyclist about his British heritage in a closing scene underline a second important irony in the play's title: the equation of the hospital with the failing welfare-state economy of contemporary England.

A third level of theatricality, providing the same kind of bridge between two dramatic levels as the teacher skit in *A Day in the Death of Joe Egg*, exists in the figure of Barnet, a hospital orderly. After his first entrance, in which the lowest man in the hospital, an orderly assigned not to attending the sick but to preparing the dead, has cajoled the ward's patients into good humor, Barnet begins to narrate the story of Staff Nurse Norton—not to the patients but to the theater audience. Barnet, beneath and beyond the hospital's concerns, also delivers a series of macabre monologues that serve to emphasize the difference between conventional representations of hospital life and its grim realities; for example, a comic rundown of his duties serves to mask the disappearance of Rees, one of the most endearing patients, so that his death seems like a successful magic trick. Barnet even provides a running commentary counterpointing the climax of the Nurse Norton melodrama, a spectacular kidney transplant, with the weary, unsuccessful attempts of the hospital staff to resuscitate Foster, another important sympathetic character. At the end of the play, Barnet appears surprisingly in blackface, a device that stresses his purely theatrical identity, and asserts that the audience members are themselves patients of a kind in the national health, not immune to the terrible suffering and humiliation that have befallen those in the hospital ward.

The National Health offers a broader scope on the problems of mercy killing and ethical responsibility explored by *A Day in the Death of Joe Egg*, pointing out that these are not mere personal problems but political issues. Biographical material has been reconstituted in both plays to achieve a layered, communicative structure that allows Nichols' characteristically ironic voice to emerge. The audience is encouraged to use one level of the play's action to see through others, and so the apparently simple situations and language of the plays take on a hidden depth, acquiring an unusual richness in their ability to encourage emotional response. Nichols' next few plays, though sometimes very successful, accomplish less, either because they address a limited range of concerns or because they employ less compelling theatrical techniques.

Forget-Me-Not Lane limits itself almost exclusively to Nichols' troubled memories of his family life. He uses a very flexible theatrical structure, with scenes shifting through three broad time periods, fluidly moving onstage and offstage through a series of hidden doors that constitute the only setting. In *Forget-Me-Not Lane*, this theatrical structure, with its Nichols-like author/narrator providing the usual direct address, serves also to facilitate a more important thesis about the structure of the family. Nichols views the family as a kind of trap, where heredity and the following of role models cause the mistakes of the parents to be repeated by their children, even when such patterns are acknowledged and challenged. The play juxtaposes scenes selected from Nichols' childhood to others from his early married years and his mature years as a parent—the time near his own father's death. Actors double roles, enacting similar events in each time frame to underline the patterns of familial repetition. Nichols deftly orchestrates the shifting scenes, incorporating material from five or more television plays while building slowly to the revelation of the father's death—the son's response to that death. Because the play is so scrupulously attentive to detail, the specific voices and cultural standing of the characters are difficult to translate beyond the time and place of the first British performance. Yet, for those same reasons, Nichols scored one of his largest popular successes in the play's original long-running London production. For critics such as John Russell Taylor, who can fund its themes with a wealth of similar experiences, the play seems to be Nichols' best, summarizing the feelings of an entire generation. From the distance of another culture, however, *Forget-Me-Not Lane* seems extremely eccentric, despite the attraction of its vaudeville elements and the cleverness of its theatrical structure.

Neither Up nor Down, like *The Hooded Terror*, made only a brief appearance onstage and has remained unpublished. The next popular success for Nichols came with *Chez Nous*, the least ambitious of his major works. The play's sensational subject involves an expert on child-rearing whose fourteen-year-old daughter has a child fathered by his closest friend. The two men and their wives undergo some doubts about the choices they have made in the past, but the play fails to arouse either the deep feelings or the theatrical excitement of Nichols' best work. Though his comic touch makes the play entertaining, particularly during a late visit to the expert by two American protégés, Nichols never introduces a specific political, moral, or personal problem with the scope of the earlier works. Unlike Joe Egg, the daughter never comes onstage, and the promising thematic potential of an itinerant French-speaking vagrant is never really exploited. Like Jean Anouilh, to whom he has been compared, Nichols appears to have employed his considerable theatrical talents in some plays written purely for diversion or profit.

The Freeway is Nichols' only attempt at a *pièce à thèse*. Once again, the amount of theatrical invention has been reduced, the only variety coming from the peculiar combination of comrades who are brought together by the national traffic jam serving as the play's premise. The work's most important aspect seems to be Nichols' new emphasis on narrative invention. Unfortunately, the world he imagines and the story he tells in *The Freeway* seem simplistic in comparison to the richness of plays drawn from biographical sources. The sort of futuristic society, based on the motor car, that Nichols uses to frame the action falls somewhere between fantasy and plausibility, satisfying neither sort of expectation. The various characters, intentionally chosen to represent different strata of British society, like their counterparts in *Forget-Me-Not Lane*, tend to lose their effectiveness when shown in another cultural context. The brief run of *The Freeway* in Jonathan Miller's National Theater production was followed shortly after by *Harding's Luck*, a children's story adaptation about the transformation of a crippled child, which must also be considered a minor work.

Privates on Parade, on the other hand, marks a new phase in Nichols' development. Here, the theatrical devices of the early plays combine with the techniques of musical comedy to produce one of the playwright's most dynamic works. The material for the play, a portrait of corruption in a Malaysian service entertainment company, comes from Nichols' postwar duty with a similar RAF troupe. As in the first two stage plays, he has transformed the material, breaking it up with a number of different performance techniques, tinkering with theatrical illusion and simultaneous action and manipulating his medium for the most intense emotional effects. Steve, a leading character loosely based on Nichols, provides a bridge into direct address for the other characters when he narrates his letters home. The military also provides a situation in which a wide variety of social classes can plausibly be put together in the same setting; at the same time, the experience of military service cuts across national boundaries, so that the play is readily accessible to non-British audiences. *Privates on Parade* was extremely successful in its London production, which was once again directed by Michael Blakemore, and will probably age well.

The technical advances which Nichols makes in *Privates on Parade* come in two areas. Most obviously, the switch to a musical comedy form allows another level of action to be introduced in the songs, much like the level provided by direct address in the early plays. Moreover, the freedom of writing lyrics rather than dialogue gives Nichols the chance to comment upon the action from an authorial perspective, whether these comments are directed toward characters and actions in the play or toward the broader political questions that Nichols asks about the nature of British colonialism. The use of music clearly marks this new level of writing for the audience, so Nichols is simply able to add it to the kind of complex theatrical structure he had already employed in his first three stage plays.

The second area of technical advance comes in Nichols' decision to use a theater as the location for much of the action. This choice allows Nichols to crosscut from song numbers directly into dramatic scenes that are frequently rehearsals, creating stinging ironic laughter and dazzling suspense by capitalizing on the audience's confusion between the immediate performance in their own theater and performances that may have some place in the dramatic structure of the play. Here, Nichols splits not only the actors but also the theater building and even the normal concept of the theater. As in his earlier extended pun on the hospital's "operating theater" in *The National Health*, in *Privates on Parade* Nichols uses the conventional machinery of the English drag show to expose the brutality of the "theater of war." In this case, the hackneyed devices being exploited and ridiculed are not those of another form, television, but a juxtapositon of wartime bravado with the decadent cross-dress tradition that has been part and parcel of the popular English theater since before the time of William Shakespeare. The military comes off looking much like the kind of theater it sponsors: ridiculously outdated, empty, ineffectual, and above all, embarrassing.

Compared to *Privates on Parade*, Nichols' next play, *Born in the Gardens*, looks like a retreat. Here, the biographical materials are spread out into a larger, older family than the one so familiar from *Forget-Me-Not Lane* and the television plays. The central character, an elderly widow named Maud, resembles Nichols' mother, but there is no clear biographical parallel for the play's three children. The subject is really Bristol and how life there has changed. Consequently, Nichols chose to direct the first production himself at the Bristol Old Vic, where the slow-moving realistic play was warmly received for its local interest. *Born in the Gardens* reflects interestingly back upon the mother-child relationship in *A Day in the Death of Joe Egg* and complements the biographical plays centering on Nichols' father with an outstanding character study of the old woman. Unlike Nichols' major works, however, this play makes no attempt to explain or analyze the events as they are presented. *Born in the Gardens* shows the other side of the range Nichols has acquired, a naturalistic antithesis to the kind of flamboyant play he is most famous for writing.

Nichols followed this interesting but tangential play with one of his finest works. In *Passion Play*, Nichols took a very common, almost banal, topic, marital infidelity, and illuminated it through the clever use of a few theatrical devices. The most striking of these is his decision to introduce, at the point where each partner begins to lie to the other, a second stage figure for the character—one that the spouse cannot see or hear. Each character's double then serves as a kind of passionate alter ego: James spins off a Jim, while Eleanor acquires Nell. These new figures function like conventional whispering temptation figures, arguing in opposition to the consciences of the original characters. This device, quite old, has also been employed by modern writers such as Eugene O'Neill, Bertolt Brecht, and Brian Fricl. Nichols uses the split masterfully, overlapping scenes and dialogue where the characters contradict one another's actions to create his usual blend of comedy, bitterness, and suspense. One might even suggest that Nichols wrote the play only for the sake of the trick's theatrical potential and not out of any interest in the subject or its resolution, for he notes that the play might well end with either Nell or Eleanor leaving the house. *Passion Play* seems to lack any specific biographical parallels; Nichols' lack of commitment to the resolution probably stems from a lack of personal commitment to the material itself.

The other devices that Nichols employs show the lessons he learned from *Privates on Parade*. Rather than writing musical numbers of his own, Nichols chooses to make Eleanor a singer of classical music. This characterization allows Nichols to quote liberally from music associated with Christ's Passion and (as the punning title suggests) to ask some important questions about the relation of Christian moral norms to the challenge of human sexual desire. Similarly, Nichols makes James a restorer of modern paintings, allowing frequent allusions to art history that reinforce the same themes. For a playwright with Nichols' skill in the manipulation of audience response, such a topic provides ideal material: Temptation and passion are as universal as pledges of fidelity, and when treated with the kind of riveting theatricality that Nichols can conjure, the aesthetic response called up becomes unusually intense and fulfilling. *Passion Play*, because of its accessibility and adept use of the medium, has become Nichols' most popular work.

Poppy, the last stage work before Nichols announced his "retirement," may be the most accomplished of all of his plays. A musical comedy, *Poppy* draws on a unique set of theatrical resources to create a scathing seriocomic indictment of the imperial British opium wars. In a fairy tale gone wrong, Nichols presents the voyage of Dick Whittington, his merchant partner, his manservant, his mother, and his ward to Asia, where they propose to make their fortunes. A number of things go wrong with this ideal scenario: The fortunes will be made through a combination of evangelism and opium trading; Dick's ward, a schoolmistress who loves him, learns that she is his illegitimate half sister and becomes an opium addict; the efforts of the Chinese rulers to resist exploitation result in civil conflicts and eventually in their defeat by British gunboats. *Poppy* shows a strong commitment by Nichols to demonstrate the havoc wrought by the British empire overseas, inasmuch as the empire was built not on Christian values or on British forthrightness but on greed and deception.

The theatrical potpourri that Nichols uses to make his point is probably his most ambitious mixture ever. With a nod to W. S. Gilbert and Sir Arthur Sullivan's *The Mikado: Or, The Town of Titipu* (1885), Nichols utilizes conventional British images of the Orient in combination with the form and figures of the holiday pantomime. Unusual turns such as a 1950's-style newsreel report on nineteenth century India are deftly woven into the presentation, while the typical splitting of characters occurs in the cross-dressing of pantomime principals (Dick Whittington is a long-legged girl) and bits such as Queen Victoria's transformations into a statue of herself and a fortune figure. Story integrates with means of representation when Sally, the principal girl, is unable to marry her half brother, who is also played by a woman. The genius of the work comes in the way Nichols uses the traditional machinery of British imperial theater forms to expose the ideology of British imperialism. Tensions within the forms, such as cross-dressed stage figures and chauvinistic choruses, are exploited to reveal the decadence in the culture that created them. All this happens in a colorful spectacle that children might enjoy in the same way that they innocently enjoy a typical innuendo-ridden British pantomime. *Poppy* elevates the theme of innocence-gone-wrong to a national level and employs the materials of the nation's cherished "innocent" performances, holiday entertainments, to make its point.

Nichols' *A Piece of My Mind*, which marked his return to the stage after a five-year absence, moves his autobiographical method out of his obsessive memories of adolescence and into a concern with the struggles of a mature writer with his literary form, his personal limitations, and his rivals. Like *Forget-Me-Not Lane*, the play uses doubling of parts and shifts through time and place, movements in and out of character. The story, about a man who retires from playwriting to work on an autobiographical novel, closely parallels Nichols' life. Moreover, the rival writers bear resemblance to contemporary British playwrights Charles Wood and Tom Stoppard. The result is a Pirandellian collage of fact and fantasy, truth and fiction, that allows the technical virtuosity of Nichols to shine while underscoring it with a primary theme of failure. In *A Piece of My Mind*, Nichols continues to work with the tools and themes of his best plays, providing a balance between formalist effect and painful confession that confirms his status as a leading writer of ironic comedy.

A *Piece of My Mind* embraces Nichols' self-consciousness not only as a writer who uses personal material to write his plays but also as a figure in contemporary culture whose every word is received in the context of his prior achievements. An early scene centers on an article in a reference book, which reports that the play's hero had died of a tumor four years earlier, on April Fools' Day; as the writer in *A Piece of My Mind*, Ted, explains it to his wife, he was suffering from a depression over the opening of his last play, so he pretended to be his own executor and sent in the biosheet announcing his own death. Yet there is nothing solipsistic about the spirit of Nichols' play; the jokes are clean and humorous, the ironic self-perception as cruel and original as in any of his earlier plays. Like the late plays of Jean Anouilh, or Tom Stoppard's *The Real Thing* (pr., pb. 1983), Nichols' *A Piece of My Mind* turns the theater in upon itself to reveal the fundamental values of the people who make it and try to live with the memory of its vanished performances. The play seethes with quotations, rigged entrances and exits, and inventive bits of writing. Since it never pretends to be more than the shadow of earlier works, it becomes a remarkably vivid shadow.

The final impression of Nichols' work must include not only a high estimation of his technical abilities as a theatrical writer but also an appreciation of his traditional humanism. Nichols consistently argues for mercy in a secular world and does so in a way that typically avoids naïveté and maudlin sentiment. The laughter in his plays is not usually silly but based on a kind of intellectual recognition that there is some overlooked truth behind the way people ordinarily behave. In his domestic plays as well as his more political musical comedies, Nichols appeals for understanding rather than violence, for comprehension rather than conformity. He notes

the danger of getting seduced by laughter for its own sake. But if understanding is the end of it all, or you manage to make the audience share your world view for a moment, or give them a glimpse of things they wouldn't have seen if they hadn't gone to the theater, then you've achieved something through laughter.

With such a point of view, Nichols cannot be dismissed as a merely "commercial" writer. He has created plays that entertain, but they often draw the spectators in only to challenge them, to encourage them to face themselves and their institutions from a new, more skeptically honest and intelligent vantage point.

Other major works

NONFICTION: *Feeling You're Behind: An Autobiography*, 1984.

SCREENPLAYS: *Catch Us If You Can*, 1965 (U.S. edition, *Having a Wild Weekend*, 1965); *Georgy Girl*, 1966 (with Margaret Foster; adaptation of her novel); *Joe Egg*, 1971 (adaptation of his stage play *A Day in the Death of Joe Egg*); *The National Health*, 1972; *Privates on Parade*, 1983 (adaptation of his stage play); *Changing Places*, 1984 (adaptation of David Lodge's novel).

TELEPLAYS: *A Walk on the Grass*, 1959; *After All*, 1959 (with Bernie Cooper); *Promenade*, 1959; *Ben Spray*, 1961; *The Reception*, 1961; *The Big Boys*, 1961; *The Heart of the County*, 1962; *The Continuity Man*, 1963; *Ben Again*, 1963; *The Hooded Terror*, 1963; *The Brick Umbrella*, 1964; *When the Wind Blows*, 1965; *The Gorge*, 1968; *Majesty*, 1968 (adaptation of F. Scott Fitzgerald's short story); *Winner Takes All*, 1968 (adaptation of Evelyn Waugh's short story); *Daddy Kiss It Better*, 1969; *Hearts and Flowers*, 1970; *The Common*, 1973.

Bibliography

Bryden, Ronald. "Playwright Peter Nichols: The Comic Laureate of Bad Taste?" *The New York Times*, November 10, 1974, p. 5. Bryden and Nichols explain how the comic effects in Nichols' first stage plays are designed to help people think and feel more acutely. This article demonstrates the clarity of Nichols' thoughts about theatricality and begins to define his characteristic style.

Davison, Peter. *Contemporary Drama and the Popular Dramatic Tradition in England.* Totowa, N.J.: Barnes & Noble Books, 1982. Davison surveys the use of popular theater in Nichols' plays up to *Privates on Parade*, arguing for the complexity and value of his artistic achievement. From this essay, it seems clear that Nichols is so unusually adept at manipulating popular materials that his use of sources sometimes goes unnoticed.

Foulkes, Richard. "The Cure Is Removal of Guilt: Faith, Fidelity, and Fertility in the Plays of Peter Nichols." *Modern Drama* 29 (June, 1986): 207-215. Foulkes reviews the marital themes in *A Day in the Death of Joe Egg*, *Chez Nous*, and *Passion Play*, arguing for a common psychological pattern in all three plays' central characters. Contains strong psychological criticism, which does not reduce the author's consciousness to the same simple outline.

Miller, Brian. "Peter Nichols." In *British Television Drama*, edited by George W. Brandt. New York: Cambridge University Press, 1981. The only survey of Nichols' many excellent television plays, well researched, with a modest appraisal of the material. Nichols clearly excelled at television writing in relation to other writers, and that achievement puts his theatrical skills in a new context, arguing for the diversity of his talents.

Nichols, Peter. "Peter Nichols on His Art, Politics, and Peers: An Interview." Interview by William Demastes. *Journal of Dramatic Theory and Criticism* 3 (Fall, 1988): 101-112. Nichols answers questions about his writing, his politics, and his position in the writing community, issues similar to those that later preoccupy him in *A Piece of My Mind*. Demastes does a thorough job of positioning Nichols in relation to other English dramatists.

Schleuter, June. "Adultery Is Next to Godlessness: Dramatic Juxtaposition in Peter Nichols' *Passion Play*." *Modern Drama* 24, no. 4 (1981): 540-545. Schleuter provides a close reading of *Passion Play*'s structure and principal themes, in what is probably the most comprehensive discussion of a play by Nichols. Particularly useful are her notes on the integration of the paintings with the story and the dramatic form.

Wertheim, Albert. "The Modern British Homecoming Play." *Comparative Drama* 19, no. 2 (1985): 151-165. Considers *Born in the Gardens* in relation to themes in plays by T. S. Eliot, Harold Pinter, and David Storey. The analysis takes for granted Nichols' excellence and demonstrates the traditional quality of even his most personal writings.

Michael L. Quinn

MARSHA NORMAN

Born: Louisville, Kentucky; September 21, 1947

Principal drama

Getting Out, pr. 1977, pb. 1978; *Third and Oak*, pr. 1978, pb. 1985 (includes *The Laundromat*, pb. 1980, 1985, and *The Pool Hall*, pb. 1985); *Circus Valentine*, pr. 1979; *The Hold-up*, pr. 1980, pb. 1987; *'night, Mother*, pr. 1982, pb. 1983; *Traveler in the Dark*, pr. 1984, pb. 1988; *Sarah and Abraham*, pr. 1987; *Four Plays*, pb. 1988; *The Secret Garden*, pr. 1991; *D. Boone*, pr. 1992.

Other literary forms

Though known primarily as a playwright, Marsha Norman began her career as a journalist, writing a number of highly regarded feature articles and reviews of books, plays, and films for the *Louisville Times* in the mid-1970's. During this same period, she created and edited that newspaper's celebrated children's weekend supplement, "The Jelly Bean Journal." She has continued to write reviews as well as articles on playwrights and on women's issues. Her first novel, *The Fortune Teller*, appeared in 1987.

Achievements

Norman's abilities as a playwright were first recognized in 1977 by Jon Jory, director of the Festival of New Plays, Actors Theatre of Louisville. Her first major play, *Getting Out*, was cowinner of the Actors Theatre's playwriting prize. Norman's other awards include the John Gassner New Playwright's Medallion (1979), the George Oppenheimer *Newsday* Playwriting Award (1979), and grants from the National Endowment for the Arts, the Rockefeller Foundation, and the American Academy and Institute of Letters. Her masterwork, *'night, Mother*, won the 1983 Pulitzer Prize in drama, the prestigious Hull-Warriner Award, the Susan Smith Blackburn Prize, and four Tony Award nominations. Norman also received a Tony Award and a Drama Desk Award for her Broadway musical *The Secret Garden*. She has been playwright-in-residence at the Actors Theatre of Louisville and the Mark Taper Forum in Los Angeles and has been elected to membership in the American Academy of Achievement.

Norman is known for her ability to write compellingly about the psychic pain of ordinary, often inarticulate, and generally forgotten people. Inevitably, she seizes upon the single moment of greatest crisis in the lives of these people, that which allows them to rise to their greatest nobility. Though she is from the South, she makes every effort to create characterizations and settings that rise above regionalism to stand as contemporary and universal.

Biography

Marsha Williams Norman was born on September 21, 1947, in Louisville, Kentucky. She was a solitary child, and she inevitably cites childhood loneliness as having led to writing as a profession. Her mother, a Fundamentalist Methodist, did not believe that the local children were "good enough," and so Norman spent her childhood reading, practicing piano, and playing with "Bettering," an imaginary friend, in her Audubon Park, Kentucky, home. A high school essay entitled "Why Do Good Men Suffer?" earned first prize in a local contest and was subsequently published in the *Kentucky English Bulletin.*

Norman's earliest works, whimsical reviews and essays published in the 1970's, appeared in local newspapers. Her most widely read pieces appeared in the *Louisville Times* starting in 1976 in "The Jelly Bean Journal," a weekend children's supplement which she created for that newspaper. It was only after Jory asked her to write a serious play that Norman recalled her counseling experiences with disturbed adolescents at Kentucky Central State Hospital (perhaps also the psychological imprisonment of her own childhood) and wrote *Getting Out.* This play was staged successfully by the Actors Theatre in 1977 and enjoyed Los Angeles and New York runs. Her most widely known play, *'night, Mother*, has been translated into twenty-three languages and was produced as a film. *Third and Oak* achieved success in Louisville in its Actors Theatre production; Robert Altman directed the first half of that play, *The Laundromat*, for a Home Box Office production. *Traveler in the Dark* received mixed reviews when presented by the American Repertory Theatre in Boston, but her musical *The Secret Garden* was successful on Broadway. *Sarah and Abraham* premiered at the Actors Theatre in 1987 and was produced at the George Street Playhouse in the fall of 1991. Her later play *D. Boone* premiered in 1992 at the Actors Theatre Humana Festival.

Norman's personal life changed greatly in the late 1970's, a period corresponding to her earliest theatrical success. Her first marriage, to Michael Norman, ended in divorce in 1974, and in November, 1978, she married Dann C. Byck, Jr., a Louisville businessman with an interest in the theater. After their marriage, Byck increasingly involved himself in theatrical production and support of Norman's work. The couple moved to New York despite Norman's apprehensions that Manhattan life would make her writing more difficult; in the event, Norman's most critically acclaimed works have all been written in New York. Norman continued to serve on the boards of the New York Foundation for the Arts and the Independent Committee for Arts Policy and to carry out her responsibilities as treasurer of the Council of the Dramatists Guild. Yet she remained closely associated with the Actors Theatre of Louisville, where her plays often open.

Her work as a dramatist led Norman to write for television, and two of her teleplays, *It's the Willingness* (1980), for the Public Broadcasting Service series *Visions*, and *In Trouble at Fifteen* (1980), for the National Broadcasting Company series *Skag*, were popularly acclaimed. Indeed, it is probably true that Norman finds television such a congenial medium for her writing because of her gift in portraying the problems of ordinary and forgotten people. Though it is difficult to make definite judgments at this stage of Norman's career, it is clear that she is a playwright with an unusual gift for writing spare and taut dialogue and that her plays address the concerns of a very broad audience.

Analysis

Marsha Norman's plays often have small casts and deal with a single moment of overwhelming importance for the protagonist. The dramatic conflict centers on the recognition of this problem and its resolution. Though this does not seem very different from the pattern of classical drama, Norman's plays focus on some difficulty which relates to the inner life of the protagonist. In consequence, her dramas depend greatly on dialogue rather than stage action, physical movement, or change of scene. They are often the cathartic conversations of ordinary people, given in simple language and without learned allusions but nevertheless profound, because they mirror the unexpressed thoughts of many individuals. Normally inarticulate, often nondescript protagonists find hidden strength and depth of feeling they had never before recognized in themselves, and they face their problems with determination. The solution is often a radical one. Though the outcome may be tragic, the central character is usually personally triumphant.

Getting Out, for example, deals with the difficulties of Arlene Holsclaw, a newly released parolee who served an eight-year prison term for robbery, kidnapping, and manslaughter. Eight years have greatly changed her, but she must still come to terms with her past as well as face an uncertain future. Her past is first represented by Arlie, her younger and uncontrolled self, that part of her capable of the earlier crimes. Played by a second actress, Arlie literally invades Arlene's shabby apartment on the first day of Arlene's new freedom. Arlie is foulmouthed, crude, and defiant in contrast to Arlene's attempt to be quiet, reserved, and self-confident. The alter ego declares that Arlene is not really free, that Arlene remains a prisoner to her younger self, and that this other part of her will surface again.

Though Arlene manages to quell Arlie, she is tormented by three other symbols of her past: a guard Arlene knew in prison who is concerned only with seducing her; her mother, who succeeds in revealing that she is domineering and selfish; and a former pimp who tries to enlist Arlene's help in supporting his addiction. The drama's tension mounts as Arlene, who could be destroyed at any moment, faces each of these temptations. She realizes that "getting out," winning personal freedom, must be accomplished by oneself and that psychological prisons are the most difficult to escape. Norman always mentions in interviews the feelings of isolation and terror she had while writing the play, that *Getting Out* represented her own emotional release.

The play was much acclaimed in its 1977 Actors Theatre production in Louisville; it was voted best new play produced by a regional theater by the American Theatre Critics Association, and it was published in extract in *The Best Plays of 1977-78* (1980), the first non-New York production ever so honored. *Getting Out* was given an Off-Broadway production at Marymount-Manhattan Theatre in the Phoenix Theatre's 1978-1979 season as well as a revival in May, 1979, at the Theatre De Lys, which ran eight months with highly favorable notices.

Third and Oak comprises a pair of one-act plays which explore psychological terrain similar to that of *Getting Out.* In *The Laundromat*, a widow and a woman trapped in a loveless marriage meet by chance in a local laundromat and fall into a discussion of the ironic similarity of their lives. Both desperately need love, though neither can find it. As she would often do subsequently, Norman imposes a strict time limit on conversation and action, as long as it takes to finish a week's washing, and the commonplace setting further highlights the banality of her characters' lives. *The Pool Hall*, the second half of *Third and Oak*, takes the form of a parallel conversation between the owner of the hall and the son of a famous pool shark. It similarly deals with personal frustrations and unrealized hopes. *Third and Oak* was the major success of the Actors Theatre's 1978 season, but, more important, it marks a further development of the kinds of characterizations and situations typical in Norman's plays and anticipates the playwright's great achievement *'night, Mother.*

The simple language and ordinary women presented in *'night, Mother* contrasts with the magnitude of the question with which it deals: whether a woman presumably in control of her life can rationally and with dignity end it if she chooses. Jessie Cates is, accordingly, typical of many suicide victims. She has no compelling or overwhelming crisis in her life at the time she chooses to end it. It is simply that she recognizes her life's mediocrity and tedium. Significantly, she blames neither herself nor anyone else for the failure of her marriage or the delinquency of her son. Indeed, she calmly tells her mother, Thelma Cates, what she plans to do, not to be dissuaded but to allow Thelma to understand better why she wants to die and to satisfy her mother's last wants.

Thelma has turned off her television set on the night of her daughter's suicide, no doubt the first time she has changed her usual routine in many evenings. The irony is that it has taken the crisis of Jessie's imminent suicide to force her into frank conversation with her daughter. Apparently, Thelma's life is as unfulfilling as her daughter's, but it is clear Thelma will never take her own life. She seems content with her small house, her sweets, her insipid friendships, and the superficial contacts she has with her son and daughter-in-law. Clearly, Norman has isolated a genuine paradox of the modern world: Crisis or impending catastrophe seems required for simple conversation; communication is otherwise limited to trivialities or sacrificed to television.

Her mother learns more about Jessie in her final ninety-minute conversation with her daughter than she has in a lifetime. The modern world ironically sets a premium on time; Norman emphasizes this with onstage clocks set at real time, 8:15 P.M. at the beginning of the performance, and running to the time of Jessie's suicide just before 10:00 P.M. Jessie makes repeated references to the time, particularly when her conversation with her mother falls into trivialities or becomes repetitive. Jessie's last act is to bequeath her wristwatch to her son. She is determined to kill herself on this evening, while she is in relative control of her own life. She is, therefore, certain that it is a rational decision, not influenced by her epilepsy or depression concerning her failed marriage or delinquent son.

The play has only two characters: Jessie and Thelma. Their conversation takes place in the small living room of Thelma's house, a room filled with Thelma's possessions: magazines, candy dishes, afghans, quilts, and other examples of Thelma's needlework. The house is cluttered but comfortable, and it is clearly Thelma's: Nothing is clearly identifiable as Jessie's. She does not even own the gun with which she kills herself.

Jessie is in her late thirties or early forties and seems pale and physically unsteady. She has come through a difficult period following her illness and divorce but now seems in complete control. She is systematic and disciplined in her behavior, and the lists she writes, the pencil behind her ear, and the arrangements she makes throughout the play for Thelma's comfort serve to confirm that her decision to take her life, announced to her mother at the play's outset, is both rational and carefully considered.

Thelma is in her late fifties or early sixties and has begun to feel her age. She allows Jessie to do even the simplest tasks for her. Indeed, without realizing it, she has become inordinately dependent on her daughter. The audience, accordingly, comes to realize that the real objections Thelma has to Jessie's suicide involve her concern for herself, not her daughter. By the play's end, it is clear that Jessie, despite her younger age, shows far greater maturity than her mother.

The conversation between Thelma and Jessie which forms this play is a confrontation of life and death. While nearly all the audience obviously will choose life, it is ironic that Thelma clearly loses the argument with her daughter. She is never able to give Jessie a solid reason for continuing a life so obviously unsatisfactory.

Yet it is a tribute to Norman's skill that she allows her audience to reach its own, albeit inevitable, conclusions about Jessie and Thelma. Aside from the plot's requirement that they live somewhere outside town, Thelma's house could be in any section of the country. Though nothing is said about their educational attainments, it is clear that neither woman is intellectually inclined. Jessie has the greater sensitivity and potential, but her inability to realize this potential is the very thing that causes her suicide.

Norman writes all of her plays about largely forgotten people, individuals whose lives seem small, perhaps even mean, but who, faced with some large and overwhelming problem, rise to their own variety of eloquence. It is for this reason that Norman keeps the dialogue simple in the extreme. There are few extended speeches and little that is philosophical. She does not intend her play as a polemic on the place of suicide in the modern world, and the audience correspondingly views Jessie and Thelma as fully individualized characters. Though this violates a norm of classical tragedy, it intensifies the drama, because the audience, while not admitting the inevitability or irreversibility of Jessie's decision, remains intent on discovering just what provoked it.

Norman has always maintained that it was precisely because she had no models that she came so late to drama. Nevertheless, it is clear from her studies at New York's Center for Understanding Media that she is a serious student of the theater in addition to being one of its most important developing playwrights. Her style is taut and spare, like that of Samuel Beckett, though her settings and characters are realistic. She deals easily with psychological questions, as in *Getting Out*, in which a young woman moves easily between Arlene, her present self, and Arlie, the girl who committed the murder which sent her to prison.

Both *The Hold-up*, about would-be cowboys at the beginning of the twentieth century in New Mexico, and *Traveler in the Dark*, about a brilliant surgeon unable to cope with the death of his closest coworker, retain this close psychological scrutiny of characters in pain, using dialogue that is witty and eloquent by turns. Throughout her work, Norman shows an interest in fundamental human relationships as fired in the crucible of both familial and generational conflict. All of her characters, in their own way, are struggling to survive, to find some inner strength to cope with the disabling emotions that their situation inevitably provokes. With similarities in both themes and technique, Norman's work fits easily into the traditional canon of American drama that includes such playwrights as Lillian Hellman, Tennessee Williams, and Arthur Miller, to whom she is often compared.

Other major works

NOVEL: *The Fortune Teller*, 1987.

TELEPLAYS: *It's the Willingness*, 1980; *In Trouble at Fifteen*, 1980; *The Laundromat*, 1985.

Bibliography

Betsko, Kathleen, and Rachel Koenig, eds. *Interviews with Contemporary Women Playwrights.* New York: Beech Tree Books, 1987. The most wide-ranging and useful of the many interviews Norman has granted since winning the Pulitzer Prize in 1983. Topics include Norman's problems with critics, her move to New York, the influence of music on her work, her rules of playwriting, and her thoughts on issues of concern to feminist writers.

Dolan, Jill. *The Feminist Spectator as Critic.* Ann Arbor, Mich.: UMI Research Press, 1988. In an important work, Dolan uses Norman's *'night, Mother* to show how more traditional plays by women, through claims of universality, gain acceptance into a male-dominated canon. Dolan questions the particular precedents set for other contemporary women playwrights by Norman's mainstream success.

Hart, Lynda. "Doing Time: Hunger for Power in Marsha Norman's Plays." *Southern Quarterly* 25 (Spring, 1987): 67-79. Beginning with Norman's own comments about her work, Hart traces Norman's complex use of food and hunger imagery to capture the struggle for both nurturance and independence that her characters experience. Such image patterns are crucial to understanding the mother-daughter relationships in Norman's plays.

Keyssar, Helene. *Feminist Theatre: An Introduction to Plays of Contemporary British and American Women.* New York: Grove Press, 1985. In a chapter titled "Success and Its Limits," Keyssar considers Norman along with five other women whose work has gained recognition on the American stage. Special attention is given to *'night, Mother*, which won a Pulitzer Prize.

McDonnell, Lisa J. "Diverse Similitude: Beth Henley and Marsha Norman." *Southern Quarterly* 25 (Spring, 1987): 95-104. In an issue devoted to Southern playwrights, McDonnell examines the work of Henley and Norman, who gained recognition at the same time. Despite their similar gifts for storytelling, gothic humor, use of language, and focus on family, McDonnell finds notable differences in both the styles and world-views of the two playwrights.

Simon, John. "Theatre Chronicle: Kopit, Norman, and Shepard." *The Hudson Review* 32 (Spring, 1979): 78-88. Simon finds the link between three diverse plays that appeared in the same season—Arthur Kopit's *Wings* (pr. 1978), Sam Shepard's *Buried Child* (pr. 1978), and Norman's *Getting*

Out—in the playwrights' powerful visual imagery and exploration of fragmented selves. Simon describes *Getting Out*, with its subtle characterizations and innovative stage techniques, as an "astonishing first play."

Spencer, Jerry S. "Marsha Norman's She-Tragedies." In *Making a Spectacle: Feminist Essays on Contemporary Women's Theatre*, edited by Lynda Hart. Ann Arbor: University of Michigan Press, 1989. This article compares Norman's first three women-centered plays: *Getting Out, The Laundromat*, and *'night, Mother*. Despite the characters' differing and sometimes successful coping strategies, they are forced to act within the limited space traditionally offered women in tragedy.

_____. "Norman's *'night, Mother*: Psycho-Drama of Female Identity." *Modern Drama* 30 (September, 1987): 364-375. Attempting to account for differences in male and female reponses to *'night, Mother*, Spencer suggests that Norman's play is as much about issues particular to women as it is a play about suicide or death. Using feminist theory, Spencer closely analyzes the mother-daughter dynamic without suggesting that the play is overtly political.

Wolfe, Irmgard H. "Marsha Norman: A Classified Bibliography." *Studies in American Drama, 1945-Present* 3 (1988): 149-175. A brief general introduction to Norman, followed by an extensive bibliography of critical resources, interviews, and reviews of Norman's work through 1988. Of special interest are reviews of international and regional productions, newspaper articles and essays written by Norman, a list of unpublished screenplays, and several academic articles.

Robert J. Forman
(Updated by *Jerry S. Spencer*)

THOMAS NORTON and THOMAS SACKVILLE

Thomas Norton

Born: London, England; 1532
Died: Bedfordshire, England; March 10, 1584

Thomas Sackville

Born: Buckhurst, England; 1536
Died: London, England; April 19, 1608

Principal drama

Gorboduc, pr. 1561, pb. 1565 (authorized edition pb. 1570; also as *The Tragedy of Ferrex and Porrex*).

Other literary forms

Thomas Norton contributed verse to the miscellany of Richard Tottel, *Songs and Sonnets* (1557), one of the most widely read collections of English poetry in the entire Renaissance. In 1561, Norton translated John Calvin's final version of *Institutes of the Christian Religion*, completed only a few years before, and in 1562, he turned twenty-eight psalms into metric versions for the collection of Thomas Sternhold and John Hopkins. Norton also wrote a number of religious pamphlets. As a writer, however, he is remembered almost exclusively for his part in *Gorboduc*.

Thomas Sackville showed considerable early promise as a poet. For the second edition of the famed *A Mirror for Magistrates* (1563), Sackville provided the "Induction" and one of the tragic laments, "The Complaint of Henry, Duke of Buckingham." Both poems are in rhyme royal, a stanza of seven lines of iambic pentameter rhyming *ababbcc*.

The "Induction" recounts a Dantesque journey into Hell. As a bitterly cold night falls on a desolate winter countryside, Sackville, pondering the mutability of all living things, muses particularly on the tragic falls of great men in England and wishes that someone would describe their tragedies in order to warn the living to avoid the mistakes of the dead. Suddenly, the pitiful figure of Sorrow, a goddess, appears to lead him into the underworld, where they pass such allegorical figures as Remorse, Misery, Sleep (for whom Sackville composes some of his most beautifully poetic lines), Death, and War before reaching the area where they encounter the ghost of Henry Stafford, Duke of Buckingham. The second poem, Buckingham's lament, begins at this point; in it, the duke admits to the crimes he helped Richard III commit on his way to the throne, but he says that he turned against the tyrant and tried to overthrow him. The failure of his enterprise he furiously blames on the common people who deserted him, and he utters terrible curses against one of his own men, Humphrey Banaster, who ultimately betrayed him to Richard. Then, his energy almost spent, Buckingham warns magistrates to learn a lesson from his fall and to rule their subjects wisely and well.

Achievements

The only achievement of Norton and Sackville in drama consists of their collaboration in *Gorboduc*, first performed at one of the Inns of Court, the Inner Temple, on January 6, 1561, where it was enough of a success to gain a second performance, before Queen Elizabeth, on January 18 at Whitehall. The title page of the first printed edition (1565) credits Norton with the first three acts and Sackville with the final two. Although that volume was a piracy, most modern scholars accept the ascription with the reservation that, based on internal evidence, Sackville appears to be the more likely author of the opening scene of act 1 and Norton, the more probable author of the final scene in the play.

The influence of *Gorboduc* is evident from the fact that a second blank-verse tragedy, the *Jocasta* (pr. 1566) of George Gascoigne and Francis Kinwelmershe, appeared at one of the Inns of Court, Gray's Inn, during 1566, the next year after the initial publication of *Gorboduc*. Within the next thirty years, English writers would produce many other tragedies, and a large number of these would contain the unrhymed iambic pentameter first introduced into drama by Norton and Sackville; blank verse would also appear in hundreds of comedies, histories, and other types of plays.

In addition to being a tragedy, *Gorboduc* is also a history play, for the English accepted the story of King Gorboduc, which had been recounted in the twelfth century in Geoffrey of Monmouth's *Historia Regum Britanniae* (1148), as a factual part of their nation's past. Some scholars claim that *Gorboduc* was the first English history play, but that honor surely belongs to John Bale's *King Johan* (pb. 1538), which obviously developed from the medieval morality play tradition. The real significance of *Gorboduc* in the development of the historical drama may be that it was the first English history free from the intrusive abstractions of the morality play.

Norton has no other significant literary achievements, but Sackville does. Sackville has been the recipient of much critical praise for his writing of the "Induction" to the second edition of *A Mirror for Magistrates*, one of the most popular of Elizabethan works. The "Induction" introduces "The Complaint of Henry, Duke of Buckingham," which Sackville also penned. Although Buckingham's lament has always been considered inferior to the "Induction," it also contains a number of fine passages, such as that in which Alexander laments the death of Clitus. Praise for Sackville's poems began in his own century, and included compliments from Thomas Campion, Edmund Spenser, and many others. In more recent centuries the acclaim has continued, culminating in George Saintsbury's famous assertion that Sackville was the author of the best English poetry to appear between the death of Geoffrey Chaucer and the flowering of Spenser.

The full measure of Sackville's achievement and of his promise as a poet may be appreciated if recent theories about the date of composition for the poems are correct. Several scholars have argued for a date as early as 1554 or 1555. If they are correct, then the lavish praise of Saintsbury and others has been given to the work of a poet not yet out of his teens.

Biography

Thomas Norton, born in 1532, was a member of a wealthy London family associated with the Grocer's Company. While still quite young, he entered the household of Lord Somerset, the Protector, proving himself a very intelligent youth and serving that important nobleman well as amanuensis. Some of Norton's Calvinist ideas were formulated while he served under Somerset; as early as 1552, Norton corresponded with John Calvin.

The lives of Thomas Norton and Thomas Sackville, four years Norton's junior, touched each other several times during their careers. The first such occasion perhaps came in 1555, when they both entered the Inner Temple to study law, of which Norton later made a successful career, serving as counsel for the Stationers' Company and later as solicitor for the Merchant Taylors' Company.

Norton married twice, both times to relatives of Archbishop Thomas Cranmer: first to a daughter, Margery, then to a cousin, Alice. Cranmer was burned by the Catholics in 1556, the year after Norton had married Margery. In the latter part of his life, Norton was virulently anti-Catholic.

Norton and Sackville were associated as members of Elizabeth's first Parliament in 1558. Norton began the main period of his literary career about that time: His translation of Calvin was published in 1561; his collaboration on *Gorboduc* culminated in the performances of 1561-1562; and his verse translations of certain psalms belonged to 1562. He also wrote a few poems in Latin and some in English, as well as a number of polemical attacks against Catholics.

At various times between 1558 and 1580, Norton was a member of Parliament for Berwick and for London. Norton and Sackville both were seated in Elizabeth's second Parliament, convening in January of 1563, which wrote a new petition to request again the same things that the first Parliament had been denied: that for the good of the country Elizabeth should agree to marry and should define the succession to her Crown. Norton was a member of the committee charged with studying the question of succession, and he may even have been its chairman since his was the voice that read the committee report to the second Parliament. Norton also was the probable author of the new petition.

Norton entered Oxford in 1565, receiving a master of arts degree in 1569. In that year, he wrote an attack on the Duke of Norfolk because of the proposed marriage of the duke to Mary, Queen of Scots. Norton's religious fervor earned for him a new appointment; he was asked officially to take notes at Norfolk's trial for treason, at which Sackville was one of the men who sat in judgment.

In 1571, the City of London appointed Norton to the newly created position of Remembrancer. His hatred of Catholicism led him to Rome to gather information to be used against English Papists, and in 1581, he officially became the censor of Catholics, carrying out his task with torture and with persecution. Among others, Edmund Campion and Francis Throckmorton evidently suffered from the cruelty of the Puritan zealot who came to be known as "Rackmaster-General." Indeed, Norton's Puritan fanaticism soon led him too far: When he dared to criticize episcopacy, he was removed from office, and when he continued his attacks, he was charged with treason and imprisoned in the Tower of London for a brief time in 1583. When released, his health was broken; he died the next year at the family home, Sharpenhoe, in Bedfordshire.

Thomas Sackville was born in the parish at Buckhurst in Sussex, in 1536, the only son of Sir Richard Sackville, who was a cousin of Anne Boleyn, the mother of Queen Elizabeth. Richard Sackville, who filled important positions at court under Edward VI, Mary, and Elizabeth, sent his heir to Oxford, probably around 1551. In 1555, Sackville married Cicely Baker, daughter of a Privy Councillor. In that same year, he entered the Inner Temple, but he never took a degree as barrister. Even so, the intellectual climate at the Temple must have been pleasing to Sackville. There he began to exchange ideas with Norton, and when the two young authors finished composing a tragedy some years later, they decided to stage the first performance at the law school.

Sackville's political career evidently began in 1558, when he sat as a member of both Mary's last and Elizabeth's first Parliament. He was seated again in 1563 and by that year had evidently won the notice and the regard of Elizabeth, who requested that he be in attendance on her. Around Christmas of that year, he was in Italy, where he was imprisoned for some two weeks, evidently for speaking too openly of his Protestantism, but his friends secured his release, and he was granted an audience with the Pope. The Vatican may have hoped to use Sackville as a mediator in its relations with Elizabeth, and he seemed willing to sail for England to serve in that capacity, but on his father's urging he stayed on the Continent for some time, and nothing came of his mission.

When his father died on April 21, 1566, Sackville inherited a vast estate. On June 8, 1567, he was knighted and given the title of Baron Buckhurst.

From this point to the end of his life, he served his country in many and various capacities, and he served well. In 1571, he was sent to the French court of Charles IX, ostensibly to bear congratulations to the monarch on his wedding to Elizabeth of Austria; in fact, Sackville was also there to further negotiations for a marriage between Elizabeth and the French Duke of Anjou, and he was entrusted to carry messages between Elizabeth, Charles IX, and the Queen Mother of France, Catherine de Médicis. In 1572, he was a commissioner at the state trial of the Duke of Norfolk, who was charged with treason for his involvement with Mary, Queen of Scots. Years later, in 1586, Sackville was supposedly the officer sent to inform Mary that the sentence of execution had been levied against her. He must have performed his painful task with great kindness, for the doomed woman gave him a gift, a carving of Christ's procession to the Cross.

In 1587, Sackville was sent on the most significant political mission of his career, a mission to smooth out difficulties with the Dutch, whose relationship with England had deteriorated under the Earl of Leicester's governorship of the Low Countries. Sackville handled the difficult situation well until forced by Elizabeth to suggest that the Dutch attempt to make peace with Spain. Although disagreeing with Elizabeth on this question, he carried out her orders; predictably, the Dutch objected strenuously, and an irritated Elizabeth returned Leicester to the Netherlands, recalling Sackville in disgrace and banishing him from court. This incident marked the only time in his long career that Sackville incurred the great anger of his royal cousin. His banishment lasted only until the death of Leicester in 1588; Sackville again was the queen's trusted adviser in dealing with the Dutch in 1589, 1596, and 1598.

Honors came rapidly to Sackville after his return to the queen's favor in 1588. In 1589, he became a knight of the Order of the Garter; in 1591, he was made the Lord Chancellor of Oxford University, winning the chancellorship over a potent rival, the youthful Earl of Essex, at whose trial for treason, in 1601, Sackville, by then Lord High Treasurer and Lord High Steward of England, sat in judgment and delivered the sentence of death.

When James succeeded Elizabeth as ruler of England in 1603, honors continued for Sackville. He was appointed to the Privy Council and was made Lord High Treasurer for life. On March 13 of the next year, he was made Earl of Dorset. Still Chancellor of Oxford, he welcomed James there in August, 1605. He remained active politically for the rest of his life, dying while at the council table in Whitehall on April 19, 1608.

Sackville's funeral services were held in Westminster Abbey, where the sermon was preached by his chaplain, George Abbot, who later became Archbishop. Sackville was buried in the family chapel near the parish church in Withyam. He was survived by Cicely, with whom he had had seven children. In his will, he spoke of her with great love and kindness.

History certainly paints very different pictures of the two authors of *Gorboduc*. Norton became the bitter Calvinist master of a torture chamber, his religious fanaticism finally overpowering his good judgment. Sackville remained a moderate Anglican, respected by all for his humanity and working to the last for king and country.

Analysis

Gorboduc is an extremely important play, and its authors are two extremely interesting men. The play was the first regular English tragedy, the first English drama of any type to be written in blank verse, and one of the first English history plays. It was written in collaboration by two young, wealthy, well-educated men, trained in law, who had already served as members of Parliament. The authors performed their play before Queen Elizabeth in the troubled early years of her reign. They had no original intention of publishing their play but were forced to do so after a pirated first edition appeared with various corrupt readings. All of these factors lead to highly interesting points of analysis.

Thomas Norton and Thomas Sackville wrote *Gorboduc* with one definite purpose in mind: to offer political advice to Elizabeth Tudor, the young relative of Sackville who then sat on the throne of a country sharply divided by political and religious differences. The whole play is an urgent plea for Elizabeth to do everything in her power to keep the nation united.

To dramatize their political statements, the two playwrights made significant changes in the story told by Geoffrey of Monmouth of an ancient British king. In Geoffrey's account, when King Gorboduc grows old, his two sons, Ferrex and Porrex, both desire the Crown. Porrex kills his brother but then is slain by his own mother, Widen, in revenge for Ferrex. Civil war breaks out, and the country is torn apart, eventually being divided into five different kingdoms before it is reunited under one strong leader. The horrors of a divided kingdom and of civil war were already evident in the story, but Norton and Sackville carefully altered other details to make their political arguments clearer and more emphatic, to make their play, in effect, a mirror for one magistrate. The play stresses the necessity of a ruler's heeding wise counsel, distinguishing between flatterers and good advisers, keeping control over the unruly commons, settling all questions of succession to the throne, summoning Parliament at the proper time, and ensuring that the realm will not fall to a foreign ruler.

The political messages begin in the play as early as possible, in the well-known dumb show that precedes act 1. To the music of violins, a group of savages enters with a bundle of sticks, which they try, first individually and then with their combined strength, to break. They fail—until they begin to pull the sticks out one at a time, and then they can snap them easily. The interpretation is clear: Unity is strength; division is weakness. The act that follows contains two scenes. In the first, Queen Videna (Geoffrey's Widen) sorrowfully informs her elder and favorite son that his father plans to divide Ferrex's inheritance and give half of the realm to Porrex. The second scene shows her statement to be true. King Gorboduc, whose mind is already decided on the question, nevertheless asks three of his counselors for their opinions of his plan. The first two, Arostus and Philander, agree to the division of the country, though Philander argues that it should not happen while the king is still living. Only Eubulus, whose name means "good counselor," argues against the dangerous plan, but he is ignored by Gorboduc. After the act has ended, a chorus of four ancient sages of Britain enters to voice their condemnation of the foolish decision of the king.

The tight organizational scheme of the authors is apparent: They begin with a dumb show which clearly relates to the events in the act which follows; then, the chorus comments on the action preceding it and connects that action thematically with the dumb show. The pattern will continue for all five acts, with the exception that there is no chorus after the fifth act.

Before the second act, the music of cornets ushers in a dumb show set in a royal court. A king refuses wine offered him in a glass but accepts liquid offered in a golden goblet. The king falls dead, killed by the poison within the goblet. The dumb show indicates the difference between an honest counselor whose advice is open and plain and a bad counselor who speaks with the poison of flattery.

In act 2, another aspect of the play's structure becomes apparent: Balance and contrast, while present in act 1, are much more obvious in act 2. Again there are two scenes, and in each scene there are three characters, a prince and two advisers, one good and one bad. Ferrex listens to his bad adviser, Hermon, a flattering parasite, and decides to raise an army for defense in case his brother should attack. Dordan, a wise counselor sent by Gorboduc to stay with Ferrex, has spoken against Hermon's counsel, but to no avail. He immediately writes a letter to inform Gorboduc of his son's foolishness.

Scene 2 repeats the pattern of its predecessor. Porrex agrees with Tyndar, another flatterer, who has advised him to invade his brother's realm; they ignore the outspoken opposition of Philander, a good counselor assigned by Gorboduc to stay with Porrex. In dismay, Philander hastens to inform Gorboduc in person of Porrex's invasion plans. The chorus enters to lament that unbridled youth would neglect the good advice of able counselors and listen instead to poisonous words from flattering mouths.

Before act 3, the music shifts from the loud measures of the first two dumb shows to the softer notes of flutes. With this change, another element in the artistry of the play becomes apparent: The instruments have been selected so that the music will provide as appropriate an accompaniment to the dumb show and as appropriate a prelude to the act which follows as are possible. For example, the sad music of the flutes—which, centuries before Christ, had accompanied the elegiac verse of Greece—accompanies a group of mourners, dressed in black, who march thrice around the stage, indicating the sorrow which will soon come upon the realm. In the act that follows, first Dordan's letter and then the personal report of Philander cause Gorboduc great concern, but he still has hope that he can intercede and make peace between his sons. Then, however, the type of character who frequently bears the worst of news in classical drama, the Nuntius or messenger, rushes in to tell of Porrex's invasion of his brother's land and the act of fratricide that has resulted. Gorboduc is left to mourn the death of Ferrex. The chorus then laments the mistakes of Gorboduc and of his children which have brought black floods of mourning to the land.

The clear connection of the music with the content of the play continues throughout. For act 4, the wild music of hautboys (oboes) introduces the terrifying figures of the Furies, and before act 5 the martial music provided by drums and flutes precedes scenes of warfare. According to his chaplain, Sackville had always been interested in music; undoubtedly, the varied musical effects in the play should be credited to him.

Sackville has always been accepted as the author of act 4, and the formal parallelism which marked Norton's first three acts is no longer present. In the dumb show, each of the frighteningly ugly Furies—Alecto with a snake, Megaera with a whip, and Tisiphone with a firebrand—lashes at a king and queen who have killed their own offspring. This presentation prepares the audience for the slaying of Porrex. The typical Senecan revenge motive appears immediately; Queen Videna, distraught over the news of Ferrex's death, vows to kill her only other child.

In the following scene, Porrex appears before his father, who, although threatening dire punishment, wishes to give his son time to speak in his own defense. Porrex admits that he has killed Ferrex, but adds that he is now full of grief and guilt, so much so that he will not beg for pardon. He does remind his father, however, that the decision to grant Porrex half of the realm was Gorboduc's own and not one planted in the king's mind by Porrex. The young prince then states something not shown in earlier scenes—that Ferrex had planned to have Porrex poisoned, a plot revealed by the servant of Porrex who had been hired to do the deed. Only then did Porrex invade his brother's realm. This account is the one major example of the failure of the two parts of the play to mesh well, giving credence to the contention that composition had shifted to a second hand.

Gorboduc sends Porrex from his sight while he and his advisers determine what action he will take. The king then laments the cruelty of fate which has brought such sorrow to his old age. Arostus, in a speech which recalls Sackville's lines in the "Induction" to *A Mirror for Magistrates*, reminds Gorboduc that all the joys of life are fleeting; in man's life, only death is a certainty. They are interrupted by a horror-stricken servant, Marcella, who tells them that Videna has stabbed and killed Porrex. The grief of the servant and her affection for Porrex contrast with the cold viciousness and hatred of the woman who killed him. Marcella's anguished speech continues at length and closes the scene.

The chorus emphasizes the idea of Nemesis. A brother has slain a brother; Jove, greatly offended, has sent the Furies to exact vengeance by making Videna kill Porrex. The play's artistry suffers here, for the choric comment meshes imperfectly with the dumb show, in which the Furies were punishing parents who had killed their children. Furthermore, the chorus makes no mention of an uprising by the common people, and this could not have been interpreted from the action of the dumb show itself, though the commentary in the printed edition lists such an uprising as one of the things signified in the dumb show. The fact that the pirated edition of 1565 led Norton and Sackville into print in 1570 may have provided them with the opportunity to insist in print upon an interpretation that would not have been understood by anyone who had watched one of the performances several years earlier.

Before act 5, the drums and flutes signal the approach of soldiers, who actually discharge their weapons before the audience. Obviously the show signals war, in this case a civil war which will rage in Britain for half a century.

The play may be charged with a lack of unity because of the handling of the fifth act. Neither Gorboduc nor Videna appears; their deaths are reported in the seventh line. Since Ferrex and Porrex have died earlier, no member of the royal family is left to bring unity into the final act. In fact, Eubulus is the only character from the opening portions of the play who appears at the beginning of the final act, though later Arostus will appear. All of the other characters in act 5 are appearing for the first time.

After the murders of Ferrex and Porrex, the common people, horrified by the atrocities within the royal family, have rebelled and slaughtered both Videna and Gorboduc. Eubulus has reason to fear what actions might be committed next by the masses, in whom he has never placed any trust. With the help of some honest lords, Eubulus puts down the rebellion, but trouble immediately flares again when one ambitious nobleman, Fergus, raises an army and tries to seize the throne of a kingdom that as yet has no king clearly and rightfully placed on its throne. As Eubulus prepares to deal with the new danger, he speaks angrily against rulers who do not listen to good advice, and he anachronistically laments that Parliament had not been summoned and that the question of succession to the throne had not been clearly determined. The play has made its essential points over and over again: The land must not be divided, a ruler must listen to the good advice of wise counselors, Parliament should be called, and the succession to the throne should be incontrovertibly settled. Norton and Sackville were saying to Elizabeth what her Parliament of 1558 had already said to her and what her Parliament of 1563 would quickly say to her again.

Since *Gorboduc* is a tragedy, since the Roman Stoic Seneca is the model for much early Renaissance tragedy, and since Seneca's tragedies were being translated at the time (Jasper Heywood's translation of *Thyestes* had appeared in 1560—with a preface referring to both Norton and Sackville as poets), it is natural to assume that *Gorboduc* must have been influenced by Seneca. Nevertheless, the extent of the Senecan influence has been the subject of long debate. In 1893, John W. Cunliffe argued that the debt to Seneca was obvious in almost every aspect of the play, but over the next few decades some more moderate voices maintained that the case for Senecan influence was being overstated. The extreme opposite of Cunliffe's position was reached in 1939, when Howard Baker presented his staggering argument that almost everything in *Gorboduc* could be traced to native English medieval dramatic traditions and that any influence of Seneca was virtually nonexistent. The truth undoubtedly lies somewhere between the views of Cunliffe and Baker.

The presence of Seneca possibly may be seen in the revenge motive of the play, in the division into five acts with a chorus appearing between the acts to summarize the significance of what has just happened, in the appearance of the Nuntius, in several rhetorical devices, and in the presence of a number of sententious passages. The dumb shows, however, certainly stem from influences other than Seneca, and it should be noted that the play does not observe the classical unities of time, place, and action. In fact, the fifth act is but weakly related to the preceding four, for Gorboduc and his entire family are dead before the fifth act begins and the act seems to exist primarily to provide the advisers and certain lords an opportunity to pronounce the major political theories of the play.

Except for the choruses, *Gorboduc* is written in blank verse. Norton and Sackville often have been criticized for their verse, and certainly it seems inferior when compared with the lines of greater poets writing thirty or forty years later, but when the language of *Gorboduc* is compared with the verse of other plays written in the 1550's and 1560's, it fares very well indeed. Admittedly, in some passages, particularly the long individual speeches, the carefully measured accents make the verse stiff and tedious, but the very first few lines of the opening scene indicate the smooth and successful movement of which the poets were capable.

One of the reasons why the blank verse seems wooden and uninteresting is that it is being made to serve rhetorical purposes. The play abounds with rhetorical devices, and the flow of the verse is often sacrificed for alliteration, antithesis, repetition, and other rhetorical ends. The syntactic balance within individual passages is particularly noticeable. Another factor which causes dissatisfaction with the verse is its lack of metaphor; indeed, there is virtually no imagery in the poetry of the play. Finally, all of the choruses are written in rhyme; the poets generally use a six-line iambic pentameter stanza for the choric passages, but there is a considerable amount of variation.

In the final analysis, *Gorboduc* seems a remarkably successful effort. Norton and Sackville wanted to express certain specific political messages, and the play conveys those clearly and emphatically. The play contains many excellent artistic touches—in organization, in visual effect, and in its music. Only the heaviness of the style has prevented greater appreciation of the play by modern readers, and the style was no barrier to the enjoyment of Renaissance audiences, as is indicated by the compliment paid to it by one of the most discriminating minds of the age, Sir Philip Sidney, who praised it highly in *The Defence of Poesie* (1595).

Strangely, for both Norton and Sackville, *Gorboduc* represented the beginning and the end of their work in drama and, in fact, of their creative literary efforts in general. For Norton, a career in law and his passionate involvement in the religious disputes of the time would occupy the remaining years of his life, and no other of his writings would prove lasting. For Sackville, the peak of accomplishment represented by *Gorboduc* would be followed by more success in 1563, with the publication of the second edition of *A Mirror for Magistrates*, but Sackville's portions of that work had evidently been written some years earlier. After the literary acclaim early in his life, Sackville would enjoy a long and successful career of almost fifty years, but that career was dedicated to the service of the realm rather than the service of the Muses.

Other major works

POETRY (by Sackville): "Induction," in *A Mirror for Magistrates*, 1563 (second edition); "The Complaint of Henry, Duke of Buckingham," in *A Mirror for Magistrates*, 1563.

Bibliography
Baker, Howard. *Induction to Tragedy: A Study in a Development of Form in "Gorboduc," "The Spanish Tragedy," and "Titus Andronicus."* University: Louisiana State University Press, 1939. This standard work considers the tragic form from two viewpoints: artistry and moral significance. Baker discusses the authorship question of *Gorboduc* and the possible Senecan influence and also considers native English dramatic influences to be very strong. Pays some attention to the historical criticism of the play.

Berlin, Normand. *Thomas Sackville.* New York: Twayne, 1974. Contains discussions of Sackville's life and his work on *A Mirror for Magistrates*, in addition to a substantial chapter on *Gorboduc*, which precedes a plea that Sackville should be more appreciated for his substantial artistic merits. Investigates *Gorboduc* for its political intent, for the mixture of Senecan and native influences, and for the likely division of parts between the coauthors. Useful annotated bibliography.

Clemen, Wolfgang. *English Tragedy Before Shakespeare: The Development of Dramatic Speech.* Translated by T. S. Dorsch. London: Methuen, 1961. In this study of the "set speech," the author finds *Gorboduc* weakened by the lack of correlation between speech and characterization or speech and action; he considers the moral and political viewpoints to be the only purposes for the speeches.

Watt, Homer A. *"Gorboduc": Or, Ferrex and Porrex.* Madison: University of Wisconsin Press, 1910. Watt presents evidence from two opposing factions, one arguing that the play is Senecan and literary, the other believing it to be English and political. He stresses the importance of Nemesis in Seneca, calls the play's sententiousness Senecan in origin, and notes parallel passages with Seneca. Contains some disagreement with Howard Baker's volume (above).

Whall, Helen M. *To Instruct and Delight: Didactic Method in Five Tudor Dramas.* New York: Garland, 1988. Finds *Gorboduc* consciously designed for artistic effects and its authors—unlike John Bale in *King Johan* (pb. 1538)—unsatisfied with simply delivering a powerful message. Shows evidence of their artistic concerns in the elaborate dumb shows, the patterned divisions of the five acts, and their innovative verse. Compares *Gorboduc* frequently with *King Johan.*

Howard L. Ford

SEAN O'CASEY
John Casey

Born: Dublin, Ireland; March 30, 1880
Died: Torquay, England; September 18, 1964

Principal drama

The Shadow of a Gunman, pr. 1923, pb. 1925; *Cathleen Listens In*, pr. 1923, pb. 1962 (one act); *Juno and the Paycock*, pr. 1924, pb. 1925; *Nannie's Night Out*, pr. 1924, pb. 1962 (one act); *Two Plays*, pb. 1925 (includes *The Shadow of a Gunman* and *Juno and the Paycock*); *The Plough and the Stars*, pr., pb. 1926; *The Silver Tassie*, pb. 1928, pr. 1929; *Within the Gates*, pb. 1933, pr. 1934; *A Pound on Demand*, pb. 1934, pr. 1947 (one act); *The End of the Beginning*, pb. 1934, pr. 1937 (one act); *Windfalls*, pb. 1934 (includes *A Pound on Demand*, *The End of the Beginning*, essays, poems, stories); *Five Irish Plays*, pb. 1935; *The Star Turns Red*, pr., pb. 1940; *Purple Dust*, pb. 1940, pr. 1944; *Red Roses for Me*, pb. 1942, pr. 1943; *Oak Leaves and Lavender: Or, A World on Wallpaper*, pb. 1946, pr. 1947; *Cock-a-Doodle Dandy*, pr., pb. 1949; *Collected Plays*, pb. 1949-1951 (4 volumes; includes *Cock-a-Doodle Dandy*, *Bedtime Story*, *Hall of Healing*, *Time to Go*); *Bedtime Story*, pb. 1951, pr. 1952; *Hall of Healing*, pr. 1951, pr. 1952 (one act); *Time to Go*, pb. 1951, pr. 1952 (one act); *The Bishop's Bonfire*, pr., pb. 1955; *Selected Plays of Sean O'Casey*, pb. 1956; *The Drums of Father Ned*, pr. 1959, pb. 1960; *Behind the Green Curtains*, pb. 1961, pr. 1962; *Figure in the Night*, pb. 1961, pr. 1962 (one act); *The Moon Shines on Kylenamoe*, pb. 1961, pr. 1962 (one act); *Feathers from the Green Crow: Sean O'Casey, 1905-1925*, pb. 1962 (includes *Cathleen Listens In*, *Nannie's Night Out*, essays, poems, stories); *Three More Plays*, pb. 1965; *Five One-Act Plays*, pb. 1990.

Other literary forms

Along with his drama, Sean O'Casey wrote verse, political tracts, historical sketches, essays, dramatic criticism, short stories, and an extensive six-volume autobiography: *I Knock at the Door* (1939), *Pictures in the Hallway* (1942), *Drums Under the Windows* (1945), *Inishfallen, Fare Thee Well* (1949), *Rose and Crown* (1952), and *Sunset and Evening Star* (1954). The autobiography is also available in a two-volume edition, *Mirror in My House* (1956). Early in his career, O'Casey published two volumes of poetry: *Songs of the Wren* (1918) and *More Wren Songs* (1918). His political pamphlets include *The Story of Thomas Ashe* (1918), *The Sacrifice of Thomas Ashe* (1918), and *The Story of the Irish Citizen Army* (1919). O'Casey's two essay collections are *The Flying Wasp* (1937) and *The Green Crow* (1956). His essays, criticism, short stories, and verse have been collected in several anthologies, including *Windfalls*, *Feathers from the Green*

Crow: Sean O'Casey, 1905-1925, Under a Colored Cap (1963), and *Blasts and Benedictions* (1967).

Achievements

Poet, playwright, essayist, and short-story writer, Sean O'Casey stands as one of the major figures of the Irish Renaissance. Though he began his career as a playwright late in life, he still managed to complete more than twenty plays, a six-volume autobiography, and numerous short stories and essays before his death in 1964. Along with the works of John Millington Synge, Lady Augusta Gregory, and William Butler Yeats, his plays sustained the Abbey Theatre during its early years, accounting for its greatest commercial successes, and they are still among the most popular works in the Abbey Theatre's repertory.

During his career, O'Casey moved beyond the confines of dramatic realism to create a new style of expressionism in Anglo-Irish theater. In this regard, he is among the most original and innovative of modern European playwrights. Perhaps only the epic realism of Bertolt Brecht's works rivals the sheer spectacle and vitality of O'Casey's stage. Though his early plays have continued in repertory, these later plays, especially, deserve to be performed more often, despite the demands of their Irish dialect and their variety of song-and-dance material. That they are not reflects the impoverishment of the modern stage, for O'Casey was a master of theatrical entertainment.

Biography

The youngest child in a large Irish Protestant family of modest means, Sean O'Casey was born John Casey in Dublin on March 30, 1880. He was the third child in his family to be named John, since two of his siblings with that name had died in infancy. Later, in his twenties, after he had become an Irish nationalist and a member of the Gaelic League, he adopted the Gaelic version of his name, Sean O'Cathasaigh (pronounced O'Casey). O'Casey's father, Michael Casey, who came from a farming family in Limerick, worked as a clerk for the Anglican Irish Church Missions. He came to Dublin as a young man and married Susan Archer, of a respectable auctioneer's family. Michael Casey was a literate man with a good library of English classics, while O'Casey's mother was a woman of great fortitude and devotion to her children, especially her youngest, whom she sheltered because of his physical frailty and a severe eye affliction, which left his vision permanently impaired. Even in the difficult period after her husband's death, she maintained her respectability and encouraged her children to enter professions.

Michael Casey died after a protracted illness on September 6, 1886, when his youngest son was only six. With the loss of his income, the family started a gradual decline into poverty. The Caseys were forced to move to cheaper lodgings in a Dublin dockside neighborhood. There, O'Casey started to associate with working-class Catholic boys who attended the local parochial school. He had been enrolled at St. Mary's National School, where his sister Isabella taught, but when he reached the age of fourteen, his schooling came to an end. His family needed the extra income, so he began to work as a stock boy with a Dublin hardware firm. Though out of school, O'Casey continued his interest in books, and he certainly learned to read before the age of sixteen, contrary to what he later reported to Lady Gregory.

O'Casey became active in the Church of Ireland during this time and was confirmed at the age of seventeen. In his free time, he read William Shakespeare and the Irish playwright Dion Boucicault. He also attended the Mechanics' Theatre with his brother Isaac and even acted in at least one production. His love of drama was strengthened by these early productions, and after the group was later reorganized as the Abbey Theatre, he would see two of his early plays produced there in 1923.

In 1902, O'Casey began work as a laborer on the Great Northern Railway of Ireland, where he was employed for the next ten years. His budding interest in Irish nationalism led him to join the Gaelic League, learn the Irish language, and change his name. Within a short time, he was also a member of the Irish Republican Brotherhood. Through these associations, O'Casey began to shape his identity as Irish nationalist, laborer, and political activist. His interest in writing also emerged as he joined the St. Lawrence O'Toole Club, a local literary society. Above all, he forged the commitment to Irish nationalism that would occupy him for the next twenty years.

O'Casey joined the Irish Transport and General Workers Union in 1909, and was dismissed from his job later that year for refusing to sign a nonstrike pledge during the railway strike. Left unemployed, he turned increasingly to politics while he supported himself as a laborer in the building trade. From his perspective, socialism began to look attractive as an alternative to British economic domination of Ireland. The six-month Dublin labor lockout of 1913 hardened his political views, as he helped to organize a relief fund for destitute families. Becoming more militant, he drafted part of the constitution for the Irish Citizen Army, though recuperation from an operation and personal doubts kept him from taking part in the week-long insurrection of Easter, 1916. Instead, he wrote poems, pamphlets, and broadsides in support of the Irish cause.

His mother and sister died in 1918, leaving O'Casey to board temporarily with the family of his brother Michael. This period marked a low point in O'Casey's fortunes, since he was out of work and was forced to accept the charity of others. Yet he was determined to write. In 1921, while living in a small flat, he started work on his three Dublin plays: *The Shadow of a Gunman*, *Juno and the Paycock*, and *The Plough and the Stars*. O'Casey reached the age of forty-three before *The Shadow of a Gunman* was finally produced, in April, 1923, but his career as a playwright had finally begun. *Juno and the Paycock* followed in March, 1924, and *The Plough and the Stars*, two years later.

O'Casey's Dublin play, *The Plough and the Stars*, presented such an unflattering view of the Easter Week uprising of 1916 that the audience rioted when it opened at the Abbey Theatre in February, 1926. Yeats stood up before the mob and defended the play, but O'Casey was embittered by its hostile reception and decided shortly afterward to leave Ireland for voluntary exile in England.

In 1926, O'Casey won the Hawthornden Prize for *Juno and the Paycock*, and he left for London that spring to accept the award in person. There, he hoped to find greater artistic freedom as a playwright. During his first three years in London, he was introduced to George Bernard Shaw, had his portrait painted by Augustus John, and met the talented and attractive actress Eileen Reynolds (stage name Carey), whom he married on September 23, 1927. They were to enjoy a long and mutually supportive marriage for thirty-seven years, with their three children, Breon, Niall, and Shivaun. Marriage and life in London apparently had a salutary effect on O'Casey's imagination, for he began to work almost immediately after their marriage on the expressionistic play *The Silver Tassie*, which marked a clear departure from his earlier work.

O'Casey had been attracted to socialism as early as 1911, during the Irish railway strike, but the economic hardships of the 1930's and the rise of Fascism drove him further to the left, to the point of tacitly accepting Communism and serving as a member of the advisory board of the London *Daily Worker*. He also became increasingly anticlerical in regard to Ireland, viewing the Catholic prelacy as the oppressor of the Irish people. After World War II, O'Casey spoke out vigorously in favor of the Soviet Union. He opposed the arms race and urged nuclear disarmament.

In 1954, O'Casey moved with his family from London to the resort town of St. Marychurch, Torquay, in Devon. There, in 1956, the family suffered a deep personal loss when the younger son, Niall, died of leukemia. In his mid-seventies when this misfortune occurred, virtually blind and suffering from constant pain, O'Casey still possessed the strength of character to write a moving tribute to his son, "Under a Greenwood Tree He Died," and to continue his playwriting. Friends remembered him from these last years as a thin, sharp-faced man with a gay spirit and an enchanting Irish brogue, who was usually dressed in a warm turtleneck sweater and one of the brightly colored caps that his daughter had knit for him.

The last decade of O'Casey's life showed an increasing American interest in his work and brought him numerous awards and honors, most of which he declined, including an appointment as Commander of the Order of the British Empire and several honorary doctorates from the Universities of Durham and Exeter and from Trinity College, Dublin. His eightieth birthday was celebrated with much fanfare. After suffering a heart attack, Sean O'Casey died in Torquay on September 18, 1964, at the age of eighty-four.

Analysis

In "O'Casey's Credo," an essay that appeared in *The New York Times* and was written in 1958 for the opening of an American production of *Cock-a-Doodle Dandy*, Sean O'Casey remarked that "the first thing I try to do is to make a play live: live as a part of life, and live in its own right as a work of drama." This concern with the vitality of his plays has marked O'Casey's craftsmanship as a playwright throughout his career. "Every character, every life," he continued, "[has] something to say, comic or serious, and to say it well [is] not an easy thing to do." To express this vitality through his characters' actions and dialogue was O'Casey's goal as a dramatist. All of his plays share the blend of comic, serious, and poetic imagination that O'Casey believed should meld in any play worth staging.

O'Casey's plays fall into three periods: the early naturalistic tragicomedies, the expressionistic plays of the middle period, and the exuberant, satiric comedies that mark his later work.

O'Casey was forty-three years old when his first play, *The Shadow of a Gunman*, was accepted by the Abbey Theatre. Behind him lay four apprentice plays and more than twenty years of hard experience in Dublin as a laborer, nationalist, and political organizer. He might easily have failed to develop his talent but for the encouragement of Lady Gregory, Yeats, and Lennox Robinson, who read his early scripts and urged him to continue writing. O'Casey was drawn to the theater as a social medium—as the best way for him to express the impact on Dublin's poor of Ireland's struggle for independence.

O'Casey's first play, *The Shadow of a Gunman*, opened at the Abbey Theatre in April, 1923, and ran for only a few performances, but its modest success encouraged O'Casey to submit *Juno and the Paycock* and *The Plough and the Stars* within the next three years. O'Casey had lived through the bitter period when Ireland was torn first by insurrection and later by the bloody struggle between the Irish Republican Army and the notorious Black and Tans. In these plays, his Dublin trilogy, he expresses disillusionment and bitterness about the way in which the Irish struggle for independence degenerated into fratricidal bloodshed. Together, these plays present a chronicle history of the Irish conflict between 1916 and 1921. Naturalistic in style and approach, they are noted, as critics have remarked, for their tragicomic tone, their vivid depictions of Dublin tenement dwellers, and their lively and colorful speech.

The second period of O'Casey's playwriting career began after he left Dublin for London in 1926. Up to this point, he had been an Irish playwright writing for a national theater, but the response to *The Plough and the Stars*, which provoked a riot at the Abbey Theatre when it opened, may have led him to recognize the limitations of conventional dramatic realism. Seeking ways to expand his artistic vision, O'Casey turned to the expressionistic mode in his next play, *The Silver Tassie*. Inspired by a London coal vendor's song, this ambitious play about World War I incorporates songs, chants, ritualistic scenes, allegorized characters, and stylized sets. The play's action alternates between Dublin and the front as O'Casey depicts the cost of war for all of the young men who departed as heroes and returned as cripples and invalids.

Like Synge before him, O'Casey opened new possibilities for Irish theater, but unfortunately, the Abbey Theatre was unwilling to accept his stylistic innovations. When O'Casey submitted *The Silver Tassie* to the Abbey Theatre in 1928, Yeats rejected it with a sharply worded reply that initiated a bitter exchange before the two were finally reconciled in 1935. Yeats attacked the play for its alleged introduction of propaganda into the theater, for, despite his own experiments with Japanese Nō theater, he was curiously unreceptive to O'Casey's attempts to move beyond dramatic realism. O'Casey did not aspire to a "pure" art of theater or cherish a dramatic theory, as did Yeats. Instead, he merely intended to expand the range of tragicomedy using the devices of expressionism. He hoped to use the exuberance of music-hall entertainment—its melodrama, boisterous comedy, burlesque, and farce—to animate serious drama, just as Shakespeare had woven comic interludes into even his most somber tragedies.

After the rejection of *The Silver Tassie* by the Abbey Theatre, O'Casey turned to a London producer to stage the play. Henceforth, he was to be a playwright without a permanent theater, often forced to publish his plays before they were staged and to depend upon commercial productions of varying quality. Though *The Silver Tassie* enjoyed only a mixed success, O'Casey was committed to expressionism as an artistic direction, and his plays during the next decade show the gradual development of this style. The 1930's were a period of diversity for O'Casey. Besides writing several one-act plays and the full-length "morality play" *Within the Gates*, he published drama reviews and short stories and began his six-volume autobiography. In his drama reviews and criticism, O'Casey defended other contemporary, experimental playwrights and called for the use of a wider range of theatrical techniques and for a drama criticism receptive to these innovations. He attacked the British critics' taste for the light drawing-room comedies of Noël Coward and the general lack of variety in the London theater. By this time he had also become a committed left-wing thinker who actively sympathized with Communist causes. His political ideology is evident in two plays of this period, _The Star Turns Red_ and _Oak Leaves and Lavender_. Unfortunately, art and politics did not mix well for O'Casey, and these are largely inferior works.

Perhaps O'Casey came to realize the limits of ideological drama, or he may simply have grown tired of the war theme, for in the most successful plays of his middle period, he returned to an Irish setting, combining expressionistic techniques with traditional Irish characters, scenes, songs, and material. Also written during the war years, _Purple Dust_ and _Red Roses for Me_ show the refinement of expressionistic techniques that O'Casey had introduced in _The Silver Tassie_ almost fifteen years earlier. These two plays demonstrate the range and quality of O'Casey's mature lyric imagination as he animates his stage with the song, pageantry, and spectacle of the Elizabethan theater. As he later observed about his plays, "Like [James] Joyce, it is only through an Irish scene that my imagination can weave a way."

The third period of O'Casey's career reflects a further enhancement of his artistic vision through a series of exuberant comic fantasies dramatizing the conflict between the affirmative and repressive forces in Irish culture. Here, he sharpened his critique of the provincialism, clericalism, materialism, and restrictive religious morality that he perceived in modern Irish life. Starting with _Cock-a-Doodle Dandy_, which O'Casey regarded as his favorite, and continuing with _The Bishop's Bonfire_, _The Drums of Father Ned_, and _Behind the Green Curtains_, the plays of this period mark the height of his mature achievement. In these late plays, O'Casey perfected his distinctive blend of broad comedy, farce, song, fantasy, dance, satire, and melodrama. As his favorite dramatists, Shakespeare and Boucicault, had done before him, O'Casey made his plays infinitely richer and more varied than conventional realistic drama. His expressionism became a medium for his lyricism and gaiety of spirit. This determination to broaden the range of contemporary theater perhaps marks O'Casey's most distinctive contribution to the modern stage.

O'Casey's first play to be accepted by the Abbey Theatre, _The Shadow of a Gunman_, is a two-act tragicomedy set in a Dublin tenement during the May, 1920, struggle between the Irish Republican Army (IRA) and the British Black and Tans. Two hapless young Irishmen, Seumas Shields (a Catholic peddler) and Donal Davoren (a poet manqué) are drawn into the guerrilla warfare when other residents mistake them for IRA fighters and a friend accidentally leaves a bag of terrorist bombs in their rooms. Davoren, the would-be poet, enjoys the hero-worship of his neighbors and the affection of young Minnie Powell, while he writes poor imitations of Percy Bysshe Shelley and pretends to be an insurgent. O'Casey uses the contrast between the self-deceiving appearance and the reality of the two men to debunk romantic myths of Irish heroism and valor. Shields and Davoren are both antiheroes, ordinary men who instinctively shun violence and try to live the semblance of normal lives amid the conflict. This antiheroic theme is the source of both comedy and pathos, for while Shields and Davoren act as cowards, Minnie behaves heroically. In act 2, when British soldiers arrive to search the apartments for snipers or weapons, she volunteers to hide the bag of bombs in her room and is discovered and captured. Sacrificing herself for a sham ideal, she is shot while trying to escape from the British, as Shields and Davoren, who form "the shadow of a gunman," cower in their rooms, terrified of the gunfire.

Juno and the Paycock is set in 1922 during the period of continued civil war after the Irish Free State had been established. The scene is once again a Dublin tenement, and the play depicts the misfortunes of the Boyle family, impoverished Dubliners temporarily lifted out of their squalor by a spurious legacy, which they quickly squander. This three-act tragicomedy parallels domestic and civil chaos; the Boyles struggle against the disintegration of their family, while outside the provisional Irish Republican Army continues its resistance against the Dublin government. "Captain" Jack Boyle and "Joxer" Daley are among O'Casey's most memorable characters. The Captain struts from apartment to pub, accompanied by the ingratiating Joxer, embellishing upon his past adventures, complaining about his hard luck, and deftly avoiding responsibility, while his wife, Juno, struggles both to work and to keep house. As the play progresses, their crippled son, Johnny, becomes an IRA informer, and their daughter, Mary, falls in love with the young lawyer who brings the family news of their supposed inheritance. Despite these misfortunes, the play generates rich humor from the garrulous, irresponsible behavior of the Captain and Joxer, who belong to a long tradition of the stage Irishman and the braggart soldier. Once their inheritance is discovered to be a sham, the family's fortunes swiftly disintegrate, as their furniture is repossessed, Johnny is shot by the IRA, and Mary is left pregnant and deserted by her lover. By the end of the play, bitter and defeated, Juno and Mary mourn Johnny's death, while the Captain and Joxer stagger in, drunk and lugubrious, to lament "the terrible state o' chassis" of the world.

The title for O'Casey's *The Plough and the Stars* is taken from the original flag of the Irish Citizen Army, with its working-class symbols, but the focus is once again the folly and futility of war. This four-act tragicomedy is set before and during the Easter, 1916, uprising in Dublin and dramatizes the mixed motives of idealism, vanity, and folly that inspired Irish nationalism. The action in the play alternates between a Dublin boardinghouse and the streets and pubs of the city. It dramatizes the trauma of war in separating a young couple, Jack and Nora Clitheroe, recently married. When the call for the uprising takes place, Jack hurries to join his compatriots, while

Nora desperately tries to prevent him from leaving and then wanders through the strife-torn city in search of him. After the battle, the city is filled with looters, and O'Casey creates some memorable scenes of rioters fighting over their plunder. The various boarders at the Clitheroes' boardinghouse represent differing attitudes toward the insurrection, from patriotism to scorn. By the end of the play, Dublin is in flames and Jack has died heroically, although Nora, who has lost her baby, cannot be told. Her neighbor, the Unionist Bessie Burgess, is fatally shot by the British while nursing Nora, and the play ends with British soldiers drinking tea in the rooms they have just ransacked.

In style and technique, *The Silver Tassie* marks a clear departure from O'Casey's earlier plays. Though he retains the tragicomic mode, he turns from a realistic to an expressionistic mode to convey the horrors of modern warfare. Symbols and abstractions of war bode large in this play, particularly in act 2, as O'Casey attempts to move his art beyond dramatic realism to a more poetic theater. The protagonist, Harry Heegan, leaves for the front in act 1 after he has won the Silver Tassie, or victory cup, for his Avondale Football Club. He departs as a hero, victorious and in love with Jessie Taite, and returns a crippled, embittered veteran, having lost his youth, vitality, and love. Act 2 invokes the carnage of the front through chant and ritual; an allegorical figure, the Croucher, dominates the action, while Harry is wounded in battle. Act 3 shifts to the army hospital during Harry's recuperation from his injuries, and act 4 brings him back to a dance at the Avondale Football Club. Now a wheelchair invalid, and having lost Jessie to his friend Barney, he drinks the bitter cup of loss and smashes the Silver Tassie on the floor. The dramatic action is quite simple, but O'Casey's expressionistic treatment makes this a powerful and compelling play.

After a period of unsuccessful propaganda plays, O'Casey's next significant play was *Purple Dust*. He called the play a "wayward comedy," though perhaps it is closer in form to a rollicking farce—a humorous confrontation between the English and the Irish national characters reminiscent of Shaw's *John Bull's Other Island* (pr. 1904, pb. 1907). The play is set in the Irish countryside, where two wealthy English dupes, Cyril Poges and Basil Stokes, try to restore a dilapidated Tudor mansion in Clune na Geera. O'Casey's "stage Englishmen" are thwarted by their bungling mismanagement and by the unpredictable Irish weather. By the end of the play, their young Irish mistresses have run off with two Irish workmen and the mansion is about to be destroyed by a flood. Once again, the English are defeated in their attempt to dominate Ireland economically, and, as the title suggests, the pair are left in the ruins of their romantic and extravagant obsession with the "purple dust" of Tudor Ireland.

The most autobiographical of O'Casey's plays, *Red Roses for Me*, presents a romantic, nostalgic evocation of his early manhood in Dublin. The protagonist, Ayamonn Breydon, is a young Protestant railway worker who helps organize a strike in the Dublin yards to win a small wage increase. Ayamonn is in love with a timid Catholic girl, Sheila Moorneen, who, along with Ayamonn's mother, begs him to give up the strike, but Ayamonn is determined that the strike will occur, and he is killed in the labor violence that follows. Before his death, however, he has enjoyed a moment of ecstatic vision, as, from a bridge across the Liffey, he envisions Dublin transfigured from its drab dullness to a golden radiance. This magnificent scene and the rich language of the play save it from becoming a mere propaganda piece for the cause of Labour.

O'Casey often remarked that he considered *Cock-a-Doodle Dandy* his best play, although it is by no means the easiest to produce. Reminiscent of the fantastic comedies of Aristophanes, this play features a life-size apocalyptic Cock who comes to banish religious bigotry and puritanism from the small Irish village of Nyadnanave, inciting a series of magical and mysterious events. The village priest and older men are sure the Cock represents some malign spirit, though the young women, especially, are attracted to it. O'Casey himself commented that "the Cock, of course, is the joyful, active spirit of life as it weaves a way through the Irish scene." In three long scenes, the play presents a parable of the Irish spirit in conflict, torn between the powers of affirmation and negation, as the puritanical Father Domineer musters the village forces of superstition, ignorance, and fear to suppress dance and merriment and, ultimately, to banish the most attractive young women from the region. Unfortunately, the enchantment of the Cock does not prevail in this play, although O'Casey implies that the spirit of human joy is irrepressible.

O'Casey continues his anticlerical theme in *The Bishop's Bonfire*, a satirical farce in which Bishop Bill Mullarky's visit to his hometown is marked by a ritual book-burning of objectionable literature. The forces of piety and respectability are once more in control, as Councillor Reiligan, the richest man in the village, prepares his house to welcome the Bishop, while both the upper and lower classes celebrate the homecoming in their own ways. The pompous Reiligan also interferes with his daughters' happiness by preventing them from marrying the men they love because he thinks these men are not respectable enough. Much of the play is farcical or melodramatic, particularly the death scene at the end of the play, in which Fooraun Reiligan is shot by her suitor, Manus Moanroe, when she discovers that he is stealing church funds from her house. Her suicide note absolves him, however, as the sight of burning books welcomes the bishop home.

O'Casey's continuing satire of Irish morality irritated many of his compatriots, and the controversy surrounding his next play, *The Drums of Father Ned*, seems like a parody of the play itself in a strange instance of life imitating art. Set in the village of Doonavale during the Tostal, or national arts festival, the play depicts the healing of an old feud between two prosperous families, the Binningtons and the McGilligans, when their son and daughter fall in love during play rehearsals. A short "Prerumble," or one-act prelude, reenacts the feud between Alderman Binnington and Councillor McGilligan, enemies since the Irish Civil War, who will talk with each other only about business matters. Through the evocative power of the "drums" of Father Ned, a life-affirming country priest, the families are reconciled, and joy and love of life are restored to the village of Doonavale during the Tostal celebration. Ironically, this seemingly innocuous comedy was scheduled to be performed at the 1958 Dublin Tostal until it was withdrawn at the behest of the Archbishop of Dublin, who refused to celebrate Mass at the festival if works by O'Casey, Joyce, or Samuel Beckett were performed. The spirit of negation prevailed, unfortunately, and the festival continued without the works of its three principal Irish artists.

In his long and productive career, O'Casey reanimated the Anglo-Irish theater with a blend of tragicomedy, fantasy, and farce that drew from Elizabethan drama, the music hall, and expressionism to create a vibrant and innovative form of dramatic theater. Though his plays have been criticized for lacking a "pure" dramatic form, his vigorous mixture of theatrical elements has stood in marked contrast to other trends in contemporary theater through its sheer power of entertainment and affirmation. Sean O'Casey had the creative power and vision to transcend the limitations of dramatic theory. His genius was for theatrical vitality rather than pure dramatic art. As Ireland's preeminent modern playwright, O'Casey deserves to have his works performed more often beyond the Irish and English stage.

Other major works

POETRY: *Songs of the Wren*, 1918; *More Wren Songs*, 1918.

NONFICTION: *The Story of Thomas Ashe*, 1918; *The Sacrifice of Thomas Ashe*, 1918; *The Story of the Irish Citizen Army*, 1919; *The Flying Wasp*, 1937; *I Knock at the Door*, 1939 (autobiography); *Pictures in the Hallway*, 1942 (autobiography); *Drums Under the Windows*, 1945 (autobiography); *Inishfallen, Fare Thee Well*, 1949 (autobiography); *Rose and Crown*, 1952 (autobiography); *Sunset and Evening Star*, 1954 (autobiography); *Mirror in My House*, 1956 (2 volumes; reissue of 6-volume autobiography); *The Green Crow*, 1956; *Under a Colored Cap*, 1963; *Blasts and Benedictions*, 1967; *The Letters of Sean O'Casey*, 1975, 1978 (3 volumes; David Krause, editor).

MISCELLANEOUS: *Windfalls*, 1934 (includes essays, plays, poems, stories); *Feathers from the Green Crow: Sean O'Casey, 1905-1925*, 1962 (includes essays, plays, poems, stories); *The Sean O'Casey Reader: Plays, Autobiographies, Opinions*, 1968 (Brooks Atkinson, editor).

Bibliography

Ayling, Ronald, and Michael J. Durkan. *Sean O'Casey: A Bibliography.* London: Macmillan, 1978. This volume is considered to be the standard bibliographic source on O'Casey's work and the critical reaction to it.

Krause, David. *Sean O'Casey: The Man and His Work.* 2d ed. New York: Macmillan, 1975. An enlarged edition of an earlier and useful scholarly study. Krause examines O'Casey's life, drama, and experiences in the theatrical world.

Mikhail, E. H. *Sean O'Casey and His Critics: An Annotated Bibliography.* Metuchen, N.J.: Scarecrow Press, 1985. Mikhail's bibliography is the finest later survey of available sources on Ireland's most celebrated playwright.

Mitchell, Jack. *The Essential O'Casey: A Study of the Twelve Major Plays of Sean O'Casey.* New York: International Publishers, 1980. This volume provides a handy summary of O'Casey's most popular works.

O'Casey, Sean. *Mirror in My House.* New York: Macmillan, 1956. This collection of O'Casey's six earlier autobiographies is most revealing for its portraits of lower-class Protestant Dublin life.

O'Connor, Garry. *Sean O'Casey: A Life.* New York: Atheneum, 1988. The best and most readable biography, especially useful on the playwright's rise, through self-education and life as a Dublin laborer, to a major role in the 1916 Easter Rebellion and his Abbey Theatre productions.

Andrew J. Angyal
(Updated by *Peter C. Holloran*)

CLIFFORD ODETS

Born: Philadelphia, Pennsylvania; July 18, 1906
Died: Los Angeles, California; August 14, 1963

Principal drama

Waiting for Lefty, pr., pb. 1935 (one act); *Till the Day I Die*, pr., pb. 1935; *Awake and Sing*, pr., pb. 1935; *Paradise Lost*, pr. 1935, pb. 1936; *I Can't Sleep*, pr. 1935, pb. 1936; *Golden Boy*, pr., pb. 1937; *Rocket to the Moon*, pr. 1938, pb. 1939; *Night Music*, pr., pb. 1940; *Clash by Night*, pr. 1941, pb. 1942; *The Russian People*, pr. 1942, pb. 1946 (adaptation of Konstantin Simonov's play *The Russians*); *The Big Knife*, pr., pb. 1949; *The Country Girl*, pr. 1950, pb. 1951; *The Flowering Peach*, pr., pb. 1954.

Other literary forms

Clifford Odets is also known for his screenplays, which include *The General Died at Dawn* (1936), an adaptation of Charles G. Booth's novel; *Blockade* (1938); *None but the Lonely Heart* (1944), an adaptation of Richard Llewellyn's novel; *Deadline at Dawn* (1946), an adaptation of William Irish's novel; *Humoresque* (1946), an adaptation of Fanny Hurst's story, with Zachary Gold; *The Sweet Smell of Success* (1957), an adaptation, with Ernest Lehman, of Lehman's novel; *The Story on Page One* (1960); and *Wild in the Country* (1961), an adaptation of J. R. Salamanca's novel *The Lost Country*.

Achievements

In the spring of 1935, Clifford Odets, a young playwright thitherto unknown, had the heady experience of seeing three of his plays produced in New York. Overnight, he was hailed as the rising star of American drama. *Waiting for Lefty*, a timely tour de force dealing specifically with the strike of New York taxicab drivers but more broadly with the stressful socioeconomic situation in which many working people found themselves during the Great Depression, was a pioneering effort in proletarian drama which made its point by presenting six vignettes around a controlling theme and by involving the audience directly in the play's action—it is the audience that gives the strike call in the play's dramatically intense ending. By March, 1935, the play had been brought to Broadway to play as part of a double bill with *Till the Day I Die*, written quickly as an accompaniment to it. By July, 1935, *Waiting for Lefty* had been performed in thirty cities across the United States.

On February 19, 1935, the Group Theatre brought *Awake and Sing* to Broadway some weeks after *Waiting for Lefty* had first gained its widespread popular acclaim, and this warm play of middle-class Jewish family life clearly established its author as a significant and effective playwright.

If ever a dramatist were right for his time, the young Odets was right for the 1930's. A nonconformist with a strong sense of outrage at social injustice, Odets drifted into various acting and radio jobs after he dropped out of high school at age seventeen. During this period, Odets learned a great deal about the struggle to survive and about theater. It was his association with the Group Theatre that gave Odets an identity, a satisfying surrogate family, and the motivation that he had until then been lacking. The Group Theatre, an outgrowth of the Depression, was to become the compelling force in the spirit and structure of Odets' best work, the plays from *Waiting for Lefty* through *Paradise Lost*, excluding only the somewhat inconsequential *Till the Day I Die*. His plays reflected the philosophy of the Group Theatre that there should be no stars; in these early plays, Odets discovered and experimented with the theme of nonfulfillment, which was to be the controlling theme of most of his writing.

The Depression gave Odets a strong subject, and when it ended, he had difficulty finding subjects about which he could write with the force and conviction of his early work. The Odets who could convincingly argue the case of young lovers unable to marry because of the economic pressures of the Depression was a much less persuasive social protester when, more than a decade later, in *The Big Knife*, he attacked Hollywood's exploitation of Charlie Castle, an actor who had a fourteen-year contract for four million dollars. The social conditions out of which Odets' best artistic achievement grew had largely ceased to exist by 1940, and he was never able to find another theme with which he could identify so fully or in quite the same way as he had with the themes that the Depression provided him. While his last three plays are dramatically sound and compelling, Odets was always forced to work in his own enormous shadow, and his public demanded more of him than he could deliver in his later years.

Biography

Clifford Odets was born in Philadelphia to a twenty-year-old Lithuanian immigrant, Louis J. Odets, and his nineteen-year-old wife, Pearl Geisinger Odets, who had come to the United States from Romania, often called "Austria" by the Geisingers. Odets was the first of three children, and he was closer in many ways to his Aunt Esther and her husband than he was to his sickly, chronically depressed mother and somewhat combative father. "Tante Esther," as he called her, had been just enough older than her sister Pearl when they arrived in the United States that she remembered Yiddish and was able to speak it. Her husband, Israel Rossman, read Yiddish newspapers, and in the Rossman household, the young Odets was exposed to cadences of language which were absent from his parents' home and which he was to use effectively in dialogue throughout his career. Indeed,

Odets was more successful than any playwright of his time in capturing the speech cadences and intonations of Jewish Americans.

Odets' father rose quickly to middle-class status. By the early 1920's, Louis Odets was owner of a print shop in the Bronx. As the fortunes of the family improved, however, Odets began to feel spiritually alienated from the bourgeois values of his parents. He was moving gradually into what would be his vocation by affiliating himself with such theatrical groups as the Drawing-Room Players, Harry Kemp's Poets' Theatre, the Mae Desmond Stock Company, and, for a short time in 1929, the Theatre Guild. It was not until 1931, however, that he found his spiritual home in the newly formed Group Theatre. His writing was to be shaped by the philosophy of the Group Theatre, in which, as Harold Clurman writes in *The Fervent Years*, "there were to be no stars ... not for the negative purpose of avoiding distinction, but because all distinction ... was to be embodied in the production as a whole." Odets' plays, reflecting this philosophy, generally contain no starring roles, but rather six or eight substantial roles of essentially equal importance.

With his meteoric rise to fame in 1935, Odets' commitment to the Group Theatre grew, and as the Group faced financial difficulties, Odets reluctantly became a Hollywood screenwriter, primarily to earn enough money to keep it from financial collapse. Some argue that Odets compromised his talent by writing for the screen, that he was never again able to write with the force and the conviction that he had demonstrated before "selling out" to Hollywood. While it is evident that he never again wrote so well as he had in the 1930's, it is overly simplistic to attribute Odets' artistic decline to any single causal factor; the times in which he lived and crucial events in his own life, including his 1937 marriage to and subsequent divorce in 1941 from Austrian film star Luise Rainer, both contributed to Odets' artistic decline in the early 1940's.

Odets' middle range of plays—*Rocket to the Moon, Night Music*, and *Clash by Night*—deal largely with questions of love, personal isolation, and nonfulfillment. None reaches the artistic level of the earlier plays. In the seven-year hiatus between *Clash by Night* and the 1949 production of *The Big Knife*, Odets produced three screenplays and an adaptation of Konstantin Simonov's *The Russians*, a propaganda piece. Odets was unable to recapture in his later plays the freshness and the authentic social anger of his early plays.

When he was called before the House Committee on Un-American Activities in 1952, Odets admitted to having been a member of the Communist Party "from toward the end of 1934 to the middle of 1935, covering anywhere from six to eight months." Never a very convinced Party member, Odets favored having a third major political party in the United States but was quickly disenchanted with the rigidity of the Communist Party and dismissed it as a reasonable vehicle for dealing with the social problems that perplexed him.

Odets' last stage play, *The Flowering Peach*, reflects its author's newly found interest in the biblical heritage of the Jewish people. A redaction of the Noah story, *The Flowering Peach* is warm and sensitive, reminiscent in its family orientation of *Awake and Sing*. It is a play of resignation rather than of revolution.

In the last decade of his life, Odets produced little, although in the last year of his life he was working on an ambitious project to write four of the thirteen scripts for *The Richard Boone Show*, a dramatic television series. Odets had completed three of the four scripts he was to write before he succumbed to cancer in Los Angeles on August 14, 1963. The year after Odets' death, the musical version of *Golden Boy*, on which he had been working with William Gibson, reached Broadway.

Analysis

In an interview with Arthur Wagner conducted two years before Clifford Odets' death but not published in *Harper's Magazine* until September of 1966, Odets told Wagner, "The question is really not one of knowing how to write so much as knowing how to connect with yourself so that the writing is, so to speak, born affiliated with yourself." When he was dealing with the pressing social problems of the 1930's, which were times of great national pain that spilled over into the lives of individuals and into the conduct of families, Odets was connecting with himself. He was writing from deep personal conviction intensified by moral outrage at a society that could do no better for its members than to allow the economic and social dissolution that the Depression brought.

Economic and social determinism is significantly present in all of Odets' major plays, and *Waiting for Lefty* is no exception. Despite its brevity, it makes eloquent statements on a broad range of topics, ranging from family life to anti-Semitism to collective bargaining to the ecological irresponsibility of capitalist producers of poison gas. The overwhelming question posed by the play is whether workers should have control over their own destinies, a question that recurs in Odets' later plays. While the last curtain leaves no doubt about the answer Odets proposes, it is clear that the social and economic pressure under which his characters are laboring will not magically disappear.

As often happens with social drama, *Waiting for Lefty*, which Brooks Atkinson called "fiercely dramatic in the theater," has become, as Michael Mendelsohn writes, "as dead as last year's newspaper." This earliest of Odets' plays, an agitprop piece written in great haste to be presented at workers' meetings, was to catapult its author into public recognition and to offer him the opportunity to become a successful Broadway playwright.

Waiting for Lefty was intended to be a play about "the stormbirds of the working class"; the play is more accurately described as being about "declassed members of the middle class," as John Howard Lawson contends. The principals in the play are from various walks of life. They have two things in common: They are taxicab drivers, and they earn their living in this way because the Depression has made it impossible for them to follow other pursuits. The drivers and those close to them are examples of men with thwarted ambitions and broken dreams; external economic forces are determining their lives. They meet to consider whether they should strike, and as the strike is discussed, various drivers tell their stories in the several vignettes of which the play is composed. Mendelsohn rightly perceives that the play succeeds dramatically because of its "interplay between personal lives and collective action." Odets was himself middle-class, his audiences were middle-class, and the play is essentially middle-class, despite Odets' polemics to the contrary. It is this which accounts for the play's initial success with its audiences. A middle-class audience could feel empathy with middle-class protagonists who had been brought to the level of the working class by the Depression.

Waiting for Lefty, which plays in less than an hour, was too short to be taken to Broadway as an evening's entertainment. The play and its writer were in great demand with all sorts of political groups, and the publicity generated by the play made producers eager to bring it to Broadway, where *Awake and Sing* had just opened. In order to round out an evening of theater, Odets wrote *Till the Day I Die*, one of the early anti-Nazi plays to appear on Broadway. The play, which focuses on the situation of Communists in Adolf Hitler's Germany, is somewhat trivial, although in it one can recognize the beginning of themes that Odets was to develop later. For example, the protagonist, Ernst Tausig, is brought in for questioning by the storm troopers, who smash his right hand with a rifle butt. This leads eventually to amputation, a particularly difficult outcome for Ernst, who is a violinist. (Similarly, in *Golden Boy*, Joe Bonaparte is a promising violinist, but he destroys his hands by becoming a prizewinning boxer, led into this activity by economic necessity rather than by choice.) Ernst Tausig commits suicide, finally, and if any ray of hope is offered, it is a questionable one: Ernst's mistress, Tilly, is pregnant and presumably will produce a child who will carry on. What this child is likely to become in Hitler's Germany is doubtful. *Till the Day I Die* was dashed off in five days, and the play is less than convincing. As a curtain opener for *Waiting for Lefty*, it served its commercial purposes at the expense of artistic integrity; its value is historical rather than artistic.

The backdrop of the Depression pervades *Awake and Sing*. Those who expected another play with the political fervor and intense anger of *Waiting for Lefty* found instead that *Awake and Sing* was an accurate view of Jewish family life and of the effect of the Depression on three generations of the Berger family, all living under one roof. The play focuses primarily on the two members of the youngest generation, Ralph and Hennie. Both are thwarted because of the economic pressures under which they live. Hennie is trapped in a marriage contrived by her mother, who cannot bear the thought of her daughter mothering an illegitimate child. Her brother, Ralph, the idealist, can proclaim, "We don't want life printed on dollar bills," but his whole existence is so economically determined that he has little control over his life. The grandfather, Jacob, also an idealist, complains, "This is a house? Marx said it—abolish such families." Jacob commits suicide in the end, leaving to Ralph the small legacy that his insurance policy will provide: a slender but unconvincing thread of hope. Bessie Berger, the mother of the household, lives in fear that her family will collapse and her home be taken away: "They threw out a family on Dawson Street today. All the furniture on the sidewalk. A fine old woman with gray hair." Ever concerned with appearances, Bessie proclaims ingenuously, "I like my house to look respectable," and acts to keep it that way no matter what deceptions she must engage in to maintain the appearance. Odets is at his best in *Awake and Sing*. He is close to his blood ties: He knows his characters, and the play exudes authenticity.

Speaking of *Awake and Sing*, Odets said that his "interest was not in the presentation of an individual's problems, but in those of a whole class." One must bear this statement in mind when approaching *Paradise Lost*, in which the trials visited upon the Gordon family are so numerous and so close together in time that they put one in mind of the most melodramatic of soap operas. In this play, which, like *Awake and Sing*, is Chekhovian in its characterization and structure, Odets deals with an upper-middle-class family caught in the grip of the Depression.

As the threat of economic annihilation closes in on the Gordons, Leo, the father, loses his business, largely through the deception of an unscrupulous partner. One of his sons, Julie, is dying of encephalitis. The other son, Ben, a former Olympic runner, is felled by a policeman's bullets in a chase following a robbery he has committed in order to get money for his wife and family. Leo's daughter, Pearl, frustrated in her musical and personal ambitions, becomes a virtual recluse. Ultimately, the family is evicted when Leo's business plunges into bankruptcy.

Odets considered *Paradise Lost* his most profound play. Most of the critics did not agree, with even such perceptive commentators as Joseph Wood Krutch suggesting that the play was a mere burlesque of *Awake and Sing*. Few could see through the melodrama and sentimentality of *Paradise Lost* to what Odets was struggling to communicate. Harold Clurman, writing in his introduction to the published version of the play, contends quite correctly that it is about middle-class people who have the "bewildering perception that everything [they intimately believe] is being denied by the actual conditions of contemporary society." Metaphorically, the play, like *Waiting for Lefty* and *Awake and Sing*, is about an entire class of people who are being wiped out by the Depression. The Bergers represent the lower range of this class; the Gordons, the upper range. The middle class, upper or lower, is being dragged down by economic conditions over which they have no control. As in most of his plays, Odets is writing in *Paradise Lost* about blocked aspirations. The theme of nonfulfillment controls the play, whose only shred of hope comes in Leo's final lengthy oration, which, in the face of such encompassing despair, is somewhat out of place and unconvincing.

The play, nevertheless, has strong vignettes, the best of which are found in the portrayal of Sam Katz, Leo's dishonest business partner. Sam, sexually impotent, blames his long-suffering wife for their childlessness. Sam's impotence can be taken to represent a general lack of the strength and will that might enable him to live as he desires. His wife-mother, Bertha, endures his taunts and his humiliation, comforting him at the end and calling him "a good boy." In Sam and Bertha, Odets was beginning to develop the characters who emerged more fully developed as Ben and Belle in *Rocket to the Moon* and who reappeared in a somewhat different form in *The Country Girl*. His concern with a weak man in a childless marriage to a woman whose maternal feelings are directed at her spouse pervades these three plays.

In *Golden Boy*, Joe Bonaparte's artistic nature and his desire to be a concert violinist are at odds with the economic realities of his life. Bonaparte goes into boxing to make money, and in so doing, he ruins his sensitive hands and destroys any possibility that he might ultimately achieve his artistic goal. On a metaphoric level, Odets is suggesting quite cynically a philosophy that Moe Axelrod espoused in *Awake and Sing*: "One thing to get another." Life kills the dreamer, the artist, in the same way that Odets' father had done everything in his power to make his son practical, to kill the dreamer in him.

Harold Clurman called *Golden Boy* Odets' most subjective play. Odets held the play in some contempt, claiming to have written the play to be a hit in order to keep the Group Theatre together. *Golden Boy*, however, shows commendable control and artistic maturation. If one can overcome the early incongruity of a boxer who is also a sensitive violinist, the rest of the play is plausible and well made. Joe Bonaparte, the "golden boy" of the play's title, falls victim to what Gerald Weales calls "the disintegration brought on by success." Joe makes the difficult decision to abandon his musical career in order to pursue a career in championship boxing. Ironically, he wins the championship fight but, in so doing, kills his opponent and forecloses all hope of returning to his music.

Joe grows increasingly alienated from his society as he realizes that he has sold out. His trainer cautions him, "Your heart ain't in fighting . . . your *hate* is." Joe changes in the course of the play from a youth who is sensitive about being cross-eyed to a necessarily hardened figure: Sensitivity, an asset for a musician, is a liability for a boxer. Ultimately, Joe becomes a piece of property (this theme recurs forcefully in *The Big Knife*). Joe gets his Duesenberg, a clear and visible symbol of economic success, but he dies when the car crashes, a conclusion with a dramatic impact not unlike that left upon audiences who learn at the end of *Waiting for Lefty* that Lefty has been found shot to death in an alley. Whereas the news of Lefty's death forces the taxicab drivers to rise to action, the news of Joe Bonaparte's death leaves audiences with a dull, pervasive ache for the human condition.

Golden Boy was Odets' first drama to underplay the Yiddish-English dialect of his earlier work. In this departure, one sees a playwright trying to broaden his range, trying to reduce his dependence on his Jewish heritage. *Rocket to the Moon*, *Night Music*, and *Clash by Night* represented a new direction for Odets. The years in which these plays were written were those during which Odets was married to and divorced from Luise Rainer, and the plays themselves are much concerned with questions of love and marriage. *Night Music* is concerned with young love and the effects of economic uncertainty upon it, while the other two are concerned with romantic triangles. Odets is tentative in these plays. His personal concerns have shifted from those of an artist struggling to establish himself and to survive during the Depression to those of someone who is concerned primarily with the tensions that two people experience in a love relationship and in marriage.

Rocket to the Moon is an unfocused drama about the tedious dalliance of a middle-aged dentist with Cleo, his receptionist. Unfortunately, Odets allowed himself to be sidetracked in this play, concentrating more on Ben Stark, the dentist, than on Cleo, the receptionist, who could have been drawn with sufficient psychological complexity to bring some intensity into the drama. The sensitivity with which Odets portrayed Sam and Bertha Katz in *Paradise Lost* was not repeated in *Rocket to the Moon*, although Ben and Belle indisputably resemble Sam and Bertha. This play is at best tawdry and represents an artistic setback for its author. Odets was at this time able neither to distance himself sufficiently from his own problems to practice his profession at its highest level, nor to use his own suffering and confusion to enrich his art. Some of Odets' remarkable ability to sketch characters is, nevertheless, evident in *Rocket to the Moon*. Belle's father, Mr. Prince, is drawn with great skill, and in him one sees a bit of what Odets was beginning to fancy himself to be—someone who had gained material security but who was essentially unloved. When Mr. Prince suggests that Cleo might marry him, she rejects the offer, saying, "Next week

I'll buy myself a dog."

The theme of *Night Music* is homelessness. Steve Takis, the protagonist, is known as "Suitcase Steve" because he always carries a suitcase with him and constantly moves from place to place. He has been sent East on an incredible errand to pick up two apes for a Hollywood film studio and to accompany them back to the West Coast. One of the apes snatches a gold locket from Fay Tucker, the police become involved, and Steve is arrested and then released, his apes being held as security. He approaches Fay with indignation for the trouble she has caused him, and, predictably, the two fall in love. The play's most sympathetic character, Detective A. L. Rosenberg, helps the couple, but Rosenberg, the symbol of good in a hostile world, is dying of cancer. The play's didacticism overcomes its warmth and its occasional gentle tenderness. The symbols are heavy-handed, and the interesting themes of personal isolation, homelessness, and loneliness, which had been themes of some prominence in all of Odets' earlier plays, here seem completely trivial.

Clash by Night was written as Odets' marriage fell apart and as the Group Theatre was reaching the point of disbanding. Between the time the play opened out of town and the time it opened on Broadway, the Japanese had bombed Pearl Harbor and national attention was on more serious matters than the sordid love triangle around which this play revolves. *Clash by Night* is about Mae Wilenski and her lackluster husband, Jerry. Mae is bored with her life, and before the end of act 1, she is involved in a love affair with Earl Pfeiffer, a boarder in the Wilenski household. The action plays out quite slowly, each act being interlarded with echoes of Odets' social fervor; in a subplot, for example, Joe and Peggy have been engaged for two years and are unable to marry because Joe works only three days a week, a situation rather unconvincing to audiences in a society gearing up for war and recruiting every available able-bodied citizen to work in defense jobs. Ultimately, Jerry is led by jealousy to murder Earl, an interesting outcome in this love triangle involving two men and a woman as opposed to the two women-one man triangle in *Rocket to the Moon*. Whereas Belle takes Ben back, perhaps to nurture him but more likely to torture him for the rest of his days, Jerry must strike out in a manly way and seek vengeance through killing his rival.

A seven-year gap separated *Clash by Night* from Odets' next Broadway production, *The Big Knife*. The play focuses on Hollywood's exploitation of Charlie Castle, an actor who has just been offered a fourteen-year movie contract worth four million dollars. Charlie, however, does not wish to sign: Like Joe Bonaparte in *Golden Boy*, he is in danger of becoming merely a piece of property, and Charlie recoils from allowing the studio to own him. The complication is that Charlie was involved in a fatal hit-and-run accident for which he and the studio have permitted his publicity man, Buddy Bliss, to take the rap. The studio now attempts to force Charlie to sign the contract under threat of revealing the real facts of the accident. In a sense, Odets was back to arguing the worker-management conflict with which he first dealt in *Waiting for Lefty*; the argument against management is somewhat less convincing, however, when management is paying the worker as handsomely as it is here, even though the principle may be similar.

The play sheds some light on the false standards of Hollywood society, presenting interesting scenes that spotlight such realities of Hollywood life as the control that gossip columnists have over actors' lives. Charlie Castle calls free speech "the highest-priced luxury in this country today," and he attacks the superficiality of Hollywood relationships by saying, "I'll bet you don't know why we all wear these beautiful, expensive ties in Hollywood. . . . It's a military tactic—we hope you won't notice our faces." Odets thus gave vent to the resentment that had been growing in him during the decade since he first came to Hollywood as a screenwriter. *The Big Knife* is tightly structured, and its dramatic intensity is at times superb, but its basic premise is difficult to accept, and Charlie Castle's suicide at the end is more melodramatic than artistically valid.

The Country Girl followed *The Big Knife* in 1950, and in it Odets revived some of the controlling ideas of his earlier plays. The protagonist, Frank Elgin, is an aging actor who has fallen on hard times, largely because of his alcoholism, brought about by the accidental death of his young son, for which he blames himself. Frank's wife, Georgie, is a wife-mother recalling Bertha Katz and Belle Stark. Bernie Dodd, a director, has given Frank one last chance for a comeback. He insists that if Frank begins drinking again, he will dismiss him immediately. Bernie, who first detests Georgie, later is strongly attracted to her, creating a love triangle. This love triangle differs from Odets' previous ones, however, in that Georgie and Bernie are ironically united in their efforts to rehabilitate Frank. The psychological complexity of the play makes it conceptually stronger than *Rocket to the Moon* or *Clash by Night*.

In numerous rewrites, the role of Georgie was drastically changed from that of a nagging wife to that of a firm but understanding and supportive marriage partner. The love relationship that grows between Georgie and Bernie is the timeworn love-hate relationship. Frank remains largely oblivious to it until near the end of the last act. In the end, despite lapses along the way, Frank succeeds in acting his part well and in paving the way for the comeback toward which he has been struggling. The role of Frank provides a challenging vehicle for an actor to play a weak, insecure character, a pathological liar who successfully undergoes a difficult rehabilitation. Still, Frank's triumph at the end, accompanied by Georgie's decision to stay with him, leaves doubts in the minds of the audience. Throughout the play, Georgie's relationship to Frank has been based upon her providing strength for a weak husband. If Frank has overcome his weakness, one must seriously question whether the relationship will give Georgie what she needs. If he has not overcome his weakness, then they are back exactly where they began. Odets himself viewed *The Country Girl* as a theater piece and disparaged the play's artistry, although he was pleased with certain technical aspects of it, especially the much-revised ending.

In his last play, *The Flowering Peach*, Odets returned to his blood sources. The family in the play, reminiscent of the Bergers in *Awake and Sing*, speak in the Yiddish-English dialect of Odets' earlier characters. *The Flowering Peach* is a version of the Noah story and largely concerns Noah, to whom God appears in a dream, predicting the Flood; Noah's attempts to build the Ark; and his conflicts with his son, Japheth, who, even when he comes to believe the truth of his father's dream, refuses to enter the Ark as a protest against a cruel God who would destroy the earth. Japheth finds himself on the Ark only because his father knocks him out and has him carried aboard. Once there, the father-son conflict, the conflict between faith and reason, again erupts. Japeth is convinced that the Ark should have a rudder; his father is equally convinced that God will direct the Ark as He intends.

The Flowering Peach is a warm and satisfying play. In it, Odets again explores the family as a unit, and he does so with sensitivity and with a sentimentality that, in this play, is not unbecoming. The dialogue is easy and natural, and tensions are reduced by the inclusion of amusing wisecracks. *The Flowering Peach* was nominated for the Pulitzer Prize, the first time that such recognition had come to an Odets play, but the Pulitzer's Advisory Board overruled the jurors and gave the prize for the 1954-1955 season to Tennessee Williams for his *Cat on a Hot Tin Roof. The Flowering Peach*, a play of great affirmation, has yet to receive the recognition that it deserves.

Odets wrote to Eugene Gross, "Nothing moves me so much as human aspirations blocked, nothing enrages me like waste. I am for use as opposed to abuse." All of his plays, with the possible exception of *The Flowering Peach*, have a deep and controlling concern with the question of blocked aspirations, and this persistent concern with a universal human problem gives Odets' work a lasting value, despite the dated topical themes of many of his plays.

Other major works

NONFICTION: *The Time Is Ripe: The 1940 Journal of Clifford Odets*, 1988.

SCREENPLAYS: *The General Died at Dawn*, 1936 (adaptation of Charles G. Booth's novel); *Blockade*, 1938; *None but the Lonely Heart*, 1944 (adaptation of Richard Llewellyn's novel); *Deadline at Dawn*, 1946 (adaptation of William Irish's novel); *Humoresque*, 1946 (with Zachary Gold; adaptation of Fannie Hurst's story); *The Sweet Smell of Success*, 1957 (with Ernest Lehman; adaptation of Lehman's novel); *The Story on Page One*, 1960 (directed by Odets); *Wild in the Country*, 1961 (adaptation of J. R. Salamanca's novel *The Lost Country*).

Bibliography

Cooperman, Robert. *Clifford Odets: An Annotated Bibliography, 1935-1989.* Westport, Conn.: Meckler, 1990. A useful bibliographic essay evaluates the listed entries, which are divided into primary works (plays, screenplays, teleplays, articles, journals, and diaries), critical studies (on individual plays and politics, and on the Group Theatre), and information on the House Committee on Un-American Activities. Includes a brief chronology and an index.

Demastes, William W. *Clifford Odets: A Research and Production Sourcebook.* New York: Greenwood Press, 1991. The book's main feature consists of summaries of characters, plots, and overviews of the critical reception of Odets' stage and radio plays. Includes a brief chronology, a biographical essay, a bibliography of Odets' primary works (with unpublished archival sources), an annotated secondary bibliography (1935-1990), a list of major productions, and an index.

Miller, Gabriel. *Clifford Odets.* New York: Continuum, 1989. Critical of the narrow interpretations of Odets as a political playwright of the 1930's, Miller focuses primarily on the published plays, arranged thematically around several "visions": Chekovian, tragic, romantic, melodramatic, and political. The interest centers on both experimentation with form and the evolution of Odets' "significant thematic and social concerns." Index.

_____, ed. *Critical Essays on Clifford Odets.* Boston: G. K. Hall, 1991. This anthology includes ten reviews of Odets' productions (from *Waiting for Lefty* to *The Flowering Peach*), two 1930's evaluations of Odets, and three interviews with Odets, dating from the 1950's and 1960's, and a collection of essays, most reprinted from earlier books. The introduction provides an evaluative chronological overview of primary and secondary sources.

Odets, Clifford. *The Time Is Ripe: The 1940 Journal of Clifford Odets.* New York: Grove Press, 1988. In 1940, Odets was immersed in profound change: After six successful plays, *Night Music* failed, his first marriage ended, and the Group Theatre was collapsing. A preface by his son Walt, an introduction by William Gibson (who focuses on Odets' preoccupation with form in his life and art), and supplementary biographical sketches all aid readers in understanding the fascinating journal entries.

R. Baird Shuman
(Updated by *Elsie Galbreath Haley*)

EUGENE O'NEILL

Born: New York, New York; October 16, 1888
Died: Boston, Massachusetts; November 27, 1953

Principal drama

Chris Christophersen, wr. 1919, pb. 1982 (revised as *Anna Christie*); *Beyond the Horizon*, pr. 1920, pb. 1921; *The Emperor Jones*, pr. 1920, pb. 1921; *Anna Christie*, pr. 1921, pb. 1923; *The Hairy Ape*, pr. 1922, pb. 1923; *All God's Chillun Got Wings*, pr., pb. 1924; *Complete Works*, pb. 1924 (2 volumes); *Desire Under the Elms*, pr. 1924, pb. 1925; *The Great God Brown*, pr., pb. 1926; *Lazarus Laughed*, pb. 1927, pr. 1928; *Strange Interlude*, pr., pb. 1928; *Mourning Becomes Electra*, pr., pb. 1931 (includes *Homecoming*, *The Hunted*, *The Haunted*); *Nine Plays*, pb. 1932; *Ah, Wilderness!*, pr., pb. 1933; *Plays*, pb. 1941 (3 volumes), pb. 1955 (revised); *The Iceman Cometh*, pr., pb. 1946; *A Moon for the Misbegotten*, pr. 1947, pb. 1952; *Long Day's Journey into Night*, pr., pb. 1956; *Later Plays*, pb. 1967; *The Calms of Capricorn*, pb. 1981 (with Donald Gallup); *The Complete Plays*, pb. 1988 (3 volumes).

Other literary forms

Although primarily known for his plays, Eugene O'Neill also wrote poetry and a large amount of correspondence, collected in several volumes and published posthumously. Among these are *"The Theatre We Worked For": The Letters of Eugene O'Neill to Kenneth MacGowan* (1982), edited by Jackson R. Bryer and Ruth M. Alvarez and containing an introductory essay by Travis Bogard; *"Love and Admiration and Respect": The O'Neill-Commins Correspondence* (1986), edited by Dorothy Commins; and *"As Ever, Gene": The Letters of Eugene O'Neill to George Jean Nathan* (1987), edited by Nancy L. Roberts and Arthur W. Roberts. O'Neill's poems were published in *Poems, 1912-1944* (1979) and were edited by Donald Gallup. His unpublished or unfamiliar writings were published in *The Unknown O'Neill* (1988), edited by Travis Bogard.

Achievements

O'Neill has been called, rightly, the father of modern American drama, not only because he was the first major American playwright but also because of the influence of his work on the development of American theater and on other dramatists. In addition to achieving both popular success and critical acclaim in America, O'Neill has achieved an international reputation; produced throughout the world, his plays are the subject of countless critical books and articles. In many of his plays, O'Neill employed traditional themes such as the quest, while in others he treated subjects that had gone largely unexamined on the American stage, particularly subjects concerning human psychology. Although many of his works are now universally acclaimed, initial critical reaction to the emotional content of some of these plays was mixed. In addition to breaking new ground in theme and subject matter, O'Neill was innovative in his use of technical elements of the theater; he experimented with such devices as masks, "asides," and even the stage itself as vehicles to further theme. Moreover, in an effort to achieve for the drama the broad temporal spectrum of the novel, he experimented with dramatic time, presenting two of his works in trilogies of nine acts each. Although some of O'Neill's dramatic and theatrical experiments were less well received than others, his reputation is now secure; his plays continue to be widely produced throughout the world, both on the stage and on film, because they speak to the human experience that is shared by all.

Biography

Eugene Gladstone O'Neill's parents were James O'Neill, an actor imprisoned by the material success of his role as the Count of Monte Cristo, and Ellen Quinlan O'Neill, a romantic and idealistic woman similarly trapped for much of her life by an addiction to morphine. The complex psychologies of O'Neill's parents and his brother, and the relationships among all the family members figure significantly as subjects of many of O'Neill's best plays, particularly *Long Day's Journey into Night.* Educated in Catholic schools, O'Neill entered Princeton University in 1906 but left before a year was over. His travels in 1910 and 1911 to South America and England provided background for his early plays of the sea, several of which he wrote during a six-month hospitalization for tuberculosis in 1912. The following year, he participated in George Pierce Baker's Workshop 47 at Harvard University, where he formally studied playwriting. O'Neill was married three times: to Kathleen Jenkins in 1909, to Agnes Boulton in 1918, and to Carlotta Monterey in 1929. He had three children, Eugene, Jr., who was born to the first marriage and who committed suicide in 1950, and Shane and Oona, who were born to the second marriage. O'Neill won four Pulitzer Prizes for his plays: in 1920 for *Beyond the Horizon*, in 1922 for *Anna Christie*, in 1928 for *Strange Interlude*, and in 1957 for *Long Day's Journey into Night.* In 1936, he was awarded the Nobel Prize in Literature. Although ill for the last seventeen years of his life, O'Neill wrote several of his finest plays during that period.

Analysis

Although Eugene O'Neill was fortunate in having several of his earliest plays produced, his first real success was *The Emperor Jones*, produced by the Provincetown Players in 1920. The play was an immense success for the small theater, for O'Neill, and for Charles Gilpin, who performed as America's first black tragic hero in a role later played by Paul Robeson. Devoted to the final hours in the life of Brutus Jones, an ex-convict who, in the course of two years, comes to be emperor of an island in the West Indies, O'Neill's expressionist play won immediate acclaim, both popular and critical.

The form of the play is particularly interesting, for it is composed essentially of one act with eight scenes. The six interior monologue scenes take place in the forest and in Jones's mind and are peopled by the ghosts and phantoms that plague Jones. These six scenes are enveloped by opening and closing scenes which occur outside the forest and which present real characters. The movement of the play is thus a journey from the civilized world into the primitive world of the forest and of the mind, and a journey for Jones to self-knowledge and to death.

The play's expository opening scene reveals that Jones, who arrived on the island two years earlier as a stowaway and who has come to rule the island, has exploited the natives; has enriched himself by manipulation, thievery, and cruel taxation; and has, as a consequence, become so hated that the natives have withdrawn into the hills to stage a revolution. Jones believes, however, that he is prepared for all possibilities: Should he need to escape suddenly, he has hidden food and has learned the paths of the forest; he has also removed vast amounts of money from the island to a safe place. As he explains, he has learned from white people to steal big, and he proudly asserts that he makes his own good luck by using his brain. Jones has, moreover, created among the islanders a mystique and a mythology for himself; distancing himself completely from the natives, whom he terms "bush niggers" and to whom he feels vastly superior, Jones has propagated the myth that he is magically protected from lead bullets and can be killed only by one of silver. Furthermore, having made for himself a silver bullet which he carries as the sixth in his gun, he has spread the companion tale that he is invulnerable to native assaults, since he is the only man big enough to kill himself. Having learned that the natives are rebelling, he congratulates himself on his precautions, boasts about how easy it is to outwit them, and makes his way to the forest through which he must go that night in order to meet the boat which will take him to safety.

When, in the second scene, Jones reaches the edge of the forest, the audience begins to see some of O'Neill's experimental techniques. The edge of the forest, O'Neill tells the audience, is a "wall of darkness dividing the world," a point at which Jones begins to understand the uselessness of his precautions: He cannot find his store of food, and, more important, he is not even sure where he is, exactly. When the little Formless Fears appear, amorphous, black, child-size shapes which, with low sounds of laughter, advance writhingly toward him, he is terrified and fires a shot at them. He reveals his thought processes through a continuing monologue, a technique that seems to reflect the influence of August Strindberg on O'Neill. Jones's monologue, which continues throughout the six forest scenes, reveals at this point his fear at having disclosed his location and his determination to make it through the forest. In addition, he begins to have, within his monologue, a dialogue with himself, a dialogue that symbolically suggests a duality within him, a dissociation between mind and body and between outer bravado and inner fear. The steadily increasing beat of the drum, which had begun with his departure from the palace in the first act, reflects Jones's heightened emotional state and conveys not only the buildup of tension in him but also that in the distant natives.

This first forest scene and the five which follow present a series of vignettes that derive both from Jones's own life and mind and from the racial memory, or collective unconscious. Having first encountered the Formless Fears, he comes next upon Jeff, the Pullman porter he killed with a razor in a fight over a crap game and for whose death he went to prison; both furious and terrified, Jones fires his second bullet into the ghost, who disappears as the drumbeat's tempo once again increases. When, in the fourth scene, Jones reaches a wide road which he does not recognize, his outer appearance is beginning to deteriorate: His glorious uniform is torn and dirty, and he removes his coat and his spurs for comfort. Castigating himself for his belief in ghosts, he reminds himself that he is civilized, not like "dese ign'rent black niggers heah." He is nearly paralyzed with fright, however, when he sees another apparition, a chain gang with a guard who forces Jones to join the prisoners. When the guard beats Jones with his whip, Jones, reenacting his actual break from prison, fires his third bullet into the guard's back.

These first three forest scenes, concerned with aspects of Jones's own life, represent troublesome elements from his individual consciousness. Making him aware of the evil to which he has committed himself, they are important stages in his journey to self-knowledge. Moreover, they indicate, beyond a doubt, the true criminality of his nature. The following scenes, concerned with aspects of his racial memory, present elements that are part of the collective unconscious and thereby reveal some of the cultural forces that have made him what he is.

In the fifth scene, in a clearing in the forest, Jones comes upon a dead stump which looks like an auction block. His appearance further deteriorating, his pants torn and ragged, he removes his battered shoes; the outer symbols of his exalted position, and of his difference from the natives, are virtually gone. As he sends an agonized prayer to Jesus, admitting his wrongdoing and acknowledging that as Emperor he is getting "mighty low," he is suddenly surrounded by a group of Southern aristocrats of the 1850's who are waiting for a group of slaves to come in. To Jones's utter horror, the auctioneer compels Jones to stand on the auction block; when he is bought, Jones, suddenly coming to life and resisting this treatment, angrily pulls out his gun and fires at both the auctioneer and his purchaser, using his last two lead bullets, as the drum quickens and the scene fades.

The sixth scene goes back to a time preceding the fifth; Jones finds himself in a clearing so overhung by trees that it appears as the hold of a ship. By this time, Jones's clothes have been so torn that he is wearing only a loincloth. Discovering that he is among two rows of blacks who moan desolately as they sway back and forth, Jones finds himself inadvertently joining in their chorus of despair, crying out even more loudly than they. Having used all of his lead bullets, he has nothing with which to dispatch them, since he needs his silver bullet for luck, for self-preservation. He is obliged, then, as he was obliged to recommit his crimes, to enter into the racial experience of slavery, to feel the grief and desperation of his ancestors. Unable to disperse this scene, Jones simply walks into the seventh and last of the forest scenes, which takes him to an even earlier time. Coming upon an ancient altar by the river, Jones instinctively bows, even as he wonders why he does so. Although he prays for the Christian God's protection, what appears is a witch doctor whose dance and incantations hypnotize Jones and force his participation in an ancient and mysterious ritual. O'Neill's stage directions indicate that Jones is expected at this point to sacrifice himself to the forces of evil, to the forces that have governed his life and that are now represented by a huge crocodile emerging from the river. Urged onward by the witch doctor and unable to stop himself from moving toward the crocodile, Jones, in a last act of desperate defiance, shoots the crocodile with his last bullet—the silver bullet.

The last act at the edge of the forest, an act which serves as an epilogue, is almost anticlimactic, describing how the natives enter the forest to kill the dazed Jones, who has wandered back (full circle) to the spot where he entered. The audience knows, however, that Jones has symbolically killed himself, destroying his evil and his identity with his own silver bullet. It is, moreover, particularly appropriate that the natives shoot Jones with silver bullets, bullets they have made out of melted money.

The journey into the forest has been for Jones a journey to death, but it has also been a journey to understanding. He has come not only to understand the evil of his own life but also to destroy it symbolically by destroying the crocodile with the bullet that affirms his identity. In effect, he is obliged to confront his true nature when the structure he has created for himself collapses. He has also come, however, to understand both his membership in his race and his connection with those natives to whom he felt so superior; by being forced to undergo the primitive experiences of his people, he is able to move from individuation into the group, into an awareness of the experiences common to his race. He is able to return, by means of this backward and inward journey, to his essential self, the self he had denied out of greed and egotism.

O'Neill in this way presents Jones as both a criminal and a victim, as a man whose own character and personality help to create his fate but whose racial and cultural experiences have also shaped him. Part of the play's tragedy, though, is that the knowledge Jones gains is insufficient to save his life; nevertheless, as the trader, Smithers, concludes at the end of the play, the Emperor Jones "died in the 'eighth o' style, any'ow."

With this play, O'Neill established himself as an important and innovative American playwright. The play is also notable for its lack of autobiographical elements; it is an imaginative creation based upon a blend of folktale and psychology that permitted O'Neill to enter the racial memory of another.

A play differing considerably in kind is *Desire Under the Elms*, first performed by the Provincetown Players in 1924 and perhaps one of O'Neill's most representative works. It reflects a number of the influences that worked significantly upon him, including the Bible and classical mythology; it treats several of his favorite subjects, including the tension-ridden family, antimaterialism, and individuals' participation in creating their own fate; and, although the play was initially received with considerable skepticism and disapproval (it was banned in both Boston and England), its critical reputation and its popular acceptance have steadily increased with time, and it continues to be produced for appreciative contemporary audiences.

The play is set on a New England farm in the mid-nineteenth century, a thematically important setting. Just as the New England land is rocky, unyielding, and difficult to manage, so is old Ephraim Cabot, who owns the farm, and so is the Puritan ethos which governs the lives of this patriarch and those around him. Accompanying this symbolism of hardness and coldness in the land and in Ephraim is the emotional symbolism associated with the farmhouse: O'Neill's set directions specify that the farmhouse is flanked by "two enormous elms" that "brood oppressively over the house," that "appear to protect and at the same time subdue," and that possess "a sinister maternity in their aspect, a crushing, jealous absorption." Clearly symbolic of Ephraim's dead second wife, and typifying both her physical and mental exhaustion and her unavenged spirit, the elms are also symbolic of the restrictive nature of New England farm life; in signifying that restriction, they are symbolic also of Ephraim, who exercises a jealous and unrelentingly selfish control over everything and everyone within his reach.

When the play opens, Ephraim is away from the farm on a trip, during which he marries Abbie Putnam, a young widow. By means of the marriage, Ephraim can prove his continuing virility and vigor and, he believes, achieve his paramount desire: to perpetuate his power and his hold over the land. His three grown sons, Simeon and Peter, children of Ephraim's first wife, and the sensitive Eben, son of Ephraim's second wife, dislike and distrust their father and recognize that his marriage to Abbie ensures that none of them will satisfy their desire to inherit the farm. One of the French naturalist writers whose work influenced O'Neill was Émile Zola, and this play seems to be particularly evocative of Zola's *La Terre* in dealing with the human greed for land. This shared desire for land, however, is not the only desire with which the play is concerned. Ephraim, who sees himself as an extension of the Old Testament God, desires to maintain his power forever; Abbie, who marries because of her initial desire for security, comes later to desire love instead, as does Eben, who initially desires revenge upon his father for working his mother to death. Although Simeon and Peter also hope for a share in the farm, they are happy to accept Eben's offer to buy them off, realizing that their expectations, because of their father's new marriage, will probably go unrealized.

The play establishes in the first act the many violent tensions existing between father and son. Blaming his father for the death of his mother, Eben also believes his father is cheating him out of the farm. Moreover, although Eben insists that he is like his mother and denies any similarity to his father, and although Ephraim likewise considers his son weak and spineless, it is one of the play's ironies that father and son are in fact much alike, as indicated symbolically by the fact that both patronize the same local prostitute. More significant, however, both father and son are governed by strong emotions: Both are quick to anger, stubborn, vengeful, proud, and hard, and both are the victims of seething animal passions that are covered by only a thin veneer of civilization. The psychologically normal conflict between any father and son is thus intensified by their temperamental similarities, and when Abbie, the catalyst, appears as the stepmother who is closer in age to son than to father, the stage is indeed set for a depiction of violent emotions that result in great tragedy.

Because they both desire the farm, Abbie and Eben initially hate and mistrust each other, but their harsh and cruel behavior toward each other is counterpointed by a growing physical desire between them, a reflection, perhaps, of O'Neill's interest in the classical myths of Oedipus and Phaedra. O'Neill's use of a divided set permits the audience to watch this desire growing as they see simultaneously into the bedroom of Eben, as he moves half-unconsciously toward the wall beyond which Abbie stands, and into the bedroom of Ephraim and Abbie, where they continue to hope for the son who will fulfill Ephraim's desire and ensure Abbie's security. As the obvious but unspoken passion between Abbie and Eben mounts and the house grows correspondingly cold, Ephraim is driven to find solace in the barn, among the animals, where it is warm—an opportunity which Abbie uses to seduce Eben in the parlor, where the restless spirit of Eben's mother seems to be concentrated.

This lovemaking between stepmother and son, teetering as it does on the brink of incest, was, as one might expect, an aspect of the play to which censors objected. Abbie is, after all, Eben's stepmother, and she uses her "maternal" relationship to Eben as a means of seduction. At the same time that she vows to kiss him "pure," as if she were his mother, she passionately blurts out that loving him like a mother "hain't enuf," and that "it's got to be that and more." As O'Neill explains in his stage directions, there is in her "a horribly frank mixture of lust and mother love." One further motive for Abbie which O'Neill leaves uncertain is her need to produce a son for Ephraim; it is one of the fine ambiguities of the play that we are unable to decide whether Abbie seduces Eben out of greed for the land, out of maternal caring, out of physical lust, or out of genuine love for him. Eben is moved by similarly discordant motives, by both a real desire for Abbie and a desire to avenge his mother by taking his father's woman; he senses his mother's spirit leaving the house and returning to her grave, finally at peace. Eben indicates his understanding of and his satisfaction with the retributive nature of this act the next morning when he offers his hand to his father, remarking to the uncomprehending Ephraim that they are now "quits."

Yet, despite the deliberate calculation with which this love affair begins, Abbie and Eben come in time genuinely to love each other. What was initially, at least in part, a mutually self-serving and opportunistic seduction results in the first warm human relationship the farm has seen. There is, however, no way for the drama to end happily, even though, at the beginning of the third act, all have attained what they at one time desired: Ephraim has a son to prove his virility, Abbie has earned the farm by providing that son, and Eben has avenged his mother. These desires are, to Abbie and Eben, at least, no longer of prime importance, and the party Ephraim gives to celebrate the birth of "his" son serves as an ironic backdrop to the play's tragic climax.

Ephraim, flushed with liquor and pride at producing a son at seventy-six and oblivious to the knowing sneers of the townspeople, in a brutal physical and emotional confrontation with Eben gloats that Abbie wanted a child only to preempt Eben's claim to the farm. Believing that Abbie has seduced him only in order to become pregnant and cheat him, Eben turns violently against her, telling her that he hates her and wishes their son dead. The half-crazed Abbie, hysterically wishing to restore the time when Eben loved her and confusedly identifying the child as the cause of Eben's present hate, smothers the child in its cradle in an appalling inversion of the myth of Medea: Whereas Medea murders her children as an act of revenge against her faithless husband, Abbie murders her child in order to recapture the lost love of Eben. Eben, however, does not respond with love, but with horror and revulsion, and he runs for the sheriff to arrest her. Returning before the sheriff, Eben in a change of heart acknowledges his own guilt and reaffirms his love for Abbie. The play ends with their mutual expression of love as they are taken off by the sheriff, who ironically remarks, with admiration, that "it's a jim-dandy farm."

The play seems, then, to be unmitigatedly naturalistic and pessimistic as the lovers go off to be hanged and as Ephraim is left alone with his farm. Yet O'Neill poses the possibility of a spiritual victory in the play: Although the desire to possess has dominated their lives, Abbie and Eben are freed of that desire at the end—even though their victory is to be short-lived. It is also possible to see a victory over the forces of evil embodied in Puritanism and in the New England patriarchal society, because, even though Eben reacts initially to his father's announcement and to the baby's murder with all the violent self-rightousness one would expect of his father, he comes to transcend this attitude and to acknowledge both his love for Abbie and his own guilt. Although Abbie and Eben have lost everything in the worldly sense, in finding love and faith in each other they do perhaps escape, however briefly and symbolically, from the brooding, confining New England elms.

In this play, O'Neill seems to return to the naturalism that informed his early plays of the sea. His characters are presented as bewildered, struggling beings, blown about like leaves in the gutter, compelled by the external forces of fate, chance, and environment and by the internal workings of their physical nature. It is indeed difficult for these characters to win, but for O'Neill, the salient point is that, in struggling, his characters can transcend their fate.

The critics, who had difficulty with *Desire Under the Elms* because of its objectionable subject matter, were also troubled by *The Iceman Cometh*, but for different reasons; many considered the latter play unhealthy, pessimistic, and morbid in its depiction of the wasted lives of the habitués of Harry Hope's New York saloon, modeled after those in which O'Neill spent considerable time in 1911 and in 1914-1919. A key theme in the play, and a recurring theme in O'Neill's dramas, is the power and the necessity of illusion to give meaning to life. O'Neill develops this theme through expository conversation and monologues, since there is very little onstage action during the two-day period that the play's four acts encompass. Containing both comic and tragic elements, the play, set in 1912, takes place entirely in the back room of Harry Hope's bar, where the regulars gather.

The play opens upon a gathering of regulars to await the arrival of Hickey, a hardware salesman who is the most successful among them and who comes to the bar for periodic drunks, particularly on the occasion of Harry Hope's birthday, when he funds a great drunken party for the regulars. Himself unfaithful to his wife, Hickey maintains a running gag that his apparently saintly wife must, in his absence, be having an affair with the iceman. Hickey and all the other characters live in a world of illusion, a world which ignores today: They all look backward to yesterday, to what they once were or to what their rosy rewriting of history now tells them they once were, just as they look forward to an equally rosy and improbable tomorrow. The illusion that they all have a future is part of the pipe dream each has, a pipe dream essential to their lives which helps them "keep up the appearances of life." Although these people really have, in Robert Frost's words, "nothing to look backward to with pride" and "nothing to look forward to with hope," they somehow manage to live, to survive in the bleak, drunken world they inhabit, because they possess the illusion that they have a yesterday about which they can feel pride and a tomorrow about which they can hope. That illusion enables them to ignore the dark reality that is their today. Moreover, because they understand one another's illusions and accept them, they can be sympathetic and tolerant of one another's failings as well as of their own.

Among the characters who frequent the bar are Larry Slade, an elderly anarchist who believes he is uninvolved in life and who claims he wants only to die; Joe Mott, a black man who plans to open a gambling house one day; Piet Wetjoen, a former Boer War commander who believes he can return home; Pat McGloin, who plans to return soon to the police force; Harry Hope, a former Tammany politician who believes he will someday leave his saloon and walk around the ward; Willie Oban, previously of Harvard Law School, who plans one day to go to the District Attorney and get a law job; Rocky, the night bartender, who, because he works as a bartender, believes that he is not a pimp, even though he "manages" and takes money from two prostitutes; Margie and Pearl, Rocky's two "girls," who make the fine distinction that they are tarts but not whores—because they don't have a pimp; Chuck, the day bartender, who believes he will go on the wagon, marry Cora, and buy a farm in the country; and Cora, who shares Chuck's dream and who also believes that he will forgive her for making her living as a prostitute. Into the circle of regulars comes the eighteen-year-old Don Parritt, whose mother, part of the anarchist movement, is on trial out West for a bombing.

Although many of these regulars stay up all night in the saloon to await Hickey, his arrival is disappointing and strangely troubling: When he appears, he is not the same as before. For one thing, he fails to make his usual joke about his wife and the iceman, and for another, he no longer drinks; he explains that he no longer needs it since he threw away "the damned lying pipe dream" that had made him feel miserable. Moreover, he wants very much to save his friends by persuading them to be honest, to stop lying about themselves, and to stop kidding themselves about their tomorrows. He believes that by giving up their illusions, they can attain peace and contentment, and he systematically embarks on a campaign to make them admit the truth about their pasts and to do immediately what they have always said they will do in the future—even though Hickey knows that they will fail. Hickey insists that if one faces reality and kills one's dreams, then those dreams will not be there to nag or to cause guilt, not haunted by yesterday and not fooling oneself about tomorrow. Then, Hickey believes, his friends will have peace, as he does.

As a result of his campaign, however, the friendly and tolerant atmosphere of the bar wears dangerously thin as the friends, stripped of their protective illusions and their defense mechanisms, become not only sober but also nervous, irritable, and belligerent with one another. Harry's birthday party is a flop, spoiled by fights and bad feeling and finally by Hickey's announcement that his wife is dead. Moreover, the peace that Hickey predicts will come, as an effect of facing reality, does not, even though the characters, with varying degrees of reluctance, attempt to give up their dreams, to leave the bar—actually as well as symbolically—and to face reality. Instead of providing them with peace, the act of facing reality robs them of tolerance for one another and therefore of companionship, of tolerance for themselves and therefore of self-respect, of hope for the future and therefore of happiness. As a result of Hickey's efforts to save them from their illusions, as a result of his forcing them to face their tomorrows and to fail, the habitués of Harry Hope's bar are miserable—quarrelsome, despondent, and hateful toward themselves and one another. Even alcohol loses its kick; it seems to have "no life in it," and they can no longer even pass out.

Hickey is genuinely puzzled by these results, since his expectation was that, once they had "killed tomorrow," they would have "licked the game of life." The play's fourth act, which begins by further demonstrating the unpleasantness that has derived from exposure to reality, centers upon Hickey's revelation of his new philosophy and how he acted out this philosophy in his marriage, finally murdering his wife. He killed her, he says, to give her peace by ending her pipe dream that he would one day be better, that he would stop drinking and whoring. Continually making vows to her that he was unable to keep, he was then obliged to feel guilty because his wife was continually hurt and disappointed. Juxtaposed to Hickey's story of love and guilt is Parritt's parallel narrative disclosing his betrayal of his mother. The two stories reach a climax when Parritt confesses that he betrayed the movement because he hated his mother as Hickey confesses that after killing his wife he laughed and called her a "damned bitch." Unable to live with what he has admitted, Hickey seizes upon the explanation that he must have been insane—insane, that is, to laugh at his wife's death, because everyone surely knows that he has always loved her, and if he laughed at her death, then he must have been insane.

The other characters seize upon this explanation as well, because it means they can disregard what he has said before, reestablish their illusions, and thereby once again live with one another and themselves. Don Parritt, however, apparently unable to live with his betrayal of his mother and the reality that his betrayal was motivated by hate, commits suicide by jumping off the fire escape, as, in a sense, does Hickey by calling the police to come for him. He and Parritt, facing the reality about themselves, must destroy themselves because of the pain of that reality. In truth, Hickey hated his wife because she represented his conscience, because although she always forgave him, she also always expected him to try to be better, which he simply did not wish to do. When for one brief moment he admits the truth, that he wanted and was glad to be free of the burden of this conscience, he is unable to live with that truth and he immediately rationalizes that he must have been insane. He thus proves that illusion is, in fact, necessary, in order to accept oneself and in order to live not only with others in the world but also with the reality that death, the iceman, does indeed "cometh."

The play, then, while pessimistic in delineating human weaknesses, seems to hold out the possibility that those weaknesses can be transcended so long as life exists. O'Neill suggests that, in order for life to exist, there must be hope—and hope, very often, is created from illusion. Although Hickey is termed a "nihilist" at one point in the play, he serves, through the dramatic revelation of his own example, to reinforce the necessity, and the positive power, of illusion.

O'Neill has often been criticized for his choice of characters, for their aberrant psychologies, and for their emotionalism. Certainly he dealt with emotions, but he did so because he believed that emotions were a better guide than thoughts in the search for truth. The struggles of his characters frequently take place, therefore, within themselves, so that there is little real action performed on the stage. Victories, consequently, are in the mind, not quantifiable. The ephemeral nature of such victories has been, for some critics, insufficient.

The popularity of O'Neill's work, however, continues to grow. His plays have been performed throughout the world and transformed into film and opera because they concern truths of human existence. For O'Neill, life *is* a tragedy—but human beings have the resources with which to confront it. The dramatic presentation of that struggle was O'Neill's lifework.

Other major works

POETRY: *Poems, 1912-1944*, 1979 (edited by Donald Gallup).

NONFICTION: *"The Theatre We Worked For": The Letters of Eugene O'Neill to Kenneth MacGowan*, 1982 (edited by Jackson R. Bryer and Ruth M. Alvarez); *"Love and Admiration and Respect": The O'Neill-*

Commins Correspondence, 1986 (edited by Dorothy Commins); *"As Ever, Gene": The Letters of Eugene O'Neill to George Jean Nathan*, 1987 (edited by Nancy L. Roberts and Arthur W. Roberts); *Selected Letters of Eugene O'Neill*, 1988 (edited by Travis Bogard and Jackson R. Bryer).

MISCELLANEOUS: *The Unknown O'Neill: Unpublished or Unfamiliar Writings of Eugene O'Neill*, 1988 (edited by Travis Bogard).

Bibliography

Bloom, Harold, ed. *Eugene O'Neill.* New York: Chelsea House, 1987. As part of the Modern Critical Views series, this collection includes essays by Lionel Trilling, Doris Falk, Arnold Goldman, Robert Lee, Travis Boyard, Thomas Van Laan, Jean Chathia, C. W. Bigsby, and Michael Manheim, arranged in chronological order by their original publication dates. Bloom describes them as representative of the "best criticism available." The theoretical slant is thematic and philosophical, with detailed characters and plot analyses. Contains a brief bibliography.

Floyd, Virginia, ed. *Eugene O'Neill: A World View.* New York: Frederick Ungar, 1979. This collection of essays considers O'Neill's European reception, American themes, and performers' views of his work. The eclectic approach provides an interesting tribute, with speculation about the future of O'Neill in theater history. Notes, index, and bibliography.

Moorton, Richard F., Jr., ed. *Eugene O'Neill's Century.* New York: Greenwood Press, 1991. This collection includes excerpts from more than seventeen plays and collected notes, as well as articles ranging from Spencer Golub's semiotic analysis of *Long Day's Journey into Night* to biographical and psychological analyses by Lowell Swortzell, Jane Torrey, Georgia Nugent, Jeffrey Elliott Sands, and Linda Herr. Some essays focus on how and why O'Neill's extensive stage directions have influenced dramatic practice. Six pages of works cited and thirteen pages of index are useful for scholars.

Ranald, Margaret Loftus. *The Eugene O'Neill Companion.* Westport, Conn.: Greenwood Press, 1984. The author has arranged in alphabetical order a complete compendium of plays, synopses, production histories, characters, personal and professional acquaintances, and critical analysis. Three appendices include a chronology of plays, adaptations, and a critical overview. Twenty-eight pages of notes and thirty-seven index pages make this work an invaluable, encyclopedia resource and guide to further study of O'Neill's work.

Robinson, James A. *Eugene O'Neill and Oriental Thought: A Divided Vision.* Carbondale: Southern Illinois University Press, 1982. Taking a philosophical approach to O'Neill's work, Robinson's 186-page work is a scholarly, detailed analysis of possible connections between O'Neill's plays and oriental mysticism, particularly Hindu, Buddhist, and Taoist belief systems. The bibliography and index offer more information on philosophy and religions of the East than on O'Neill, but Robinson's analysis of individual plays, such as *The Great God Brown, Lazarus Laughed, The Iceman Cometh*, and *Long Day's Journey into Night*, sheds new light on the often-stated view of O'Neill's drama as "religious" and "romantic."

Sheaffer, Louis. *O'Neill.* 2 vols. Boston: Little, Brown, 1968-1973. This two-part biography is considered the most complete work on O'Neill's life, and it stands as a model for the genre of literary biography. Including recollections by a variety of O'Neill's colleagues and friends, this work reads smoothly and effectively combines scholarship and human interest. Generally acknowledged as both sympathetic and trustworthy. Notes, index.

Wainscott, Ronald H. *Staging O'Neill: The Experimental Years, 1920-1934.* New Haven, Conn.: Yale University Press, 1988. This highly scholarly yet accessible historical work chronicles the production of O'Neill's plays and the profound influence of his work on American theater practice. Written in a lively style, it is the most detailed work of its kind on O'Neill, although others may have greater scope.

Evelyn S. Newlyn
(Updated by *Rebecca Bell-Metereau*)

JOE ORTON

Born: Leicester, England; January 1, 1933
Died: London, England; August 9, 1967

Principal drama

The Ruffian on the Stair, pr. 1964 (radio play), pr. 1966 (staged), pb. 1967 (one act); *Entertaining Mr. Sloane*, pr., pb. 1964; *The Good and Faithful Servant*, wr. 1964, pr. 1967 (staged and televised), pb. 1970 (one act); *Loot*, pr. 1965, pb. 1967; *The Erpingham Camp*, pr. 1966 (televised), pr. 1967 (staged), pb. 1967 (one act); *Funeral Games*, pr. 1968 (televised), pr. 1970 (staged), pb. 1970 (as television script) (one act); *What the Butler Saw*, pr., pb. 1969; *The Complete Plays*, pb. 1976.

Other literary forms

Joe Orton's novel *Head to Toe* (originally entitled "The Vision of Gombold Proval") was published posthumously in 1971. *Up Against It*, a screenplay written for the Beatles, was published in 1979, although it was never produced. He also collaborated on several novels with Kenneth Halliwell, entitled "The Last Days of Sodom," "Priapus in the Shrubbery," and "The Mechanical Womb"; these were never published.

Achievements

Orton's meteoric rise as a dramatist during the mid-1960's in Britain was the result of the unique and frequently outrageous tone and style of his plays. Called "the master farceur of his age" by John Lahr and "the Oscar Wilde of Welfare State gentility" by Ronald Bryden, Orton made a radical break with the currently popular naturalistic drama of John Osborne and Arnold Wesker. He was instead influenced by Samuel Beckett and Harold Pinter, although he rapidly moved away from Pinter's "comedy of menace" to experiment with farce and the brittle epigrammatic style of Oscar Wilde. The verbal wit, aggressive sexuality, and black humor of his dramas created a new critical term, "Ortonesque," to describe his own style and that of his imitators. The critical reaction to Orton's drama was and remains mixed; the middle-class audiences that Orton worked so hard to affront frequently reacted with horror and shock to his plays, as did many reviewers. Playwrights as varied as Pinter and Terence Rattigan, however, were impressed by Orton. *Loot* won the best play of 1966 award from the *Evening Standard* and was voted the best play of 1966 by *Plays and Players*. Orton's body of work is small, consisting of four one-act plays and three full-length dramas, but he gained an international reputation before his premature death. At the time of his murder, he had begun work on a play tentatively entitled "Prick Up Your Ears," a farce about King Edward VII's coronation.

Biography

John Kingsley Orton (who later changed his name to Joe Orton to avoid any confusion with playwright John Osborne) was born to William and Elsie Orton in a working-class area of Leicester, England. After failing the eleven-plus examination, he enrolled in Clark's College, a commercial school where one of his teachers described him as "semiliterate." Seeing the theater as a way to escape the drudgery of the menial jobs he was forced to take, Orton joined the Leicester Dramatic Society in 1949 and acted in several small roles in other amateur theatrical groups. In 1950, he was accepted to study at the Royal Academy of Dramatic Art, which he entered in 1951. It was there that he met a fellow student-actor, Kenneth Halliwell, who became Orton's friend, lover, and roommate for the rest of his life.

After receiving his diploma from the Royal Academy of Dramatic Art, Orton worked briefly as an assistant stage manager for the Ipswich Repertory Company and then rejoined Kenneth Halliwell in London in 1953. They began collaborating on a series of novels, all of which were turned down for publication. In 1959, Orton, aided by Halliwell, began stealing and defacing books from the Islington and Hampstead libraries. Orton, who would remove the photographs and illustrations from the books and then replace them with his own creations, would also write false blurbs and summaries; after replacing the books on the shelves, he would stand and watch people's reactions to his pranks. In 1962, Orton and Halliwell were arrested and convicted of theft and malicious damage, and both men were sentenced to six months in jail. The jail sentence was a turning point in Orton's life, for it brought him a new sense of detachment from his own writing that had been lacking before this experience; after his release, he began writing plays and no longer collaborated to any great degree with Halliwell.

Orton's sudden fame and fortune during his brief career from 1963 to 1967 put a tremendous strain on his relationship with Kenneth Halliwell, who, older and better educated than Orton, had considered himself the real creative artist. Deeply resentful of Orton's literary success and sexual promiscuity, Halliwell became more and more deeply depressed and neurotic. On August 9, 1967, a chauffeur who had come to drive Orton to an appointment to discuss his screenplay, *Up Against It*, discovered the bodies of Orton and Halliwell. Halliwell had beaten Orton to death with hammer blows to his head and then committed suicide with sleeping pills. Orton's murder, which was so similar in fashion to many of the events of his plays, made him even more famous in death than in life. The details of Orton's life and career may be found in Lahr's superb critical biography, published in 1978, entitled, *Prick Up Your Ears: The Biography of Joe Orton*.

Analysis

Joe Orton's career was launched by the British Broadcasting Corporation's acceptance of his first play, *The Ruffian on the Stair*. By the time the drama was broadcast in 1964, however, Orton had already achieved fame with the successful West End production of *Entertaining Mr. Sloane*. Orton revised *The Ruffian on the Stair* for its stage production in 1966; the revised version is less derivative of Harold Pinter's *The Room* (pr. 1957), although it still shows Orton's early debt to Pinter's techniques.

This one-act play involves three characters: Joyce, a former prostitute; Mike, a thief; and Wilson, the "intruder" who arrives at Joyce and Mike's apartment ostensibly searching for a room to rent. During the course of the play, Wilson reveals that he has had a homosexual relationship with his own brother, whom Mike has recently killed. Wilson's plan is to force Mike to kill him by pretending to sleep with Joyce; in this way, he hopes that Mike will be brought to justice for the murder. Wilson's plan succeeds, and the drama concludes with Mike comforting Joyce, who is weeping not over Wilson's murder but over the death of her goldfish. The play shows Orton, still strongly influenced by Pinter, moving toward the kind of verbal style that would characterize *Entertaining Mr. Sloane*—a style in which characters use media-influenced language to mask their real thoughts and emotions. The emotional sterility of the characters is reflected in the debased, meaningless language of cliché and the popular press, which they use almost exclusively. Although the play suffers from an ending that appears to be arbitrarily forced upon the action, *The Ruffian on the Stair* does show Orton's talent with dialogue and his ability to create a degree of emotional tension among his characters.

Orton's first full-length drama was *Entertaining Mr. Sloane*, a three-act play which showed that the playwright had made important advancements beyond *The Ruffian on the Stair*. In much firmer control of his material in this play, Orton perfected his characters' use of media-influenced language and cliché. In addition, he was able to construct a relationship among the characters that made the play's ending believable and inevitable, a problem he had been unable to solve satisfactorily in *The Ruffian on the Stair*.

In *Entertaining Mr. Sloane*, Kath and Ed, Kath's brother, battle for control and possession of Sloane, Kath's young lodger. The double meaning of the play's title becomes clear as the play progresses, for the insidious Sloane is at first wooed and entertained by Kath and Ed and later must provide entertainment in the form of sexual favors for both of them when they become witnesses to his second murder. At the beginning of the play, Sloane takes a room in Kath's house, where she lives with her father, Kemp. Kemp soon recognizes Sloane as the young man who murdered his employer two years earlier. Kath, a middle-aged woman who coyly plays the role of Sloane's "Mamma" while brazenly seducing him at the end of the first act, soon finds herself pregnant by Sloane. Sloane is also being pursued, in a less obvious fashion, by Ed, who gives him a job as his chauffeur. When Kemp threatens to expose Sloane as a murderer, Sloane accidentally kills him and is then at the mercy of Kath and Ed, who both want to possess him exclusively. The brother and sister finally agree to share Sloane, each taking him for six months at a time. Sloane, who at the play's beginning was able to control Kath and Ed completely, is quickly reduced to an object.

Orton insisted that the play should be acted as realistically as possible so that the characters would not degenerate into caricatures or stereotypes. "What I wanted to do in *Sloane*," said Orton, "was to break down all the sexual compartments that people have." Kath and Ed are deadly serious about their designs on the young lodger, and Orton resisted the two male leads being played as effeminate homosexuals, just as he did not wish Kath to be played as a nymphomaniac. Instead, the play is about individual personalities who are constantly maneuvering in their attempts to gain power. Despite the play's realism, however, *Entertaining Mr. Sloane* is, like several of Orton's later dramas, reflexive in the sense that the characters are aware of their own theatricality. Orton also uses the rhetoric of the detective film in the play, just as he would parody the genre of farce in later dramas.

Present throughout the play is Orton's fascination with a debased language that functions to obscure the characters' real thoughts and deeds. John Lahr argues that Orton's dialogue reveals the "sensory overload" of the effects of the media on the individual—what he calls "an eclectic brew of rhythms and idioms which captured and commented on the mutation of language." *Entertaining Mr. Sloane* is the best example of Orton's search for what he described as his "collage" literary style: His characters mix the language of newspaper headlines, scandal sheets, advertising, and cliché in a comical and meaningless speech which nevertheless manages to communicate their obsessions and desires. Pinter's influence is still present in *Entertaining Mr. Sloane*, but Orton's success with the play led him in new directions as a dramatist. His work became increasingly more outrageous and farcical as a result of the self-confidence he gained because of the success of *Entertaining Mr. Sloane*.

Orton's next play, *The Good and Faithful Servant*, was written in 1964 and appeared on television and stage in 1967. It was Orton's first full-scale attack on authority and convention, represented in this case by the company from which the main character, Buchanan, is retiring after fifty years of service. At the time of his retirement, Buchanan is stripped of his uniform and given an electric clock and toaster, neither of which works. Buchanan also encounters Edith Anderson, an elderly maid who is working for the firm and who turns out to have given birth to their illegitimate twins many years ago. The one-act play concerns Buchanan's adjustment to his retirement, his marriage to Edith, and the relationship between his grandson, Ray, and Debbie, who is pregnant with Ray's illegitimate child.

Buchanan's broken-down physical condition is reflective of what his life-long service to the company has given him. Although he claims to have led "a useful and constructive life," he breaks down coughing at the end of this statement and, in addition to needing glasses and a hearing aid, has also lost an arm in the service of the firm. Buchanan's pitiful reverence for the company is shared by the other employees. Edith is thrilled because she was able to sweep out the canteen one day in the distant past, and Buchanan states that the "high point" of his life came when he appeared in the company's magazine. He also reverentially mentions that he was "almost Staff" and actually opened the door to the chairman of the board on one occasion. Buchanan's death at the end of the play, which occurs after his disillusionment with the party for the elderly, which culminates in his smashing of the toaster and clock with a hammer, is ironically counterpointed by Ray's induction into the corporate life after having been forced by the company's representative, Mrs. Vealfoy, into marrying Debbie. Just as illegitimacy is handed down from generation to generation in the play, so is the grinding and mindless service to a corporation which remains an abstraction to its employees.

Mrs. Vealfoy is the voice both of the corporate mentality and the social conformity which it uses to manipulate its workers. She advises Ray to "say 'yes' as often as possible. . . . I always do. . . . Always," and she organizes the darkly comic party for the retired workers in scene 16, forcing the dispirited elderly people to sing songs containing the word "happy" while a woman collapses and dies in the background. Mrs. Vealfoy's genial intrusiveness and blind faith in the rightness of the company's policies structure *The Good and Faithful Servant*, which is Orton's most naturalistic assault on the world of authority and convention that he would lampoon in a much more anarchic and farcical style in his later drama.

In his novel *Head to Toe*, Orton said that "To be destructive, words had to be irrefutable. . . . Print was less effective than the spoken word because the blast was greater; eyes could ignore, slide past, dangerous verbs or nouns. But if you could lock the enemy into a room somewhere and fire the sentences at them, you would get a sort of seismic disturbance." Not surprisingly, Orton turned from fiction to the theater, where he could attack his audience directly with words, for Orton considered his audience to be his enemy. He chose farce as the most appropriate genre to create a "seismic disturbance," to disturb his audience's conventions and expectations. *Loot* was the first full-length play in which he allowed his taste for anarchic farce a free rein, and if it sometimes too exuberantly celebrates a farcical, outrageous, and topsy-turvy world of madness and corruption, it also shows Orton discovering the proper vehicle for his talent. Farce, observes John Lahr, is an act of "literary aggression," and Orton used farce in order to vent his own anger and to assault a society which he believed to be hypocritical and stultifying. In his farces, he sought what he called in *Head to Toe* a "particularly dangerous collection of words" which could "explode," creating "shock waves [which] were capable of killing centuries afterwards."

In *Loot*, Orton mercilessly lampoons authority, represented most clearly in the play by Detective Truscott. Truscott, who comes to the home of Mr. McLeavy, whose wife has just died, is investigating a theft in which Hal, McLeavy's son, has been involved. McLeavy, the only character in the play with any real respect for authority, is also the only "innocent" character; ironically, it is McLeavy who at the play's conclusion is arrested for a "crime" which Truscott refuses to define.

McLeavy's faith in authority is naïve and pitiful. Early in the play, he says that he likes "to be of assistance to authority" and that public servants can be relied on to behave themselves: "As a good citizen I ignore the stories which bring officialdom into disrepute." All the events of the play work to underscore the irony of McLeavy's blind trust in "officialdom," and his statement in act 2 that "my personal freedom must be sacrificed" so that Truscott can continue with his investigation becomes chillingly significant later in the play. McLeavy's amazement at his own arrest at the conclusion of the play leads to his incredulous comment, "You can't do this. I've always been a law-abiding citizen. The police are for the protection of ordinary people." Truscott's reply, that he does not understand where McLeavy has picked up "such slogans," sums up Orton's view of authority and justice: The conventional law and order of society is merely a mask for corruption, intolerance, and irrationality. As a result, most of the play's references to authority are couched in clichés which render the characters' speeches ludicrous. Fay, the young nurse who has just murdered McLeavy's wife for her money, reacts similarly to McLeavy when she is threatened with arrest: "I'm innocent till I'm proved guilty. This is a free country. The law is impartial." Truscott's response is reminiscent of his reply to McLeavy: "Who's been filling your head with that rubbish?"

As *What the Butler Saw* would later parody farce, *Loot* parodies the detective novel and film. Truscott's comical conclusion that Fay shot her husband at the Hermitage Private Hotel because one of her wedding rings has a roughness associated with "powder burns and salt" shows Orton mocking the detective story's emphasis on rational thinking and deductive reasoning. The world of *Loot* is instead one of madness and illogic in which relationships among people alter rapidly; there is no core of stability or predictability. McLeavy finally asks Truscott, "Is the world mad? Tell me it's not"; his question is answered by Truscott's statement that "I'm not paid to quarrel with accepted facts." *Loot* shows that mysteries cannot be solved, for mysteries only lead to further mystification: Truscott tells the group that "the process by which the police arrive at the solution to a mystery is, in itself, a mystery." In *Loot*, the plot becomes more rather than less complicated as it progresses; the true "criminals" are allowed to go free while the "detective" becomes part of the crime. Fay's final statement in the play, "We must keep up appearances," articulates an important theme: The world is composed of masks, false identities, and lies which exist not to conceal reality but to compensate for its nonexistence. There are only appearances, and the characters who can most effectively manipulate appearance are the most successful. McLeavy's worship of authority reflects his ignorance of appearances; he assumes that those in power are what they claim to be, and he pays the price.

In *The Erpingham Camp*, Orton continues to attack authority and convention and to develop the brilliantly epigrammatic style that culminated in *What the Butler Saw*. Much less naturalistic even than *Loot*, *The Erpingham Camp* is a one-act play composed of eleven short scenes. Its setting is a holiday camp in which chaos and anarchy erupt in what initially appears to be a rigidly organized situation controlled by the proud entrepreneur Erpingham. He is the major symbol of authority in the play and, like Orton's other authority figures, has false notions about the predictability and rational nature of the world. Early in the play, he tells an employee, "We live in a rational world, Riley"; the rest of the drama functions to destroy the validity of this statement.

Problems begin when Riley, who is organizing an evening of entertainment, slaps Eileen, a pregnant woman who is screaming hysterically. Although Riley's action is an attempt to make her stop screaming, a melee ensues and the campers begin, in Erpingham's phrase, to "destroy property," which results in Erpingham's refusing to feed them an evening meal. "We've no time for hedonists here. My camp is a pure camp," Erpingham has said earlier, and he tries to punish his "underlings" in an effort to control their behavior. Erpingham, whose usual advice in any situation is to "consult the manual," is unable to understand or deal with the campers' rage and replies to their pleas for food with the statement, "You have no rights. You have certain privileges which can be withdrawn. I am withdrawing them."

Physical and verbal violence breaks out after this incident, with two groups of campers battling for their own "approach" to the situation. Lou and Ted, a right-wing young couple who claim to have met outside the Young Conservatives, call for moderation, remaining "within the law," and adherence to "page twenty of the Civil Defense Booklet." Kenny and Eileen, a working-class couple resentful of Lou and Ted's "advantages," instead want to take the "means of supply" into their own hands and encourage the campers to break into the food stores, screaming, "Have a bash, I say. Have a bash for the pregnant woman next door!"

The play becomes increasingly anarchic and unrealistic until it concludes with Erpingham's falling to his death down a hole in the floor. Attending at the funeral is the Padre, who has just returned from a court appearance in which he has been accused of molesting a young girl and who ironically notes, "As the little foxes gnaw at the roots of the vine, so anarchy weakens the fibers of society." The play ends with one of Orton's most famous epigrams, the Padre's statement that "it's Life that defeats the Christian Church. She's always been well-equipped to deal with Death." Although his themes in this play are similar to the dramas of the past, particularly the attacks on political and clerical authority, convention, and corruption, *The Erpingham Camp* shows Orton's increasing confidence in his ability to write anarchic farce in the epigrammatic style and was an important step in his movement away from naturalistic drama.

Orton's last completed drama, *What the Butler Saw*, was not performed until after his death, and as a result the play did not undergo final rewrites by the playwright. Nevertheless, *What the Butler Saw* is Orton's most accomplished work. The play is a celebration of irrationality that also parodies the farce form by comically exaggerating its structure and characteristics: An Absurdist genre is parodically made even more absurd. C. W. E. Bigsby suggests that the "byzantine complexities of the plot of *What the Butler Saw* can be seen as a deliberate attempt to parody the very structure of farce itself," and certainly the play's intricate plot makes summary almost impossible.

Like Orton's earlier work, *What the Butler Saw* attacks authority and tradition. In this drama, Dr. Rance, a government representative who has come to Dr. Prentice's mental clinic to be "given details" about its operations, at first appears to be the voice of conventional authority that wishes to suppress the forces of chaos. Although Rance represents the "Commissioners," however, he is also a spokesman for unreason, mentioning to Dr. Prentice that he is a representative of "Her Majesty's Government. Your immediate superiors in madness," and opining that "the higher reaches of the Civil Service are recruited entirely from corpses or madmen." In *What the Butler Saw*, Orton's questioning of authority goes beyond that of religious or governmental institutions; here, he tries to destroy the very foundations of logic, reason, and predictability upon which his audience's assumptions are based.

One of the most important themes of the play is the very thin line of demarcation between the sane and the insane. The setting is a madhouse in which no actual "insane" patients ever appear; rather, it is the ostensibly sane inhabitants, particularly the psychologists, who are mad. Rance tells the policeman Match that they are in a madhouse where "unusual behavior" is the prerogative of everyone: "We've no privileged class here. It's democratic lunacy we practice." "Democratic lunacy" aptly describes the world of *What the Butler Saw*, in which sanity and insanity are relative conditions that depend entirely upon perspective. "The sane appear as strange to the mad as the mad to the sane," Rance tells Dr. Prentice in a statement that echoes the play's epigraph, drawn from Cyril Tourneur's play *The Revenger's Tragedy* (pr. 1606-1607): "Surely we're all mad people, and they/ Whom we think are, are not." Rance tells Mrs. Prentice that her husband's behavior is "so ridiculous one might suspect him of being sane," a Wildean paradox that sums up Orton's view that sanity and insanity are actually mirror images of one another.

In this play, sanity is dependent upon a rejection of all evidence of reality; Rance, after denying that the blood on Mrs. Prentice's hand is "real" while admitting that he sees it, says, "I'm a scientist. I state facts, I cannot be expected to provide explanations. Reject any para-normal phenomena. It's the only way to remain sane." Because reality *is* madness, sanity can exist only when reality is denied. In a sense, however, madness is to be preferred to sanity, for Rance tells Geraldine Barclay that the fact that her mind has "given way" will be an invaluable aid in her efforts to "come to terms with twentieth century living." In a world where irrationality and farcical absurdity rule, the most effective defense is insanity.

Orton's characters also lack any firm sense of their individual identities. Identities and sexes are exchanged with dizzying rapidity, with the result that the characters begin to lose their sense of who and what they are. Nicholas Beckett, in an attempt to verify his own existence, tells Rance, "If [my] pain is real I must be real," a statement Rance counters with the observation that "I'd rather not get involved in metaphysical speculation." Rance prefers to construct elaborate and illogical premises upon which he bases even more outrageously illogical theories, at one point noting his own "law" that the "relations of apparitions are also apparitions." In *What the Butler Saw*, characters are much like "apparitions" who disappear and reemerge as different people; lacking any core of intrinsic identity, they are capable of endless psychic transformations. This lack of immutable identity, however, is not necessarily a negative characteristic: Like madness, fluidity of identity is a means of survival.

What the Butler Saw posits a universe in which irrationality must rule because all premises are illogical, erroneous, or nonexistent. Rance's comically incorrect "theories" about the reasons for Geraldine Barclay's neuroses and Dr. Prentice's madness are blatant fictions that have, as he is well aware, no relationship to reality. In the play, there is no actual "reality" because there is no truth. Geraldine asserts to Dr. Prentice, "We must tell the truth!" and is answered, "That's a thoroughly defeatist attitude." Rance's repeated admonishments to characters to "face facts" is ironic in this context, and near the end of the play, he admits to Geraldine, who is still trying to discover the "truth" about her situation, "It's much too late to tell the truth," a statement that could have been uttered at the play's beginning.

Indeed, Rance is adept at creating theories that satisfy his imagination much more than any simple truth could. When confronted with an actual "fact," such as Dr. Prentice's attack on Mrs. Prentice, he dismisses it by saying, "Oh, that was a mere physical act with no special psychological significance." Rance, entranced with Freudian symbols and theoretical interpretations, sees the madness around him as culminating in the "final chapters" of his planned documentary novel, which will include "incest, buggery, outrageous women, and strange love-cults catering to depraved appetites. All the fashionable bric-a-brac"—a list that also describes Joe Orton's dramatic world. Rance's fictive reworking of the "plot" of the drama is similar to the artistic process, and Orton the dramatist creates a character who imaginatively and fictively revels in the madness around him, just as Orton used his own chaotic life-style as fodder for his art. His early death ended a career that had, perhaps, only begun to approach its maturity. It is impossible to speculate, given his rapid development as a playwright, in which directions he might have gone.

Other major works

NOVEL: *Head to Toe*, 1971.
NONFICTION: *The Orton Diaries*, 1986 (edited by John Lahr).
SCREENPLAY: *Up Against It*, 1979.

Bibliography

Bigsby, C. W. E. *Joe Orton.* London: Methuen, 1982. This brief study contends that Orton developed a style of anarchic farce that was deliberately subversive, not only of the authority figures appearing in his plays but also of language itself and conventionalities of plot and character. Bigsby also relates Orton's work to developments in postmodern literature and contemporary art. Notes, bibliography.

Charney, Maurice. *Joe Orton.* London: Macmillan, 1984. This introductory overview of Orton's oeuvre concisely assesses not only all of his plays but also his novel *Head to Toe* and his unproduced screenplay for the Beatles, *Up Against It.* The final chapter offers a useful definition of "the Ortonesque." Photographs, notes, bibliography.

Hutchings, William. "Joe Orton's Jacobean Assimilations in *What the Butler Saw.*" In *Farce*, edited by James Redmond. Cambridge, England: Cambridge University Press, 1988. Although this intertextual study focuses exclusively on Orton's last play as an embodiment of a fundamentally Jacobean perspective, its demonstration of the extensiveness of Orton's reading and the nature of his literary assimilations is germane to his other works as well. Hutchings also defends Orton's insistence on copious bloodshed at the end of *What the Butler Saw*, though this scene is often omitted from productions of the play.

Lahr, John. *Prick Up Your Ears: The Biography of Joe Orton.* New York: Alfred A. Knopf, 1978. This definitive biography of the playwright, based in part on Orton's diaries, is indispensable to any study of Orton's work. It is not only a readable, detailed study of his life but also an insightful critical appreciation of the plays. The biography was the basis of a feature film of the same name, directed by Stephen Frears and released in 1987. Photographs, notes.

Taylor, John Russell. "Joe Orton." In *The Second Wave: British Drama of the Sixties.* London: Eyre Methuen, 1971. Rev. ed. London: Eyre Methuen, 1978. This overview emphasizes the unique comic disparity between the outrageous happenings of Orton's plays and the polished, unflappable, epigrammatic style in which the characters speak of them. Taylor, however, disparages the posthumously produced *What the Butler Saw* as inchoate and little more than a rough draft, though most other critics (including John Lahr) consider it Orton's masterpiece. Bibliography of playscripts.

Worth, Katharine J. *Revolutions in Modern English Drama.* London: G. Bell & Sons, 1972. Reprinted as "Form and Style in the Plays of Joe Orton." In *Modern British Dramatists: New Perspectives*, edited by John Russell Brown. Englewood, Cliffs, N.J.: Prentice-Hall, 1984. Worth points out Orton's relationship to such Victorian predecessors as Oscar Wilde, Arthur Wing Pinero, and Lewis Carroll, particularly in his preoccupation with the clergy and the police. She also details the structural similarities between *What the Butler Saw* and Wilde's *The Importance of Being Earnest* (pr. 1895, pb. 1899) and notes the Pinteresque elements of his earlier plays.

Angela Hague
(Revised by *William Hutchings*)

JOHN OSBORNE

Born: London, England; December 12, 1929

Principal drama

Look Back in Anger, pr. 1956, pb. 1957; *The Entertainer*, pr., pb. 1957 (music by John Addison); *Epitaph for George Dillon*, pr., pb. 1958 (with Anthony Creighton); *The World of Paul Slickey*, pr., pb. 1959 (music by Christopher Whelen); *Luther*, pr., pb. 1961; *Plays for England: The Blood of the Bambergs and Under Plain Cover*, pr. 1962, pb. 1963; *Inadmissible Evidence*, pr. 1964, pb. 1965; *A Bond Honored*, pr., pb. 1966 (adaptation of Lope de Vega's play, *La fianza satistecna*); *A Patriot for Me*, pr., pb. 1966; *The Hotel in Amsterdam*, pr., pb. 1968; *Time Present*, pr., pb. 1968; *A Sense of Detachment*, pr. 1972, pb. 1973; *Hedda Gabler*, pr., pb. 1972 (adaptation of Henrik Ibsen's play); *A Place Calling Itself Rome*, pb. 1973 (adaptation of William Shakespeare's play *Coriolanus*); *Four Plays*, pb. 1973; *The Picture of Dorian Gray*, pb. 1973, pr. 1975 (adaptation of Oscar Wilde's novel); *West of Suez*, pr., pb. 1973; *Watch It Come Down*, pb. 1975, pr. 1976; *Déjàvu*, pb. 1991, pr. 1992.

Other literary forms

John Osborne's considerable output includes, besides his plays, a comparatively unsuccessful musical comedy about a gossip columnist with a dual personality, *The World of Paul Slickey*, and a series of dramatic scripts for television: *A Subject of Scandal and Concern* (1960, originally *A Matter of Scandal and Concern*); *The Right Prospectus* (1970); *Very Like a Whale* (1971); *The Gift of Friendship* (1972); *Ms.: Or, Jill and Jack* (1974, later published as *Jill and Jack*); *The End of Me Old Cigar* (1975); *Try a Little Tenderness* (1978); and *You're Not Watching Me, Mummy* (1980). He has adapted several plays and a novel for the stage and has written the screenplays for several of his own plays. His adaptation of *Tom Jones* (1963) from Henry Fielding's novel earned for him an Academy Award in 1964. He has also written *A Better Class of Person: An Autobiography, 1929-1956* (1981), and the second volume, entitled *Almost a Gentleman* (1991), covering his life to 1966.

Achievements

Osborne's most generous critics credit him with having transformed the English stage on a single night: May 8, 1956, when *Look Back in Anger* opened at the Royal Court Theatre. He is celebrated as the principal voice among England's "angry young men" of the 1950's and 1960's, who railed vindictively against Edwardian dinosaurs and the empty-headed bourgeoisie; it should be noted, however, that his antiheroes rebel against their own frustrations and futility more than they do in the service of any substantial social or political reform. Indeed, they betray their envy of the stability and the "historical legitimacy" of the very generation they condemn. Perhaps Osborne's most profound influence has been his leadership in bringing authenticity into contemporary English theater; a member of what has loosely been defined as the "Kitchen-Sink" school, he helped institute a new receptivity to social issues, naturalistic characterization, and the vernacular, thereby revitalizing a theater scene which had been dominated by the verse elevations of T. S. Eliot and Christopher Fry and the commercial conventionality of Terence Rattigan.

In addition to his achievements as a playwright, Osborne is also an accomplished actor, director, and screenwriter. Testimonies to his popular and critical successes include three *Evening Standard* awards (1956, 1965, 1968), two New York Drama Critics Circle Awards (1958, 1965), a Tony (1963), and an Oscar (1964). Over the past few years, Osborne has devoted much of his energy to television plays for the British Broadcasting Corporation. Although some see this as a confirmation of dwindling artistic resources, Osborne's reputation as a prime mover of the postwar English stage is secure. He has created some of the most arresting roles in twentieth century drama, and his career-long indictment of complacency is evident in every "lesson of feeling" he has delivered to his audiences.

Biography

John Osborne grew up in Fulham, Ventnor, and Surrey, leading a suburban childhood in somewhat less dire circumstances than one's preconception of Jimmy Porter's alter-ego would lead one to expect. In fact, every class subtlety between "upper-lower" and "lower-middle" was represented in his own extended family; Osborne's recently published autobiography traces, with a gusto bordering on the vengeful, the Welsh and Cockney sides of his family, and characterizes, in the spirit of English low comedy, their attempts to sustain outworn Edwardian amenities after having "come down in the world." His father was an advertising copywriter who suffered long spells of illness, and his mother was a barmaid, but the family tree included many connections to the music hall and the theater. (Grandfather Grove, for example, would be revived in the form of Billy Rice in *The Entertainer*.)

Osborne was an only child, rather sickly and bookish. His most vivid memories of adolescence include listening in the air-raid shelter to German bombers and suffering the abuse of bullies at school. Eventually, he went to a boarding school, St. Michael's, and after being expelled for striking back at the headmaster, turned toward journalism as a reporter for a trade journal, *Gas World*. After a failed engagement, he joined a struggling touring company, with which he gained his first experience in acting and playwriting, including an artistic and sexual collaboration with an older actress. The most important result of this picaresque period for the young Osborne was that he realized his ear for speech and developed his ambition to write for the stage. The early 1950's led him into the vital world of provincial repertory—the background for *Epitaph for George Dillon*—and ultimately, to the acceptance of *Look Back in Anger* by George Devine and the English Stage Company. Thus began a prolific career which has established Osborne as an influence on the style and subject of contemporary English theater, rivaled only by Harold Pinter. He has been married four times, to Pamela Lane (1951-1957), actress Mary Ure (1957-1963), writer Penelope Gilliat (1963-1968), and actress Jill Bennett, whom he married in 1968. He has one child. Osborne is a member of the Royal Society of Arts and in 1970, he received an honorary doctorate from the Royal College of Art in London.

In the mid-1970's, after two decades of steady production for the stage, Osborne substantially reduced his playwriting, though he continued to turn out television dramas. Other than occasional adaptations, such as the 1991 televised revision (produced as a stage work in 1975) of Oscar Wilde's *The Picture of Dorian Gray* and an hour-long profile on British television's South Bank Show, Osborne was not highly visible on the theater scene in the 1980's. His 1992 play, *Déjàvu*, which opened at the Comedy Theater in London to mixed reviews, was his first major new work to appear on the London stage in more than fifteen years. The 1991 publication of the second volume of Osborne's autobiography, *Almost a Gentleman*, brought his memoirs up to the mid-1960's and kept his name in the news for a short time.

Analysis

When the much-heralded John Osborne hero tears into an entire generation and yet has no prospect for viable change, he discovers his own nakedness and vulnerability. He is inevitably a man in limbo, caught between nostalgia for the settled order of the past and hope for an idealized future he cannot possibly identify. His rage is directed against his own inadequacy, not simply against that of his society. Because it is ineffectual, protesting against the ills of society becomes primarily a ritual complaint of the self against its own limitations.

Look Back in Anger is less specifically about rebellion than it is about the inertia that overcomes someone when he feels helpless to rebel. To excuse his own inanition, Jimmy Porter cries that there are no "good, brave causes left"; in fact, he daily rails against dozens of enemies—the bomb, advertisers, the church, politicians, aristocrats, cinema audiences, and others—until one realizes that the problem is that there are *too many* causes worth fighting for, and their sheer magnitude renders Jimmy impotent. His anger, his irreverence, and his castigating wit are all an imposture, an attempt to shield himself from his failure to take meaningful action. While he pricks the illusions and damns the lethargy of those around him, he himself holds fast to the sense that only he suffers, that his anger betokens spiritual superiority over Alison, who irons incessantly and who only desires peace, and over Cliff, who buries his head in the newspaper and who only desires comfortable seclusion in the Porters' flat. However justifiable his charges against the other characters, Jimmy's anger is less a mark of privilege than it is a standing joke—part of the "Sunday ritual."

Jimmy at times seems almost envious of those he attacks. The man for whom he professes the greatest resentment, Colonel Redfern, is an illusion-ridden, displaced Edwardian whom Jimmy prefers to see as the tyrannical father from whose clutches he saved Alison; nevertheless, the colonel at least had a golden age, whereas Jimmy agitates in a vacuum. Similarly, Helena, Alison's posh actress-friend, inspires in Jimmy equal portions of spite and sexual desire; he not only brings this officious snob down from her pedestal, but also makes a place for her in his home after Alison's departure. Even Alison's political brother, Nigel, "the chinless wonder," whose vagueness Jimmy loves to attack, reflects on Jimmy's personal lack of commitment.

The point is that Jimmy cannot afford to see himself as in any way implicated by his own attacks. He resents everyone else's desperate evasion of suffering—he goes so far as to wish that Alison should witness the death of a baby, thereby unwittingly previewing her fate—but he, too, tends to leave the scene at times of crisis, going off to play his horn in the other room, for example, when Alison returns to confront the "traitorous" Helena. At this crucial juncture, Helena decides to opt out of the mess; rather than risk dirtying her soul, she spouts convenient clichés about doing the decent thing and thus escapes her guilt. Alison's return is itself a compromise made in order to reaffirm the only security she has ever had. To say that Jimmy Porter proves any more willing to handle the pain and difficulty of being alive, however, is to ignore the fact that his has been an exclusive self-interest throughout the play. He is childishly arrogant rather than righteously indignant. So long as some woman is there to iron his clothes, he will not be bothered about his responsibilities to either Alison or Helena. (After all, he reasons, by leaving him, they have betrayed his "love," and so they deserve little more than scorn.) The image that concludes the play—Jimmy and Alison huddled together in a game of bears and squirrels—marks a final repudiation of the complications of adult life. "Let's pretend we're human" is Jimmy's original suggestion at the beginning of *Look Back in Anger*, but the consequences of human thought and feeling are too great; only within the limited arrangement of a "brainless" love game can either of them function at the end of the play.

Look Back in Anger portrays a world that lacks opportunities for meaningful achievement. Jimmy Porter loses his glibness and sarcasm as the "cruel steel traps" of the world close in upon him; he trades in his anger for anesthesia. Ironically, even more obsolete than Colonel Redfern's visions of bygone days is Jimmy's own anger; Helena suggests that he really belongs "in the middle of the French Revolution," when glory was available. Jimmy Porter, who embodies the failures of his society, can support no cause other than that of the self in retreat. An impotent reformer and would-be martyr, he is consumed by a burning rage that finds no outlet.

Osborne's society is one that seems immune to creativity and inimical to full humanity. In *The Entertainer*, Archie Rice looks back upon the past nobility of the music hall (his is now a tawdry striptease joint) and forward to the barren legacy he has to offer his alienated children, and he wonders where all the "real people" have gone. Like Colonel Redfern, he is an anachronism, a personification of degraded values, as exemplified by his adherence to a dead art. He lacks even the satisfaction of the dying Billy Rice, who can at least withdraw into memories of free pudding with a pint of beer and respectable women in elegant dresses. Instead, Archie must console himself as best he can with a pitiful affair, his "little round world of light" on stage, and the conviction that at least he has "had a go at life."

The music hall structure of "turns" on a bill is imitated in the structure of the play itself. In this way, the story of the Rice family becomes an elaborate sketch, including overture, comic patter, heartrending interludes, and skits of love and death. Like the music hall, which has been corrupted by nudity and obscenity, the family unit, once a bastion of British dignity, has fallen upon hard times: Phoebe, Archie's wife, indulges her husband's adulteries and failures and seeks shelter in local movie houses (another degraded art form); his son Frank is a conscientious objector who can only manage a "relationship substitute" with his father; his daughter Jean is also estranged from her parents, as she nurses the pain of a failed engagement and teaches an art class to children she loathes. In short, the younger generation is embittered by an inheritance of disappointment and ruined values; Archie is incapable of communicating with them naturally and openly; he chooses, rather, to relate to them through a contrived performance, as he would to one of his vulgar audiences. In the place of intimacy, there is cajolement and manipulation, so that it becomes impossible for characters to distinguish sincerity from routine, confession from monologue.

"Everybody's all right," croons Archie, and the central tension of *The Entertainer* is that between his efforts to sustain happiness, Britishness, the welfare state, and the state of his private little world, all by sheer theatricality, and the steady deconstruction of those myths. The final blows are the deaths of Billy Rice and young Mick, the one seeming to pass away out of his own irrelevance to the contemporary world, and the other, killed in an otherworldly war. The result is shell shock. All that Archie can turn to is a quiet drink and a few awkward old songs in the faded spotlight. Like *Look Back in Anger*, which concludes with a desperate desire for mindless retreat, *The Entertainer* shows the responses to crisis as the familiar patter and the old soft shoe.

Luther was both a departure from and an expansion of familiar themes for Osborne. The move from contemporary middle-class England to six-teenth century Germany makes *Luther* seem an anomalous experiment, but Osborne is once again concerned with the psychology of a sensitive man who prefers to escape the world rather than cope with the burden of mammoth causes that he finds overwhelming. Luther is a direct ancestor of Jimmy Porter: He is frightened by the implications of his own anger. The realization of God's enormous task sends him into an epileptic fit. By embracing a monastic alternative, Luther can rationalize, at least temporarily, his divestment of the trappings and complications of secular life in the protective bosom of the Lord. The Augustinian order is the religious equivalent for the psychological refuges in Osborne's previous plays.

It is not God alone who castigates Luther for his retreat. Luther's father, a practical and rather blasphemous man of the world, argues that his son, who could have been a fine lawyer, has chosen to run away from such a challenge and is now "abusing his youth with fear and humiliation." Luther's response is that his father is narrow-minded and blind to the glory of God, but the indictment still plagues Luther. The other brothers, too, laugh at the intensity of his "over-stimulated conscience"; Brother Weinand says Luther always speaks "as if lightning were just about to strike" behind him. Even Luther's sleep is infested by demons, and his days are soured by constipation and vomiting. Having entered the monastery to find security and certainty, Luther is instead faced with weakness and doubt; not only does he fail to forge his soul into a human equivalent of sanctuary, but also he finds his worst traits are exaggerated within this restricted arena. As Staupitz will advise him years later, his fanaticism does not guarantee the order's potency; it simply renders it ridiculous. It is paranoia, not faith, that underlies Luther's devotion.

One can appreciate the fact that, despite Luther's ultimate role as world-shaker, he is not a social revolutionary. He consistently sides with the forces of law and order during the Peasants' Revolt; although he prefers to drink to his own conscience instead of to the Pope, he is equally disdainful of the "empty" rampage of revolution, which he deems an affront to what is truly Christian. In short, Luther has never learned the last tool of good works—to hate his own will—and his one-man crusade in the play is not so much against Satan as it is against the devilish fears in his own heart. It is ironic, then, that Luther contributes to the dismantling of the fortress which Cajetan calls a representation of the perfect unity of the world, since Luther has never desired anything more than its unassailable safety. As he tries to bargain with God, he insists, "This cause is not mine but yours. For myself, I've no business to be dealing with the great lords of the world. I want to be still, in peace, and alone." *Luther* concludes with the hero crawling into a substitute sanctuary, in the form of marriage to a nun, Katherina von Bora. One is left with a weary man cradling his sleeping son in his arms and praying that God grant both of them sweet dreams. Luther is no different from Osborne's wholly fictional creations in that he is the one who appears to be most afflicted by the fires he has ignited; the fact that Luther is far more successful in having an effect on the world at large than is Jimmy Porter does not free him from the sense that all he has "ever managed to do is convert everything into stench and dying and peril."

Inadmissible Evidence resumes Osborne's contention that one can suffer more personal damage from one's own attempts to insulate oneself than from those things—a hostile world, a guilty past, or simply other people— from which he desires insulation. Bill Maitland is an attorney who undergoes a play-long cross-examination about the quality of his own life. Although his detestation of computerized, deculturalized, dehumanized society may in part explain his callousness and conceit, it does not justify his personal inadequacies or his inability to maintain meaningful relationships. The most damaging evidence against him is that, however virulently he argues that the world has discarded him, he appears to be the instrument of his own isolation, and this is what he cannot admit to himself.

The play records Maitland's last hours in a process of collapse. It opens in a "dream-court," in which he conducts an anxious, helpless defense; when he awakens to his real world, he is no longer capable of handling the trials there. Like so many of Osborne's main characters, Maitland turns to rhetoric to defend himself and to convince himself of his own existence. With a lawyer's expertise, he spins convoluted monologues; he proposes to obscure, if he cannot eliminate, the ambiguous "wicked, bawdy and scandalous object" of which he stands accused: a life lived at a distance. Indeed, *Inadmissible Evidence* has the effect of a one-man play, for Maitland is so manipulative and exploitative that other characters in the play are reduced to two-dimensional fact files; they exist solely as embodiments of reactions toward Maitland. Their limited existence is a result of his incapacity for engaging in relationships of any real complexity or depth. What he sees as betrayal by his friends and family—one by one they appear in his office or call up to confirm their desertion—is, from another perspective, Maitland's steady disappearance into solipsism. Having treated everyone with the same cynical caution, he grows to feel more and more "like something in a capsule in space, weightless, unable to touch anything or do anything, like a groping baby in a removed, putrefying womb." He is losing the control he once exerted over people both sexually and professionally, and now he cannot stem the tide of their retreat. Eventually, not even taxis notice him; even the newspapers feature the replacement of lawyers by computers that will render them obsolete. Ironically, the sentence for the crime of a practiced detachment is a suffocating anonymity.

Maitland's last clients serve as the most effective witnesses for the "prosecution." The women who complain of the callousness and the adulteries of their men come for legal counsel, but their function in the play is to force Maitland to recognize his own crimes in those of their men. (That all the women are played by one actress seems to insist on their symbolic status; they represent a single indictment.) Maitland can no longer escape into his work, for his work presents further evidence against him. He becomes indistinguishable from his last client, the self-consumed Mr. Maples, who also wants to avoid the ugly issues he has helped to create for himself.

The play ends in plea bargaining. It is no longer possible to keep from being "found out" (his fear in the opening dream sequence), so Maitland considers changing his plea to guilty in order possibly to mitigate the judgment against him. Perhaps he can salvage something by warning his daughter not to make the same mistakes and messes he did. Unfortunately, it may simply be too late to avoid his sentence; after all, can his daughter take to heart the didactic instruction of a man who has shown her nothing but insincerity? *Inadmissible Evidence* leaves one with the image of a man repenting his sins in solitary confinement.

Osborne has never deserted the theme of life's failure to measure up to human desires, and of people's unwitting contribution to that failure by virtue of the self-interest that underlies their complaints. Thus, for example, does Pamela in *Time Present* take up the gauntlet from Jimmy Porter, ridiculing the tawdriness and banality of the 1960's, the drugs, hippies, happenings and the need to be "cool," with the same fervor that Jimmy railed against the uninspiring prospects of life in the 1950's. Osborne's most recent approach to this theme, however, has been from the point of view of the conservative forces which were the target of the younger heroes of his earlier plays. This approach is not so much the inevitable by-product of an aging playwright's political reassessment as it is a change of focus which intensifies his argument; in other words, the materially comfortable Establishment and the stolid aristocracy are as dissatisfied as the disenfranchised younger generation. In *West of Suez*, the first play designating this new focus, the shift from self-righteous anger to anxious unsettledness denotes not only nostalgia for the past and dissatisfaction with the present, but also, a fear of the future.

West of Suez examines yet another cramped refuge: In this case, it is the garden of a villa in the West Indies meant to serve as a retreat from the "cold, uncertain tides and striving pavements. And the marriage of anxieties." What had been intended as a reservation for the vestiges of the old

British Empire is instead proof of its degradation. The Suez Canal is closed; the dreams of the empire it once exemplified are choked. The fiction cannot survive unless those who maintain it do so miles away from the reality, "in the West, among the non-descripts of the Bahamas."

Like their literary predecessors, Colonel Redfern and Billy Rice, the nostalgia-ridden members of this "exclusive circle" have been trivialized into comedy. A brigadier is reduced to domestic chores; the aged writer, Wyatt Gillman, gives an interview "like a wounded imperial bull being baited by a member of the lesser breeds"; social gatherings are contaminated by hippies, homosexuals, and tourists. The only defense against this invasion is boorish prejudice, which the traditionalists exhibit throughout the play.

The offspring of their obsolescence, represented by Edward and Frederica, are saddled with a useless legacy, and their marriage encompasses the tension and disappointment of people who must live vicariously on other people's distant memories. Edward immerses himself in pathology because it affords him uncompromised detachment, and Frederica finds her self-possession in a kind of sneering sophistication. Their conversations are nothing more than highly stylized verbal exercises designed to take their minds off the supreme boredom of their lives. In a sense, they aspire to the state of blissful self-importance of Wyatt Gillman, the extreme version of which must be senility. Modern life is not something in which they would choose to involve themselves, but their island home is no escape from vulgarity. Tourists litter the place, cheapening it with their very presence, and the native blacks are charmless and sullen. Finally, there is the anarchist-hippie Jed, something of a reincarnation of Jimmy Porter, who lambastes the befuddled aristocrats with curses and threats of violence. His heavy-handed assault summarizes their ineffectuality, their pathetic irrelevance to the real world; it also demonstrates the ugliness of that world, and almost justifies aristocratic stereotypes of the undignified lower classes. The response of Wyatt Gillman to all of this is to ask to go to bed, but there is no hiding from Jed's vicious prophecy. Wyatt is murdered at the end of *West of Suez* by a band of natives. Nothing is sacred anymore, especially not the memory of colonial power and prestige. Wyatt's children, friends, and associates, all of whom have staked claims in a world which no longer exists, stand over his corpse in stupefaction.

In 1992, Osborne returned to the London stage with *Déjàvu*, which brought *Look Back in Anger*'s Jimmy Porter back to life after two and a half decades. In *Déjàvu*, Jimmy, now a middle-aged drunk, still vents his spleen at all those around him; few critics, though, thought that the new incarnation matched the power of the original.

Every Osborne play deals with reality's raids upon self-esteem. His characters, even those who are most hostile to outworn conventions, are all in search of some private realm where they can operate with distinction. Sadly, that very search, which leads to isolation and denies communication, is as important a contributor to the contemporary malaise as is any governing body or social system. Angry young men and scornful old men, alike, feel disaffiliated and frustrated by the meager roles they occupy, but their greatest failure comes from not making a commitment to anything other than the justification of those feelings. Osborne writes of a world which is immune to meaningful achievement. The degree to which his characters can move beyond complaint toward some constructive alternative that welcomes other people is the best measure of their heroism.

Other major works

NONFICTION: *A Better Class of Person: An Autobiography, 1929-1956*, 1981; *Almost a Gentleman: An Autobiography, Volume Two: 1955-1966*, 1991.

SCREENPLAYS: *Look Back in Anger*, 1959 (with Nigel Kneale); *The Entertainer*, 1960 (with Kneale); *Tom Jones*, 1963 (adaptation of Henry Fielding's novel); *Inadmissible Evidence*, 1968; *The Charge of the Light Brigade*, 1968 (with Charles Wood).

TELEPLAYS: *A Subject of Scandal and Concern*, 1960 (originally as *A Matter of Scandal and Concern*); *The Right Prospectus*, 1970; *Very Like a Whale*, 1971; *The Gift of Friendship*, 1972; *Ms.: Or, Jill and Jack*, 1974; *The End of Me Old Cigar*, 1975; *Try a Little Tenderness*, 1978; *You're Not Watching Me, Mummy*, 1980; *Very Like a Whale*, 1980; *A Better Class of Person*, 1985; *God Rot Tunbridge Wells*, 1985.

Bibliography

Banham, Martin. *Osborne.* Edinburgh, Scotland: Oliver & Boyd, 1969. Contains discerning essays on *Look Back in Anger*, *The Entertainer*, and nine other plays, discussed around the thesis statement that "most of Osborne's targets are very clearly observed, defined, and, through his frontal assault, shaken to their foundations." Rich with material for further inquiry, especially when compared with later work. Complemented by a list of first British productions and a select bibliography.

Brien, Alan. "Snot or Not?" Review of *Almost a Gentleman. New Statesman Society* 4 (November 15, 1991): 47. In this review of Osborne's second volume of his autobiography, Brien's premise is that an "autobiography is not history. It is a form of entertainment." He finds Osborne's work hostile but valuable. Brien was one of the few defenders of Osborne's aggressively straightforward second volume.

Ferrar, Harold. *John Osborne.* New York: Columbia University Press, 1973. This booklet on Osborne's first fifteen years of output notes that Jimmy Porter (in *Look Back in Anger*) is a portrait of "the body politic: one either defensively dismisses him or confronts the political implications of his protest and the social etiology of his anguish." Discusses *A Bond Honored*, *The Hotel in Amsterdam*, and other more obscure works. Brief select bibliography.

Hayman, Ronald. *John Osborne.* New York: Frederick Ungar, 1972. The World Dramatists series specializes in a factual overview, with play-by-play chapters, copious notes on stage productions, cast lists (here, both of London and New York premieres and productions), and a careful chronology. The introduction speaks of Osborne's ability to "epitomize something important about England today, not just by expressing moods and stating attitudes but by summing up the condition that the country is in, almost personifying it." Index.

Hinchliffe, Arnold P. *British Theatre, 1950-1970.* Totowa, N.J.: Rowman & Littlefield, 1974. The best book for putting Osborne in the context of the total revolutionary movement in British and European theater, and written when the movement was preparing for the second wave of playwrights. Particularly articulate on European influences, the Theater of the Absurd, and the relation of a national theater to the themes of Osborne and his contemporaries. Select bibliography but no index.

_____. *John Osborne.* Boston: Twayne, 1984. A general introduction to Osborne, with an oddly dated discussion of his most influential works, and not much new. While this series generally finds writers on the rise, this study is almost a respectful retrospective of someone long gone, which Osborne is not. Chronology, index, and bibliography.

Osborne, John. *Almost a Gentleman.* New York: E. P. Dutton, 1991. The second volume of Osborne's autobiography (the first, *A Better Class of Person*, was published in 1981) takes the reader to 1966 with considerable one-sided detail and with candor and grimness. Controversy about his disregard of the sensitivities of persons still alive, notably his fourth wife, raged in the news media for several months after its publication. Index.

Arthur M. Saltzman
(Updated by *Thomas J. Taylor*
and *Robert McClenaghan*)

THOMAS OTWAY

Born: Trotton, England; March 3, 1652
Died: London, England; April 14, 1685

Principal drama

Alcibiades, pr., pb. 1675; *Don Carlos, Prince of Spain*, pr., pb. 1676; *Titus and Berenice*, pr. 1676, pb. 1677 (adaptation of Jean Racine's play *Bérénice); The Cheats of Scapin*, pr. 1676, pb. 1677 (adaptation of Molière's play *Les Fourberies de Scapin); Friendship in Fashion*, pr., pb. 1678; *The History and Fall of Caius Marius*, pr. 1679, pb. 1680; *The Orphan: Or, The Unhappy Marriage*, pr., pb. 1680; *The Soldier's Fortune*, pr. 1680, pb. 1681; *Venice Preserved: Or, A Plot Discovered*, pr., pb. 1682; *The Atheist: Or, The Second Part of the Soldier's Fortune*, pr. 1683, pb. 1684.

Other literary forms

The writings of Thomas Otway, apart from his plays, are of minor significance. His two most substantial poetic efforts were his first published poem, *The Poet's Complaint of His Muse* (1680), and the posthumously published *Windsor Castle* (1685). The former poem, despite claims made for its autobiographical and political interest, is a disjointed effort that shifts from a seemingly personal apologia to an allegorized presentation of the Popish Plot and the Exclusion Crisis. *Windsor Castle* consists of a mélange of devices, drawn from elegy, topographical poetry, and Restoration advice-to-the-painter poetry, occasioned by the death of Charles II. The rest of Otway's poetry is in typical Restoration modes: dramatic prologues and epilogues, translations (of Ovid and Horace), a commendatory poem (addressed to Thomas Creech upon his translation of Lucretius), and a verse epistle (to Richard Duke). Published posthumously were his prose translation from the French, *The History of the Triumvirates,* in 1686, and a group of love letters, supposedly written by Otway to the actress Elizabeth Barry, in 1697.

Achievements

A proper measure of Otway's achievement as a dramatist can be taken neither from the current critical reputation of his heroic plays, tragedies, and comedies nor from the success of these works in his own time but, rather, must take into account a popularity and influence which continued through the early nineteenth century. *Don Carlos, Prince of Spain, The Orphan*, and *Venice Preserved* were among the most popular of Restoration plays; only by comparison with these plays could Otway's comedies be considered unsuccessful. It is true that his comedies were dropped from the repertory of the London theaters early in the eighteenth century, but this fact reflects a change in taste for which Otway himself might have been partly responsible: It is possible to detect a gradual translation of the affective techniques that characterize Otway's tragedies into the comedies of the late seventeenth and early eighteenth centuries. The frequent revivals of *The Orphan* and *Venice Preserved* suggest these plays' persistent influence and confirm Otway's high standing in English drama. Joseph Addison in *The Spectator* (1711-1712, 1714) anticipated many later comments when he wrote that "Otway has followed Nature in the Language of his Tragedy, and therefore shines in the Passionate Parts, more than any of our English poets." A renewed appreciation of Otway's plays followed from the general revival of critical and scholarly interest in Restoration drama in the 1920's. Most subsequent study has concentrated upon *The Orphan* and *Venice Preserved* but, unfortunately, critical interest has rarely led to theatrical production. Harold Pinter, however, has spoken for the dramatic accessibility of *Venice Preserved* to modern audiences, and critics have supplied groundwork for a more extensive treatment of Otway's dramatic production.

Biography

Thomas Otway was born March 3, 1652, in Trotton, Sussex, the son of Humphrey Otway, an Anglican clergyman of distinguished family and of Royalist sympathies, and Elizabeth Otway, of whom little is known. Otway briefly attended Winchester College before entering Oxford University in May, 1669; he left the university in 1671 without taking a degree, perhaps because of the death of his father. Sometime after leaving Oxford, Otway made his way to London, where, at the Duke's Theatre, he was given a role in Aphra Behn's play *The Forced Marriage: Or, The Jealous Bridegroom.* His performance was a failure; nevertheless, he may for a time have found some marginal employment as an actor. In any event, by 1675, the year in which his first play, *Alcibiades,* was presented at Dorset Garden, he was devoting himself to the financially insecure profession of playwriting. Despite some early theatrical success (notably the extremely popular *Don Carlos, Prince of Spain*), the uncertainty of his fortunes and of patronage by members of the royal court probably led to his decision to join the English forces in Flanders in 1678. Even though Otway received a commission, his military career was brief: The army was recalled from Flanders early in 1679 and disbanded in June. This expedition having improved his fortunes not at all, Otway returned to writing, and thereupon followed his most concentrated period of literary production. The plays *The History and Fall of Caius Marius*, *The Orphan*, and *The Soldier's Fortune*, and the poem *The Poet's Complaint of His Muse*, were either first produced or first published within the year. He was granted a master of arts degree by St. John's College, Cambridge University, in 1680, and, at about this time, he may have been tutor to one of Charles II's illegitimate chil-

dren by Nell Gwyn. Nevertheless, Otway seems to have slipped into a state
of poverty which the production of his later plays, *Venice Preserved* and
The Atheist, did little to relieve. Although the circumstances of Otway's
death in London on April 14, 1685, became the stuff of legend, they remain uncertain.

Analysis

In his *Lives of the English Poets,* Samuel Johnson says of Thomas
Otway's *The Orphan* that "its whole power is upon the affections; for it is
not written with much comprehension of thought or elegance of expression.
But, if the heart is interested, many other beauties may be wanting, yet
not be missed." For one accustomed to Johnson's judicial manner of literary evaluation, his praise of the play rises above the qualifications with
which it is voiced. Although Johnson is here addressing himself to only one
of Otway's plays, the quality upon which he fastens—the ability to elicit an
affective response through the representation of the passions—is one that
was fitfully apparent even in *Alcibiades* and at least as forcefully realized in
Venice Preserved. Indeed, in *Venice Preserved,* Johnson discovered a
greater virility, if not an elegance, of expression, but this new strength of
Otway's imagery and language could not overcome his qualms regarding
"the want of morality in the original design, and the despicable scenes of
vile comedy with which he has diversified his tragic action." Pathos is the
play's sole saving grace; that Otway's "original design" was in fact altered
in eighteenth century theatrical productions so that the offensive comic
scenes were deleted suggests that Johnson stood very much with his age in
his refusal to accept the "thought" which was expressed in *Venice Preserved.* While the pathetic character of Otway's plays remains a matter of
critical interest, respect must also be given to those elements of Otway's
work that were considered anomalous in the period of Johnson—his seeming immorality, his comic cynicism, and his tragic despair—in order to
understand fully the attitudes that informed not only his heroic plays and
tragedies but also the comedies (and the comic episodes of *Venice Preserved*), which Johnson dismissed.

The characteristic strengths of Otway's plays seem to depend more upon
the force of their original conception than upon the art with which they are
executed. Too often, Otway seems simply unwilling to improve upon his
first designs. Certainly such a nearly complete lapse of dramatic sense as is
seen in the opening exposition of *The Orphan* could have been prevented
by even the most cursory reading of François Hédelin, Abbé d'Aubignac's
La Pratique du théâtre (1657), a contemporary French dramatic treatise. At
other times, Otway's original conception, however deficient, seems incapable of being altered without sacrificing its intended effect. To use the example of *The Orphan* again, there appears to be a lack of motivation in

Castalio's concealing of his marriage to Monimia from the rest of his family, particularly from his brother, Polydore. That the brothers are rivals in love seems less important than the violation of Castalio's vows of absolute friendship for his brother by his withholding of the truth. Without Polydore's misunderstanding of the situation, however, there could be no tragedy, at least not the kind that Otway intended. Motivation for Castalio's behavior would perhaps be necessary in a tragedy of character, but the focus of the tragedy of *The Orphan,* as in other Otway plays, is not upon individual character so much as upon the inveterate frailty of human intentions and the circumstances by which human ideals are defeated.

Earlier in the Restoration period, the ideals of honor, love, and friendship were given heroic affirmation in the plays of John Dryden and Roger Boyle, Earl of Orrery. Even in his later tragedies, so formally different from these heroic plays, Otway typically does not take the position of denying that these ideals are worthy of desire—indeed, the pathos of his plays would be lost if he did—but of casting doubt upon their power to determine actions. The influence of the heroic tradition upon Otway persists to the last of his serious plays in the tendency to conceive of dramatic character as representing the radical expression of human possibility, but, instead of being employed to glorify human potential, this mode of characterization is used to indicate man's pathetic inability to realize his aspirations. Further, Otway was able to rely upon the continued urgency of the heroic play's thematic concerns to direct attention, in a dramatically concise and forceful manner, to his own iconoclasm. The writing of comedy in no way lightened Otway's vision of the human situation, but, because the world represented is closer to the mean of everyday experience, the substance of his comedies may seem trivial in comparison with his heroic plays and tragedies. A comparison of *The Orphan* with *Friendship in Fashion,* however, would also serve to indicate the presence in the comedy of the two thematic motifs, friendship and love, which are the dominant concerns of the later tragedy, and the power of *Friendship in Fashion* to disturb the most commonly held notions of Restoration comedy suggests that Otway approached the conventions of the comedy of manners not with delight but with something close to moral repugnance. Otway, then, looks to a common area of experience in both dramatic modes, exploiting alike the forms and conventions of comic and serious plays.

The high road of the Restoration heroic play is that represented in John Dryden's proselytizing of a dramatic practice based upon an epic analogy. His two-part drama produced between 1670 and 1671, *The Conquest of Granada by the Spaniards,* has been considered the apotheosis of his theory of the heroic play, but his earlier play, *Tyrannic Love: Or, The Royal Martyr* (pr. 1669), was more remarkable for its extravagance of language, character, and situation and its accompanying use of theatrical spectacle than for any truly epic qualities. Elkanah Settle's extraordinarily successful 1671 production, *The Empress of Morocco,* and Nathaniel Lee's *The Tragedy of Nero, Emperor of Rome* (pr. 1674) resemble both of Dryden's plays in the use of rhymed couplets as their basic verse form and in the portrayal of "heroic" love, but they exploit the theatrical values of *Tyrannic Love* rather than the epic tendencies of *The Conquest of Granada by the Spaniards.* *The Tragedy of Nero, Emperor of Rome* is of particular interest in regard to *Alcibiades,* and not merely because it was Lee's own initial dramatic effort: The choice of classical subject, the fictional elaboration upon the facts of history, and the indiscriminate letting of the blood of both protagonists and villains in a manner reminiscent of the Jacobean theater are common to the two plays. Both the plays make use of dramatic sensationalism; *The Empress of Morocco* had previously shown that theatric capital could be made of a blatantly melodramatic approach to the heroic play in which action was forwarded by villainy and lust.

Viewed against the perspective supplied by the repertory of Restoration playhouses, the plot of *Alcibiades* contains no surprises. The plot is built upon a single incident drawn from Plutarch—Alcibiades' expulsion from Athens following a night of drunken sacrilege—but the action of the play begins not with the event itself but with its report to the woman to whom he is betrothed, Timandra. This brief scene of exposition concludes with Timandra's rejection of the love of Theramnes, the man who supplanted Alcibiades as Athenian general. The remaining action of the play takes place about the camp of the King of Sparta, where Alcibiades had taken himself upon his expulsion from Athens. There, the Spartan king's granting of the title of General to Alcibiades; the secret resentment and desire for revenge of Tissaphernes, the Spartan he replaces; the Spartan queen's sudden, violent passion for Alcibiades; the appearance of Timandra; the victory over the Athenians; and the capture of Theramnes supply more than the necessary means of spasmodically forwarding the action of the play toward its bloody conclusion, in which the only major character left alive is Patroclus, who is the son of Tissaphernes but nevertheless a loyal friend of Alcibiades.

Little can be said for the artistic merit of *Alcibiades.* In part, the weakness of its dramatic organization might be simply explained by Otway's failure to amalgamate those materials he had freely and rather too copiously borrowed; nevertheless, *Alcibiades* yet has something of the characteristic tenor of the later plays, and it is possible to find in it an anticipation of the sorts of problems of form and characterization with which Otway, by the very nature of the kind of drama that he was attempting to write, was later forced to confront.

The titular character of *Alcibiades* is a major dramatic liability. The historical character from Plutarch is almost completely lost from sight, and

Otway never quite squares his presentation of Alcibiades the martial figure with Alcibiades the sensitive lover. Further, the character of Alcibiades is weakened not merely by the disjunction of his characterization but also by his situation within the plot. Although he is at the center of all the various actions of the play, he is a character more acted upon than acting. His military triumph over Athens and Theramnes and the killing of his rival in the act of ravishing Timandra were obviously intended to establish his heroic credibility, but the latter action serves only to precipitate the catastrophe of the play—the murder of the king and of Timandra and the suicide of Alcibiades. It is by the forces of lust, deceit, and revenge that the two lovers, Alcibiades and Timandra, are made vulnerable (although it is not as a necessary consequence that they are doomed). That Timandra's vulnerability seems more emphatic and compelling has much to do with contemporary dramatic and social stereotypes of feminine behavior; from the first scene, however, her articulation of the vulnerability of love places her closer to the realities of the play than is Alcibiades. The burden of these fears is realized not only in *Alcibiades* but also in later plays by Otway: Loyalty and love cannot survive the way of the world. She and her lover serve as exemplars of this fact. There is, however, a definite irony, one that Otway may not have fully intended, in the situation which forces Alcibiades to suicide: The "heroic" self-absorption that prevents his admitting any real danger to himself, even when Tissaphernes' designs are revealed by Patroclus, also renders him incapable of recognizing the peril to Timandra represented by the queen. The force of his love seems rather too summarily expressed by his suicide. Timandra, on the other hand, has only one role, that of the loved one, and from this role the expression of her fears seems naturally to follow. Moreover, her anticipation of the sad worldly fate of her love for Alcibiades is joined in a corrupt Neoplatonic manner to the belief that their love will find its true reward in an afterlife together. The unusual prominence given to this notion in *Alcibiades*, even as it diminishes its tragic effect, constitutes the most powerful formal demand for the sacrifice of the lovers.

The villainy of Tissaphernes and of Deidama, the Queen of Sparta, although in the end self-defeating, is nevertheless efficient in its decimation of the *dramatis personae* of *Alcibiades*, and the characterization of Deidama is a gesture in the direction of the heroic fashion of sensually motivated villainesses. Some traces of this dramatic type remain in the Duchess of Eboli in *Don Carlos, Prince of Spain*. Yet even though she aids in the machinations against the prince, it is her husband, Rui-Gomez, who is clearly the central figure in the plot. Reflection upon the role of Rui-Gomez suggests some of the changes in dramatic conception which, in the streamlining of the heroic apparatus, made *Don Carlos, Prince of Spain* a markedly better play than *Alcibiades*. The action of *Don Carlos, Prince of*

Spain, like that of *Alcibiades*, entails the pursuit of revenge; in the earlier play, however, there exists another major motivating force, the queen's desire for Alcibiades. Although Tissaphernes and the queen are brought together in the murder of the king, the need for some coordination or subordination of their purposes is realized too late in the play. In *Don Carlos, Prince of Spain*, the malevolence of Rui-Gomez, even as it exploits and infects the other characters, is used to concentrate and direct the play's action. Since Rui-Gomez does not attempt anything so crude as assassination, there is no need for him to follow Tissaphernes' almost ludicrous course of failed attempts at murder in order that his revenge might be protracted to the length of the play. Rather, because the revenge of Rui-Gomez is to be effected through the jealousy of King Philip, each stay in his scheme seems only to increase its potential yield, until only the death of his son and wife can satisfy the king's maddened sense of injury.

This concurrent dilation and intensification of the act of revenge resembles the action of Shakespeare's *Othello* (pr. 1604), as Rui-Gomez resembles Iago. Iago may have also had a part in the conception of Tissaphernes, but the earlier character is so much an epitome of villainy that any particular touches drawn from Shakespeare are lost in generality. The influence of Iago upon the characterization of Rui-Gomez is sharply rendered; the effect is to draw the character into a more particular and probable dramatic world than that inhabited by Tissaphernes. J. C. Ghosh overstated the case for *Don Carlos, Prince of Spain* when, in the introduction to his edition of the works of Otway, he said that "the characters are not the bloated abstractions of the heroic play, but real flesh and blood"; yet within the dramatic limits of the heroic form, Otway managed to give his characters touches of life which were absent from *Alcibiades*. The action of *Don Carlos, Prince of Spain*, however, does not approach the dramatic and moral concentration of *Othello*. The focus of the play is not so much upon the victim of jealousy, the king, as upon those characters who suffer on account of his jealousy—his son, Don Carlos, and his recently married queen. The result would be analogous to an *Othello* more concerned with the fate of Desdemona than with the victimizing of the Moor. As a consequence of the play's design, none of the characters is allowed the intense moral and psychological regard which is given to Othello.

The love of Carlos and the queen, moreover, is represented not as wrong but as unfortunate, and moral evaluation in the play does not depend so much upon the nature of particular actions as upon their association with the almost schematically opposed guilt and innocence of Rui-Gomez and the queen. Thus, the king, once he is made to realize the treachery of Rui-Gomez's counsel, must be allowed the full weight of the forgiveness by his dying queen and his son, allowing him a share in the pathetic emotions of the play's conclusion. Even the anomalous moral position of Don Juan, whose naturalism is reminiscent of Edmund in Shakespeare's *King Lear* (pr. c. 1605-1606) and near to the contemporary libertinism of John Wilmot, Earl of Rochester, is accommodated more by his allegiance to Don Carlos than by his representation as an *honnête homme*. (It must be noticed, however, that the blunt sexuality of his relationship with Eboli, which is not disguised by the preciosity of its expression, serves as a negative counterpoint to the ideal quality of the love of Carlos and the queen.) Don Carlos himself is not so absolute a paragon as the queen. The method in which the vacillation of Carlos' sense of filial duty is made external in his design to defect to the rebels in Flanders adds a hint of moral complexity that aids in forwarding the plot yet, in the end, does not inhibit the pathetic capability of his character. Carlos' plan to go to Flanders ultimately condemns him in the eyes of his father. It is also an indication of his heroic aspirations, but, most important, it is an attempt to escape the emotional agony of his passion for the queen. The catastrophe of the play follows almost the same destructive pattern as does that of *Alcibiades*. That Otway could boast in his preface to *Don Carlos, Prince of Spain* that the play "never fail'd to draw Tears from the Eyes of the Auditors" is a result of his ability to enunciate fully the pity of a love which does not capitulate to the accidents of fate but is destroyed by them.

In his prefatory discussion of the pathos of *Don Carlos, Prince of Spain*, Otway made reference to Jean Racine's *Bérénice* (pr. 1670), and in 1676, his adaptations of this play and of Molière's *Les Fourberies de Scapin* (pr. 1671) were combined in a single night's entertainment at the Duke's Theatre. Otway's three acts of *Titus and Berenice*, although faithful to Racine's plot and the tendency of his language, are nevertheless an extremely compressed redaction of the original. While the alternation of emotional states remains, the adaptation's compression short-circuits the sustained dramatic logic of Racine's play, and yet, considering the remarkable efficiency of the heroic couplets of *Don Carlos, Prince of Spain*, Otway's verses seem slack in comparison with Racine's French Alexandrines. Otway's *Titus and Berenice* is similar to the shortened versions of Shakespeare which were produced in the eighteenth century: It supplies the bare bones of the action but little of the quality of the original.

Otway, in fact, made use of Shakespearean materials in *The History and Fall of Caius Marius*, the first of his plays produced after his return from Flanders. Otway openly admitted his Shakespearean borrowings in the prologue to the play, and, until 1744, *The History and Fall of Caius Marius* replaced Shakespeare's *Romeo and Juliet* (pr. c. 1595-1596) in the repertory of the London theaters. Indeed, what little modern critical interest there has been in *The History and Fall of Caius Marius* has tended to concentrate upon its indebtedness to *Romeo and Juliet*, but a refashioning of Shakespeare's love story constitutes only a part of Otway's drama. A more various use of Shakespearean techniques is evident in that portion of the play which represented a historical parallel to current political events in England. Otway's lovers are separated and ultimately destroyed not as a result of the private feuding of their families, but because of their fathers' engagement in the political antagonisms of the Marian civil war. Even though Otway employed Plutarch with more integrity than in *Alcibiades*, his purpose was not simply to dramatize episodes from the life of Caius Marius. Similarly, although his dramatic prologues and epilogues, along with *The Poet's Complaint of His Muse*, proclaim his staunch allegiance to the Duke of York, he did not simply allegorize the events of the Exclusion Crisis from a Royalist perspective. Rather, the play uses its historical materials to portray the miseries of civil war, a condition seen by many Royalists as the inevitable consequence of the attempt to exclude the Catholic duke from succession to the English throne. Monarchy could not, without blatant anachronism, be introduced into a treatment of the Marian civil war, but the sort of stabilizing, ordering influence which Royalists credited the monarchy as having upon the social economy of England is conspicuously absent from the dramatic world of the play. In *The History and Fall of Caius Marius*, political ambition and factional strife are allowed free play in a Hobbesian nightmare of naked self-interest. Caius Marius himself establishes the keynote of the play when he expresses his desire "to be Great, unequall'd, and alone." His ambition functions without regard for the Roman commonwealth or for those human values that are evident in his son's love for Lavinia, the daughter of his political rival. In exposing the hypocrisy of his patriotism, Otway no doubt intended that it should count against those politicians, the first to be called "Whigs," who claimed that their support of Exclusion was in the best interest of the nation, but that *The History and Fall of Caius Marius* was a play of narrow political regard and application is denied by its continued theatrical production in the changed political circumstances of the years following the accession of William and Mary.

In such a dramatic context, for which Shakespeare's history plays, English and Roman, seem a model, the claustrophobic intensity of Shakespeare's treatment of the ill-fated love of Romeo and Juliet was impossible. Instead, Otway used the story as a counter in which the destruction of the love of Marius' son and Metullus' daughter, insofar as it is a symbol of social collapse, serves a wider function than do the similar catastrophes of *Alcibiades* and *Don Carlos, Prince of Spain*. *The History and Fall of Caius Marius* should perhaps be considered a play which marks a transition in Otway's dramatic work. While the use of blank verse in *The History and Fall of Caius Marius* (and of prose in its comic sections) is suggestive of other of Otway's departures from the practice of his heroic plays, the extended focus of the play is nothing like that of the painfully constricted tragedy *The Orphan,* which followed within a year.

Although Otway's first full-length comedy, *Friendship in Fashion*, is recognizably a product of its dramatic environment, it cannot be made to sit comfortably with William Wycherley's *The Country Wife* (pr. 1675) or Sir George Etherege's *The Man of Mode* (pr. 1676) as a comedy of manners. It is neither a matter of subject—the title of Otway's play accurately describes its social focus, and sex was as much at the forefront of its action as in the two plays of Etherege and Wycherley—nor a matter of dramatic form so much as of emphasis, a different attitude taken to the form as it existed. Otway exploits its satiric potential at the expense of that comic brilliance of surface, which at times has been considered the Restoration comedy of manners' only claim to critical redemption. *Friendship in Fashion*, in fact, has as much (if not more) in common with Wycherley's *The Plain Dealer* (pr. 1676), a play which has been similarly resistant to narrowly prescriptive notions of the comedy of manners, as with his earlier *The Country Wife* (although Otway borrows a character, or at least a name, Mrs. Squeamish, from that play). Yet even *The Plain Dealer*, while pointing in the satiric direction of *Friendship in Fashion*, does not go as far. Both plays are concerned with the betrayal of trust, but Otway does not allow a figure such as Fidelia or the reminiscence of the romantic pattern of Shakespeare's *Twelfth Night* (pr. c. 1600-1602) to obstruct his indictment of love and friendship in its current fashion. The misanthropy of Manly is shown by Wycherley to be in excess of the whole of the play's facts; an unstable but nevertheless a crucial distance is thus established between Manly's perspective and that of the play. There is no such figure as Manly in Otway's play, and there is no ground for ambiguity in its meaning. *Friendship in Fashion* offers the grim sort of entertainment that a Manly might have found in having his views affirmed.

In *Friendship in Fashion,* the cynical, manipulative rake figure was not displaced from the center of the play's action, as he had been in Wycherley's last comedy. Rather, Otway removed the rake both from his position of social power and from his dominant dramatic status. *Friendship in Fashion* seems an almost precise inversion of the dramatic pattern of *The Man of Mode*: The action of the play represents the progressive loss of control of Otway's rake, Goodvile, over his social domain. Goodvile's attempt to combine a rake's career with marriage makes him vulnerable, but it is, significantly, Goodvile's violation of his friendships that is made to seem the effective cause of his cuckoldry, which, in turn, is made palatable by Otway's complete degradation of his rake. Goodvile not only is morally unattractive but also lacks charm and wit. Indeed, the other major characters of the play are responded to, not on account of their personal characteristics or in terms of their adherence to more or less ideal social or amatory values, but almost purely in respect to their opposition to Goodvile and their frustration of his designs. The play obviously pursues dramatic unity in the compression of its events; there is a coordinate compression, or collapse, of social values.

Just as *Friendship in Fashion* depended upon the comedy of manners, *The Soldier's Fortune* refined and enlarged the pattern of contemporary farce. The play contains the constitutive figures of sexual farce—the lover, the boorish husband, and the willing wife—and its action depicts the frustration and delay of the sexual engagement of the soldier, Beaugard, with Lady Dunce, but both in characterization and in the tenor of its action, *The Soldier's Fortune* exceeds the limits of farce. The play is heavily weighted with matters that retard a blithe depiction of cuckoldry. Otway is concerned with the subject of unhappy marriage here, as in his other comedies, as something more than grist for the mill of comic invention. The disaffection of Lady Dunce for her husband, Sir Davy, is not represented simply as the pettish response of a willful, sexually frustrated young woman to confinement by an old and unattractive husband, as it would have been in farce. On the contrary, Otway does much to elevate the character of Lady Dunce—she is shown to be clever, discerning, even sensitive—and the fact that her emotional involvement with Beaugard antedated her enforced marriage to Sir Davy extenuates her pursuit of Beaugard and her adultery. In short, her incompatibility with Sir Davy is more than sexual, and her marriage is made to seem a form of injustice.

A sense of injustice is also evident in Beaugard's complaints against his fortune. Forced to leave London (and Lady Dunce) to become a soldier, he is still almost beggared after his departure. The grievances of Beaugard and his military companion Courtine take them into the position of being outsiders upon the scene of London, and, from the beginning, *The Soldier's Fortune* is leavened by their acerbic commentary. In this commentary, which distends the dramatic shape of the play, it is tempting to see a reflection of Otway's own experience and attitudes; nevertheless, it is made to serve a dramatic purpose, reinforcing, for example, the apposition of Beaugard and Sir Davy. Beaugard's unrewarded loyalty is in complete contrast with the prosperity of Sir Davy's disaffection with the king. Indeed, the political context in which the play was written exerted a forceful, albeit intermittent, influence. Sir Davy's plan to murder Beaugard and his subsequent disposal of Beaugard's body have a parodic relationship to the Whig version of the events of the Popish Plot, and, fueled by prior allusions to Shakespeare's *Macbeth* (pr. c. 1605-1606), the obsessiveness, the frenzy, and the utter disregard for even the comic conventions of human behavior at the play's conclusion are in apparent similitude to the contemporary state of England.

At the end, when Beaugard has finally obtained sexual possession of Lady Dunce, there is little sense of either delight or permanence in the arrangement. Throughout the play, Sir Jolly Jumble, an impotent, bisexual pimp and voyeur, has served them as a go-between, and his involvement is enough to limit the romantic implications of their relationship. The concurrent courtship and marriage of Courtine and Sylvia that function as an underplot to the main action represent a romantic possibility denied to Beaugard and Lady Dunce, despite the hesitation and even the cynicism that results from the pair's lack of faith in the institution of marriage.

Otway's last play, *The Atheist*, a "second part" of *The Soldier's Fortune*, was probably written for the same reason as was the second of Aphra Behn's *Rover* plays: to capitalize on the theatrical success of the original. Beaugard, in the earlier *The Soldier's Fortune*, was the same type of character as the "Rover" Willmore; *The Atheist* was of the same dramatic kind as the *Rover* plays. In the dramatic extravagance of their use of cloaks and daggers and nighttime intrigue, these plays have more in common with the "Spanish" plays of the early years of the Restoration than with the social comedies of the 1670's. Yet the one aspect of *The Atheist* which is an actual sequel to the events of *The Soldier's Fortune*—the treatment of the marriage of Courtine and Sylvia—establishes a thematic link with Otway's earlier comedies. Courtine has reached the nadir of Goodvile's dissatisfaction with marriage, but his attempts to escape its bonds are complete in their lack of success. His situation is contrasted with that of his brother-in-arms, Beaugard, who by the death of an uncle has achieved a fortune totally unencumbered by the demands of marriage. He, it seems, has entered into a rake's paradise of financial and emotional freedom. That Beaugard freely marries a widow who had echoed his consistent objections to marriage suggests, however, that in *The Atheist*, Otway, for once in his comedies, acceded to the satisfaction of a dramatic formula and a romantic pattern. Moreover, both Daredevil, the "atheist" of the title, and Beaugard's father bear a potential for thematic complication which is never realized in the play. Instead, they supply local dramatic interest in the manner of "humours" characters; they are intrinsically entertaining. Otway's increased allowance of the claim of comic entertainment in *The Atheist* may have constituted a recognition that he had exhausted a particular comic vein and may therefore have been an attempt to write a dramatically richer, perhaps a more Shakespearean comedy; it may, on the other hand, have been simply meretricious.

Otway's personal disappointment in the rewards of military service may have been reflected in *The Soldier's Fortune*. In *The Orphan*, produced earlier in the same year, the uncertainty of virtue's reward at court is the reason given by Acasto, himself a disillusioned courtier, for the continued rustication of his twin sons, Castalio and Polydore. Eric Rothstein speaks of the influence which the naturalism of Restoration comedy had upon *The Orphan*, while the play's subtitle, *The Unhappy Marriage*, suggests a tragic treatment of one of the topics of *Friendship in Fashion*, and the dramatic prominence of the friendship of the two brothers points to another form of thematic continuity. Although *The Orphan* does not represent a formal assault upon heroic ideals as such, its depiction of the corruption of a rural idyll denies that sense of pastoral whose function in the late heroic play, according to Rothstein, was as "a counterpoise to dismal actualities, a psychological possibility of vacationing forever from corrupt courts, the contests of ambition, the dangers of martial glory, the deceitful lures of fortune." Moral corruption in *Friendship in Fashion* seems the common, but local, condition of fashionable life; the tragic power of *The Orphan* results from the unaccommodated recognition of a corruption that, in its adherence to a world so much closer to the pure facts of man's nature, is made to seem almost universal.

The central dramatic fact of *The Orphan* is Polydore's taking the place of his brother Castalio on his wedding night with Monimia, their father's ward. Although the act itself is only technically incestuous, it registers the shattering of all the chains of social relationships which have, by various means, been fused into a familial pattern. At the beginning of the play, Acasto's servants mention that Monimia is only his ward and Serina, his only daughter, but in the remainder of *The Orphan*, this distinction is often blurred. Serina's character is remarkable only for its lack of prominence. Indeed, the high point of Serina's dramatic existence begins with her being greeted by Monimia's brother, Chamont, as "another sister." The sudden efflorescence of his love for her and its allowance by Acasto does not, however, divert Chamont from an overwrought and morbid concern for his sister. Moreover, the strangely unmotivated secrecy of Calisto's dealings with Monimia tends to imply that their marriage represents some manner of violation beyond that of the trust of his father and brother. Thus, the celebration in act 2 of his king's birthday by Acasto, divorced from the changes of courtly fortune and content in the security of his newly extended family, achieves a full measure of dramatic irony. Chamont has come from the court, but it is not he who contaminates Acasto's world; corruption is already present in his sons.

Critics have been disturbed (or, more accurately, distracted) by the problem of how Polydore, confined by his father to a country retreat, could have learned the language of a fashionable sexual cynicism. Too strict a conception of dramatic verisimilitude obscures Otway's point: Otway was here using the diction of libertinism, as in the characterization of Don John in *Don Carlos, Prince of Spain*, primarily in order to express a sexual attitude, not a coherent philosophy. It is not, perhaps, an accident of language that "venery" is a word which comprehends Polydore's hunting of the boar as well as his sexual pursuit of Monimia. Polydore's sexual attitude is the efficient cause of the play's tragic dilemma, but not the formal ground of its tragic significance. Otway, both here and in *Venice Preserved*, suggests that the actions determining tragedy are neither matters of simple moral choice nor the products of moral intention. The sensibility evident in Polydore's relationship with his brother, and his regret for his crime, while they offer no protection against, or relief from, the fact of moral pollution, are at the center of the play's pathos. Since the play is uninhibited by sustained and explicit moral judgment, there exists an almost total freedom of response to the emotional dilemmas of the characters. To suggest, however, that pathetic response is the play's only dramatic concern is to ignore the power of the play's moral analysis, a power that resides not in judgment but in recognition.

The dramatic progress of *Venice Preserved* is sustained by the series of shifting moral, political, and personal oppositions that confront Jaffeir, the play's central character. While the extensive use of peripeteia as a dramatic device may seem to recall the heroic play, its significance has been radically altered. Peripeteia was employed in Dryden's heroic plays to register the heroic self-consistency of his protagonists in the face of changing fortune; in *Venice Preserved*, it is the impossibility of moral integrity which is the point of the vacillations in the dramatic action, since Jaffeir is implicated in all of them. The initial, domestic antagonism of Jaffeir and his father-in-law, Priuli, is projected, through the agency of Jaffeir's friend Pierre, into his joining in a conspiracy against the entire senatorial order of which Priuli is a member. Priuli had considered Jaffeir's marriage with his daughter, Belvidira, a betrayal of trust; Jaffeir now leaves Belvidira with the conspirators as a pledge of his faithfulness to their cause. Consequently, the first countermovement of the play begins, not as might have been expected, in the initiation of the revolt, but with Jaffeir's learning of the attempted seduction of his wife by Renault, the oldest and the most morally repugnant of the conspirators. On the tide of his emotional reaction, Belvidira is able to lead her husband to the betrayal of the conspiracy. Although the main conspirators have already been apprehended by the time of his betrayal, thus undercutting the public significance of Jaffeir's action, this fact does not diminish his consciousness of guilt. There is no possible resolution of the conflict of love and honor, because these concepts no longer exist as moral ideals capable of being reconciled, as in Dryden's heroic plays. Jaffeir is forced to choose between life with Belvidira or death with his friend Pierre. He chooses death.

Every human relationship, every political act in *Venice Preserved* seems tainted by sexual motivation. Even the friendship of Jaffeir and Pierre is at times represented in imagery which is unequivocally sexual. This pandemic sexuality cooperates in the representation of the action to constrict the moral vision of the play, and, insofar as *Venice Preserved* bears a general political significance, it is that the world of politics reflects this fundamental moral ambiguity. Thus, the so-called Nicky-Nacky scenes must be seen as more than a satiric, political attack (though they are that) upon Anthony Cooper, Earl of Shaftesbury, perhaps the most important of the Whig leaders during the Exclusion Crisis, or, in dramatic terms, as merely more or less offensive bits of comic relief. Otway's presentation of the perverse sexual relationship of Antonio, himself a senator, with Aquilina, formerly a mistress to Pierre, so precisely echoes and counterpoints the action on the "serious" level of the play that a sense of dramatic equivalence is established which qualifies the audience's understanding of both the senators and the conspirators.

Venice Preserved is the best known of Otway's plays, perhaps because it is the most accessible to modern audiences. In a sense, the public and private dimensions of *The History and Fall of Caius Marius* and *The Orphan* are made to converge in the series of contradictory stances that Jaffeir is forced to adopt. Even though the oppositions that Jaffeir faces are fully articulated, they are perplexed and problematic. Jaffeir, like Antony in Dryden's *All for Love: Or, The World Well Lost* (pr. 1677), decides upon death as the resolution of conflict, but, since his dramatic existence is so much closer to the mean of human experience, his death cannot be considered an act of romantic transcendence. In *Venice Preserved*, even more completely than in *All for Love*, the death of the central character represents a tragic denial of life.

Other major works

POETRY: *The Poet's Complaint of His Muse*, 1680; *Windsor Castle*, 1685.
TRANSLATION: *The History of the Triumvirates*, 1686.
MISCELLANEOUS: *Thomas Otway*, 1903; *The Complete Works of Thomas Otway*, 1926 (3 volumes); *The Works of Thomas Otway: Plays, Poems, and Love-Letters*, 1932, 1968 (2 volumes; J. C. Ghosh, editor).

Bibliography

Ham, Roswell Gray. *Otway and Lee: Biography from a Baroque Age.* New Haven, Conn.: Yale University Press, 1931. This volume is an excellent study of two Restoration dramatists whose careers ran parallel on the turbulent London stage. A chapter entitled "Shakespeare and Otway" studies Otway's indebtedness to his famous predecessor, and an appreciative chapter, "Venice Preserved," examines that play and the reasons for its success.
Johnson, Samuel. *Lives of the English Poets.* Edited by George Birkbeck Hill. Vol. 1. Oxford, England: Clarendon Press, 1905. Johnson comments briefly on some of the works and moralizes typically on the life: "Want of morals or of decency did not in those days exclude any man from the company of the wealthy and the gay if he brought with him any powers

of entertainment." Hill's notes are excellent.

Noel, Roden. Introduction to *Thomas Otway.* New York: Charles Scribner's Sons, 1903. Noel includes *Don Carlos, Prince of Spain, The Orphan, The Soldier's Fortune,* and *Venice Preserved.* In his introduction, Noel compares Otway to the Greek tragedians and analyzes the four plays he has chosen. An appendix prints six letters supposed to have been written to the actress Elizabeth Barry.

Otway, Thomas. *The Complete Works of Thomas Otway.* Edited by Montague Summers. 3 vols. London: Nonesuch Press, 1926. Reprint. New York: AMS Press, 1967. Summers' long introduction is informative and readable in its gossipy, anecdotal approach. The explanatory notes are brisk, and the source notes are rich with references. Should be compared with J. C. Ghosh's two-volume edition (1932).

Pollard, Hazel M. Batzer. *From Heroics to Sentimentalism: A Study of Thomas Otway's Tragedies.* Salzburg: Institut für Englische Sprache und Literatur, Universität Salzburg, 1974. Pollard traces the development in Otway's tragedies away from the heroic tragedies of his time toward the mounting psychology of sentimentalism. Among the discussions are "*Caius Marius*: Emancipation from the Heroic" and "*The Orphan*: Domestic Tragedy."

Taylor, Aline Mackenzie. *Next to Shakespeare: Otway's "Venice Preserv'd" and "The Orphan" and Their History on the London Stage.* Durham, N.C.: Duke University Press, 1950. An invaluable account of the stage histories of these two plays, with a list of performances, an excellent bibliography, an essay on Otway's reputation, and an index of actors.

Warner, Kerstin P. *Thomas Otway.* Boston: Twayne, 1982. A fine overview in the format of the Twayne series. A chronology is followed by a biographical sketch and chapters on Otway's political views, Otway's first plays (1675-1678), the playwright's "peak season" (1678-1680), and a chapter entitled "After the Playhouses Merged (1682-1683)." A succinct annotated bibliography completes this essential work.

James E. Maloney
(Updated by *Frank Day*)

ROCHELLE OWENS
Rochelle Bass

Born: Brooklyn, New York; April 2, 1936

Principal drama
Futz, pb. 1961, pr. 1965, pb. 1968 (revised; music by Tom O'Horgan); *The String Game*, pr. 1965, pb. 1968; *Istanboul*, pr. 1965, pb. 1968; *Homo*, pr. 1966, pb. 1968; *Beclch*, pr. 1966, pb. 1968; *Farmer's Almanac*, pr. 1968, pb. 1974; *Futz and What Came After*, pb. 1968 (includes *Beclch, Homo, The String Game, Istanboul*); *The Queen of Greece*, pr. 1969; *Kontraption*, pb. 1971, pr. 1978 (one act); *The Karl Marx Play*, pb. 1971 (one act; in *The Best Short Plays of 1971*, Stanley Richards, editor), pr. 1973, pb. 1974 (revised as two acts; music by Galt MacDermot); *He Wants Shih!*, pb. 1972, pr. 1975 (one act); *The Karl Marx Play and Others*, pb. 1974 (includes *Kontraption, He Wants Shih!, Farmer's Almanac, Coconut Folk-singer, O. K. Certaldo*); *Emma Instigated Me*, pb. 1976, pr. 1977 (expanded); *Mountain Rites*, pb. 1978 (one act); *Chucky's Hunch*, pr. 1981; *Who Do You Want, Peire Vidal?*, pr. 1982, pb. 1986.

Other literary forms
Rochelle Owens began writing as a poet and has published several volumes of poetry as well as poems in various journals and small magazines. Her poetry is lyric and metaphysical, depending heavily upon juxtapositions that often involve fairly wide leaps between ideas or attitudes. In addition to conventional poetic devices, Owens makes considerable use of typographical devices: The spacing between words, phrases, and lines is important both to the sense and to the rhythm of her verse, and she often uses capitalization and punctuation (or the lack of it) in an arresting way, sometimes forming unusual patterns upon the page with words or parts of words. These appear to be voice cues, and her voice is, as Toby Olson has written (in a symposium devoted to Owens' work), the controlling element of her poetry. Wit and humor are also essential ingredients, but Owens is by no means a poet of the intellect only; her poetry conveys emotion and sensuality as she probes deeply into her subject, expressing her discoveries energetically if not always with the greatest lucidity.

Owens writes about a variety of subjects, but her chief interests are political and humanistic, combined, for example, in "Purple Worms of Vengeance," a poem that contrasts a fat, gluttonous congressman with a poor Chicano child. In the same volume—a collection of her verse from 1961 to 1971 entitled *I Am the Babe of Joseph Stalin's Daughter* (1972)—are a number of poems about her "Deebler Woman," such as "Deebler Woman's Thoughts on the Nature of the Universe," which is a working woman's meditation upon her lot in life and the pleasure she gets from going to the movies: "the movies don't/ really tell it/ honestly/ but I like it." "Radiant Heat," dedicated to her husband, is a moving love lyric about how, through the "radiant heat" of two bodies, true contact is achieved. "Song of the Loving Father of the Stuffed Son" captures the real agony, partly expressed in jokes, felt by an affluent Jewish lawyer whose son is a Cuban-loving Marxist. Owens' Jewishness does not express itself in modish self-hate; she is entirely capable of satiric attacks against Jewish anti-Zionists and others, as in "A Poem for Jewish Collaborators Who Betray Their Ancestral Homeland Israel" or "The Camel Smiles at the Ignorance of the Assimilated Man." Beneath the political, social, or economic concerns, however, is the fundamental human one: "I love my family! I want them to laugh!" cries Karl Marx, even as he recognizes "I am the coming judgment!" ("The Voluminous Agony of Karl Marx"). Owens expands on these themes in one of her most celebrated dramas, *The Karl Marx Play.*

In her later poetry, as in her dramatic work, Owens has continued to experiment with form and content. She sums up her own efforts succinctly and accurately in her note to her poetry collection *Shemuel* (1979): "Imagination is generator of the word as act/event. In *Shemuel* the journey begun in *The Joe 82 Creation Poems* [1974] and *The Joe Chronicles II* [1978] continues to explore through patterns of force the conjunction of the old and the new, the spiritual and the physical."

Achievements

Throughout her career, Owens has received support for her writing from major foundations. In 1965, she received grants from the Rockefeller Office for Advanced Drama Research and the Ford Foundation. The next year she won a Creative Artists Public Service grant, and in 1968 she was awarded a Yale University Drama School fellowship. She received a Guggenheim Fellowship in 1971 and a National Endowment for the Arts grant in 1974, followed by a Rockefeller grant in 1975. Her plays have won or been nominated for Obie Awards in 1967 and 1973. Critics have generally shown interest in her plays, which have been reviewed in *The New York Times* as well as *The Village Voice*, often with sympathy and sensitivity, despite their unconventional subject matter and sometimes surrealist manner. Her first successful play, *Futz*, was made into a motion picture by Tom O'Horgan, who directed several of Owens' plays and who also wrote music for them. She is recognized as a major talent among Off-Broadway playwrights, and she is a founding member of the New York Theatre Strategy. Several of her plays were first produced by Café La Mama, either in New York or in Europe, where her work has attracted a considerable amount of critical attention, both favorable and unfavorable. Owens is a member of the Dramatists Guild, of the New Dramatists Committee, of the American Society of Composers, Authors, and Publishers, and of the Authors Guild.

Biography

Rochelle Owens was born Rochelle Bass, daughter of Maxwell and Molly (Adler) Bass. She later took the name Owens, presumably in admiration of the famous athlete Jesse Owens, about whom she wrote a poem in which she refers to him as her father.

Owens' real father was a postal clerk. Reared in Brooklyn, Rochelle was educated in New York City public schools and was graduated from Lafayette High School in 1953. She began writing poetry early. When George Economou saw "Groshl Monkeys Horses" in a 1960 issue of *Yugen*, he invited her to submit some of her poems to *Trobar*, which he had just begun editing with Robert Kelly. She sent him a packet of verse, many of the poems appearing in *Trobar* (II), including "Humble humble pinati." Trobar Press also brought out her first book of poems, *Not Be Essence That Cannot Be* (1961), simultaneously with Paul Blackburn's *The Nets*. In 1962, Owens and Economou were married, and many of her books subsequently have been dedicated to her husband, a poet in his own right, who has also appeared in some of her plays (he played the Robed Man, for example, in *Istanboul*).

Although written several years earlier, *Futz* was first produced by the Tyrone Guthrie Workshop in Minneapolis on October 10, 1965, where it played for a single performance. Later revised, it was produced in New York by the Café La Mama Theatre Troupe on March 1, 1967. During this period, several other plays were produced in New York and elsewhere. On February 12, 1965, the Judson Poets Theatre produced *The String Game*, and on September 12, *Istanboul*. Andre Gregory produced *Beclch* at the Theatre of the Living Arts with the Southwark Theatre Company in Philadelphia on December 20, 1966. The controversial production was at least in part responsible for the termination of relations between Gregory and the Theatre of the Living Arts.

By then, Owens' association with Café La Mama had already begun, and *Homo* was taken on tour, to Europe in the summer of 1966, where it played in Stockholm, and later in New York. Tom O'Horgan's production of *Futz* followed early the next year and was made into a film by Commonwealth United in 1969, O'Horgan again directing and Owens contributing additional dialogue for the screenplay. Portions of *The String Game* and *Beclch* were televised by the Columbia and Public broadcasting systems. On April 12, 1969, Café La Mama staged two plays: *The Queen of Greece*, a curtain raiser, and *Homo*.

Owens continued writing poetry during this period and began giving readings of her verse throughout the United States, including appearances at universities such as Princeton and Columbia. She has made several recordings, reading both her own verse and some of the primitive and archaic poetry that has obviously influenced her writing.

In the 1970's, several new plays by Owens were produced, most notably *The Karl Marx Play*, which opened at the American Place Theatre in New York on March 16, 1973. For this production, the original one-act version, first published in Stanley Richards' *The Best Short Plays of 1971*, was revised and expanded to a two-act play. The music for the play was composed and directed by Galt MacDermot, with Mel Shapiro in charge of overall direction. The production was honored by the New York Drama Critics Circle. *He Wants Shih!* opened the spring season of Theatre Strategy at the Gate Theater in New York on April 1, 1975, and in 1977 the American Place Theatre performed *Emma Instigated Me* as a work-in-progress, expanded from the original version published in 1976. *Chucky's Hunch*, a play for a single actor, first opened Off-Off-Broadway at the Theater for the New City on March 22, 1981, with Kevin O'Connor. It was revived, again with O'Connor, on February 18, 1982, when it opened at the Harold Clurman Theater in New York. Later in the same year, *Who Do You Want, Peire Vidal?* opened at the Theater for the New City on May 8.

Rochelle Owens thus continues to be a vital force in American experimental theater. Her chief interests remain poetry and drama, and doubtless each nourishes the other. She has written several unpublished works, including the play "Three Front" (1990) and the radio play "A Guerre Trois" (1991), and she has written and produced video works, such as "Oklahoma Too" (1987). Her reading performances at the Museum of Modern Art, the Guggenheim Museum, and the Whitney Museum are popular with the artistic community of New York. "Creativity, idealism and mental concentration have enabled me to pursue the world of ideas, transforming itself always into art," she notes in her *Who's Who in America* entry.

Analysis

Futz was Rochelle Owens' first play to attract significant critical attention. It is about a gentle farmer, Cy Futz, in love with his sow, Amanda. He lives alone and raises vegetables for himself and his sow, but the people of the community will not leave him alone. Majorie Satz, the town whore, fancies him and finally inveigles him into a three-way sexual encounter with her and his pig, but Cy prefers Amanda.

Cy's amorous devotion to his pig has unfortunate consequences for Oscar Loop, who hears the grunts and groans coming from Cy's barn. The sounds and sight of Cy's lovemaking antagonize Oscar to the point that he murders randy Ann Fox, whom he has brought with him and with whom he is engaging in some amorous activity of his own: He is driven insane by the idea of evil and his need to wipe it out. Oscar is arrested for the murder, and subsequently Sheriff Tom Sluck and Bill Marjoram come to arrest Cy, too. Meanwhile, Majorie has become worse than ever, upsetting the Satz family so much that her brother Ned resolves to take matters into his own hands and vindicate the family's loss of honor.

In jail immediately before his execution, Oscar is visited by his mother, who gives an account of her son's conception and birth. Oscar is obviously mad, thinking that the "spice-seed insects" he gives his mother have miraculous powers. The suggestions of incestuous feelings between them are quite broad, but Mrs. Loop seems interested mostly in her position of respectability and as an object of sorrow in the community.

Neither Oscar's execution nor Cy's murder by Brother Ned has any effect on the sexual mores of the community. Two characters, Buford and Sugford, take Majorie (in a "whorey mood") with them to a field. Majorie suggests that she and her friends kill Cy's pig, offering to do it herself when they demur. They go as Brother Ned prepares to kill Cy because, he says, "You make my brains red!"

Futz thus dramatizes and satirizes some of the worst aspects of humankind's vicious animal nature and counterpoints them to its gentler manifestations. Cy intends no harm to anyone and asks only to be left alone. The members of his community find his bestiality intolerable but are oblivious to the far more damaging consequences of their own animality toward one another, as in Oscar Loop's treatment of Ann Fox, or in her treatment of him (she leads him on shamelessly, unwittingly preparing the scene for her own murder). The scenes in the field between Majorie and Buford and Sugford are devoid of any of the feelings that Cy has for Amanda; likewise, Mrs. Loop's feelings for her son are a perversion of genuine motherly love. Nothing softens the conclusion of the play: Owens intends that the full force of human brutality should be felt, and it is.

Clive Barnes, in a review that appeared in *The New York Times* in October, 1968, called *Futz* a conventional play about an unconventional subject. The rapid alternation of scenes is hardly novel, and neither is the use of a narrator, who gives stage directions that are dispensable and makes choral comments that are not. The music and dance of the production in New York by O'Horgan doubtless filled out the play, which by itself can hardly take up an evening.

The String Game, Owens' next play, is similarly conventional in structure and in theme as well; only its setting is novel: Greenland. A group of Eskimo are sitting around in a hut playing the string game, guessing at the patterns or pictures that the string makes, usually erotic ones. Father Bontempo, a Maltese priest who is with them, tries to get their minds off sex. He objects to their customs of wife exchange, adult breast-feeding, and other heathenish practices. For their part, the Eskimo cannot understand Bontempo's objections to what they regard as natural behavior.

Cecil, a half-breed (he is half German), also tries to get the Eskimo interested in something else—business. He suggests various schemes, such as a herring factory, the manufacture of clay pipes, and so on, to help them get ahead. Personally very ambitious, he is baffled by the lack of ambition among the others and enlists Father Bontempo's aid in a plan to involve everyone in a shoe-selling business about which he learns from a match-book cover. At first, the Eskimo resist, seeing nothing creative about this venture as compared to the string game; in any case, they are comfortable enough with their government checks. Under Bontempo's persuasion, however, they acquiesce, though still with misgivings. They recognize only too well how "it's the outer world that wants to change the inner one. The foreign influences." When Bontempo dies, choking on the pasta and sauce with which Cecil had bribed him, the shoe-selling scheme dies with him. The Eskimo throw Cecil out and resume the string game.

The evils of foreign influences are dramatized in *Istanboul* and *Homo* as well. In *Istanboul*, set in fifteenth century Constantinople, the crusaders Godfrigh and Baldwin try to make a commercial deal with Saint Mary of Egypt, while Godfrigh's wife, Alice, and her friend Gertrude compete for the favor of the Byzantine dancer, Leo, also desired by two native women, Mary and Zoe. A robed man watches most of the action of the play in silence. In a religious/sexual frenzy, Saint Mary cuts off Godfrigh's leg, which results in Godfrigh's death and Alice's widowhood. The play ends as Alice lies in bed with Leo, an hour before the Saracens arrive to overthrow Byzantine rule.

If effetism, decadence, religious ecstasy and corruption, and the mutual attraction and repulsion of East and West are major themes in *Istanboul*, white European racism and greed are the themes of *Homo*. Bernice is the blonde bitch-goddess worshiped by the horse-man and the Asiatics in the play, while Elizabeth, a fiftyish, fleshy European female, is abused by Asiatic workmen but is also adored by them, especially when she gives them her sugarcoated fingers to suck. Thus, competition is set up between Bernice (the goddess) and Elizabeth (the mother archetype), objects of primal masculine drives. Elizabeth's husband, the Dutch merchant Gelderen, is also abused by Asiatics, officials who allow him to do business at the price of self-abasement. The time shifts between the mid-nineteenth century and the present, and the so-called Asiatics may actually be played (the stage directions tell us) by Mediterranean types, who speak much better English than Gelderen. Owens thus does not depend upon mere verisimilitude to drive home her satiric point about cultural imperialism or to dramatize her themes.

Beclch (pronounced Bek-lek) is one of Owens' most ambitious and difficult plays and her first full-length one. Here she strikingly unveils the violence, lust, sadism, and brutality that she sees at the heart of perverted human nature. Beclch is a power-maddened woman living in Africa, manipulating Yago and others to satisfy her desire to rule supreme among the poor specimens of humankind that surround her. She is unleashed passion personified, finding no reason at all to keep her impulses in check. Succeeding in making her husband, Yago, king through means both cruel and disgusting as well as (to him) extremely painful, she later becomes bored and persuades him to die by self-strangulation, whereupon she becomes queen. She plans to marry her lover Jose, but he recognizes her for what she is, refuses to participate fully in her activities, and eventually runs away, leaving her husbandless and thus ripe for ritual slaughter. Her depravity is best expressed by her words as she faces death: "I hope I drool like an animal."

From all accounts, *Beclch* was a failure, if an interesting one in some respects. Lavishly produced in New York after its original opening in Philadelphia, it was condemned even by usually sympathetic critics, such as Clive Barnes, who found the play badly written or at least badly played and reeking of bad taste. Julius Novick commented on the play's failure finally to shock because it overshot its mark. If excess is its theme, it should not have been allowed to drown in its own excesses.

Plenitude is also a quality of *The Karl Marx Play*, but here Owens exercises firmer control over her material, even as she allows her innate lyricism full expression. Owens all but abandons traditional concepts of plot in favor of a representation of Karl Marx, the man and the historical figure, surrounded by family, friends, and—in the anachronistic character of Leadbelly (Huddie Ledbetter, 1888-1949), the famed black American blues singer—a nagging and insistent conscience. Like the biblical Job, Marx suffers from boils and must force himself finally to go to the British Museum and write his famous *Das Kapital*. He has reveries about his romantic and aristocratic wife, Jenny von Westphalen, and he thinks of her voluptuous breasts when he should be concocting his theories on economics. Indeed, one of the running jokes in the play is that Marx hates economics and must be driven to write his treatise. His friend and supporter, Friedrich Engels, also emerges as a comical figure. Very *mittel European*, as the stage directions indicate, he speaks with a German accent and, as the heir to his family's manufacturing concern, provides the funds on which Marx and his family live. The language throughout the play is vivid, idiomatic according to character, and often raunchy. Songs are frequent and help to emphasize the essential lyric quality of the drama; in fact, the play opens with Leadbelly singing a kind of hymn. Hymns, however, are by no means the chief kind of song the audience hears.

In keeping with its lyric approach to drama, *The Karl Marx Play* moves back and forth in time easily: One must not look for linear development here. Owens' exuberance is not confusing but refreshing and enlivening,

aided by Galt MacDermot's music. *The Karl Marx Play* received many favorable reviews, vindicating Owens' intentions; she says in her author's note:

> The play evolved out of investigations of the circumstances and events, factual and
> imaginary, of the life of Karl Marx. It is a play with music whose story is told as much
> by its imagery and tonal "meanings" as it is by its plot. It is a theatrical experiencing of
> the extreme humanness of Karl Marx, a vision of the man's spirit and fate.

The experiments of Owens' poetry pay off handsomely in this work, which,
one critic has said, is as much about the creative process as about Karl
Marx. Marxism has never appeared less doctrinaire than it does here,
thanks to the humanity that Owens reveals underlying the historical facts.

As restless in dramatic experiments as she is in her verse, Owens has
continued to explore the frontiers of her art in other plays, such as
Kontraption and *He Wants Shih!* The latter was begun as early as 1967 but
waited for eight years to be produced. Written partly in a kind of pseudo-
Chinese, it is one of Owens' most richly poetic dramas; the Chinese words
act as images and enhance through sound and rhythm other aspects of the
diction. The play's multiply punning title is ambiguous; in a note, Owens
says that *Shih* is pronounced *shur* and means "Law, Command, Poetry."
Lan, the young Emperor of China and the last of the Manchu Dynasty,
strives for complete self-fulfillment to the extent that he is willing to
surrender all worldly responsibility in his quest. That quest, Owens says in
her author's note, is "toward the supernatural . . . toward an ultimate transformation: the means of entering the Unseen by force, of driving his way
into the Power over the world." Instructed by his tutor, a monk named
Feng, Lan recognizes the male-female duality within himself and actively
courts his half brother, Bok. He also loves the Princess Ling. While China
is beset by civil war and foreign invasion, Lan pursues his own goals, longing to answer questions of being and becoming. He is more interested in
learning magic tricks and acrobatics than in fighting battles; indeed, he advocates disarmament. According to critic Bonnie Marranca, Lan embodies
both the Buddhist thought that informs the play and Neo-Confucian
teachings on the infinite number of principles, or laws, that make up the
universe. By the final scene, having killed Princess Ling with a golden dart,
he transforms himself into both Lan-He and Lan-She, male and female,
and carries on a dialogue with him/herself, dancing and singing as appropriate. Ultimately, however, Lan is a tragic figure: Dethroned and imprisoned, he is murdered by rough Chinese soldiers at the end of the play in
an ecstasy of self-abasement and poetry.

Reminiscent of Vladimir and Estragon in Samuel Beckett's *Waiting for
Godot* (pb. 1952), Hortten and Abdal—the chief characters in Owens'
Kontraption—are friends living in an Absurdist world in which reality and
fantasy freely interchange. Their love-hate relationship oscillates between

deep devotion and vigorous attacks. Abdal appears most violent and is punished shortly after he suffocates Mr. Strauss, an Albanian/German laundryman who has asked only to sit down and rest for a while, entertaining them with tales of Gastour, his fantasy ideal of himself as a he-man surrounded by lovely ladies. The master deity of the play's universe, a Chemist, appears and transforms Abdal from "an agreeable bald man" smelling of myrrh and sweet herbs (his own conception of himself) to a square-shaped contraption from the neck down, part mechanical, part animal. Justifying this action, the Chemist says, "I smelled his fear, his longing!" A symbol of technology gone awry, the Chemist boasts that he has now made Abdal into a perfect man, "a blending of nature and graceful art."

Gradually, Abdal recovers from his shocked state and begins dancing and singing. At first, Hortten is impressed with his friend's new form and being, but the alternation of devotion and name-calling in their relationship quickly returns, along with more fantasies and the haunting memory of Mr. Strauss. The fantasies are mostly erotic ones and arouse the passions of the two friends. The Chemist reappears and forbids grief: "We put grief in a mudhole!" he declares. At the end, Abdal dies and ascends to heaven, leaving Hortten in intense despair, imploring his friend to come down to him, promising him food and water and good times again in the summer. "There's nothing up there! In the sky!" he cries, berating himself for not nailing Abdal down while he had the chance.

In her introduction to *The Karl Marx Play and Others*, Owens proclaims that she writes "so that God will not hate you." By portraying our "visceral anguish," as in *Kontraption*, she reveals humanity in its deepest agonies, but she also believes in human joy and its recovery, as in the lighter one-act play *O.K. Certaldo*. "Authentic theatre," she says, "is always oscillating between joyousness and fiendishness." In her later plays, such as *Emma Instigated Me* and *What Do You Want, Peire Vidal?*, she continues to reject theater as entertainment in favor of experimentation. "We are extremists," she says of herself and of similar playwrights, "and attempt both in our lives and in our art to explore aesthetic possibilities and to become more open to the profound, endless dimensions of creating art." Only in *Chucky's Hunch*, an epistolary drama written for a single actor, does Owens appear to concede anything (but not much) to traditional conceptions of theater. This successful play, with Kevin O'Connor playing Chucky in both New York productions, was quickly followed by the boldly conceived *What Do You Want, Peire Vidal?*, suggesting that Rochelle Owens has surrendered nothing of her integrity as an innovative dramatist.

Other major works

SHORT FICTION: *The Girl on the Garage Wall*, 1962; *The Obscenities of Reva Cigarnik*, 1963.

POETRY: *Not Be Essence That Cannot Be*, 1961; *Four Young Lady Poets*, 1962 (with others; LeRoi Jones, editor); *Salt and Core*, 1968; *I Am the Babe of Joseph Stalin's Daughter*, 1972; *Poems from Joe's Garage*, 1973; *The Joe 82 Creation Poems*, 1974; *Poems*, 1974; *The Joe Chronicles II*, 1978; *Shemuel*, 1979; *Constructs*, 1985; *W. C. Fields in French Light*, 1986; *How Much Paint Does the Painting Need*, 1988.

SCREENPLAY: *Futz*, 1969 (adaptation of her play).

ANTHOLOGY: *Spontaneous Combustion: Eight New American Plays*, 1972 (editor).

Bibliography

Cohn, Ruby. *Dialogue in American Drama*. Bloomington: Indiana University Press, 1971. In a longer discussion of major playwrights, Cohn separates Owens as one of the "poets at play." Provides a strong discussion of *Futz*, *Homo*, and *Beclch* ("suggesting beak, belch, cluck, lick—all resonant of animals") and concentrates on how Owens "renders her cruelty mainly through language."

Marranca, Bonnie, and Gautam Dasgupta. *American Playwrights: A Critical Survey*. New York: Drama Book Specialists, 1981. Contains a chapter on Owens, beginning with her poetic output and continuing into a discussion of *Futz*, and an analysis of the "ethnopoetics" and the poetic language inherent in *Beclch*, *Kontraption*, and *The Karl Marx Play*. Most of Owens' plays are set in Africa, Greenland, Europe, and China, but *Futz* and *Emma Instigated Me* have American settings. Of *Kontraption*, Marranca says: "The characters . . . are conjurers of words as well as visions—and the Word is made Flesh."

Murray, Timothy. "The Play of Letters: Possession and Writing in *Chucky's Hunch*." In *Feminine Focus: The New Women Playwrights*, edited by Enoch Brater. New York: Oxford University Press, 1989. Putting "play" in quotation marks, Murray examines in this postmodern linguistic analysis the writing strategies of Owens in her 1981 play: "The primary [strategy] continually positions Chucky's silent and disgusted interlocutors . . . vis-à-vis a crisis of reception posed by his narrative presence." Contains a long essay, divided by sections entitled "Self-Restoration," "Oozing Signs, Early Memories," "Primal Digressions," and "Rebirth or Lack?" Notes.

Novick, Julius. *Beyond Broadway: The Quest for Permanent Theatres*. New York: Hill & Wang, 1968. In a chapter treating André Gregory and the East Coast theaters (Washington to Philadelphia), Owens' play *Beclch* is discussed in Artaudian terms. Owens, says Novick, in her attempt to shock, "generated a feeling of adolescent eagerness that was at odds with the somber impression she was trying to convey." Good discussion of the relation of experimental theater to its audience.

Olauson, Judith. *The American Woman Playwright: A View of Criticism and Characterization.* Troy, N.Y.: Witston Publishing, 1981. A feminist reevaluation of traditional literary views of women, divided by decades (Owens is in the 1960-1970 period with Megan Terry, Myrna Lamb, and others), this study sees Owens as "a proponent of the 'underground theatre' movement and insists that modern times require a new artistic response." Owens portrays her two main female characters in *Futz* as predators. No index.

Jay Halio
(Updated by *Thomas J. Taylor*)

JOHN PATRICK
John Patrick Goggan

Born: Louisville, Kentucky; May 17, 1905

Principal drama

Hell Freezes Over, pr. 1935; *The Story of Mary Surratt*, wr. 1940, pr., pb. 1947; *The Willow and I*, pr. 1942, pb. 1943; *The Hasty Heart*, pr., pb. 1945; *The Curious Savage*, pr. 1950, pb. 1951; *Lo and Behold!*, pr. 1951, pb. 1952; *The Teahouse of the August Moon*, pr. 1953, pb. 1954 (adaptation of Vern Sneider's novel); *Good as Gold*, 1957; *Everybody Loves Opal*, pr. 1961, pb. 1962; *Love Is a Time of Day*, pr. 1969, pb. 1970; *Lovely Ladies, Kind Gentlemen*, pr. 1970 (music, lyrics by Stan Freeman and Franklin Underwood); *Opal Is a Diamond*, pr. 1971, pb. 1972; *Anybody Out There?*, pb. 1972; *Opal's Husband*, pr., pb. 1975; *Noah's Animal: A Musical Allegory*, pr. 1975, pb. 1976; *Opal's Million Dollar Duck*, pr. 1979, pb. 1980; *The Girls of the Garden Club*, pr. 1979, pb. 1980; *People*, pb. 1980; *That's Not My Father!*, pb. 1980; *That's Not My Mother!*, pb. 1980.

Other literary forms

In addition to his plays, John Patrick is the author of more than thirty screenplays, more than one thousand radio plays for the series *Cecil and Sally* (1929-1933), and a television play, *The Small Miracle* (1972), with Arthur Dales, from the novel by Paul Gallico. It is worth noting that many of Patrick's best-known screenplays are those adapted from novels or plays. *Look Out, Mr. Moto* (1937) and *Mr. Moto Takes a Chance* (1938), written with others, were taken from the detective novels of John P. Marquand. *The President's Lady* (1953), *Three Coins in a Fountain* (1954), *Love Is a Many-Splendored Thing* (1955), *Les Girls* (1957), and *Some Came Running* (1958) were based on novels by Irving Stone, John H. Secondari, Han Suyin, Vera Caspary, and James Jones, respectively. The Philip Barry play *The Philadelphia Story* (pr. 1939) provided the basis for *High Society* (1956), while *The World of Susie Wong* (1960), and *The Teahouse of the August Moon* (1956) were adapted from novels by, respectively, Richard Mason and Vern Sneider, and plays by, respectively, Paul Osborn and John Patrick himself. Patrick is also noted for radio dramatizations of novels, and his adaptations for that medium doubtless contributed to the sure grasp of dramatic structure that distinguishes Patrick's stage plays.

Achievements

John Patrick is one of the most prolific American dramatic writers on record. While his plays range in genre, subject matter, and setting from wartime or postwar experiences in foreign lands to domestic situations and murder mysteries, the majority of them emerge as comedies and evidence both their author's superior craftsmanship and his marked talent for the comic genre.

Patrick's most accomplished and enduring work is *The Teahouse of the August Moon*. One of the greatest critical and popular success in the history of the American theater, the play garnered in 1954 the Pulitzer Prize for Drama, the New York Drama Critics Circle Award for Best American Play of the Broadway season, the Tony Award, the Donaldson Award, and the Aegis Club Award. Less spectacular in their success yet also notable are *The Hasty Heart*, a serious play set in wartime and popular with audiences and critics in the 1945 Broadway and London seasons, and *The Curious Savage*, a comedy whose regional popularity (it has been a staple of community theater playbills over the years) has far exceeded and outlasted its restrained reception in New York in 1950. All three plays are interlaced with gentle humor and a compassionate view of the human condition, but it is for *The Teahouse of the August Moon* that Patrick will be remembered. A fine craftsman and a productive journeyman playwright in the best sense of the term, Patrick surpassed himself in that play, giving American theater one of its best comedies.

In addition to awards won for *The Teahouse of the August Moon*, Patrick won the Screenwriters Guild Award and the Foreign Correspondents Award for the 1957 musical screenplay *Les Girls*, with Gene Kelly and Cole Porter songs, which was presented as a command performance for Queen Elizabeth II. Patrick also received an honorary doctorate in fine arts from Baldwin Wallace College in Berea, Ohio.

Biography

John Patrick was born John Patrick Goggan on May 17, 1905, in Louisville, Kentucky. Following a rift with his parents, which he has not publicly discussed, Patrick spent a portion of his youth living with relatives and attending boarding schools such as St. Mary's Seminary in La Porte, Texas, and St. Edward's College in Austin, Texas. Later he attended Holy Cross College in New Orleans and was a summer school student at Harvard and Columbia universities. In the early 1930's, Patrick began a career in San Francisco as a scriptwriter for the National Broadcasting Company, where he authored numerous radio scripts and earned a reputation for his radio dramatizations of novels.

In 1935, Patrick's first play, a melodrama entitled *Hell Freezes Over*, concerning polar explorers whose dirigible crash-lands in the Antarctic, was produced on Broadway; the production was the directorial debut of Joshua Logan, who went on to gain fame as director of *South Pacific* (1949) and many other Broadway musicals. *Hell Freezes Over* closed after an unfavorable reception, causing critic George Jean Nathan to remark that its playwright should be thrown back to Hollywood. Perhaps taking his cue from Nathan, a talent scout secured for Patrick a Hollywood contract. Returning to California, Patrick developed his craft by writing thirty or more screenplays between 1936 and 1968 for such studios as Metro-Goldwyn-Mayer and Twentieth Century-Fox.

Leaving Hollywood (to which he would often return for screenwriting assignments) in the late 1930's, Patrick established himself in Boston. It was there that he wrote "The Gentle Ghost," a drama about the woman hanged for complicity in Abraham Lincoln's assassination, which appeared on Broadway in 1947 as *The Story of Mary Surratt.* During this period, Patrick also completed *The Willow and I*, a psychological drama about two sisters competing for the love of the same man and destroying him in the process, which opened in New York in 1942. Neither of the two plays was a box office success.

In 1942, Patrick joined the American Field Service, serving overseas as a captain with a British ambulance unit in Egypt, India, Burma, and Syria. He drew on this experience in *The Hasty Heart*, which centers on a dour and terminally ill Scottish sergeant in a British military hospital in Southeast Asia; the play enjoyed both critical and popular success in the 1945 Broadway season. The fruits of his first stage success permitted Patrick to purchase a sixty-five-acre farm in Rockland County, New York, which he appropriately called Hasty Hill. There he lived casually as a gentleman farmer, raised sheep, remained unmarried, and continued to write. In a 1950's interview with Harry Gilroy for *The New York Times Magazine*, he said that strenuous physical activity keeps one aware of life's basic values and that one "can't lead a push-button life and be a writer."

Turning to comedy, Patrick wrote *The Curious Savage*, whose heroine is a wealthy eccentric widow, and *Lo and Behold!*, a comedy-fantasy about a solitude-loving writer who, after stipulating in his will that his house be kept vacant as a sanctuary, returns as a ghost to find it occupied by three incompatible spirits. Both comedies had short runs on Broadway, but the former has enjoyed lasting popularity with community theater audiences. Following these plays, Patrick created his most successful comedy, *The Teahouse of the August Moon*, which won many awards and established his reputation as an American dramatist. Patrick rewrote it as a screenplay and later as a short-lived musical entitled *Lovely Ladies, Kind Gentlemen*, with music and lyrics by Stan Freeman and Franklin Underwood.

Patrick is also the author of a number of comedies that, while attaining neither Broadway acclaim nor, in some cases, New York productions, have proved popular with regional theaters. For example, *The Hasty Heart* was successfully performed at the Berkshire Theatre Festival Mainstage in August of 1990; *Opal Is a Diamond*, "as entertainingly silly as the silliest sitcom," was presented by the Arena Players of Baltimore, Maryland, in

March of 1991. The Group Repertory Theatre of Los Angeles produced *The Curious Savage*, "this pallid American chestnut," in October of 1991.

Analysis

A versatile, prolific playwright, John Patrick has been most successful as a writer of comedy. His comic plays, like the best of his serious ones, are, in the main, marked by cleverly conceived situations, well-drawn characters, effective dialogue, and an overall sense of solid craftsmanship. Patrick's comedies are imbued with charm and humor, wit, a gentle satirizing of misguided conventional attitudes or behavior, and a compassionate view of the human species and its frailties. Implicit is a comic view of the world that sees the need for compromise and mutual understanding, however different from one another people may be.

While Patrick is not ostensibly a "theme" writer, his most effective plays reveal commonalities of theme. In these plays can often be found a sympathetic major character who, by virtue of culture, behavior, or association, is considered an outsider by members of an establishment presumably motivated by conventional and rational standards of judgment, and who meets with misunderstanding or a lack of compassion from that group. In some instances, the outsider's nature makes group acceptance difficult. An encounter occurs between these disparate forces, resulting in a clash from which emerges the realization (on the part of some but seldom all of the characters concerned) of people's need to accept and treat one another with understanding and kindness. Interwoven in such a situational pattern are several interrelated themes: people's need to realize their interdependency with others, however great the differences; the urgency for compassionate understanding and truly rational judgment in human affairs despite pressures to the contrary; and the need to comprehend and value the person who marches to a different drummer. The subsequent examination of three of Patrick's plays will discover, in varying degrees, these characteristic themes and patterns.

The Curious Savage, Patrick's first comedy, tells a fanciful tale about a widow, left millions by her deceased husband, whose adult stepchildren have her committed to a private sanatorium because she insists on endowing a foundation that will enable people to finance their daydreams. The widow, Mrs. Savage, decides in her last years to indulge all the foolish whims she has suppressed in a lifetime of self-denial. In the sanatorium, the gently eccentric but sane Mrs. Savage is greeted by a compassionate staff and by pleasant inmates with such harmless idiosyncracies as fibbing about imagined careers and reading only month-old newspapers (vulnerable men and women who cannot cope with life and require the affectionate understanding that their new arrival can provide). As she comes to know her companions, Mrs. Savage finds them more attractive than her own sane but greedy family. When the latter learn that their stepmother has transformed the family's financial assets into negotiable securities, which she has hidden, they take active steps to find and seize them. After the members of the Savage family have been sent by the wily Mrs. Savage on a wild-goose chase and have been humiliated by performing ridiculous acts in pursuit of the bonds, they angrily threaten to transfer their stepmother to a public mental institution and never release her. Forced to reveal the hiding place of the bonds, Mrs. Savage receives the united help of the institution's kindly staff and fellow inmates in ultimately outwitting her family; she is free to use her money as she will. The institution's doctor, realizing her sanity, tells her she is free to go. After the inmates throw a farewell party in which each demonstrates Mrs. Savage's beneficial influence by acting out the fulfillment of a hopeless dream for something never realized, she reluctantly bids her friends good-bye and departs to the harshness of the world outside. The neglected virtues of kindness and affection have not been entirely lost in a world largely motivated by greed and callousness.

Reminiscent of Jean Giraudoux's *The Madwoman of Chaillot* (pr. 1945), the comedy's charmingly irrational characters, and its central figure in particular, are treated with affectionate humor and are solidly supported by a cleverly constructed plot. While the rational "villains," Mrs. Savage's stepchildren, are treated somewhat too stridently, they make excellent foils for the "irrational" characters and contribute effectively to the drama's comic complications. *The Curious Savage* is a minor work in comparison with the two following plays to be discussed, yet it permits a fuller view of the scope of Patrick's work while also reflecting characteristic themes and patterns.

Patrick's World War II experiences as an ambulance driver with the British Army in Southeast Asia furnished the background for *The Hasty Heart*, a serious comedy with none of the farcical characterizations and action of *The Curious Savage*. Prominent, however, is the figure of the outsider. The action is set in the convalescent ward of a British military hospital behind the Assam-Burma front. A distinctive and convivial company of five convalescent soldiers—an American, an Australian, an Englishman, a New Zealander, and an African Basuto who knows no English—find their tranquillity and good-natured banter disrupted by the arrival of a dour and seemingly healthy Scottish sergeant, Lachlen McLachlen, who is unaware that an operation for a wound has left him with one defective kidney, which will soon fail. A colonel keeps this information from the Scot but imparts it to the five men and to their efficient young nurse, Sister Margaret, asking them to gladden the Scot's last six weeks of life. Their assignment is not an easy one. The young sergeant, whom the men call Lachie, is friendless, distrustful, and antisocial, hard-used by life and hardened by war. Pridefully asserting an uncompromising independence and demand for privacy, Lachie persistently frustrates the men's attempts to befriend him. All of his life, Lachie, who is an orphan, has obstinately repressed the "hasty heart" that accepts and gives fellowship and understanding. Patrick skillfully carries the story this far by the end of the first act. The playwright introduces a group of individualized characters, economically supplies the essential exposition, and establishes the classic dramatic pattern in which a situation of initial equilibrium is thrown out of balance by the incursion of a disturbing force or catalytic agent.

As the action progresses in the final two acts, occurring two weeks after act 1, Lachie's misanthropic sullenness is melted when his wardmates, urged by Sister Margaret to renew their hitherto abortive attempts at friendship, present him on his birthday with a kilt that he has long coveted. This act breaks through the hard crust of suspicion and pride in which the Scot has encased himself. Engulfing himself in a whole new world of fellowship, the taciturn Lachie starts talking nonstop, invites his new mates to pay a peacetime visit to the farm in Scotland in which he has invested, and even shyly proposes marriage to Sister Margaret, who accepts him. At this point, the author introduces a complication leading to the crisis of the play. Lachie learns the truth of his fatal condition, suspects that the friendship extended to him was simply pity in disguise, and rejects his new companions. Ultimately, however, he realizes the value of friendship and again embraces his wardmates' goodwill, resolving to spend his last days with them rather than in Scotland without friends. That act of final acceptance demonstrates Patrick's premise: the importance of a man's acknowledgment of his dependence on others.

Not unlike the typical Molière comedy in which an unreasonable man (be he miser or hypochondriac) is surrounded by reasonable people who eventually pull the former into the circle of society, *The Hasty Heart* displays an outsider at first eschewing the proffered understanding and friendship of a group but eventually coming to trust and value them. There is a warmth and humor to the play, sustained by the good nature and wit of the men, that lends a correctly comic perspective to a serious subject and keeps sentimentality within proper bounds. *The Hasty Heart* demonstrated Patrick's growth as a dramatist, able to deal incisively with plot structure and with the effect of inner states of mind on conduct and character. The drama earned considerable Broadway success in 1945 before it was made into a motion picture.

Patrick's award-winning comedy *The Teahouse of the August Moon*, like *The Hasty Heart*, centers on soldiers in a foreign setting. Based on a novel by Vern Sneider, the play is an amusing satire on the efforts of the American Army of Occupation, following World War II, to bring democracy to the people of Okinawa. A young captain, Fisby, with a record of past failure in the military, is assigned to the remote Okinawan village of Tobiki to teach democracy to the natives and make them self-supporting. His commanding officer, a stiff-necked simpleton named Colonel Purdy, demands strict enforcement of Plan B, which calls for the formation of native industry, municipal government, a Ladies League for Democratic Action, and the building of a schoolhouse in the shape of the Pentagon. The young officer, aided by a wily native interpreter named Sakini, attempts to meet his stipulated objectives but at first fails to take into account the traditions and mores of the much-occupied Okinawans, who are experienced in surviving under conquerors. Nor is he prepared to contend with the villagers' ingenuous charm. Within a short time, Fisby finds himself the master of an attractive geisha and, adhering to the democratic principle of the will of the majority, allows the materials sent to him for a schoolhouse to be used to build the teahouse that the male villagers have longed for; he also agrees to the native women's demands for geisha lessons, lipstick, and perfume. Moreover, he encourages the impoverished village to sell its only marketable item, potato brandy, to all the surrounding army and navy officers' clubs—an enterprise astoundingly enriching to the local economy.

Relaxing into village life, Fisby "goes native," as does an army psychiatrist with a yen for organic gardening who has been sent to check up on him. When Fisby's increasingly suspicious commanding officer inopportunely visits the village at the opening of the teahouse, he is outraged at such unorthodox practices and orders the teahouse and the brandy stills to be destroyed. The order is seemingly obeyed, but the resultant mood of despair changes when word arrives from the Pentagon that Congress has received reports that Tobiki is the most progressive village on the island. Colonel Purdy, who has feared demotion, now stands to win unearned credit for Fisby's methods if a soon-to-arrive congressional committee can be impressed. Happily, the teahouse and stills have only been hidden by the villagers and are swiftly reassembled; Captain Fisby is exonerated for his first success. Although East is East and West is West, both have learned from each other. American capitalistic get-up-and-go has brought prosperity to the village, while the kindly people of Tobiki have taught the occupying Americans "the wisdom of gracious acceptance."

Interwoven into the fabric of the drama is the well-made play structure, with its establishment of a problem (the democratization of Tobiki) progressively developed by causally connected and conflict-laden incidents leading to a major crisis (the ordered destruction of the teahouse) and resolution (the exoneration of Captain Fisby's methods and the meeting of East and West). Within three acts and eleven scenes, the carefully constructed linear plot takes the protagonist Fisby through a series of difficult but comedic attempts to achieve his major objective. Even though shifts of locale and parallel scenes (as when Colonel Purdy at General Headquarters is seen talking on the telephone to Fisby in Tobiki) are called for, these are accomplished swiftly and fluently; crucial in this respect is the conception of Sakini as a frame character who orders locales to be progressively revealed by commanding the raising and lowering of an inner curtain of bamboo panels.

Both characters and scenes are introduced by Sakini, who functions as a character-narrator akin to the Stage Manager in Thornton Wilder's *Our Town* (pr. 1938) or the *waki* figure of the Japanese Nō play. Sakini comments on the action to the audience and connects the scenes while also participating in the action, establishing a friendly rapport between actor and audience and lending a nonrealistic style—borrowed from the Oriental theater—to the realistic mode of the episodes. In addition, he establishes the wryly satiric perspective according to which the action and its characters are to be viewed.

The Teahouse of the August Moon is John Patrick's masterwork, representing the pinnacle of his achievement as a craftsman of the American theater.

Other major works

SCREENPLAYS: *Educating Father*, 1936 (with Katherine Kavanaugh and Edward T. Lowe); *15 Maiden Lane*, 1936 (with others); *High Tension*, 1936 (with others); *36 Hours to Live*, 1936 (with Lou Breslow); *Big Town Girl*, 1937 (with others); *Born Reckless*, 1937 (with others); *Dangerously Yours*, 1937 (with Breslow); *The Holy Terror*, 1937 (with Breslow); *Look Out, Mr. Moto*, 1937 (with others); *Midnight Taxi*, 1937 (with Breslow); *One Mile from Heaven*, 1937 (with others); *Sing and Be Happy*, 1937 (with Breslow and Ben Markson); *Time Out for Romance*, 1937 (with others); *Battle of Broadway*, 1938 (with Breslow); *International Settlement*, 1938 (with others); *Up the River Heaven*, 1938 (with Breslow and Maurine Watkins); *Mr. Moto Takes a Chance*, 1938 (with others); *Enchantment*, 1948; *The President's Lady*, 1953 (based on Irving Stone's novel); *Three Coins in a Fountain*, 1954 (based on John H. Secondari's novel); *Love Is a Many-Splendored Thing*, 1955 (based on Han Suyin's novel); *High Society*, 1956 (based on Philip Barry's play *The Philadelphia Story*); *The Teahouse of the August Moon*, 1956 (adaptation of Vern Sneider's novel and Patrick's play); *Les Girls*, 1957 (with Vera Caspary; based on Caspary's novel); *Some Came Running*, 1958 (with Arthur Sheekman; based on James Jones's novel); *The World of Susie Wong*, 1960 (adaptation of Richard Mason's novel and Paul Osborn's play); *The Main Attraction*, 1962; *Gigot*, 1962 (with Jackie Gleason); *The Shoes of the Fisherman*, 1968 (with James Kennaway).

TELEPLAY: *The Small Miracle*, 1972 (with Arthur Dales; adaptation of Paul Gallico's novel).

RADIO PLAYS: *Cecil and Sally*, pr. 1929-1933 (series; 11,000 scripts).

Bibliography

Atkinson, Brooks. *The Teahouse of the August Moon.* Review of *The Teahouse of the August Moon. The New York Times*, October 16, 1953, p. 32. Patrick's most successful play opened at the Martin Beck Theatre on October 15, 1953, a "light and sagacious comedy . . . ingratiating." "The form is inventive and familiar . . . the point of view is droll," Atkinson states. He praises Patrick as a stylist for the "piece of erotic make-believe in a style as intimate as a fairy story."

——————. "Theatre: *Good as Gold.*" Review of *Good as Gold. The New York Times*, March 8, 1957, p. 22. "Basing his study of political science on a book by Alfred Toombs, John Patrick says that the number of taxes we pay is foolish," notes Atkinson in this review of *Good as Gold.* Patrick's playwriting, according to Atkinson, indicates "a refreshing lack of reverence for the people who process and implement our society," but "he does not drive straight on through the entire evening in the key of the opening scenes."

Borak, Jeffrey. "Compelling 'Heart' at BTF." *Berkshire Eagle* (Pittsfield, Mass.), August 17, 1990. "This is tough material to play," says Borak of *The Hasty Heart*, adding that "the emotional transitions here are far too abrupt and convenient." Provides a strong discussion of characters, especially Lachlen and Margaret, and gives credit to director Richard Dunlap for giving "unsentimental attention to detail in both the staging and the playing of Patrick's wartime romance."

Coleman, Robert. "'Teahouse' a Smash Hit, Rich in Comedy." *Daily Mirror* (New York), October 16, 1953. Coleman praises Patrick's "first-rate script" of *The Teahouse of the August Moon*, which was an adaptation of Vern Sneider's novel. "Beautifully blends satire, robust comedy, drama and heart . . . even a dash of human and practical philosophy," he states. David Wayne is singled out for his work as Sakini, the role that Marlon Brando played in the film version.

Watts, Richard, Jr. "A Thoroughly Delightful Comedy." Review of *The Teahouse of the August Moon. Post* (New York), October 16, 1953. Watts calls the play "[w]arm, charming . . . a wise, gently satirical and beautifully understanding dramatic fantasy" about East and West. Provides a longer discussion of the play's themes and structure than most reviews offer of this "gay, smiling tribute to the human spirit and the capacity of mankind for mutual understanding."

Christian H. Moe
(Updated by *Thomas J. Taylor*)

ROBERT PATRICK
Robert Patrick O'Connor

Born: Kilgore, Texas; September 27, 1937

Principal drama

The Haunted Host, pr. 1964, pb. 1972; *Lights, Camera, Action*, pr. 1967, pb. 1972; *Cornered*, pr. 1967; *Help, I Am*, pr. 1967, pb. 1972; *Still-Love*, pr., pb. 1967; *Camera Obscura*, pb. 1968; *Preggin and Liss*, pr. 1968, pb. 1972; *Salvation Army*, pr. 1968; *Fog*, pr. 1969, pb. 1971; *I Came to New York to Write*, pr. 1969, pb. 1972; *Joyce Dynel*, pr. 1969, pb. 1972; *Lily of the Valley of the Dolls*, pr. 1969; *One Person*, pr. 1969, pb. 1972; *The Actor and the Invader*, pr. 1969, pb. 1972; *The Golden Circle*, pb. 1970, pr. 1972; *Hymen and Carbuncle*, pr. 1970, pb. 1980; *La Répétition*, pr. 1970, pb. 1972; *The Golden Animal*, pr. 1970; *The Richest Girl in the World Finds Happiness*, pr. 1970, pb. 1972; *A Christmas Carol*, pr. 1971; *The Arnold Bliss Show*, pr., pb. 1972 (originally as *Presenting Arnold Bliss*, pr. 1969); *Robert Patrick's Cheep Theatricks!*, pb. 1972 (includes *I Came to New York to Write*; *The Haunted Host*; *Joyce Dynel*; *Cornered*; *Still-Love*; *Lights, Camera, Action*; *Help, I am*; *The Arnold Bliss Show*; *One Person*; *Preggin and Liss*; *The Richest Girl in the World Finds Happiness*); *The Arnold Bliss Show*, pr., pb. 1972 (in *Robert Patrick's Cheep Theatricks!*; includes *The Arnold Bliss Show*, *The Actor and the Invader*, *La Répétition*, *Arnold's Big Break*); *Play-by-Play: A Spectacle of Ourselves*, pr. 1972 (revised, pr., pb. 1975); *Ludwig and Wagner*, pr. 1972, pb. 1979; *Judas*, pr. 1973, pb. 1979; *Simultaneous Transmissions*, pr. 1973, pb. 1974 (one act); *Kennedy's Children*, pr. 1973, pb. 1975; *Cleaning House*, pr. 1973, pb. 1978; *One Man, One Woman*, pb. 1975; *My Cup Ranneth Over*, pr. 1978, pb. 1979; *Mutual Benefit Life*, pr. 1978, pb. 1979; *T-Shirts*, pr. 1978, pb. 1979; *Diaghilev and Nijinsky*, pb. 1979, pr. 1981; *Mercy Drop and Other Plays*, pb. 1980; *Michelangelo's Models*, pr. 1981; *Blue Is for Boys*, pr. 1983; *Fairy Tale*, pr. 1984; *Odd Number*, pr. 1984; *Sit-Com*, pr. 1984; *50's 60's 70's 80's*, pr. 1984 (includes *Odd Number*, *Fog*, *Fairy Tale*, *Sit-Com*); *No Trojan Women*, pr. 1985; *Explanation of a Xmas Wedding*, pr. 1987; *Untold Decades: Seven Comedies of Gay Romance*, pb. 1988.

Other literary forms

Robert Patrick has contributed poetry to several small magazines and has written articles for a number of periodicals, usually with a focus on theater, but he is known primarily for his plays.

Achievements

Robert Patrick has one of the most fertile imaginations in the contemporary American theater, impulsively freewheeling and continually surprising. Because his career has remained considerably Off-Broadway, except for his best-known play, *Kennedy's Children*, he has not had to succumb to conventional Broadway formulas and has been able to give his imagination free rein. His dramatic oeuvre is filled with fresh, often startling ideas and striking images, all in the service of dynamic theater, rarely in familiar realistic and naturalistic traditions. Instead, for example, he creates satiric, often surrealistic farces such as *The Arnold Bliss Show*, which mocks the ambitions and struggles of the young actor on his way to fame and fortune, however much he may have to "sell out." Patrick also creates brilliant stage metaphors, as in the brief but effective one-act *Simultaneous Transmissions*, in which United States-Soviet relations (or those of any opposing nations) are represented by two families on opposite sides of the stage. The two sets of parents simultaneously instruct their sons in the proper attitude of distrust, hostility, and aggression regarding the other family, until the play ends with the sons blindly destroying each other's families.

Patrick has also experimented with dramatic form, as in the alternating monologues of *Kennedy's Children*. Occasionally an experiment of his has anticipated a far more famous work of several years later. For example, Patrick's *Still-Love*, like Harold Pinter's *Betrayal* (pr. 1978), traces a love affair backward in time, though somewhat more effectively; even some scenes are broken up so that the audience views the events of one particular encounter in reverse order. In this play, Patrick involves the audience intensely, not so much in figuring out what has happened (that is, what they will discover as the play moves backward in time), but rather in looking ahead from the present scene onstage to the earlier scenes that transpire at a later time, to recall the outcome of specific events or snippets of dialogue. Moreover, Patrick's manipulation of stage props and costume changes is masterful (and a stage manager's headache) in getting the audience to think about the story and the characters' relationship.

Patrick likewise preceded Harvey Fierstein in presenting a one-person monologue in which a character not only talks to a number of other people who are present only by implication, but also performs a number of intimate actions. Fierstein's remarkable back-room bar scene in *Torch Song Trilogy* (pr. 1978-1979), in which Arnold, onstage alone, describes a sexual encounter as he experiences it, may be indebted to Patrick's *One Person*, which Fierstein, whose career also started Off-Broadway, is likely to have seen or at least read before writing his own tremendously successful and unconventional work.

Fierstein is certainly indebted to Patrick for helping to open the theater's closet doors on the subject of homosexuality. In Patrick's plays dealing with gay characters, homosexuality is not really an issue. Mart Crowley's *The Boys in the Band* (pr. 1968) may have introduced the subject to Broadway audiences in a frank way, while *Torch Song Trilogy* progressed to a stronger sense of gay pride and self-assurance when it came to Broadway in 1982, but Patrick, even in 1964, was presenting a gay man in *The Haunted Host* who was completely at ease with his homosexuality and quite unapologetic about it. The story concerns an exorcism, whereby Jay, a blocked playwright haunted by the ghost of his dead lover, proceeds to free himself of the past and resume his own creativity. Jay's homosexuality is simply a given, needing no explanation or defense.

Patrick's other plays dealing with gay people also focus on individuals' particular concerns, such as loneliness, sexual betrayal, or a dissolving (or beginning) love affair. Mere coming-out stories can get repetitious, Patrick believes; finding many other stories that are apropos of gay life, he seeks to present a wide range of them. In an interview in *The Advocate* in October, 1984, he said, "I seem to be expected to write grim, serious plays about gay persecution. That's fine; I've done that and there are others doing it. I am determined to give gay people a rich, dramatic literature, including romances, comedies, musicals."

Biography

Born in Texas in 1937, Robert Patrick O'Connor, as well as being part Native American, was a product of the Dust Bowl. He and his two older sisters spent their childhood moving around the Southwest with a father who worked as a rigger in the oil fields and a mother who waited on tables. Of greater influence, however, was the popular culture of Patrick's childhood, especially motion pictures, which find their way into many of his plays in references to specific films and stars as well as in familiar story lines and such devices as song-and-dance numbers.

After three years at Eastern New Mexico University and a stint in the United States Air Force, Patrick traveled to New York in 1961. There he wandered by chance into a rehearsal at the Caffé Cino, founded and run by Joe Cino. He thought that all the repetition common to a rehearsal was part of the real play, and he became entranced with such a new method of theater. He stayed with Caffé Cino until 1968, when Cino committed suicide.

Unlike many playwrights, Patrick came to writing through practical experience in the theater. He spent three years in the Off-Off-Broadway milieu of Caffé Cino, waiting on tables, running errands, and eventually stage-managing, before his first play was produced there. In fact, Joe Cino wanted him to stick with stage-managing, at which he excelled, rather than take a risk with playwriting. Fortunately, another budding young playwright, Lanford Wilson, persuaded Cino to consider Patrick's work, and *The Haunted Host* was produced in 1964.

Although many of Patrick's contemporaries, including Wilson, Sam

Shepard, and David Rabe, are far better known, Patrick has remained loyal to his roots—the grass-roots kind of theater where everyone is involved in all aspects of production. He resigned from his position as artistic director of the Fifth Estate Theatre in Hollywood when Actors' Equity began to propose potentially restrictive measures on Los Angeles' Equity Waiver theaters, threatening the "let's put on a show" feeling that Patrick was familiar with and favored. After all, the company of theater people whose duties are not strictly divided has a long and honorable history; William Shakespeare himself, as a member of the Lord Chamberlain's Company, not only wrote—often with specific actors in mind—but also acted and certainly staged his own work and the plays of others. Patrick may have been alluding to the theater of Elizabethan England when he entitled his 1972 collection of plays *Robert Patrick's Cheep Theatricks!* The spelling not only suggests the archaic spelling of Shakespeare's time but also, as is common with Patrick, constitutes a clever pun on the word "tricks," revealing the element of play so important to his concept of theater. Patrick has frequently attached himself to specific theaters, for varying periods of time, in order to work more fully with the plays and the companies. He has been particularly associated with the Old Reliable Theatre Tavern in New York, the Fifth Estate in Hollywood, and La Mama in Hollywood and New York, as well as theaters in other cities.

Patrick is Off-Off-Broadway's most produced playwright, but that has not necessarily meant financial success. He has supported himself and his talent with jobs as a dishwasher, an autopsy typist, an accounts receivable correspondent, an astrologer, and a reporter. In 1973, he left New York for Los Angeles, disillusioned with the commercialization and stagnation of Off-Off-Broadway. With *Kennedy's Children*, however, he gained both fame and welcome royalties from the United States and abroad. In fact, that play, the only one of his plays to be produced on Broadway, has been translated into sixty languages.

Among Patrick's honors are the *Show Business* Best Off-Off-Broadway Playwright Award for *Joyce Dynel*, *Fog*, and *Salvation Army*; the Glasgow Citizens' Theatre World Play Writing Award for *Kennedy's Children*; the Omni One-Act Award; and Rockefeller and New York State Creative Artist Public Service grants. His work has appeared in numerous publications and anthologies, and on television.

Around 1978, Patrick started spending a considerable amount of time traveling to high schools and colleges, presenting workshops and classes, and advocating alternative life views among the student production repertories. He won the International Thespian Society's highest award for "service to theater and to youth" in 1979, an award of which he is very proud. He began curtailing his travels in 1988, because, he said, "I felt I wasn't really making a difference. . . . I would visit, do workshops and they [high schools and colleges] were still having the kids perform *Hello Dolly*. I decided I was their token liberal, to assuage their guilt."

Patrick voiced his objections in *The New York Times* to *En attendant Godot* (pb. 1952, pr. 1953; *Waiting for Godot*, pb. 1954, pr. 1955) and Samuel Beckett, whom he called "a charming writer of lugubrious skits, completely inflated," when Beckett's play was revived on Broadway in 1988. In 1991, two of Patrick's short plays were performed at the Actors Playhouse in New York to good reviews. *The Haunted Host* was revived with Harvey Fierstein in the major role; it was followed by *Pouf Positive*, a monologue that Fierstein performed.

Analysis

Robert Patrick's preoccupation as a dramatist with the theme of illusion versus reality may be attributed in part to his experience as a gay man in a society which largely prefers that homosexuality be hidden; in part to a childhood spent riding around Depression and post-Depression Texas as his parents were looking for work, while he turned the dials on a silent Motorola radio and made up programs with his sisters; and in part to other forms of popular culture in which he immersed himself, including paperback books, glossy magazines, and motion pictures. Whatever the source, his plays are filled with illusions—illusions that are frequently deadly but can also be life-giving.

Many of America's greatest plays have dealt with the theme of illusion versus reality—from Tennessee Williams' Amanda Wingfield with her dreams of gentlemen callers, Laura with her glass menagerie, and Blanche DuBois on her streetcar named "Desire," to Arthur Miller's starry-eyed salesman Willy Loman with his impossible plans for his sons, to Edward Albee's George and Martha in *Who's Afraid of Virginia Woolf?* with their imaginary son. For some of these characters, the puncturing of illusion brings a tragic end, while for others it allows a hopeful renewal. Patrick's characters respond similarly, but Patrick's concern is rather a further twist on the theme: He generally carries characters not merely into a recognition of illusion but also beyond, into appreciation of the need for illusion. This is not a tragic understanding—that is, that people are crippled because of their reliance on illusion, like Blanche or Mary Tyrone—but rather a tranquil acceptance of the fact that illusion is not merely a crutch for the mentally unbalanced but is present to a degree in every human being's existence. This is one of the central truths of *Kennedy's Children*: The play reveals the many realities present in a single historical era, and not merely one for each of the five characters, but a complex of different realities for each of them.

Kennedy's Children presents the interweaving monologues of five diverse individuals in a bar, each recalling his or her experience of the 1960's from the perspective of the present, February 14, 1974. Each began with hopes and dreams, optimism and vitality; each has been disillusioned and depleted in some way. Patrick has said that the play is about the loss of heroes, and indeed, it suggests the importance of finding heroism and dreams in oneself rather than in the myths of popular culture.

Carla is probably the most poignant character, building her illusions on the image of Marilyn Monroe. Like two of the other characters, she came to New York in the 1960's as a teenager (one of "Kennedy's children") with dreams of success. Her dreams, she discovers, are shared by millions of others, and her own life becomes a tangle of lofty ideals and harsh realities, all of which she seeks to reconcile through rationalizations. Her illusions come crashing down when she realizes that the symbols of glamour and sex in the 1970's are the artificially perfected body of Raquel Welch and the complete artifice of drag queens. Somehow the surface has become all-important, an illusion overpowering her loftier dreams of inspiring the masses with her own beauty and glamour. Which is the deeper reality, which the frailer illusion? Does Carla kill herself because her brand of glamour has become obsolete, or is it rather that she is unable to reconcile herself to a world of such contradictory realities?

Sparger is an actor, but he never becomes caught up in the illusions of the stage. His approach is that of the cynical realist, well aware of the pretentiousness and insincerity of the underground theater movement (virtually identical with Off-Off-Broadway, quite familiar to Patrick). Yet perhaps Sparger's very cynicism, as he describes the preoccupation with sex and lack of serious artistry motivating the movement, is itself delusion. Was it all merely a mockery? Was there no value in the antiestablishment, nonconformist productions in which he has participated? Theater life is one of Patrick's favorite themes, and he punctures many of the glamorous notions connected with it, showing the venality of the actors and others involved. Yet Patrick clearly believes in its power and its value, as the seriousness of much of his work demonstrates.

In the characters of Rona, the hippie-revolutionary, and Mark, the Vietnam War veteran, Patrick embodies the most serious sides of the 1960's. Each of them has arrived at 1974 quite lost, their high ideals revealed as inadequate for coping with the realities of life. All the movements in which Rona has participated (a bit unrealistically perhaps, but appropriately for effective symbolic representation)—from civil rights to antiwar, from Berkeley's Free Speech movement to rebellion in drugs, dress, and rock music—seem to have culminated in apathy and drug or alcohol dependency for her and her offstage husband, himself a former revolutionary. When she tells him that action and leaders are needed now, he asks ironically, with a sense of despairing futility, "Who do you want me to *kill*? What do you want me to be: Lee Harvey Oswald?"

Mark is one of the saddest casualties of the 1960's, his mind strung out by drugs and the shocks of war. As he reads from his diary of his Vietnam War experiences, he proceeds through the multiple meanings that confront him—and the multiple contradictions (a Robert Patrick hallmark). Humankind should be unified, he believes—but not, he says, in the way that the Communist Vietcong would do this. His friend Chick tells him how important it is not to take sides, in order to save his own hide and not involve himself in another person's war. Yet Mark's mind has become so numbed that when Chick moves to kill a Vietcong about to attack Mark, Mark kills Chick in return, because Chick has taken sides. What is the proper role or belief for a soldier? How do thoughts and feelings and philosophies fit into the midst of war? Which illusion is least delusory, closest to reality—or is that question utterly unanswerable?

It is Wanda who most extensively makes the connection with John F. Kennedy, as she proceeds through her recollections, first of his assassination, then of his impact upon her, the era he embodied, his wife, Jackie, and finally the complete oblivion into which he has fallen in the lives and minds of the "subnormal" children with whom she is now working as she pursues her teaching license. Even though she is well aware of the criticisms people have made of both Jack and Jackie, aware of the short memories of people around her, she retains her idealism, her belief in Camelot. She is keeping his memory alive by becoming a teacher. She has not succumbed to disillusionment; she can be aware of reality, but she finds no reason to abandon an illusion that provides a standard by which to live. This is what the other characters have not comprehended.

Kennedy's Children, like many of Patrick's plays, suggests that reality depends upon the individual's perceptions of it. Why not, Patrick seems to ask, give the mind positive images, illusions of beauty and love, rather than images that will lead only to despair? Consequently, many of Patrick's plays are comic romps with happy endings, such as *Blue Is for Boys*, in which boy gets boy five times over, with all ten characters happily matched at the end. Patrick is doing nothing more serious in that play than offering the same kind of wish fulfillment represented by traditional romantic comedies dating back to Shakespeare's *As You Like It* and *Much Ado About Nothing*.

Yet other plays by Patrick, seemingly more frivolous works, including the outrageous "The Loves of the Artists" trilogy (*Hymen and Carbuncle, Ludwig and Wagner, Diaghilev and Nijinsky*) and the varied *50's 60's 70's 80's* tetralogy, provide keen insights into a wide variety of homosexual relationships. A single short play such as *Fog* (the *60's* segment), for example, can be at once comic and satiric, offering a complex presentation of illusion and reality laced with multiple ironies. In *Fog*, two gay men meet (in a sense) in Central Park during a heavy fog which prevents their seeing each other. The fog allows each to create for the other the reality he prefers for himself: the gorgeous "Stud," in his twenties, presents himself as an unattractive, seventeen-year-old writer whose only attraction is his mind, while the effeminate "Fag" presents himself as an attractive man who belittles the value of looks. Both, it seems, have recently left the same party, the Fag in fact looking for the Stud, as the Stud soon realizes in their conversation, though never letting on, choosing rather to expound on the party guests' shallow emphasis on beauty. Later, when briefly lighting a match, the Fag discovers the Stud's true identity, but he, in turn, does not let on, and together they proceed into the bushes for a sexual encounter, each thinking the other imagines him as someone different. The Fag is getting what he wants, but is the Stud? Will he not fault the Fag for his falsehood, or will he simply acknowledge his own as they both proceed to laugh about it, having each indulged in his own deception, created his own image, his own reality? Perhaps the play is simply a shrewd look at the complicated games of contemporary sex and love.

These games and intricate knots of feelings and relationships are explored throughout Patrick's work, in a wide range of homosexual and heterosexual characters. Some plays, such as *Cleaning House*, present characters who can see so many sides of an issue that they cannot decide what they really want. Other plays, such as *T-Shirts* and *My Cup Ranneth Over*, present characters who cover up their hurts with a barrage of gags and one-liners. Sometimes, in fact, elaborate puns and joke sequences come so fast and furiously as to leave the audience behind, and some viewers might find the humor strained. Yet much of Patrick's work has been highly popular with audiences, in the tradition of Neil Simon and Jean Kerr (a writer for whom Patrick has expressed much admiration).

One of Patrick's few wholly serious plays is *Judas*, also one of his most powerful. Like *Kennedy's Children*, *Judas* is a play with many realities— that is, with no single illusion to destroy. Also like *Kennedy's Children*, its topic (Jesus' last days) evokes in audience members their own perspectives and interpretations, the conceptions of reality which they hold when they enter the theater. The story line is familiar, but it is susceptible to numerous retellings in fresh approaches, as in Tim Rice and Andrew Lloyd Webber's rock opera *Jesus Christ Superstar* (1970), Pier Paolo Pasolini's film *The Gospel According to St. Matthew* (1964), or even Patrick's own earlier work *Joyce Dynel*.

Despite its title, the play's focus is actually upon Pilate. The ambience of the play is strictly late twentieth century, with Pilate in a business suit and Jesus in work clothes, and the dialogue uses very little direct quotation from the Bible, conveying less the feeling of a biblical epic than of a contemporary political drama.

Patrick presents Pilate as a counterpart to Jesus; Pilate has his own "disciples"—Judas the Jew and Klautus, his Roman assistant—whom he is instructing in proper thought and behavior for government service with Rome. At the end of the play, Pilate, too, is betrayed, not by Judas but, like Jesus, by his own countryman, Klautus, who discovers that his master's highest allegiance is not to Rome after all. Pilate, in fact, comes to believe in Jesus' images of a better world, even if it means denouncing Rome. Pilate is a pragmatist, but he believes above all in truth. Patrick avoids the temptation of having Pilate voice his great question to Jesus from John 18:38—"What is truth?"—for it is amply implicit throughout his discussion with Jesus. What Pilate comes to discover is Jesus' truth—the kingdom of Heaven within—as humanity's highest goal. Though he cannot transcend the sectarianism that would destroy Jesus, Pilate still believes in the inner reality as the path to good. The irony is that Pilate, too, is on his way to destruction, when Klautus discovers that he holds something in higher esteem than Rome itself.

More than any other Patrick work, this is a play of ideas in the tradition of George Bernard Shaw, with a superb theatrical sense as well. In the powerful interrogation scene, for example, which carries reverberations of the great confrontation between Christ and the Grand Inquisitor in Fyodor Dostoevski's *The Brothers Karamazov* (1879-1880), Jesus speaks not at all, while Pilate circles Him with extended pleas to save His life by denying Himself. Jesus' last words onstage, at the end of this scene—when Pilate, joined by Judas, tries to urge Jesus one last time to use a proto-Machiavellian political lie and deny His role as King of the Jews so that he might live to *become* King of the Jews—are merely those of the Lord's Prayer, through which Jesus restores Judas to his faith in Him and inspires Judas to his own act of self-sacrifice.

The true reality, according to *Judas*, *Kennedy's Children*, and many other Robert Patrick plays, is the one within, though others may consider it mere illusion. In a time when many playwrights trade in nihilism and despair, Patrick's message is one of hope.

Bibliography

Evans, Everett. "Revival Proves '60s Legacy Lives." Review of *Kennedy's Children. Chronicle* (Houston), February 5, 1992. In this review of a revival of *Kennedy's Children* at the Grassroots Theater Project, Evans finds in the play "interwoven monologues by five characters who exist in the same environment but never speak directly to one another." Evans considers, however, that the play still "asks some valid questions about mixed-up American values."

Evett, Marianne. "Playwright Robert Patrick Champions Artistic Integrity of Off-Off Broadway Theater." *Plain Dealer* (Cleveland), May 19, 1989. A good, long interview article occasioned by Patrick's classroom visits, playwriting workshops, and staged readings in Cleveland. Includes a discussion of *Judas*, which was performed at Case Western Reserve University in 1985. "Write what excites you," Patrick advises his workshop participants. He also expresses his firm belief in theater and states that "it's our only real hope of spreading any idea not already accepted." He also discusses acquired immune deficiency syndrome (AIDS).

Kirkpatrick, Melanie. "Fierstein's Gays." Review of *The Haunted Host. The Wall Street Journal*, May 7, 1991, p. A16. *The Haunted Host*, a two-person play originally performed in 1964, was staged at the La Mama Experimental Theatre Club (ETC), with raging comic Harvey Fierstein and Jason Workman. It was performed with a new play, *Pouf Positive*, a forty-minute monologue by Fierstein.

Marranca, Bonnie, and Gautam Dasgupta. *American Playwrights: A Critical Survey.* 2 vols. New York: Drama Book Specialists, 1981. Contains a chapter on "playwright-actor-director-general factotum" Robert Patrick, whose presence in the early days of Off-Off-Broadway are chronicled here, more in the analytical than the informational mode. Good recaps of the small, often one-person plays, such as *Cornered*, *Camera Obscura*, and *Help, I Am. Kennedy's Children*, itself a fragmented play, is Patrick's only full-length play to get any substantial notoriety.

Weeks, Jerome. "An Amusing but Superficial Look at Gay Life." *Morning News* (Dallas), September 10, 1991. Patrick's *Untold Decades* is compared to August Wilson's "ongoing attempt to write a drama for each decade of the black American experience." Two plays from the homosexual cycle, together dubbed "Homosexual Acts," played in Dallas to mixed reviews. The plays illustrate the tendency of homosexuals to work "their way into positions of power; and they use it for their protective advantage," Weeks says.

Scott Giantvalley
(Updated by *Thomas J. Taylor*)

JOHN HOWARD PAYNE

Born: New York, New York; June 9, 1791
Died: Tunis, North Africa; April 9, 1852

Principal drama

Julia: Or, The Wanderer, a Comedy in Five Acts, pr., pb. 1806; *Lovers'
Vows*, pb. 1809, pr. 1811 (adaptation of August von Kotzebue's play *Das
Kind der Liebe*); *Trial Without Jury: Or, The Magpie and the Maid*, pr.
1815(?), pb. 1940 (adaptation of Louis Charles Caigniez and Jean Marie
Théodore Baudouin's play *La Pie voleuse*); *Accusation: Or, The Family of
D'Anglade*, pr. 1816 (adaptation of Frédéric du Petit-Méré's play *Le Vol:
Ou, La Famille d'Anglade*); *Brutus: Or, The Fall of Tarquin*, pr., pb. 1818;
Thérèse: Or, The Orphan of Geneva, pr., pb. 1821 (adaptation of Victor
Ducange's play *Thérèse: Ou, L'Orpheline de Genève*); *Adeline, the Victim
of Seduction*, pr. 1822; *Love in Humble Life*, pr. 1822 (one act; based on
Eugène Scribe and Henri Dupin's play *Michel et Christine*); *Clari: Or, The
Maid of Milan*, pr., pb. 1823 (libretto, music by Henry R. Bishop; adapta-
tion of L. J. Milon's play *Clari: Ou, La Promesse de mariage*; also as
Angioletta); *Charles the Second: Or, The Merry Monarch*, pr., pb. 1824
(with Washington Irving; adaptation of Alexandre Duval's *La Jeunesse de
Henri V*); *Richelieu, a Domestic Tragedy*, pr., pb. 1826 (with Irving; adapta-
tion of Duval's *La Jeunesse du Duc de Richelieu: Ou, Le Lovelace Fran-
çais*; also as *The French Libertine*); *The Last Duel in Spain, and Other
Plays*, pb. 1940 (edited by Codman Hislop and W. R. Richardson); *Trial
Without Jury and Other Plays*, pb. 1940 (edited by Hislop and Richardson).

Other literary forms

Though John Howard Payne wrote some dramatic criticism and several
essays on political subjects, he is chiefly known as a dramatist.

Achievements

The achievement of John Howard Payne is difficult to gauge. His work is
admittedly derivative; much of it comprises close translations and adaptations of other dramas, mostly French. At his best, however, he was a supreme adapter. He worked with astonishing speed, producing more than
sixty plays in a career of little more than twenty years. His career, in fact,
provides fascinating insight into the life-style of the dramaturgical hack of
the early nineteenth century.

Theatrical houses of the day hungrily devoured any material, original or
adapted, which would fill seats. Plagiarism was a minor concern in an age
of uncertain and ill-defined copyright laws, and Payne thus provided a wel-

come service to theater managers and actors. Though not a creator, he was a literary carpenter, a superlative transmitter of popular drama. His knowledge of the contemporary stage and of what was dramatically effective often resulted not in slavish imitation but in the molding of a truly superior product from existing material, although that material was always suited to the popular taste rather than to the discriminating temper.

Payne's position in the history of the drama can best be understood by comparing him to a scriptwriter; he produced quick-moving melodramatic plays for a general audience that used the theater at that time as general audiences of today use television. Much of his work was entertainment that never had any pretensions to art. Payne himself admitted as much, writing in one of his prefaces that it was "almost hopeless to look to the stage of the present days for a permanent literary distinction."

A broader view of the drama in England and the United States during most of the nineteenth century suggests that Payne's admission bespoke not only his own limitations but also the relatively undistinguished record of most of the century's dramatists before the arrival of Oscar Wilde and George Bernard Shaw. On balance, one could justly claim that Payne's enormous output in itself provides the scholar with a source sufficient to gauge accurately the dramatic tastes of an age.

Biography

John Howard Payne's career in the theater began when he submitted some critical reviews to newspapers at the age of twelve. His precocious interest was so intense that he founded his own theatrical newspaper, *Thespian Mirror*, when he was fourteen. Though short-lived—issued only from December 28, 1805, to March 22, 1806—the paper gave Payne a great deal of self-confidence and a few literary contacts. At fifteen he wrote his first play, *Julia*. Though a completely conventional melodrama, the play was a modest success and so impressed his friends that they arranged to send the young playwright to Union College in Schenectady, New York. He was there only two years, however, when his family's bankruptcy forced him to return to New York City and to the pursuit of his overwhelming ambition, acting.

A genial, good-humored, handsome young man, Payne made his debut in 1809, at the age of eighteen. He played a number of roles, from Young Norval (a famous male lead in John Home's popular tragedy, *Douglas*, pr. 1756) to Hamlet. Payne, in fact, was among the first Americans to play Hamlet, and the theatrical season of 1809 was to be the time of his greatest triumph as an actor. His fame as "the American Roscius," a great Roman actor, followed him wherever he played—from Boston, Massachusetts, to Charleston, South Carolina. Whether because the novelty of his boyish good looks soon wore off or because his talent was too undisciplined or because established actors were jealous of his early success, Payne found his career stalling badly. For the rest of his life, in fact, his acting roles were irregular, and he was continually in debt.

It was during the time of his success as an actor that Payne wrote his second play, *Lovers' Vows*, an adaptation of August von Kotzebue's *Das Kind der Liebe* (pr. 1790). Payne used an English translation for his own adaptation, and though this work is not particularly noteworthy, it clearly shows Payne's early disposition toward adaptation as a quick and easy way to make money.

Meanwhile, the American theater began to fall on hard times. The public taste, never very sophisticated, was being distracted by the War of 1812 and the resulting instability of the American economy. Still in debt and harboring his great ambition to succeed on the British stage, Payne left New York for Liverpool in January, 1813. His voyage signaled a turning point in his career; he was to remain a part of the European theatrical scene for the next twenty years.

By June, 1813, Payne had played at Drury Lane, one of the two legitimate theatrical companies in England, but there, too, audiences tired of the young actor, so that by the summer of 1814, Payne was penniless and facing an uncertain future. At this point, abreast of the latest dramas of England and France, Payne turned his talent as a speedy adapter of other plays toward earning money between acting engagements, which were becoming less frequent. As he had done in the United States, so he could do in Europe; hence, in August, 1815, he translated a popular French melodrama, *La Pie voleuse* (pr. 1815), and quickly wrote an adaptation, *Trial Without Jury*. He eventually sold it to Covent Garden, the rival house of Drury Lane. There is some doubt as to whether the play was ever performed, but there is no doubt about its effect on Payne's career. The manager of Drury Lane, Douglas Kinnaird, was so impressed with both the speed and the theatrical "rightness" of Payne's adaptation that he offered the twenty-four-year-old American the opportunity to supply Drury Lane with as many adaptations of successful plays as he could turn out. Kinnaird sent Payne to Paris, where, for a brief period, Payne worked as both a translator and an adapter, a virtual literary secret agent, in the service not of the government but of Drury Lane Theatre. Payne, in fact, boasted of a "system" whereby he could provide his employer with a complete adaptation of an original French production within four days.

Kinnaird and Drury Lane, however, treated Payne poorly. He was generally underpaid for his work, derived little or no credit for it, and received few opportunities to act, still his principal ambition. Dissatisfied, he left the employ of Drury Lane and went to work for Covent Garden, for which he labored for two years with the same results.

Payne's ill treatment at the hands of theater managers such as Kinnaird and of actors such as Edmund Kean is a telling commentary on the harsh conditions of the London theater business of that period. Ironically, Payne produced his best work at this time. His *Brutus* is generally acknowledged as his finest play, though Payne himself admitted in his preface to the printed edition that he was indebted to at least seven previous plays on the same subject. Typically, he was paid poorly for it, receiving less than other playwrights customarily got for a curtain raiser. Yet, despite accusations of plagiarism, *Brutus* was to become one of the most famous tragedies in English during the entire nineteenth century. Its popularity in America was such that it held the boards for seventy years, supplying a meaty role for actors such as Edwin Forrest, Edwin Booth, and Kean.

Despite the enormous popularity of *Brutus*, Payne was still struggling against crushing debts, and when at last he despaired of fair treatment from both Drury Lane and Covent Garden, he opened his own theater at Sadler's Wells in 1820. The enterprise was a disaster; Payne's poor business sense and the failure of his own plays to draw audiences plunged him into bankruptcy, and he was arrested for debt.

From debtors' prison, Payne still managed to keep up with the latest plays from the Continent. In three days, he adapted *Thérèse*. Selling the play to Drury Lane, Payne bought his way out of prison and fled to Paris; from there, he continued to sell his adaptations of popular French dramas to the British theaters. One such play was *Clari*. A typical melodrama of little literary value, it is nevertheless a noteworthy play because it contains the song "Home Sweet Home," one of best-known ballads of the era. Payne wrote only the lyrics; the melody was based on a French or Sicilian air. In the play, it is sung by the heroine, who longs for her rural homestead rather than a life of urban dissipation. Interestingly, Payne had not been "home" for ten years, and it would be yet another decade before he returned.

In Paris, Payne renewed his friendship with Washington Irving. The two had known each other as youths in New York City, and during these later years Irving gave his old friend some financial help as well as literary contacts. For a time, they even shared the same house in Paris, collaborating on a number of plays, among them *Charles the Second*, Payne's best comedy. It clearly shows Irving's hand in the urbane wit and comic verve of such characters as Captain Copp. Like Payne's other works, *Charles the Second* is an adaptation. The plot is drawn essentially from a French comedy, although the characters and situations are made thoroughly British. The play is interesting as an example of Irving's dramatic ability.

Back in London in 1824-1825, Payne courted the newly widowed Mary Wollstonecraft Shelley, but no serious relationship seems to have developed. It is uncertain whether Payne's attentions to her were based on her beauty of mind or her bounty of pocketbook. In any event, her stated preference for Irving (unreciprocated on Irving's part) did nothing to dampen the Payne-Irving friendship.

For the next few years, Payne lived a precarious existence, still adapting dozens of plays and selling them to Drury Lane or Covent Garden. Finally, in 1832, penniless and disappointed, he returned to the United States, where he was surprised to find that he was a famous and respected man of letters. His plays had been popular in America since *Brutus*, and though he had never received royalties from any of them, dozens of his plays were running in American houses through the 1830's. The fame and prestige that he had so long sought in Europe and that had eluded him had now settled on him in the United States; on his arrival, he was treated as the conquering literary man he had wanted to be in England. He was feted in Boston and New York; benefits were given in his honor; and several of his famous plays, including *Brutus* and *Charles the Second*, as well as his "Home Sweet Home," were performed.

Payne's career as a playwright was finished; for the next few years, he busied himself with visionary schemes. The year 1835 saw him in Georgia gathering materials for a projected series of articles on the plight of the Cherokee Indians, but both the material and the magazine for which it was intended died stillborn. While in Georgia, Payne was detained for his abolitionist activities, was called a troublemaker, and was asked to leave the state.

In 1842, still penurious but well-known, Payne was appointed American consul at Tunis by President John Tyler. Recalled by the next administration, he again suffered financial difficulties until his appointment to the same post by President Millard Fillmore in 1851. He died, still in debt, in Tunis, the following year. Ironically, the man whose fame throughout the century was yoked to "Home Sweet Home" died in a foreign land, thousands of miles from his home.

Analysis

Trial Without Jury was one of John Howard Payne's first translations, his first play written or adapted in England, and the work that established his position as "supplier" for Drury Lane and, later, for Covent Garden. An adaptation of the French melodrama *La Pie voleuse*, by Louis Charles Caigniez and Jean Marie Théodore Baudouin, the play is a source of controversy among scholars. There is some evidence that Payne's play was never performed, since three other versions of the original exist in English by other adapters, including Thomas Dibdin and Isaac Pocock, both of whom were well-known hacks for Drury Lane. Aside from such scholarly discussion, however, and the interesting fact that the original version was turned into a libretto for a sparkling opera by Gioacchino Rossini, *La gazza ladra* (pr. 1817), the play is a trivial concoction that relies on a brilliantly theatrical gimmick.

Rosalie is the pretty young heroine, employed as a maid in the house-hold of Mr. Gregory, a rich farmer, and his wife, Nannette. Rosalie is in love with the Gregorys' handsome son, Henry, who is returning from a career in the army. The army is also the career of Everard, Rosalie's father. As the play opens, the Gregorys are preparing a feast to celebrate Henry's return. Rosalie is setting out the silver and plate, assisted by Coody, an honest manservant and country bumpkin. The family's pet magpie sits in an open cage above the table. While Rosalie and Coody are engaged in friendly banter, the magpie swoops down, steals a spoon, and flies away.

Eventually, the loss of the spoon is noted by Nannette, who suspects Rosalie, since other spoons have disappeared over a period of time. Mean-while, Rosalie's father, facing court-martial for insubordination, visits his daughter for the last time, asking her to sell a silver spoon of his own and to give him the money later, in the woods. Rosalie sells the spoon, but the money is afterward found on her and she is accused of the theft of the Gregorys' silver. A trial ensues; the prosecutor is a villainous magistrate who seeks vengeance on Rosalie because she had spurned his advances.

In the end, Coody spies the magpie stealing again. Following it, he re-trieves a cache of plate, silver, and money. He makes all known; Rosalie is acquitted and is pledged to Henry; her father is exonerated; and the justice is relieved of his duties, which are now given to Gregory.

A modern reader might find it difficult to understand how anything could be made of such nonsense, material more suitable to parody and comic opera than to serious drama, but the original play and its adapta-tions were quite popular in their time. Despite its foolishness, Payne's play proceeds smoothly. Further, Payne anglicizes the tone and feel of the play by a deft reliance on solid English idiom.

Though it appeared rather early in Payne's career as a playwright, *Brutus* is his finest achievement. First performed in December, 1818, the play held the stage for more than seventy years and became for many the supreme model for romantic historical tragedy. The importance of *Brutus* lies not in the creation of original characters or dramatic material, but rather in Payne's complete mastery of the art of editing, in pruning and selecting scenes and characters from among the welter of dramatic predecessors. *Brutus* brings the skill of a first-rate adapter to the verge of art. Payne's version has survived because he knew what would work dramatically. He combines, for example, the effective language of Hugh Downman's 1779 version with the effective theatricality of Richard Cumberland's contem-poraneous treatment, transposing speeches from the middle of a scene to the end, and making the action more concise and logical.

The sheer theatricality of *Brutus* is impressive. The dialogue is crisp and fast-moving. Payne eliminated many of the excesses of orotund phrasing and simplified the plot, removing subplots and scenes of protracted rhetorical passion. Simplicity, in fact, is the play's chief virtue. *Brutus* is remarkably free, for example, of melodramatic absurdity, though melodramatic elements are bound closely to the plot.

Junius Brutus, Rome's leading citizen, has been killed by Tarquin, who now rules as king, together with his queen, the ruthless Tullia. The spirit of Junius is kept alive by his son Lucius, the Brutus of the play, who has survived the Tarquins' onslaught by feigning madness. Throughout his early confrontations with Tullia and her dissolute son, Sextus, Brutus plays the fool, waiting for a propitious moment to rise up and make Rome a republic. Meanwhile, Brutus' own son, Titus, is saddened by what he believes is his father's madness; Titus keeps his own republican sentiments in check because of his love for Tullia's daughter, Tarquinia.

Brutus' propitious moment arrives when Sextus rapes a noble Roman matron, Lucretia. Lucretia kills herself, and the family seeks vengeance. Brutus abandons his pretense of madness, organizes the enemies of the Tarquins, and leads them to victory. Tullia is captured and dies on the tomb of her father (whom she had murdered), and the republic is restored. In the final dramatic scene, Titus, who has joined the Tarquins out of love for Tarquinia, is captured and brought before his father.

Titus faces Brutus without fear, asking only to be allowed to die on his own sword rather than suffer execution as a traitor. Brutus, however, must remain true to his republican principles: Though "a father's bleeding heart forgives," "the sov'reign magistrate of injured Rome" must condemn. As he gives the signal for execution, Brutus declares: "Justice is satisfied and Rome is free."

Brutus' dilemma in the concluding scene might have been dramatically powerful, but its impact is lessened because Payne provides no preparation for the conflict between paternal and national love, no scenes of intimacy between Brutus and his son to prepare for the climactic scene. The play is interesting as an example of sheer theater and controlled rhetoric, but there is in it little real characterization, little emotional charge, and thus little real tragedy.

Bibliography

Ailes, Milton E. "John Howard Payne: A Strange, Eventful History." *Frank Leslie's Popular Monthly*, December, 1899, 115-130. This short biography of Payne is particularly interesting for its account of the exhumation of Payne's remains from Tunis and their return to the United States, where they were laid to rest at ceremonies attended by then President Chester A. Arthur and his cabinet. Bandmaster John Philip Sousa and the U.S. Marine Band played Payne's "Home Sweet Home." The article clearly shows the esteem in which Payne was held even as late as 1900.

Harrison, Gabriel. *John Howard Payne: His Life and Writings.* Philadelphia: J. B. Lippincott, 1885. The definitive biography, detailing Payne's early career as child actor, his life abroad as dramatist, and his final years as editor and consul at Tunis. The study is valuable as a source of original material, such as Payne's letters and excerpts from his voluminous journals. The book also includes Payne's unpublished juvenilia and his critical reviews, and it provides estimates of Payne's character from friends.

Hewitt, Bernard. *Theatre U.S.A., 1665-1957.* New York: McGraw-Hill, 1959. This general history provides a brief but interesting account of Payne as seen by his contemporaries. The first American child actor, "Master Payne" is seen as an untutored prodigy often—as in his portrayal of young Norval—relying on melodramatic gestures and bombast. Often accused of poor judgment in his selection of material, he was still capable in a few roles of showing natural talent and power.

Hughes, Glenn. *A History of the American Theater, 1700-1950.* New York: Samuel French, 1951. Includes a brief account of notable plays by Payne, the "erstwhile" prodigy. Hughes sees *Brutus* as Payne's best work. The account primarily treats Payne's work in the context of theatrical events and news.

Overmeyer, Grace. *America's First Hamlet.* New York: New York University Press, 1958. Overmeyer re-creates Payne's career largely through views of him presented by his friends, particularly Washington Irving and Charles Lamb. The study also draws on Payne's diaries, letters, and critical reviews, and it reveals Payne's brilliant, if erratic, personality and his pioneering work in the early American theater.

Edward Fiorelli

GEORGE PEELE

Born: London, England; July 27, 1556 (baptized)
Died: London, England; November 9, 1596(?)

Principal drama

The Hunting of Cupid, wr. 1581-1585, pb. 1591 (no longer extant); *The Arraignment of Paris*, pr. c. 1584, pb. 1584; *The Battle of Alcazar*, pr. c. 1589, pb. 1594; *Edward I*, pr. c. 1590-1591, pb. 1593; *The Old Wives' Tale*, pr. c. 1591-1594, pb. 1595; *David and Bethsabe*, pr. c. 1593-1594, pb. 1599; "Mahomet and Hiren the Fair Greek," wr. before 1594 (no longer extant).

Other literary forms

George Peele's work in other literary forms consists mostly of occasional pieces celebrating public or patriotic events. Somewhat related to his dramatic works are three of the Lord Mayor of London's annual pageants: *The Device of the Pageant Borne Before Woolstone Dixi*, of 1585; the pageant of 1588 (now lost); and *Descensus Astraeae*, of 1591. "A Farewell," a short poem published in 1589, applauds an English naval expedition setting out to destroy the Spanish forces. Longer occasional poems, with their dates of publication, are *An Eclogue Gratulatory* (1589), celebrating the Earl of Essex's safe return from the same ill-fated naval expedition; *Polyhymnia* (1590), written for the Queen's Accession Day, November 17, 1590; *The Honour of the Garter* (1593), marking the Earl of Northumberland's induction into the Knights of the Garter; and *Anglorum Feriae* (printed transcript, c. 1830), written for the Queen's Accession Day, November 17, 1595. Miscellaneous pieces are the short poems "Lines to Watson" (1582) and "The Praise of Chastity" (1593) and the long poem *A Tale of Troy* (1589; revised as *The Tale of Troy*, 1604), a narrative summary.

Achievements

Peele's full achievement as a dramatist cannot now be properly assessed, because some of his work is missing. Two of his known plays are lost, and possibly others are; in addition, the extent of his collaboration with other playwrights is unknown. Peele was, however, well respected by his fellow writers, and he is one of those from whom a certain "upstart crow," William Shakespeare, was accused of stealing beautiful feathers (by Robert Greene in *Greene's Groatsworth of Wit Bought with a Million of Repentance*, 1592). Along with Greene, John Lyly, and Christopher Marlowe, Peele was one of the so-called University Wits, in whose hands Renaissance English drama was swiftly breaking out of the classical mold. No doubt, Shakespeare did build on their efforts and their risks: The University Wits, with Thomas Kyd, explored the new world of drama, and Shakespeare colonized it. Except for Marlowe, Peele was probably the most original of Shakespeare's predecessors, though some of Peele's innovations were not taken up by others (for example, biblical drama).

Peele's dramatic talent, unlike Marlowe's, was not for depicting character and conflict but for spectacle, as his writing of pageants tends to confirm. The prevailing mode in his work is narrative, expository, or poetic: Two main influences on Peele were Geoffrey Chaucer and Edmund Spenser, and one of Peele's achievements was to stake out their material for the drama. His plays embody dramatic conflicts, but the conflicts do not generate much tension; thus, his characters sometimes declaim or rant. Balancing the declamation and ranting is some attractive poetry. In addition, if the approximate dating of his plays is roughly correct, Peele improved as a dramatist as he went along, so that his best plays are his latest ones, *The Old Wives' Tale* and *David and Bethsabe*.

Biography

Many of the facts about George Peele's life are now unknown or uncertain. What little is known is to some extent eclipsed by a highly unreliable biographical source, *The Merry Conceited Jests of George Peele* (1607), which depicts him as a rascal. Published by an unknown author eleven years after Peele died, the jest book is merely a traditional collection of old pranks and tricks, here ascribed to Peele. Despite the jest book's apparently fictional nature, biographers have been unable to resist its suggestions, especially in combination with Francis Meres' statement (in *Palladis Tamia: Wit's Treasury*, 1598) that Peele died of syphilis: "As Anacreon the poet died by the pot: so George Peele by the pox." Thus, a tradition has grown up which pictures Peele variously as a wastrel, a street person, and a Bohemian who frequented the White Horse Tavern and caroused with fellow writers and University Wits.

The truth is probably more somber, or at least more sober. Peele spent much of his London childhood in the environs of Christ's Hospital, a public home for orphans and indigent old people managed by his father, James Peele, a solid middle-class citizen and author of two works on double-entry bookkeeping. Peele attended school at Christ's Hospital until his mid-teens, when he entered Christ Church College of Oxford University. Here he proceeded to earn a bachelor of arts degree in 1577 and a master of arts degree in 1579. He also became involved with drama at Christ Church College, which had a tradition of presenting plays in its large dining hall. Not only did he translate one of Euripides' plays about Iphigenia, but also he became expert at stagecraft, as indicated by his later work on London pageants and his return to Oxford in 1583 as a technical director of the Christ Church plays presented during the Count Palatine's visit. Possibly he also had another reason for returning to Oxford: In 1580, he had married a sixteen-year-old Oxford heiress, Ann Cooke, and he spent the next four years in court trying, with meager success, to collect the modest inheritance. He and Ann had one daughter, possibly more (Peele's only extant letter refers to "my eldest daughter"); there is inconclusive evidence that Ann died in 1587, that Peele remarried—taking as his second wife the widow Mary Yates in 1591—and that any other daughters could have been hers.

What is more certain is that Peele's life after Oxford was a constant struggle for money. His fine Oxford education, whose effects can be seen in the historical and mythological content of his plays, fitted him to be a gentleman, but it was a style he had difficulty maintaining. His writing probably did not bring in enough money, and if he married the widow Mary Yates, her small inheritance also came encumbered with lawsuits. Peele's state toward the end of his life is indicated in the poem *The Honour of the Garter*, wherein he describes himself as a poor poet without a patron but with many cares: "... I laid me down laden with many cares/ (My bedfellows almost these twenty years). . . ." Peele's only existing letter, dated 1595 and mentioning his "long sickness," is an appeal to Lord Burghley, Lord High Treasurer of England, for patronage; Lord Burghley, however, placed the letter in his file for cranks and crazy people.

Analysis

George Peele was an inveterate experimenter in verse form, types of drama, and subject matter. His five extant plays are extremely diverse: *The Arraignment of Paris* is a mythological pastoral with touches of a court masque; *The Battle of Alcazar* is a historical melodrama with a revenge motif; *Edward I* is a historical chronicle with elements of romantic comedy; *The Old Wives' Tale* is a folklore play; and *David and Bethsabe* is a biblical tragedy. Some of these plays are imitative, combining the influences of other writers, but the last two in particular show Peele breaking new ground. Their diversity is a tribute to Peele's academic background, which gave him the learning to range widely; at the same time, an academic stiffness permeates his work, again less so in the last two plays. The diversity and experimentation that characterize his work suggest that Peele was only completing his apprenticeship and reaching his stride as a dramatist when he died at the age of forty.

Except for *The Old Wives' Tale*, all of Peele's extant plays are concerned with politics, in particular the behavior of rulers. This interest is consistent with Peele's work in other genres, his pageants for the Lord Mayor and his occasional poems celebrating patriotic or court events. Apparently Peele identified closely with the Elizabethan political order, possibly because he saw himself playing an important role in it. To some extent, too, he was on a political bandwagon: Like all the English, he was stirred by the victory over the Spanish Armada in 1588, and the prevailing patriotic fervor accounts for his chauvinism and his anti-Catholic, anti-Spanish sentiments. Like other playwrights of the time, he no doubt was also happy with the stability under Elizabeth I and concerned about the uncertain succession after her death; thus, he wrote plays which examined the behavior of rulers and subjects and offered implicit advice to both. Even *The Old Wives' Tale* cannot entirely be exempted here, since its general admonitions about charitable behavior certainly apply to the political context.

Peele's three earliest extant plays, awkward apprentice efforts for the greater part, all take up the behavior of rulers. Of the three plays, *The Arraignment of Paris* is the least clearly political and also the best written. A veritable anthology of verse forms—fourteeners, heroic couplets, blank verse, and assorted songs—*The Arraignment of Paris*, as befits a pastoral, maintains a leisurely pace and a light touch, except for a brokenhearted nymph and the death of a lovesick shepherd. The tyranny of lovers in the play is paralleled by the tyranny of the gods, as the Trojan shepherd Paris discovers when he has to judge a beauty contest among three goddesses, Juno, Pallas, and Venus. Paris awards the prize, a golden ball, to Venus, and in consequence Juno and Pallas arraign him before a court of the gods for "indifference." The other gods treat the golden ball like the hot potato it is, and they skirt their difficulty by setting Paris free and getting Diana, the virgin goddess, to rejudge the contest. Diana neatly solves the problem by turning to the audience and handing the symbolic prize to Elizabeth I:

> In state Queen Juno's peer, for power in arms,
> And virtues of the mind Minerva's mate:
> As fair and lovely as the queen of love:
> As chaste as Diana in her chaste desires.

Peele's message is clear: The English have a good queen, one not prone to the capricious and irresponsible behavior of mere gods.

If Elizabeth I epitomizes the good ruler who "gives laws of justice and of peace," *The Battle of Alcazar* displays a variety of bad rulers. The worst of them is Muly Mahamet, the Moorish usurper of Barbary who slaughters his own uncle and brothers so that his son may succeed him. One uncle, Abdelmelec, survives and, returning to claim his rightful throne, unseats Muly Mahamet. Crying revenge, Muly Mahamet goes to Sebastian, the young King of Portugal, to ask for help, and Sebastian is rash enough to offer it. For the expedition, Sebastian gets an offer of collaboration from Philip, the Spanish king, but at the last moment, the conniving Spanish king reneges. With his modest force, Sebastian goes off to Barbary, there to die on the desert battlefield of Alcazar, along with Abdelmelec, Muly Mahamet, and most of both armies. Significantly, Sebastian is killed by his own soldiers for leading them into disaster. Suffering the same fate at the hands of his Italian mercenaries is the English adventurer Tom Stukley, sidetracked on his way to becoming the Catholic king of Ireland. In case the audience misses the point, each act is preceded by a choruslike "presenter" and a grisly dumb show—for example, "To them enter Death and three Furies, one with blood, one with dead men's heads in dishes, another with dead men's bones." Thus, in *The Battle of Alcazar*, Peele not only shows how blessed the English are in their ruler but also indulges in some typically vehement anti-Catholic propaganda.

The blank verse of *The Battle of Alcazar* is full of rant, but the language in *Edward I*, mostly a mixture of blank verse and prose, is considerably better. *Edward I* also provides relief from the wars with some pleasant scenes of comedy, romance, and Welsh rebels playing Robin Hood. The inconsistency of mood, however, causes the long play to fall apart, especially the twist into domestic tragedy at the end. There is also inconsistency of character; it is disconcerting to see Queen Elinor, at first benevolent and loving, turn out to be a torturer who suckles a poisonous snake at the breast of the Lord Mayor's wife. Then King Edward, hitherto an ideal exemplar of kingly behavior, poses as a French friar in order to hear Elinor's secret deathbed confession of infidelities with his brother (on her wedding day) and with a friar. One is reminded of Peele's penchant for spectacle when the earth at Charing Green opens up and swallows the evil queen:

> QUEEN: Gape, earth, and swallow me, and let my soul
> Sink down to Hell if I were author of
> That woman's tragedy. Oh, Joan! Help, Joan,
> Thy mother sinks!

Unfortunately, the earth spits her forth again at Potter's Hive, in time for this queen of Spanish origin to decimate her English royal family.

For unknown reasons, the first edition of *The Old Wives' Tale* indicated only that the play was "written by G.P." Perhaps the initials G.P. were readily identifiable at the time; in any event, the author was not identified in print as George Peele until 1782, by Isaac Reed in his *Biographia Dramatica*. Reed's identification has not been much disputed, since internal evidence of language and style points to Peele as author; so also does the play's unrestrained experimentation in content and form.

Indeed, most commentators stress the play's uniqueness among extant Renaissance English drama: its wild mix of folkloric elements. The play is not as original, however, as this mix makes it first appear. The idea of dramatizing folklore could have been suggested by almost any village mumming or old gammer such as the one in the play. It was also only a short step from dramatizing classical mythology to dramatizing native folklore; here, as in his other plays, Peele made heavy use of sources, except here the sources were likely oral rather than written. In form, too, the play's compact action, suitable for folk material, is reminiscent of medieval drama, while the music and spectacle suggest the sophisticated influence of the court masque. Still, Peele's daring use of folkloric elements opened a rich lode for Shakespeare and other dramatists, helped to bridge the gap between classical and native drama, and helped to legitimate certain "low" material for later romantic comedy.

Some features of the play still seem strikingly new, even modern. One such feature is the dignity accorded the "young master's" retainers, however comically lost, and the old peasant couple, Clunch and Madge, who take the retainers in for the night. In his humble cottage, Clunch the "smith leads a life as merry as a king with Madge his wife." Madge provides the evening's entertainment with her old wives' tale; she is not one of the "rude mechanicals" out of Shakespeare's *A Midsummer Night's Dream*, a play perhaps inspired by *The Old Wives' Tale*. Another notable feature is the association of folklore with the night, with the world of dreams, the irrational, and the supernatural. Here the archetypes flow fast and furiously: the conjurer, the abducted maiden, the quest, the two brothers, the two sisters, the man-bear standing at the crossroads, the grateful dead, the heads in the well, and on and on. Finally, a related feature, familiar to modern audiences from Hollywood's cinematic fade, is the merging of the old lady's spoken narrative into dramatization. As in a modern psychological drama, this convention suggests that the play-within-the-play is taking place in her mind, or at least through her words.

The experimentation in content and form carries over into the play's mix of prose, blank verse, rhymed verse, and songs. As in most Renaissance work, there is a great deal of punning and play with language (including Latin). There is parody of other writers, of Petrarchan conventions, and of the folkloric mode. There is much sexual innuendo, especially in the folklore material.

Some commentators have found only confusion in this mixture of styles, but at least two themes stand out clearly and simply in *The Old Wives' Tale*. First, the old wife tells her tale to entertain her guests. Her purpose suggests that a story—and, by extension, art in general—need be nothing more than pleasant playing, which is a value in itself, a human gesture in a human context, a gift more sustaining than the bread and pudding which the guests refuse. The second theme, related to the first, is suggested by the father of the two sisters, Lampriscus, who pleads with the bear-man Erestus "for charity," "for neighborhood or brotherhood." Erestus gives Lampriscus charity, as he does other characters, in the form of his oracles. Throughout the play-within-the-play, those characters who show charity or "brotherhood" are rewarded, while those who are uncharitable also get their deserts. Even in the framing action, the theme of charity is enforced by Clunch and Madge's hospitality to the lost retainers, by the old wife who shares her food, her fire, and her imagination.

There is no doubt that *David and Bethsabe*, the only biblical play among extant English Renaissance drama, is Peele's work, but there is evidence that the text is corrupt (for example, in one startling textual fragment, Absalom bounces forth, alive and well, after he has just writhed through one of those sensational and prolonged Elizabethan deaths). It is thus uncertain whether one should criticize Peele or a corrupt text for occasional instances of awkward or obscure imagery and action. Such imagery may be a result of Peele's striving for a biblical richness, which he sometimes achieves (with the help of his source) but which he sometimes inflates into purple passages or bombast. Any awkward action may be attributable to Peele's condensation of time and action here, as in *The Old Wives' Tale*. Despite the play's tendency toward long speeches, events move rapidly, covering the David-Bethsabe affair, the incest of Amnon and Thamar, and the rebellion of Absalom. During this time, Salomon is born to David and Bethsabe, grows to a youth, and begins spouting his traditional wisdom. The rambling plot is held together by an Aeschylean curse wherein the evils visited upon David's children are presumably caused by the sins of the father, in particular his affair with Bethsabe. With his many wives and concubines and his close relationship to God, David may have reminded contemporary audiences of Henry VIII, Elizabeth I's father.

Aside from the sometimes rich blank verse, the sordid action, and the plot's biblical basis, the play's main attraction is the conjunction of theology, politics, and character, though modern audiences might find the theme offensive. David is depicted as an Asian tyrant whose greatness is measured by his self-indulgence; hence, it is natural in the play to see outward events as an extension of his ego. He forces himself on Bethsabe, sends her soldier-husband Urias into the front lines to die, appears at the siege of Rabbah in time to take credit for the victory, and orders all the town's inhabitants slaughtered. Then, for his sins, punishment is visited on his children: Amnon forces himself on Thamar, Absalom kills Amnon, and Absalom is killed in a rebellion against David. Modern audiences might view Absalom as a force for reform, but they would be wrong. Absalom's vanity makes him an unworthy successor to David; instead, the wise Salomon, son of David and Bethsabe, is the next chosen one. In rebelling against David, proud Absalom has also tried to usurp the authority of God, whose prerogative it is to punish chosen ones. The proper role of subjects is illustrated by the submissive Bethsabe and the sycophantic Urias. In all of English Renaissance drama, one could hardly find a more enthusiastic endorsement of the divine right of kings.

David and Bethsabe, like much of Peele's work, shows that the playwright was more than a budding sycophant himself. A member of the London middle class who worked his way up from a Christ's Hospital scholar to an Oxford gentleman to a University Wit and would-be court hanger-on, Peele identified with the greatness of the ruling class in his writing. When he was not offering outright flattery to the queen and members of the nobility, he was usually giving implicit advice on the proper behavior of rulers and subjects. He apparently felt that, as a writer, a volunteer poet laureate, he played an important part in the ruling order. It is therefore ironic that the Lord High Treasurer of England scorned his dying plea for patronage; it is also ironic that Peele should be best remembered for *The Old Wives' Tale*, a play which dignifies humble people.

Other major works

POETRY: *An Eclogue Gratulatory*, 1589; *A Tale of Troy*, 1589 (revised as *The Tale of Troy*, 1604); *Polyhymnia*, 1590; *The Honour of the Garter*, 1593; *Anglorum Feriae*, c. 1830 (written c. 1595).

MISCELLANEOUS: *The Life and Works of George Peele*, 1952-1970 (3 volumes; Charles Tyler Prouty et al., editors).

Bibliography

Braunmuller, A. R. *George Peele*. Boston: Twayne, 1983. An attempt to rebuild Peele's reputation by noting how thoroughly he studied the folk motifs used in *The Old Wives' Tale* and how frequently he rearranged historical facts for *The Battle of Alcazar* and *Edward I* to relate those plays to current political concerns. Asserts that Peele is a careful artist worthy of reexamination as one learns more about Elizabethan art and thought.

Clemen, Wolfgang. *English Tragedy Before Shakespeare: The Development of Dramatic Speech*. Translated by T. S. Dorsch. London: Methuen, 1961. Peele's five extant plays are analyzed in turn. Clemen concludes that Peele had considerable gifts for poetic expression and could create effective dramatic moments, but he lacked a talent for consistency in characterization or plot structure. Emphasis on Peele's language and the set speeches in his plays.

Dreher, G. K. *Samples from the Love of King David and Fair Bethsabe*. Chicago: Adams Press, 1980. This unusual brief volume relates passages from the play *David and Bethsabe* to their biblical sources, followed by commentary on these passages.

Horne, David H. *The Life and Minor Works of George Peele*. 1952. Reprint. Westport, Conn.: Greenwood Press, 1978. A lengthy study of Peele's life and family backgrounds, with some historical and critical information about the plays. Contains illustrations and references from public records concerning the Peele family. Informative and readable.

Hunter, G. K. *Lyly and Peele*. London: Longmans, Green, 1968. This thin volume, although containing only some ten pages on Peele, provides comments on every play. Peele is seen as highly patriotic, using Christopher Marlowe's style and Marlowe's flamboyant actor, Edward Alleyn, to express his views. Comments on Peele's stylistic decorum and his varying use of language to suit the audience and/or subject matter. Hunter states that Peele could reach members of the audience because he knew and shared their assumptions.

Peele, George. *The Life and Works of George Peele.* Edited by Charles Tyler Prouty. 3 vols. New Haven, Conn.: Yale University Press, 1952-1970. Volume 1 consists of the Horne study listed above. Volume 2 contains lengthy introductions, to Frank S. Hook and John Yoklavich, respectively, to *Edward I* and *The Battle of Alcazar.* Volume 3 contains similar introductions: by R. M. Benbow for *The Arraignment of Paris*, Elmer Blistein for *David and Bethsabe*, and Frank S. Hook for *The Old Wives' Tale.* Authoritative.

_____. *The Old Wives Tale.* Edited by Patricia Binnie. Baltimore: The Johns Hopkins University Press, 1980. This effective general introduction to the text of Peele's most famous play provides basic information on the evidence of Peele's authorship, the date of the play, and its sources. Contains a brief consideration of some critical views of the play and its stage history.

Harold Branam
(Updated by *Howard L. Ford*)

ARTHUR WING PINERO

Born: London, England; May 24, 1855
Died: London, England; November 23, 1934

Principal drama

£200 a Year, pr. 1877; *Two Can Play at That Game*, pr. 1877; *La Comète: Or, Two Hearts*, pr. 1878; *Daisy's Escape*, pr. 1879; *Bygones*, pr. 1880; *Hester's Mystery*, pr. 1880, pb. 1893; *The Money Spinner*, pr. 1880, pb. 1900; *Imprudence*, pr. 1881; *The Squire*, pr., pb. 1881; *Girls and Boys*, pr. 1882; *Lords and Commons*, pr. 1883; *The Rector*, pr. 1883; *The Rocket*, pr. 1883, pb. 1905; *Low Water*, pr. 1884, pb. 1905; *The Ironmaster*, pr. 1884 (adapted from George Ohnet's play *Le Maître de forges*); *In Chancery*, pr. 1884, pb. 1905; *The Magistrate*, pr. 1885, pb. 1892; *Mayfair*, pr. 1885 (adapted from Victorien Sardou's play *Maison neuve*); *The Hobby Horse*, pr. 1886, pb. 1892; *The School Mistress*, pr. 1886, pb. 1894; *Dandy Dick*, pr. 1887, pb. 1893; *Sweet Lavender*, pr. 1888, pb. 1893; *The Weaker Sex*, pr. 1888, pb. 1894; *The Profligate*, pr. 1889, pb. 1892; *The Cabinet Minister*, pr. 1890, pb. 1891; *The Plays of Arthur W. Pinero*, pb. 1891-1915 (25 volumes); *Lady Bountiful*, pr. 1891, pb. 1892; *The Times*, pr., pb. 1891; *The Amazons*, pr. 1893, pb. 1905; *The Second Mrs. Tanqueray*, pr. 1893, pb. 1895; *The Benefit of the Doubt*, pr. 1895, pb. 1896; *The Notorious Mrs. Ebbsmith*, pr., pb. 1895; *The Princess and the Butterfly: Or, The Fantastics*, pr. 1897, pb. 1898; *The Beauty Stone*, pr., pb. 1898 (libretto, with J. Comyns Carr; music by Sir Arthur Sullivan); *Trelawny of the "Wells,"* pr., pb. 1898; *The Gay Lord Quex*, pr. 1899, pb. 1900; *Iris,* pr. 1901, pb. 1902; *Letty,* pr. 1903, pb. 1904; *A Wife Without a Smile*, pr. 1904, pb. 1905; *His House in Order*, pr., pb. 1906; *The Thunderbolt*, pr. 1908, pb. 1909; *Mid-Channel*, pr. 1909, pb. 1910; *Preserving Mr. Panmure*, pr. 1911, pb. 1912; *The "Mind the Paint" Girl*, pr. 1912, pb. 1913; *The Widow of Wasdale Head*, pr. 1912, pb. 1924; *Playgoers*, pr., pb. 1913; *The Big Drum*, pr., pb. 1915; *Mr. Livermore's Dream*, pr. 1917; *Social Plays*, pb. 1917-1922 (4 volumes); *The Freaks: An Idyll of Suburbia*, pr. 1918, pb. 1922; *Monica's Blue Boy*, pb. 1918 (ballet-pantomime; music by Frederick Cowen); *Quick Work*, pr. 1919; *A Seat in the Park*, pr., pb. 1922; *The Enchanted Cottage*, pr., pb. 1922; *A Private Room*, pr., pb. 1928; *Dr. Harmer's Holiday*, pr. 1930, pb. 1931; *A Cold June*, pr. 1932.

Other literary forms

Unlike his great contemporary George Bernard Shaw, Arthur Wing Pinero wrote very little other than plays. His nondramatic works consist of less than a dozen essays and the collected letters. The essays contain comments on theatrical technique, appreciations and criticisms of his fellow ¬laywrights, retrospective accounts of the late nineteenth century London stage, and vignettes of his own life in the theater. The letters constitute a more substantial document; written in a style which varies from the businesslike to the witty and urbane, they provide invaluable glimpses of London theatrical life during the several decades in which Pinero was a dominant figure in British drama.

Achievements

During his extraordinarily productive career, Pinero wrote more than fifty plays, nearly all of which were produced and most of which were popular successes. Although his reputation is no longer what it once was, during the last two decades of the nineteenth century and the first decade of the twentieth he was one of Britain's most acclaimed playwrights. His prolific output was the financial mainstay of many a London theater, and his plays brought him both great wealth and international fame. The foremost performers of his day acted the roles he created, often achieving triumphs which they could never again equal. Nothing in the career of Edward Terry, for example, could match his popularity as Dick Phenyl, the amiable drunkard of *Sweet Lavender*.

Pinero achieved success in a variety of dramatic forms. He wrote a series of farces for the Court Theatre which brought that institution from the brink of financial collapse to immediate prosperity. The first of these, *The Magistrate*, set a London record by running for more than three hundred consecutive performances. The play is still occasionally revived, a retitled version having been produced in London as recently as 1983. His sentimental comedies were also immensely popular, especially *Sweet Lavender*, which outdid even *The Magistrate* with an unprecedented first run of 684 performances. More historically important were Pinero's problem plays, which demonstrated that drama with a serious social purpose could succeed on the nineteenth century British stage. Such plays as *The Profligate*, *The Second Mrs. Tanqueray*, and *The Notorious Mrs. Ebbsmith* lack the intellectual subtlety and dramatic power of the works of Shaw, but they did help to prepare the way for Shaw. Although Pinero never challenged his audience's social assumptions as directly as Shaw did, he showed that British playgoers were willing to think as well as to be entertained.

Another of Pinero's accomplishments was his successful advocacy, along with Henry Arthur Jones, of dramatic realism. An admirer from his youth of Thomas William Robertson's cup-and-saucer drama, Pinero wrote in a colloquial rather than a declamatory style and avoided extreme melodramatic flourishes. Like Robertson, he drew his characters and plots from ordinary life, especially the life of the upper-middle class. He made meticulous use of place references and of speech mannerisms to establish dramatic verisimilitude, and because of its greater naturalness for the performance of social drama, he preferred the three-walled-box stage to all other arrangements. As director of his own plays, he insisted that his actors avoid artificiality in the delivery of their lines, a practice which helped rid the theater of its last vestiges of bombast. Pinero's determination that his plays not be distorted during their preparation for performance induced him, in fact, to exert complete directorial control over the final product, and the key place of the director in modern theater owes much to Pinero's thoroughness.

The extreme care with which Pinero created his realistic effects did not preclude the occurrence in his plays of sentimental and sensational moments reminiscent of melodrama. Indeed, sentiment and surprise are vital elements in most, if not all, of Pinero's works, but these elements develop with a logical inevitability from character portrayal and plot construction rather than springing up, as they so often do in melodrama, with inappropriate suddenness. Unfortunately, the plot construction necessary to bring about some of the effects at which Pinero aimed is not as realistic as other aspects of his writing, and his plots often seem contrived. In imitation of Eugène Scribe, Victorien Sardou, and Alexander Dumas, *fils*, Pinero was a writer of well-made plays, plays which Shaw compared to "cats'-cradles, clockwork mice, mechanical rabbits, and the like." Such plays relied heavily on compressed exposition through convenient exchanges of letters and unlikely conversations between characters. Their well-made plots contained obtrusive foreshadowings of later events, especially of the startling, but carefully prepared-for, plot reversal. They then moved to their inevitable denouement, in which every plot complication was resolved and every uncertainty clarified.

Although Pinero's fusion of realism, sentiment, and plot contrivance may sound like an unpromising amalgam, the craftsmanship with which he drew these elements together suited the taste of his audiences well enough to make him the most popular playwright in the English-speaking world for more than two decades and to earn for him, in 1909, a knighthood—the second to be granted to a playwright for his contributions to the theater; no one but W. S. Gilbert had been so honored previously. Moreover, the conventions of popular theater which Pinero helped to shape are not drastically different from the conventions which exist today. It would take very little rewriting to transform *The Magistrate* into the most up-to-date of situation comedies, and it would take only slightly more effort to make *Sweet Lavender* a believable contemporary screen romance. For his considerable contributions to popular theater, then, and for his pioneering efforts in serious social drama, Pinero is worthy of more attention than he has, in the past, received.

Biography
Sir Arthur Wing Pinero was born into an upper-middle-class family in

London, England, on May 24, 1855. He was the youngest child and only son of Lucy Daines Pinero and John Daniel Pinero, a couple described by Pinero's biographer, Wilbur Dunkel, as "liberal-minded." Pinero's maternal ancestors were of long-established English stock. His paternal forebears, whose name was originally Pinheiro, were Portuguese Jewish immigrants who had arrived in England in the early eighteenth century.

Pinero's parents were frequent theatergoers, and one of his earliest memories was of attending a Grecian Theatre pantomime with his parents and his sisters, Frances and Mary. Very early, too, he discovered the wonders of Sadler's Wells, where, for a mere eighteen pence, he could indulge his growing fascination with plays and actors. His parents never objected to this fascination, but it was always understood that Arthur, like his father and his grandfather, would become a lawyer.

Because of family financial difficulties, Pinero was removed from school and began his legal apprenticeship at age ten. He worked in his father's law office, without great enthusiasm, until his father's retirement in 1870 and then found employment as a library clerk. He soon left that job to accept a position in a solicitor's office, but he felt no more interest in the law while working for his new employer in Lincoln's Inn Fields than he had felt while working for his father in Great James Street.

Meanwhile, Pinero's fascination with the theater continued to increase: He discovered Thomas William Robertson's dramas at the Prince of Wales's Theatre and became absorbed in the new theatrical realism. He learned much that would later be of great use to him from Marie Wilton's purposely understated productions of Robertson's plays, and he began to haunt the street outside the David Garrick Club in hopes of catching an occasional glimpse of the performers he so much admired. He wrote plays which no theater manager would produce, took elocution lessons that intensified his interest in the actor's art, and decided finally to seek a theatrical career of his own.

In 1874, soon after the death of his father, Pinero became an extra with the Edinburgh Theatre Royal. A year later, he moved on to Liverpool, where Wilkie Collins saw him and secured for him a part in his newest play, *Miss Gwilt*, which opened at the Globe Theatre, London, in April of 1876. Henry Irving liked Pinero's unpretentious style of acting and offered him the role of Claudius in a Lyceum Theatre tour of William Shakespeare's *Hamlet*. Pinero accepted the part and spent most of the next five years performing in various Lyceum Theatre productions.

Pinero also succeeded for the first time in having one of his own plays produced. In October of 1877, *£200 a Year* was performed as a curtain raiser at the Globe Theatre, which borrowed him back from the Lyceum for the evening to play the male lead. During the next three years, five more of his plays were produced, with varying degrees of success, followed at last by his first undeniable hit, *The Money Spinner*, which opened in Manchester during November of 1880 and moved to London the following January. His next several plays also turned a profit, and he retired from acting in 1882 to dedicate himself fully to the creation of new works for the stage.

Pinero's work habits were almost compulsive in their regularity, and even after marrying Myra Holme, a widowed actress, in 1883, he refused to deviate from his accustomed writing schedule. Between teatime and breakfast, he wrote and slept, a routine which he maintained with stubborn perseverance and which helped him turn out an amazing number of plays. Many of these early efforts were farces, farce being the first dramatic form of which Pinero was an acknowledged master. *The Rocket* and *In Chancery*, which premiered in December of 1883 and December of 1884 respectively, brought Pinero considerable success, but it was with the opening of *The Magistrate*, the first of the Court farces, on March 21, 1885, that his reputation soared. During the next several years, he supplied the Court Theatre with four more farces, *The School Mistress*, *Dandy Dick*, *The Cabinet Minister*, and *The Amazons*, all of which were resoundingly popular.

In this same period, Pinero was also writing sentimental comedies and had begun to experiment with the problem play. *Sweet Lavender* commenced its record first run on March 21, 1888, and the more modestly successful but equally sentimental *Lady Bountiful* opened on March 7, 1891. The first of the significant problem plays, *The Profligate*, premiered in the spring of 1889 and caused a considerable critical stir. The play was hailed for its daring treatment of a serious social theme, and hope was expressed that further plays of the same sort, from Pinero or from others, might soon appear.

This hope was realized on May 27, 1893, with the premiere of *The Second Mrs. Tanqueray*, Pinero's most acclaimed play. Pinero had dedicated a year of his life to putting the play together and another several months to getting it staged. Despite Pinero's prodigious reputation, none of the London theater managers was at first willing to touch it. Finally, with some reluctance, George Alexander accepted it for production at the St. James's Theatre and cast an unknown actress, Mrs. Patrick Campbell, in the title role of Paula Tanqueray. In a part which was later to provide triumphs for Sarah Bernhardt, Eleonora Duse, and Ethel Barrymore, Mrs. Campbell was brilliant, and the play was an unqualified critical and popular success. It was compared favorably to Dumas' *Camille* (pr. 1852) and was declared to be superior to every English drama since the time of Richard Brinsley Sheridan.

For the next fifteen years, Pinero was at the top of his profession. Theaters clamored for his work, his plays were performed throughout the world, and nearly everything he wrote gained an enthusiastic reception.

There were occasional failures, such as *The Princess and the Butterfly* and the ill-advised Sir Arthur Sullivan collaboration, *The Beauty Stone*, but the successes far outnumbered the infrequent lapses. When Pinero's knighthood was announced in 1909, there were few to cavil. After all, his two most recent plays, *His House in Order* (which earned for him an astounding £50,000) and *The Thunderbolt*, were among his very best works, and the immediately following *Mid-Channel* was equally fine.

Preserving Mr. Panmure, however, was not so fine, and The *"Mind the Paint" Girl* was booed. The materials Pinero was shaping were not so very different from those he had used in the past, but he had begun to lose his craftsman's touch, and his audience's interests had begun to shift in ways he could not understand. He was becoming old-fashioned, and try as he might, he could never regain the knack for creating successful plays.

The last twenty-five years of Pinero's life were marked by a gradual decline. He wrote fewer and fewer plays, and they received less and less attention. He remained financially prosperous, but he was no longer the theatrical lion that he had once been. The death of his wife in 1919 reduced his creative energies still more, and when he died in London on November 23, 1934, it had been many years since he had experienced a theatrical triumph.

Analysis

Because of its earnest self-importance and prudish restrictiveness, Victorian England was as ripe for comic deflation as the Rome of Plautus, and few of his contemporaries were as skillful as Arthur Wing Pinero at producing subversive, farcical laughter. In the typical Pinero farce, the young and uninhibited gain the upper hand over their proper, authoritarian elders with dazzling ease. In the course of the play, the well established and the vain, the powerful and the pompous are teased and tormented until nothing remains of their cherished propriety but a sheepish grin. All of this is accomplished without rancor, however, and even the figures of fun are treated with warmhearted sympathy.

In *The Magistrate*, the primary victims of comic deflation are the mock-heroically named Aeneas Posket, a stuffy but charitable police magistrate who fills his household with those convicted in his court, and his deceiving second wife, Agatha. The instigator of their discomfiture is Agatha's delightfully irresponsible son, Cis Farringdon. The unlikely premise on which the plot depends is that, out of vanity and a desire to catch a second husband, Agatha has subtracted five years from her own age and five years from that of her son, thereby convincing both Aeneas and Cis that she is thirty-one and that Cis is fourteen. As she explains to her sister Charlotte in one of Pinero's contrived expository dialogues, "If I am only thirty-one now, my boy couldn't have been born nineteen years ago, and if he could, he oughtn't to have been, because, on my own showing, I wasn't married till four years later." Because she lives in a society which has taught her that no man is likely to propose to a middle-aged woman and that no respectable woman has a child out of wedlock, Agatha has set a trap both for herself and for her unsuspecting husband.

The trap is sprung by Cis, who, despite believing himself to be fourteen, cannot help acting nineteen. He flirts with his sixteen-year-old music teacher, gambles quite skillfully, and lures his dignified stepfather, at a key moment, into a night of carousing. The carousing is made possible through Pinero's use of another of his favorite plot contrivances, the fortuitous arrival of important letters. One of these letters announces an upcoming visit by Colonel Lukyn, a friend of Agatha's first husband, who will be sure to expose Agatha's deceit unless she intercepts him. A second letter informs Agatha of the sickness of a friend, Lady Adelaide Jenkins, which gives Agatha the excuse she needs to leave the house in quest of Colonel Lukyn. A third contains an overdue bill for charges incurred by Cis and his friends at the Hotel des Princes, a bill that Cis decides to manipulate his stepfather into paying. The fourth, whose significance in Pinero's jigsaw puzzle plot becomes clear only later in the play, declares the intention of Charlotte's straitlaced, sententious fiancé, Captain Horace Vale, to break off their engagement because of the impulsive Charlotte's flirtation with another man.

What the characters are unaware of is that all of them are headed for the same place, the Hotel des Princes, where the intricately prepared comic reversal awaits them. Cis is there to get his bill paid for him and to have a good time; Aeneas is there to see his wondrous new fourteen-year-old son in his unlikely natural habitat; Colonel Lukyn is there to visit old haunts; Captain Vale is there because he knows Colonel Lukyn; Agatha is there to plead for Lukyn's silence; and Charlotte is there because Agatha is.

Pinero milks the scenes that follow for all of their humorous possibilities, and in the process, he puts his dignified characters through absurd torments. The proper Captain Vale, for example, is asked to step onto a rickety balcony during a torrential rainstorm when Agatha and Charlotte request a private meeting with the colonel. He later creeps back into the room, soaked to the skin and wearing a bedraggled, oversized hat, mistakenly handed to him by Lukyn, and hides behind a curtain. In the meantime, the colonel has peppered his speech with so many babbling asides about his poor friend on the balcony that Agatha suspects him of suffering the aftereffects of sunstroke. Nevertheless, she does win his pledge to keep her secret, and the three sit down to dinner, while the grumbling, half-starved captain acts as a disembodied waiter from behind the curtain.

After an absurd discovery scene in which Vale converses from his hiding place with the principals visible to the audience, Pinero begins the true humbling of his characters. As Vale and Charlotte attempt a reconciliation and as the infuriated Agatha realizes for the first time that the voices from the next room are those of her husband and her son—both of whom, like Agatha herself, have lied about their plans for the evening—the hotel is raided for serving food and drink after-hours. Aeneas, the ostensible up-holder of the laws, and Cis escape by leaping through a window and falling through a roof, while the magistrate's wife and her three companions are dragged off to jail.

After several hours of running from the authorities, Aeneas again be-comes a figure of authority himself and prepares, as best he can, to judge the wrongdoings of others. What a shock it is, however, when he finds that the first case before him involves his wife's friend, Colonel Lukyn, and three of Lukyn's comrades. In a face-to-face interview with the colonel before the trial begins, Aeneas refuses to give special treatment to any of the four, not even the two ladies, and he exclaims, in righteous indignation, "I am listening, sir, to the guiding voice of Mrs. Posket—that newly-made wife still blushing from the embarrassment of her second marriage, and that voice says, 'Strike for the sanctity of hearth and home, for the credit of the wives of England—no mercy!'" The result is that he hears the four malefactors plead guilty to exactly the crime he himself has committed and sentences them to seven days in jail, at the very moment that his wife, who has lied about her identity, pulls back her veil.

In a play of this sort, in which self-righteousness and rigid social conven-tions are held up to ridicule, the appropriate conclusion is a liberating re-laxation of the rules, and Pinero chooses just such a conclusion for *The Magistrate*. Mr. Bullamy, Aeneas' fellow magistrate, finds a way of skirting the letter of the law and secures the prisoners' release; the warring parties, much chastened by their experiences, are reconciled; and every concealed truth is revealed. Pinero even makes use of that most ancient symbol of reconciliation, a marriage, to bring the play to an end. Aeneas agrees to bless the upcoming union of the music teacher and Cis, who was fourteen yesterday but is nineteen today, especially if the two will accept his gift of a thousand pounds and take themselves off to Canada.

Pinero's most successful sentimental comedy, *Sweet Lavender*, also makes use of ego deflation to bring its characters to their senses, but here laugh-ter is less important than pathos for winning the audience's approval of the playwright's resolution of his plot. The play centers on one of the themes dealt with in *The Magistrate*, the sometimes rocky progress of love, but *Sweet Lavender* manages to explore much more dangerous ground without giving the impression of considering controversial materials. Essentially, the play asks whether one should follow the dictates of one's heart or the ex-pectations of society when choosing a spouse; the emphatic, and un-abashedly maudlin, answer is that, if it is sensitive to innocence and virtue, the heart is the better guide.

The exposition is again handled through convenient conversations, but this time with less artificiality than in *The Magistrate*. From these conversations, the audience learns that Clement Hale, a law student and the adopted son of wealthy banker Geoffrey Wedderburn, is sharing rooms with Dick Phenyl, a drunken but kindly barrister, and that Clement loves Lavender Rolt, the young daughter of housekeeper Ruth Rolt. He has not yet told Lavender of his love, and Dick Phenyl is convinced that such a declaration would destroy Clement's future. The simple, poverty-stricken young lady is an unworthy match for Clement, he argues, and Mr. Wedderburn expects Clement to marry his niece, Minnie Gilfillian. Dick himself is very familiar with poverty and failure and would hate to see his young friend ruin his own expectations.

From Lavender's first entrance, however, Pinero makes it clear that she and Clement are destined for each other and that whatever snobbishness interferes with their union is unjust and must be overcome. Barriers of rank and wealth are of no consequence when two people are as well matched as Clement and Lavender, and the audience is in perfect sympathy with the two lovers when Clement, early in the play, proposes marriage and Lavender accepts him. Their decision to marry is so obviously right that the Wedderburns and anyone who sides with them must be convinced of their error in resisting such a perfect union.

Dick Phenyl is the first to be won over. An impractical romantic himself, and for that very reason an admirable character, he quickly succumbs to the sentiment of the situation and acts as the lovers' ally. Minnie becomes a collaborator with equal ease; her love for Clement is more nearly sisterly affection than passion, and besides, she herself is too busy flouting social conventions by playing the coquette with an upstart American to worry about a lost match with Clement.

Mr. Wedderburn and his sister, Mrs. Gilfillian, are more stubborn in their interference, and it is only after both have been humbled that the marriage can occur. In one of his most extreme reversal scenes, Pinero has Wedderburn deliver an ultimatum to Clement to abandon Lavender or be cut off without a cent at the very moment when his own ruin is about to be announced. Barely has Clement reaffirmed his loyalty to Lavender and Wedderburn cursed him as a penniless fool when Dick Phenyl carries in a telegram which tells of the collapse of Mr. Wedderburn's bank. At the same instant, Ruth Rolt appears at the door, and Wedderburn stares at her in shock. He has just been using himself as an example of a man who escaped the consequences of an improvident love affair by leaving the woman he loved; that woman was Ruth.

In fact, the young lady whom Wedderburn has branded as unworthy of his stepson is Wedderburn's own daughter, and the poverty for which he despised her becomes, temporarily, his own. Mrs. Gilfillian, who performs the housekeeping tasks once taken care of by the Rolts, is also drawn down, by necessity, to the level of those whom she has scorned. Both learn respect for their erstwhile inferiors and drop all objection to Clement's marriage to Lavender. Mrs. Rolt, who had taken Lavender away out of fear that her daughter would either enter an incestuous marriage or have to be told the closely guarded secret of her illegitimacy, also relents when she discovers that Clement is an adopted son and that Mr. Wedderburn, who still loves her, will never reveal the truth. Finally, Dick Phenyl crowns the play's triumphant ending when he announces that he has it in his power to restore Mr. Wedderburn's bank to solvency. He knew of the bank's collapse because he had been informed of his unexpected inheritance of the estate of his Uncle George, all of whose money had been placed in Mr. Wedderburn's bank. By withdrawing his claim to the money, he can put the bank back on its feet. With this announcement, the play comes to its ecstatic conclusion.

Despite the play's popular success, Pinero was well aware that *Sweet Lavender* is artistically flawed. It slips perilously close to pure melodrama, and its fairy-tale ending is outrageously contrived. Shakespearean comedy contains elements as unlikely as those found here, but as many commentators have pointed out, such plays as *The Winter's Tale* (pr. c.1610-1611) and *As You Like It* (pr. c.1599-1600) make no claims to verisimilitude, whereas *Sweet Lavender* purports to be realistic. The incompatibility which exists between its real and its contrived elements hurts the play's artistic integrity.

Nevertheless, *Sweet Lavender* does contain elements of serious drama, however flawed it may be. In its contrast of happy and unhappy couples, it attempts to make a statement about male sexual irresponsibility and about the double standard which allows such irresponsibility to flourish. The victimizing male is forced to see the consequences of his insensitivity to the abandoned female, and he feels appropriately ashamed. A more idealistic male is then permitted to right the wrongs of the past by treating the virginal female with proper love and respect.

Such a neatly symmetrical combination of parts, however, is not often reflective of the complexities and compromises of real life. Of much deeper human interest is the use Pinero makes of the same four character types in his fascinating, but again flawed, problem play, *The Profligate*. Here, innocence is married to experience, and the virginal female to the victimizing male, while the idealistic male and the abandoned female move into and out of their lives, sometimes in troublesome ways.

Hugh Murray, a thirty-year-old solicitor, is selflessly in love with Leslie Brundenell, a naïve but charming schoolgirl. Unfortunately for Hugh, "a pale, thoughtful, resolute-looking man," Leslie has fallen in love with the gallant and worldly Dunstan Renshaw, the sort of man that Hugh himself admits to be more often successful with the ladies than men of his own kind. Leslie and Dunstan are to be married, and Hugh has agreed to be best man at their wedding, but he has second thoughts about his participation in the ceremony when Dunstan's friend Lord Dangars drops by to pick up his latest divorce decree. After all, how could the friend of such a libertine as Dangars, a friend whose past is probably as shameful as Dangars' own, behave honorably toward the innocent Miss Brundenell? Hugh will not actively interfere with the young couple's union, but he will also not help it take place.

Almost as soon as the wedding party departs, Janet Preece appears, a woman in search of her seducer. He had called himself Lawrence Kenward when he had known her in the country, but Janet is well aware that that name was as false as the man himself. She wants Hugh Murray to help her find him, and when he guesses the man's identity, he agrees.

If the audience is unfamiliar enough with Pinero's use of foreshadowing not to have discovered that Lawrence Kenward is Dunstan Renshaw, Murray makes that fact explicit during a later conversation with Renshaw. Leslie and Dunstan have been living together blissfully in an Italian villa for several weeks when Murray arrives to warn Renshaw of his danger. He has compromised his professional ethics for a month by concealing what he knows from Janet Preece, but the secret will soon be out, and for Leslie's sake, Dunstan had best be prepared.

Unfortunately, when the secret does come out, Dunstan is not the least prepared, and the results are disastrous. In a series of coincidences as unlikely as the events which bring the characters in *The Magistrate* together at the Hotel des Princes, Janet, Leslie, Dunstan, and Lord Dangars suddenly find themselves in a distressing confrontation at the Italian villa. Janet has been stranded at the villa by her former employer and has confessed her sordid past to the kindly Leslie, who has nursed her through a serious illness. Soon thereafter, Dunstan returns from a visit with Lord Dangars. Dangars has accompanied Dunstan to the villa, since Dangars' latest fiancée, who is Leslie's closest friend and the daughter of Janet's former employer, is staying there. When Janet sees the two approaching, she shouts, "It's the man—the man!" and Leslie's imagination does the rest. In order to protect her affianced friend, she prepares for Lord Dangars' unmasking and unmasks her own husband instead. Despite Dunstan's pleas for mercy, Leslie leaves him, and Dunstan commits suicide.

This summary of events seems to support the frequently enunciated interpretation of the play as an attack on the double standard, which makes its point by punishing the erring male as severely as the more conventional moral tale punishes the erring female. According to this view, then, men ought to guard their honor as diligently as women do, for who knows what the eventual consequences of sin may be? Such an interpretation undervalues the play's complexity.

First, Dunstan is not destroyed by his sin but by the moral rigidity of his wife. Dunstan has been cruel in his abandoning of Janet Preece, and it was his lust that led him astray, but he has changed since that premarital adventure and has become worthy of Leslie's love. Because of her own upbringing as an overprotected Victorian young lady, however, Leslie cannot see this and classes Dunstan with the play's one true profligate, Lord Dangars. So serious is this inability to discriminate, in fact, that, in the moment of her greatest distress over the discovery of Dunstan's past, Leslie loses the power to protect her close friend from the truly dangerous male, and Dangars escorts his reluctant fiancée from the stage. Furthermore, human sexuality is not as one-sided as Leslie assumes, and in a startling confession toward the end of the play, Janet admits to having been the sexual aggressor in her affair with Dunstan, a confession which Leslie dismisses without considering its implications. She does finally forgive Dunstan, however, and in the final scene of the play, she exhibits a sadder but deeper humanity than she possessed at the play's beginning. Unfortunately, the man to whom she speaks her forgiveness has already taken his life.

The dialogue in *The Profligate* is too wooden and a number of the scenes too sensational for the play to be a fully successful work of art. In *The Second Mrs. Tanqueray*, Pinero largely solved such aesthetic problems to produce what is generally regarded as his masterpiece. The play again concerns Victorian sexual mores, and it again centers on the confrontation between innocence and experience, with innocence once more learning the lesson of tolerance and humanity too late.

In the play's opening act, which contains some of Pinero's most skillfully handled exposition and foreshadowing, Aubrey Tanqueray is bidding a tentative farewell to the friends of his single life, to whom he announces that tomorrow he will be married for the second time. The first Mrs. Tanqueray had been "one of your cold sort . . . all marble arms and black velvet." She had had no lack of Victorian respectability, but sexually, "She *was* an iceberg! As for kissing, the mere contact would have given him chapped lips." The second Mrs. Tanqueray will be different; just how different is implied by Aubrey's uncertainty that his friends will continue to socialize with him after the marriage has occurred. It is also implied by the discomfort with which he listens to the account given by his best friend, Cayley Drummle, of Sir George Orreyed's marriage to a woman of low repute. The best people will cut him dead, Cayley asserts. The man should have known better.

At the end of the act, when the men have left, the audience is introduced directly to the future Paula Tanqueray and indirectly to her pure and innocent opposite, Aubrey's daughter Ellean. Paula, who has been the mistress of many men, has arrived at an outrageously late hour to deliver a letter to Aubrey containing an account of her various sexual escapades. She wants Aubrey to enter married life with no illusions about his wife's past, but Aubrey assures her that he has no doubts about the wisdom of marrying her and gallantly burns the letter. She begs him to be sure, very sure, of what he feels; reminds him of the suicide of one of her close friends; and leaves him for the evening. He then opens a letter from his daughter, who has treated him with the same bloodless coldness as her mother had done before her, and discovers that Ellean has suddenly decided to leave the convent in which she has been educated in order to come home to her father. The potential difficulties of this decision are immediately obvious. How can such a creature of the spirit as Ellean and such a creature of the flesh as Paula be brought under the same roof without tragic results? How, in the age of Victoria, can the soul and the body be reconciled?

The confrontation between the two women develops gradually and occurs, ironically enough, after they appear to have made peace. During the first days of their acquaintance, Paula is constantly attempting to win Ellean's friendship and is constantly being treated with a maddening, dutiful politeness. Paula's self-respect is totally dependent on being accepted and understood by Aubrey's virginal daughter, a fact of which Aubrey himself is partially aware, and when that acceptance and understanding are not forthcoming, Paula lashes out at those around her. As Aubrey had feared, he and Paula have not been received into polite society, and their ostracism has intensified Paula's contradictory feelings of shame and anger. She wants very much to be an untainted woman, and despite the power of her personality, a power that sometimes suggests a Phaedra or a Hedda Gabler, she has a deep need for approval. If Ellean, the embodiment of the purity she herself had once possessed, can love her, all will be well.

For that to occur, however, each woman needs to learn something about the other's attitude toward human relationships. That reeducation takes place for Ellean when she accompanies Aubrey's friend, Mrs. Cortelyon, on a trip to Paris, a trip that Paula mistakenly assumes is intended to separate her forever from her stepdaughter. Paula's own reeducation occurs when, in retaliation for the carrying off of Ellean and in direct defiance of her husband's wishes, she invites the Orreyeds to visit. Lady Orreyed had been a close friend during their days as mistresses to the wealthy, and Paula has frequently expressed a desire to see her again.

What she sees, however, is a vulgar gold digger who has married a stupid drunkard and who seems well on her way to bankrupting him. The married Paula Tanqueray is no more like Lady Orreyed than the married Dunstan Renshaw is like Lord Dangars, but after watching Lady Orreyed in action, Paula can hardly fail to see why anyone whose situation even superficially resembles Lady Orreyed's might have difficulty winning her way into the hearts of the respectable and the well-to-do. Sexual prudery is part of the problem, but not the whole problem.

The more drastic transformation has taken place in Ellean. This cold, spiritual young lady has experienced a sexual awakening, and the drives which have determined so much of Paula's life are suddenly comprehensible to her. While in Paris, she has fallen in love. The young man is reputed to have had a wild youth, but he has since performed an act of heroism in India, and no one is more dashing and handsome. She now understands and accepts Paula, or seems to, and she kisses her in acknowledgment of their shared womanhood. At last, Paula is happy.

Then the catastrophe occurs. Ellean's sweetheart was once Paula's sweetheart, and out of a false sense of duty, Paula informs Aubrey. Aubrey forbids Ellean to see him again, and Ellean guesses the reason; her love for Paula becomes hatred. In response, Paula surrenders to the sense of worthlessness that society has tried for so long to force upon her and kills herself. Ellean hears "the fall" of this fallen woman's body and runs to tell her father, crying out as she does so, "But I know—I helped to kill her. If I had only been merciful!"

The Second Mrs. Tanqueray exhibits Pinero's talents at their best, but it also suggests why Pinero is not praised today as enthusiastically as he once was. His craftsmanship is there for all to see, no matter in which literary epoch they live, but his serious social statements come through in their full power only when one is familiar with their Victorian context. His pronouncements lack the ring of lasting truth of the words of a Shakespeare or a Shaw, whatever he might have taught his Victorian (and later his Edwardian) audiences. Nevertheless, he helped to prepare the way for modern English social drama, and he perfected many of the techniques of modern popular drama, accomplishments which assure his place in British dramatic history.

Other major works

NONFICTION: *The Collected Letters of Sir Arthur Pinero*, 1974 (J. P. Wearing, editor).

Bibliography

Beerbohm, Max. *Around Theatres.* London: Rupert Hart-Davies, 1953. A collection of theater pieces by one of England's most brilliant and perceptive writers and cartoonists. Contains reviews of four Pinero plays, *The School Mistress*, *Iris*, *Letty*, and *The Notorious Mrs. Ebbsmith*, valuable precisely because Beerbohm wrote them after he succeeded George Bernard Shaw as drama critic for the *Saturday Review*. They give the modern reader a sense of how Pinero's audiences received his plays in his own day. Beerbohm, in following Pinero's development as a dramatist, gives him high marks for the later plays.

Dunkel, Wilbur Dwight. *Sir Arthur Pinero: A Critical Biography.* Chicago:

University of Chicago Press, 1941. This huge volume traces the beginnings of Pinero's theatrical career at the age of nineteen. He became an actor despite the opposition of his solicitor-father who had expected him to follow the legal profession. The actor Henry Irving encouraged him to write for the stage, and after producing a few curtain raisers, he launched a career that lasted more than thirty years. Like his fellow author Henry Arthur Jones, Pinero strove for greater realism in the theater and was a pioneer in the new drama that was to come to its flowering with George Bernard Shaw and John Galsworthy.

Fyfe, Henry Hamilton. *Arthur Wing Pinero, Playwright: A Study.* London: Greening, 1902. An early appreciation of Pinero's contribution to the theater, showing the influence of playwright Thomas William Robertson on his work. Although Henrik Ibsen was deemed too radical a thinker for the English stage (only George Bernard Shaw embraced him unequivocally), Pinero, like Robertson, was interested in creating dramas that came to be known as "problem plays." Subjects such as the woman with a past (*The Second Mrs. Tanqueray*) or conflicts in marriage (*The Notorious Mrs. Ebbsmith* and *Mid-Channel*) struck a new note in the theater even if, as Shaw insisted, the plays never offered honest solutions.

Pinero, Arthur Wing. *The Collected Letters of Sir Arthur Pinero.* Edited by J. P. Wearing. Minneapolis: University of Minnesota Press, 1974. A treasure trove of information in the form of letters from Pinero to his fellow authors Henry Arthur Jones and George Bernard Shaw, to critic William Archer, to producer Augustin Daly, and to actor George Alexander. This volume helps the reader set a clear idea of Pinero's working methods, his deep involvement in the productions of all of his plays, and his understanding of the theater's function.

Shaw, G. B. *Dramatic Opinions and Essays.* 2 vols. New York: Brentano's, 1907. These reviews, published when Shaw was still a drama critic, remain the most perceptive ever written about Pinero. Despite Pinero's extraordinary popularity, Shaw exposed the conventionality of the playwright's ideas and his inability to come to grips with the situations he had created. It was partly because of Shaw's impatience with the timidity of Pinero's approach that he launched his own career as a dramatist, *Mrs. Warren's Profession* (pb. 1898, pr. 1902) being Shaw's answer to Pinero's *The Second Mrs. Tanqueray.*

Robert H. O'Connor
(Updated by *Mildred C. Kuner*)

HAROLD PINTER

Born: London, England; October 10, 1930

Principal drama

The Room, pr. 1957, pb. 1960 (one act); *The Birthday Party*, pr. 1958, pb. 1960; *The Dumb Waiter*, pr. 1959 (in German), pr. 1960 (in English), pb. 1960 (one act); *The Caretaker*, pr., pb. 1960; *The Collection*, pr. 1961, pb. 1963; *The Lover*, pr., pb. 1963 (one act); *The Homecoming*, pr., pb. 1965; *Tea Party*, pb. 1965, pr. 1965 (televised), pr. 1968 (staged); *The Basement*, pb. 1967, pr. 1967 (televised), pr. 1968 (staged); *Landscape*, pb. 1968, pr. 1968 (radio play), pr. 1969 (staged) (one act); *Silence*, pr., pb. 1969 (one act); *Old Times*, pr., pb. 1971; *No Man's Land*, pr., pb. 1975; *Plays*, pb. 1975-1981 (4 volumes); *Betrayal*, pr., pb. 1978; *The Hothouse*, pr., pb. 1980 (wr. 1958); *Family Voices*, pr., pb. 1981; *Other Places: Three Plays*, pr., pb. 1982 (includes *Family Voices*, *Victoria Station*, and *A Kind of Alaska*; a revised version produced in 1984 includes *One for the Road* and deletes *Family Voices*); *Mountain Language*, pr., pb. 1988; *The New World Order*, pr. 1991.

Other literary forms

Before writing drama, Harold Pinter published poetry (collected in *Poems*, 1968) and a few short stories in magazines. He has also written screenplays based on his own work and the fiction of other writers.

Achievements

Harold Pinter is sometimes associated with the generation of British playwrights who emerged in the 1950's, known as the "Angry Young Men." His first plays, with their dingy, working-class settings and surface naturalism, seemed to link Pinter with this group, but only the surface of his plays is naturalistic, and most of a Pinter play takes place beneath the surface. His closest affinities are with a movement more centrally important in the recent history of drama, the Theater of the Absurd. As a young man, before he started writing plays, the novels of Franz Kafka and Samuel Beckett made a great impression on Pinter: "When I read them it rang a bell, that's all, within me." Like Kafka, Pinter portrays the absurdity of human existence with a loving attention to detail that creates the deceptive naturalism of his surfaces. It is particularly with the meticulously rendered, tape-recorder-accurate language of his characters that Pinter pulls the naturalistic and Absurdist strands of his drama altogether. The language of his characters, bumbling, repetitive, circular, is actually more realistic—more like actual human speech—than the precise and rhetorically patterned dialogue found in what is considered to be "realistic" drama. Yet that actual language of human beings, when isolated on the stage, underlines the absurdity of human aspirations and becomes both wonderfully comic and pathetic as it marks the stages of human beings' inability to communicate what is most important to them. Pinter, however, is more than an accurate recorder of speech; he is also a poet. The language of his characters, for all of their inarticulateness, is finally profoundly communicative of the human condition. What makes Pinter the most important recent British dramatist is his consummate skill as a dramatist; the fact that in language and pattern he is a poet, especially a poet of contemporary language, both its spoken expression and its expressive silences; and his existential insight into human beings' place in the universe, which connects him with the most profound writers and thinkers of his time.

Biography

Harold Pinter was born October 10, 1930, in Hackney, East London, the son of a hardworking Jewish tailor whose business eventually failed. Pinter grew up in a run-down working-class area, full of railroad yards and bad-smelling factories. When World War II broke out in 1939, Pinter, like most London children, was evacuated to the countryside to be safe from the German bombing. Living in the countryside or by the sea was not, for Pinter, as idyllic as it might have been: "I was quite a morose little boy." He returned to London before the end of the war and remembers seeing V-2 rockets flying overhead and his backyard in flames. After the war ended, the violence did not cease; anti-Semitism was strong in his neighborhood, and Jews were frequently threatened. Perhaps these early brushes with war and violence decided him; when he was eighteen and eligible for National Service, he declared himself a conscientious objector. He was afraid he would be jailed, but in fact, he was merely fined. In grammar school (the term, in England, for what would be called high school in the United States), he was a sprinter and set a record for the hundred-yard dash. He was also an actor in school plays, playing Macbeth and Romeo, and he received a grant in 1948 to study acting at the Royal Academy of Dramatic Art. He did not stay long, however, and spent the next year tramping the streets. He published a few poems in literary magazines (he was only nineteen when the first were published) and got an acting job with a Shakespearean company touring Ireland; other acting jobs followed. He met the actress Vivien Merchant and married her in 1956; she was to perform in a number of his plays.

In 1957, a friend of Pinter who was studying directing at Bristol University told him he needed a play, and Pinter wrote *The Room* for him in four afternoons. The play was performed and was favorably reviewed by Harold

Hobson in the *Sunday Times*. Pinter seemed to have found himself. Immediately after writing *The Room*, he wrote *The Birthday Party* and *The Dumb Waiter*. The plays were performed, and though Harold Hobson continued to champion him, many drama critics gave the plays scathing reviews. *The Birthday Party* closed after a week. In the following years, though Pinter's plays continued to be attacked, they also continued to be revived and performed, and his work began to receive considerable critical attention.

Since his first early commercial success, *The Caretaker*, Pinter has become a productive and versatile writer for stage and screen, as well as a political activist and spokesperson for the arts in general. He has won many awards, including the *Evening Standard* Award (1960, for *The Caretaker*), the Italia Prize (1963, for the television version of *The Lover*), the British Film Academy Award (1965, for *The Pumpkin Eater*), and the Common Wealth Award (1981). He has a long list of honorary degrees, and he was elected an Honorary Fellow in the Modern Language Association in 1970.

In 1989, he came to the United States to direct his play *Mountain Language*. Directing his own and others' work and acting in such touring shows as *Old Times* (with Liv Ullmann, in 1986), he has become very well respected in the theater community. His film work includes, in addition to adaptations of his plays, *The Handmaid's Tale* (1990; adapted from Margaret Atwood's novel), *The Heat of the Day* (1990; based on Elizabeth Bowen's novel), and original works such as *Reunion* (1989).

Politically and culturally, Pinter protested the imprisonment of writers through his activities with the International Association of Poets, Playwrights, Editors, Essayists, and Novelists (PEN Club), donated proceeds to Václav Havel, protested against the Margaret Thatcher government in Great Britain and U.S. involvement in Central and South America, founded the Arts for Nicaragua Fund, delivered a speech by Salman Rushdie while the writer was in hiding, and raised funds for famine relief in Ethiopia. In 1990, he organized a celebration in honor of Samuel Beckett at the National Theatre.

Analysis

Harold Pinter's first play, *The Room*, contained a number of features that were to become his hallmarks. The play is set in a single small room, the characters warm and secure within but threatened by cold and death from without. *The Room* is overtly symbolic, more so than Pinter's later work, but the setting and characters are, for the most part, realistic. Rose sits in the cheap flat making endless cups of tea, wrapping a muffler around her man before she lets him go out into the cold; her husband, Bert, drives a van. Under the naturalistic veneer, however, the play has a murky, almost expressionistic atmosphere. The room is Rose's living space on earth. If she stays within, she is warm and safe. Outside, it is so cold it is "murder," she says. She opens the door, and there, waiting to come in, is the new generation, a young couple named Mr. and Mrs. Sands (the sands of time? Mr. Sands's name is Tod, which in German means "death"). They are looking for an apartment and have heard that Rose's apartment is empty. "This room is occupied," she insists, obviously upset at this pre-monition of her departure. A man has been staying in the basement. She imagines it to be wet and cold there, a place where no one would stand much of a chance. The man wants to see her. Again the door opens, to reveal a terrifying intruder from the outside. He comes in. He is a black man—the color of death—and he is blind, tapping in with his stick, blind as death is when claiming its victims from the ranks of the good or the bad. "Your father wants you to come home," he tells her. Rose's husband comes in at this moment, shrieks "Lice!" and immediately attacks the man, tipping him out of his chair and kicking him in the head until he is motion-less. On the naturalistic level of the play, the action seems motivated by racist hatred, perhaps, but at the symbolic level, Bert seems to have recog-nized death and instinctively engages it in battle, as later Pinter characters kick out violently against their fate. It is, however, to no avail: Rose has been struck blind, already infected by her approaching death.

While this summary stresses the symbolic dimension of the play, it is Pinter's genius to achieve such symbolic resonance at the same time that he maintains an eerily naturalistic surface—although less so in this first play than in later plays. Critics have objected to the heavy-handedness, the overt symbolism, of the blind black man, and characters with similar roles in later plays are more subtly drawn.

The Birthday Party was Pinter's first full-length play; in effect, it is a much fuller and more skillful working out of the elements already present in *The Room*. The scene once more is restricted to a single room, the din-ing room of a seedy seaside guesthouse. Meg, the landlady, and Petey, her husband, who has a menial job outside the hotel, resemble Rose and her husband of *The Room*. Meg is especially like Rose in her suffocating moth-erliness. In this play, however, she is no longer the main character. That role has been taken by Stanley, the only boarder of the house, who has been there for a year. He is pinned to the house, afraid to go out, feeling that intruders from outside are menacing bringers of death. Although he is in his late thirties, he is being kept by Meg as a spoiled little boy. He sleeps late in the morning, and when he comes down to breakfast, he com-plains querulously about everything she fixes for him. He is unshaved and unwashed, still wearing his pajamas. What is enacted symbolically by his refusing to leave the house is his fear of going out and engaging life, his fear that an acceptance of life—meaning going outside, having a job, having normal sexual relations with a woman his age—would also mean accepting his eventual death. He is refusing to live in an absurd world which exacts so high a price for life. It is an untenable position, and his refusal to live as an adult human being has left him a wrinkled and aging child. Further, it does him no good to remain in the house: If he does not go out into the world, the world will come in to him. In fact, he hears that two men have come to town and that they are going to stay at the guesthouse. He knows at once that they have come for him and is thrown into a panic. In the meantime, Meg decides that it is his birthday and gives him a present. The unintentionally chilling reminder of his aging is cut across by the present itself, a child's toy drum, which Stan begins beating frenziedly as the first act ends.

The symbolic action, though more complex, resembles that of *The Room*: What is new is the much finer texture of the realistic surface of the play. The relationship between Stan and his surrogate mother, Meg, beautifully handled, is both comic and sad—comic because it is ridiculous for this nearly middle-aged man to be mothered so excessively and to behave so much like a spoiled child; sad because one believes in both Meg and Stan as human beings. Both comedy and pathos, realism and symbolic undercurrents, grow out of the fully developed language of the dialogue. Its richness, its circumlocution—all elements that have come to be called "Pinteresque"—are evident even in this early play.

It is obvious that the two men who come, Goldberg and McCann, have indeed come for Stan. There is no concealment between them and Stan. He is rude to them and tries to order them out. They make it equally clear to him that he is not to leave the premises. McCann is gloomy and taciturn; Goldberg, the senior partner, is glib and falsely jovial. His language is a wonderfully comic—and sinister—blend of politicians' clichés, shallow philosophy, and gangster argot. There is a brilliant scene when they first confront Stan, cross-examining him with a dizzying landslide of insane questions ("Why did you kill your wife? . . . Why did you never get married? . . . Why do you pick your nose?") that finally leaves him screaming, and he kicks Goldberg in the stomach, just as the husband in *The Room* kicks the blind black man. It is too late, however, for they have already taken his glasses, and he has had his first taste of the blindness of death.

Meg comes in, and they stop scuffling, the two henchmen putting on a show of joviality. They begin to have a birthday party for Stan. Lulu, a pretty but rather vulgar young woman, is invited. Lulu in the past has frequently invited Stan to go outside walking with her, but he has refused. She and Goldberg hit it off together, and she ends up in his lap kissing him as everyone at the party drinks heavily. They begin a drunken game of blindman's buff—"If you're touched, then you're blind"—and the recurring image of blindness serves as a foretaste of death. McCann, wearing the blindfold, comes over and touches Stan, so that it is Stan's turn to be "blind." To make sure, McCann breaks Stan's glasses. The drunken Stan stumbles over to Meg and suddenly begins strangling her. They rush over to stop him, and suddenly the power goes out. In the darkness, Stan rushes around, avoiding them, giggling. The terrified Lulu faints, and when someone briefly turns on a flashlight, the audience sees that Stan has Lulu spread-eagled on the table and is on top of her. With his mortality approaching him anyway, Stan, buoyed up by drink, makes a desperate effort to get out of the house, out of his entrapment in sterile childhood. He struggles to strangle the mother who is suffocating him and to have a sexual relationship with an appropriate female—a taste of the life he has denied himself in order to escape paying the debt, death. It is too late. In the morning, a nearly catatonic Stan is brought downstairs by the two henchmen. He has been washed and shaved and dressed in a suit, as if for burial. A black limousine waits outside the door. Petey, Meg's husband, makes a halfhearted attempt to save Stan from the henchmen, but to still his protests, they need only invite him to come along. One is reminded of the medieval morality play *Everyman*. When Death is carrying off Everyman, Everyman's friends and family promise to be true to him and help him in any way, but the moment they are invited to come with him, they find some excuse to stay behind.

The play in some ways points one back to other possible intentions in *The Room*. Perhaps Rose, like Stan, has denied life. Afraid to go out in the cold, she does not escape having the cold come in after her. What she has lost is the pleasure she might have had in actively engaging life. Her husband, for example, comes home after a cold, wintry day out driving his van and talks with almost sexual relish about the pleasure he has had in masterfully controlling his van through all the dangers of his route.

The Dumb Waiter has much in common with *The Room* and *The Birthday Party*. Again, the setting is a single room in which the characters sit, nervously waiting for an ominous presence from the outside. The two characters are a pair of assassins, sent from place to place, job to job, to kill people. They are, then, rather like McCann and Goldberg of *The Birthday Party*. What is interesting is that the cast of *The Birthday Party* has been collapsed into only these two, for they are not only the killers who come from outside, they are also the victims who wait nervously inside. While they wait in an anonymous room for their final directions on their new job, a job in which everything begins to go wrong, they pass the time by talking. The conversation ranges from reports of what one character is reading in the paper to discussions of how to prepare their tea, but in this oblique fashion it begins circling around to much more pressing speculations on the nature of their lives, questions with which these semiliterate thugs are poorly equipped to deal. The dialogue is quite comical at first, the verbal sparring between the two Cockneys handled with Pinter's customary assurance, but the play is also witty in a more intellectual, allusive manner.

In the opening scene, a number of direct allusions are made to Beckett's play, *Waiting for Godot* (pb. 1952). There is, for example, a great deal of comic business made over putting on and taking off shoes and shaking things out of them, and at one point a character walks to the apron, looks over the audience, and says, "I wouldn't like to live in this dump." Ben and Gus (like Didi and Gogo) are waiting, with varying amounts of patience and impatience, for the arrival of a mysterious presence to reveal the meaning of things to them—the person who makes all the arrangements and sends them out on their jobs. Also Beckettian is the way an entire life is described in the most minimal terms: "I mean, you come into a place when it's still dark, you come into a room you've never seen before, you sleep all day, you do your job, and then you go away in the night." The many parallels are intentional: *The Dumb Waiter* is Pinter's urban, Cockney version of *Waiting for Godot*. In *Waiting for Godot*, there was at least a tree; here, there is only a squalid room, with no windows, in the basement of an old restaurant. The two characters do not have any intellectual or poetic aspirations, as do the two characters representing mankind in Beckett's play. In Beckett's play, Godot's name suggests at least a remnant of belief in a benevolent, loving God—if only by parody. *The Dumb Waiter* lacks even such a remnant. The name of Gus and Ben's boss, Wilson, is deliberately lacking in any allegorical resonance. Further, Wilson is depicted as being increasingly arbitrary in his treatment of them, even though they have been faithful and pride themselves on their reliability. If God exists in this contemporary world, he is God as a Fascist.

Early in the play, mysteriously, an envelope slides under the outside door. It contains twelve matches. Is a benevolent power giving them fire, the great civilizing agent, to help them stave off chaos? They use the matches to light a fire under their kettle, but a moment later, the gas fails, and they have no tea. It is not benevolence, but the power of chance, which rules their absurd world, as soon becomes manifest. There is a dumbwaiter in the room. A tray comes down to them from upstairs. They open the dumbwaiter and take it out. There is a message, ordering an elaborate meal. They do not know what to do, and a moment later the tray goes back upstairs. They are quite worried. When it comes down again, ordering an even more elaborate meal, they desperately fill it with everything they have—biscuits, tea, potato chips. A message comes down telling them that it is not good enough.

Earlier in the play, Ben had read to Gus items from the newspaper, accounts of bizarre accidents and killings, and they had been astounded that such things could go on. The popular press represented their access—from their safe room—to the absurd goings-on in the arbitrary world outside. They try to go back to remarking on the news items now, but they are no longer really interested in the news from outside, because now the absurd has invaded their safe room. They have passed all of their tests, they have been reliable and faithful on the job—yet absurdity is still with them. Their good behavior has not, after all, been able to save them. Ben, the senior partner, falls back on what has been successful for him before: He follows instructions more and more rigidly, becoming increasingly punctilious over the least detail of formal instructions. Gus, who from the beginning has shown himself to be more sensitive, reacts in a quite different way. He begins questioning the absurdity; he begins, to Ben's horror, to question authority. His first questions have to do with his job. He does not have the luxury of being a guiltless victim, such as the two tramps in *Waiting for Godot*. He lives in his modern society by being a part of its violence. Others die that he may live and hold his place in the world. This has already been bothering him, and when he finds out that on top of his burden of guilt, he will not even be treated fairly by authority, he begins to rebel; he criticizes Ben, his superior, and even shouts angrily up the dumbwaiter shaft. He wanders offstage left to get a glass of water. Then Ben is notified by the authority that the person he is to kill is coming in the door at stage right (to the audience's left). He shouts for Gus, his partner, to come help him. The door at stage right flies open. Ben levels his revolver. It is Gus, thrust in, his coat and tie and revolver stripped from him, to stand there, stooped and awkward; he slowly looks up to meet Ben's eyes. The play ends there, but it is clear that Ben, who, faced with absurdity, reacts by following orders all the more unquestioningly, will shoot his partner. He will be the ostensible winner, the survivor, although in an absurd world, what can really be won? He will in the end be nothing. When Gus spoke earlier about coming in at night, doing a job, and leaving at night— a realistic statement but also a metaphor of man's life—he went on to say that he wanted a window, a bit of a view, before he left. His perceptions of absurdity and guilt, a first step toward moral choice, constitute his bit of a view, his wresting of some meaning out of life.

The Caretaker, generally considered to be Pinter's greatest play, is in many ways an even more complex permutation of the elements that were developed in the first few plays. Though *The Caretaker* is much more realistic on the surface than the earlier plays and has much less overt violence, it retains its tie with Absurdist theater in the fact that it readily lends itself to allegorical interpretation. The setting, again, is a single room, and, once more, it is made clear that at least a degree of security exists within the room, and that outside, in the endlessly rainy weather, there is little chance for survival. Davies, the old tramp, is the man struggling to stay in the room, but he is ultimately thrown out to his destruction. The two young men, the brothers Aston and Mick, though in much more subtle and complex ways, occupy the role of the killers. It is they who throw Davies out.

The setting is a run-down room in an old house, with a leaky roof and piles of miscellaneous junk stacked everywhere. As the scene opens, Mick, the younger brother, is scrutinizing the room. He hears a door slam and voices offstage, and he quietly exits. Aston, the older brother, enters. He has brought Davies, the old tramp, along. It is revealed that Aston had found him in a fight, had saved him from a bad beating, and is now taking him into his house and giving him a place to sleep. Davies is the worst kind of garrulous old man, puffed up with self-importance, constantly justifying himself, and running down everyone else, especially blacks and aliens. Aston seems kindly, ingenuous, almost a bit simple. Davies, who is wearing old sandals, says he needs shoes. Aston immediately rummages through his things and brings out a solid pair of shoes to give him. Davies regards them very critically and rejects them as too narrow, throwing them aside.

In a nice bit of theatercraft on Pinter's part, the audience initially tends to see the play from the kindly Aston's point of view and wonders why he has taken in this tiresome and ungrateful old bum. Very shortly, however, as Aston begins to act more strangely and as his brother Mick shows his own erratic and unpredictable behavior, the audience slowly realizes that it is seeing the play from Davies' point of view—that Davies, disagreeable as he is, is Everyman.

Davies, who is shabby and bad-smelling, continues truculently to insist on his personal worth. He evidently does this no matter what the cost. He lost his job, which he sorely needed, and got in the fight, which might have killed him, because he was asked to carry out a bucket of slops when he had been hired to sweep up. He also values himself for not being a black or an alien and therefore, he believes, having a higher place in the scheme of things. He is rude and choosy when Aston offers him gifts. Obviously, however, these are all pathetic attempts by a man with nothing to preserve but a certain dignity. When Aston goes out the next morning, Davies is incredulous that Aston lets him remain behind, actually trusting him in the room alone. In other words, Davies knows that his position is low, but he desperately wants to keep it above the very bottom. It is all he has left.

Aston, though apparently kindly, is very strange. He goes out every day and buys more worthless junk to pile up in the room. He is constantly tinkering with electric appliances, though obviously without a clue as to how to fix them. He plans eventually to fix up the room but obviously, from day to day, is accomplishing nothing. When he leaves, Mick comes in. If Aston is slow in everything he does, Mick is dazzlingly quick. He deluges Davies with torrents of language, holds Davies completely in his power, and torments him with words—threats alternating with attractive-sounding offers. It is his house, it turns out, in which Aston merely lives. Both Mick and Aston, at different times, offer Davies the job of being caretaker of the house. The offer is tempting. Davies keeps saying he needs shoes so he can get down to Sidcup and pick up his papers, get his life sorted out. Yet as he refuses offers of shoes, it becomes clear that he does not want to go; he wants to remain in this room, which, for all of its shortcomings, is at least out of the rain. One night, in a long monologue, the usually taciturn Aston tells Davies about the time he was committed to an asylum and given shock treatment. Davies, who knows that he is himself near the bottom, only marginally above the blacks, now decides that, being sane, he is also above Aston. Although Aston has befriended him and put him up, and Mick has only offered him extravagant promises, Davies decides he will be Mick's man and perhaps work to ease out Aston.

Aston has been waking Davies up in the middle of the night, complaining that his muttering and groaning make it impossible to sleep. Davies is fed up with this treatment, and the next time Aston wakes him up, Davies explodes and tells him that he is crazy and should go back to the asylum, and that he, Davies, and Mick will start running things—perhaps Aston had better leave. It is a typical outburst from Davies, overstepping himself, but he relies on Mick—though Mick has been erratic and unpredictable in the past—to back him up. At this point, Aston tells Davies that he had better look for a place somewhere else, and Davies is forced to leave. Davies comes back the next day to the room when only Mick is there, but Mick turns on him savagely, and Davies realizes he has been had. Aston comes in, and Mick exits. All Davies' truculence is gone, and he begs Aston to take him back, but Aston ignores him, and it is clear that Davies must depart.

The play is moving enough only on its surface, by turns comic, ominous, perhaps even approaching the tragic. It does not remain at the surface, however, but pushes toward allegorical interpretation. There are many possible readings of the play, none of which necessarily excludes the others. Martin Esslin, in *The Peopled Wound: The Work of Harold Pinter* (1970), sees the play as an Oedipal confrontation: The father lords it over the sons while he has the power, but when he gets too old to defend himself, their covert antagonism against him comes to the surface, and they destroy him, throwing out the old generation so that the new generation has room in which to live. An even older archetype, however, might fit the play more closely. A kindly God puts together a world for man and invites him to come live in it. Man, rather than being grateful, as he ought, becomes puffed up with self-importance and lets a tempting Satan (Mick) convince him that he, mankind, is the equal of God; as a result, he is thrown out of his paradise. Pinter has updated his allegory. It is a rather trashy and run-down paradise, a Cockney paradise in a London slum. Obviously, the temptation and fall, the ejection from paradise, is a pattern that can be read into many stories. There is evidence in the text, however, that Pinter intended this particular reading. Aston is referred to in terms that would suggest such an interpretation. "There was someone walking about on the roof the other night," Davies says. "It must have been him." Aston, of course, is the giver of all necessary things—a roof, money, bread. When Davies wakes in the morning, he is startled to find that Aston is sitting smiling at him. Davies, characteristically, immediately begins complaining that Aston's gifts are not enough. Aston gives him bread but no knife with which to cut it (reminiscent of Wilson, in *The Dumb Waiter*, sending the two men matches to light the stove but providing no gas for the stove); gives him shoes with unmatching shoelaces; and does not give him a clock.

Aston's curious life history suggests an identification with Christ. He tells Davies that he used to talk to everyone, and he thought they listened, and that it was all right. He used to have hallucinations, in which he would see everything very clearly. When he had something to say, he would tell the others, but some lie got spread about him, and they took him away, and gave him shock treatment (the Crucifixion?), after which he was no longer able to work or get his thoughts together. After his long confessional monologue to Davies, Aston seldom speaks to him again, and Davies feels deserted. In suggestive words, Davies says: "Christ! That bastard, he ain't even listening to me!" By this time, Davies has also deserted Aston. He listens to Mick, forgetting Mick's previous bad treatment of him and forgetting Aston's many kindnesses to him.

It is a hopeless situation for Davies, because Aston does indeed seem feckless and unstable; Mick seems to own the world now, and in a world of increasing absurdity, Davies has to make his decision, has to struggle for survival and some sort of existential sense of personal value. In the final scene before Davies' expulsion, Mick and Aston meet briefly and smile faintly, and there is almost, for the moment, the hint of collusion between them, as if God and the Devil worked in concert to destroy mankind, as if, working together, they were indeed the two hit men sent out to annihilate man after his brief sojourn in an absurd world.

The Caretaker carries to full maturity the themes and techniques which Pinter first adumbrated in *The Room* and developed over his next few plays. With its characters, its allegory, and its brilliant language and stagecraft, it is a quintessentially Pinteresque play, the perfection of all he was feeling his way toward as a playwright. Thereafter, he had to change direction if he were going to avoid merely imitating himself. He felt increasingly that he "couldn't any longer stay in the room with this bunch of people who opened doors and came in and went out." He changed his milieu, writing plays with middle-class characters, leaving behind the Cockney language of the first plays but demonstrating that he had just as accurate an ear for the absurdities and banalities of middle-class speech and could hear just as clearly what was trying to be said under the affectations of its language. With plays such as *Landscape* and *Silence*, he began working with more lyric kinds of language. With later plays such as *One for the Road*, *Mountain Language*, and *The New World Order*, Pinter began writing overtly political works that reflected his growing activism as a self-styled "citizen of the world." In each new direction he has taken, he has continued to show that the essence of Pinter is not one or another easily imitated mannerism, but rather his poetic brilliance with language, his flawless stagecraft, and his insights into the human condition.

Other major works

NOVEL: *The Dwarfs*, 1990.

POETRY: *Poems*, 1968 (Alan Clodd, editor); *I Know the Place*, 1979.

SCREENPLAYS: *The Servant*, 1963; *The Guest*, 1964; *The Pumpkin Eater*, 1964; *The Quiller Memorandum*, 1966 (adaptation of Adam Hall's novel); *Accident*, 1967; *The Birthday Party*, 1968 (adaptation of his play); *The Go-between*, 1971; *The Homecoming*, 1971 (adaptation of his play); *The Last Tycoon*, 1976 (adaptation of F. Scott Fitzgerald's novel); *Proust: A Screenplay*, 1977; *The French Lieutenant's Woman*, 1981 (adaptation of John Fowles's novel); *Betrayal*, 1983 (adaptation of his play); *Turtle Diary*, 1985; *Reunion*, 1989; *The Handmaid's Tale*, 1990 (adaptation of Margaret Atwood's novel); *The Heat of the Day*, 1990 (adaptation of Elizabeth Bowen's novel); *The Comfort of Strangers*, 1991.

MISCELLANEOUS: *Poems and Prose*, 1949-1977, 1978, 1986 (revised as *Collected Poems and Prose*).

Bibliography

Burkman, Katherine H. *The Dramatic World of Harold Pinter: Its Basis in Ritual.* Columbus: Ohio State University Press, 1971. A fairly early study dealing with mythic structures in the stylized staging of Pinter's work, especially *The Birthday Party* (viewed as an agon) and *The Caretaker*, "a poignant portrayal of man's self-destructive nature, his seeming compulsion to live his life in the image of the cruel ritual of the priesthood of Nemi." Much on Themis, Sir James George Frazer's *The Golden Bough* (1890-1915), and similar fertile but sphinxlike areas of inquiry. Bibliography and index.

Dukore, Bernard F. *Harold Pinter.* 2d ed. London: Macmillan, 1988. An updating of Dukore's earlier 1982 work, this study serves as a condensation of the essential critical vision: the sense of menace, the acknowledgment of the absurd, struggles with realism, the nature of power, the place of memory. Notes Pinter's "minimalist theorizing," which "resonates widely." Bibliography; index of proper names and play titles.

Gale, Steven H. *Butter's Going Up: A Critical Analysis of Harold Pinter's*

Work. Durham, N.C.: Duke University Press, 1977. After a brief biographical chapter, Gale examines "the comedies of menace," a group of Pinter's plays that "collectively . . . defines the themes and establishes the techniques which will be basic in all of his works." Following chapters analyze the metaphor of "the room" and sum up Pinter's writing patterns over a long and varied career. Contains lists of first performances, casts and directors, productions directed by Pinter, and several other valuable appendices. Strong chronology, annotated bibliography (including select reviews), and index. Exhaustive and authoritative.

Gordon, Lois, ed. *Harold Pinter: A Casebook.* New York: Garland, 1990. Honoring Pinter on his sixtieth birthday, this collection of insightful essays is a good source for later plays and revisionist criticism on earlier plays. Best is Gordon's "observation," full of contemporary information, of Pinter's 1989 visit to the United States, where the playwright came to stage *Mountain Language*, among other projects. Appendix of photographs from Pauline Flanagan's collection, select bibliography, and valuable index to all articles.

Merritt, Susan Hollis. *Pinter in Play: Critical Strategies and the Plays of Harold Pinter.* Durham, N.C.: Duke University Press, 1990. Centering her discussion on "criticism as strategy" and comparing criticism to "playing" in Pinter's work, Merritt puts a postmodern twist to her study. Divided into "Perspectives on Pinter's Critical Evolution," "Some Strategies of Pinter Critics," and "Social Relations of Critical and Cultural Change," this work is a major statement, sophisticated and astute. Supplemented by a list of works cited and an index.

Quigley, Austin E. *The Pinter Problem.* Princeton, N.J.: Princeton University Press, 1975. This early study of Pinter's "problems of identity, illusion, menace, and verification" is the first to examine the contradiction between the concrete and the abstract approaches to understanding Pinter's work, up to *Landscape.* Bibliography, but very skimpy index of proper names only.

Thompson, David T. *Pinter: The Player's Playwright.* New York: Schocken Books, 1985. Taking a performance approach, and starting from Pinter's own acting career, this short but information-packed work helps get the plays off the page and onto the stage. Subtleties of movement and dialogue, and Pinter's concentration on "the positioning of characters" in the stage picture, are well discussed, with theatrical examples throughout. Claims more attention should be paid to stage directions. Includes a list of plays acted by Pinter in the 1950's and a good index.

Norman Lavers
(Updated by *Thomas J. Taylor*)

JAMES ROBINSON PLANCHÉ

Born: London, England; February 27, 1796
Died: London, England; May 30, 1880

Principal drama

Amoroso, King of Little Britain, pr., pb. 1818 (music by Tom Cooke); *The Vampire: Or, The Bride of the Isles*, pr., pb. 1820 (adaptation of a French melodrama); *Kenilworth Castle: Or, The Days of Queen Bess*, pr. 1821; *The Pirate*, pr., pb. 1822; *Cortez: Or, The Conquest of Mexico*, pr., pb. 1823 (libretto; music by William Reeve); *Der Freischütz: Or, The Black Huntsman of Bohemia*, pr. 1824, pb. 1825 (music by B. Livius; based on J. F. Kind's opera); *Success: Or, A Hit if You Like It*, pr. 1825, pb. 1879; *Oberon: Or, The Elf-King's Oath*, pr., pb. 1826 (libretto; music by Carl Maria von Weber); *Charles XII: Or, The Siege of Stralsund*, pr. 1828, pb. 1830; *The Mason of Buda*, pr., pb. 1828 (libretto; music by George Rodwell); *Der Vampyr*, pr. 1829 (libretto; music by Heinrich Marschner; adaptation of his play); *Olympic Revels: Or, Prometheus and Pandora*, pr. 1831, pb. 1834 (with Charles Dance); *Olympic Devils: Or, Orpheus and Eurydice*, pr. 1831, pb. 1836 (with Dance); *The Paphian Bower: Or, Venus and Adonis*, pr. 1832, pb. 1879 (with Dance); *The Deep, Deep Sea: Or, Perseus and Andromeda*, pr., pb. 1833 (with Dance); *Secret Service*, pr., pb. 1834; *The Two Figaros*, pr. 1836, pb. 1837; *The Child of the Wreck*, pr. 1837, pb. 1859 (music by Cooke); *Caractacus*, pr. 1837 (adaptation of Francis Beaumont and John Fletcher's play *Bonduca*; music by Michael Balfe); *Puss in Boots*, pr., pb. 1837 (with Dance); *The Drama's Levee: Or, A Peep at the Past*, pr. 1838, pb. 1879; *Blue Beard*, pr., pb. 1839 (with Dance); *The Garrick Fever*, pr. 1839, pb. 1855; *Beauty and the Beast*, pr., pb. 1841; *The White Cat*, pr., pb. 1842 (music by J. H. Tully); *The Drama at Home: Or, An Evening with Puff*, pr., pb. 1844; *Queen Mary's Bower*, pr. 1846, pb. 1847; *The Jacobite*, pr. 1847, pb. 1852; *The Island of Jewels*, pr. 1849, pb. 1850; *A Day of Reckoning*, pr. 1850, pb. 1852; *My Lord and My Lady: Or, It Might Have Been Worse*, pb. 1852, pr. 1861; *Mr. Buckstone's Ascent of Mount Parnassus*, pr. 1853, pb. 1879; *The Camp at the Olympic*, pr. 1853, pb. 1854; *Mr. Buckstone's Voyage Round the Globe (in Leicester Square)*, pr. 1854, pb. 1879; *The Knights of the Round Table*, pr. 1854; *The New Haymarket Spring Meeting*, pr. 1855, pb. 1879; *Orpheus in the Haymarket*, pr. 1865, pb. 1879 (music by Jacques Offenbach); *King Christmas*, pr. 1871, pb. 1879 (masque, one act); *Babil and Bijou*, pr. 1872 (with Dion Boucicault); *The Extravaganzas of Planché*, pb. 1879 (5 volumes); *Plays*, pb. 1985 (Donald Roy, editor).

Other literary forms

James Robinson Planché's literary versatility extended well beyond the theater. He was an inveterate traveler, recounting one of his many Continental journeys in his *Descent of the Danube from Ratisbon to Vienna* (1828); he was also an antiquarian and a historian, and his *History of British Costume* (1834) and *A Cyclopaedia of Costume: Or, Dictionary of Dress* (1876-1879) became standard reference works for theatrical costumers. Furthermore, Planché's two-volume history, *The Conqueror and His Companions* (1874), was considered "definitive" in his own day. Always adept at languages, Planché also translated, edited, or adapted works by French, Spanish, Italian, and German authors, including, in 1853, a translation of E.T.A. Hoffmann's *Nussknacker und Mausekönig* and, in 1855 and 1858, translations of the seventeenth century fairy tales of the Countess d'Aulnoy.

When Planché was asked to write about his extraordinarily long and successful theatrical career, the result was his informative and witty *Recollections and Reflections* (1872), which offers invaluable insights into nineteenth century theatrical practices. Planché was concerned, however, not only with the theater's past but also with its future. Shortly before his death, he published a pamphlet, *Suggestions for Establishing an English Art Theatre* (1879); this proposed theater was to produce plays of merit without regard for commercial considerations. Five volumes of Planché's extravaganzas were also published in 1879. His songs and poems appeared posthumously in 1881.

Achievements

By his own count, Planché wrote seventy-two original plays, ten of those in collaboration with Charles Dance. He adapted or translated an additional 104 plays. Thus, Planché's pen produced some 176 stage entertainments, embracing such diverse genres as historical drama, melodrama, comedy, farce, burlesque, extravaganza, opera libretto, and revue.

Planché's achievements were not limited to playwriting. His antiquarian interests, especially his passion for the history of British costume, led him in 1823 to persuade Charles Kemble, then manager of Covent Garden Theatre, to stage William Shakespeare's *King John* with historically correct costuming instead of the contemporary dress that had been customary. Kemble's production was an unprecedented success. Similarly, in 1831, Planché persuaded Madame Vestris (Lucia Elizabeth Bartolozzi), chief actress and manager of the Olympic Theatre, to stage his burlesque *Olympic Revels* with authentic costuming. Again, Planché's innovation was remarkably successful.

Planché was also adept at stagecraft, especially set design and scene painting. For his production of *The Vampire*, he invented the "vampire trap," which enabled an actor to come and go through seemingly solid scenery. Indeed, when Madame Vestris became manager of the Lyceum

Theatre in 1847, Planché wrote for that theater and supervised its scenery.

Shortly before his death, Planché published his *Suggestions for Establishing an English Art Theatre*, a theater "not wholly controlled by the predominant taste of the public." Although he did not live to see his project realized, Planché was responsible for two other important reforms. In 1828, an unauthorized performance of Planché's popular historical drama, *Charles XII*, led him to seek legal protection. Five years later, in 1833, Parliament, as a result of the efforts of Planché's friend Sir Edward Bulwer-Lytton, passed the Dramatic Authors Act, providing fines for appropriating a play without the consent of its author. Similarly, in 1829 Planché sued George Rodwell, who was about to publish the lyrics to Planché's operetta *The Mason of Buda*, without payment to the author. Planché won his suit and thereby broke the custom of publishers paying royalties to the composer of the music for an operetta but nothing to the writer of the lyrics, which were considered of little value. Thus, Planché's reforms and innovations touched almost every aspect of nineteenth century theater, much of whose history can be discerned from his works alone.

Biography

James Robinson Planché, son of Jacques Planché, a watchmaker, and Catherine Emily Planché (his father's cousin), was born in London on February 27, 1796. In his youth, Planché studied geometry and perspective— arts he later applied to his stagecraft. His apprenticeship to a bookseller also enabled him to read widely.

Planché began his theatrical career as an amateur actor at several private theaters. At twenty-two, he wrote his first play, *Amoroso, King of Little Britain*, which was staged successfully at Drury Lane on April 21, 1818. From that date until 1872, one or more new entertainments by Planché appeared on the London stage nearly every year.

Planché's diverse talents led to his supervising the music at Vauxhall Gardens during the 1826-1827 season. In 1830, he managed the Adelphi Theatre, and in 1831, he began his long association with Madame Vestris, first at the Olympic Theatre and later at the Lyceum. Planché not only wrote for her theaters but also designed and decorated their sets; meanwhile, he also wrote and staged entertainments for many other theaters, including the Haymarket.

Although Planché's first love was the theater, his second was antiquarianism. He was elected to the Society of Antiquaries in 1829 and also helped found the British Archaeological Association in 1843. From 1866 to 1871, he held the post of Somerset Herald. Indeed, Planché's expertise eventually led to his being permitted to arrange chronologically the collection of armor in the Tower of London.

In 1821, Planché married Elizabeth St. George, herself a dramatist. The couple had two daughters, Katherine Frances and Matilda Anne. Planché died on May 30, 1880.

Analysis

In his *Recollections and Reflections*, James Robinson Planché categorized contemporary English drama as "mere amusement." Although critical of this situation, Planché both capitalized on and contributed to it. Indeed, he was the master of nearly every popular dramatic form of his day, including the melodrama.

The melodrama had been popular in England since the end of the eighteenth century. The term literally means "musical drama," and thus songs and sometimes dances were often an integral part of the entertainment. Songs were also necessary to circumvent the theatrical licensing regulations of Planché's day, which placed many restrictions on the kinds of dramatic fare the minor London theaters were able to offer. Although the nineteenth century enjoyed several specific varieties of melodrama (such as the nautical or the Gothic), exotic settings, excessive emotions, and extravagant dialogue characterized the genre as a whole.

One of Planché's early melodramas was *The Vampire*, which Planché adapted from a French melodrama, *Le Vampire*, at the invitation of Samuel James Arnold, then proprietor of the Lyceum Theatre. Indeed, it was Arnold who refused to allow Planché to change the play's setting from Scotland, "where the [vampire] superstition never existed," to somewhere in Eastern Europe.

This "Romantic Melo-Drama," as Planché called his play, consists of two acts and an "Introductory Vision"—the latter set in the moonlit interior of "the Basaltic Caverns of Staffa." Lady Margaret, soon to be wed to the Earl of Marsden (the vampire), is sleeping fitfully. Unda, the Spirit of the Flood, and Ariel, the Spirit of the Air, recount the vampire legend and try to warn Margaret of her danger by raising a vision of the vampire, who emerges from a nearby tomb, springs at Margaret, and then "sinks again, shuddering." Planché's invention of the so-called vampire trap enabled T. P. Cooke, as the vampire, to repeat his spectacular exit at the end of the play.

The action of *The Vampire* is confined to Lady Margaret's wedding day. Neither she nor her family is aware that her fiancé Ruthven is a vampire who must wed a virgin bride and drink her blood before the moon sets or forever vanish into nothingness. Although Ruthven loves Margaret and tries to forestall their wedding by eloping with a servant girl, his plans are thwarted, and he presses for an immediate ceremony. Margaret's father at first consents, but later he reflects on two miraculous reappearances of Ruthven, each after Ruthven has supposedly been killed, and concludes that Ruthven himself must be the legendary vampire. Margaret's father tries to prevent the wedding, but Ruthven discredits his warnings as the ravings of a madman. To Ruthven's distress, however, Margaret promises to humor her father and heed his plea not to marry until after the moon has set. As the moon sets, the desperate Ruthven draws a dagger and attempts to seize his bride but is disarmed by Margaret's father and his servants. With a peal of thunder overhead, the lost Ruthven falls to the ground and vanishes forever.

Although Planché often condemned the public's preference for a theater of "mere amusement," he succeeded more often than any other of his contemporaries in catering to that preference. Planché himself attested that *The Vampire* became one of the most popular plays of its day. Its curious Scottish vampire-villain, its suspenseful though contrivance-ridden plot, its Gothic setting, and its spectacular vampire trap precisely suited public tastes. In 1829, Planché converted his melodrama into a libretto for the German opera *Der Vampyr*, changing its location to Hungary and substituting a "Wallachian Boyard" for the play's "Scotch chieftain." Planché also designed costumes that were, in his own words, "novel as well as correct." Taken together, these two "vampire" works testify to Planché's talents as playwright, translator, set and costume designer, librettist, and theatrical entrepreneur.

One of Planché's most successful ventures into what he termed "historical drama" was *Charles XII*. The play's title character, the Swedish King Charles XII (1682-1718), was renowned for his obsession with war. Not having been content to rule his own country, he had attacked Denmark, Saxony, and Poland before finally being defeated by the Russians at Poltava in 1709. As Samuel Johnson later observed, "the name at which the World grew pale" would henceforth be used only "to point a Moral, or adorn a Tale"—in this case, Planché's drama.

Planché's *Charles XII* avoids the moral ambiguities of the king's military escapades, using war only as a background menace that sometimes threatens to intrude into the play's comedy. Instead, the focus is on Charles's incognito visit to an inn kept by a Mr. Firmann, who is really one Major Vanberg, unjustly convicted of treason and under Charles's own death sentence. Charles is both charming and charmed, especially by the innkeeper's daughter Ulrica, who in turn is in love with Gustavus, one of Charles's officers. Charles has come to the town in search of Adam Brock, the play's liveliest and most popular character. Brock, something of a good-humored philosopher, had earlier lent money to the king, who now comes to repay him and cancel the debt. Brock's daughter Eudiga is in love with a Colonel Reichal, and when the king uses that name for his alias, Brock assumes he has come to propose to his daughter. The ensuing comic confusions are finally straightened out when Charles reveals his identity. Potentially tragic complications soon follow. Triptolymus Muddlewerk, a clerk and a busybody, reveals Vanberg's identity. Brock, who had earlier refused the king's debt repayment, claims Vanberg's life instead and later clears Vanberg's name as well, leaving Charles still indebted to him. Eudiga and Ulrica are united with their fiancés, and Charles returns to his war.

Unlike the sensationalism of *The Vampire*, characterization is the strength of *Charles XII*. Charles, momentarily removed from his primary obsession, exhibits all the charm, wit, and repartee of the cultivated eighteenth century gentleman. Likewise, Adam Brock maintains his composure and especially his good humor whether he is dealing with the machinations of Muddlewerk, kneeling before his newly discovered king, or saving Vanberg's life. Eudiga and Ulrica resemble the spirited heroines of eighteenth century comedy, while the meddling Muddlewerk is straight out of the humors tradition. Nevertheless, *Charles XII* also anticipates George Bernard Shaw's *The Man of Destiny* (pr. 1897). Planché's Charles is no more "historical" than is Shaw's Napoleon. Both playwrights depict the softer side of a military hero: Shaw to deflate the pretensions of authority, Planché to show what happens when the softer values predominate, even if only for a moment. Charles's tragedy is that he cannot sustain those values beyond the moment. Unlike Adam Brock, he cannot synthesize honor and courage with a peaceable disposition—a misfortune in a private man, a disaster in a public one.

In addition to his forays into historical drama and melodrama, Planché also experimented with burlesque, a form that treats a lofty subject in a lowly manner. The first of Planché's classical burlesques, *Olympic Revels*, which opened at the Olympic Theatre on January 3, 1831, became, in Planché's words, "the first of a series which enjoyed the favour of the public for upwards of thirty years." *Olympic Revels* retells the myth of the title characters in doggerel verse, often laced with puns. Jupiter is angry with Prometheus for "making creatures out of clay beneath us" and especially for heating their passions with "pilfered coals" from Jupiter's "kitchen range." Jupiter proposes to punish Prometheus by giving him the gift of a woman, Pandora, newly forged by Vulcan himself. With Pandora comes a mysterious casket and Jupiter's injunction not to open it. A jealous Juno also gives her the gift of curiosity. Pandora soon opens the box, from which immediately issue "fiends of every description." Jupiter punishes Pandora by turning her into "an ugly old maid" while Prometheus is condemned "to die of a liver complaint." Both are reprieved, however, when Hope arises out of Pandora's box to pardon them and provide the conventional happy ending. The play concludes with an appeal to the audience to "fill with patrons all Pandora's boxes."

Olympic Revels derives its title both from its classical subject and from the name of the Olympic Theatre where it was performed. Indeed, Madame Vestris, manager of the Olympic, chose Planché's play to open her new theater. Before the play began, she delivered an address to her audience, promising them joy, mirth, song, whim, fancy, humor, wit, music, and vaudeville from France. *Olympic Revels* itself comes close to fulfilling most of those promises. In the tradition of eighteenth century ballad opera, the action was interrupted by songs whose original lyrics were set to popular tunes. Planché, however, departed from the convention of presenting burlesques using outlandish costumes. Instead, he insisted on classically correct costumes, dressing Prometheus, he says, in a "Phrygian cap, tunic, and trousers" instead of "in a red jacket and nankeens, with a pinafore all besmeared with lollipop."

Planché, in his *Recollections and Reflections*, confesses that the idea for his *Olympic Revels* came from *The Sun Poker*, by George Colman the younger. Planché had originally written his burlesque several years earlier but had been unable to produce it. He then suggested to Dance, with whom he had previously collaborated, that they revise the piece and present it to Madame Vestris. Its overwhelming success inspired Planché's similar treatment of the Orpheus and Eurydice myth a year later in *Olympic Devils*, which was nearly as well received as its predecessor.

Planché's fascination with fairy tales led him not only to translate but also to dramatize many of them, including one of his most popular, *The Island of Jewels*, which opened December 26, 1849, at the Lyceum Theatre. Laidronetta, daughter of the King and Queen of Pharitale, has been made ugly by a spell cast by the wicked fairy, Margotine, who was accidentally overlooked and thus not invited to Laidronetta's christening. While lamenting that her ugliness prevents anyone from loving her, Laidronetta is interrupted by a large, green serpent—himself a victim of Margotine's spells—who declares his love for Laidronetta and then disappears when she faints. Later, she and her servant are shipwrecked on the Island of Jewels—a fabulously wealthy land governed by the mysterious King Emerald. The king, carried about in a covered sedan chair, offers his hand and his kingdom to Laidronetta if she will marry him sight unseen. She at first agrees, but, prompted by her beautiful and envious sister, she peeks at her intended bridegroom, who is none other than the green serpent. Margotine reappears to threaten both of them, but her power is finally broken by the intervention of the good fairy Benevolentia and by Laidronetta's unselfish choice to give happiness to the serpent at the cost of having to remain forever ugly. The serpent is transformed into King Emerald, who immediately weds Laidronetta, while Margotine is condemned to live tormented by her "own bad spirits." The fairy extravaganza concludes with the maxim: "If mortals would by happy here below,/ The surest way is making others so!"

Planché's play is a tour de force of pun and parody. For example, the King of Pharitale, distraught over his daughter's supposed loss of a kingdom, begins to recite King Lear's "Blow winds and crack your cheeks" when the rains come and the thought strikes him that he is "a king more rained upon than reigning." A moment later, the king shouts: "I tax not you, ye elements, you pay/ No duty under schedules D or A. . . ." Nevertheless, under the foolery there lies a nugget of truth, for *The Island of Jewels* underscores the folly of judging by appearances, both individually and as a country. The irony, though, is that the play itself was finally to be judged chiefly by appearances, for its costumes and scenery were so elaborate that they overshadowed everything else. "It was not," Planché himself complains, "the precise tissue of absurdity I had calculated for effect. . . ." Indeed, "calculated absurdity"—the satirist's ability to create a controlled chaos that looks beyond the appearances of order—accounts for much of Planché's theatrical success.

Planché was to use this talent to its fullest in his dramatic revues—a form whose freedom allowed him to satirize the popular entertainments of his day, usually those running at competing theaters. *Mr. Buckstone's Ascent of Mount Parnassus*, for example, pokes fun at specific genres, such as the Italian opera, at specific plays, such as Dion Boucicault's *The Corsican Brothers* (pr. 1848), and at specific theaters, such as Drury Lane and the Lyceum. It even satirizes the contemporary craze for dramatic adaptations of Harriet Beecher Stowe's *Uncle Tom's Cabin* (1852), which were appearing at many of the London playhouses.

Planché's protagonist is Mr. John Buckstone, "Sole Lessee and Manager" of the Haymarket Theatre, who acted the part himself. As the play opens, Mr. Buckstone is contemplating a pile of manuscripts, attempting to choose the most profitable entertainment for his theater. As he is reading "Arsenic: a Tragedy in fifteen acts,/ and forty tableaux, founded upon facts," the Spirits of Fashion and Fortune appear and suggest that Mr. Buckstone emulate Mr. Albert Smith's *The Spirit of Mount Blanc*—a combination travelogue and display of scene painting currently appearing at the Egyptian Hall. Mr. Buckstone eventually returns to this suggestion, but not before he has heard an aria from an Italian opera, has talked with the spirits of Drury Lane and the Lyceum, and has considered scenes from *The Corsican Brothers* and George L. Aiken's *Uncle Tom's Cabin* (pr. 1852).

Observing that Fortune has its ups and downs, Mr. Buckstone determines that he will go "up or down something wonderful" and selects Mount Parnassus, home of the classical Muses, since "nobody lately has gone high up there." With the aid of his scene painter, Mr. Buckstone presents a series of views beginning with Mount Parnassus, followed by the Greek villages of Crisso and Delphi and concluding with the summit of Parnassus upon which Phoebus Apollo is enthroned. Throughout these proceedings, the Muses appear and comment on contemporary corruptions of their arts. Euterpe, for example, laments that her "ancient concerts" have been displaced by the "discords and sharps" of "rival operas." Urania bemoans the star system, which emphasized individual actors at the expense of the ensemble, and Mr. Buckstone himself calls it "the ruin of the stage." Nevertheless, he vows to continue his climb until he can learn from Apollo in person "those fine arts [which] may the drama raise." His final plea is for his audience's "assent" to assure his "ascent."

Planché was an admirer of the eighteenth century dramatic satirists, and *Mr. Buckstone's Ascent of Mount Parnassus* is the descendant of such pieces as Henry Fielding's *The Author's Farce* (pr. 1730), in which emblematic representations of the "pleasures of the town" contest for the honor of being declared the Goddess of Nonsense's most devoted servant. Indeed, both Fielding and Planché capitalized on the dramatic revue's episodic plot structure, which conveniently permits the presentation of diverse topical material and the easy removal of or substitution for some or all of that material whenever it needs to be updated. More important, however, the dramatic revue constitutes a form of criticism in and of itself because it uses the conventions of its own medium to challenge those same conventions and sometimes to change them.

Despite Planché's criticism of popular dramatic forms, the majority of his own works were written to satisfy commercial dictates. Indeed, his instincts for what would work on the stage of his era were remarkably acute (a talent also shared by his most direct dramatic descendant, W. S. Gilbert). Although content with the personal profitability of the popular theater, Planché was never content with the status quo. He attempted to change the English stage by experimenting with new dramatic forms and theatrical techniques; by presenting satiric, sentimental, or sensational plays with an underlying serious point; and by proposing the establishment of an "English Art Theatre" to revive "the masterpieces of the last three centuries" in a theater where commercialism would be subordinated to the highest production standards. Like his own Mr. Buckstone, Planché never quite reached the summit of Parnassus, but he did enjoy the "assent" of his audience. The result of his creative efforts was 176 dramatic entertainments and perhaps the most successful career of any nineteenth century playwright.

Other major works

NONFICTION: *Descent of the Danube from Ratisbon to Vienna*, 1828; *History of British Costume*, 1834; *Recollections and Reflections*, 1872; *The Conqueror and His Companions*, 1874 (2 volumes); *A Cyclopaedia of Costume: Or, Dictionary of Dress*, 1876-1879; *Suggestions for Establishing an English Art Theatre*, 1879.

TRANSLATIONS: *King Nutcracker*, 1853 (of E. T. A. Hoffmann's *Nussknacker und Mausekönig*); *Fairy Tales*, 1855 (of the Countess d'Aulnoy's fairy tales); *Four-and-Twenty Fairy Tales*, 1858 (of d'Aulnoy's fairy tales).

MISCELLANEOUS: *Songs and Poems from 1819 to 1879*, 1881.

Bibliography
Booth, Michael, et al. *The Revels History of Drama in English, 1750-1880.* Vol. 6. London: Methuen, 1976. Richly illustrated with portraits of important theatrical personalities and drawings of the innovative stagecraft of the early nineteenth century, this readable survey considers Planché among the most important playwrights between 1810 and 1850. His combination of witty dialogue, melodramatic plots, and burlesque themes anticipated—and occasionally influenced—the comic opera of W. S. Gilbert and Sir Arthur Sullivan. Contains a thorough bibliography of primary sources on the Georgian and Victorian theaters.
Clinton-Baddeley, V. C. *The Burlesque Tradition in the English Theatre After 1660.* London: Methuen, 1952. This short, readable account, written by a producer of burlesque, traces the development of the genre from its origin in the Restoration. The author locates Planché in a tradition of theatrical experimentation that reinvigorates and reinterprets the conventions of a previous generation to make way for a new age of vigorous growth. The book is well illustrated and offers detailed notes and an extensive bibliography.
Emeljanow, Victor. "Dramatic Forms and Their Theatrical Context." In *Victorian Popular Dramatists.* Boston: Twayne, 1987. Planché is one of many dramatists upon whose work Emeljanow comments as he investigates the paradox of Victorian theater: Its audiences grew and its technical expertise increased even as the literary quality of the drama declined—not only in Great Britain but also throughout the English-speaking countries worldwide.
Jenkins, Anthony. "Breaking Through the Darkness." In *The Making of Victorian Drama.* Cambridge, England: Cambridge University Press, 1991. This important study touches briefly upon Planché but offers an enlightening, introductory account of the rise of realistic, spectacular stage production of the sort at which Planché excelled. Jenkins details the crucial role of the Olympic Theatre in breaking the patent theater monopoly under the direction of Planché's sometime coentrepreneur, Madame Vestris (Lucia Elizabeth Bartolozzi).
Nicoll, Allardyce. *A History of English Drama, 1660-1900.* 6 vols. Cambridge, England: Cambridge University Press, 1959-1962. Planché is frequently mentioned in Nicoll's account of "illegitimate drama," by which is meant melodrama, farce, burlesque, burletta, and extravaganzas. Nicoll has little sympathy for Planché or any other writer who experimented outside conventional comedy and tragedy, but he provides an exhaustive list of Planché's prolific output between 1818 and 1850.
White, Eric Walter. *A History of English Opera.* London: Faber & Faber, 1983. An expanded version of White's earlier *The Rise of English Opera* (1951). Aimed at a general audience, *A History of English Opera* is a

readable and sympathetic account of an art form that Nicoll derides as "illegitimate drama." Although this volume traces opera from the early 1660's through the 1980's, it devotes generous attention to Planché and other Victorian practitioners, mainly through anecdotes about personalities and performances rather than the analysis of texts.

Valerie C. Rudolph
(Updated by *Robert M. Otten*)

J. B. PRIESTLEY

Born: Bradford, England; September 13, 1894
Died: Stratford-upon-Avon, England; August 14, 1984

Principal drama

The Good Companions, pr. 1931, pb. 1935 (adaptation of his novel, with Edward Knoblock); *Dangerous Corner*, pr., pb. 1932; *The Roundabout*, pr. 1932, pb. 1933; *Laburnum Grove*, pr. 1933, pb. 1934; *Eden End*, pr., pb. 1934; *Cornelius*, pr., pb. 1935; *Duet in Floodlight*, pr., pb. 1935; *Bees on the Boat Deck*, pr., pb. 1936; *Spring Tide*, pr., pb. 1936 (with George Billam); *People at Sea*, pr., pb. 1937; *Time and the Conways*, pr., pb. 1937; *I Have Been Here Before*, pr., pb. 1937; *Music at Night*, pr. 1938, pb. 1947; *Mystery at Greenfingers*, pr., pb. 1938; *When We Are Married*, pr., pb. 1938; *Johnson over Jordan*, pr., pb. 1939; *The Long Mirror*, pr., pb. 1940; *Goodnight, Children*, pr., pb. 1942; *They Came to a City*, pr. 1943, pb. 1944; *Desert Highway*, pr., pb. 1944; *The Golden Fleece*, pr. 1944, pb. 1948; *How Are They at Home?*, pr., pb. 1944; *An Inspector Calls*, pr. 1946, pb. 1947; *Ever Since Paradise*, pr. 1946, pb. 1950; *The Linden Tree*, pr. 1947, pb. 1948; *The Rose and Crown*, pb. 1947 (one act); *The High Toby*, pb. 1948 (for puppet theater); *Home Is Tomorrow*, pr. 1948, pb. 1949; *The Plays of J. B. Priestley*, pb. 1948-1950 (3 volumes); *Summer Day's Dream*, pr. 1949, pb. 1950; *Bright Shadow*, pr., pb. 1950; *Seven Plays of J. B. Priestley*, pb. 1950; *Dragon's Mouth*, pr., pb. 1952 (with Jacquetta Hawkes); *Treasure on Pelican*, pr. 1952, pb. 1953; *Mother's Day*, pb. 1953 (one act); *Private Rooms*, pb. 1953 (one act); *Try It Again*, pb. 1953 (one act); *A Glass of Bitter*, pb. 1954 (one act); *The White Countess*, pr. 1954 (with Hawkes); *The Scandalous Affair of Mr. Kettle and Mrs. Moon*, pr., pb. 1955; *These Our Actors*, pr. 1956; *The Glass Cage*, pr. 1957, pb. 1958; *The Pavilion of Masks*, pr. 1963; *A Severed Head*, pr. 1963 (with Iris Murdoch; adaptation of Murdoch's novel).

Other literary forms

J. B. Priestley's plays may be his most lasting contribution to literature, yet as a consummate man of letters he mastered many genres in a canon comprising nearly two hundred works. Beginning his writing career as critic and essayist on subjects ranging from William Shakespeare to Thomas Love Peacock, from the art of conversation to political theory, Priestley became a household name in 1929 with the extraordinarily popular success of *The Good Companions*, a picaresque novel about a concert party, which, translated into many languages, was an international best-seller. In all, he wrote more than thirty novels, eighteen books of essays and auto-biography, numerous works of social commentary and history, accounts of his travels, philosophical conjectures on the nature of time, even morale-boosting propaganda during World War II, as well as an occasional screenplay and an opera libretto. Poetry was the only genre he neglected, after publishing, at his own expense, a single slim volume of verse in 1918, *The Chapman of Rhymes*. He was a popular professional writer, vitally concerned with every aspect of human life, and no subject escaped his scrutiny. As a result, the gruff, pipe-smoking Yorkshireman held a unique position in English letters as a highly respected sage who was also a man of the people.

For more than half a century, he remained loyal to a single publishing house, William Heinemann Ltd., which brought out nearly all of his massive output in various genres. Heinemann published single editions of most of his plays as well as thematically linked collections of two, three, and four plays. Heinemann's major collection of his drama, comprising twenty-one of his plays, both comedies and dramas, was published as *The Plays of J. B. Priestley* in three volumes from 1948 to 1950.

Achievements

Priestley's achievements as a dramatist outshine his work as a novelist. If he was a mainstream figure, albeit a minor one, in a vastly rich period of the English novel, in drama he was the single serious English writer of the first half of the twentieth century, bridging the gap between George Bernard Shaw and John Osborne. Only Sean O'Casey, an Irishman like Shaw, had a reputation as dramatist greater than Priestley's in the same period. The plays of John Galsworthy were quickly dated, while much of the work of Sir James Barrie, aside from the 1904 production of the immortal *Peter Pan*, was too cloying to survive its own generation. The plays of W. Somerset Maugham and Noël Coward may have been more successful with contemporary audiences, but they remain monuments to triviality rather than attempts to illuminate the plight of twentieth century humankind.

Priestley's focus was England and the Englishman, not the aristocrats and idle wastrels who people Maugham's and Coward's elegant drawing rooms but the middle classes, the workers—the backbone of the country, England's defenders and its hope for a workable future. Priestley was an optimist who believed that human beings working in and for the community can overcome any obstacle. A Socialist, he firmly believed throughout a long career that the golden world in which he grew up before World War I could be reestablished once people rid themselves of sloth and greed and willingly accept responsibility for others. If his view now seems at times overly romantic, it was fueled by a belief in quasi-scientific theory of the coexistence of all time, popularized by J. W. Dunne in *An Experiment with Time* (1927), and was tempered by a clear-sightedness concerning his compatriots' failings, which may have caused a decline in his popularity at home after World War II at the same time that his plays were embraced in the Communist world. Not long before his death, he called himself "a cautious optimist" and had yet to give up on his compatriots.

After attempting comedies of manners in such works as *The Roundabout* and *Duet in Floodlight* but rejecting the mode as a shallow one, Priestley revealed that the influences upon his drama were more Continental than native. Specifically, he attempted to demonstrate, like Henrik Ibsen, that the present is the inevitable result of the deeds and actions of one's past. The present, in turn, inevitably colors the future. Here, too, the reader can detect the effect of theorizing about time as a fourth dimension in which human beings live. The single most important influence upon Priestley's drama, however, was Anton Chekhov. Like Chekhov's, Priestley's best plays capture and sustain an elegiac atmosphere in which imperfect individuals lose their way but also touch others and their families with love. Again like Chekhov, the dramatist could love his characters despite their failings, but unlike Chekhov, Priestley did not always successfully universalize his situations. Whereas *The Cherry Orchard* becomes a metaphor reaching beyond Russia to evoke a world, *Eden End* remains a view of provincial England. As a result, Priestley never touched American audiences as he did his own people. Nevertheless, in such plays as *Eden End*, *Cornelius*, and *The Linden Tree*, Priestley evoked a sense of loss more subtly than any dramatist since Chekhov.

Exploring the family circle in such early plays as *Laburnum Grove* and *Eden End*, Priestley eventually widened his focus to the nation as family in *They Came to a City* and *How Are They at Home?* and inevitably to the world as family in *Home Is Tomorrow* and *Summer Day's Dream*. The unifying thread through these works is the Jungian concept of the unity of all human beings, a concept most clearly expressed in such innovative plays as *Johnson over Jordan* and *Music at Night*, works that enabled Priestley to handle time and place in the fluid manner of the Expressionists. Priestley, however, denied that his work was Expressionistic; he preferred to believe instead that his theory of coexisting time, in which persons are at all times beyond mere chronological time, proved that Expressionist "distortion" does not take place in his work.

Priestley's experimental dramas, again influenced by Continental writers, as well as his insistence upon thrusting the common person to the very center of the stage in his realistic plays, were important blows in freeing the English theater from a stultifying conservatism. Never losing sight of the fact that a dramatist must be able to entertain his audience, Priestley found the way to make audiences think as well, to face hard truths about themselves, and to confront these truths with love rather than with anger. Although the Angry Young Men who came after him mistakenly thought him to be, as Osborne has stated, an Edwardian relic, Priestley's plays are in fact precursors of their own. Their concerns were his before them, but his voice was gentler and, unlike theirs, forgiving.

Biography

Bradford, once the wool-merchandizing center of Northern England, provided the perfect atmosphere for a budding writer. A commercial hub on a more human scale than sprawling London, the city nurtured the arts. There were two theaters, two music halls, a concert hall visited by the world's most renowned musicians, play-reading societies, arts clubs, a good library, and a local paper which accepted contributions from young writers. Nearby were the Yorkshire dales, providing solace from the city's bustle. John Boynton Priestley, encouraged by his Socialist schoolmaster father and his kindly stepmother, took advantage of all that his native city had to offer. He lived a culturally rich childhood balanced by long weekend walks on the moors. The environment of his home, where his father led discussions on the arts, education, and politics, stimulated him as well. To Richard Pendlebury, his English master, Priestley attributed his awakening interest in literature and his early desire to be a writer.

Priestley furtively wrote poetry and short stories in his notebooks during the days he spent as a junior clerk in a wool firm. Unable to concentrate on commerce, he began placing his pieces in popular London weekly magazines. In 1913, he became a regular contributor to *The Bradford Pioneer*, a Labour weekly, with a cultural column he called "Round the Hearth."

World War I interrupted a tranquil, idyllic, if directionless, existence, and, in 1914, Priestley enlisted in the Duke of Wellington's West Riding Regiment. Shipped to France, he was wounded near Souchez and returned to England. In 1917, after his recuperation, he received a commission as lieutenant. Back in France, Priestley, along with several members of his Devon Regiment, was gassed. In his writing, he hardly mentioned the wartime horrors that he witnessed and suffered, yet World War I remains the key to an understanding of his work. Priestley never shed his sense of waste and loss. The war spelled an end to a simpler life which, in retrospect, always seemed to him a better life. The world he was brought up to inhabit no longer existed, and Priestley's own boyish innocence died with it. Much of his work was a romantic attempt to recapture the vitalizing spirit of an earlier time, of a world in harmony.

After three unsatisfying years at Cambridge, from 1919 to 1922, where he studied literature, history, and political science, Priestley abandoned plans for a teaching career and moved to London to try his luck as a freelance writer. At the time, he and his wife, Pat Tempest, whom he married in 1919, were expecting their first child. Aided by J. C. Squire, who ran *The London Mercury*, he established himself as essayist and critic. In 1925, after a long illness, his first wife died. A year later, he married Mary (Holland) Wyndham Lewis. As a result of the two marriages, Priestley had five children: four daughters and a son.

The almost immediate worldwide success of *The Good Companions* in 1929 made it possible for Priestley to live the life he had chosen, that of a professional writer. He began to travel widely at home and abroad to find new subjects to explore and entered the world of the commercial theater, which had seemed, until his success, too much of a risk for a family man. Beginning a new phase of his career in 1931 with the adaptation (in collaboration with Edward Knoblock) of *The Good Companions*, the novel which had won for him fame and a newfound security, Priestley achieved theatrical success on his own a year later with a well-crafted melodrama, *Dangerous Corner*, which was soon produced around the world. Shortly afterward, he formed a company for the production of his own work. In addition to writing various types of plays, Priestley occasionally directed them as well, and even acted in one, *When We Are Married*, while a leading actor was indisposed. For a time Priestley thought of himself as primarily a dramatist, but in later life he left the theater to concentrate again on novels and essays.

Priestley became one of his nation's most beloved figures during World War II, rivaling Sir Winston Churchill in popularity, with the weekly broadcasts of his "Postscripts" for the British Broadcasting Company. These began in 1940 after Dunkirk and ended the next year when the Germans launched their blitz on London. The talks stirred a nation and comforted those who, like Priestley, hoped that a better world would be the outcome of this devastating war.

In 1952, Priestley divorced his second wife and a year later married Jacquetta Hawkes, the distinguished anthropologist with whom he occasionally collaborated. The two lived in a gracious Georgian home, Kissing Tree House, in Alveston, just outside Stratford-upon-Avon. Insisting on remaining a man of the people, Priestley refused a knighthood and a life peerage. In 1973, however, he received the conferment of the Freedom of the City of Bradford. In 1977, he accepted membership in the Order of Merit, a prestigious honor limited to twenty-four living Britons, privately expressing the opinion that it had come too late to bring him satisfaction for very long. Nevertheless, Priestley lived to enjoy the honor for seven years. After a short illness in 1984, he died in his home one month before his ninetieth birthday.

Analysis

Much of J. B. Priestley's drama explores the oneness of all human beings. That notion leads the dramatist to view individuals as members of a charmed or magic circle. The circle is continually broken, but Priestley, the essential optimist, believed that the circle can and must be mended as people accept responsibility for their fellow human beings. The family, then, with its temporary victories, its too frequently dashed dreams, its individuals pulling the circle out of shape only to have it reshaped by the family's wiser members, becomes the microcosm of the world. That world, however, is continually buffeted by time. Priestley therefore viewed the family through a multiple time perspective. He was conscious of time past, time present, even future time. Occasionally he enabled an especially perceptive character to understand his place in flowing time, but he always led his audience to an awareness that all time is one. Even in an early commercial success such as the melodramatic *Dangerous Corner*, Priestley implied that a family shattered by the sordid past deeds of one of its members can find life anew. It need not be bound by the past, and a new awareness in the present may even reshape a past. The return to the beginning and a second chance for the characters of *Dangerous Corner*, though perhaps a mere theatrical gimmick in this early play, foreshadows Priestley's more thoughtful view of the Family of Man in time in *Eden End*, *Time and the Conways*, *Johnson over Jordan*, and *An Inspector Calls.*

Time provides *Eden End* its richest dimension. Eschewing the gimmickry of *Dangerous Corner's* celebrated time-twist, Priestley made extraordinary use of dramatic irony in *Eden End*, a realistic family drama set in 1912. Not only are his characters about to lose their innocence, but an entire world is also about to be plunged into the horrors of a war from which it can never recover. As characters speak of a better time to come, the audience is fully aware of darkening shadows on the horizon. Time itself evokes *Eden End's* autumnal atmosphere, making the play a threnody for a glorious but doomed world, which must inevitably give way to a material, technological advancement, spelling the end of the safe and sane values of love and loyalty and the quiet pleasures of a life lived in the service of others. As the Kirby family inevitably breaks apart, Eden comes to an end.

The widower Dr. Kirby, a general practitioner who has always longed for something more from his career, is suffering from a heart condition that will soon kill him. He has with him in Eden End, in Northern England, his younger daughter, Lilian, who serves as his housekeeper, and crotchety old Sarah, who was nurse to his three children and has been retained beyond her years of usefulness. Expected to arrive is Wilfred, the youngest of the children, home on leave from the British West Africa Company. An unexpected arrival, however, Stella, Lilian's older sister and the family prodigal, disrupts a stable family situation. Stella had left the limited horizons of Eden End to pursue an unsuccessful career as an actress. Aware now that the only happy period in her life was her youth in Eden End, she learns before the play ends that one's youth cannot be recaptured; to expect miracles is a pointless pastime. Eden End can no longer be for her the haven she has imagined, and she must return to the actress' life of tiring railway journeys, uncomfortable lodgings, and dusty dressing rooms. Before her departure, which signals a return to normalcy for the others, she attempts to rekindle the love of Geoffrey Farant, who runs a nearby estate. Lilian, however, herself interested in Geoffrey, retaliates by bringing Charlie Appleby, another second-rate actor and Stella's estranged husband, to Eden End to confront her. On learning that Stella is married, Geoffrey plans to relocate in New Zealand, inadvertently dashing the hopes of Lilian, who has for many years been quietly contemplating a home of her own with the man she loves. Reconciled, Stella and Charlie make a seemingly futile attempt to renew their life together, while Wilfred, frustrated by an aborted relationship with a local barmaid, takes his disappointment back with him to Nigeria, where he will wait patiently for his next unfulfilling leave.

Knowing that his own death is approaching, Dr. Kirby ironically comforts himself with the mistaken notion of a bright future which he believes life holds in store for his children and for the baby he has just delivered. If no dreams come true, if life holds only the promise of hardship and heartbreak in Eden End, it is left to Charlie Appleby to proclaim the reward which life offers to all. That he is inebriated at the time does not diminish the truth of his observation that life is full of wonder. Pain is part of life's wonder, and man is the richer for experiencing it, especially in those moments in which the experience is shared with others. Dr. Kirby is not the failure he believes himself to be, but a good man who has shared the life of family and community.

In a brief critical study, *Anton Chekhov* (1970), Priestley makes clear his admiration and affection for the plays of the Russian master, and in *Eden End* he demonstrates that he has been an apt pupil. Priestly's method is Chekhov's own as he sustains a mood dependent on depth of characterization and wealth of detail. Stella incorporates the qualities of Madame Ranevskaya of *The Cherry Orchard*, Nina of *The Seagull*, and Elena of *Uncle Vanya* as she tries to win the man loved by her more practical sister Lilian, who recalls *Vanya*'s Sonia and Varya of *The Cherry Orchard*. Lilian even has a brief exchange with Geoffrey Farant in which, like Varya and Lopakhin, they avoid any discussion of their personal relationship by talking about the weather instead. Wilfred is as much the idle dreamer as Gaev, while Dr. Kirby recalls a number of Chekhov's sad and wise doctors. Like old Firs, Sarah emphasizes a bewildering, rapidly changing world. She still thinks of her charges as children and fails to come to terms with the technology of motorcars and phonographs. When the others go off to the station at the play's end, Sarah, like Firs, is left behind and ignores the ringing telephone which replaces Chekhov's breaking string.

Despite the similarities, however, *Eden End* is no mere imitation of Chekhov. The play exquisitely evokes the life of provincial England in the second decade of the twentieth century, and English audiences, deeply moved by it, responded enthusiastically. The minute details of English life in another era, however, may finally work against the play's achieving universality, and it has not found favor abroad. Acknowledging that Chekhov has influenced many English dramatists, Priestley himself suggested that he and others were better for that influence. *Eden End* ranks among the finest plays of the Chekhovian mode.

Priestley, who called himself "a Time haunted man," inevitably turned again to time as the controlling factor in human life in *Time and the Conways*, a play highly influenced by the theories of Dunne. In *An Experiment with Time*, Dunne, the designer of Great Britain's first military aircraft, attempts to explain the experience of precognition, that sense of déjà vu in which human beings, through the distortion of dream, receive foreknowledge of future events displaced in time. Dunne's quasi-scientific theory provides for a series of observers within every person existing in a series of times. To a person's ordinary self, Observer One, the fourth dimension appears as time. The self within dreams, however, is Observer Two, to whom the fifth dimension appears as time. Unlike the three-dimensional outlook of Observer One, Observer Two has a four-dimensional outlook that enables him or her to receive images from the coexisting times of past and future. Part of the appeal of Dunne's so-called theory of Serialism is its provision for immortality: Observer One dies in time one but lives on within Observer Two in time two, and so on to "infinite regression." *Time and the Conways* is Priestley's rendering of abstruse theory into poignantly effective literature. Revisiting the world of his own past, he infuses it with an awareness of the effects of time on all human beings, a sense of waste and loss tempered with a note of hope and an intimation of immortality.

The play begins in 1919 in the Conway home, in a prosperous suburb of a manufacturing town, where a party is under way to celebrate Kay's twenty-first birthday. An aspiring novelist, Kay is joined by her widowed mother, five brothers and sisters, friends, and neighbors. With the war ended, all of them look forward to a bright future. Madge is eager to be part of a new Socialist order; Robin, home from the Royal Air Force, expects to make his fortune in car sales; Hazel, the family beauty, awaits her Prince Charming, while Carol, the youngest, is bursting with an overflowing sense of life. Alan, a clerk in the Rate Office and the only member of the family with no great hopes or plans, is the most contented of the lot as he savors what seems to the others to be merely a humdrum existence. Once their game of charades is over and the costumes are put away, everyone goes into the next room to hear Mrs. Conway's rendering of Robert Schumann's "Der Nussbaum." Kay, however, returns to the sitting room. She cannot let go of this moment of blissful happiness, the happiest moment any of the young Conways will ever experience. Sitting on a window seat, her head bathed in moonlight, Kay, with the special sensitivity of the artist, is about to be granted a vision of her family's future as the curtain falls on the first act.

The action of act 2 seems to be continuous as the rising curtain reveals Kay in the same position. When Alan enters and turns on the lights, however, it is obvious that several years have passed. It is again Kay's birthday, but the year is 1937, the year in which the play was written, and Kay is now forty. Act 2, as Priestley explained it, is Kay's precognition or glimpse of the future. In terms of Dunne's Serialism, her Observer Two sees what will happen to her Observer One.

Mrs. Conway, as impractical as Madame Ranevskaya, has called her children together to discuss her financial difficulties but has attempted to turn the homecoming into a party. Her children, however, are not in a party mood this time. Kay, no celebrated novelist, merely a hack journalist, is involved in an unhappy affair with a married man. Madge is an embittered schoolmistress, and Robin is unable to hold on to a job. He has frittered away much of the family funds and has deserted his wife and children. Hazel, too, has changed. Married to a wealthy mill owner who resents the family for snubbing him years before when he had first come to town, she is terrified of her husband. Conspicuously absent from the family group is Carol. On the threshold of life in the first act, she has been dead for sixteen years in the second.

The air is full of insult, accusation, and recrimination. Once the others have gone their separate ways, a miserable Kay tells her brother Alan that life seems pointless to her now as she remembers the happiness of their younger days. At forty, she is constantly aware of every tick of the clock, of that great devil in the universe called time. Alan, still the one stable element in the family, manages to soothe her. She is again alone at the window as the act ends.

Act 3 continues the action of act 1. Mrs. Conway can be heard singing as Kay is again discovered at the window. It is again 1919 and her twenty-first birthday. The events of act 2 have not yet taken place; life has not yet exacted its toll. Kay, however, has an awareness the others do not share. For her and for the audience, act 3 has a terrible poignancy as the carefree Conways unwittingly plant the seeds of their future unhappiness and destroy one another in ignorance and innocence. The doomed Carol tells the rest how full her life will be. She will act, paint, travel, but the point of it all, she explains with Priestley's acquiescence, is to live. Moved, Kay begins to cry and asks Alan for comforting words. As the play ends, Alan replies that one day he will have something to tell her that may comfort her.

What Kay needs to hear, what Alan will tell her in eighteen years, he has already told her at the end of Kay's precognitive vision which is act 2— that all human beings are at any moment only a cross section of their real selves. At the end of their lives, they are all of themselves in all of their times and may find themselves in yet another time which is another kind of dream. If the ideas are Dunne's, Priestley transcends theory in a profoundly moving play which affords insight into a person's plight in a bewildering age and offers an audience something to cling to in the midst of the pain of life. Pseudoscientific explanations are beside the point.

The play is no bag of tricks, as some critics have complained, with a third act where the second ought to be. Performed chronologically, the three acts would not have the meaningful impact that Priestley's dramatic irony unleashes. In *Time and the Conways*, Priestley revealed himself as innovator, liberating the stage from the limiting convention of realism, paving the way for such later works as Harold Pinter's 1971 production of *Old Times* and his 1975 production of *No Man's Land*, in which past and present coexist on the stage.

The enthusiastic acceptance and understanding of *Time and the Conways* convinced Priestley that audiences were ready for more daring experimentation, that he could challenge himself and them with the form and content of untried materials. In *Johnson over Jordan*, which he called "a biographical morality play," Priestley made maximal use of all the resources the theater offered in a drama stressing the timelessness that was one of his favorite themes. The play calls for intricate musical effects requiring a full orchestra, even ballet sequences, as characters are taken outside time and presented four-dimensionally.

Influenced by the Tibetan Book of the Dead, Priestley was especially struck by an account of the Bardo, a dreamlike state after death, filled with hallucinatory visions. *Johnson over Jordan* is an attempt to simplify the complex Bardo into a Westernized version in which Robert Johnson, an English Everyman, moves back and forth in time examining the quality of the life he has just departed.

The manager of a small business firm, Johnson cannot let go of his material concerns even after death. He wanders through a distorted landscape of documents, ledgers, and tax forms, a nightmare world with which he cannot cope. Like the officer in August Strindberg's *A Dream Play*, he becomes a schoolboy again, confused by life's contradictions, reminded of his petty deeds and thoughtless actions. Eventually he takes refuge, like Ibsen's Peer Gynt in the land of the trolls, in the Jungle Hot Spot. Here, he confronts his animal self as he mingles with men and women in grotesque, piglike masks. A mysterious figure, who, like Peer's Button Moulder, reappears throughout his spiritual journey, directs him on to the Inn at the End of the World. All who have illuminated Johnson's mind and touched his heart, members of his immediate family and characters from beloved books, reappear to him through a window at the inn. He recognizes his wife, like Peer's Solveig, as Eternal Woman. His love for her, stronger than material desires, is a lasting one which makes him finally aware of life's wonders and its prosaic joys. At last Johnson, acknowledging himself a less than perfect being, is granted entry into an unknown universe.

Despite a now legendary performance by Sir Ralph Richardson, effective music by Benjamin Britten, and inventive choreography by Antony Tudor, *Johnson over Jordan* failed to find its audience. To some extent Priestley attributed that failure to the critics who dwelled on the work's Expressionistic style, frightening away its potential audience. Priestley's own view of the Expressionistic theater is that it is peopled entirely by symbolic figures and flattened characters. In the case of *Johnson over Jordan*, he believed, the realistic portrayal of the protagonist, despite the distorted trappings of his environment, made a mockery of the dreaded label. His own explanation of what he was attempting, however—to make use of objective form to present material which was deeply subjective—suggests that the work in fact derives from the Expressionist tradition. Like those of Expressionist drama, the characters, apart from Johnson himself, are types. All, Johnson among them, speak a heightened language, and the play, in its exploration of a dreamworld devoid of time and space, deals abstractly with a basic Expressionist theme—the worth of human beings. The play's very theatricality is the measure of its achievement. Without becoming a commercial success, *Johnson over Jordan* was a landmark occasion in a London theater long resistant to dynamic change. It encouraged others to press on with efforts to expand the limits of a too-confining stage.

Priestley's work for the theater during World War II expressed his lifelong theme of commitment to community. Plays such as *Desert Highway* and *How Are They at Home?* appear to have been written more from a sense of duty than from a spark of creativity, but one play of the war years stands apart from the rest. Written during the last winter of the war, *An Inspector Calls* was first performed by two Soviet theater companies in Moscow at a time when no London theater was available for its production. When it was produced at home in 1946, in a weighty production full of realistic detail, it was dismissed with indifference. Priestley believed that acclaim with which Russian audiences had greeted it resulted from a more sympathetic symbolic production. There were no walls to the set, only an illuminated acting area. The symbolic setting made the audience aware that the play concerned more than its immediate and continuous action, was in fact concerned with the history of a generation that had just come through a worldwide conflagration. Sharing with *Dangerous Corner* the form of a conventional melodrama, *An Inspector Calls* is a committed social drama that focuses on one man's family while insisting inevitably on the Family of Man.

On an evening in 1912 in an industrial city in the North Midlands, the Birlings are celebrating their daughter Sheila's engagement to Gerald

Croft. The coming wedding will signal the merger of Birling & Company and Crofts Limited. Dashing the festive mood of the occasion is the visit of an Inspector Goole, new to the district, to announce the death that evening of a young woman, Eva Smith, who swallowed a disinfectant and died in agony in the Infirmary. One by one the Birlings are shown a photograph of the girl, and each recognizes her. By the time Goole departs, everyone is implicated in the girl's death. Birling had fired her for her part in a strike at his factory; Sheila had had her discharged from a dress shop for impertinence; Croft, who knew her as Daisy Renton, had made her his mistress for a time, but she had later become pregnant by Birling's son Eric. When she had asked for assistance from a charity organization, she had been denied by the interviewing committee, chaired by Mrs. Birling. Frustrated at every turn, she had committed suicide.

The Birling children are shaken by Goole's statement that the world is full of Eva Smiths, and that everyone is responsible for his own destiny. The elder Birlings and Croft, on the other hand, are more concerned with their reputations and with covering up the scandal than they are convinced of their guilt and responsibility. It even occurs to them that they may have been shown different photos, that Eva Smith and Daisy Renton may not have been the same girl. Checking with the police a few minutes later, they are overjoyed to learn that there is no Inspector Goole on the force and that no girl has died in the infirmary. Believing that they have been the victims of an elaborate hoax, they prepare to carry on as before, much to the dismay of Sheila and Eric. Suddenly the phone rings, and Birling reports his telephone conversation to the others. The police have just informed him that a girl has died on the way to the Infirmary after swallowing disinfectant. An inspector is on his way to ask some questions. The curtain abruptly falls on five stunned characters.

In one of Priestley's tautest and best-crafted works, what seems to be a realistic drama suddenly moves outside time. No particular time theory is under illustration here. Instead, time reinforces the notion that human beings must take responsibility for their actions and their consequences. In the present, individuals prepare their future. Even Inspector Goole is taken outside time. Is he police officer or imposter? Perhaps he is the very embodiment of the Birlings' collective guilt, which has been called forth by their need to account for their actions.

Like *Eden End*, *An Inspector Calls* is set in 1912, enabling the dramatist to make astonishing use of dramatic irony. The Birlings' world, like the Kirbys', is about to disintegrate. The Kirbys were victims of their own innocence, but the Birlings, no innocents, have caused the demise of their comfortable world through a lack of compassion, a disregard for those members of their community less fortunate than themselves. Priestley added a further dimension to the play, which he wrote as World War II was ending, by setting it on the eve of World War I. When will humankind benefit, he was asking, from the lessons of the past?

Priestley's wartime despair eventually gave way to a cautious optimism, despite the uncertainties of the future, in such later plays as *Summer Day's Dream* and *The Linden Tree*. After collaborating with Iris Murdoch on a successful adaptation of her novel *A Severed Head* in 1963, he abandoned the theater. The National Theatre celebrated Priestley's eightieth birthday with a production of *Eden End* in 1974, and in the decade before his death there were major revivals in London of *Laburnum Grove* and *Dangerous Corner*. Throughout Great Britain and the rest of the world, his plays continue to be revived today, spreading his lifelong belief that human beings are basically good and must, one day, come to their senses.

Other major works

NOVELS: *Adam in Moonshine*, 1927; *Benighted*, 1927; *The Good Companions*, 1929; *Farthing Hall*, 1929 (with Hugh Walpole); *Angel Pavement*, 1930; *Faraway*, 1932; *I'll Tell You Everything*, 1933 (with George Bullett); *Wonder Hero*, 1933; *They Walk in the City: The Lovers in the Stone Forest*, 1936; *The Doomsday Men: An Adventure*, 1938; *Let the People Sing*, 1939; *Blackout in Gretley: A Story of—and for—Wartime*, 1942; *Daylight on Saturday: A Novel About an Aircraft Factory*, 1943; *Three Men in New Suits*, 1945; *Bright Day*, 1946; *Jenny Villiers: A Story of the Theatre*, 1947; *Festival at Farbridge*, 1951 (published in the United States as *Festival*); *Low Notes on a High Level: A Frolic*, 1954; *The Magicians*, 1954; *Saturn over the Water: An Account of His Adventures in London, South America, and Australia by Tim Bedford, Painter, Edited with Some Preliminary and Concluding Remarks by Henry Sulgrave and Here Presented to the Reading Public*, 1961; *The Thirty-first of June: A Tale of True Love, Enterprise, and Progress in the Arthurian and ad-Atomic Ages*, 1961; *The Shape of Sleep: A Topical Tale*, 1962; *Sir Michael and Sir George: A Tale of COMSA and DISCUS and the New Elizabethans*, 1964 (also known as *Sir Michael and Sir George: A Comedy of New Elizabethans*); *Lost Empires: Being Richard Herncastle's Account of His Life on the Variety Stage from November, 1913, to August, 1914, Together with a Prologue and Epilogue*, 1965; *Salt Is Leaving*, 1966; *It's an Old Country*, 1967; *The Image Men: Out of Town and London End*, 1968; *The Carfitt Crisis*, 1975; *Found, Lost, Found: Or, The English Way of Life*, 1976; *My Three Favorite Novels*, 1978.

SHORT FICTION: *The Town Major of Miraucourt*, 1930; *Going Up: Stories and Sketches*, 1950; *The Other Place and Other Stories of the Same Sort*, 1953; *The Carfitt Crisis and Two Other Stories*, 1975.

POETRY: *The Chapman of Rhymes*, 1918.

NONFICTION: *Brief Diversions: Being Tales, Travesties, and Epigrams*, 1922; *Papers from Lilliput*, 1922; *I for One*, 1923; *Figures in Modern Litera-*

ture, 1924; *Essayist Past and Present: A Selection of English Essays*, 1925 (edited); *Fools and Philosophers: A Gallery of Comic Figures from English Literature*, 1925 (published in the United States as *The English Comic Characters*); *Tom Moore's Diary: A Selection*, 1925 (edited); *The Book of Bodley Head Verse*, 1926 (edited); *George Meredith*, 1926; *Talking: An Essay*, 1926; *The English Novel*, 1927, 1935, 1974; *Open House: A Book of Essays*, 1927; *Thomas Love Peacock*, 1927; *Too Many People and Other Reflections*, 1928; *Apes and Angels: A Book of Essays*, 1928; *The Balconinny and Other Essays*, 1929 (published in the United States as *The Balconinny*, 1931); *English Humour*, 1929, 1976; *The Female Spectator: Selections from Mrs. Eliza Heywood's Periodical, 1744-1746*, 1929 (edited); *The Lost Generation: An Armistice Day Article*, 1932; *Self-Selected Essays*, 1932; *Albert Goes Through*, 1933; *English Journey: Being a Rambling but Truthful Account of What One Man Saw and Heard and Felt and Thought During a Journey Through England During the Autumn of the Year 1933*, 1934; *Four-in-Hand*, 1934; *Midnight on the Desert: A Chapter of Autobiography*, 1937 (published in the United States as *Midnight on the Desert: Being an Excursion into Autobiography During a Winter in America, 1935-1936*); *Rain upon Godshill: A Further Chapter of Autobiography*, 1939; *Our Nation's Heritage*, 1939 (edited); *Britain Speaks*, 1940; *Postscripts*, 1940 (radio talks); *Out of the People*, 1941; *Britain at War*, 1942; *British Women Go to War*, 1943; *The Man-Power Story*, 1943; *Here Are Your Answers*, 1944; *The New Citizen*, 1944; *Letter to a Returning Serviceman*, 1945; *Russian Journey*, 1946; *The Secret Dream: An Essay on Britain, America, and Russia*, 1946; *The Arts Under Socialism: Being a Lecture Given to the Fabian Society, with a Postscript on What Government Should Do for the Arts Here and Now*, 1947; *Scenes of London Life, from "Sketches by Boz" by Charles Dickens*, 1947 (edited); *Theatre Outlook*, 1947; *Delight*, 1949; *Journey down a Rainbow*, 1955 (with Jacquetta Hawkes); *All About Ourselves and Other Essays*, 1956; *The Writer in a Changing Society*, 1956; *The Art of the Dramatist: A Lecture Together with Appendices and Discursive Notes*, 1957; *The Best of Leacock*, 1957 (edited); *The Bodley Head Leacock*, 1957; *Thoughts in the Wilderness*, 1957; *Topside: Or, The Future of England, a Dialogue*, 1958; *The Story of Theatre*, 1959; *Four English Novels*, 1960 (edited); *Literature and Western Man*, 1960; *William Hazlitt*, 1960; *Four English Biographies*, 1961 (edited); *Charles Dickens: A Pictorial Biography*, 1962; *Margin Released: A Writer's Reminiscences and Reflections*, 1962; *Adventures in English Literature*, 1963 (edited); *The English Comic Characters*, 1963; *Man and Time*, 1964; *An Everyman Anthology*, 1966 (edited); *The Moments and Other Pieces*, 1966; *All England Listened: J. B. Priestley's Wartime Broadcasts*, 1968; *Essays of Five Decades*, 1968 (Susan Cooper, editor); *Trumpets over the Sea: Being a Rambling and Egotistical Account of the London Symphony Orchestra's Engagement at Daytona*

Beach, Florida, in July-August, 1967, 1968; *The Prince of Pleasure and His Regency, 1811-1820*, 1969; *Anton Chekhov*, 1970; *The Edwardians*, 1970; *Over the Long High Wall: Some Reflections and Speculations on Life, Death, and Time*, 1972; *Victoria's Heyday*, 1972; *The English*, 1973; *Outcries and Asides*, 1974; *A Visit to New Zealand, Particular Pleasures: Being a Personal Record of Some Varied Arts and Many Different Artists*, 1974; *The Happy Dream: An Essay*, 1976; *Instead of the Trees*, 1977 (autobiography).

SCREENPLAY: *Last Holiday*, 1950.

CHILDREN'S LITERATURE: *Snoggle*, 1972.

Bibliography

Atkins, John. *J. B. Priestley: The Last of the Sages.* New York: Riverrun Press, 1981. Priestley's extraordinary outputs defies analysis in any depth in a single volume with a wide focus on all the genres with which the prolific writer dealt. Atkin's attempt to illustrate Priestley's development as essayist, critic, novelist, dramatist, autobiographer, social commentator, historian, and travel writer in a "leap-frogging method" leads inevitably to overlapping and repetition. The 309-page book is most useful on the political, social, and economic background of the late 1920's and 1930's, the period of Priestley's most significant contributions to literature.

Braine, John. *J. B. Priestley.* London: Weidenfeld & Nicolson, 1978. An appreciative, informal assessment of Priestley's major works in various genres, written by a successful novelist with an unusual point of view. Braine knew Priestley's world intimately, and both writers were natives of Bradford.

Brome, Vincent. *J. B. Priestley.* London: Hamish Hamilton, 1988. In a full-scale biography (486 pages) written after Priestley's death, Brome offers an affectionate but candid portrait of the writer in public and private life. Brome rightly argues that the prolific writer has been denied his proper niche by overly harsh critics who do not deal fairly with those who write for a wide, general audience. Brome points to the popularization of Carl Jung's theories as an important aspect of Priestley's work.

DeVitis, A. A., and Albert E. Kalson. *J. B. Priestley.* Boston: Twayne, 1980. After a biographical chapter that includes a discussion of Priestley's time theories, the 257-page book divides into two sections, the first half dealing with Priestley as novelist, the latter half dealing with Priestley as dramatist. All Priestley's works in the two genres are discussed, the more significant ones in some detail. The volume, which underscores Priestley's view that humankind must work in harmony as a community, includes a chronology of the important events in the writer's life and a useful bibliography.

Klein, Holger. *J. B. Priestley's Plays.* New York: St. Martin's Press, 1988.

Klein states that his goal is "to further an understanding" of Priestley's "dramatic objectives and methods," but his seeming inability to differentiate between Priestley the serious dramatist (*Eden End, Time and the Conways*) and Priestley the occasional hack working to order (*Mystery at Greenfingers*) occasionally invalidates his findings in the confusing first section of the book that deals with dramatic structure. Klein's 315-page study is more useful in its latter half in its discussion of Priestley's ideas concerning contemporary issues, pointing especially to *The Linden Tree* as the dramatists condemnation of Great Britain's post-World War II malaise.

Lloyd Evans, Gareth. *J. B. Priestley: The Dramatist.* London: Heinemann, 1964. Devoted entirely to Priestley's plays, this book was published long before Priestley stopped writing, but it provides in-depth analyses of the dramatist's finest contributions to the genre. Offering praise where it is deserved, Lloyd Evans is not blind to Priestley's occasional shortcomings, faulting dialogue that sometimes "does not penetrate deep into the recesses" of the characters' minds and feelings, but instead "reports."

Albert E. Kalson

DAVID RABE

Born: Dubuque, Iowa; March 10, 1940

Principal drama

Sticks and Bones, pr. 1969, pb. 1972; *The Basic Training of Pavlo Hummel*, pr. 1971, pb. 1973; *The Orphan*, pr. 1973, pb. 1975; *In the Boom Boom Room*, pr. 1974, pb. 1975 (originally as *Boom Boom Room*, pr. 1973); *The Burning*, pr. 1974; *Streamers*, pr. 1976, pb. 1977; *Goose and Tomtom*, pr. 1982, pb. 1986; *Hurlyburly*, pr. 1984, pb. 1985; *Those the River Keeps*, pr. 1991.

Other literary forms

David Rabe is known primarily for his plays and screenplays.

Achievements

While the aesthetic effectiveness of Rabe's dramas remains a matter for discussion and debate, it is an easier task to place his work within the context of his twentieth century contemporaries and their concerns. Modern drama asserts, among other fundamental precepts, that the notion of heroism is outdated and that the principle of the individual's alienation from the community provides the normative social standard. In his plays of disorder, violence, and lack of choice—in his "war" plays, in other words—Rabe conforms to the prevailing tradition as he addresses both psychological and political issues.

Like Eugene O'Neill, Tennessee Williams, and Arthur Miller, Rabe works on both the symbolic, or nonrealistic, and the naturalistic, or realistic, levels. Like Edward Albee, he uses surrealist or absurdist elements as he explores the implications of the failure of human contact, the enervation of American social values, the interplay between past and present, and the overwhelming finality of death. His misfits, like those of Lanford Wilson, endure a course of failure that he ordains for them, and Rabe attempts, as does Arthur Kopit, to chart their psychological landscapes as they struggle with the perennial question of identity. As Sam Shepard reveals the distorted, destructive fabric of family relationships and the commercialized corruption of American society, so does Rabe attempt to account for the same bewildering phenomena.

Although Rabe's characters exist too firmly in an abstracted, topical dimension, his ritualistic evocation of their alienated conditions functions, in an inverse manner, to call attention to their need for genuine human interaction. If he is not as successful as many of his contemporaries in sustaining dialogue with his audience, if the impact of his works is not as likely to endure, still, in his plays David Rabe asks significant questions.

Rabe has been the recipient of many awards. *The Basic Training of Pavlo Hummel* received the Obie Award, the Drama Desk Award, and the award of the Variety Critics Poll. The Outer Circle Critics Award and the New York Drama Critics Circle citation went to *Sticks and Bones*. Rabe received the National Institute of Arts and Letters Award in 1974 and a second award from the prestigious New York Drama Critics Circle in 1976 for *Streamers*.

Biography

David Rabe was born on March 10, 1940, in Dubuque, Iowa, where he attended Roman Catholic parochial schools. He began to write short stories and plays while an undergraduate at Loras College, a Catholic institution in Dubuque, from which he was graduated in 1962 with a B.A. in English. He was drafted into the army in 1965 and served with a hospital support unit at Long Binh, South Vietnam; while he did not go into actual combat himself, he observed many casualties. After his discharge in early 1967, he resumed his interrupted graduate studies at Villanova University and earned a master's degree in 1968. While at Villanova, he wrote the draft scripts of *The Basic Training of Pavlo Hummel* and *Sticks and Bones*, inspired by his experiences of Vietnam and then of America as encountered by a returned Vietnam veteran. Under the auspices of Joseph Papp's New York Shakespeare Festival, *The Basic Training of Pavlo Hummel* opened in New York at the Public Theatre on May 20, 1971, with *Sticks and Bones* following, also at the Public Theatre, on November 7 of the same year. With these productions, Rabe was saluted by many critics as a most promising young dramatist.

Rabe's third play, *The Orphan*, a puzzling retelling of the dramas of Aeschylus that made repeated allusions to Vietnam, was roundly criticized. With his fourth play, *In the Boom Boom Room* (originally produced in 1973 as *Boom Boom Room* and later revised and retitled), Rabe turned his focus away from the Vietnam experience to depict the life of a young go-go dancer, but the play received a lukewarm response. In 1976, though, Rabe returned to the Vietnam War as the setting for *Streamers*, which again brought him wide praise.

Rabe's long professional relationship with Joseph Papp and the Public Theatre in New York was jeopardized in 1982, when a production of *Goose and Tomtom* was put into rehearsal at the Public Theatre but was disavowed by Rabe because of aesthetic differences in interpretation. "I despaired of it," said Rabe, when Papp misinterpreted the relationship between the two title characters.

Despite the critical and commercial success of *Hurlyburly* on Broadway in 1984, it did not receive any major awards (although Judith Ivey won a Tony Award for her performance in the play). Rabe was dissatisfied with

Mike Nichols' direction of the production and reworked the play for a later production (1989) under his own direction. After six years of silence, except for screenplay work such as *Casualties of War* (1989), Rabe's play *Those the River Keeps* was produced in 1991 by the McCarter Theatre. It continues the story of Phil, the main character of *Hurlyburly*.

Rabe is married to actress Jill Clayburgh, who starred in the 1982 *I'm Dancing As Fast As I Can*, a Rabe screenplay.

Analysis

The body of work which David Rabe has produced thus far is closely linked thematically to the late 1960's and early 1970's in America. He expresses this turbulent era of the debilitating war in Vietnam, racial strife in the streets, the horrific murders by Charles Manson's clan, the puzzling generation gap, and the confusing sexual revolution as a dramatic world of violent confrontation. For the individual living in this setting, its most salient features are racial and sexual turmoil, family disintegration, social isolation, and personal inarticulateness. Whether the scene is an army barracks room, a middle-class American home, the ancient Greece of Aeschylus' *Oresteia*, or a slimy bar in Philadelphia, Rabe's characters live on a metaphoric battlefield. His plays, then, are war plays, and his protagonists lose their separate struggles with dispiriting inevitability. The chaos of their lives is figured, institutionalized, and sometimes justified by ritualistic activities that are symbolic of their alienation and lack of choice rather than of the communal experience and support that ritual ordinarily celebrates.

The title of *Streamers* suggests the bleak vision of Rabe's work: A "streamer" is a parachute which unexpectedly fails to open, a fragile ribbon of silk that simply trails the unlucky jumper as he plummets toward his death. As he leaps out of the secure womb of the airplane, he is born, after a few seconds, into a brief life characterized by the terror of circumstance, the rule of irrationality, and the absence of alternatives to the destruction awaiting him. There is no possibility of introspection or insight and no reality except for the unambiguous fact of personal annihilation. Like the parachutist, the main characters in Rabe's plays are hurriedly discovering death.

Although *The Basic Training of Pavlo Hummel*, *Sticks and Bones*, and *Streamers*, with their episodes of ritualistic violence, are often referred to as Rabe's "Vietnam trilogy," only the first includes actual combat, and that only briefly. Rabe uses the war in Vietnam as a generalized background for his presentation of the violence endemic to American life. In response to critics who proposed the "antiwar" label as an appropriate description of his work, Rabe asserted that he expected to achieve no political effect but simply sought to identify and diagnose the informing cultural and social phenomena around him.

In *The Basic Training of Pavlo Hummel*, the time-honored ritual of army basic training generates the controlling metaphor: the four-beat cadence of a basic training company's marching and singing, the formal dance of bayonet practice, the impending trainee proficiency test. Into this arena the classic loser Pavlo enters, leaving his dreary existence behind and seeking the clear confirmation of physical courage and sexual virility which he expects military heroism to afford him. The two-act play opens with Pavlo's ironic, nonheroic death in a Saigon whorehouse, following an argument with an army sergeant over a prostitute. The play then flashes back to portray the stages of Pavlo's journey to this grim end. The drill sergeant's tower, a constant reminder of army ritual, commands the stage.

Unfortunately for Pavlo, his pathetic expectations of army life clash with everything the audience sees about the army and the war. His enthusiasm for a career as an army "lifer" and his desire to excel in the community that is superficially symbolized by army ritual actually exclude him from his fellow draftees and from a realistic perspective on the war itself. As a foil to almost everyone else in the play, Pavlo is most clearly exemplified by his consistent naïveté and stupid fervor. For example, he persistently volunteers for menial duties and eagerly performs supplemental physical training. He takes solitary bayonet and port arms practice when he should be in formation and anxiously studies the conduct manual for the upcoming proficiency test.

In act 2, Pavlo enjoys the sexual experience that eluded him on his leave, despite his snappy dress uniform. The sergeant drills the men on one side of the stage as Pavlo makes four-beat love to Yen on the other. Reluctantly serving as a medic in a field hospital, Pavlo refuses to comprehend the vivid example of a soldier blown into a living stump. Only after he is actually wounded in combat does Pavlo recognize the vicious truth of the infantryman's plight on the field. Whereas he formerly associated acts of violence in the barracks or on the battlefield with an affirmation of manhood, Pavlo simply wants to go home after he is wounded for the third time. Rewarded, instead, with a Purple Heart, he retreats to the whorehouse for a dalliance with Yen and the assignation with the grenade that finally kills him.

From start to finish, Pavlo Hummel is doomed—as trainee, medic, or combat infantryman. Army ritual overtly offers community, song, and some humor as both a mask and an excuse for the violence which awaits Pavlo. Life for the enlisted man in Vietnam, however, actually means every man for himself. The interweaving of past and present, the use of simultaneous action, and the play's surrealist and absurdist elements demonstrate Pavlo's self-centered confusion and his failure to develop. In some respects, he is so one-dimensional that it is difficult to maintain sympathy for him.

Like *The Basic Training of Pavlo Hummel*, *Sticks and Bones* begins with the ending, the ritualistic suicide of the protagonist David, a blinded Vietnam veteran. Shockingly, his father, mother, and younger brother encourage and assist him in this act. As Pavlo's army "family" rebuffs him, so do Ozzie, Harriet, and Ricky reject David. Unlike Pavlo, however, David denies his family, too; they mutually repel one another. In his naming of the characters, Rabe parodies the popular situation comedy *The Adventures of Ozzie and Harriet*: This middle-class American family is the antithesis of the television Nelsons.

The ritual matter of *Sticks and Bones* arises from what Rabe considers the symbols of modern American culture: racism and television. Both destroy communication and, thus, indicate the mutual alienation of David and his family. Television offers a desirable fantasy life redolent of money and materialism. Related to sexual fear and insecurity, racism answers the need to feel superior to some group. From the instant when David is virtually delivered home, he and his family are strangers to one another. Ozzie even considers checking his son's dental records to verify his identity.

Although he is physically blind, David's moral vision has been expanded by his experiences in Vietnam and also by his sense of guilt over the Vietnamese girl, Zung, whom he loved but, typically, deserted. A symbol of continuity between his past and present, the wraith-like Zung appears intermittently throughout the play and, until the climax, is "seen" by David only. She embodies the immediate motivation for the mission he assumes in his parents' home, as their moral blindness is exemplified by virulent racial and sexual prejudice. Their contempt for the Vietnamese recalls that of the soldiers in *The Basic Training of Pavlo Hummel* in its perverted preoccupation with sex. Neither Ozzie nor Harriet can tolerate the notion that David might have engendered children with yellow faces and, worse, that he might have brought them home. Both in the field and at home, Rabe charges, the Vietnamese are despised by the Americans who profess to help them.

David's abrasive presence and his withering accusations cause his parents' superficial veneer of middle-class respectability to blister and peel away. Ozzie is deeply troubled that his combat experience has been confined to his safe childhood, when he regularly beat up "Ole Fat Kramer." During World War II, his army service consisted of truck maintenance. Operating as a catalytic agent, then, David releases his father's suppressed capacity for violence. Zung becomes visible to Ozzie, who, refusing to "see" her, nevertheless strangles her. Rick suggests that David should cut his wrists, and Harriet provides pans and towels so that the blood will not stain the carpet. With this ritualistic self-sacrifice, David is exorcised from the mainstream of the middle-class consciousness and can pose no further challenge to the self-deluded but triumphant American way of life.

In this grotesque family portrait, Rabe demonstrates that domestic violence is as terrible as the military violence in Vietnam. Through language and action, he indicates the irreconcilable division within the family and charges that racism was a basic cause of the war in Vietnam. The polarization of the family, concurrently, is a source of the play's most disabling flaw. The dramatist would have his audience simplistically concede that a blinded Vietnam veteran, by definition, possesses greater moral stature than his family, that he is entitled, because of his combat experiences, to instruct them in moral concerns. David's sufferings, however, have not enhanced his capacity for understanding and compassion, the requisites for the moral stature he assumes, but have only refined his ability to hate. Like Ozzie, Harriet, and Rick, David remains a cipher despite the truth of much of his indictment of American life.

Additionally, the names of the characters finally detract from Rabe's message as well because their names isolate them from the audience. The television Nelson clan, in all its saccharine perfection, is so one-dimensional a target that the playwright's generalizations about middle-class America become increasingly difficult to accept. Nevertheless, taken in conjunction with *The Basic Training of Pavlo Hummel*, *Sticks and Bones* presents a disturbing portrayal of the divisive features of American military and domestic experience in the late 1960's.

The Orphan is Rabe's most intellectually complex play, but it is marred by thematic diffuseness. Instead of using modern war as the background, the playwright employs Aeschylus' *Oresteia*, with its informing theme of violence within the family, as a framework for his consideration of the related phenomena of Vietnam and My Lai, governmental apathy, commercial obsession, and the Manson murders. As in *Sticks and Bones*, the source of all corruption resides in the family. Touchstones of modern American culture are sex, drugs, business, and killing. The rigid progression of cause to effect enslaves men, and past becomes present as men and women seem literally born to kill.

Murder is so common that it achieves the status of ritual, its rites observable in governmental policy statements, the entrails of birds, current scientific explanations, and hallucinatory drug rampages—all the same and all unavoidable. As a part of this ritual, language itself becomes automatic and thus debased: It helps to isolate people from one another by preserving the gaping distinctions between them. As such, it, too, is a blunt instrument of destruction.

Act 1 concerns the sacrifice of Iphegenia over the impassioned opposition of Clytemnestra 1 and the resultant murder of Agamemnon by Clytemnestra 2 and Aegisthus; act 2 entails Orestes' revenge upon his mother and her lover. From the tub in which Agamemnon is slaughtered, Orestes is born in act 2, blood-soaked and wrapped in the placenta-like net in which his father died: Life's violent course is ordained from the moment of birth. In this same tub, the bound Clytemnestras—their simultaneous presence indicative of the identity between past and present—will be killed by Orestes. The womb, then, greatly resembles a grave.

Orestes' revenge against Aegisthus reiterates both the Manson murders and the My Lai massacre; depravity and murder are nearly sanctified by their regularity in this world. Tainted by violence, Orestes is left literally suspended between the uncaring gods of heaven and the waiting Furies on earth, abandoned and deluded.

Although *The Orphan* makes provocative statements about modern American society, it founders upon its diffusion of images and upon its categorical statement that America is a murderous wasteland. If Orestes' revenge is justifiable according to the myth, then the Manson murders and My Lai cannot be explained according to the same criterion. The audience withdraws because, to an even greater extent than in *The Basic Training of Pavlo Hummel* and *Sticks and Bones*, the characters are totally manipulated in the service of the prevailing doctrine. Without alternative or ambiguity, they and *The Orphan* become morally artificial and intellectually confused. The spurting gore undercuts its own effect.

With *In the Boom Boom Room*, the scene shifts to a deteriorating, neon-lit section of Philadelphia in the mid-1960's. Once more, sex, violence, racism, self-deception, and inarticulateness are the interrelated themes. Although Vietnam is not a factor in this play, the characters live in an urban jungle where the strong defeat and brutalize the weak. Chrissy, an aspiring go-go dancer who wants to become good enough to succeed in New York, is doomed in her struggle for individuality because she is a vulnerable woman in a man's world. Ironically, the lives of the various men in Chrissy's sphere are as rigidly circumscribed and hopeless as hers.

Chrissy is Rabe's only female protagonist, but she has much in common with her male counterparts. Past and present intermingle to show that she is victimized by everyone she knows: her parents, her boyfriends, her lover, her homosexual neighbor, and the bisexual dance captain at the Boom Boom Room. Like Rabe's other protagonists, she has little self-awareness.

With their associations of physical and mental imprisonment, spiritual isolation, and sexual exhibitionism, the go-go cages provide the continuous backdrop for the action. The controlling metaphor—and the ritual—grows out of the animalistic, solitary go-go dance itself. To be able to perform the Monkey and the Jerk fluidly and sensually will enable Chrissy to transfer to the elite realm of the go-go world, but the names of these dances symbolize the degradation that is her actual present and her future lot. Everyone wants something from her, most often sex, but no one loves her, starting with the mother who nearly aborted her.

A thief and a drunk like her father, Chrissy's brutal, emotionally impotent lover, Al, destroys her professional hopes and, concomitantly, her ability to order her life. In an argument suffused with the sexism and racism also fundamental to *The Basic Training of Pavlo Hummel* and *Sticks and Bones*, Al beats Chrissy bloody. In the final scene of the play, she has come to New York, but as a masked topless dancer. She is completely anonymous, alone, and dehumanized.

In the Boom Boom Room is like *The Orphan* in its consistent despair about the human condition, but it lacks the intellectual gamesmanship which is the major interest of *The Orphan*. Rabe's reflections on violence in modern America as seen through an Oresteian glass invite the audience—or more effectively, perhaps, the reader—to become sufficiently engaged by his philosophical comparisons between ancient and contemporary, mythical and mundane to treat them skeptically. The action of *In the Boom Boom Room*, however, adheres to a static, linear structure in which Chrissy does not develop as a personality but in which the quality of her life inexorably deteriorates. Although it is finally difficult to sympathize with Pavlo and David, one can discern a measure of conflict and vitality in their lives. Chrissy never has a chance.

Rabe returns to the thematic background of the American experience in Vietnam in *Streamers*, his most persuasive play because it is his most straightforward. It concentrates exclusively upon the interactions of four young army enlisted men, each of whom exemplifies a different facet of American society. Foregoing the flashbacks and the special effects of his earlier plays, Rabe here achieves sustained focus: The four characters form a desperate Family of Man in the barracks room.

Their clashing ideas about war, sex, and racism transform this barracks crucible into a battlefield upon which violence is as certain, and as deadly, as the violence which awaits them in Vietnam. Their metaphorical parachutes have failed to open, and the matter of the play chronicles their fall to earth, streamers floating uselessly above them. Two older sergeants, Cokes and Rooney, one suffering from leukemia and the other an alcoholic, represent the general way that the four recruits are destined to go. As the exhausted members of the previous generation of cannon fodder, they introduce the song, set to the tune of Stephen Foster's "Beautiful Dreamer," which provides the ritualistic foundation of the play: "Beautiful streamer,/ Open for me,/ The sky is above me,/ But no canopy."

Like the parachutist and like Rabe's other characters, Roger, Billy, Richie, and Carlyle have no control over their lives. For them, there is no escape from the barracks except through violence. If they survive the battlefield in the barracks, then the elephant traps in Vietnam loom before them. Isolated from the external world, they find no philosophical, racial, or sexual comradeship within the army either.

For example, Cokes and Rooney are embittered career men whose prolonged experiences of combat in World War II cause them simultaneously to envy and despise the two-year recruits. Blacks, represented by Roger and Carlyle, and whites, represented by Billy and Richie, live together warily, with ready recourse to a switchblade or an epithet. The homosexual Richie belongs to the army's least visible, most defensive, minority. Rabe clearly establishes these categories within the army of the Vietnam era, but he succeeds in transcending them to an extent that he does not achieve in *The Basic Training of Pavlo Hummel* and *Sticks and Bones*: The army in *Streamers* is a credible microcosm of American society at large.

Roger and Billy, black and white, exemplify the conventional middle-class stance. They ambitiously want to leave this holding company and get into the real army, yet it is understandably difficult for them to absorb the fierce prospect of Vietnam into their lives. Carlyle is a ghetto black terrified of the deadly fate which the army obviously, and casually, reserves for him, and Richie is a spoiled white in the process of adjusting to his homosexuality. They constitute a counterpoint to Roger and Billy, and their personal relationship inspires the crisis. Carlyle is the patented Rabean grenade who shatters the delicate equilibrium achieved by the other three; in this sense, his function resembles that of Pavlo and David. Alienated by his race, education, and social status, Carlyle loathes American society in general and the war in particular.

The two outcasts, Carlyle and Richie, deserted by their fathers and by conventional society, connect in a sexual relationship born as much from lonely despair as from physical craving. Roger can accept this situation, while Billy, on the other hand, is enraged by this desecration of his barracks "house." His aggressive cries of outrage abruptly end as Carlyle repeatedly stabs him in the stomach in a fatal parody of the sexual act. The drunken Rooney literally stumbles into the fight's aftermath and inadvertently becomes Carlyle's next victim. As in all of Rabe's plays, mindless violence prevails.

Richie and Roger, white and black, homosexual and heterosexual, have survived the barracks, but Vietnam, with its myriad opportunities for the unanticipated situations which produce streamers, awaits. If they survive Vietnam, there is always, as *Sticks and Bones* reveals, the home front.

There are no simple explanations for the characters' motivations and actions in *Streamers*, and thus Rabe surpasses his previous work. He blends the themes of war, sex, racism, family, and resultant chaos without relying upon a schematic, predictable plot, exhibited at its least effective in *In the Boom Boom Room*.

Although *Streamers* is a sounder play, structurally, than Rabe's prior dramas, it partakes of a full measure of their informing cynicism and despair. In all of his plays through *Streamers*, the dramatist establishes some expression of ritual as a reflection of disorder. Men live in a world so irrational that there is virtually no order to subvert. This ethos contributes much to the spectacular, bloody stageworthiness of the plays and is, further, a direct function of their topicality. Their effectiveness depends crucially on an audience's knowledge, appreciation, and, preferably, experience of American political, social, and cultural history in the mid- and late 1960's and early 1970's.

This topicality is the source of both the strength and the weakness of Rabe's plays. For those who lived through the Vietnam era, the plays have a visceral, emotional impact that compensates, to some degree, for the stylization of the characters, their lack of alternatives, and their failure to develop. At the same time, however, like Rabe's characters, the plays become victims of this topical concentration. With the exception of *Streamers*, they cannot transcend their particular time and place.

Rabe's *Hurlyburly* appeared in New York in 1984 to general critical acclaim. This play marks both a continuation from and a break with his artistic past. The battlefield moves from Vietnam to the vicious jungle of Hollywood, but the prevailing violence and the fragmentation of the characters' lives preclude the need for even a gesture toward the sort of ironic ritual which pervades his earlier plays.

The bungalow shared by Eddie and Mickey, two casting directors, provides a drug-inspired arena for the testing conflicts which are acted out between the male characters and, even more hideously, for their brutal expressions of fear and hatred for the various women who pliantly stumble into their lives. The world of *Hurlyburly* lacks moral focus of any sort. As Rabe stated in an interview in *The New York Times* that accompanied the play's opening, the contemporary scene offers "philosophies that aren't philosophies, answers that aren't answers, one pharmaceutical solution after another." Repellently dazzling as the play's language is, it reiterates the playwright's recurring theme: the willed failure to communicate, to care.

Those the River Keeps focuses on the character Phil, an ex-convict who had also appeared as a struggling actor in *Hurlyburly*. In *Those the River Keeps*, Phil is confronted by an acquaintance from his criminal past who attempts to lure him back to a life of crime. Rabe once described the play as an "invitation/seduction" and remarked cryptically, "It's literal in one way, and in another way it's not."

Rabe's intense, critical reflections on the interrelatedness of war, sex, racism, the family, past, and present as they define the contemporary American battlefield are frequently provocative. His dramatic world of streamers is, however, all of a piece. Lacking complexity and nuance, it only sporadically achieves, beyond the transitory moment, the sustained dialogue between dramatist and playgoer or reader that is the essence of great art.

Other major works

SCREENPLAYS: *I'm Dancing As Fast As I Can*, 1982 (based on the novel by Barbara Gordon); *Streamers*, 1983 (based on his play of the same name); *Casualties of War*, 1989.

Bibliography

Bigsby, C. W. E. *Beyond Broadway*. Vol. 3 in *A Critical Introduction to Twentieth-Century American Drama*. Cambridge, England: Cambridge University Press, 1985. The introduction to part 5, "The Theatre of Commitment," includes a long discussion of Rabe's work. Bigsby is respectful of the power and importance of Rabe's work through *Streamers*. He says that Rabe's Vietnam plays are less "about war than about loneliness and self-betrayal; less an account of political perfidy than of the failure of private morality."

Cohn, Ruby. *New American Dramatists, 1960-1990*. 2d ed. New York: St. Martin's Press, 1991. Cohn once called this chapter "Narrower Straits" but renamed it "Roaming Around" to point at an orientation away from Broadway conventions in the plays of Rabe, Ronald Ribman, John Guare, and David Hwang. Notes the revision of the early version of *In the Boom Boom Room* in 1986 but is silent regarding the hiatus from *Hurlyburly* to 1990.

Herman, William. *Understanding Contemporary American Drama*. Columbia: University of South Carolina Press, 1987. Places *Hurlyburly* in the Shakespearean context of despair as an aftereffect of war. Discusses some individual works at length but calls others "a small body of less assured and less coherent drama," including Rabe's favorite, *Goose and Tomtom*. Good bibliography of primary and secondary sources.

Kolin, Philip C. *David Rabe: A Stage History and a Primary and Secondary Bibliography*. New York: Garland, 1988. The first source for factual information and continuing study of the playwright, including a chronology of productions. The secondary bibliography is valuable for pursuing criticism on individual plays and reviews of first productions.

Savran, David. *In Their Own Words: Contemporary American Playwrights*. New York: Theatre Communications Group, 1988. Rabe is interviewed here in 1986 after the success and anguish of *Hurlyburly*. The brief biographical notes include discussions of his writing habits, his relations with directors, and his problems with Mike Nichols' direction of *Hurlyburly*.

Zinman, Toby Silverman, ed. *David Rabe: A Casebook*. New York: Garland, 1991. Contains nineteen articles, including an interview. Separate chapters provide Rabe's comments on Vietnam, *Streamers*, *Sticks and Bones*, and *Goose and Tomtom*.

Janet S. Hertzbach
(Updated by *Thomas J. Taylor*
and *Robert McClenaghan*)

TERENCE RATTIGAN

Born: London, England; June 10, 1911
Died: Bermuda; November 30, 1977

Principal drama

First Episode, pr. 1933 (with Philip Heimann); *French Without Tears*, pr. 1936, pb. 1937; *Flare Path*, pr., pb. 1942; *While the Sun Shines*, pr. 1943, pb. 1944; *Love in Idleness*, pr. 1944, pb. 1945 (also as *O Mistress Mine*, pr., pb. 1946); *The Winslow Boy*, pr., pb. 1946; *Playbill: The Browning Version and Harlequinade*, pr. 1948, pb. 1949 (2 one-acts); *Adventure Story*, pr. 1949, pb. 1950; *The Deep Blue Sea*, pr., pb. 1952; *The Collected Plays of Terence Rattigan*, pb. 1953-1978 (4 volumes; Hamish Hamilton, editor); *The Sleeping Prince*, pr. 1953, pb. 1954; *Separate Tables: Table by the Window and Table Number Seven*, pr. 1954, pb. 1955 (2 playlets; commonly known as *Separate Tables*); *Ross*, pr., pb. 1960; *A Bequest to the Nation*, pr., pb. 1970 (adaptation of Rattigan's teleplay *Nelson*, pr. 1964); *In Praise of Love: Before Dawn and After Lydia*, pb. 1973, pr. 1974 (as *In Praise of Love*); *The Winslow Boy*, pb. 1973; *Cause Célèbre*, pr. 1977, pb. 1978 (adaptation of his radio play); *Plays*, pb. 1981-1985 (2 volumes).

Other literary forms

Terence Rattigan wrote many screenplays, including a number of adaptations of his own plays. For the film of *The Browning Version*, he won the 1951 Cannes Film Festival Award for best screenplay. In 1958, the screenplay of *Separate Tables*, adapted from Rattigan's play in collaboration with John Gay, was nominated for an Academy Award. The triumvirate of Rattigan, cowriter/producer Anatole de Grunwald, and director Anthony Asquith created a number of films, including *Quiet Wedding* (1941, based on Esther McCracken's play), *English Without Tears* (1944, based on *French Without Tears*; also as *Her Man Gilbey*), *The Way to the Stars* (1945; also as *Johnny in the Clouds*, 1946), *While the Sun Shines* (1946, adapted from Rattigan's play), and *The Winslow Boy* (1948, adapted from Rattigan's play). These films were significant contributions to Great Britain's postwar film renaissance. *The Sound Barrier* (1952; also as *Breaking the Sound Barrier*), from Rattigan's screenplay, is considered by some aficionados the finest film ever made about aviation. His best-known films are probably *Separate Tables* (for which David Niven won an Academy Award as Best Actor), *The Prince and the Showgirl* (1957, starring Marilyn Monroe and Sir Laurence Olivier in the adaptation of Rattigan's stage comedy *The Sleeping Prince*), and *The VIPs* (1963, with an all-star cast headed by Elizabeth Taylor and Richard Burton).

Of Rattigan's seven original television scripts and one radio script, *The*

Final Test (1951) was released as a film in 1954; *Nelson—A Portrait in Miniature* (1964) was adapted as the play *A Bequest to the Nation* in 1970, with the film version appearing in 1973 under that title; and the radio script *Cause Célèbre* (1975) was adapted for the stage.

Rattigan also wrote numerous theoretical essays. Most important to his career were "Concerning the Play of Ideas" and "The Play of Ideas," both published in 1950 in *The New Statesman and Nation*, and the prefaces he wrote for the first three volumes of *The Collected Plays*, published by Hamish Hamilton. In *The New Statesman and Nation*, Rattigan defended story and character—as opposed to intellectual debate and propagandizing—as the timeless values of drama; he was rebutted, wholly or partly, by James Bridie, Benn Levy, Peter Ustinov, Sean O'Casey, Christopher Fry, and George Bernard Shaw. In his second and third prefaces, Rattigan invented a prototypical theatergoer, Aunt Edna, intended as a humorous salute to the good common sense of audiences throughout the ages but attacked as evidence of his own pandering to lowbrow sensibilities. His theoretical essays are too gentlemanly in tone to persuade with the sheer moral fervor of Shaw's, yet Rattigan was as sincere in his convictions and as true to his own values. His championship of the craft of playwriting and of the judgment of the dedicated theatergoer, his exploration in his first preface of the significance of dramatic implication, his musings in American newspaper articles on why plays suffer a "sea change" when produced in foreign countries, and his concept of the "farce of character" (in a 1947 *Strand* magazine article) are all valuable contributions to the literature of dramatic theory.

Achievements

The first author ever to have had two plays (*French Without Tears* and *While the Sun Shines*) run for more than one thousand performances each on London's West End, Rattigan was one of the most commercially successful playwrights in theater history. With striking versatility, he achieved his goal of moving audiences to laughter or tears in romantic comedy, comedy of manners, farce, fantasy, history plays, courtroom drama, and dramas about troubled middle-class characters. He also attracted many of the finest acting and directing talents of his period. Roles in Rattigan plays made stars of such young actors as Rex Harrison, Paul Scofield, and Kenneth More, and enhanced the careers of such luminaries as Peggy Ashcroft, Sir Laurence Olivier, Sir Alec Guinness, Margaret Sullivan, Margaret Leighton, and Alfred Lunt and Lynn Fontanne (a couple who had enjoyed the longest run of their stage careers in the American version of *Love in Idleness*).

Rattigan's success, however, was often held against him by critics, who did not bother to look beyond the polished surfaces of his plays. Failing to grasp the depth of psychological insight and the serious themes which usually characterized even his light comedies, most critics rated him as a good boulevard playwright at best. During the 1950's and the 1960's, the heyday of the Angry Young Men and the Theater of the Absurd, Rattigan's work was derided as representing the establishment culture that younger playwrights and critics sought to demolish. London revivals of five of his plays between 1970 and 1977, the year of Rattigan's death, led to a greater appreciation of his worth. With the widely hailed National Theatre's production of *Playbill* in 1980 and the Roundabout Theatre Company's acclaimed New York revivals of *The Winslow Boy* in 1980 and *The Browning Version* in 1982, Rattigan began to be recognized as an artist of high stature.

Biography

Terence Mervyn Rattigan was born in Kensington, London, on June 10, 1911, to William Frank and Vera Houston Rattigan, ten days before the coronation of George V. His father, a career diplomat, was a minor functionary in the coronation and his mother missed the ceremony because of her confinement. Forty-two years later, when Rattigan wrote his sophisticated fantasy *The Sleeping Prince* as a *pièce d'occasion* for Elizabeth II's coronation, he said that he used George V's coronation for the background of the play as a present to his mother for having missed the real thing.

Both of Rattigan's parents came from distinguished families of Irish lawyers, a heritage that fascinated Rattigan and showed itself not only in the characters of the lawyers in *The Winslow Boy* and *Cause Célèbre* but also in such scenes as the hotel residents' "trial" of Major Pollock in *Table Number Seven*. Rattigan's father, who failed in his own career and was pensioned off in 1922, hoped that Rattigan would find a career in the diplomatic service.

From early boyhood, however, when his parents first took him to the theater, Rattigan was determined to be a playwright. He hoarded his allowance and sneaked off to the theater, began writing plays at eleven, and read plays avidly while on scholarship at Harrow from 1925 to 1930. At Oxford on a history scholarship, he acted, wrote criticism for the *Cherwell*, and collaborated with fellow student Philip Heimann on a play about Oxonian high jinks and their sad consequences, *First Episode*, which enjoyed respectful reviews and a brief run on the West End in the 1933-1934 season. On the strength of this success, he persuaded his father to give him a modest allowance to enable him to write for two years, at the end of which he either would be a successful playwright or would bow to his parents' wishes for his career.

Rattigan's Oxford years were far from wasted; his reading of history helped inspire his studies of Alexander the Great (*Adventure Story*, 1949),

T. E. Lawrence (*Ross*), and Lord Nelson (*A Bequest to the Nation*), and summers spent taking language courses in Germany and France prompted *French Without Tears*, whose spectacular success enabled Rattigan to win his career gamble with his father. From then until the last decade of his life, even though he suffered his share of flops and personal sorrows, Rattigan was depicted in the press as fortune's favorite, an image enlarged by his exceptional good looks and elegant life-style.

Virtually all of Rattigan's work was influenced directly or indirectly by his personal experience. Several of his wartime plays and film scripts, for example, grew out of his service as a Royal Air Force flight lieutenant. *In Praise of Love* was dually inspired by his friendship with Rex Harrison and Harrison's wife, Kay Kendall, when she was dying of leukemia and by a false diagnosis of leukemia in Rattigan himself in 1962. Examples of more pervasive influences are his parents' unhappy marriage, his attempts to love and be loyal to both his mother and his father, and his own homosexuality. Rattigan's comedies and dramas often feature compassionate portraits of mismatched couples, bewildered youths in contention with their elders, and individuals tortured by sexual repression, deviation, or frustration. Rattigan's protagonists generally meet their problems with the dignity and courage that he brought to his own life, particularly during his two-year battle with bone cancer. After a self-imposed seven-year exile to write film scripts during the period of his greatest vilification by younger critics and colleagues, Rattigan lived to see himself welcomed back into the British theater community with his knighthood in 1971, the beginning of his artistic renaissance through revivals of his earlier plays, and the positive reception of a new work, *Cause Célèbre*, only months before his death.

Analysis

In a 1962 *Theatre Arts* interview, Terence Rattigan told John Simon that playwrights were born Ibsenites or Chekhovians and that he was the former longing to be the latter. In fact, he blended the influences of both. Like Henrik Ibsen in his problem plays, Rattigan reshaped the Scribean well-made play to his own ends, imbuing it with psychological complexity and moral passion. Unlike Ibsen, he seldom allowed his characters to debate ideas and issues, taking instead a firm stand against ideological drama. Like Anton Chekhov, Rattigan focused on the personal problems of predominantly middle-class characters who are left with no neat solutions; his comedies end with a respite instead of a celebration; his dramas, with a delicate balance of losses and gains. Rattigan's characters are, like Chekhov's, bound in a rich tapestry: Their fates are to varying degrees interrelated, but their essential aloneness is poignantly conveyed. Unlike Ibsen or Chekhov, Rattigan was not a radical innovator, and as yet there is no evidence of his direct influence on successors. Each of Rattigan's plays displays innovative touches, however, and the body of his work reveals an artist with a distinct personal vision which he expressed in both the content and the form of his plays.

Rattigan's attacks upon doctrinaire drama and his dismissal by most critics as an ideologically empty playwright are ironic, for his work is deeply ideological. His pervading theme is a passionate defense of the most oppressed minority throughout history: the individual. In a 1982 *Contemporary Review* retrospective, a writer recalled Rattigan's saying: "People should care about people, and I've some doubts that the ideologists do. They may care about the starving millions, but they're not worried too much about those millions' particular concerns." Rattigan was.

All but three of his plays are set in the twentieth century, most in the period from the 1930's to the 1960's. Rattigan captured the bewilderment of people living in a world without a firm moral and social structure to give them a sense of place and security. Theirs is a stark existence where confusion and loneliness predominate, compounded by stale ideas and conventions. The philosophical idea Rattigan implicitly condemned throughout his work was the mind-body dichotomy, or the belief that human beings' physical and spiritual natures are irreconcilable, that one can be satisfied only at the expense of the other, and that spiritual love is superior to physical love. The social conventions Rattigan most abhorred were the prohibition against expressing emotion and the ostracism of individuals for deviating from various norms. His plays show that the individual's best resources are self-reliance and self-respect, understanding and compassion for others, and the healing bonds of kindness and friendship.

Rattigan's characters are influenced by outside factors, but all have a range of choice in their values and actions. His plots delineate the cause-and-effect relationship between the nature of the values that individuals pursue, evade, or betray and their psychological and existential well-being. The form of a Rattigan play is determined by and inseparable from its content. In a *Daily Telegraph* tribute after the playwright's death, William Douglas-Home likened the beauty of Rattigan's structures to those of classical architecture and the symphony. The *Contemporary Review* writer stated that Rattigan's plays have "'good bones'—a prime requisite for aging well." The sinews of his plays are his extraordinarily rich dialogue— naturalistic but so precisely stylized that a few simple words can, as Harold Hobson frequently pointed out, convey a world of meaning. Rattigan's personal signature on the form and content of his work may be seen by surveying one play from each of the five decades of his playwriting career.

Even when one recalls that Rattigan had been writing plays diligently from the age of eleven, the artistic wholeness of *French Without Tears*, his first produced solo effort, seems remarkable. In varying degrees, the characteristics of his body of work are all present in this early work.

The innovative element of this romantic comedy is Rattigan's reversal of the cliché of a femme fatale who turns friends into enemies. At a small language program in France, several young Englishmen try to learn French while one student's alluring sister, Diana, tries to distract them. She entraps Kit, much to the distress of the French tutor's daughter, Jacqueline, and then entices a newly arrived, more mature naval commander. Alan, a diplomat's son yearning to be a novelist (an autobiographical touch), feigns indifference to Diana, cheers Kit, and ridicules the Commander. In a scene reminiscent of the Elyot-Victor clash in Noël Coward's *Private Lives* (pr. 1930), Kit and the Commander fight until they discover that Diana has used the same "line" on them. They unite in friendship, accompanied by Alan, and confront Diana with her perfidy. She confounds them all by declaring that she really loves Alan. Kit turns to Jacqueline and Diana chases Alan as he, taking the Commander's advice, bolts to London to tell his father that he is taking up writing instead of diplomacy. While structured on the Chekhovian model of short scenes between groups of characters, building up a central situation through accumulation of detail, the plot has the vitality of a mixed-doubles grudge match in tennis, with changes of partners topped by one player taking off after the referee.

The play examines the relationship of love and sex at a depth unusual in light comedy. Alan and Kit are caught in the mind-body dichotomy, desiring an attractive girl with little character and feeling only friendship for the plainer but more worthy Jacqueline. At the end, she and Kit decide timidly to see if love and friendship, sex and liking, can mix. For all of his sophisticated airs, Alan is a little English gentleman who can sail only calm waters; he feels comfortable in friendship with Jacqueline but panics over Diana, afraid of sex and of having his emotions aroused.

Friendship is a bond bridging social and economic gaps and changing people's lives throughout Rattigan's work. When they stop fighting with the Commander, Kit and Alan discover that he is not the stodgy figure they mocked but a sensitive and sensible man. This revelation is also an instance of Rattigan showing characters as individuals, not types. He accomplishes this with Diana in a sequence in which she admits to Jacqueline that she cannot give up the chase because she knows that men can only love but never like her.

Rattigan's use of dramatic implication is illustrated by a short scene in which Alan describes the plot of his rejected novel to Kit and the Commander. His story not only mirrors the conflict between his listeners and its resolution, but also foreshadows the war clouds gathering around the students—a point reinforced by other touches in the play. Historically, the comedy is a sunny look at the youth of a generation soon to fight World War II. Rattigan's biographers, Michael Darlow and Gillian Hodson, cite *French Without Tears* as the best comedy of the 1930's and the representative British play of that decade.

In spite of the success of his war drama *Flare Path*, his comedy of manners and romance *Love in Idleness*, and his courtroom-like drama set entirely in a drawing room, *The Winslow Boy*, Rattigan had difficulty finding a producer for *Playbill*. Most managements thought bills of one-acts commercial folly. T. C. Worsley noted in a *London Magazine* essay that Rattigan's defense of the artistic integrity of the one-act form and his reintroduction of it to the West End after the war proved boons to his successors.

Though *The Browning Version* and *Harlequinade* are often produced separately, their coupling in *Playbill* represents an artistic design. The overall structure is psychological, encompassing studies of vastly different personalities—the severely repressed and the flamboyantly theatrical. They are embodied in plots ingeniously similar enough—in each play, errors from the past press upon the protagonists—to highlight the contrast between psychologies.

The Browning Version, which won the Ellen Terry Award for best play of 1948, probes a psychological state which Rattigan had used as a leitmotif of characterization in his earlier plays. As Kay Nolte Smith pointed out in a 1971 *Objectivist* essay, the drama's theme is the tragedy of emotional repression. This is Rattigan's most original theme, and a difficult one to dramatize. His genius lay in making the causes and effects of repression intelligible and dramatic in a classically severe plot, without the use of soliloquy, of a narrator or *raisonneur* figure to offer explanations, or even of the word "repression."

The setting is the living room of a schoolmaster's apartment at a British boy's school. Andrew Crocker-Harris, once a brilliant and idealistic Greek master but now a dessicated pedant, is retiring early because of ill health. Visits by his young successor, the Headmaster, a pupil, and a colleague, and constant taunts by his sexually and socially frustrated wife, recall Crocker-Harris to his hopes and failures as a teacher and as a husband. Two gestures of kindness—the pupil's parting gift of Robert Browning's version of Aeschylus' *Agamemnon* and the colleague's offer of friendship— help Crocker-Harris to overcome what he calls his state of being a spiritual corpse, to break with his wife and to assert himself to the Headmaster. The play's penultimate line, when Crocker-Harris claims from the Headmaster his right to speak last at a school ceremony, "I am of opinion that occasionally an anti-climax can be surprisingly effective," is a characteristic Rattigan understatement, conveying his protagonist's recovery of self-respect in a simple phrase. Reviewing a 1976 London revival in the *Sunday Times*, Harold Hobson called *The Browning Version* "a masterpiece if ever there was one, the best one-act in the language."

Crocker-Harris was inspired partly by Rattigan's Greek master at Harrow. The famed acting team playing an aging Romeo and Juliet, whose dress rehearsal is interrupted by unwelcome visitors in *Harlequinade*, bore resemblances to Alfred Lunt and Lynn Fontanne with whom Rattigan had worked so closely on *Love in Idleness*. The focus is on the Romeo, a quintessential actor-manager oblivious of events outside the theater, who embodies Rattigan's theory that farce may be based on character. The comedy has been compared favorably with George Villiers' *The Rehearsal*, Richard Brinsley Sheridan's *The Critic*, and Arthur Wing Pinero's *Trelawny of the "Wells"* as a classic play about theater life.

Though usually cited as one of Rattigan's finest works, *The Deep Blue Sea* has yet to be fully appreciated. Eleven years before the women's movement began with the publication of Betty Friedan's *The Feminine Mystique* (1963), Rattigan produced a prescient drama about the effects of a woman's "raised consciousness."

The play is structured like a thriller, beginning with a landlady's discovery of Hester Collyer, unconscious from a suicide attempt, in a run-down London boardinghouse. Hester no longer feels worthy or desirous of living; gradually, the action reveals why. Daughter of a clergyman, wife of a judge honored with knighthood, she has fallen passionately in love with a feckless younger man and run off with him. A war pilot who has never found an equivalent challenge in civilian life, Freddie Page loves Hester in his way but is incapable of returning her ardor sexually or emotionally, and determines to leave rather than ruin Hester's life further. Hester's loving husband, Sir William, views her attachment as an ignoble but pardonable sex obsession and wants her to return to being his companionable wife.

Hester's sexual awakening with Freddie has released her need for more intense relationships than either man can offer. She feels deep shame at the pain she has caused, terror at the prospect of losing Freddie, and anger at the religious and societal view—pressed by her background, Sir William, and a young neighbor—that spiritual love is superior to physical. Another neighbor, a former doctor who lost his license and bears his disgrace with dignity, is able from his perspective as a social outcast to help Hester view herself as a worthy individual. In the end, after saying goodbye to her husband and lover, Hester takes her first step toward independence by lighting the gas heater she may still decide to use to escape life. *The Deep Blue Sea* was ahead of its time not only in Rattigan's sympathetic portrait of a woman who must virtually start life again almost at middle age, but also in his equally compassionate portrayals of men who are bewildered, wounded, and threatened by women's changing needs.

Rattigan applied principles of craftsmanship from the well-made play to the epic form with impressive results. Although his portraits of Alexander the Great in *Adventure Story* and T. E. Lawrence in *Ross* are marred by earnest but ultimately unconvincing attempts to explain each man's motivations, Rattigan captures the personal charisma of both figures and the sweep of their lives through world history with narrative mastery.

Like *Adventure Story*, *Ross* traces the psychological destruction of a brilliant military leader. The first three scenes dramatize Lawrence's attempt to find peace after World War I as a Royal Air Force aircraftman enlisted under the pseudonym of Ross. Recognized and awaiting expulsion, he drifts into a malarial dream which becomes a bridge to scenes depicting the wartime exploits that made him famous but sickened him spiritually. He is torn by exulting in his triumphs while wading through carnage to achieve them, and then destroyed psychologically by being awakened to his homosexual and masochistic tendencies in his (offstage) beating and rape by Turkish soldiers. Lawrence had trusted in the supremacy of his will and cannot face the realization that behind his will are not strength and integrity but inclinations that shame him. In the end, he decides to seek sanctuary in the service again under another assumed name.

In terms of Rattigan's attempt to integrate an expansive narrative structure with a comprehensive character study, *Ross* is his most complex and ambitious play. There is a density in its texture because of the sheer weight of material it encompasses. Rattigan had to explain the British, Arab, and Turkish positions during the World War I Middle Eastern conflict while simultaneously exploring the inner conflicts of a character who is both a man of action and a deeply repressed, tormented intellectual. Without narration, Rattigan was able to organize his mass of material in theatrical terms, judiciously balancing humor, suspense, and pathos.

The last third of *In Praise of Love*, Rattigan's penultimate play, contains some of his finest writing. About an Eastern European war refugee dying of leukemia, her apparently callous British husband, their sensitive son, and an old family friend, the work is structured as a psychological suspense story. Two-thirds of the play are devoted to creating a negative picture of the husband as a childish, boorish, selfish man. The wife confides her illness to the friend because she fears boring her husband, as she thinks she once bored him with her refugee tales, and tries to reconcile the contentious husband and son, both of whom she adores. In a *coup de théâtre*, the husband is forced to tell the friend that he has known of his wife's illness all along and is determined to keep it from her lest she relive her wartime anticipation of death at any moment. His callousness, once a habit, is now a mask he dons to foster the illusion that all is normal. He finds the mask torturous to wear because he has realized how much he loves his wife, and cannot tell her. He remarks that the English people's worst vice is their refusal to admit to their emotions.

Rattigan's condemnation of emotional repression is explicit in *In Praise of Love*, but particularly noteworthy in the play is the most daring use he ever made of implication. Rattigan's dramas are all dotted with comic dialogue and business which further his goals without undercutting the seriousness of his subjects. With *In Praise of Love*, he used comic dialogue and action throughout to build a picture of a household under almost unbearable emotional pressure, a household in which characters use banter to mask their own feelings and to try to spare the feelings of others. The contrast between the characters' veneer and the depth of their love and grief is profoundly poignant.

Upon Rattigan's death in 1977, the *Guardian's* Michael Billington, representative of a post-Angry-Young-Man generation of theater critics, maintained that Rattigan was misunderstood as an exemplar of the cool and gentlemanly school of English playwriting: "The real truth is that his plays are a remorseless attack on English emotional inhibition, and a moving plea for affection and kindness and understanding in the everyday business of life. . . . Few dramatists [in the twentieth] century have written with more understanding about the human heart." Giving evidence that this revaluation is not confined to British critics, Susan Rusinko concludes in her 1983 study of Rattigan for Twayne's English Authors series: "Polished without being slick, natural without untidiness, Rattigan's art has given firm shape to the mid-twentieth century mainstream of English life, chronicling the sweeping changes in the moods and attitudes of the time, as [did] Chekhov for his time."

Other major works

SCREENPLAYS: *Quiet Wedding*, 1941 (based on Esther McCracken's play); *English Without Tears*, 1944 (with Anatole de Grunwald; also known as *Her Man Gilbey*); *The Way to the Stars*, 1945 (with de Grunwald; also known as *Johnny in the Clouds*); *While the Sun Shines*, 1946; *The Winslow Boy*, 1948 (with de Grunwald); *Bond Street*, 1948; *Brighton Rock*, 1948 (later as *Young Scarface;* with Graham Greene; based on Greene's novel); *The Browning Version*, 1951; *The Sound Barrier*, 1952 (also known as *Breaking the Sound Barrier*); *The Final Test*, 1954; *The Prince and the Showgirl*, 1957 (adaptation of *The Sleeping Prince*); *Separate Tables*, 1958 (with John Gay; adaptation of Rattigan's play); *The VIPs*, 1963; *The Yellow Rolls-Royce*, 1965; *A Bequest to the Nation*, 1973.

TELEPLAYS: *The Final Test*, 1951; *Heart to Heart*, 1964; *Nelson—A Portrait in Miniature*, 1964.

RADIO PLAY: *Cause Célèbre*, 1975.

Bibliography

Curtis, Anthony. "Professional Man and Boy." Review of *The Browning Version. Plays and Players* 25 (February, 1978): 21-23. A review of a 1975 revival of what is generally regarded as Rattigan's best play, *The Browning Version*, in the context of a memoir that captures the life-affirming, movingly informative overview of Rattigan's work, particularly his positive reception by younger playwrights such as David Rudkin.

Darlow, Michael, and Gillian Hodson. *Terence Rattigan: The Man and His Work.* London: Quartet Books, 1979. A 360-page critical biography, thoroughly researched, using archives from the British Broadcasting Corporation. In this eminently readable narrative of Rattigan, his plays, and their times—all three led inexorably to one another—the authors write with authority and with permission from Rattigan to reveal much of what he had been unable to write about directly in his own plays. Includes photographs, a bibliography, a list of British and American opening dates and casts, and an index.

Hill, Holly. "Rattigan's Renaissance." *Contemporary Review* 240 (January, 1982): 37-42. A review by an acquaintance of the playwright of a revival of interest in Rattigan's plays in the 1980's, stressing the basis for his universality so that even a demanding critic, John Simon, confesses to having underrated Rattigan during the latter's life.

Rusinko, Susan. *Terence Rattigan.* Boston: Twayne, 1983. A chronological summary-analysis of the complete stage, film, and television plays, analyzing Rattigan's major plays, from his early sunny comedies to his later dramas about dysfunctional families in a dysfunctional society. Rattigan's themes of the rights of the individual, the emotional and sexual needs denied by prevailing repressive attitudes, and the necessarily oblique expression—sometimes Chekhovian in style—are threads that run through the play analyses. Photograph, chronology, bibliography, index.

_____. "Terence Rattigan." *British Dramatists Since World War II*, edited by Stanley Weintraub. Vol. 13 in *Dictionary of Literary Biography.* Detroit: Gale Research, 1982. Remains the most comprehensive short introduction to Rattigan's themes and style. Includes photographs, a chronology, and a bibliography.

Smith, Kay Nolte. "Terence Rattigan." *Objectivist* 9 (March, 1971): 9-15. An introduction to the artistry of Rattigan as a romantic playwright whose dramas are "beautifully clear and purposeful and unique." Looking forward to his next play (which turned out to be his last), Smith deals during his lifetime with a topic not given serious treatment until after his death in 1977.

Worsley, T. C. "Rattigan and His Critics." *London Magazine* 11 (September, 1964): 60-72. A spirited, overly defensive attack on Rattigan's hostile critics. Worsley nevertheless provides a valuable historical overview of the bases for drama criticism in a time during revolutionary changes on the British stage.

Young, B. A. *The Rattigan Version: The Theatre of Character.* New York: Atheneum, 1988. A personal memoir by an author who knew Rattigan. Leisurely in pace and impressionistic in style, it raises some questions, as in the descriptions of Rattigan's manner of throwing "his dialogue down on the page, caring only for its gist rather than its style." The author assumes a certain familiarity by the reader with Rattigan and the English stage. Includes index, cast lists, and photographs that tell their own story.

Holly Hill
(Updated by *Susan Rusinko*)

JAMES REANEY

Born: Stratford, Ontario, Canada; September 1, 1926

Principal drama

Night-Blooming Cereus, wr. 1952, pr. 1959 (radio play), pr. 1960 (staged), pb. 1962 (libretto); *The Sun and the Moon*, wr. 1959, pb. 1962, pr. 1965; *The Killdeer*, pr. 1960, pb. 1962 (pr. 1970, pb. 1972, revised); *One-Man Masque*, pr. 1960, pb. 1962; *The Easter Egg*, pr. 1962, pb. 1972; *Names and Nicknames*, pr. 1963, pb. 1969; *Let's Make a Carol*, pr. 1964, pb. 1965 (music by John Beckwith); *Applebutter*, pr. 1965, pb. 1973 (puppet play); *The Shivaree*, wr. 1965, pb. 1978, pr. 1982 (libretto; music by Beckwith); *Listen to the Wind*, pr. 1966, pb. 1972; *Ignoramus*, pr. 1966, pb. 1973; *Colours in the Dark*, pr. 1967, pb. 1969; *Three Desks*, pr. 1967, pb. 1972; *Geography Match*, pr. 1967, pb. 1973; *The Donnellys: Part I Sticks & Stones*, wr. 1968-1972, pr. 1973, pb. 1975; *The Donnellys: Part II St Nicholas Hotel Wm Donnelly Prop.*, wr. 1968-1973, pr. 1974, pb. 1976; *The Donnellys: Part III Handcuffs*, wr. 1968-1974, pr. 1975, pb. 1977; *All the Bees and All the Keys*, pr. 1973, pb. 1976 (music by Beckwith); *Baldoon*, pr., pb. 1976 (with C. H. "Marty" Gervais); *The Dismissal*, wr. 1976-1977, pr. 1977, pb. 1978; *Wacousta!*, pr. 1978, pb. 1979; *King Whistle*, pr. 1979; *Antler River*, pr. 1980; *Gyroscope*, pr. 1981, pb. 1983; *The Canadian Brothers*, pr. 1983, pb. 1984; *The Donnellys*, pb. 1983 (includes the Donnelly trilogy).

Other literary forms

Since the late 1940's, when James Reaney first distinguished himself as one of Canada's most provocative writers, he has amassed an impressive list of publications in all areas of creative and scholarly writing. In addition to more than twenty-five plays produced onstage, on radio, and on television, Reaney has written four volumes of award-winning poetry (*The Red Heart*, 1949; *A Suit of Nettles*, 1958; *Twelve Letters to a Small Town*, 1962; *The Dance of Death at London, Ontario*, 1963). His individual pieces, published in a wide variety of literary magazines and academic journals, have been collected into three separate volumes by editor Germaine Warkentin (*Poems*, 1972; *Selected Shorter Poems*, 1975; *Selected Longer Poems*, 1976). With composer John Beckwith, Reaney developed skills as a librettist, setting his poetry to Beckwith's music for radio broadcast in the late 1950's and early 1960's.

Like his drama, much of Reaney's poetry concerns the power of language as a redemptive catalyst in a corrupt and evil world. Geographically set in his native region of southwestern Ontario, his poetry is essentially lyric pastoral with characters, situations, and the landscape transformed by the imagery and such diverse poetic structures as eclogues, dialogue, and prosaic narrative. Reaney's poetry is a testament to his fascination with the musical patterns of rhyme and rhythm, demonstrating the author's talent for iambic pentameter, doggerel, rhyming couplets, blank verse, and lyric stanzas.

Reaney's short stories, written between 1946 and 1955, are also set in small-town Ontario. Young women with disturbing and unresolved emotional conflicts dominate the action of these stories. Beneath the calm, romantic façade of domesticity, Reaney's heroines hide a passionate intensity, which is revealed in the often surprising climaxes to the stories. One juvenile novel and a journal of the cross-country tour of the Donnelly trilogy fill out his creative dossier.

Reaney is also a highly respected professor of literature with numerous academic publications covering a variety of scholarly and literary topics.

Achievements

A distinguished poet, playwright, and scholar, Reaney has won three Governor General's Awards for poetry and drama, as well as a Chalmer's Award for drama. His first major dramatic work, *The Killdeer*, collected five of the top awards at the Dominion Drama Festival in 1960 for Reaney, Pamela Terry (director), the designer, and two performers. The numerous awards and accolades garnered during his career are but one measure of Reaney's impact on modern Canadian literature. The success of *The Killdeer* thrust Reaney into the limelight of a small, elite group of contemporary Canadian writers who had a marked effect on the growth of professional theater (and dramatic literature) in Canada.

Reaney has been involved in theatrical production since his high school days, and the sheer number of plays that he has written and had produced (more than twenty-five) is an enormous achievement in a country whose theatrical traditions began to reach maturity more than twenty years after he began writing drama. One of his early goals was to provide Canadians with a portrait of their own, unique experiences. As he said in a 1977 interview with *University of Western Ontario News*, "We need new plays, and Ontario is a very fascinating place."

Reaney understood that it was essential to develop actors, directors, and creative support-staff simultaneously with the evolution of his writing style—artists whose diverse approaches to theater would enhance his writing. To this end, he established the Listeners' Workshops, which began at the Alphacentre in London, Ontario, in 1967. The workshops were a joint project of many in the artistic community who believed that performers need to relearn how to play and to be inventive in the way children are as they engage in make-believe. Children and adults, amateurs and professionals all participated in the Saturday morning sessions, directed by

Reaney, which explored sound, music, movement, poetry, play, myth, and magic in an effort to develop a vibrant ensemble theater. The freedom of imagination which evolved in the workshops redefined for Reaney the meaning of ensemble playing. From the workshops grew a core of fiercely loyal, creative people who ultimately formed the nucleus of the NDWT Company, the troupe with which Reaney worked on the Donnelly trilogy.

The success of the trilogy was unlike anything that had happened before in Canadian theater. Over a period of three years, each of the three plays was a huge box-office and critical success when it was first presented in Toronto. Even more remarkable was the reception of the trilogy tour across eight of the ten provinces—proving that Canadian audiences were as interested in poetry, drama, and local history as was the author. In 1975, Reaney and the NDWT Company took the three plays from coast to coast, ending the tour in Toronto, where all three plays were presented again. Audiences in Toronto had the opportunity to see the entire trilogy performed in one day (each play is more than three and a half hours long) with a break for lunch and dinner. This once-in-a-lifetime opportunity sold out. The experience of the tour has been recorded in Reaney's book *Fourteen Barrels from Sea to Sea* (1977). With the tour complete, Reaney was awarded the Order of Canada in 1975.

Besides the significant contribution that Reaney has made to Canadian literature, he has also been influential in his role as teacher. Through his children's literature, his courses in creative writing, and his Listeners' Workshops, Reaney has led a new generation of young Canadians to an appreciation of poetry, drama, and their own unique history.

Biography

James Crerar Reaney, born in 1926 on a small farm in Fundamentalist southwestern Ontario (about ninety miles from the major cultural center of Toronto), grew up in a family and a community that was predominantly Irish and Scottish. The family broke with the conventional teachings of their congregation, Gospel Hall, and conducted prayer meetings at home. As Reaney grew older, he was sent to attend an Interdenominational Sunday school and later a combination Presbyterian and Congregational Sunday school, where the evangelical nature of the teachings had a dramatic effect on his imagination. The gothic tones and melodrama of the church teachings are clearly evident in his early plays *The Killdeer*, *The Sun and the Moon*, and *Listen to the Wind*.

By the time Reaney was graduated from high school, he was an accomplished musician and linguist. On a scholarship, he moved to Toronto to study Greek and Latin at the country's most distinguished college, the University of Toronto. It was during his study of classical languages that Reaney began his exploration of the alphabet and his fascination with the creative possibilities of a flexible language. He began to experiment with word lists as a way of developing an inventory of life, imagination, and experience; these word lists grew into volumes of highly acclaimed poetry. The underlying concept of the word catalogs is an iconography of the imagination—a concept which came to fruition with the founding of an unusual literary journal, *Alphabet*, published from 1960 to 1971. Reaney's experimentation with language as an integral part of dramatic structure is demonstrated in his 1967 play *Colours in the Dark* but shows itself in its most mature form in the Donnelly trilogy, written between 1968 and 1974. The trilogy brought Reaney national acclaim as one of Canada's foremost playwrights.

By 1947, Reaney had already achieved national notoriety as a provocative young talent with the publication of his short story "The Box Social" in the July 19, 1947, issue of *New Liberty Magazine*. This macabre story, which tells of a young man whose girlfriend presents him with a stillborn fetus during a church social, set the tone for much of his early writing. Reaney's world is an unsettling mixture of good and evil where pastoral romance, rural realism, and strong strains of melodrama are held together by the common thread of childhood experience—simultaneously innocent and corrupt.

While completing his M.A. at the University of Toronto in 1949, Reaney published his first volume of poetry, *The Red Heart*, which won the Governor General's Award, the most prestigious literary prize in Canada (comparable to the Pulitzer Prize). It was also during this time that the young writer came under the influence of Northrop Frye, the internationally acclaimed scholar and literary critic whose pioneering study of William Blake, *Fearful Symmetry* (1947), was to revolutionize modern literary analysis. Although Reaney was not yet a student of Frye, he was very much a part of the literary elite at the university who were preoccupied with discussion and analysis of Frye's important work. *Fearful Symmetry* provided Reaney with an archetypal vision of the Bible which became the impetus for much of the imagery and metaphor in both his poetry and drama. As Ross Woodman says in his excellent introduction to *James Reaney* (1971), Frye's work transformed "in a comprehensive and systematic way Reaney's earlier evangelical world into a literary one."

With his M.A. completed and the Governor General's Award in hand, Reaney accepted a position at the University of Manitoba in Winnipeg (the gateway to the Canadian West) to teach English and creative writing. The years in Winnipeg (until 1956) were difficult for Reaney, who felt isolated from the creative activity of southern Ontario, but it was also a time when he forged important friendships with people such as stage director John Hirsch (who later founded the Manitoba Theatre Centre, one of Canada's leading performing arts facilities) and playwright Tom Hendry. Both men, along with Keith Turnbull of the NDWT Company, would have an important influence on Reaney's development as a dramatist.

It was also during this period that Reaney began writing librettos for composer John Beckwith, whom he had met as an undergraduate at the University of Toronto. Their first coproduction, *Night-Blooming Cereus*, was also Reaney's initial attempt at dramatic writing and was produced on radio by the Canadian Broadcasting Corporation (CBC) in 1959 and staged in 1960.

Each summer during the Winnipeg years, Reaney returned to Stratford to write and to take part in an important cultural event in his hometown. Internationally famous actor/director/producer Tyrone Guthrie had come to Stratford (from London, England) to found the Stratford Shakespeare Festival. The festival began in a large marquee in the early 1950's and had grown by the late 1960's to encompass the Festival Theatre (a Shakespearean thrust stage), the Avon Theatre (a proscenium arch theater), and the Third Stage (a flexible, experimental space). Reaney's participation in the formative years of the Stratford experiment solidified his desire to write for the stage. His first attempt at a full-length play, "The Rules of Joy" (later rewritten and retitled *The Sun and the Moon*), was conceived with the Festival Theatre stage in mind, but it was not until 1967 that the festival commissioned Reaney to write a major work for the Stratford stage. *Colours in the Dark*, which was performed at the Avon Theatre in 1967, was not only a watershed piece in Reaney's evolution as a dramatist but also a celebration of the nation itself—written to commemorate Canada's one hundredth birthday.

At home in Stratford for Christmas of 1951, Reaney married Colleen Thibaudeau, an accomplished poet of Irish and Acadian French background whom he had met during his years at the University of Toronto. Both had been members of a small literary group at the university, and Reaney respected both her accomplishments and her advice on his writing. Thibaudeau, whose poetic style was very different than his, had a substantial impact on the tone and quality of Reaney's writing. The often negative view of marriage and family life presented in his early works changed and mellowed after their marriage and the birth of their first son, James Stewart, in 1953. The Reaneys' had another son, John Andrew, in 1954, and a daughter, Susan Alice, in 1959. While Reaney was in rehearsal with one of his most romantic plays, *Listen to the Wind*, John Andrew died at the age of eleven. The published version of *Listen to the Wind* is dedicated to Reaney's son.

In 1956, Reaney took a two-year sabbatical from the University of Manitoba and returned to the University of Toronto in 1956 to write his doctoral thesis, "The Influence of Spenser on Yeats." He enrolled in Northrop Frye's course on literary symbolism and finally came under the direct influence of the great scholar when Frye became Reaney's thesis supervisor. His studies with Frye brought together the many facets of literature and myth which Reaney had been exploring for decades. His love of nursery rhymes, fairy tales, and all other literary paraphernalia of childhood began to take on a new meaning: Childhood fantasy, evangelism, and the magic of pastoral romance merged with marionettes, children's games, and his growing understanding of the many possibilities of stage business. Reaney, who had bicycled more than one hundred miles to see the opening of Walt Disney's *Fantasia* (1940), was on the brink of creating his own very personal vocabulary for poetry and drama.

With his doctorate completed, Reaney returned to Winnipeg and to the business of teaching and writing. In 1958, his second volume of poetry, *A Suit of Nettles*, was greeted with critical enthusiasm and, in 1959, a second Governor General's Award. In Winnipeg, Reaney began work on his first major play, *The Killdeer*, the story of an emotionally retarded young man and the young lovers who help him reach both maturity and reality. Reaney had difficulty restraining the narrative to fit the dramatic structure. He sent the play to Toronto to his friend Pamela Terry (who was later to marry composer Beckwith), and with her assistance the play was rewritten and finally produced, with Terry as director, in 1960. This first version of *The Killdeer* won five awards at the Dominion Drama Festival, and in 1962, the play and Reaney's radio poem, *Twelve Letters to a Small Town*, won for him a third Governor General's Award.

The year of *The Killdeer* was a new beginning. Reaney began dedicating more and more time to his dramatic writing. He returned from Winnipeg and accepted a professorship at the University of Western Ontario, in London, Ontario. The year 1960 also saw the first volume of *Alphabet: A Semiannual Devoted to the Iconography of the Imagination* and the flourishing of his scholarly writings in such esteemed academic and literary journals as *Tamarack Review*, *Canadian Literature*, *Canadian Forum*, and the *University of Toronto Quarterly*.

Reaney continued to write both poetry and plays. In the mid-1960's, he was particularly influenced by a performance of the Peking Opera, where mime, movement, and masks replaced traditional properties and stage sets. Fascinated by the circuslike nature of the production, Reaney assimilated the experience and began work on his major opus, the Donnelly trilogy, which was to take nearly ten years to complete. The story of an outcast Irish family in rural Ontario at the turn of the century, the Donnelly plays brought to fruition the various threads of poetry, music, drama, dance, documentary, mime, circus, and magic which appear in embryonic form in the early plays. In 1974, *The Donnellys: Part II St Nicholas Hotel Wm Donnelly Prop.*, the second of the three Donnelly plays, won the Chalmers Award for Drama, the outstanding prize for stage writing in Canada. In the wake of this success, Reaney turned increasingly to dramas focused on the history and culture of southwestern Ontario, but such plays as *Wacousta!* and *The Canadian Brothers* met with mixed receptions.

Analysis

"William Blake's poetry" says Reaney . . . "is the kind of ideal I have in which there's painting and dance and rhythm and poetry and sound, a whole world on various levels. . . . I'm not interested in writing a play that's two dimensional. It's got to have references to your whole psyche."

James Reaney had fulfilled his vision of multidimensional drama in his masterpiece, the Donnelly trilogy, by the time he made this statement in 1976. In retrospect, one can see that it is a vision equally applicable to his earliest attempts at stage drama.

The original three-act version of *The Killdeer*, produced by the University College Alumnae Association in Toronto in 1960, brought Reaney national acclaim as a playwright. This work is an excellent model for investigating the Reaney universe of themes, symbols, characters, and techniques common throughout his drama. A study of *The Killdeer* has this to recommend it as well: The play was rewritten in a more economical two-act version in 1968 at a time when Reaney began mulling the task of turning the legend of the Black Donnellys into a major stage presentation, a project which took nearly ten years of writing and research to complete.

Both versions of *The Killdeer* share elements of romance, mystery, and melodrama. In the original three-act version, the structure of the play hints strongly of a "well-made play" formula, with a third-act trial scene in which a *deus ex machina* figure delivers previously unknown evidence that resolves the plot complications.

The story concerns two families who are inextricably bound through generations of greed, lust, love, and murder. At the center of attention are two innocents—a young boy, Eli, who raises angora rabbits, and a girl, Rebecca, who delivers farm eggs to the townsfolk. Rebecca and Eli are about to marry. They are the offspring of two half sisters and share a common history of horror. Eli's mother, Madam Fay, is responsible for the death of Rebecca's mother and brothers, and her own husband, who was Eli's father, and she is also responsible for the mental breakdown of Rebecca's father. Both youngsters have grown up essentially as orphans (a favorite Reaney character-type). Rebecca's hope is that their marriage will be "love's solution to the puzzle of hatred." As she says, "Eli and I will untie the evil knot."

Unbeknown to Rebecca, she and Eli are trapped in separate but intersecting worlds of malevolence and horror that threaten to destroy the beneficent, regenerative power they represent. A hired man named Clifford, who has reared Eli, plots to destroy them both. Rebecca's other dilemma is that she is in love with Harry Gardner, a young bank clerk whose life is dominated by his overpowering mother, just as Rebecca's life is dominated by her sense of duty. What is common to all is that they cannot follow their true instincts; circumstances that are the legacy of the previous generation force each character into a loveless, death-in-life existence which leads irrevocably to violent death.

As in all Reaney plays, the strong narrative line of *The Killdeer* implies that his primary concern is to resolve the mystery and to allow virtue to triumph, but a close examination of his works reveals another purpose. Reaney is interested in exploring the subtext, the subconscious realm of imagination and instinct; he probes inside the human and social psyche, looking beneath the surface of settings that are often romantic, pastoral, and idyllic. There, he finds greed, lust, hatred, malice, and fear, but also love.

Appropriately, the first characters that one meets in *The Killdeer* are Mrs. Gardner and Madam Fay—two mothers, starkly contrasting types. Reaney is both fascinated and repelled by the power of motherhood. Typical of most of Reaney's married women, Mrs. Gardner and Madam Fay are widows who stand alone against the world. They are strong personalities, powerful obstacles in the way of their children's happiness and development into adulthood.

Mrs. Gardner is a typical small-town, churchgoing woman whose veneer of good manners conceals her narrow-mindedness, her ambition, and her fascination with things sinful and evil. She has dominated her son into a state of compliance and despair. Madam Fay, at the other end of the spectrum, is the local bad girl, talking tough, feeling nothing but contempt for the holier-than-thou townsfolk. She has knowledge of the real world and therefore no use for its false pretenses to civility and manners. She wears her sordid past as if it were a badge of honor.

Madam Fay is an interestingly drawn character (of a type that recurs throughout Reaney's works): She appears to have no sense of right and wrong, no guilt. She is in no way the conventional "whore with a heart of gold." She admits responsibility for the deaths of her half sister, two nephews, and husband. She reveals that she abandoned her own son and cares nothing for him. She laughs at her part in the mental breakdown of her illicit lover. Yet despite her confessions, the viewer is intrigued rather than repulsed by her character, wanting to know the motivation behind such action; thus, the author creates the curiosity which moves the play along to its dramatic conclusion.

In addition to the dominating hypocrite (Mrs. Gardner) and the demoniac yet honest primitive (Madam Fay), the play presents other character-types that recur throughout Reaney's works. Rebecca is exactly what one would expect of the heroine of a melodrama and much more—she is candid, untainted, naïve, loving, calm, brave, loyal, and bright. Most important, she is an orphan, and like the other orphans of Reaney's world (including Madam Fay), she is independent, intelligent, and self-sufficient. Like Polly in *The Easter Egg* and Susan Kingbird in *The Sun and the Moon* (two other young heroines), when confronted with the necessity to sacrifice her own needs for the betterment of those around her, Rebecca is willing to make the sacrifice—made with no hint of martyrdom or melodrama, as one might expect. Reaney seems to be saying that such women are necessary to absolve the play world of the sins of the other characters. To ensure ultimate justice, none of his heroines has to live long with her sacrifice: Justice is restored by the end of the play.

Two more significant figures are introduced before the canvas is complete. Eli, the unwilling bridegroom, and his mentor-tormentor, Clifford, one of Reaney's finest villains, appear next. Eli is half man, half child, emotionally stunted by the traumatic experiences of his past and mesmerized by Clifford's evil. Clifford has forced Eli into the marriage as a way of getting possession of Rebecca and her land. Eli is the ultimate battered and abused child. His real tragedy is that he is intelligent and perceptive enough to understand Clifford's machinations, but he does not have the power to stop him.

Eli's powerlessness is important. He is as trapped by his history as Harry Gardner is by his mother's conditioning. Eli and others like him (Kenneth in *The Easter Egg*, Andrew Kingbird in *The Sun and the Moon*, and Rogue in *Listen to the Wind*) are all trapped in a limbo between adolescence and manhood. Such characters need to be freed by the power of love, the power of language, the power of knowledge. In contrast to these brutalized and immature male characters, Reaney presents female characters who, despite common histories of childhood neglect and abuse, have grown to be mature and self-reliant. Repeatedly in Reaney's plays, the maturation of male characters is facilitated by the strength of female characters.

In 1968, Reaney rewrote *The Killdeer*, telescoping the action and characters into two acts and making considerable changes in the plot line. Technically, the second version is more adventurous: Flashbacks, choruses, significant properties, and clarified symbols dominate the stage directions. The revision demonstrates that Reaney had gained considerable confidence in the interim between the two versions, teaching himself to simplify the poetry, the plot, and the stage business. He allows his characters to be more explicit, adding a sense of urgency and eliminating much of the melodramatic formula of the first version. What feels confessional in the first version becomes exciting, forthright dialogue in the second version. By looking at the two versions in combination, one can see much of the landscape of what has come to be known as Reaneyland. Both his thematic concerns and his fascination with developing a new, exciting vocabulary of stagecraft are manifest here, as are his striking character-types.

The revision of *The Killdeer* was an important step toward achieving an unencumbered drama. As Reaney's stagecraft began to match his poetic skills and his visionary gift, as in such works as *Colours in the Dark*, *Listen to the Wind*, and the Donnelly trilogy, he began to experiment more and more with structure, language, and imagery, following his conviction that drama should be a process of dreaming.

Listen to the Wind, which premiered in 1966, before the revision of *The Killdeer*, is one of Reaney's most popular and successful plays. It was this work that brought him together with Keith Turnbull, the director who has made a significant contribution to Reaney's career. *Listen to the Wind* is symbolic, romantic, and melodramatic. It depends on a play-within-a-play device which allows two separate yet similar worlds to intersect. Significantly, it developed out of the Listeners' Workshops, where the ability to "pretend" was the most important talent necessary for the participants, both actors and audience.

The play is set in rural southwestern Ontario in the 1930's. A young boy, Owen, is confined to bed by a serious and mysterious illness. At the same time, he is burdened by the knowledge that his parents' marriage has come to an end. Thus, his malaise is both physical and spiritual. He is visited, for the summer, by three female cousins who want to cure both his body and his soul. The children decide to produce a play, *The Saga of Caresfoot Court*, in the hope that the adults not only will be entertained but also will get involved and therefore resolve their problems. Owen's life parallels the life of the saga's heroine, Angela: Both are surrounded by a terrifying world of indifference, neglect, and violence; both are innocent and naïve, overwhelmed by the evil around them.

The Caresfoot Court play focuses on Angela's corruption in a debased world; her life attests the dictum that the sins of the parents are visited upon the children. Owen tries to avoid Angela's fate by writing alternative endings for the play—a happy and a tragic conclusion. Thus, he attempts to determine events in the real world (his parents' divorce) by controlling the internal fantasy, wherein everything, including parental reconciliation, is possible.

Particularly noteworthy is the manner in which the play proper and the play-within-a-play interact, illuminating each other. As Jay Macpherson observed in a 1966 article in *Canadian Forum*, "They do so through numerous cross-references in image and situation, and through the revelation of the capacities of the characters of the outer story by the roles they play in the inner one. . . . While the outer story is slight, gentle, and touching, the inner one consists of a series of explosive confrontations."

The device of using a play-within-a-play also allows Reaney to present both sides of the story at once—a technique that he used again in a more radical form in the medicine show of the Donnelly plays. This device juxtaposes Owen's reality to the deeply sentimental world of the inner play; it is also Owen's way of "listening to the wind." The play was a giant leap forward in the development of Reaney's craftsmanship. One sees here the beginning of a theater that relies on minimal directions, few properties, and a large cast, and one that requires the audience to be an active participant in the creative process. It is a dramatic world in which past and present are no longer clearly delineated.

To re-create Victorian England, in the play-within-a-play Reaney employed a brilliant theatrical device borrowed from ancient Greece, the chorus—in this play, composed of children—which can create anything possible within the scope of the audience's imagination by chanting, singing, stomping, clapping, miming, dancing, and generally acting out, or making believe. This device led Reaney to a turning point in his career: *Colours in the Dark*, a landmark play, produced at the Stratford Festival in 1967. Reaney himself described the work as "a play box"; it is a collage of images, colors, objects (toys), songs, dances, myths, symbols, and sounds, culminating in the "existence poem" that is the central image of the play and the focus of its structure.

Colours in the Dark demands much of an audience. There is overlapping dialogue, and the same actors play several different parts. Multiscreen images are projected behind the action as the plot unravels in a linear and historically chronological fashion. To hold the many scenes together, the playwright uses scene codes—codes which arc held up on banners labeling them by color and a related word. White is Sunday, but it is also a flower, a type of music, and a symbol of innocence and goodness. Color, word, and symbol are signposts to the action of each scene.

Colours in the Dark is Reaney's testament to the power of language. It proposes that there are many nontraditional ways of interpreting the world. The story begins with a game in which a child is blindfolded so that he will have to develop other senses to guide him through the matrix of life. Without the use of his eyes, he must depend on touch, smell, sound, and imagination—leading the audience to the experience of synesthetic knowledge, whereby sensory perception creates a new vocabulary of equivalents, breaking down boundaries between word, symbol, and image. What *Colours in the Dark* achieves is a recapitulation of the history of civilization in the life of a single individual. It is a kaleidoscope that proves "our ancestors are we, our descendants are us, and so on like a sea."

Reaney's masterpiece, the Donnelly trilogy, was a logical next step. In it one sees much that has developed directly from *Colours in the Dark*: catalogs of names, the use of local color, important chorus sections, the juxtaposition of the real and absurd worlds, and much more. The trilogy is truly the fulfillment of Reaney's artistic vision. In it, with help from Keith Turnbull and a talented, loyal crew of actors and technicians, he was able to synthesize poetry, dance, music, and movement to create a powerfully unified theater experience.

All three plays, *The Donnellys: Part I Sticks & Stones*, *The Donnellys: Part II St Nicholas Hotel Wm Donnelly Prop.*, and *The Donnellys: Part III Handcuffs*, are consistent in their style of presentation, although each has separate symbols: sticks and stones, wheels and tops, grains and seeds. Reaney deliberately uses familiar props, stage furnishings, and styles in all three plays. The best description of this technique comes from critic Urjo Kareda in his review in *The Toronto Star* on November 26, 1973:

> The 11 performers, always present, using beautiful props which are always on view, work through choric chanting, songs, children's games, soliloquies, plays-within-plays, indirect narration, mime and even marionettes to express Reaney's collage of history. The play has an exceptionally simple and evocative range of symbols and imagery; like the props, they are chosen from a common experience. The seven sons are represented by seven white shirts hanging on a line; horizontal country roads are seen as vertical ladders; the lieutenant-governor and his lady are dolls; a greedy fat woman is her "darling little laundry stove"; the Donnellys themselves are the solid stones, while their enemies are the dry, crackling sticks.

In the Donnelly trilogy, Reaney achieved the dream first hinted at in *The Killdeer*: He found a way to make his universal themes pertinent to the real history of the people in his community. The poetic language of the three plays reverberates with musical structures of duet, trio, and quartet. The structure is interwoven with symbol, myth, and significant props. Most important, Reaney's vision has grown to accommodate documented, historical truth. What results is a smooth, rich mixture of language, action, structure, and stagecraft—a theater in which everything can be something.

Other major works

SHORT FICTION: "Clay Hole," 1946; "The Elevator," 1946; "The Book in the Tree," 1947; "Mr. Whur: A Metamorphosis," 1947; "The Box Social," 1947; "Afternoon Moon," 1948; "The Young Necrophiles," 1948; "The Bully," 1952; "Dear Metronome," 1952; "To the Secret City: From a Winnipeg Sketch Book," 1954; "Winnipeg Sketches," 1955.

POETRY: *The Red Heart*, 1949; *A Suit of Nettles*, 1958; *Twelve Letters to a Small Town*, 1962; *The Dance of Death at London, Ontario*, 1963; *Poems*, 1972 (Germaine Warkentin, editor); *Selected Shorter Poems*, 1975 (Germaine Warkentin, editor); *Selected Longer Poems*, 1976 (Germaine Warkentin, editor); *Imprecations: The Art of Swearing*, 1984; *Performance: Poems*, 1990.

NONFICTION: "The Influence of Spenser on Yeats," 1958 (Ph.D. thesis); "The Canadian Imagination," 1959 (in *Poetry*); "Isabella Valancy Crawford," 1959; *Alphabet: A Semiannual Devoted to the Iconography of the Imagination*, 1960-1971 (20 volumes); "The Canadian Poets' Predicament," 1962 (in *Masks of Poetry*); "An Evening with Babble and Doodle," 1962; "Ten Miles High on a Song," 1966 (in *The Globe and Mail* newspaper); *Ten Years at Play*, 1969; *Fourteen Barrels from Sea to Sea*, 1977; "Some Critics Are Music Teachers," 1982 (in *Centre and Labyrinth: Essays in Honour of Northrop Frye*); "Digesting the Bible," 1982 (in *Saturday Night Magazine*).

TELEPLAY: *An Evening Without James Reaney*, 1960.

RADIO PLAYS: *The Great Lakes Suite*, 1950; *Message to Winnipeg*, 1959; *Poet and City—Winnipeg*, 1960; *The Journals and Letters of William Blake*, 1961; *Wednesday's Child*, 1962; *Canada Dot—Canada Dash*, 1965-1967 (in 3 parts).

CHILDREN'S LITERATURE: *The Boy with an R in His Hand*, 1965; *Take the Big Picture*, 1986.

Bibliography

Lee, Alvin. "A Turn to the Stage: Reaney's Dramatic Verse." In *Dramatists in Canada: Selected Essays*, edited by William H. New. Vancouver: University of British Columbia Press, 1972. Offers "a description of the major writings . . . in an attempt to show something of his [Reaney's] development as a verse dramatist." Deals with *The Red Heart*, *A Suit of Nettles* (briefly), and the chamber opera *Night-Blooming Cereus.* Long discussion of *The Killdeer* and *The Easter Egg.*

Parker, Gerald. "The Key Word . . . Is 'Listen': James Reaney's 'Sonic Environment.'" *Mosaic* 14 (Fall, 1981): 1-14. This article on the Donnelly trilogy is a model of Reaney's use of "the sonic environment through various forms of instrumentation and vocal gesture." Examines a large part of Reaney's dramatic work, praising "the preoccupation with the theatrical values of sound" and Reaney's appreciation of filmic and operatic techniques. Notes provide a bibliography for further inquiry.

Reaney, James. *Masks of Childhood.* Toronto: New Press, 1972. An afterword, by editor Brian Parker, accompanies this edition of three plays, *The Easter Egg*, *Three Desks*, and *The Killdeer*. Parker sees "the interplay of man and child" as the central idea in Reaney's work. A brief but informative analysis of the three plays is followed by a chronology of plays and works for radio.

Tait, Michael. "Everything Is Something: James Reaney's *Colours in the Dark.*" In *Dramatists in Canada: Selected Essays*, edited by William H. New. Vancouver: University of British Columbia Press, 1972. Tait concentrates on *Colours in the Dark*, produced at the Stratford Festival in 1967, and finds much of merit in his "attempt to define some of Reaney's strengths as a dramatist, and more particularly, those qualities of *Colours* which set it apart from earlier, less successful stage pieces." He

finds Reaney's play "*sui generis*, a luminous structure . . . lyric in subjective intensity of mood; dramatic in the articulation of large conflicts;
epic in its breadth of statement."

—————————. "The Limits of Innocence: James Reaney's Theatre." In
Dramatists in Canada: Selected Essays, edited by William H. New. Vancouver: University of British Columbia Press, 1972. An alternative, more
critical view than Alvin Lee's essay (above) in the same collection. Tait
claims that "a pattern of striking imagery, in the absence of plausible
characterization and coherent action, is not enough to hold any play together." After more of the same criticism, he concludes: "No one else
has his capacity to write for the stage at once so badly and so well."

Eleanor R. Goldhar
(Updated by *Thomas J. Taylor*)

RONALD RIBMAN

Born: New York, New York; May 28, 1932

Principal drama

Harry, Noon and Night, pr. 1965, pb. 1967; *The Journey of the Fifth Horse*, pr. 1966, pb. 1967 (based in part on Ivan Turgenev's short story "The Diary of a Superfluous Man"); *The Ceremony of Innocence*, pr. 1967, pb. 1968; *Passing Through from Exotic Places*, pr. 1969, pb. 1970 (includes three one-acts, *The Son Who Hunted Tigers in Jakarta*, *Sunstroke*, and *The Burial of Esposito*); *Fingernails Blue as Flowers*, pr. 1971, pb. 1973; *A Break in the Skin*, pr. 1972; *The Poison Tree*, pr. 1973, pb. 1977; *Cold Storage*, pr. 1977, pb. 1978; *Buck*, pr., pb. 1983; *Sweet Table at the Richelieu*, pr. 1987, pb. 1992; *The Cannibal Masque*, pr. 1987; *A Serpent's Egg*, pr. 1987; *The Rug Merchants of Chaos*, pr. 1991, pb. 1992; *The Dream of the Red Spider*, pr. 1993.

Other literary forms

Ronald Ribman has worked extensively as a screenwriter, both for film and for television. Among those scripts that have been produced are *The Final War of Olly Winter*, an original television play produced by CBS in 1967; *The Angel Levine*, a screenplay written with William Gunn and based on a story by Bernard Malamud, produced by United Artists in 1970; and *Seize the Day*, a teleplay based on the novel by Saul Bellow, produced by PBS in 1987. Three of Ribman's stage plays have also been adapted for television: *The Journey of the Fifth Horse* for NET in 1966 and for the Canadian Broadcasting Company in 1969, *The Ceremony of Innocence* for NET in 1972 and for Granada Television in London in 1974, and *Cold Storage* for the Entertainment Channel in 1983.

Achievements

Since the beginning of his career in the late 1960's, Ribman has been recognized by a relatively small number of discriminating critics, and by foundations dedicated to improving the literary merit of the American theater, as one of the most significant voices of the stage, one that rings out with poetry in the face of the prosaic norm that values language itself: a language that emphasizes the beauty and fluidity of words. Though *The Journey of the Fifth Horse* was savaged by the mainstream critics, it received the Obie Award for the best Off-Broadway play of the 1965-1966 season. *The Final War of Olly Winter* was nominated for five Emmy Awards; *The Poison Tree* won the Straw Hat Award for Best New Play in 1973, and *Cold Storage* won the Hull-Warriner Award of the Dramatists Guild in 1977. *The Rug Merchants of Chaos* was the winner of an award from the Kennedy

Center Fund for New American Plays. Ribman received Rockefeller grants in 1966 and 1968, and in 1975 the Rockefeller Foundation awarded him a fellowship "in recognition of his sustained contribution to American theatre." He has also been awarded a Guggenheim Foundation grant in 1970, and National Endowment for the Arts fellowships in 1973 and 1986-1987.

Biography

Ronald Burt Ribman was born in New York City on May 28, 1932, the son of Samuel M. Ribman, a lawyer, and Rosa Lerner Ribman. As a teenager he took an aptitude test that indicated that he should be a writer, but it made no sense to him; at that time he despised all forms of literature. His earliest career choice was science. "I was the worst chemistry major in the history of Brooklyn College," he has said. "Things bubbled strangely and blew up in my retorts." He abandoned science, and for his sophomore year he transferred to the University of Pittsburgh, where in 1954 he received his bachelor's degree in business administration.

Soon after graduation he was drafted. To while away the long hours off duty while he was stationed in Germany, he began to write: long letters at first, and then poetry. "I wrote a lot of terrible poems which they broadcast over the Armed Forces Network, which led to all kinds of suspicions about me—whether I was the right kind of gung-ho military material the Army was looking for."

Upon his discharge, he started working at one of his father's business concerns, a coal brokerage in Pennsylvania. He continued to write—short stories as well as poetry—and decided to apply to the graduate school at the University of Pittsburgh to study the very subject he had once despised above all others, English literature. He supported his application with copies of his recent writing and was accepted. (His writing was returned with a critical comment: "Mr. Ribman has a penchant for the bizarre, which a few writing courses that stress concrete imagery will take out of him.") After earning his M.Litt. in 1958, he was accepted for doctoral work at the Universities of Edinburgh and Minnesota. "Faced with a choice, I of course picked the wrong one." After "one freezing quarter" in Minnesota, he returned to "Pitt," where he earned his Ph.D., with a dissertation on John Keats, in 1962. He then entered the academic world as an assistant professor of English at Otterbein College in Westerville, Ohio. This career lasted only one year. He resigned to devote himself full-time to writing, which he has done ever since.

In New York, Ribman collaborated with his father on an article about the poor treatment indigent defendants were getting in the federal court system; the piece appeared in *Harper's*. He was thus a published writer, but he had not yet discovered his form. That discovery came while he was watching an amateur production of Edward Albee's *The Sandbox* (1960) in Johnstown,

Pennsylvania. It hit him rather suddenly: "I'm a playwright. That's what I am. I recognize myself now."

Ribman wrote a one-act play called "Day of the Games," and sent it to the American Place Theatre in New York. The artistic director, Wynn Handman, came across it while slogging through a stack of manuscripts one Saturday morning in 1963, and it leaped out at him. "It was the language: fantastic, actable language, rich, evocative, poetic." He immediately telephoned Ribman and asked him to write a companion piece that would fill up an evening of theater.

The "companion piece" turned out to be a full-length play, *Harry, Noon and Night*, which was staged as the second major production in the American Place Theatre's first season, with two then-unknown actors in the leads, Joel Grey and Dustin Hoffman. Another Off-Broadway production followed immediately, with Robert Blake in the cast. In 1966, the American Place Theatre produced Ribman's second full-length play, *The Journey of the Fifth Horse*, with Hoffman as Zoditch and Michael Tolan as Chulkaturin.

A number of critics—among them Robert Brustein, Martin Gottfried, and Gerald Weales—immediately identified Ribman as one of the few playwrights who represented the future of American playwriting and a rejection of the relatively mindless fare that was becoming the staple of Broadway. Mainstream critics have never embraced him, though, and only two of his plays have been produced on Broadway: *The Poison Tree* in 1976 and *Cold Storage* in 1977. Most of his subsequent plays have been produced by Handman at the American Place Theatre and by Brustein at the Yale Repertory Theatre in New Haven, Connecticut, and the American Repertory Theatre in Cambridge, Massachusetts.

Ribman has refused to create his plays according to any notion of what an audience might want to see. "The thing for me that has always been the most difficult," he has said,

> is to be faithful to my own creative instincts, to what I want to do. There are powerful market forces out there that push you into more conservative directions because more conservative directions are what pay. To be true to yourself means that if you are going to find your authentic, individual voice you may at first be pushed aside because it doesn't sound like anyone else, and if it doesn't sound like anyone else they don't know what to do with it. It's been said that we are all born originals, but most of us die as copies. That's what an artist must avoid.

Ronald Ribman lives and writes in South Salem, New York, with his wife, Alice Rosen, a nurse, whom he married on August 27, 1967. They have two children, James and Elana.

Analysis

Ronald Ribman is a virtuoso of style. The shape of his imagination is protean, its colors those of a chameleon. He has the ability to project himself, from play to play, into different locales, times, levels of reality and fantasy, and to sound, against all odds, persuasive, consistent, compelling.

Each of his plays adopts a different approach to the question of how reality is to be refracted through the playwright's prism before being presented to the audience. He can write snappy, amusing dialogue, and he can adopt the tone of a parable: simple, lapidary, but suggestive. He can hew very close to realism, but at other times he approaches surrealism, jumping back and forth in time, presenting different levels of fantasy and reality simultaneously, with a poet's eye and ear journeying deep into the thickets of the imaginary to create new worlds—worlds that resemble our own but differ in time, locale, and in their idiosyncratic approaches to reality.

As a result of this virtuosity, it is difficult to identify Ribman with any one particular style. "Some writers," he has said,

> are very fortunate in that they find the vein, the seam in their mind that they can mine right at the beginning and they just keep hacking away at it. I keep finding it and I keep losing it and keep picking it up somewhere else. People have told me, "None of your plays looks like the one that went before. They all look very different from each other." That's because I'm mining different areas.

Nevertheless, there are certain themes and patterns that have recurred from play to play throughout his career, preoccupations and threads of consistency that tie together all the disparate forms of his protean shape. One of these is an interest in the process of victimization, in which, frequently, the victim and the victimizer reverse roles; both are revealed as no more than clowns, and the conflict itself as nothing more than an absurd game.

Often the characters and the plots are created with a bizarre, dreamlike logic, a grotesque, nightmarish quality. Sometimes the fevered imagination of one character seems to create the rest of the cast, as distorted reflections of his fears or preoccupations; they speak and act as if they had never felt the inhibitions of civilization, as if they were capable of keeping nothing inside, as if every unspeakable thought had to emerge immediately—as if, in fact, they had no insides, as if their insides were all on the surface. Grotesque images and incidents appear, too, that are distorted images of what is disturbing the protagonist.

Characters often speak past one another, rather than to one another. They misunderstand one another, and so make it easy for the audience to misunderstand them. In fact, as Ribman himself has often insisted, the plays are ambiguous; there are no single meanings, and each will and should be understood in a number of different ways. Their exact natures are as difficult to seize as Proteus. Ribman's poetry, then, is not simply a matter of rich, supple language; it is also a matter of poetic ambiguity, of ineffability.

One other recurring concern of Ribman is his preoccupation with the persistence of the past in the present—a recognition that all people carry a heavy baggage of seeds, each of which began sprouting at a different time in the past, and never stopped shooting out tendrils: a bag of memories which can never simply be dumped. The figure that embodies this preoccupation, in play after play, is a character who seldom appears onstage: the lost one, the dear one who has disappeared, never to be recovered. He has often been swept away in a horrifying instant, a moment that can never be forgotten, that will always live in the present but can never be reversed.

Harry, Noon and Night, the first of Ribman's plays to be produced, is set in Munich in 1955, during the American occupation. Each of the three scenes of this black comedy is essentially a confrontation between two people. In the first, Harry, posing as an impossibly inept journalist, is interviewing a thick-witted soldier in a bar while both of them fondle a local prostitute. The interview is a wild, improvisatory put-on; the soldier submits to all of Harry's addled questions because Harry promises to give him money for the girl when it is over, but the audience never learns Harry's reason for going through this charade.

In the second scene, the audience meets Immanuel, Harry's insectlike roommate (and bedmate), in their chaotic, filthy apartment; he is conducting a similar put-on of Harry's brother Archer, a gung-ho Air Force gunner during the war, now a can-do Ohio businessman. Harry is an artist who has abandoned the sugary, commercial pictorial realism he learned at home in favor of an ugly, inchoate expressionism that he has never succeeded in selling; Archer has come to fetch him home. Immanuel conducts a masterful put-on of Archer, posing alternately, and successfully, as a student of philosophy, a raging queen, and a vendor of religious relics, and befuddling him with fish scales, dry-cleaning fluid, talcum powder, and an overflowing toilet. In the last scene, Harry returns to the apartment to pack his bags to meet Archer at the train station, but causes such an uproar—he ties Immanuel up in the bedding and assaults the neighbors—that he is arrested and misses the train.

The plot is as chaotic as Harry's life and art, but through it, by indirection, the audience begins to see relationships and histories; it is never made clear exactly what Harry's problem is, or what his youth with Archer was like, but, subtly, a picture emerges. The one image that emerges most clearly is that of Moko the failure clown, whom Archer had brought Harry to see at the circus; Archer had found him hilarious, but Harry had seen only his pain.

One of the clowns in *The Journey of the Fifth Horse* is Chulkaturin, an impoverished landowner in czarist Russia, whose story is adapted from Ivan Turgenev's short story "Dnevnik lishnyago cheloveka" ("The Diary of a Superfluous Man"). Dying at the age of twenty-eight, Chulkaturin confides to his diary that he has never really lived, never succeeded in love, or indeed in making any impression at all on his fellowman. Ribman creates another clown as counterpoint to Chulkaturin: Zoditch, the lowly first reader in a publishing house, whose task it is to evaluate the manuscript of Chulkaturin's diary. As he reads the diary in his miserable rooming house, Chulkaturin's story comes to life, and Zoditch peoples it with analogous characters from his own loveless, pointless existence. In the end, Zoditch, dripping with scorn for Chulkaturin—especially for those qualities that resemble his own—rejects the manuscript and consigns him to oblivion.

Throughout the play, scenes from Chulkaturin's diary alternate with scenes from Zoditch's life and fantasies. This interweaving of plots and levels of reality is quite ingenious, but the technical ingenuity only enhances the pain and ludicrousness of the two protagonists. It is a bittersweet play, its laughter tinged with death. One of its most remarkable aspects is the way Ribman, through his mastery of language, convincingly creates two separate levels of nineteenth century Russian society.

His leap of imagination is even greater in *The Ceremony of Innocence.* This play was written, in a sense, as a response to the war in Vietnam, but the story that Ribman tells is a fanciful revision of the history of Ethelred the Unready, King of England in the eleventh century. Ribmán creates a sense of war as an entity unto itself, with its own momentum and a tenacious hold upon the minds and spirits of the people. Ethelred (who is generally seen by historians in a harsher light) is depicted as standing alone for peace, for common prosperity and the spread of literacy, and for justice; appalled at the prejudice and treachery of his court—even his son and his mother—toward the Danes, he simply refuses, as a matter of principle, to take the field at the head of his troops in defense of England.

Ribman begins his play with Ethelred's refusal to meet with the Earls of Sussex and Kent and the Bishop of London, who have come to his retreat on the Isle of Wight to importune him to do battle. His refusal seems bull-headed, a bit deranged, and positively untenable—especially in that the subject matter inevitably calls to mind William Shakespeare's histories, in which the welfare of the English throne is assumed to be the greatest good. The playwright then leaps backward a full year to reveal the underpinnings of Ethelred's convictions; then he works forward to the last scene, which is set a few hours after the first; and by the end of the play Ribman has managed to justify, both ethically and emotionally, the king's refusal to lead his country into war even in defense of its borders. Ribman's achievement is all the more remarkable in that he creates a persuasive language for his characters, a diction that mixes some of the direct, prosaic idiom of modern American speech with Elizabethan locutions—a factitious language that, in less skillful hands, might have come across as clumsy or downright silly, but which Ribman wields into an eloquent sort of poetry.

The linguistic audacity of *The Poison Tree* is very different, but no less perilous, and no less successful; Ribman sets the play in a prison, for the most part among black prisoners, and writes for them a number of varieties of black dialect. (A few years earlier, in 1967, another white writer, William Styron, had been excoriated for using black dialect—and, indeed, for daring to imagine the workings of a black man's mind—in *The Confessions of Nat Turner*, 1967.) The racism of the white prisoners and guards is a palpable, oppressive force throughout the play, but it is only one of a number of oppressions wearing away at the souls of prisoners and guards alike.

The play begins with the murder of a white guard by a black prisoner. The victim, his neck snapped, falls into the arms of another guard, Di Santis. He becomes obsessed with the senseless loss of his comrade, and, through direct violence and covert manipulation, he wreaks a terrible vengeance on the innocent as well as on the guilty. In the end, though, the tables are turned again, and the victimizer becomes the victim.

In *Cold Storage*, Ribman's most successful play commercially, the language is very close to his own natural speech: modern New York. In technique, it is his most realistic, straightforward play. It dares, though, to forge snappy comedy from a situation of inevitable catastrophe; set on the roof garden of a hospital, it presents the relationship between two patients: an old man who is dying and a prosperous middle-aged designer who may have cancer.

Buck, also set in modern New York, is somewhat more complex stylistically. It concerns a television director who is hired to make sleazy exploitation tapes for a cable channel but gets so involved in trying to create a true picture of the realities he is restaging that the scenes he films take on a life of their own.

Sweet Table at the Richelieu is set in a mysterious, elegant spa in an unspecified (though probably Germanic) corner of Europe. It consists of nothing but an after-dinner conversation among the guests; the guests, however, are a most curious, nightmarish assemblage of Eurotrash, and the discussion is brutal, feral, flaying—more direct, probing, and yet poetical than any real-life chitchat could ever be. Among the guests are a widowed baroness avid to enforce the prerogatives of her rank despite the humiliations of a more democratic age; a half-man, half-beast clairvoyant; a best-selling American author of pulp novels and her lover, a Moroccan given to violent fantasies; and a French Lothario who constantly humiliates his wife, who is always hanging on his neck. The presiding figure is Dr. Atmos, a cheerful but treacherous unlicensed physician who attracts guests to the Richelieu with promises of eternal youth.

The central character, Jeanine Cendrars, is a Pennsylvania woman who speaks very little. Early in the play, the audience learns that her marriage is in trouble, and toward the end Dr. Atmos, who dabbles in psychology as well as in rejuvenation, reveals to all that she is haunted by the loss of a child who was swept from her side on a boat by a wave during a moment of inattention.

While the other characters are intent on obliterating their pasts, Jeanine clings tenaciously to the image of her lost child, keeping him alive in her mind. In fact, the entire play can be seen as an emanation of her mind, and all the other characters as dream-figures brought to palpable form as combatants in her struggle with a tragic past that remains ever present.

The Cannibal Masque and *A Serpent's Egg* are one-act plays that were conceived to form a trilogy with *Sweet Table at the Richelieu*. Each of the three plays has for its central image people eating: in *Sweet Table at the Richelieu*, a cornucopia of sweets from a groaning board; in *The Cannibal Masque*, a fat pork dinner in the midst of a famine in Bavaria in 1923; and in *A Serpent's Egg* (set some thirty years later), a skimpy picnic on a German mountainside under the greedy eye of a rapacious landowner. While the longer play deals with excess through luxuriant verbiage, the one-acts are spare and parabolic, like little allegories of inhuman victimization, but each with a sudden shift of fortunes.

Though there are similarities with *Sweet Table at the Richelieu*, the other plays in the trilogy are very different in form and feel. Indeed, one of the most curious aspects of Ribman's playwriting career is its diversity, the breadth of imagination that puts him into so many different times, places, idioms, and styles. "I think of Keats," he has said, "who likened a career to the sun which gradually rises, reaches its zenith, and gradually sets. A playwright produces a body of work—he doesn't just produce one or two plays—because what he's doing is mining his life, and a life encompasses more than one or two plays." Ronald Ribman has mined many different veins of his life—a life of imagination as well as experience, rich in words, emotions, and fantasies—and has produced a body of work that reveals the absurd and often grotesque mixture of comedy and tragedy, reality and dream, that constitutes human existence.

Other major works

SCREENPLAY: *The Angel Levine*, 1970 (with William Gunn; based on a story by Bernard Malamud).

TELEPLAYS: *The Final War of Olly Winter*, 1967; *The Most Beautiful Fish*, 1969; *Seize the Day*, 1987 (based on Saul Bellow's novel); *The Sunset Gang*, 1991.

Bibliography

Brustein, Robert. "Journey and Arrival of a Playwright." In *The Third Theater*. New York: Alfred A. Knopf, 1969. In this discussion of *The Journey of the Fifth Horse*, Brustein, who was the drama critic for *The New Republic*, highlights the flexibility of Ribman's language, which can move from evocative tenderness to stinging rebuke. He also praises the way the dramatist suggests the hidden affinities of his two central characters, men who, at first glance, seem worlds apart.

Gottfried, Martin. *Opening Nights: Theater Criticism of the Sixties.* New York: G. P. Putnam's Sons, 1969. Theater critic Gottfried reviews *The Journey of the Fifth Horse* and compares it favorably to a contemporary British drama. Gottfried gives Ribman high marks for his fluid use of structure and his compassion for those tormented by loneliness.

_____. *A Theater Divided: The Postwar American Stage.* Boston: Little, Brown, 1967. In this work, Gottfried argues that the American theater after World War II was divided between left (liberal) and right (conservative) wings, each contesting the shape of drama in the United States. Ironically enough, though, the critic notes that Ribman's works were rejected by both camps. Even if, as Gottfried states, *Harry, Noon and Night* was "the best new American play produced anywhere in New York that year," it divided the critics because it proved unassimilable to fashionable viewpoints.

Lamont, Rosette C. "Murderous Enactments: The Media's Presence in the Drama." *Modern Drama* 28 (1985): 148-161. This essay analyzes how plays by Ribman and Janusz Glowacki present the mass media as violator of people's selfhood and sense of community. In Ribman's play *Buck*, "the true villains are the media and society; the circulation of money, as well as need and avarice, generates violence." In such an outlook, according to Lamont, one sees a reversal of the optimistic picture of technology that appeared in earlier generations of modern dramatists, as in the work of the Surrealists.

Weales, Gerald. *The Jumping-Off Place: American Drama in the 1960's.* New York: Macmillan, 1969. Comparing Ribman's three earliest plays, Weales finds the greatest strength to be in the first two. While they are idiosyncratic, they are full of surprises, feeling, and black comedy. In the first, *Harry, Noon and Night*, Ribman is able to "transform a potentially conventional character and situation into a statement about human beings that transcends the specific."

Jonathan Marks
(Updated by *James Feast*)

ELMER RICE
Elmer Leopold Reizenstein

Born: New York, New York; September 28, 1892
Died: Southampton, England; May 8, 1967

Principal drama

On Trial, pr. 1914, pb. 1919; *The Passing of Chow-Chow*, pr. 1915, pb. 1925 (one act); *The Iron Cross*, wr. 1915, pr. 1917, pb. 1965; *The House in Blind Alley*, wr. 1916, pb. 1932; *Wake Up, Jonathan*, pr. 1921, pb. 1928 (with Hatcher Hughes); *The Adding Machine*, pr., pb. 1923; *The Subway*, wr. 1923, pr., pb. 1929; *Street Scene*, pr., pb. 1929; *See Naples and Die*, pr. 1929, pb. 1930; *The Left Bank*, pr., pb. 1931; *Counsellor-at-Law*, pr., pb. 1931; *The Black Sheep*, pr. 1932, pb. 1938; *We, the People*, pr., pb. 1933; *Judgment Day*, pr., pb. 1934; *Between Two Worlds*, pr. 1934, pb. 1935; *Not for Children*, pr., pb. 1935, pr., pb. 1951 (revised); *American Landscape*, pr. 1938, pb. 1939; *Two on an Island*, pr., pb. 1940; *Flight to the West*, pr. 1940, pb. 1941; *A New Life*, pr. 1943, pb. 1944; *Dream Girl*, pr. 1945, pb. 1946; *Street Scene*, pr. 1947, pb. 1948 (libretto; adaptation of his play; music by Kurt Weill, lyrics by Langston Hughes); *Seven Plays*, pb. 1950; *The Grand Tour*, pr. 1951, pb. 1952; *Love Among the Ruins*, wr. 1951, pr., pb. 1963; *The Winner*, pr., pb. 1954; *Cue for Passion*, pr. 1958, pb. 1959; *Court of Last Resort*, pb. 1985.

Other literary forms

Elmer Rice was a versatile and prolific writer. Not only was he a serious dramatist, with more than thirty published plays to his credit at the time of his death, but also he was a novelist of some skill. In 1930, he published *A Voyage to Purilia*, a satire on Hollywood based on his experiences there during his stint as a writer for Samuel Goldwyn shortly after World War I. In the novel, Rice satirizes the shortcomings and triteness of the movie industry. That the book was accepted for serialization in *The New Yorker* attests Rice's skill as a stylist and craftsman. Rice's second novel, *Imperial City* (1937), was written during his four-year retirement from the theater. The work examines the variegated pattern of New York City life and offers a panoramic view of that fascinating metropolis. Rice was praised for the completeness of his depiction.

In his third and final novel, *The Show Must Go On* (1949), Rice drew on his experiences in the theater world. The book received some acclaim, both in the United States and in England, and has been translated into several foreign languages.

Rice is not remembered for his success as a screenwriter. He did, however, work in Hollywood after World War I and again in the 1930's, and still later in the 1940's. In the 1930's, Rice was hired by Universal to serve as scenarist for the film version of his own play *Counsellor-at-Law*. In the late 1940's, Rice agreed to do a screenplay based on *Earth and High Heaven* (1944), a novel by a Canadian writer, Gwethalyn Graham. The screenplay was completed, but the film was never made.

Rice also published a wide-ranging book on the theater, entitled *The Living Theatre* (1959). In it, he distinguishes the theater from the drama and covers such other areas as the status of the theater in Japan, England, and the Soviet Union; the beginnings of the theater in the United States and its growth; the Federal Theatre Project; commercialism in the arts; and censorship.

Finally, in 1963, Rice published his autobiography, *Minority Report*, which is fascinating reading for any student of modern American drama.

Achievements

Ever an innovator, ever seeking to improve the quality of the American theater, Rice began his Broadway career with a play, *On Trial*, that used the flashback technique for the first time on an American stage. The use of the technique created a production problem, the solution to which required yet another innovation. In order to shift scenes rapidly from various interior settings to a permanent courtroom setting, as required by the play, a two-platform stage had to be developed. In due course this was accomplished, and the device, called a jackknife stage, was introduced for the first time to the American theatergoing public. This development was a boon to playwrights, to whom it offered greater freedom and flexibility in choosing settings.

Rice was responsible for a number of other innovations. In *A New Life*, he was the first American playwright to present a birth scene in full view of the audience, shattering a long-observed taboo and leading the way for other American dramatists. In *The Winner*, Rice again broke with tradition: For the role of the judge who presides over a hearing involving a contested will, Rice chose an African American, Frederick O'Neal. This was a departure from the accepted practice of casting black people only in subordinate, menial, or other stereotypical parts. For casting a black person in an unconventional role, and thus opening up the American theater to racial equality, Rice was presented with the Canada Lee Foundation Award.

The most prestigious award Rice received as a playwright was the Pulitzer Prize. This was accorded him for his precedent-shattering play *Street Scene*. It was such a departure from the standard stage fare of the time that some thought it was not a play at all. There were simply too many characters, too many stories to be followed, Rice was told; the play would not be able to hold the attention of the audience. Nevertheless, when Rice persisted in his "folly," and finally found a producer, the play turned out to be his greatest hit—commercially as well as critically. It ran for 601 performances and was later produced in Europe, South America, Australia, New Zealand, the Near East, the Far East, and South Africa. Again it shows Rice's penchant for innovation: He introduced to the stage a dramatist's version of the collective novel.

Rice's disenchantment with the rampant commercialism of the American theater, its cliché-ridden plots, and its appeal to the puerile instincts of theatergoers caused him to become involved with organizations that were attempting to improve the quality of American theater fare. To that end, he contributed both financial support and advice to the Group Theatre, the Theatre Union, and the Theatre Alliance; he helped in the organization of the latter. On the whole, the purpose of these groups was to produce plays of social significance, to increase and make more important the contribution of those creative individuals—playwrights, directors, actors, and others—involved in putting on plays, and generally to improve the quality of American drama.

To the same end, Rice and four other successful and highly regarded American dramatists—Maxwell Anderson, S. N. Behrman, Sidney Howard, and Robert E. Sherwood—founded the Playwrights' Company in 1938. Its purpose was to extirpate the purely commercial influences of producers and theater owners by having the playwrights themselves furnish the money for producing plays. In this way, dramas of high quality—plays that might not otherwise be produced because of financial considerations—could be staged. The Playwrights' Company was a successful enterprise that survived for more than twenty years.

With the advent of the Depression, Rice became concerned with the price of theater admission tickets, which were no longer affordable to a large segment of the public. This problem compounded another one: the unemployment of many theater workers, unemployment that threatened to become permanent as the Depression spread and deepened. Rice's response to this crisis was to call for some sort of government sponsorship. His leadership here resulted in the formation of the Federal Theatre Project, the genesis of which was his letter to Harry Hopkins in 1935. The Federal Theatre priced tickets at a dollar or less, and sometimes gave them away. The effect was to build up a theater audience for the future and to provide employment for vast numbers of professional theater workers. Thus, Rice was in some measure responsible for keeping the American theater going during a critical period in its history.

Biography

Elmer Rice was born Elmer Leopold Reizenstein, in an apartment on Ninetieth Street in New York City, in 1892. It was a name he kept until the first production of his play, written in collaboration with Hatcher Hughes, *Wake Up, Jonathan*, in 1921. On opening night, the program listed the playwright for the first time under his newly assumed pen name, Elmer L. Rice.

Rice attended public schools in New York but had to drop out after his sophomore year in high school because his parents could no longer afford to support him. Jobs were hard to get, but Rice finally secured employment as a filing clerk in a law office. Though he did not really wish to become a lawyer, he decided that it was the only career open to him and enrolled in the New York Law School. There he found that classes bored him, and he began bringing reading materials to class to relieve the tedium. The classes were two hours long, and Rice discovered that he could read a play in that length of time. Thus, plays became his preferred reading material. In this way, he developed and nurtured his interest in the drama.

In 1913, Rice took and passed the bar examination, but he soon became appalled by legal ethics and decided that the practice of law was not for him. At this point, he had already written three plays: "A Defection from Grace," "The Seventh Commandment," and *The Passing of Chow-Chow.* The first two, written in collaboration with Frank Harris, a fellow law clerk, have never been published or produced; the third, a solo effort, was entered in a one-act-play contest sponsored by Columbia University in 1915 and won the aspiring playwright a silver cup. With his apprenticeship over, Rice was ready for Broadway.

Rice's first professionally produced play, *On Trial*, opened in New York on August 19, 1914. It was a blockbuster. The play ran for 365 performances, then went on the road to play in numerous cities throughout the United States. Later, it was performed abroad: in Europe, in South Africa, in South America, in Central America, and in the Far East. Eventually, it was made into a film.

During the remainder of the 1920's, Rice demonstrated his versatility and revealed his penchant for using the drama to expose the major social and economic diseases of his day. For example, in *The Iron Cross*, written in 1915 but not performed until 1917, Rice, a pacifist, excoriated the glorification of war. He also attacked in this work the puritanical element in American society and the distorted view of sex that it has produced.

In *The House in Blind Alley*, Rice considered some of the evils of the American economic system; in particular, he inveighed against the inclusion of children in the work force. The play was written in 1916 but has never been produced.

In the 1920's, Rice was at his best; it was during this period that his two greatest plays were produced. *The Adding Machine* and *Street Scene* are at least minor classics of the American theater. Although Rice continued to produce work at a prolific rate during this period, most of the plays he completed were collaborations, one-acts, or adaptations; the lone exceptions were *See Naples and Die* and *The Subway*, both produced in 1929.

During the 1930's, Rice was unable to maintain the high standard that he had set with his two masterpieces, *The Adding Machine* and *Street Scene*. His best drama of this period is undoubtedly *Counsellor-at-Law*, but that play, good as it is, hardly approaches the artistic merit of the two earlier ones. It was during the Depression years, however, that Rice was most effective as a social critic. In such plays as *The Black Sheep* and *The Left Bank*, Rice deplored the status of the creative artist in American society; in *We, the People* and in *American Landscape*, he lamented the plight of the American worker during this economically chaotic period; in *Judgment Day* and in *Between Two Worlds*, he attacked totalitarianism.

In the war years, Rice continued to write prolifically: Between 1940 and 1945, he had four plays produced. *Two on an Island*, a comedy, depicts the struggles of an aspiring young playwright and an embryonic actress to achieve success on Broadway. *Flight to the West* is another attack on Fascism. Rice's next play, *A New Life*, also expressed his desire that freedom and liberty flourish. Instead of the Nazis, however, it is dictatorial grandparents who are the recipients of the playwright's wrath. Rice concluded the period as he began it, with a comedy: *Dream Girl*, Rice's greatest commercial success since *Counsellor-at-Law*, is reminiscent of James Thurber's short story "The Secret Life of Walter Mitty."

Rice's first dramatic production of the postwar years, unless one counts his writing of the libretto for the musical version of his 1929 hit *Street Scene* and a revised version of his 1935 drama *Not for Children*, was *The Grand Tour*. One must not assume, however, that his energies were diminished. In addition to the libretto, he had written a novel, *The Show Must Go On*, and had taken two trips abroad, one of which provided him with the setting for a later play. Moreover, he hurled himself into several controversies involving censorship, or attempted censorship, of a number of movies. Finally, in the early 1950's, he was to be found defending the civil liberties threatened by the excesses of the House Committee on Un-American Activities and by McCarthyism.

The Grand Tour, principally a love story, also treats extensively materialism as a negative factor in American life. It is not one of Rice's better dramas. *The Grand Tour* was followed three years later by *The Winner*. Like its predecessor, it is not one of the playwright's serious plays, though it does point out the hypocrisy that is to be found everywhere in American society. The fragility of American marital relationships, another Rice staple, also receives its share of attention. One might add that the play revealed that Rice's low opinion of lawyers, first indicated when he gave up the practice of law, had not changed for the better. *Cue for Passion* reached the stage in 1958. It is William Shakespeare's *Hamlet*, converted to modern times and reeking with twentieth century psychology.

The playwright's last play to reach the stage, though only in a college production with Rice employed in an advisory capacity, was *Love Among the Ruins*, written twelve years earlier. In it, Rice deals with the death of love in the postwar world.

To the list of Rice's accomplishments between 1945 and his death in 1967, one must add *The Living Theatre*, a book of essays that reveals Rice's views on world theater, and much about his principles and practices as a dramatist. Then, too, there is his autobiography, *Minority Report*, which not only offers many insights into Rice the man and Rice the playwright but also serves as a history of the American theater between 1914 and 1963.

Analysis

Elmer Rice is unquestionably a major American playwright. His durability—his first play was produced in 1914, his last in 1963—and the sheer scope of his output ensure his stature in the history of American drama. Like many writers who came to maturity in the 1920's and the 1930's, he combined a dedication to art and craftsmanship with a commitment to social reform. In his autobiography, Rice mentions his particular attraction to works of literature that unmask the evils of society. This predilection serves to explain his preference for such dramatists as Henrik Ibsen, George Bernard Shaw, and August Strindberg. Of this group, it was Shaw with whom Rice most felt an affinity. Like Shaw, Rice believed that it was the playwright's duty to improve society by exposing its false values and hypocrisies. In this pursuit, virtually all of his attention was focused on America and Americans. Even when Rice's plays are set abroad, it is principally the weaknesses of Americans and of American society that he lays bare. Though he employed a variety of dramatic forms, and though his work covers a wide range of subject matter, his oeuvre is consistent in at least one respect: All of his dramas reveal his perennial engagement with improving the quality of American life by uncovering its many imperfections.

The Adding Machine, Rice's first masterwork, represented a departure from the realism of his earlier plays. In it, he adapted to the American stage the devices of German Expressionism; indeed, *The Adding Machine* is quite possibly the best full-length Expressionistic play by an American dramatist. The play had its genesis in Rice's visit to the Ford Motor Company's plant in Detroit, quickly followed by his tour of the Chicago stockyards. These firsthand observations of industrialization left Rice appalled. He watched in some horror the robotlike actions of workers who were obliged to perform their monotonous tasks while hovering over a relentless conveyer belt. Some time later, after a period of germination, Rice wrote, in the remarkable time of seventeen days, the play based upon his observation of the effect of the machine age upon humankind.

Expressionism, a technique for making inner experience concrete, is exemplified in the play in a number of ways: in the externalization of thought processes; in the treatment of the characters, who are numbered instead of named to indicate their dehumanization and loss of individuality; in the rows of numbers that decorate the wallpaper, signifying the ascendance of a quantified society.

Although *The Adding Machine* represented a departure in both form and technique from Rice's previous work, he remained the social critic he had always been. Among the targets of the play are hypocrisy, the depersonalization of the modern business world, bigotry, the impersonality of the law, and Puritanism.

The hypocrisy that permeates American life is demonstrated by Rice through his depiction of his protagonist, Zero, and Zero's wife. Zero, who has taken delight in watching a prostitute who neglects to pull the shade across her window even when she is not dressed, finally reports her to the police. Although he deplores her lack of modesty and her extravagant use of makeup, he later regrets that he had not taken advantage of his wife's absence to pay the prostitute a visit.

For her part, Mrs. Zero claims that she prefers movies that portray highly moral, wholesome love stories, but in the dialogue that follows, one discerns that Mrs. Zero's real predilection is for love stories that incorporate risqué scenes—scenes that may be cut before the movies reach the neighborhood theaters where she can see them.

To Rice, the business world is a competitive one where human beings and human values get short shrift. In such a world, there is little room for personal considerations. This depersonalization of relationships is shown both in Zero's boss's failure to know Zero's name—even though he has been his employee for twenty-five years—and his lack of concern for the consequences that await a man fired at an advanced age with no warning.

Racial bigotry, a frequent subject in Rice's drama, and sexism also receive attention in *The Adding Machine*. Early in the play, the Zeros host a party. Those who attend all dress alike, have the same tastes, share the same views and prejudices. If business conditions are bad, it is because of foreign agitators; women's suffrage is ridiculous; a woman's place is in the home; women have no business meddling in politics.

Rice's disenchantment with the legal profession, expressed when he refused to practice law shortly after receiving his degree and passing the bar examination, is revealed again here. Rice believed that the spirit of the law should be paramount, not the letter. He believed that in practice, however, the reverse is true. Thus, Rice finds the courts to be impersonal, even indifferent to those whose fates they determine—an attitude embodied by the judge in the courtroom scene, who is nothing but an impassive automaton. Similarly, Rice's belief that justice does not always prevail and that court cases are frequently won by trickery, theatrics, and obscuration is exemplified by Zero's lawyer's insistence that the blood on the murder weapon is red ink, even though Zero fully admits to his guilt and wishes to be punished. Later, Zero complains about court procedure that requires yes or no answers. Some questions necessitate more complex answers if justice is to be served.

The deleterious effects of Puritanism on the American psyche are revealed by Zero and Shrdlu, whom Zero (who has been executed for murder) meets in the afterlife. Shrdlu is also a murderer: He has killed his mother, and his conscience demands that he suffer the torture of the damned in hell for his unspeakable crime. What has happened to justice, to morality, that he should be permitted to spend eternity in the Elysian Fields? Schooled in a puritanical tradition, he cannot accept forgiveness and a happier fate, and he insists on eternal punishment.

Zero, imbued, like Shrdlu, with the Puritan morality of his earthly existence, cannot understand a heaven that admits murderers. Moreover, he is shaken by his discovery that he is living in the midst of drunkards, thieves, vagabonds, and adulterers. Unable to reconcile this knowledge with his own ingrained ideas about what is respectable, Zero is consigned to return to Earth to begin life anew in another identity.

Though *The Adding Machine* was neither a critical nor a commercial success when it first appeared in 1923, it is now highly esteemed and often performed; Rice himself compiled a list showing that between 1958 and 1963, *The Adding Machine* had a total of ninety-two productions. Today, more than a half century after its first performance, with machines encroaching at an ever-increasing rate upon territory previously held by human beings, the play remains relevant.

In *Street Scene*, Rice's second major work, the playwright returned to realism with a vengeance. To convey the sounds associated with the New York City setting of his play—automobile horns, squealing brakes, steamboat whistles—Rice recorded them, then put the records on two record players started a minute apart during the performance so as to duplicate the overlapping effect of heavy traffic and other assorted noises of the busy metropolis. Not satisfied with the unrealistic sound of footsteps moving across a wooden stage that purported to be a city street, Rice had a thin layer of cement placed upon the boards. Finally, and on a different level, Rice increased the play's authenticity by drawing his characters from a rich diversity of national and ethnic backgrounds.

In this play, Rice sought to reveal the lives and problems of various families living in an apartment house in a lower-middle-class neighborhood in New York. His realistic depiction of character and circumstance, however, does not prevent him from mounting the soapbox to decry the inadequacies of America's social and economic system.

To begin with the latter, Rice focuses on organized charity, which is a concomitant of the capitalistic system, since under capitalism there will always be those who are unable to support themselves and who have no other source of aid. In the 1920's, accepting charity was considered demeaning, and those who had to depend upon it—often through no fault of their own—were considered inferior. Rice, with his strong socialistic bent, sought to point out the unfairness of such an attitude and to invoke sympathy for its victims.

Thus, in *Street Scene*, the playwright's depiction of charity's representative, Miss Simpson, is highly critical. He begins by describing her as an unattractive spinster and then heightens the unfavorable impression by having her upbraid the small, timid, bewildered Mrs. Hildebrand for spending charity money to take her two children to the movies. That these two children cling to their mother in fear of the austere Miss Simpson only increases the audience's sympathy for the Hildebrands and one's dislike for Miss Simpson and the charity she represents.

There are other flaws in the American economic system, Rice would have us know. His spokesman here is Abraham Kaplan, who is appalled by the eviction of the Hildebrands by their landlord. The institution of private property, which places those without property at the mercy of the property-owning classes, is the real culprit, Kaplan contends.

Then, broadening the scope of his diatribe, he laments the status of the worker, whom he calls a wage slave, at the mercy of the all-powerful leaders of industry. Although these sentiments sound Marxist, one must not assume that Rice was a Communist: He was merely pointing out the need for social reform.

Racial bigotry, a ubiquitous element in American society, and one which Rice abhorred, is also treated in *Street Scene*; the play's mixture of Italian, Swedish, Irish, and Jewish characters provides Rice with an excellent opportunity for comment. At the same time, Rice, ever cognizant of the plight of women in American society, provides a sympathetic portrait of Mrs. Maurrant, one of the casualties of the virulent gossip of the bigoted Joneses. Though she is engaged in an adulterous relationship with Steve Sankey, the neighborhood collector for the milk company, Mrs. Maurrant is portrayed as a victim rather than a victimizer. Rice shows her to be a compassionate, loving woman joined in an unhappy marriage to a man who cannot satisfy her emotional needs and who treats her as though she were his personal property rather than a human being.

As a playwright, Rice followed in the footsteps of such earlier dramatists as Ibsen and Shaw. Like them, he was a social reformer, often in the vanguard of his contemporaries. Both for his contributions toward social betterment and for his multifaceted efforts to improve the quality of the American theater, Rice is deserving of a high place in his nation's literary history.

Other major works

NOVELS: *A Voyage to Purilia*, 1930; *Imperial City*, 1937; *The Show Must Go On*, 1949.

NONFICTION: *The Living Theatre*, 1959; *Minority Report*, 1963.

Bibliography

Durham, Frank. *Elmer Rice.* New York: Twayne, 1970. Durham's book progresses chronologically through Rice's work, first in farce, then in realist melodrama, through Expressionism and naturalism, propaganda plays, and finally through the period of psychological and symbolic drama. Durham writes in a readable fashion, perhaps somewhat worshipful in tone of Rice's ethical qualities and his ability to turn types into real characters with his "vivid, life-giving touch." Offers detailed analyses of all Rice's work, as well as nineteen pages of notes, bibliography, and index.

Hogan, Robert. *The Independence of Elmer Rice.* Carbondale: Southern Illinois University Press, 1965. Hogan offers a comparative analysis, discussing Rice's connection to Honoré de Balzac, Émile Zola, Marcel Proust, William Faulkner, Clifford Odets, Tennessee Williams, Eugene O'Neill, and others. His appreciation for Rice is evident with the statement that Rice "is rivalled in our theatre only by O'Neill." Hogan adds that "as a master of every kind of plot structure he probably stands alone." While this evaluation may be a bit hyperbolic at times, biased in Rice's favor, Hogan provides extensive analysis of major and lesser known works, as well as fourteen pages of notes, bibliography, and index.

Krutch, Joseph Wood. *The American Drama Since 1918: An Informal History.* Rev. ed. New York: George Braziller, 1957. Krutch praises *Street Scene* as Rice's best work, commenting that "no contemporary dramatist has (or rather had) a keener ear or a shrewder eye." He further remarks on Rice's ability to catch "the rhythm of everyday speech" and gestures. In a regretful tone, he describes Rice's decline into explaining theories rather than creating the kind of vision he had when he first produced *The Adding Machine.*

Levin, Meyer. "Elmer Rice." *Theatre Arts Monthly* 16 (January, 1932): 54-62. Levin analyzes Rice's "power to create people—however negative they may be." He places *The Adding Machine* within the Expressionist traditions, stating that it "bears direct comparison with the best products of the expressionist years." His analysis of *Street Scene* acknowledges Rice's desire to put "real people" in his plays. Levin is nevertheless critical of Rice for being too dexterous, perhaps even "bored by the theatre," despite or perhaps because of his technical gifts.

Palmieri, Anthony F. R. *Elmer Rice: A Playwright's Vision of America.* Rutherford, N.J.: Fairleigh Dickinson University Press, 1980. Palmieri argues that "Rice's greatest strength is related to his chief failing." His reformer's impulse leads at times to didactic or propagandistic writing. Palmieri details how Rice struggled against censorship and strove to make the theater an agent of social change, being one of the first to attack such evils as child labor and Nazism. This fair yet sympathetic assessment reveals Rice's place in American drama as an innovator in such works as *The Adding Machine*, *Street Scene*, *We, the People*, *A New Life*, *The Winner*, *Wake Up, Jonathan*, *The Subway*, *Judgment Day*, *Between Two Worlds*, and *American Landscape*. Palmieri's index and ten-page bibliography offer the most extensive available background on Rice.

Anthony F. R. Palmieri
(Updated by *Rebecca Bell-Metereau*)

LYNN RIGGS

Born: Claremore, Cherokee Nation (now Oklahoma); August 31, 1899
Died: New York, New York; June 30, 1954

Principal drama

Knives from Syria, pr. 1925, pb. 1927 (one act); *Big Lake*, pr., pb. 1927;
Rancor, pr. 1927; *A Lantern to See By*, pb. 1928, pr. 1930; *Sump'n Like
Wings*, pb. 1928, pr. 1939; *Roadside*, pr., pb. 1930; *Green Grow the Lilacs*,
pr., pb. 1931; *Russet Mantle*, pr., pb. 1936; *The Cherokee Night*, pr., pb.
1936; *A World Elsewhere*, pb. 1939; *The Year of Pilar*, wr. 1940, pb. 1947;
The Cream in the Well, pr., pb. 1941; *Dark Encounter*, pb. 1947; *Laughter
from a Cloud*, pr. 1947; *Hang on to Love*, pb. 1948; *Borned in Texas*, pr.
1950 (revision of *Roadside*); *Toward the Western Sky*, pr., pb. 1951 (music
by Nathan Kroll).

Other literary forms

In addition to writing more than twenty plays, Lynn Riggs was the
author of many poems, which appeared in such periodicals as *Poetry: A
Magazine of Verse* (edited by Harriet Monroe), *The Smart Set* (edited by
H. L. Mencken), and *The Nation*. A number of these poems were collected
and published in a volume entitled *The Iron Dish* (1930). Riggs also
authored screenplays in Hollywood for Metro-Goldwyn-Mayer, including
Laughing Boy (1933), *Delay in the Sun* (1935), *Garden of Allah* (1936),
and, perhaps most notably, *The Plainsman* (1936), on which he collaborated with Waldemar Young and Harold Lamb.

Achievements

Riggs achieved early recognition from such notable theatrical authorities
as Barrett H. Clark and Arthur Hopkins, both of whom championed his
work, although most later critics labeled him a minor regionalist. When
Clark was speaking of Riggs's first full-length production for the commercial stage, *Big Lake*, he called Riggs "one of the few native dramatists who
can take the material of our everyday life and mould it into forms of stir-
ring beauty." Speaking of *Green Grow the Lilacs*, Hopkins said that "Riggs
caught our fading glory and left it for posterity." It was this play and the
comic *Russet Mantle* that were Riggs's greatest commercial successes for
the stage during his lifetime, although he continued to write for the theater
until 1951. His chief posthumous claim to fame has been as the author of
Green Grow the Lilacs, which provided the basic text for the epoch-making
Richard Rodgers and Oscar Hammerstein musical *Oklahoma!* (1943). As
tastes change, however, so do literary reputations, and it may be that, as
interest in regional and ethnic literature and in plays about women

increases, Riggs's work will come to be more highly regarded.

As noted by critic Richard Watts, Jr., Riggs's plays are "invariably rich and lyric folk [dramas, with] true feeling for atmosphere and period." "He wrote of people he had known," said his colleague Joseph Benton, "entwining their foibles, weaknesses and strengths, their garrulous chatterings and grass-roots wisdoms throughout his plays." Of Cherokee extraction, growing up the son of a farmer in Oklahoma in its earliest days as a state, Riggs wrote of the disappointed expectations and compromised human values that resulted among simple farm people from their conflicts with the changing values of American society. Perhaps his outstanding characteristics as an American playwright are his unwillingness to write cheap or empty plays, his facility with strong situations, his ability to write powerful two-person scenes, his appreciation for the genuine folk music of his region, and his gift for expressing the lyricism half-consciously felt and beautifully revealed in the lives of humble and ordinary people.

Biography

When Lynn Riggs was born in 1899, Claremore was still part of the Indian territory that was later incorporated into the state of Oklahoma. Son of an Indian farmer, he enjoyed the simple amusements and "play parties" of his neighbors as well as their unselfconscious folk traditions. He did various odd jobs in his youth, first as an itinerant farmhand and cowpuncher and then as a singer at the local movie house. Later, he traveled around the country, working as a proofreader on a newspaper in San Francisco, as a clerk in the book section of Macy's department store in New York City, and as a newspaper reporter in Tulsa. At the age of twenty-one, Riggs enrolled in the University of Oklahoma as a music major, later changing his major to English so that he could qualify for a readership position. He continued to hold the position of second tenor in the solo quartet organized by the university, which toured in a professional summer Chautauqua and minstrel show. He had two farces, *Cuckoo* and *Honeymoon*, produced at school while he was still an undergraduate.

Riggs's dramatic successes at the university and his early one-act *Knives from Syria*, with its Ali Hakim-like peddler character, all showed originality and humor, and he was encouraged to continue playwriting. The production of the full-length *Big Lake* by the American Laboratory Theatre attracted some critical attention and won for Riggs a Guggenheim Fellowship. In 1928, Riggs resided in France, where he wrote *Green Grow the Lilacs* and much of *Roadside*, which was produced by Arthur Hopkins and starred Ralph Bellamy as Texas. At this point, Riggs was considered one of America's most promising playwrights, but critics qualified their praise. By 1936, when *Russet Mantle* succeeded as a comedy, although it had been conceived as a serious work, reviewers were generalizing about Riggs's failure to master the needs of the theater in terms of probability of plotting and characterization. They seemed to believe that Riggs's promise had somehow missed fire. During this period, Riggs was working with some success as a screenwriter.

Riggs was inducted into the United States Army in 1942, serving in the Army Air Corps, and his plays of the 1940's reflect his concern with the international chaos that rocked that era. His last work produced on Broadway was the 1950 *Borned in Texas*, a revision of the 1930 *Roadside*; in 1951, he wrote a "music play" on commission from Western Reserve University to celebrate the school's one hundred twenty-fifth anniversary. He was working on his first novel when he died of stomach cancer at the age of fifty-four. Riggs was survived by a sister and several brothers; there is no evidence that he ever married. A memorial for him was erected in the town of Claremore, Oklahoma, in 1958, and the library at Rogers University in Claremore has a collection of materials both by and about him.

Analysis

Lynn Riggs is known almost exclusively as a regional dramatist in the tradition of Susan Glaspell and Paul Green, but his work is more varied in both content and style than this label would suggest. For example, it is accurate to call Riggs an ethnic regionalist, but only if one includes the Cherokees in *The Cherokee Night*; the Hispanics in *The Year of Pilar*, *A World Elsewhere*, and *Laughter from a Cloud*; the farmers and ranchers of *Green Grow the Lilacs*; and braggart frontiersmen in *Roadside* as ethnic groups associated with Riggs. A favorite theme deals with the attempts, in Arthur Hopkins' words, to show "beauty in rebellion... now successful self-assertion, now frustration—usually girlhood or womanhood fighting for the right to self, for adventure, for love." This theme finds expression not only in the lightly sketched romance between Curly and Laurey in the well-known *Green Grow the Lilacs*, but also in almost all Riggs's other plays, which include tragedies, comedies, and two naturalistic studies of uneducated, lower-class women.

Stylistically, Laurey's dream ballet in *Oklahoma!* is a natural extension of elements already present in *Green Grow the Lilacs*, where Riggs successfully portrays Jeeter's perverse and lurid lust while remaining almost within a naturalistic framework. The authentic folk songs in this, as well as several other of his plays, typify his desire to extend the stage's bounds beyond realism. Thus, most of his plays are infused with a poetic diction that goes far beyond naturalistic speech, as in *Roadside*, or deal with highly melodramatic situations that reflect deep, unconscious drives, as in *The Cream in the Well*, or move overtly beyond naturalism in setting, language, situation, or onstage use of supernatural elements, as does *The Cherokee Night*.

Riggs's plays demonstrate various kinds and strands of excellence, mixed with a number of structural problems. His poetic gift surfaces whenever the beauty of the natural world is invoked. This sensitivity to natural beauty, for example, resulted in the charming opening stage directions for *Green Grow the Lilacs*, which were translated into the lyrics of the title song in *Oklahoma!* In a number of his plays, Riggs uses songs and poetic diction in situations of heightened emotion. The same desire for lyricism finds expression in the effective use of scenic elements, such as the mountains in *Laughter from a Cloud*. In the play that Riggs himself considered his best, *The Cherokee Night*, a Cherokee burial ground looms in the background of each scene, dominating the stage action in an effective symbolic statement.

The Cherokee Night, however, also illustrates Riggs's weaknesses as a playwright. The play has strong moments and a significant, fresh theme, but the characters are present more to illustrate the theme than to exist on their own, while the structure (the play's seven scenes are not in chronological order) lacks clarity. Another play that illustrates Riggs's weaknesses as well as his strengths is *The Cream in the Well*, a story of incest which is based on the premise that an intelligent, sensitive woman may yet be a despoiler of all of those around her because of the secret desires which poison her and her brother's life. Aware that individual scenes showed real power, reviewers nevertheless asked why this melodramatic, contrived plot had been chosen. The theme of incest is a powerful element in *A Lantern to See By* as well and lurks in the background of *Sump'n Like Wings*. It is doubtful that Riggs chose the theme in order to write a successful play. Rather, this was a serious playwright who was wrestling with a theme that engaged him.

The Riggs protagonist searching for love is more often female than male, an emancipated woman, struggling to make some sort of active life for herself in which she will not be dependent on the superior strength or initiative of a man. It seems as though those plays end happily in which both the man and his "womern" agree on a common set of values—either mutually accepting the division into traditional, sharply defined masculine and feminine roles or both being willing to adjust to the newer emancipation of women—while those plays end unhappily in which some external condition or some restlessness within the characters forces an irresolvable confrontation over traditional values. It should not be assumed that Riggs was trying to assert the superiority of traditional values. He understood that the forces causing change were irresistible, and he was trying to chart what happened as people tried to accommodate such changes.

Riggs was one of thirty-three playwrights who responded to a questionnaire from W. David Sievers, who was researching his book *Freud on Broadway* (1955). Riggs said that he had read some of Sigmund Freud's work, that he felt his plays were "doing the same thing" as analysts did, and that "he had sought for dramatic devices to dramatize the workings of

the unconscious. . . ." The need of Riggs's characters to express their libidi-
nous impulses—a need that seemed overstrained to some reviewers and
critics—is insistent throughout his plays. In *Dark Encounter*, for example,
the heroine, Gail Atwood, seems to have fallen in love with three different
men (although engaged to marry Ancil Bingham, she becomes involved
sexually with Teek and Karl on day one and day two of the play, respectively), while Riggs portrays her throughout as a sensitive and sympathetic
character. Similarly, in *Russet Mantle*, Kay spends night one with one man
and night two with another without losing Riggs's sympathy.

The first group of plays written by Riggs, dating from the 1925 *Knives
from Syria* through the 1931 *Green Grow the Lilacs*, are studies of young
people struggling to find themselves within the context of the kind of harsh
farm environment made familiar by Eugene O'Neill in *Desire Under the
Elms* (pr. 1924), which the early, tragic *A Lantern to See By* resembles.

In *A Lantern to See By*, John Harmon, the father of six living sons,
treats his wife as a child breeder and servant. Only the youngest boy,
Jodie, seems to have any sensitivity to his mother's situation. When Jodie
tries to protect her, the father almost deliberately misinterprets his motives
and beats him with an iron bar. In act 2, the mother dies after her eleventh
childbirth, and a neighbor's daughter, Annie Marble, comes to do the
mother's work for the family. Jodie sees a potential for both mothering and
loving in Annie. He falls in love with her, whereas she is willing to make
use of his infatuation. She tells him that to win her he must take her away
to the big city—Muskogee—which she had admired on a visit to a friend.
Jodie leaves to take a job so that he can earn enough money to start his
own life with Annie. Meanwhile, act 2 ends with Annie accepting John
Harmon's advances. Act 3 opens a month later on the evening of a play
party at the Harmons'. Annie is asking for her salary of eight dollars a
month, plus the unspecified amount promised for her "extra services" to
her employer. Harmon puts off the payment, rightly fearing that she will
leave as soon as she gets the money. Then Jodie arrives, angry because his
employer, his father's friend, had said he would pay Jodie's wages only to
John Harmon. Learning of the situation between his father and Annie,
Jodie becomes even angrier, and he kills his father offstage with an iron
bar. The play ends as the neighbors speculate over Jodie's fate and the
audience learns that Annie's goal was to reach a friend in Muskogee, a
prostitute, and join her in her chosen occupation.

This naturalistic tragedy of lower-class farm life, with its theme of father
and son fighting first over the mother and then her replacement, was
clearly indebted to O'Neill's farm play. Taken on its own, Riggs's play is an
effective drama. The father is a driven man, though without the religious
ecstasy of O'Neill's Ephraim Cabot, and his crude energy provides an
effective contrast to Jodie's poetic sensitivity. Less complex and melodra-

matic than *Desire Under the Elms*, it is more squalid, as is its companion piece, *Sump'n Like Wings*.

In *Sump'n Like Wings*, the protagonist is a young girl, Willie, whose mother has tried to keep her "good" not by moral persuasion but by locking her up, for example, when she goes swimming with some boys. Finally, Willie rebels and runs off with a ne'er-do-well. Riggs makes no attempt to glamorize Willie or her environment. She gets into the kinds of trouble endemic to such situations (a baby that dies, a husband who simply takes off, never to be seen again). Though a kindly uncle offers help, Willie declares that she must learn to stand on her own. She refuses his offer of a refuge and ends the play alone, trying to put a lock on her door so that strange men will not be able to enter her room whenever they choose.

The audience is intended to see Willie's determination to earn her own way as a victory; she is trying to grow up and become responsible for herself without giving up her right to express her own sexuality. This theme is developed in parallel through an extended conversation in act 1 between Willie and Elvie Rapp, an odd young vagabond whose bold sexuality has gotten her into trouble but which is sympathetically presented by Riggs. Writing in 1936, drama historian Arthur Hobson Quinn deplored Riggs's choice of a protagonist such as Willie, saying that she "escapes from the deadly hotel life not into anything worthwhile, but only into the world of her own desires, which are entirely selfish." Since Willie's is a "narrow soul," this play, like its heroine, is a "little one." From a more modern perspective, the play can be seen, rather, as an early attempt to deal with the theme of overt female sexuality—a theme that is still likely to raise the hackles of some male critics.

The issue of healthy versus neurotic sexuality again underlies the seemingly simple *Green Grow the Lilacs*. The attraction of Curly and Laurey for each other, like the attraction of Texas and Hannie in *Roadside* (which seems to be a more broadly drawn caricature of some of the same themes as are found in *Green Grow the Lilacs*), is set in a context in which people pair off as a part of the fecund natural world. As the opening stage directions say, "men, cattle in a meadow, blades of the young corn, streams" give off "a visible golden emanation." Curly is associated with the outdoors and nature, both by his rhapsodic appreciation of its beauty in several long speeches which serve no other dramatic function, and by his job as a cowboy. Laurey, too, is part of nature. When Curly tells her he loves her, it is by describing how he saw her while she was growing up: first, "a little tyke" "pickin' blackberries"; next, riding "a little gray filly of Blue Starr's"; then, the year before, when she had been "out a-pickin' flowers" and "had a whole armful of Sweet Williams and wild roses and morning glories." In contrast, Jeeter, the hired hand on Aunt Eller's and Laurey's farm, lives "in a dark hole bent over a table a-fingerin' a pack of cards 's greasy 's a ole tin spoon." Laurey has made the mistake of being kind to Jeeter when he was ill, and his feelings of inferiority, his fascination with sadistic tales of sexual obsession, murder, and revenge, lead to his sexual advances on and threats to Laurey.

Laurey is afraid not to go to the play party with Jeeter, imagining that he might burn down her home in revenge, but when he goes too far at the play party, seizing and threatening her, she sends him off, relying on Curly. They soon agree to marry, but their wedding night is marred by the locals, who set on them to tease them in a "shivoree" (defined by Riggs as a bawdy, communitywide marriage celebration). Then Jeeter emerges from the crowd, setting fire to the haystack holding the young couple. He and Curly fight, and Jeeter is accidentally impaled on his own knife. Curly is arrested but breaks out of jail before the hearing that will determine his fate; in the play's last scene, he visits his bride, who assures him, "I'll put up with everything now. You don't need to worry about me no more." There is an implied happy ending, but there is not the onstage trial and freeing of Curly that occurs in *Oklahoma!*

There are other differences between the play and the adaptation. Riggs used traditional folk songs, whereas Rodgers and Hammerstein wrote the many famous songs, including "People Will Say We're in Love," "The Surrey with the Fringe on Top," and "Oh, What a Beautiful Morning," which enrich the musical. In Riggs's play, Ado Annie has no steady beaux. She comes to visit Laurey with the peddler, who is unnamed, but her significant role in the musical, as well as her fiancé, Will, do not exist in the play. Jeeter, Curly, and Aunt Eller are the play's chief figures. Laurey starts out as somewhat of a spoiled child who is taught by Aunt Eller that she's "got to look at all the good on one side and all the bad on the other, and say: 'Well, all right, then!' to both of 'em."

In his introduction to the play, Riggs explained his intention to use "the simplest of stories." His play could have been subtitled "An Old Song," he wrote. He wanted to illustrate his characters' "quaintness, their sadness, their robustness, their simplicity, their hearty or bawdy humors, their sentimentalities, their melodrama, their touching sweetness." His success cannot be measured by the fate of the play. Although it was produced by the prestigious Theatre Guild with Franchot Tone as Curly, Helen Westley as Aunt Eller, June Walker as Laurey, and Lee Strasberg as the peddler, it ran for only sixty-four performances. In the musical version, however, it ran for more than five years and was one of the American theater's truly great events.

Russet Mantle, first produced in 1936, was Riggs's biggest hit. Ironically, although he intended it as a serious study of love versus convention and the materialistic values of American society, the minor character provided as comic relief came to dominate the play. It was produced as a comedy and thus provided an effective balance between Riggs's interests and Broadway standards. In the play, Kay Rowley and her mother visit Kay's retired aunt and uncle living in New Mexico. Kay spends her first night there in bed with a cowboy whom she has met that day. Kay's scandalized aunt and uncle try to discipline her, while Kay's mother, Effie, who is the comic creation largely responsible for the play's success, wants to know none of the details, so she will not have to be upset. The audience learns that the aunt did not marry the poor boy she loved in her youth but settled for financial security with her present husband. Their marriage, then, is an empty one, and their scandalized reaction to Kay's sexual aggressiveness may mask their own dissatisfaction. A young poet named John comes to the farm seeking a job and is hired. He sees through Kay's pose of pseudosophistication, and the two have a love affair. When Kay's pregnancy is discovered, she refuses to name the father, but John is delighted to acknowledge the child. Their hosts now threaten to throw them out into the harsh Depression world which has been evoked by John's job search and Kay's talk of "Riot squads, strikebreakers, nausea gas, bayonets and starvation! And voices crying out, for what? A little bread, a little sun, a little peace and delight." For their part, the young people are ready to go out into the world together, having affirmed the primacy of true love over convention. In the last line of the play, however, the aunt suggests that she and her husband talk things over before ejecting the young couple, implying that they may find a way to help their niece, even though they disapprove of her behavior.

Critics particularly enjoyed Effie Rowley, and the play enjoyed a good run of more than one hundred performances. Riggs's other 1936 effort, *The Cherokee Night*, a serious statement, fared very poorly with reviewers when performed by the Federal Theatre Project, yet this unique play deserves discussion.

Each of the seven scenes of *The Cherokee Night* is separately titled and constructed so that it can be performed independently of the others. Yet the point of the play, that the Cherokees have become weak, materialistic, and immoral as a result of abandoning their cultural heritage and mixing through intermarriage with the whites, is made most effectively by implication through seeing the entire play and realizing the relationship between the various scenes. The play's structure may well owe some elements to O'Neill's *The Emperor Jones* (pr. 1920), in which supernatural elements and racial memory are similarly implied, and effective use is also made of a drumbeat, but *The Emperor Jones* proceeds in a straight chronology (backward through time) in its supernatural scenes and prepares the audience for the supernaturalism by establishing Jones's superstition and by introducing the transitional symbol of the silver bullet. *The Cherokee Night* lacks that clarity of structure. The chronological order is confusing as the scenes take place, severally, in 1915, 1927, 1931, 1906, 1913, 1919, and 1895.

Brooks Atkinson claimed that the play was "pushing into real poetic trag-edy," that this "story of a world that has lost its heritage . . . is the universal complaint." At the same time, like other reviewers, Atkinson complained of the play's incoherence, and there was, no doubt, much confusion among audiences because of the demands the play made on their attention. Whether audiences today would be equally bewildered, when flashbacks and flash-forwards have become commonplace in films, is an open question.

In the play's first scene, "Sixty-seven Arrowheads," a desultory picnic of bickering, young, half-breed Cherokees is interrupted by the entrance of the Cherokee Jim Talbert. He tells them that he has been digging for arrowheads, the relics of the once proud nation whose burial ground they have chosen for their picnic site. He wants them to remember their heri-tage, but they drive him, and it, off and out of their minds as the mound begins to glow in the gathering darkness. In the subsequent scenes, with the symbol of the burial ground always present, the picnickers are seen at various points in their lives. One becomes a prostitute, another becomes rich by denying her heritage entirely, another becomes a murderer. A fourth becomes a parasite, wasting his time in aimless joyriding, living off a land grant given to an Osage woman instead of earning his own. Two scenes (4 and 5) imply the supernatural. In the last scene, a full-blooded Cherokee, Gray Wolf, says to the dying criminal, "You though—like my boy. He's dead. He was half white, like you. They killed him, had to kill him! Not *enough* Indian. The mixture."

Although not all Riggs's various concerns would captivate modern audi-ences, there is no question that he deserves a place in the history of Amer-ican drama. Perhaps theater historian Alan S. Downer said it best when he praised Riggs for "the freshness and poetry of the speech and the warm humanity of the characters." His plays invoke the American tradition of love of nature, simplicity, and decency, at war with the complexities of modern life. The plays have value in helping to preserve that tradition.

Other major works

POETRY: *The Iron Dish*, 1930.

SCREENPLAYS: *Laughing Boy*, 1933; *Delay in the Sun*, 1935; *Garden of Allah*, 1936; *The Plainsman*, 1936 (with Waldemar Young and Harold Lamb).

Bibliography

Braunlich, Phyllis. *Haunted by Home: The Life and Letters of Lynn Riggs.* Norman: University of Oklahoma Press, 1988. In this important biogra-phy and critical analysis of Riggs's works, Braunlich discusses the uni-versal themes in Riggs's plays, which are all set in the early days of the

Oklahoma territory. His plays deal with the worst human frailties. Attention is given to *Green Grow the Lilacs*, upon which was based the book for the Richard Rodgers and Oscar Hammerstein musical *Oklahoma!* (1943). Illustrations, complete listing of Riggs's works, extensive bibliography, and index.

Brenton, Joseph. "Some Personal Reminiscences About Lynn Riggs." *Chronicles of Oklahoma* 34 (Autumn, 1956): 296-301. A warm remembrance of Riggs by Brenton, who knew him from his earliest college days in Oklahoma to his death in New York. Brenton places some of Riggs's major decisions and accomplishments into biographical context.

Downer, Alan S. *Fifty Years of American Drama.* Chicago: Henry Regnery, 1951. In the chapter entitled "Folk Drama," Downer suggests that *Green Grow the Lilacs*, and more important, *Roadside*, epitomize the American folk drama. The plays are distinguished above other Western melodramas by their poetry of speech, warm humanity, and characters. Index.

Erhard, Thomas. *Lynn Riggs: Southwest Playwright.* Austin, Tex.: Steck-Vaughn, 1970. This forty-four-page monograph provides an excellent biography and critical introduction to Riggs's plays. Erhard comments on the playwright's use of the territorial Oklahoma dialect and settings to tell universal stories of human drama.

Sper, Felix. *From Native Roots: A Panorama of Our Regional Drama.* Caldwell, Idaho: The Caxton Printers, 1948. Sper briefly describes the conflicts and plots of nine Riggs plays. He concludes that Riggs's use of violence, fury, incest, and murder seem to give the plays an air beyond reality. Bibliography and index.

Vera Jiji
(Updated by *Gerald S. Argetsinger*)

THOMAS WILLIAM ROBERTSON

Born: Newark-on-Trent, England; January 9, 1829
Died: London, England; February 3, 1871

Principal drama

A Night's Adventure: Or, Highways and Byways, pr. 1851 (adaptation of Edward Bulwer-Lytton's novel *Paul Clifford*); *David Garrick*, wr. c. 1857, pr. 1864, pb. 1870(?) (adaptation of Mélesville's play *Sullivan*); *The Cantab*, pr. 1861 (one act); *Constance*, pr. 1865 (libretto; music by Frederick Clay); *Society*, pr. 1865, pb. 1866; *Ours*, pr. 1866, pb. 1890; *Caste*, pr. 1867, pb. 1878; *Play*, pr. 1868, pb. 1890; *School*, pr. 1869, pb. 1874; *Home*, pr. 1869, pb. 1879 (adaptation of Émile Augier's play *L'Aventurière*); *Dreams*, pr. 1869, pb. 1875(?) (originally as *My Lady Clara*, pr. 1869); *M.P.*, pr. 1870, pb. 1890; *Not at All Jealous*, pr. 1871, pb. 1872; *War*, pr. 1871, pb. 1891; *A Row in the House*, pr. 1883; *The Principal Dramatic Works of Thomas William Robertson*, pb. 1889, 1977 (2 volumes).

Other literary forms

Thomas William Robertson was a prolific writer of periodical articles and stories before he achieved success as a playwright. None of this work is of lasting interest; none of it advances theories of dramaturgy. Robertson produced one novel of interest, *David Garrick* (1865). Four of his prose works are easily accessible to modern readers. "The Poor Rate Unfolds a Tale," in *Rates and Taxes and How They Were Collected*, edited by Thomas Mood and published in 1866, anticipates the play *Caste* in many important ways, including similar characters, motifs, and themes. "After Dinner," in *The Savage Club Papers* of 1867, is a spoof on marriage customs which gently suggests that neither cold calculation nor lusty romance guarantees a happy marriage. "Exceptional Experiences," in *The Savage Club Papers* of 1868, is a modestly witty essay aimed at exploding a variety of social myths: the brutality of miners, the rapacity of innkeepers, the jolliness of sailors, and the snobbishness of successful men toward their former acquaintances. Robertson's restiveness about the unfairness of stereotyping is characteristic of his plays as well. His introduction to *Artemus Ward's Panorama* (1869) is essentially an effusion memorializing his friend, the American humorist Charles Farrar Browne.

Achievements

The front matter of *The Principal Dramatic Works of Thomas William Robertson* lists forty-seven plays, all but fourteen of them published. Of the total, *The Principal Dramatic Works of Thomas William Robertson* reproduces sixteen. Except for the plays *David Garrick*, a highly successful potboiler adapted from Mélesville's *Sullivan*, and *Dreams* (retitled version of *My Lady Clara*), a somewhat less successful one, Robertson's reputation rests on the six plays produced at the Prince of Wales's Theatres: *Society*, *Ours*, *Caste*, *Play*, *School*, and *M.P.* These plays form the body of a dramatic revolution whose reality is universally recognized but whose extent has not been finally set. Robertson teamed with sympathetic managers, Sir Squire and Marie Wilton Bancroft, to achieve a new sort of production. It featured ensemble acting, which emphasized the totality of the dramatic situation and eschewed the then dominant star system. This was combined with a realistic treatment of theme and staging within a cameo theater setting. Less clear than the fact of Robertson's signal success is the extent to which he should be given credit for achieving a breakthrough from melodrama to realistic serious drama a decade and a half before Henrik Ibsen; also a matter of critical debate is his contribution to the Little Theater movement that began to sweep Europe and eventually the United States.

As early as 1875, an anonymous critic for the magazine *Temple Bar* gave Robertson credit for revitalizing British drama and exerting a continuing influence after his death. This anonymous critic asserted that Robertson's success was in part a result of his novel treatment of social conflicts in a manner drawn from life; Robertson's skills as a stage manager, the critic said, were also crucial to his success. This early evaluation of Robertson's career anticipated the boundaries of much subsequent criticism.

George Bernard Shaw took two occasions to refer to Robertson's work in passing. In the first, he used a recently revived production of *Caste* as a club with which to hammer Arthur Wing Pincro's *The Second Mrs. Tanqueray* (pr. 1893), observing that a comparison of Pinero's characters, in the matter of realism, to those of *Caste* would be as absurd as a comparison of *Caste*'s realism with that of Ibsen's *A Doll's House* (pr. 1879). In a hardly less restrained mood, Shaw declared in another essay, "Mr. John Hare," that young people seeing *Caste* for the first time in 1884 could form no clear idea of the extent of its impact upon their fathers, who had spent a lifetime watching dramas whose staging was so far removed from natural representation that a production of Giuseppe Verdi's opera *La Traviata* might be considered "photographically realistic" in comparison.

Shaw's most extensive consideration of Robertson's achievement came in "Robertson Redivivus." He described *Caste* as an epoch-making play, newly revived. While he conceded that the epoch and the play were both "very little," he suggested that few critics encountered more than two plays of such importance in a lifetime. Shaw pointed out, as have most subsequent critics, that Robertson's new, realistic characters were, in fact, the old stage types very thinly "humanized": the stage swell, the Dickensian caricature of a rogue, the sentimental hero and heroine, and the conventional haughty mother. Still, Shaw noted, even the swell and the haughty mother were indeed humanized, compared with their counterparts on the stage in the 1860's. He held that Robertson gave sympathetic qualities to characters previously treated as "beyond redemption."

Less kind than Shaw, W. Wilding Jones wrote in "Robertson as a Dramatist," published in 1897, that Robertson's plays owed their success to the strength of their actors, to Robertson's good sense in keeping the plays short enough not to try the audience's patience, to bright dialogue and concise structure, and to the novelty of seeing a play of "home manufacture" on a stage dominated by French adaptations.

Cecil Ferard Armstrong's "Thomas William Robertson," published in 1913, was probably the first serious and extensive critical approach to Robertson's life and plays. Armstrong, too, argued that *Caste* began two revolutions, but not the revolutions identified by his predecessors. The first he defined as the innovation of highly professional London companies which, being sent on tour, doomed the old-fashioned provincial stock companies. The second he defined as the establishment of international dramatic copyright laws, triggered by a fuss over a pirated edition appearing before the New York production of *Caste*. Armstrong refused to acclaim Robertson as a writer who understood the society he undertook to reform, but in compensation, he declared that in the process of keeping "his garden [plays] very neat, and tidy, and pretty," he "uprooted a host of noxious weeds."

In contrast, during the centennial year of Robertson's birth, 1929, Harrison Dale declared, in an article in *Contemporary Review*, that the history of modern drama begins with Robertson. His work, Dale said, was a "miracle of freshness" beyond the experience of contemporary audiences. For Dale, Robertson's strongest point as a playwright was his ability to see "light as well as shadow." Dale came close to ascribing an overarching philosophy to Robertson in asserting that Robertson both "knew vice" and "believed in the existence of virtue."

In the same year, Frank A. Rahill opened his assessment of Robertson's work on a much less sympathetic centenary note. In the *Theatre Arts Monthly*, he argued that Robertson's "modern social comedy" was an isolated incident, confined to a single theater, and that, failing to take root, its influence had all but disappeared within a decade. He characterized Robertson's point of view as "pure, unadulterated Victorian cant." After suggesting that Charles Matthew anticipated Robertson's innovations in understated acting, that Dion Boucicault actually preceded Robertson in attention to stage business techniques, and that Charles Fechter took precedence in introducing improved set construction and manipulation, Rahill rather surprisingly declared that the production of Robertson's play *Society* signaled the birth of realism and that modern British theater "dates as legitimately from Robertson's plays as from Ibsen's."

The outstanding modern Robertson scholar is Maynard Savin, whose critical biography *Thomas William Robertson: His Plays and Stagecraft* appeared in 1950. He argued that previous criticism had reduced Robertson to a mere link between the "theatrical claptrap" of the early nineteenth century and the dramatic revival of its last two decades. Savin was willing to accept the reduction of Robertson's role from that of a revolutionary to that of a transitional figure but argued for the genuine contribution he believed Robertson's leadership had made. Far from seeing Robertson as an imitator of Augustin Eugène Scribe's "well-made play," he saw him as one who mastered the form and then struggled to escape its restrictions. While accepting the proposition that other attempts at realism preceded Robertson's, Savin argued that Robertson succeeded in synthesizing the contributions of playwright, director, actor, and stage designer to achieve "a theatre united in aim." The elements working against Robertson were, according to Savin, a monopoly of management, commercialization of playwriting, censorship (a problem against which Shaw fulminated but which he did not raise in estimating Robertson's problems), and what he termed "the decadent resurgence of the poetic tradition."

In a minor vein, Savin took note of Robertson's skill in having two conversations going forward on the stage simultaneously. The technique allows for dramatic contrasts and a great deal of character-highlighting. Although Savin did not say so, this technique also allows an unusual opportunity to intensify dramatic irony, by means of which the audience is put into possession of knowledge denied to the characters. Savin also discussed Robertson's constant use of the tableau and double tableaux. In the former, the action is held suspended at a point of heightened dramatic interest for a moment before the curtain is dropped. If the audience reaction warrants, the curtain is raised again to reveal that the characters have taken the next logical step suggested by the action. The trick was common enough in the nineteenth century theater and may be viewed either as one of the outworn conventions to which Robertson clung or as a clever, popular, and theatrically effective technique, not unlike the cinematic practice of freezing the action in intense situations, especially at the end of a film.

Still, Savin was under no illusion about the limitations of Robertson's realism. He remarked that a combination of very superficial realism and the conventions of the melodrama "cheated" Robertson's audiences into believing that they had seen a mirror "held up to nature." Among these conventions, Savin identified the following: The nature of woman was held to be either frail or self-sacrificing, with love being regarded as holy and secret; the English class system was represented as both natural and desirable (Robertson distrusted, even rejected, political power for ordinary people; upward mobility, he held, could be permitted safely only to the morally virtuous); militarism was glorified, and soldiers were invariably splendid fellows—notions that permeate most of even his best plays. Robertson's obsession with these unexamined conventions, Savin argued, smothered his "creative energy" and revealed him as merely a rebel against theatrical conventions, not against the more deadly Victorian conventions. Even so, Savin insisted that Robertson's efforts cleared the way for the emergence of the problem play and of the evolution of realism into naturalism.

Allardyce Nicoll, whose judgments can rarely be safely ignored, observed, in *Late Nineteenth Century Drama, 1850-1900* (1962), that several men have been credited with the introduction of stage managing in the modern sense of directing, including Robertson and Bancroft, W. S. Gilbert, and Boucicault. He also noted that Gilbert gave full credit to Robertson in his *Green-Room Recollections* (1896). Nicoll ultimately attached great importance to Robertson's collaboration with Lady Bancroft, which, he concluded, elevated plays from "merely virtuoso entertainments" to "artistic unities," with realism of action coordinated with realism in staging. Nicoll also praised Robertson's comparatively natural dialogue, a virtue he felt is often hidden from modern readers by the elements of sentimentalizing and moralizing which Robertson retained. To the charge that Robertson continued to make use of the older character-types, Nicoll responded that Robertson's reintroduction to the theater of individually conceived characters was a great contribution to the revival of good drama. Less acceptable is Nicoll's notion that Robertson introduced genuinely serious themes into his plays and attempted a balanced view of his entire society, a task of which Robertson was not capable either philosophically or intellectually. Still, Nicoll's placement of Robertson, not first in merit among playwrights of the past but "first in time among the dramatic writers of the present," is a stand to be reckoned with.

Errol Durbach, in his 1972 article "Remembering Tom Robertson (1829-1871)," observed that Robertson combined "emotional impulses" with opposing "social" ones, which was a major contribution to the English comedy of domestic realism. Certainly the technique is still in use by John Osborne, Tom Stoppard, and many others. Durbach concluded that Robertson's plays tend to support the status quo and suggested that the popularity of Arthur Wing Pinero's *Trelawny of the "Wells"* (pr. 1898) established the myth of Robertson as a revolutionary. Durbach then concluded rather oddly that Robertson brought drama to "a point from which significant European drama might develop."

The penultimate estimate may well belong to Hans Otto Thieme, who argued, in *Das englishe Drama im 18 und 19 Jahrhundert: Interpretationen* (1976), that without doubt, Robertson's new drama swept aside old conventions and, with its realism and its focus on central themes, aided the movement from society drama to the problem play and social drama, despite the necessity for Robertson to master the art of feigned reality.

A critical consensus of sorts emerges. It seems that Robertson was an innovator who was willing to use whatever means were necessary to achieve an intellectually honest drama during a time which could boast of little integrity in that art. His plays show that he was willing to refurbish old techniques and character-types to achieve his end: an intellectually significant play, highly entertaining, produced in a setting that imitated reality by actors who were willing to subordinate their roles to the overall needs of the play. That he was not always clear about these goals, that he produced potboilers along with significant drama throughout the glory years, is demonstrated well enough by the plays themselves. Even so, considering that, except for the aid of the Bancrofts and the support of a few friends, he struggled alone for most of his career, it is rather astonishing that in a period of almost universal decadence, he produced even a half dozen plays that were hailed by contemporary audiences as marvels and remain readable today. That he was the best of his theatrically none-too-impressive time is clear; that he was the first considerable writer of modern drama in Britain is at least arguable.

Biography

Biographical materials for Thomas William Robertson's life necessarily begin with the "Memoir" to *The Principal Dramatic Works of Thomas William Robertson* by his son, T. W. Robertson, and with the two Bancroft memoirs of 1889 and 1909. Additional material is to be found in *Dame Madge Kendal, by Herself* (1933), by Robertson's sister, a famous actress. Savin's *Thomas William Robertson: His Plays and Stagecraft* offers a very useful short critical biography as well as a list of secondary sources. Among the earliest of these is T. Edgar Pemberton's *The Life and Writings of T. W. Robertson* (1893). Cecil Ferard Armstrong produced a largely derivative but solid and readable biography in his essay "Thomas William Robertson," a very fine condensed overview of Robertson's life and works. His conclusions are sensible and humane and provide an excellent initiation for the Robertsonian neophyte without being the less valuable to scholars.

Robertson's life was bound up in the theater from beginning to end. For several generations, his family had been actors and managers in the old theater circuits in the north of England. As a young child, he appeared in bit parts before being sent off, under the care of his actress-poet great-aunt, Fanny Maria Robertson, to attend such undistinguished schools as Henry Young's Spalding Academy in 1836 and Moore's School at Whittlesea in 1841. He seems to have been a normal, fun-loving child, inclined to be frail of health.

At the age of fourteen or fifteen, Robertson rejoined the family acting company based in Lincoln. There he gained practical experience in all aspects of the theater business except playwriting itself. During all of this activity, Robertson found time to continue studying under the supervision of his father, who was a cultured literary man. The regimen included mastering French, a skill which later would prove useful in translating and adapting French plays for the English stage, a process which contributed much to Robertson's understanding of the playwright's business.

In 1848, the family business was in a bad way, and Robertson went to London to seek his fortune. As things went badly, Robertson involved himself in an escapade which haunted him the rest of his life. He simply dropped out of sight for six weeks, to the distress of his family, spending the time miserably in Utrecht, the Netherlands, as a sort of assistant teacher. The mutual antipathy he felt for a fellow assistant teacher eventually surfaced in the character of Krux in the play *School.*

In 1851, Robertson met H. J. Byron, who became a lifelong friend. Together they produced a dramatic fiasco which attracted a single spectator who ultimately demanded his money back. The pair also made an abortive attempt to enlist in the Horse Guards. Meanwhile, Robertson free-lanced articles, adapted plays for a publisher, Thomas Hailes Lacy, and saw the production of an early play, *A Night's Adventure,* at the Olympia. In 1854, he found steady work as a prompter at the Lyceum Theatre.

By 1855, Robertson was back with the family troupe, which proceeded to get itself stranded in Paris when their production of William Shakespeare's *Macbeth* folded. Later that year, he met an actress, Elizabeth Burton, at the Queen's Theatre (later called the Prince of Wales's), inelegantly known to members of the trade as "the Dust Hole." They were married on August 27, 1856. A son, Thomas William Shafto Robertson, was born December 2, 1857, and a daughter, Betty, died in infancy in 1858.

An acting tour of Ireland followed the marriage, after which Robertson plunged once more into the bohemian life of the backwaters of literary London, acting occasionally and seeing some minor plays and farces produced. He became a member of two clubs, the Savage Club in 1861 and, later, the Arundel. His cronies there included other literary figures, among them the younger Tom Hood and W. S. Gilbert. The bohemian life of the Savage figured realistically in the play *Society.*

On February 14, 1861, Robertson achieved success with his farce *The Cantab* at the Strand Theatre and became drama critic for *The Illustrated Times* at about the same time. In 1863, he wrote a novel, *David Garrick.* In 1864, he produced the play *David Garrick,* an adaptation of a French play, Mélesville's *Sullivan.* The "drunken scene" was reckoned a *coup de théâtre* by Robertson's contemporaries. The play's production in April at the Haymarket was Robertson's first considerable dramatic success.

On May 8, 1865, *Society* opened in Liverpool. In the late summer, on August 14, Robertson's first wife died. She had been loving and supportive, and her loss was a terrible blow. Meanwhile, Byron, who had arranged the Liverpool engagement of *Society,* found London managers unreceptive to the play. John Baldwin Buckstone, a crusty actor-manager, pronounced it "rubbish." After much maneuvering, Byron succeeded in interesting the Bancrofts, the actor-managers of the small, newly refitted and renamed Prince of Wales's Theatre on Tottingham Court Road, and *Society* opened there November 11, 1865.

From this point onward, Robertson's life of Bohemian penury was over. The play was an immediate success with its first London run of 150 nights. Robertson, for the first time, had theater owners who agreed entirely with his notions of acting, setting, and stage management. Triumph followed triumph with productions of *Ours, Caste, Play, School,* and *M.P.,* all at the Prince of Wales's. In 1867, Robertson had four other plays running in London, and in the glory year of 1869, he had six plays on the London stage and one each in Liverpool and Manchester.

In the midst of this triumph, Robertson married again, this time to a charming German woman, Rosetta Feist, in Frankfurt, Germany, on October 17, 1867. Never an especially well man, though generally described as robust, Robertson's health declined with the onset of success. His last years were marked by increasingly painful bouts of lung disease, heroic efforts to continue to write and direct, and a nagging sense that, in spite of his obvious success, his work was middling and would not survive.

Robertson died on February 3, 1871, and was buried six days later in Abney Park Cemetery, attended by, among others of note, Tom Hood, Dion Boucicault, and Squire Bancroft.

Analysis

Maynard Savin was unquestionably right in dubbing many of Thomas William Robertson's plays "potboilers." Robertson spent much of his life as a literary hack, turning a pound the best way he could, when he could. He continued to grind out inferior work even during the period of his greatest success, 1865 and after. Two late plays, produced in 1871 and 1883 respectively, are cases in point: *Not at All Jealous* (Court Theatre) and *A Row in the House* (Toole's Theatre). The first is simply a running farce centered on jealousy and mistaken identity, puns and concealment. The other is equally mechanical, being a farce in which an uncle sorts out the confusion created among three couples by jealousy. In it, Robertson uses his famous double-dialogue technique but fails to achieve freshness.

David Garrick is theatrically better than either and shares many characteristics with Robertson's best work. Savin observed that Robertson worked in this play as an adapter rather than as a mere translator and was encouraged by the play's success to trust his own originality. The play is essentially a dramatization of an old chestnut: the man who pretends drunkenness to shock the prudish. To that business, however, Robertson attached a theme which became his trademark, the vulgar snobbery of the newly rich mercantile class which allowed itself to sneer at "mere" actors, as well as a situation, the tender love between two sensitive persons, which also became a recurring feature of his plays. While the tradition of the well-made play is present in some force, that of the farce is not. In the end, the class conflict between the snobbery of the city and that of the theater is reconciled, and the reconciliation is confirmed by a marriage between two superior people.

The last of the better potboilers, and perhaps Robertson's most underestimated drama, is *Dreams,* which was staged under the title *My Lady Clara* in Liverpool before coming to London as *Dreams* at the Gaiety Theatre on March 27, 1869. That Robertson thought highly of *Dreams* is suggested in a headnote of the published acting version, which indicated that it should be played as a comedy, not as a melodrama. The relative seriousness of two of its themes supports his view. The first and lesser theme turns on the difficulties a young man encounters in trying to establish himself as a composer of music in England, a difficulty parallel to that encountered by Robertson in establishing himself as a writer. The second is an extended examination of the merits and demerits of a social system based upon caste. The conclusion, as usual, is that caste is a good thing which should be challenged only by superior merit. While Savin dismissed the play as "a rusty excrescence scraped up from the bottom of the pot," that estimation is extreme at best. A melodramatic interpretation, exaggerating the more sensational features of the play, would certainly be possible, and some such consideration must have led to Robertson's caveat at the beginning of the script. It is also possible, however, that a troupe, playing as an ensemble and employing Robertson's by then established understated method of acting, could achieve something delicate, if not entirely fragile.

Even Robertson's best plays, four of which will be considered here, are far from perfect. In some ways, they could be said not to merit attention from modern readers who have available not only the superb dramas of the past but also those of the twentieth century, the best of which make even Ibsen's work seem quaint, timid, and old-fashioned. Be this as it may, Robertson's plays are still very readable. If this is so, the odds are that, in skillful hands, they are still good theater and even have some claim to treating serious themes seriously. That they can be treated thematically without much need for plot summary is another clue to their continuing value.

Society, Robertson's first play in London's Prince of Wales's Theatre, followed a year after the success of *David Garrick.* The play examines the place of wealth in the marriages of the upper-middle classes, the repulsiveness of the newly moneyed social climber, and the plight of the impoverished gentry. The play was celebrated for the novelty of its low-key love scenes set in a realistically staged park (leaves actually fell), for its accurate portrayal of the lives of journalists, and for the "Owl's Roost" scenes, set in a club modeled after the Savage Club, in which the journalists and other bohemians enjoy themselves.

In regard to dynastic marriage, an old aunt advises her niece to marry for money and thereby restore the honor of the family. She argues that sentiment is the province of servant girls who romance policemen, a pastime beneath a lady. In her view, a commonplace person with an uncommonplace purse is better than the reverse. Later, this theme is picked up in the "Owl's Roost" when the rejected lover quotes from Alfred, Lord Tennyson's "Locksley Hall": "Thou are mated to a clown. . . ." Later in the play, the heroine rejects a marriage of convenience in a speech worthy of Ibsen or Shaw. She will not prostitute herself to a man she despises for the privilege of dressing herself at his expense and controlling his household, leading a life "that is a daily lie." Neither will she share the poverty of a man who does not treat her as an equal and has doubted her. All is sorted out in the end, and after the misunderstandings are cleared away, the deserving young lovers are rewarded with each other. As one might expect, in the final outcome, the impoverished young man turns out to be wealthy after all.

After opening in Liverpool, *Ours* began a 250-night run at London's Prince of Wales's Theatre on November 26, 1866. Jingoistic to the hilt, the play not only reflects Robertson's often noticed penchant for things military but also demonstrates his instinct for what will appeal to his audience—in this case, a sentimental feeling for the local regiment (hence the title) and a probably genuine patriotic feeling that is also clearly sentimental. The list of characters includes many stock figures from the old melodrama: a comic sergeant, a bouncing girl, an eccentric noblewoman, and a noble foreigner.

The plot is simple enough. Several English women, incredibly, follow their lovers and husbands to the Crimea and manage a reunion in a hut just behind the lines. Two realistic bits of business drew strong admiration: Snow blows in each time the outer door is opened, and Mary makes a roly-poly pudding onstage, converting military equipment into kitchen utensils in the process. Even more impressive is the departure of the regiment at the close of act 2. The movements of the troops offstage, complete with shouted orders, band music, and the sound of marching feet, all with modulations of volume indicating their changes of position, form the background against which the actors onstage react to the departure.

In addition to the theme of patriotism, the nature of love and marriage and its appropriateness at various social levels is explored. The sergeant must leave family behind, wife and children alike. For him, this is merely an inconvenience, because the gentry will see them through. Mary's problem is more serious; she is an impoverished gentlewoman who prefers her relative independence as a paid companion, a demeaning enough position, to marrying simply for the sake of escape. At one point, Mary argues, in a burst of sarcasm, that society makes it a duty for a woman to marry in order to subjugate a man. Blanche, who is not impoverished, is likewise under pressure to marry a prince because he is a good match in spite of the difference in their ages. In the sorting out, everyone either stabilizes a threatened marriage, withdraws from an inappropriate courtship, or is matched with a suitable partner. Even Mary finds a husband she can respect.

School is not genuinely autobiographical, although the character of the evil teacher, Krux, was drawn from Robertson's unhappy Utrecht experience. The benevolent Dr. Sutcliffe and his foolish, jealous wife run an institution for young ladies which cannot much resemble the penurious Dutch one. *School* is also not entirely original; Robertson drew freely on Roderick Benedix's German play *Aschenbrödel* (1868) and used the Cinderella motif as a charming framing device.

The plot turns on the adventures of Bella, a sort of pupil-teacher who is unjustly turned out because of the obsessive jealousy of Mrs. Sutcliffe and the talebearing of Krux. To everyone's horror, she disappears for six weeks just at the point when her long-lost grandfather shows up to claim her. Right on cue, Bella reappears with her "prince" as a Cinderella bride. Comic justice is satisfied with the thrashing, offstage, of the villainous Krux, while romantic justice is fulfilled at the curtain with the splendid Lord Beaufoy fitting a glass slipper on the foot of the virtuous Bella.

School depends upon big scenes for its impact. They begin with Bella's reading the Cinderella story aloud to the assembled girls. Another centers on the school examination, with its nonsensical questions followed by Krux's tyrannizing over the girls after the guests leave the stage. Perhaps as whimsical a scene as any in Robertson's work is the scene in which Lord Beaufoy insists upon carrying the milk jug for Bella, an act far beneath his station and accountable only by eccentricity or love. That Robertson substitutes strong scenes for careful plotting is clear and surely identifies the play as more nearly fantasy than realism. This is not surprising, since, for Robertson, plot meant the marshaling of events with an eye to surprise and intensifying effect, rather than action growing logically out of situation and character. In this, he more closely resembles Oscar Wilde than he does Ibsen or Shaw.

Caste, which opened at the Prince of Wales's Theatre on April 6, 1867, is a triumph of theatrical craftsmanship. In spite of its reputation as a thematic play, a forerunner of realism and a British anticipation of Ibsen, it is nothing of the sort. It is, however, exactly what Robertson's development as writer-manager suggests he meant it to be—a basically sentimental play, expertly cast and produced, to which his audience could respond with appreciation and applause. All the old situations are there, as well as all the old stereotyped characters. For stereotypes, there are the aristocratic, snobbish mother-in-law, the Marquise de St. Maur; her love-smitten and wholesome son, George D'Alroy; the military swell, Captain Hawtree; the nearly saintly, certainly virtuous woman and wife, Esther Eccles; and the madcap girl, Esther's sister, Polly. There is also the Dickensian eccentric, Sam Gerridge, the pipe fitter who is courting Polly, and the roaring, drunken father, who is a lamb before the gentry and who harks back to Shakespeare's Sir Toby Belch and forward to Shaw's Alfred Doolittle. For situations, there is the aristocrat's love affair and secret marriage to a lower-class woman who has suffered in order to support her drunken, sometimes brutal, and always unappreciative father, and who will suffer to support her supposedly orphaned boy.

There is also a cradle scene in which the villain, in this case the unprincipled Eccles, steals a jewel from the baby, a variation of the thieving Gypsy routine. Finally, there is the stock motif of the soldier, supposedly lost in battle, who miraculously turns up again when things are darkest to save the day. That Robertson was able to present such threadbare situations so freshly that his jaded audiences mistook them for something new and significant is itself remarkable. Thus, the enthusiasm and feistiness of Sam Gerridge was taken for the sturdy independence of the respectable working class; the socialistic jargon of Eccles seemed to be in its proper place, in the mouth of a drunken shirker; and the nobility and virtue of George and Esther was seen not only as a triumph of youth over old age, a long-standing comic motif, but also as a daring challenge to the caste system under which many of the audience—the wealthy middle classes who hoped to rise—writhed. In retrospect, the whole show is given away. George is not, after all, a very great aristocrat, although his mama is. Captain Hawtree, if not quite a cad, is at best a social climber who does not quite belong. When his own suit for the hand of a titled lady is rejected for that of a potential marquis, he quite understands. In the denouement, all the couples are sorted into their proper social levels, except Esther, whose virtues place her above caste. While the revelation that Robertson's social revolution was hardly more than a dramatic ploy cannot be said to destroy the play, it does bring the play into focus. With its pathos, its wit, its occasions of boisterous comedy, and its web of tensions and cross-tensions, all realistically mounted and understated in presentation in an intimate theater, *Caste* confirms that Robertson had orchestrated the techniques which would pave the way for the influx of genuine realism a decade later.

Robertson, then, was a playwright who knew his craft completely, who had luck in his friends and wives, who was fortunate enough to find managers who would give his ideas scope, and who adapted more than he innovated in preparing the English stage for its modern renaissance.

Other major work

NOVEL: *David Garrick*, 1865.

Bibliography

Armstrong, Cecil Ferard. *Shakespeare to Shaw: Studies in the Life's Work of Six Dramatists of the English Stage.* Freeport, N.Y.: Books for Libraries Press, 1968. The early significance of Robertson is established as he is assessed with William Shakespeare, William Congreve, Richard Brinsley Sheridan, Arthur Wing Pinero, and George Bernard Shaw as the best of English playwrights. A brief literary biography shows the development of the writer in conjunction with the major events of his life. Robertson's plays must be studied in their historical context to see how he returned drama to its rightful place in art.

Dale, Harrison. "Tom Robertson: A Centenary Criticism." *Contemporary Review* 135 (April, 1929): 356-361. Dale reassesses Robertson's accomplishments on the occasion of his centennial. Even though the work is faulty by modern standards, it marked a turning point in English comedy. Robertson's "cup-and-saucer" drama, with its realistic, domestic interior which now draws sneers, drew applause and acclaim from his contemporary audience.

Durbach, Errol. "Remembering Tom Robertson (1829-1871)." *Educational Theatre Journal* 24 (October, 1972): 284-288. A retrospective of Robertson's contributions to the theater on the occasion of the centennial of his death. His contemporaries praised his drama for its freshness, nature, and humanity. Although Robertson is almost forgotten, he was revolutionary in his day and provided a point from which significant European drama could develop.

Nicoll, Allardyce. *British Drama.* 6th ed. London: Harrap, 1978. Nicoll describes how Robertson created a new "cup-and-saucer" drama where he invited people to bring their "fireside concerns" to the playhouse and look upon reality. Robertson was successful in bringing life back into the theater. He was influential in showing how to write characters who speak in natural tones and in showing how to write about themes.

Pemberton, T. Edgar. *The Life and Writings of T. W. Robertson.* London: Richard Bentley and Son, 1893. The standard biography of Robertson, tracing his life and literary development. Robertson's son provided pertinent family information to Pemberton, who offers no literary criticism of the plays. Instead, he invites his audience to judge the works for themselves, as they were still standards on the London stage. Index.

Savin, Maynard. *Thomas William Robertson: His Plays and Stagecraft.* Providence, R.I.: Brown University, 1950. This biography and critical analysis of the plays explores why Robertson's early evaluations as a revolutionary were later tempered to that of merely transitional significance. Savin places Robertson's works into the context of mid-Victorian theater to demonstrate his remarkable achievement, in spite of its weaknesses, in leading the English theater into realism. Chronology and bibliography.

Tydeman, William, ed. Introduction to *Plays by Tom Robertson.* New York: Cambridge University Press, 1982. Tydeman demonstrates why Robertson's plays were so acclaimed in their day, even though they were based on features whose lasting merits have failed. He also claims that the plays have since been vastly underrated. He draws attention to the features in the best of those genteel, optimistic comedies that enable them to endure for modern audiences. Illustrations, chronology, and bibliography.

B. G. Knepper
(Updated by *Gerald S. Argetsinger*)

LENNOX ROBINSON

Born: Douglas, Ireland; October 4, 1886
Died: Dublin, Ireland; October 14, 1958

Principal drama

The Clancy Name, pr. 1908, pb. 1909 (one act); *The Cross Roads*, pr., pb. 1909; *The Lesson of His Life*, pr. 1909; *Harvest*, pr. 1910, pb. 1911; *Patriots*, pr., pb. 1912; *The Dreamers*, pr., pb. 1915; *The White-Headed Boy*, pr. 1916, pb. 1921; *The Lost Leader*, pr., pb. 1918; *Crabbed Youth and Age*, pr. 1922, pb. 1924; *The Round Table*, pr. 1922, pb. 1924; *Never the Time and the Place*, pr., pb. 1924 (one act); *Portrait*, pr. 1925, pb. 1926; *The White Blackbird*, pr. 1925, pb. 1926; *The Big House: Four Scenes in Its Life*, pr. 1926, pb. 1928; *The Far-off Hills*, pr. 1928, pb. 1931; *Plays*, pb. 1928; *Give a Dog*, pb. 1928, pr. 1929; *Ever the Twain*, pr. 1929, pb. 1930; *The Critic*, pr. 1931 (modernization of Richard Brinsley Sheridan's play); *All's Over Then?*, pr. 1932, pb. 1935; *Drama at Inish*, pr., pb. 1933 (also known as *Is Life Worth Living?*); *Church Street*, pr. 1934, pb. 1935 (one act); *When Lovely Woman*, pr. 1936; *Killycreggs in Twilight*, pr. 1937, pb. 1939; *Bird's Nest*, pr. 1938, pb. 1939; *Let Well Alone*, pr. 1940 (radio play), pr. 1941 (staged), pb. 1941; *Roly Poly*, pr. 1940 (adaptation of Guy de Maupassant's story "Boule de suif"); *Forget Me Not*, pr. 1941; *The Lucky Finger*, pr. 1948, pb. 1949; *The Demon Lover*, pr. 1954; *Selected Plays*, pb. 1982.

Other literary forms

Lennox Robinson's nondramatic writings are of interest only because of the insights they provide into his development as a nationalist and man of the theater. Central in this regard are two volumes of autobiography, *Three Homes* (1938) and *Curtain Up* (1942), and *A Young Man from the South* (1917), published as a novel but little more than a fictionalized autobiography. In the last of these, Willie Powell, the hero, is a Protestant Anglo-Irishman from southwest Cork, a physically weak fellow who has become a successful dramatist (writing plays that are like Robinson's). As a result of a confrontation between nationalists and unionists, Powell reappraises his commitment to nationalist extremism and decides to seek more reasonable outlets for his patriotism. The book is a lucid portrait of the social, intellectual, and political milieu of Ireland in the decade leading up to the Easter Rebellion, but it is not much of a novel. From the same period and of interest for similar reasons is the 1918 collection of political sketches, *Dark Days*. These pieces give Robinson's reactions to Ireland's troubles and show how his growing nationalism was tempered by doubts about the extremist methods of the Sinn Féiners. The attitudes and problems that Robinson dramatized in *The Big House* in 1926 emerged for the first time in such earlier nondramatic works as *A Young Man from the South* and *Dark Days*.

Achievements

Robinson's relationship with Dublin's Abbey Theatre spanned half a century, beginning in 1908 when his first play, *The Clancy Name*, was presented there. During this period, he was one of the theater's most prolific dramatists; its manager for a time; a producer, director, and board member; and author of an officially commissioned Abbey history. The most prominent of the Irish playwrights known as the Cork Realists, Robinson helped chart the course of the theater during the period that included World War I and the height of Ireland's political turbulence, leading the transformation of the literary theater of the Abbey's founders into a realistic one.

In addition to his work for the Abbey, Robinson also acted in productions of the Dublin Drama League, of which he was a founder; edited collections of Irish poetry; wrote drama criticism and other articles for newspapers; and turned out a novel, two volumes of autobiography, short stories, and two biographies. A frequent judge at amateur drama festivals throughout Ireland, he also lectured in the United States, China, and on the Continent. Both at home and abroad, he was widely recognized for several decades not only as one of Ireland's leading playwrights and theatrical figures but also as an important all-around man of letters.

Robinson's most enduring achievement is his dramatic oeuvre, thirty plays written between 1908 and 1954. Among these, the conventional comedies and realistic dramas were his most popular works. *The White-Headed Boy*, his first full-length comedy, was an immediate Abbey success and gained for him an international reputation. His second most successful play, *The Far-off Hills*, also a comedy, focuses upon provincial life and satirizes foibles of the Irish character. His most notable serious work is *The Big House*, which dramatizes the tragedy of Anglo-Irish Protestants in a Catholic country during the tumultuous period following World War I; this play and others of its type have echoes of Henrik Ibsen, a major influence on Robinson as on most of his Abbey contemporaries. Robinson also ventured into political drama: *Patriots*, *The Dreamers*, and *The Lost Leader* all reflect William Butler Yeats's political views. Though Robinson's major contributions to the Irish drama were as a realist, he shows the influence of Eugene O'Neill in the expressionistic *Ever the Twain*, and in *Church Street*, he employs techniques and themes of Luigi Pirandello. Further, while Abbey manager, he introduced Dublin audiences to plays by such non-Irish dramatists as Gerhart Hauptmann, August Strindberg, and Rabindranath Tagore.

While Robinson possessed some of Yeats's romantic idealism, he followed more closely in the footsteps of such realists in the Irish Literary Renaissance as Padraic Colum, John Millington Synge, and Lady Augusta Gregory, and his contemporaries so admired his early plays that they also wrote morbidly realistic peasant dramas. T. C. Murray's *Birthright* (pr. 1910) is one such, and A. P. Wilson, Robinson's successor as Abbey manager, said that ninety-five percent of the manuscripts he received were of this type. Perhaps second only to Lady Gregory as the most prolific twentieth century Irish dramatist, Robinson was much more versatile than his sometime mentor and during his long career provided the Abbey and other Dublin stages with comic and serious plays that remain penetrating studies not only of his compatriots but also of the human condition. While not a dramatist of the first rank, Robinson indeed may be, as a biographer has characterized him, "a modern Goldsmith."

Biography

Esmé Stuart Lennox Robinson was born on October 4, 1886, in Douglas, southeast of Cork, to Andrew Craig and Emily Jones Robinson, Anglo-Irish Protestants. He was the youngest of seven children. His father, who had been a stockbroker, was ordained a minister of the Church of Ireland in 1892 at the age of fifty and given a parish in Kinsale, County Cork, where the family lived until he was transferred in 1900 to Ballymoney in West Cork. In the same year, young Robinson, who had been tutored at home, began attending Bandon Grammar School for Protestants, but this formal education ended in a year because of his ill health, and his father again became his tutor. Robinson long after wrote of how, during this period, he devoted himself "to music, to rough shooting, and fishing, to reading, to a little boyish writing." He recalled, too, how he and a cousin started *Contributions*, a monthly magazine which ran for three years: "At first many relatives and friends contributed; later they fell away, and my cousin and I had to write it all ourselves under a bewildering variety of *noms-de-plume*." During this period in his late teens, Robinson also became friendly with a Catholic family connected to the nationalist Daniel O'Connell and began to stray from his family's unionist sentiments.

The landmark event in Robinson's progress toward identification with the cause of Irish nationalism and the theater as vocation occurred in August, 1907, when he saw a performance at the Cork Opera House of Yeats's *Cathleen ni Houlihan* and *The Hour Glass* (pr. 1903) and Lady Gregory's *The Jackdaw* (pr. 1907) and *The Rising of the Moon* (pb. 1904). He wrote years later: "Certain natural emotions and stirrings . . . were crystallized for ever by *Kathleen ni houlihan*. . . . Those two hours in the pit of the Opera House in Cork made me an Irish dramatist."

The first product of his new vocation was *The Clancy Name*, a one-act play based on a story by his sister; it was produced at the Abbey on October 8, 1908, "a play as harsh as the stones of West Cork, as realistic as the midden in front of an Irish farm house," according to Robinson (who reacted to criticism of the harshness by rewriting the tragic melodrama for the next Abbey season). His second work, *The Cross Roads*, opened on April 1, 1909; a full-length problem play with overtones of Ibsen, it was well received by the Abbey's audiences mainly because the actors—Sara Allgood, Maire O'Neill, and Arthur Sinclair—obscured its defects (which Robinson unsuccessfully attempted to correct for a 1910 production).

Recognizing Robinson's talent, Yeats and Lady Gregory made him the Abbey's producer and manager late in 1909, and to prepare him for the responsibilities, they sent him to London early the next year to see plays, observe rehearsals, and get to know such luminaries as George Bernard Shaw and Harley Granville-Barker. As manager, Robinson was an arbitrator of disputes among actors and promoter of the Abbey; he also directed plays, including some of his own; and he led the troupe on its 1911 and 1913 American tours. Upon returning from the latter one, he resigned his post, mainly because of conflicts with Lady Gregory that stemmed from Abbey financial matters, but also because he wanted more time to write. The next year, he joined the Carnegie United Kingdom Trust as an organizer and developer of libraries, a position he held until 1919, while continuing to write plays, a novel, short stories, and newspaper and magazine articles. During this period, his nationalism emerged in political sketches published as *Dark Days* as well as in the novel *A Young Man from the South* and in *The Lost Leader*, a play dealing with Charles S. Parnell (and which also reveals Robinson's growing interest in Spiritualism and psychic phenomena). In 1919, he returned to the Abbey as manager and presided over the theater for four years at a time of financial stress (which led the government in 1924 to recognize the Abbey as the official National Theatre of Ireland and to grant it a subsidy) and artistic advances (with playwrights Brinsley MacNamara, George Shiels, and Sean O'Casey being introduced to its audiences).

When Robinson again was free of Abbey administrative responsibilities, he was able to devote more time to the Dublin Drama League, and after marrying Dorothy Travers Smith (an Abbey scene designer) in 1931, he began to make lecture tours of the United States and to teach and direct on American campuses. His last trip to the United States was in 1947-1948; upon his return, Trinity College, Dublin, awarded him an honorary doctor of literature degree. Though his health was failing, he continued to direct and write plays (his last, *The Demon Lover*, a reworking of a 1914 manuscript, was produced in 1954), to judge amateur theatricals, to write a weekly newspaper column, and to represent Ireland at gatherings in China and Norway. He died on October 14, 1958, and is buried in St. Patrick's Cathedral, Dublin.

Analysis

The White-Headed Boy, Lennox Robinson's masterpiece, was first presented at the Abbey on December 13, 1916. A gentle satire of his compatriots with a plot and characters that are wholly complementary, it may have autobiographical origins, since Robinson's own frail health as a youth caused his mother to be overprotective and to treat him (like Denis in the play, a youngest son) as her pet, or "whiteheaded boy." He previously had used the theme in his first play, *The Clancy Name*, in which a doting mother orchestrates a marriage for her only son and then shields him—and the family name as well—after he accidentally kills a man.

Though Robinson later lamented that everyone had overlooked his political intent in *The White-Headed Boy*, his humorous asides to the reader and stage directions in Irish idiom demonstrate that laughter, not allegory, was his primary goal. The action begins with the Geoghegans—a widowed mother, two sons, three daughters, and a visiting aunt—awaiting the return of Denis, the third and youngest son, from Dublin, where he has been studying medicine and has twice failed his examination. All expect a triumphant homecoming this time, however, and Mrs. Geoghegan looks forward to Denis' becoming a Dublin doctor, not "one of your common dispensaries, hat in hand to every guardian in the country"; but while family members sacrificed so the mother's favorite could get an education, Denis wasted his allowance on horse races and neglected his work. When a telegram comes for him ("Hard luck. Geoghegan's Hope also ran. Sorry, Flanagan"), brother George, the family breadwinner, correctly interprets it as reporting that Denis has failed a third time, and all except Mrs. Geoghegan agree that they no longer will subsidize the prodigal.

When Denis returns, he at first appears to be vain and irresponsible; told of this third examination failure, he reacts indifferently: "Isn't that a beastly nuisance? I'm not surprised; I guessed I hadn't got it." He had not wanted to be a doctor after all, but had allowed himself to be led by his mother's misguided expectations for him and hope of enhanced reputation for the family. When brother George offers him passage to Canada as a final familial gesture, Denis retorts:

> I never asked to be sent to College; I never asked to have all this money spent on me. I'd have been content to live here with the rest of you—Yes, I'm different now, but whose fault is that? It's not mine. Who was it made me out to be so clever; who insisted on making a doctor of me, or sending me to Trinity? It was all of you.

He shows more spunk and good sense when George also offers to pay passage to Canada for Delia Duffy, Denis' fiancée: "Thank you for nothing. I'm asking no money from you, and I've no intention of asking Delia to come out and rough it in Canada. She wasn't brought up to that sort of thing." Jilting Delia, however, arouses the wrath of her father, who threat-

ens to sue for breach of contract. This prospect and its possible consequences frighten the family into frenetic attempts to forestall public shame,
and Duffy reaps a harvest as George, Mrs. Geoghegan, and Aunt Ellen
offer him payoffs and Aunt Ellen (who years earlier had rejected him) also
agrees to become his wife. Ironically, though all had intended to rid themselves of the burden of Denis, they remain in his thrall.

Delia and Denis, meanwhile, confound the schemers by marrying; further, instead of emigrating to Canada, Denis gets a job in Ballycolman as a
laborer on a work crew. Duffy and the Geoghegans are shocked; says
George, "Think what everyone will say of you, and what sort of name will
they put on us to say we drove you out on the road!" Again, reputation is
a prime consideration, and they offer Denis the payoffs previously tendered
to Duffy, but Denis wants independence: "I only want to be able to do
what I like with my own life—to be free." He agrees, nevertheless, to go
to Kilmurray and manage a cooperative shop, the latest enterprise of rich
Aunt Ellen, and he accepts the family's money, the prospect of Aunt
Ellen's estate, and Delia's promise to look after everything: "An easy life,
no responsibility, money in your pocket, something to grumble at—What
more do you want?"

Robinson said that *The White-Headed Boy* "is political from beginning
to end, though I don't suppose six people have recognised the fact." It is
easy to miss, for the play moves briskly through a series of comical situations, with the second-act wooing scene between Aunt Ellen and old Duffy
a comic classic. It is Duffy who expresses the political theme. He is "one
of the solidest men in Ballycolman, Chairman of the District Council,
Chairman of the Race committee, and a member of every Committee and
every League in the village," and he mocks Denis' desire for independence: "Free? . . . Bedad, isn't he like old Ireland asking for freedom, and
we're like the fools of Englishmen offering him every bloody thing except
the one thing? . . . Do Denis, do like a darling boy, go out to Kilmurray
and manage the shop."

Denis (like Ireland) desires the freedom to chart his own course, but the
family (like England) assumes that financial support will suffice. "Will I
never be free from you?" Denis asks, but he acquiesces in almost the same
breath. Futile though his assertion of self-determination may seem, at least
he marries; the prospects for his brothers and sisters, however, are bleaker,
their dreams of marriage and careers still mere illusions at the final curtain. Robinson's satiric portrayal of ineffectual Irishmen trapped by their
environment and sense of inadequacy is softened by his whimsical handling
of their conflicts and problems, and given the tense political situation in
Dublin in 1916, perhaps it is just as well that almost everyone missed the
subtle allegory and serious intent of *The White-Headed Boy.*

There are no such hidden purposes in *The Far-off Hills*, which opened at the Abbey on October 22, 1928, and was Robinson's first three-act comedy of Irish life since *The White-Headed Boy* in 1916. A lighthearted portrayal of the marriage game, it has its roots in the same provincial background as that of the earlier plays but ends on a more optimistic note, for all the characters (except the fickle servant Ellen) realize their ambitions. Though its spirit, characters, and milieu are Irish, the central motif of woman as matchmaker may come from Serafín and Joaquín Álvarez Quintero, four of whose plays were translated by Helen and Harley Granville-Barker and published in 1927. Robinson particularly liked *The Women Have Their Way*, which was presented at the Abbey a few weeks after *The Far-off Hills* premiered.

In this second most successful of Robinson's plays, the Clancy family, like the Geoghegans of *The White-Headed Boy*, is overseen by a woman, in this instance the eldest daughter, Marian, who puts off becoming a nun because of her widowered father's blindness. Severe in demeanor, she is a strict disciplinarian who reins in her exuberant younger sisters but fails to gain similar control over Patrick Clancy's drinking, smoking, and socializing with cronies. The girls Ducky and Pet, however, plot to get their father married so Marian will be free to enter the convent and they will be rid of her stern control. Susie Tynan, an eligible old flame of Clancy, is available and willing, so the girls' plan succeeds, but Marian then decides to postpone going to the convent until the girls are older, primarily because she has begun to have doubts about a religious vocation. When Pierce Hegarty, Susie Tynan's nephew, calls her a pretty girl, for example, "she drifts to a mirror and does something to her hair," and later, when Harold Mahony, another young man, loses his wife, Marian invites him to propose to her, but the gloomy pessimist turns her down. Ambitious and personable Pierce is a better man, however, and, encouraged by Pet and Ducky, he eventually prevails. Patrick Clancy delivers the valedictory: "This little room is as full of happiness as an egg is full of meat. Marian dear, Pierce . . . good luck, God bless you both."

The blind father is married to a woman who will tolerate his drinking, smoking, and cronies; Marian, no longer a tyrant, is soon to be wed; and the younger girls have freed themselves from unwanted control. Everyone, in other words, discovers that though far-off hills beckon, those closer to home may be just as verdant. The message of this play, then, is more optimistic than that which most Irish plays deliver, and though some have remarked about a padded plot, the seemingly irrelevant farcical interludes contribute significantly to the play's pervasive blitheness of spirit as well as providing opportunities for character development.

Though in his plays he ranged far and wide in subject matter and form, Robinson regularly returned to what he called "this strange Irish thing, the commanding force in my life." He wrote in the manner of O'Neill and Pirandello, and he adapted Richard Brinsley Sheridan and Guy de Maupassant, but he was at his best in plays that have, as one critic put it, "their inspiration in the warp and woof of Irish life."

Robinson's third most successful play deals with the "Irish thing" in a serious manner. *The Big House: Four Scenes in Its Life* opened at the Abbey on September 6, 1926; as its title suggests, Robinson focuses upon a favorite Anglo-Irish literary theme, the decay and destruction of the Big Houses, aristocratic country homes of Protestant families whose forebears had come from England as long ago as the seventeenth century but were still regarded—and saw themselves—as different from their Irish Catholic neighbors. The decline of the Big Houses and the departure of many Anglo-Irish families were inevitable when the conflict between the Irish and the English reached its peak following World War I, and a number of the estates were destroyed by nationalists as reprisals for actions of the government, but as early as 1912, Synge had written: "If a playwright chose to go through the Irish country houses he would find material, it is very likely, for many gloomy plays that would turn on the decaying of these old families." In his 1931 biography of Bryan Cooper, an Anglo-Irish landlord, Robinson recalls his reaction to a decaying Big House:

> Perhaps . . . in that Georgian house or sham Gothic castle there remained an old father and mother and a couple of aged daughters. The house was too large for their needs or too large for their purse and what reason was there for clinging to it? Meanwhile the old house was too full of memories of past greatness, too full of memories of boys who had shot rabbits in the long summer evenings.

A decade later, he wrote in his autobiography of the same experience: "I fell into a reverie and spoke no word until we reached home. A play of mine was born then." *The Big House* is a lament on the passing of an old order that Robinson admired, and at the same time it rallies the young Anglo-Irish to a dynamic commitment to Protestantism and their country.

The play is set at Ballydonal House, County Cork, ancestral home of the Alcocks, atypical Anglo-Irish landlords in that they have not lapsed into penury or decadence (unlike the O'Neills, with whom Robinson contrasts them). Mr. Alcock has devoted himself to public service for years, but he continues to remain apart from his Catholic neighbors, though without Mrs. Alcock's overt sense of alienation.

The first scene takes place in 1918 on Armistice Day, with the Alcocks celebrating the end of a war in which two of their sons served. Reginald, the elder, died, but they await the return of Ulick, the younger. With them is their daughter Kate and a visiting English officer, Montgomery Despard, who served with Reginald and met Kate in London, where he fell in love with her. Despard, who sees the atypicality of Ballydonal House— "It doesn't seem to be so awfully Irish . . . the way it's run, and—everything"—asks Kate to marry him and come to London, but she is unwilling. She is committed to Ballydonal House and dreams of running it with Ulick after the war: "Reggie wouldn't have cared if he had dragged Ballydonal down. But Ulick and I do care—tremendously. We're going to hold our heads above water, hold Ballydonal above water, proudly and decently." So strong is Ulick's tie to the estate, she says, that "I see him sometimes when he's not here at all," the most recent vision having occurred three evenings before: "That was just when the armistice had begun to seem inevitable. He was dreaming it all over you see, he was dreaming he was home." The vision was a prescient one, for a telegram arrives with news that Ulick was killed three days earlier.

The next scene takes place in 1921 during the terror wrought by the Republicans and the Black and Tans. The O'Neills, burned out, have left for England (where Irish refugees, Mrs. Alcock supposes, "will soon become as *distingué* as the Russians"), and Mrs. Alcock wants to join them ("I know that we're living in a community of criminal lunatics and that the sooner we get out of it the better"), but Mr. Alcock intends to stay until he is "put out . . . burned out . . . or starved out." To avenge an ambush the night before, the Black and Tans have shot Maggie Leahy, who had been Kate's childhood nurse. Kate, who has been working to overcome the alienation between the Anglo-Irish and the Irish Catholics, returns from Maggie's wake to report that despite her efforts ("I threw a bridge across the gulf and ran across it"), she remained an outsider, "different, away from them. . . . Yes, there was religion to make me feel outside but lots of other things too; education, I suppose, and tradition and—and everything that makes me me and them them." Though she always has felt this separation, she "thought it could be broken down." Alcock tells her that she never will be like the neighbors: "It will be always 'them' and 'us.'" Later, while alone, Kate is surprised by a drunk Despard, now a member of the Auxiliary Police, whose men are searching for nationalists. He proposes to her, but she again rejects him, and the scene ends with a solitary Despard firing his revolver at the voice of Ulick he thinks he hears, as if the protective spirit of Ballydonal has begun to haunt him, too.

Two years later, the Alcocks, almost destitute, have closed off most of the house. Kate, who had taken a job in London, returns, unable to stay away from "country-houses going up in flames, senators being kidnapped and all kinds of thrilling goings-on." Her report of the financial and social successes of the O'Neills in London contrasts vividly with the Alcocks' stoic endurance and Kate's rejection of the "sentimental play-acting" of London life and her decision to return, to "criticize and dislike Irish people—some of them—and be either a Free Stater or a Republican." The family reunion is interrupted when three Republicans come to blow up Ballydonal House in retaliation for the execution of a young Republican by the Free State

government, ironically the very fellow whose life Mr. Alcock had been trying to save.

The next morning, the family gathers in the aftermath of the destruction
to retrieve some possessions. Mr. and Mrs. Alcock will go to England after
all: Mrs. Alcock is happy to return home after more than two decades in a
foreign country; he is relieved that the turmoil will be part of his past,
though he still cannot understand the aspirations that have fostered it.
Kate, however, will try to shape a new life amid the ruins, renouncing her
"poor attempt to pretend" that she was not different from her compatriots
and quoting Yeats: "We must glory in our difference, be as proud of it as
they are of theirs." Her intentions notwithstanding, she remains tied to the
past, for a vision of Ulick appears at the end of the play, smiling with
apparent satisfaction at his sister's heroic resolve. Sean O'Casey's *Juno and
the Paycock* (pr. 1924) and *The Plough and the Stars* (pr. 1926, seven
months prior to the *The Big House*) dramatize the political upheavals from
the perspective of Dubliners. Robinson's play provides a realistic portrait of
a different aspect of the era: the tragedy of an Ascendancy family.

Robinson's real strength was in his comedies, with their brilliant technique, sharp observation, and deft touch. In *The White-Headed Boy* and
The Far-off Hills, he created his masterworks. Although he never attained
the stature of a first-rank dramatist, Robinson's contribution to the Irish
national theater was crucial, for he did much to create a climate favorable
to the development of indigenous talent.

Other major works

NOVEL: *A Young Man from the South*, 1917.

SHORT FICTION: *Eight Short Stories*, 1919.

NONFICTION: *Dark Days*, 1918; *Bryan Cooper*, 1931; *Three Homes*, 1938;
Curtain Up, 1942; *Towards an Appreciation of the Theatre*, 1945; *Pictures
in a Theatre: A Conversation Piece*, 1946; *Palette and Plough*, 1948; *Ireland's Abbey Theatre*, 1951.

Bibliography

Hogan, Robert. *After the Irish Renaissance: A Critical History of the Irish
    Drama Since "The Plough and the Stars."* Minneapolis: University of
    Minnesota Press, 1967. An overview of Irish theater from 1926 to 1965.
    The study situates Robinson's career in the context of the prevailing the-
    atrical traditions and practices of the day. Includes an analysis of Robin-
    son's plays as well as a separate discussion of Robinson's most important
    works. Contains a substantial bibiography.
Hunt, Hugh. *The Abbey: Ireland's National Theatre, 1904-1978.* New York:
    Columbia University Press, 1979. This history of the Abbey Theatre by
    one of its former directors contains an account of Robinson's two signifi-

cant connections with that institution. Describes Robinson's years as a director and examines his work as a playwright. Includes a complete listing of Abbey Theatre productions.

Journal of Irish Literature 9 (January, 1980). This special Lennox Robinson issue contains hitherto fugitive and unpublished materials. Perhaps the most important item is the controversial short story "The Madonna of Slieve Dun." In addition to another short story, a full-length play entitled *The Red Sock*, written pseudonymously by Robinson, is published here for the first time. Also contains an article on Robinson's relationship with William Butler Yeats.

O'Neill, Michael J. *Lennox Robinson.* Boston: Twayne, 1964. This study provides a thematic approach to Robinson's wide-ranging and productive career, including his nondramatic writings. The biographical material is related to the development of the playwright's themes and techniques. Contains a detailed chronology that functions both as a bibliography and as a calendar of productions of Robinson's plays.

Robinson, Lennox. *Lennox Robinson: Selected Plays.* Edited by Christopher Murray. Washington, D.C.: Catholic University of America Press, 1982. Contains Robinson's most important dramatic works: *Patriots, The White-Headed Boy, Crabbed Youth and Age, The Big House, Drama at Inish,* and *Church Street.* The editor's introduction judiciously evaluates Robinson's themes, dramaturgy, and the development of his playwriting career. Includes a bibliography of Robinson's plays and other works.

Gerald H. Strauss
(Updated by *George O'Brien*)

OLA ROTIMI

Born: Sapele, Nigeria; April 13, 1938

Principal drama

To Stir the God of Iron, pr. 1963; *Our Husband Has Gone Mad Again*, pr. 1966, pb. 1974; *The Gods Are Not to Blame*, pr. 1968, pb. 1971 (adaptation of Sophocles' play *Oedipus Rex*); *Kurunmi*, pr. 1969, pb. 1971; *The Prodigal*, pr. 1969; *Ovonramwen Nogbaisi*, pr. 1971, pb. 1974; *Holding Talks*, pb. 1979; *If*, pr. 1979, pb. 1983; *Hopes of the Living Dead*, pr. 1985, pb. 1988.

Other literary forms

Ola Rotimi is noted only for his plays, although he has also written critical articles on Nigerian theater.

Achievements

Rotimi is one of Nigeria's and Africa's foremost dramatists, both a theatrical teacher and an entertainer as well as a playwright. Two of Rotimi's plays, *Kurunmi* and *Ovonramwen Nogbaisi*, are historical tragedies that recapture pivotal moments in the history of the Yoruba people and the glorious empire of Benin. Three other plays, *Our Husband Has Gone Mad Again*, *If*, and the unproduced and unpublished "When the Dead Awaken," constitute a dramatic sociopolitical trilogy, an extended inquiry into the themes of struggle and integrity of leadership. In these plays, as in others, Rotimi warns his people to beware of political charlatans who have continued to lead postindependence Nigeria to one poor harvest after another. Official and unofficial corruption on such a massive scale that the traditional African sense of community has been sacrificed to personal greed, personal power, and personal self-glorification—this is one dominant subject of Rotimi's plays. *The Gods Are Not to Blame*, first presented at the Ife Festival of the Arts in 1968, has as its theme that the real source of the Nigerian Civil War (1967-1970) was mutual ethnic distrust among Nigerian people, not the great political gods of the world, the United States and the Soviet Union as well as France and England.

The Gods Are Not to Blame was awarded first prize in the African Arts/Arts d'Afrique playwriting contest in 1969. The politico-domestic comedy *Our Husband Has Gone Mad Again*, written in 1965, when Rotimi was in his final year as a graduate student of playwriting and dramatic literature at Yale University, was honored as Yale Major Play of the Year.

Rotimi's plays are often filled with dance, mime, music, and song. Frequently, the songs or chants are in his native Yoruba. They offer thematic commentary on the actions of individual characters and on the destiny of the community. Like the words of the Greek chorus in the plays of Sophocles, the songs articulate the views of reason and social stability; at the same time, they are often humorous, frequently with a satiric intent. Rotimi merges the serious with the humorous in nearly all of his plays, for he believes that the dramatist must entertain as well as teach. Action in the Aristotelian sense is the essence of his drama. A distinctive characteristic of Rotimi's work among that of contemporary African playwrights is the large number of characters, singers, and dancers onstage at one time. In his plays, the stage often becomes a meeting place for large crowds. Rotimi thus seeks to re-create the spirit of communal participation that existed and still exists in traditional African ceremonies.

Along with Wole Soyinka and John Pepper Clark, Rotimi belongs to the vibrant first generation of modern Nigerian dramatists writing in English. Throughout Nigeria, their plays are continually produced. In the late twentieth century, new dramatists, inspired by Rotimi and his contemporaries, have emerged: Zulu Sofolo, Wale Ogunyemi, Femi Osofisan, Bode Sowande, and Samson Amali. Rotimi is one of the two or three most highly regarded dramatists in Africa and as such has played a major role in the development of a dramatic literature on his continent.

Biography

Emmanuel Gladstone Olawale Rotimi was born on April 13, 1938, the son of a Yoruba father from western Nigeria and an Ijaw mother from Rivers State in the Niger Delta of eastern Nigeria. His father, principal of the Engineering Training School of the Ports Authority in Lagos, often directed plays, and his mother had her own dance troupe. The young Rotimi took part in some amateur plays directed by his father, making his stage debut at the age of four. This tradition of family involvement in dramatic performance has continued to the present. Rotimi's wife, Hazel, whom he met at Boston University when they were both undergraduates, has always been involved in his plays—onstage or backstage. A talented musician in her own right, she has led the chorus in productions of *If*, while Kole Rotimi, Ola's son, has appeared in a principal role in the same play.

Ola Rotimi attended primary school in Port Harcourt in eastern Nigeria and the Methodist Boys High School in Lagos, Nigeria's capital. Capable in four languages—English, Ijaw, Yoruba, and pidgin—the playwright Rotimi has drawn on his rich linguistic heritage: Although his plays are written in English, there is a smattering of the other three languages as well, and his English is not an imitation of the language spoken in Oxford or Boston; rather, it is alive with the rhythms, the aphorisms, the pulse of Nigerian English.

From 1959 until 1966, Rotimi studied in the United States. He received a

Nigerian Federal Government scholarship to attend Boston University, where he majored in playwriting and directing, after which he attended Yale on a Rockefeller Foundation scholarship. Receiving his master of arts from Yale in 1966, he returned to Nigeria to become senior research fellow at the Institute of African Studies at the University of Ife. While living in Ife, in the heart of Yorubaland, he familiarized himself with Yoruba oral tradition, including various musical forms that he was to inculcate into his plays. During his tenure there, he directed the university theater company, the Ori-Olokun Players. This company was invited by the French government in 1971 to the World Festival of Theatre in the city of Nancy in eastern France. Rotimi left Ife and moved to the University of Port Harcourt, where he has continued to direct his plays at the University Theater, The Crab. Using both student actors and trained actors from the Arts Council of Rivers State, he has brought the vibrancy of his art to the Port Harcourt area. From 1982 to 1984, Rotimi was Dean of the Faculty of Humanities at the University of Port Harcourt, and he continued to work in the field of university teaching. His play *Hopes of the Living Dead* was first performed at the University of Port Harcourt theatre in 1985.

Rotimi speaks English, Yoruba, Ijaw, Igbo, Hausa, and Pidgin English but writes primarily in English. In 1989, at the Talawa Theatre's revival of *The Gods Are Not to Blame*, at London's Riverside Studios, Rotimi explained, "I believe that in Nigeria's multicultural situation writers should be less partisan. So I write in English. But I try all the time to use simple words and introduce the speech patterns and cadences of Yoruba villagers." His later plays, notably *If* and *Hopes of the Living Dead*, make use of Nigerian names and proverbs.

Analysis

It would not be much of an exaggeration to claim that almost everything in most traditional African societies is a form of theater. The community itself is the central actor, and the village is the stage. Wrestling matches, funerals, initiation rites, religious ceremonies—each of these rituals involves the entire community. It is not surprising, then, that in this modern time, a time which has witnessed the effulgence of written literature, African drama has been nourished by traditional sources. Contemporary writers have returned to the marketplace to be inspired by oral storytellers, whose dramatic tales are often accompanied by musicians and dancers, all of whom are engaged with the audience-community in a statement of social value. The actor and audience are both active participants in the affirmation of the community. One cannot appreciate African drama without recognizing the essence of ritual in the nature of traditional communal activity. The theatrical stage is the village meeting ground, and the dramatist cannot function apart from the society to which he belongs.

The theater of Ola Rotimi, like that of his coeval Soyinka and like that of Aristophanes and Sophocles, is rooted in ritual. Songs, chants, dance, and mime are as elemental as dialogue and monologue. In his plays, Rotimi, the contemporary artist-historian, teaches his people of their past so they can better understand the present and build a constructive future.

Rotimi's *Our Husband Has Gone Mad Again*, written in 1965, foreshadows his career as a dramatist with a sense of social responsibility. The play's protagonist, a former military major, Rahman Taslim Lejoka-Brown, takes to politics not out of feelings of patriotism but rather out of vanity. His political naïveté is matched by his marital ineptitude. When his American wife rejoins him unexpectedly, to discover two other wives whom he has married without her knowledge, the major begins to suffer major symptoms of discomfort.

Rotimi's next play, *The Gods Are Not to Blame*, was written in 1967, while the civil war was raging. The war took strength from long-standing tribal rivalries and was fostered by private political aspirations and corruption in high quarters. *The Gods Are Not to Blame* is an indictment of this Nigerian fratricide.

With the military takeover in Nigeria from 1966 to 1979, Rotimi articulated the anxieties of this period of his country's history. *Ovonramwen Nogbaisi*, *Kurunmi*, "Akassa Youmi," and *The Gods Are Not to Blame* deal with warfare, military rule, and the need for responsibility of leaders to the society. The plays also call Nigerians to a recognition of the nation's past and the need for Nigerians to be free from foreign exploitation and control. Both *Ovonramwen Nogbaisi* and the unpublished "Akassa Youmi" deal with nineteenth century confrontations between England and the Nigerian people. The former tells the story of the sacking and destruction of the capital of the great empire of Benin; the latter narrates the attack by Brassmen in the Niger Delta at the British trading outpost in Akassa. These plays tell Nigerians that their ancestors did not passively accept the tyranny of colonialism; in fact, they did all they could to resist oppression and domination. The British raped Nigeria in their quest for economic expansion. Rotimi is telling his modern audience that unless Nigeria frees herself economically from foreign control, there can only be a continuation of a national malaise based on a feeling of unworthiness. There can be no real development if European interests come first.

With the return to democracy from 1979 to 1983, Rotimi proved to be no more tolerant of civilian political abuse than he was of military abuse. The play *If*, written and produced in 1979, focuses on a landlord-politician who threatens his tenants with eviction if they do not actively support his candidacy. The play, with seventeen characters excluding the twenty children and the twenty-four-person chorus, presents juxtaposed, variegated actions. Different scenes take place simultaneously. The rapid pace of *If* is accentuated by a series of satiric songs inspired by such different sources as African-American spirituals and traditional African chants.

Rotimi has continued to experiment in his art. He has acknowledged his respect for William Shakespeare as well as for the Yoruba folk theater of Duro Lapido, and in his plays he has borrowed from diverse cultural sources. In 1979, with the publication of an absurdist drama, *Holding Talks*, a play in which characters talk and talk without achieving communication, Rotimi tried his hand at a different style, but even in this play, inspired perhaps by the techniques of Harold Pinter, Rotimi continues to be a writer involved with society, for its satire focuses on characters who fail when action is required. Thus, despite the evolution of his craft, Rotimi continues to devote his artistic life to further the interests of the majority of Nigerian people, who, since independence, have been victimized by self-seeking leaders.

Rotimi's commitment to his people and his heritage is passionately made manifest in the three-act historical tragedy *Ovonramwen Nogbaisi*, a play that tells the story—well-known to Nigerian audiences—of the brutal end of the empire of Benin.

In the fifteenth century, the empire of Benin was famous throughout West Africa. Indeed, in the mid-fifteenth century, under Oba Ewuare the Great, the fortified city of Benin, surrounded by three miles of walls, was the center of a great civilization. With organized guilds of palace artisans, the arts flourished. Most famous are the Benin bronze works, recognized today as one of the apogees of the history of art. Work in ivory and coral was also of high quality. In the sixteenth century, Oba Esigie ruled for nearly fifty years. At that time, Benin had a standing army of more than 100,000 men, and Benin City had more than thirty streets which exceeded 120 feet in width. The Yoruba Wars and the incursions of Moslems from the north led to the decline, from the mid-sixteenth century, of the once powerful empire. By the end of the nineteenth century, Benin had seen its greatest days, but its bronze art was still a testament to its greatness, and its Oba or chief, Ovonramwen, carried on the tradition of the god-ruler.

In 1897, the British destroyed the capital, captured Ovonramwen, and exiled him to Calabar in eastern Nigeria. The British account of the events leading up to the sacking of Benin City is as follows: An unarmed British trade delegation was massacred by the Oba's men; the British retaliated, destroying the capital, a center of human sacrifice and barbarousness. To save the bronze artwork, the British carried the statues and reliefs back to London, where they can be seen today in the British Museum. Rotimi tells a different story. He does not romanticize Ovonramwen. In the first act, the audience sees a leader trying to hold his empire together, struggling with rebellious chiefs and recalcitrant followers. Fear is his weapon in dealing with his people. The arrival of the British, who mask their desire to gain control of the rubber trees of Benin with treaties of friendship, leads to inevitable conflict. The royal bards chant hymns of hope, but their hopes are not to be fulfilled.

During the religious festival of Agwe, British traders—with arms— approach Benin. Warned that it is taboo to visit the Oba at this sacred time, the white men pay no attention. They are murdered by subalterns of the Oba, even though Ovonramwen had warned his subordinates to use no violence. As the second act ends. the Oba is forced to flee.

In the third act, the Oba confronts the British. He declares that British intentions in Benin were suspect. After all, had not the British captured King Jaja of Opobo when he fought to maintain control of his territory? Had not Jaja been traitorously captured at a putative peace conference and exiled to the West Indies? Oba Ovonramwen knows that the British interest in Benin is rubber, ivory, palm oil. In the end, while struggling to join guerrilla forces still combating the British, the god-chief is captured. His empire, the magnificent empire of Benin, is dead. The god-king is a mere subject of the white man. A man more sinned against than sinning must suffer the humiliation of capture, a degradation emblematic of the destiny of his people.

The play is rooted in ritual. In the first act, the prophecy of the Ifa priest of the Oracle of Oghere warns that fire and blood threaten Benin, that disaster is at hand. Despite the Oba's serious efforts to unify his people and maintain the integrity of the empire, collapse is inevitable. The chants of the bards chronicle the passage from fear to doubt to destruction. These songs and chants are derived in the main from the traditional folk-music repertoire of the Edo Cultural Group in Benin City, arranged by Osemwegie Ebohon.

In *Ovonramwen Nogbaisi*, Rotimi retells Nigerian history from Nigeria's point of view, not that of history books written by the English. He warns his people that continued economic exploitation of contemporary Nigeria by Western powers undermines the independence of "independent" Nigeria. In *The Gods Are Not to Blame*, however, Rotimi warns Nigerians that the nation cannot excuse its own failure merely by blaming foreign powers. Written in 1967 as civil war was raging in Nigeria, *The Gods Are Not to Blame* reinterprets the Oedipus myth in the light of the Nigerian situation. Certainly the causes of the civil war are many and are rooted in the time of British colonialism. The military coup of January 15, 1966, in which the Hausa leaders of the north were killed, was followed by an orgy of slaughter of Igbo people living in the north. Those Igbo who could, escaped to the safe confines of Igboland in eastern Nigeria, and on May 30, 1967, the Igbo declared that eastern Nigeria—now called Biafra—was an independent nation. Three years later, millions of deaths later, Nigeria became reunited. The war has inspired many works by Nigerian dramatists, poets, and novelists. Rotimi's *The Gods Are Not to Blame*, however, was one of the first literary responses to the conflict.

The play's protagonist, Odewale (Oedipus), the son of King Adetusa and Queen Oguola of Kutuji, grows up far from his native town. A man of an irascible nature, Odewale, like Oedipus, unwittingly slays his father, marries his mother, and in so doing pollutes the land. To save his people, he must be cleansed. There are, however, distinct differences between Odewale and Oedipus. Odewale's tragic flaw is not primarily pride; it is tribal animosity. When he attacks the old man (his father, the king) who has intruded on his farmland, Odewale is determined not to be violent, but when the old man refers to Odewale's tribe as a bush tribe, the protagonist loses all control and slays the intruder.

Throughout the play, the theme of tribalism reappears. When the village seer, Baba Fakunle, accuses Odewale of being the murderer of the former king, Odewale's immediate instinct is to see tribal bias. Odewale believes himself to be an Ikejun man among the people of Kutuje. Although it is not uncommon among Nigerian people for a member of one tribe to become head of another, Odewale chooses to see tribal resentment as the basis of any criticism directed toward him.

Rotimi alters the Oedipus story when necessary. For example, in the Nigerian cultural setting there can be no justification for a young man to strike an elder in a dispute over a right-of-way, as happens in the Greek tale. A young man who resorts to violence against an elder is justified only in very specific circumstances, one of which is if the elder has stolen or intends to steal the young man's property. This is the situation that initiates the conflict between father and son in *The Gods Are Not to Blame*.

There are, however, distinct cultural similarities between the Greek society of Sophocles and traditional Yoruba society. Like the Greeks, the Yoruba have their pantheon of gods: Ogun, Shango, Obatala. These hero-gods provide the framework for traditional Yoruba religious beliefs and moral codes and also are symbolic vehicles for aiding Yoruba men in facing the ambiguities of human tragedy. There is a sense of cosmic totality among the Yoruba as there was among the Greeks. What Soyinka calls the ritual archetype is the foundation upon which Rotimi's *The Gods Are Not to Blame* is built.

The title of the play refers ironically to the great political powers who became involved in the Nigerian War. The Biafrans blamed the Soviet Union and Great Britain for aiding the Nigerian Federalists in their attack on Biafra. The Federalists blamed France and the United States, through its charitable organizations, for supporting the Biafran's secession. Rotimi knows that ethnic distrust was the root of the conflict. Though Nigerian politicians play upon the theme of foreign control, *The Gods Are Not to*

Blame unsparingly rejects such self-serving rhetoric. In his final speech, Odewale warns the people not to blame the gods. Odewale warns those who will listen about the weakness of a man easily moved to the defense of his tribe against others. Since tribal hatred is a learned response, it can be unlearned.

The Gods Are Not to Blame was first produced by the Ori-Olokun Acting Company at the Ife Festival of the Arts in 1968; Rotimi himself played the Narrator. The rhythms of Ogun, Yoruba God of War and Iron, are never distant. The play is filled with many Yoruba proverbs and choral chants that echo principal themes. Ultimately, Rotimi is saying that when the wood insect gathers sticks, it carries them on its own head.

Rotimi has continued to warn Nigeria of the dangers that threaten the stability of society in the modern world. His dramatic trilogy examining the fate of a people in need of sociopolitical hope looks at Nigerian democracy and shudders. *Our Husband Has Gone Mad Again*, first staged at Yale University in 1966, was very popular during the hiatus from military rule that lasted from 1979 to 1983. Nigerian electioneering maneuvers seem to have changed not at all between 1966 and 1983. Party members in *Our Husband Has Gone Mad Again* are all thugs, and the politicians are nothing more than greedy charlatans interested only in instant wealth.

The political figure in *Our Husband Has Gone Mad Again* is a former military major, Rahman Taslim Lejoka-Brown. His National Liberation Party mouths slogans of freedom for the people of Nigeria, for Africa. In actuality, political freedom really means unlimited license for corruption.

Our Husband Has Gone Mad Again is a drawing-room comedy of sorts. Most of the action takes place in Lejoka-Brown's living room; his political ambition is paralleled in his private life. When the play begins, the audience learns that his sophisticated American-educated wife, Lisa, is due to arrive in Lagos. Lejoka-Brown has not told her about his two other wives, Mama Rashida and Sikira, both of whom are in the mold of market women. The play contains a very humorous scene in which Lisa, believing Sikira to be a housemaid, manages to antagonize the two other wives. They know that the newly arrived fowl needs to have her proud feathers plucked.

It is generally known in traditional Nigerian societies that if a man cannot handle his wives, he probably will not be able to handle political responsibility. Lejoka-Brown thinks that he is in control of his wives; he is not. Once the wives learn to accept one another and work together, the poor major has no chance. At the end of the play, Sikira, with the support of the market women, is to become the candidate of the National Liberation Party. Lejoka-Brown's world is turned upside down. He laments that before he became caught up in the craziness of politics, he was doing very well running his cocoa business.

Rotimi's historical plays, his comic satires, his ritualistic tragedies, and his social and political works show his versatility as a dramatist. In his plays, he borrows from traditional Yoruba sources, combining music, mime, and dance with more conventional elements of drama to offer his view of the political and psychological landscape of the country that he loves.

If examines the problems faced by ordinary Nigerians in the wake of the country's civil war. *Hopes of the Living Dead*, which has been widely acclaimed, depicts the turn-of-the-century rebellion of Nigerian lepers against their colonial rulers and expands the historical events into a metaphor for contemporary Nigerian society.

Bibliography

Banham, Martin. "Ola Rotimi: 'Humanity as My Tribesman.'" *Modern Drama* 33 (March, 1990): 67-81. Quotes at length from *If* and offers the first close critical look at *Hopes of the Living Dead*, which, Banham says, is more optimistic than *If. Hopes of the Living Dead* is based on the life of Ikoli Harcourt Whyte, a composer and leper, treated at Port Harcourt Hospital in 1924. "The strength of his [Rotimi's] work," Banham says, lies . . . in its powerful theatrical advocacy of political and social action."

Crow, Brian. "Melodrama and the 'Political Unconscious' in Two African Plays." *Ariel* 14 (July, 1983): 15-31. Compares Rotimi's *Ovonramwen Nogbaisi* with Ngugi wa Thiong'o's *The Trial of Dedan Kimathi* (pr. 1974, pb. 1976), written with Micere Githae-Mugo. Says that both "articulate and assert the immanence of good and evil in the historical conflicts that they dramatize" and invite further comparisons with traditional Western melodrama.

Lindfors, Bernth, ed. *Dem-Say: Interviews with Eight Nigerian Writers.* Austin: University of Texas African and Afro-American Studies and Research Center, 1974. Recorded at the University of Ife in 1973, the interview covers Rotimi's education in the United States, his beginnings as a playwright, the influences of Wole Soyinka and John Pepper Clark-Bekederemo on his work, and his ambitions for "a full-length massiveness in music, dance and movement lasting two whole hours . . . mobilizing a 500-man cast."

Okafor, Chinyere G. "Ola Rotimi: The Man, the Playwright, and the Producer on the Nigerian Theater Scene." *World Literature Today* 64 (Winter, 1990): 24-29. Okafor, an actress and assistant director in some of Rotimi's productions, offers firsthand knowledge of her work. She discusses Rotimi's canon and production practices, especially on dramatic spectacle, and his breaking of the proscenium arch. She says that "[m]ore good things are still expected of this renowned man of the theater."

Rotimi, Ola. "The Head Without a Cap." Interview by Adeola Solanke. *New Statesman Society* 2 (November 10, 1989): 42-43. An interview with the playwright on the occasion of the Talawa Theatre's revival of *The Gods Are Not to Blame* in 1989. Reexamines the Oedipus Rex myth as derivation of the play, quoting Rotimi's remark that "in my play the 'gods' are . . . the superpowers who control the political and economic destiny of the developing world."

Donald Burness
(Updated by *Thomas J. Taylor*)

NICHOLAS ROWE

Born: Little Barford, England; June 20, 1674
Died: London, England; December 6, 1718

Principal drama

The Ambitious Step-Mother, pr. 1700, pb. 1701; *Tamerlane*, pr. 1701, pb. 1702; *The Fair Penitent*, pr., pb. 1703 (adaptation of Philip Massinger's play *The Fatal Dowry*); *The Biter*, pr. 1704, pb. 1705; *Ulysses*, pr. 1705, pb. 1706; *The Royal Convert*, pr. 1707, pb. 1708; *The Tragedy of Jane Shore*, pr., pb. 1714; *The Tragedy of Lady Jane Gray*, pr., pb. 1715; *Dramatick Works*, pb. 1720 (2 volumes).

Other literary forms

Nicholas Rowe adapted some odes of Horace to current affairs and published many poems on public occasions. He contributed a memoir of Nicolas Boileau to a translation of Boileau's "Lutrin" in 1708, took some part in a collective rendering of Ovid's *Metamorphoses*, and published translations of work by Jean de la Bruyère in the same year. In 1709, he edited William Shakespeare's works, creating the first truly modern edition, an edition still highly respected. A highly praised translation of Lucan's *Pharsalia* was published posthumously.

Achievements

Rowe was an extremely cultivated man, well-acquainted with the classics and with French, Italian, and Spanish literature. He was esteemed as a conversationalist; Alexander Pope called him "the best of men" and seemed to delight in his society, both in London and in the country.

One of Rowe's chief achievements was his edition of Shakespeare's works, first published in 1709, generally regarded as the first attempt to edit Shakespeare in the modern sense. It was Rowe who first added a list of *dramatis personae* to each play; he was also the first to divide and number acts and scenes on rational principles, to mark the entrances and exits of the characters, and to modernize the spelling.

Hugh Blair and Samuel Johnson, also eighteenth century writers, found most of Rowe's drama too cold and too flowery, but two of his plays escaped such censure: *The Tragedy of Jane Shore* and *The Fair Penitent*. Johnson found Rowe's other literary efforts more enduring than his plays; he described Rowe's translation of Lucan as one of the greatest productions of English poetry.

The consensus among critics lies with Blair and Johnson—that of all Rowe's plays, *The Tragedy of Jane Shore* is his greatest. The tenderness and pathos of this play show how thorough and affectionate had been Rowe's study of great Elizabethan drama. The proof of Rowe's power is in the fact that such a play held the stage so long and was so popular even in an age much different from his own.

Biography

Nicholas Rowe was born in the house of his mother's father at Little Barford, Bedfordshire, in 1674. His father's family settled at Lamerton, Devonshire, and one of his ancestors is said to have been distinguished as a Crusader. His father was a London barrister of the Middle Temple and a sergeant-at-law.

After attending a private school at Highgate, Rowe was in 1688 elected a king's scholar at Westminster. Not long afterward, he was removed and entered as a student at the Middle Temple. The law, however, proved to be uncongenial. From his youth, Rowe had read widely in literature, especially that of the theater, and soon he was ambitious to try his hand as a playwright. When his father died in 1692, Rowe was enabled to follow his own inclinations.

Early in 1700, Rowe saw his first play, entitled *The Ambitious Step-Mother*, produced at Lincoln's Inn Fields. Following this success, Rowe was for some years a professional playwright and soon gained the acquaintance of the leaders of literary society of eighteenth century London, including Pope and Joseph Addison. In 1702, he published his second tragedy, *Tamerlane*, the play he valued most of those he was to write. It was common knowledge that the play was really intended to portray William III, endowed with most amiable virtues, and Louis XIV, his villainous rival. The political tone of the play made it quite popular; it became tradition to perform it annually on November 5 of each year, in celebration of the anniversary of William III's landing.

In 1703, Rowe completed *The Fair Penitent*, a sentimental tragedy adapted from Philip Massinger's *The Fatal Dowry* (pr. 1616-1619). It was produced at Lincoln's Inn Fields, and the public approved its pathos; the villain Lothario acquired a proverbial reputation. Rowe's next play, *Ulysses*, was not nearly as successful, but it did enjoy a long run at the Queen's Theatre in the Haymarket in 1705. *The Royal Convert*, produced in 1707 at the Haymarket, was based on early British history. The final lines, spoken by Ethelrede, describe the blessing anticipated from the union of England and Scotland and panegyrize Queen Anne. Several years passed before Rowe wrote again, but his next play was one of his most popular ones. When first produced at Drury Lane in February, 1714, *The Tragedy of Jane Shore* ran for nineteen nights, and it long held the stage. His last tragedy, *The Tragedy of Lady Jane Gray*, was produced on April 20, 1715, at Drury Lane.

Rowe found himself involved in politics as an ardent Whig soon after he had begun writing plays. In February, 1708, he became under secretary to the Duke of Queensberry, Secretary of State for Scotland, and held office until the duke's death in 1711. After some years of political service, Rowe obtained the recognition he sought. On August 1, 1715, he was made poet laureate in succession to Nahum Tate.

Later, Rowe produced official odes addressed to the king and eventually a collection entitled "State Poems." In 1717, he completed a verse translation of Lucan's *Pharsalia*, but the whole was not published until after his death.

Analysis

Nicholas Rowe's first play, *The Ambitious Step-Mother*, produced in 1700, continues the tradition of heroic drama. It is set against the exotic Oriental background characteristic of the type. The play opens with Arsaces, the aged Persian king, on his deathbed. Real power is in the hands of the second wife, Artemisa. He had contrived to have her first husband killed and had then wedded her. She has gained control over the king, who is infatuated with her beauty. Artemisa is determined to secure the succession of the crown for her own son, Artaban. Arsaces had sent into exile his elder son, Artaxerxes, who has now returned, demanding his right of succession. In order to make her plan succeed, Artemisa finds a supporter in a scheming courtier, Mirza, who seeks revenge because the king's son Artaxerxes rejected the offer of his daughter Cleone for his bride. Instead, Artaxerxes chose Amestris, the daughter of his counselor, Memnon.

The scheming Mirza then confides a plan for estranging Artaxerxes and Memnon, and Artemisa bars the way of Artaxerxes to his dying father's bedside. Their plot is complicated by the fact that Cleone, although rejected by Artaxerxes, is passionately in love with him and deaf to her father's desires. In the meantime, Mirza devises a plot to overpower his and the queen's enemies. Artaxerxes, Memnon, and Amestris are all seized by guards at the annual Festival of the Sun. It is Mirza's intent that Artaxerxes and Memnon shall be executed on the morrow, but he does not take into account Cleone. She dons masculine dress and offers the two prisoners the chance of escaping through Mirza's palace. Meanwhile, Amestris, confined in Mirza's palace, is sexually assaulted by Mirza. In the struggle, she stabs him with his own poniard. In one last revengeful attempt, he bids the captain of the guard to drag Amestris near him, and he stabs her. As she lies dying, Artaxerxes and Memnon enter to hear the tale of her wrongs and her last appeal to her lover. She dies, whereupon Artaxerxes stabs himself. So ends the tragedy, showing the innocent suffering along with the guilty.

Rowe's ending was severely criticized by many as too barbarous, even though he defended it on the basis of Aristotle's precept that terror and pity are the ends of tragedy. Others saw weakness in the characterization. Perhaps certain spectacular scenes made up for this deficiency, however, because the play had a good run.

Rowe's *Tamerlane*, produced in 1701, also employs the Oriental theme. Although Christopher Marlowe had written his *Tamburlaine the Great* (pr. 1587), on the same subject, there is little similarity between the two. Rowe intentionally perverts historical truth when he presents the Oriental conqueror as a prototype of the ideal political leader, William III. His dedicatory letter includes comments about how the two share courage, piety, moderation, justice, love of their subjects, and hatred of tyranny and oppression. It is evident that just as Tamerlane typifies William III, so Bajazet represents Louis XIV. The action of the play centers on Tamerlane's camp, where he is about to battle Bajazet. When the contest goes in Tamerlane's favor, he takes no personal pride in victory. He remarks, in fact, that all such pride is vain "pretence to greatness." Bajazet defies him as a dervish and declares his own conception of good rule, which in his view necessitates the ruler's thirst for more territory, this being the call of nature. Although in British terms, such ideas of sovereignty are villainous, Tamerlane nevertheless releases Bajazet and restores to him his captive queen, all of which will eventually be his undoing. Tamerlane's religious tolerance is great, also—so great, in fact, that he takes into his council the Christian Italian Prince Axalla. This act alone angers Bajazet, who wants to conquer all lands and make all people followers of Mohammet. Because he is not able to win the argument, Bajazet attempts to stab Tamerlane with a concealed dagger, an act which Tamerlane forgives as he has certain others. Bajazet is not satisfied, however, and plots with a general, Omar, who supported Tamerlane in his rise to power but who now is angry with him because Tamerlane has not allowed him to take Bajazet's daughter Selima as his bride. Selima has given her love to Axalla, and Omar, in vengeance, arrests them both. Selima's father, Bajazet, attempts to kill her, but she is saved by the arrival of Tamerlane with Axalla, who has escaped in the disguise of a slave. Another pair of lovers are not so successful. Arpasia, who had been contracted to her countryman of royal lineage, Moneses, had been forced earlier to become one of Bajazet's brides. Moneses appeals to Tamerlane to undo this terrible wrong, but Tamerlane feels that he cannot interfere. Bajazet decides to have Moneses killed, and as his henchmen struggle with Moneses and strangle him, Arpasia sinks in a fatal swoon.

Tamerlane has effective dialogue, but it is less impressive theatrically than *The Ambitious Step-Mother*. Probably the greatest weakness in the play lies in the crude contrast between the high-souled Tamerlane and the villain Bajazet. It did remain a popular play, however, evidently because of its political allegory. It was acted at various London playhouses, usually on William III's birthday, until 1749, a period of forty-eight years. Dramatically, critics generally agree, the tragedy has little to recommend it. The love scenes are either insipid or unreal. Its chief merit lies in the vigorous action of the villain, who has the bragging manliness of John Dryden's heroes; also, the unhappy love of Moneses and Arpasia anticipates the "she tragedies" which were to follow. Dr. Johnson's estimate of the play is perhaps the best criticism: "This was the tragedy which Rowe valued most, and that which probably by the help of the political auxiliaries, excited most applause; but occasional poetry must often content itself with occasional praise."

Rowe's next play, *The Fair Penitent*, written in 1703 and produced in the same year, is set in Italy. The plot involves a Genoese nobleman, Sciolto, who has taken the place of Lord Altamont's father, thrust out by his ungrateful state. Sciolto, in the opening scene, is about to give his daughter Calista in marriage to Altamont. Calista, however, is cold toward Altamont because she is secretly in love with Lothario, Altamont's enemy. She has in fact allowed Lothario to seduce her and has begged him to marry her, all in vain. When she learns of her betrothal to Altamont, she writes Lothario informing him of her situation and asking for a last meeting between them, but the letter accidentally falls into the hands of Altamont's friend, Horatio. Horatio confronts Calista with the information, but she declares that the letter was forged. She denounces Horatio as a slanderer, so he is forced then to show the letter to Altamont. Altamont, not wanting to believe the facts, strikes Horatio, and they fight until Horatio's wife, Lavinia, also Altamont's sister, runs between their swords to part the two. Shortly thereafter, Altamont surprises Lothario and Calista in a rendezvous and kills Lothario. With nothing to live for, Calista tries to kill herself by using Lothario's sword, but Altamont takes it from her. Sciolto, learning the truth, impetuously begins to slay his own daughter, but recoils. Later at night, he visits Calista where she is in mourning at Lothario's body. There, Sciolto offers his daughter a dagger, but as she lifts it, he prevents her death, because he cannot forget that she is his daughter. Altamont, too, experiences a strong passion for revenge against Calista, but like her father, controls his emotions. In the midst of this repentance, however, catastrophe erupts. Horatio comes in to announce that Sciolto has been attacked by Lothario's faction in revenge and is dying. Hearing his news, Calista stabs herself and begs Altamont's and her father's blessings.

The Fair Penitent had an even greater success than did *Tamerlane*. The play was eventually adapted into French, and all over Europe, Lothario became proverbial as the equivalent of a rake: His name entered the English language, and even today a "lothario" is a seducer. The tragedy illustrates the working theme of most of Rowe's plays: the temptation of a more or less pure woman by a libertine. Indeed, Rowe serves as the link between Thomas Otway and George Lillo as a writer of domestic tragedy. Frank J. Kearful analyzes the play's characterization thoroughly in an essay in *Papers on Language and Literature* (1966). He points out that Rowe was endeavoring to create something more than a melodrama of "unsuspecting virtue assailed by diabolical vice." By injecting issues of property and respectability into the drama, Rowe confronted his audience with the complexity of moral experience and the various kinds of moral problems they might encounter in their daily lives.

The Tragedy of Jane Shore centers on the crowning of Prince Edward and the desire of Richard of York to usurp the throne. The Duke of Gloster, a supporter of Richard, fears that Lord Hastings, a staunch Edwardite, will stand in his way if he attempts to help put Richard into power, but he very much wants to do so. Hastings is loved by fair Alicia. Jane Shore, the mistress of the late King Edward IV, is being officially deprived of her property, and Hastings enters the scene to plead for gentle treatment of her.

To make matters worse, Dumont, Jane's husband in disguise, assures her that her husband died three years ago, leaving Jane in complete grief with no one but Alicia to reassure her. Alicia, who had persuaded Hastings to intercede for Jane, tries to comfort her friend, who ironically will become her rival, for Hastings falls in love with Jane in the process.

After Alicia has comforted Jane, she leaves to greet Hastings and berates him for his recent coldness to her. Hastings admits that he has lost his love for her and is attracted to Jane. From this point on, Alicia tries to ruin Jane in every way possible. When Hastings later confesses his love to Jane, she refuses him, only to have Hastings attempt rape. Jane is saved only by the intercession of Dumont.

Now set on revenge, Alicia tries to make Gloster hostile to Hastings. She openly accuses Hastings of blocking Gloster's plans for Richard. When Jane enters later to report that Dumont has been arrested by Hastings' men, Alicia tricks her into giving Gloster the letter she has written about Hastings' supposed treachery, rather than the letter pleading for merciful treatment toward Jane. The former not only accuses Hastings but also implicates Jane Shore in the treacherous action.

Although Gloster tries to persuade Jane to get Hastings to change his mind about supporting Edward, Jane, too, is loyal to the Edwardian line and praises the steadfastness of Hastings. In response, Gloster turns Jane into the streets and arrests Hastings for high treason. Though Alicia has found her revenge, it is not sweet, because she is sorry to see her lover Hastings in prison awaiting death.

Jane, left to beg, goes to Alicia and requests sustenance, but Alicia pushes her away. Only Dumont runs to her aid. She faints when she recognizes that Dumont is really her deserted, ill-treated husband, who still loves her very much. All is not well, however, because Dumont is seized by guards and accused of aiding a traitor. He is taken to prison as Jane dies of starvation and suffering.

The Tragedy of Jane Shore enjoyed as much popularity as *The Fair Penitent*, perhaps because the moral taste of the audience was oriented toward justice for the wrongdoer. Though Jane repents and receives Dumont's blessing, she has erred by breaking the marriage vow. The play ran for several weeks and was even translated into French. Most critics regard it as Rowe's finest play.

Before Rowe ended his career as a dramatist, he penned one more play, *The Tragedy of Lady Jane Gray*. Again there is the theme of a disputed succession to the throne, but in this play, it receives the focus of attention. The issue of succession is complicated by a bitter religious feud. Edward IV is dying, and there is a rivalry for the throne between the supporters of Lady Jane and Mary, the latter being Roman Catholic. Lady Jane has been named successor by Edward, but the girl's thoughts are not on the crown but on the dying man. When Guilford Dudley promises that he will forgo a usual bridegroom's right and will join her in mourning, she consents to an immediate wedding with him. It so happens that Jane is loved also by the Earl of Pembroke, hitherto Guilford's close friend. Pembroke now denounces Guilford as a betrayer to Gardiner, Bishop of Winchester, who is Mary's chief supporter.

Soon, Jane's mother, who has forced her into a sudden marriage, tells her that she is to wear England's crown. She shudders at the very thought of being queen, but at last is persuaded to take the crown to save England from Rome's tyranny. Jane's fears are soon justified. The London crowd that had earlier supported her veers to Mary's side, and Jane finds herself in a precarious situation. Gardiner is appointed Chancellor and orders Jane and Guilford imprisoned in the Tower. There is a touch of hope for the two, because Pembroke repays an earlier kindness from Guilford and secures from Mary a pardon for Jane and her husband. The hope is short-lived, however, for Gardiner intervenes and makes the pardon conditional on their renouncing their Protestant heresy. This they refuse to do, and they must die.

The irony of this production is that even though it did not enjoy the popularity of *The Fair Penitent* or *The Tragedy of Jane Shore*, it is in one way actually a better-written play. The interest is not dispersed; it remains focused on Lady Jane. With the writing of this play, Rowe's work for the stage came to an end.

Other major works

POETRY: *Poems on Several Occasions*, 1714.

TRANSLATION: *Lucan's Pharsalis*, 1719.

MISCELLANEOUS: *The Works of Mr. William Shakespeare*, 1709 (editor, 6 volumes), 1714 (9 volumes); *The Works of Nicholas Rowe, Esq.*, 1727 (3 volumes).

Bibliography

Aikins, Janet E. "To Know Jane Shore: 'Think on All Time, Backward.'" *Papers on Language and Literature* 18 (Summer, 1982): 258-277. Provides an intriguing close reading of *The Fair Penitent* and *The Tragedy of Jane Shore*, describing the nature of the two protagonists as "static." Rowe deliberately creates passive heroines to whom events happen, rather than active individuals, to suggest the role of fate in their downfall. Consequently, he creates a tragedy that arouses "generous pity" in the audience, leading them to pardon the offenders.

Burns, Landon C. *Pity and Tears: The Tragedies of Nicholas Rowe.* Salzburg, Austria: Institut für Englische Sprache und Literatur, 1974. Examines Rowe's gradual abandonment of the style of the seventeenth century heroic play for pathos and sentimentality. Rowe gives to his villains the posturing and bravado of John Dryden's heroes, while creating realistic heroes; further, Rowe redefines the drives for both love and admiration that animate heroic characters in the earlier plays.

Canfield, Douglas. *Nicholas Rowe and Christian Tragedy.* Gainesville: University Presses of Florida, 1977. Canfield's is the first book to analyze all Rowe's tragedies. He links Rowe's use of the structuring device of the "trial" of the protagonist's faith to the Christian worldview of the period. Good bibliography and a listing of Rowe's library as found in a sale catalog published after his death.

Dammers, Richard H. "The Importance of Being Female in the Tragedies of Nicholas Rowe." *McNeese Review* 26 (1979-1980): 13-20. Examines Rowe's creation of the "religious preceptress" figure and finds that the women of his plays lead their husbands to faith and virtue. Rowe's depiction of idealized married love is a shift from the "courtship" scenes of earlier dramatists. He thus critiques his society's double standards in sexual conduct and upholds humility and fidelity for both partners.

Goldstein, Malcolm. "Pathos and Personality in the Tragedies of Nicholas Rowe." In *English Writers of the Eighteenth Century*, edited by John H. Middendorf. New York: Columbia University Press, 1971. An excellent introduction to Rowe's work, with a review of the two "types" of women characters Rowe frequently used.

Hesse, Alfred W. "Who Was Bit by Rowe's *Biter*?" *Philological Quarterly* 62 (1983): 477-485. Hesse argues that Rowe's generally unsuccessful comedy possibly satirized Elihu Yale, benefactor of Yale University, then recently returned from the Orient.

Jenkins, Anibel. *Nicholas Rowe.* Boston: Twayne, 1977. Follows the standard arrangement of the Twayne series. Jenkins provides a brief biographical summary, then analyzes Rowe's works individually. Unlike Douglas Canfield (above), she discusses Rowe's comedy *The Biter* and his editorial and poetic work.

Kearful, Frank J. "The Nature of Tragedy in Rowe's *The Fair Penitent.*" *Papers on Language and Literature* 2 (1966): 351-360. Discusses Rowe's shift from heroic drama to domestic tragedy, avoiding the sentimental treatment of character and plot common of Thomas Otway or John Banks. To essentially middle-class characters, he adds an element of moral instruction missing earlier. Kearful examines Rowe's Calista, unfaithful to her husband, yet under very real social pressures that contribute to her downfall.

John W. Crawford
(Updated by *Richard J. Sherry*)

GEORGE RYGA

Born: Deep Creek, Alberta, Canada; July 27, 1932
Died: Summerland, British Columbia, Canada; November 18, 1987

Principal drama

Indian, pr. 1962 (televised), pb. 1962, pr. 1964 (staged); *Nothing but a Man*, pr., pb. 1966; *The Ecstasy of Rita Joe*, pr. 1967, pb. 1970; *Grass and Wild Strawberries*, pr. 1969, pb. 1971; *The Ecstasy of Rita Joe and Other Plays*, pb. 1971 (includes *Indian* and *Grass and Wild Strawberries*); *Captives of the Faceless Drummer*, pr. 1971, pb. 1972 (music and lyrics by Ryga); *Sunrise on Sarah*, pr. 1972, pb. 1973 (music by Ryga); *A Portrait of Angelica*, pr. 1973, pb. 1976; *A Feast of Thunder*, pr. 1973 (music by Morris Surdin); *Paracelsus and the Hero*, pb. 1974; *Twelve Ravens for the Sun*, pr. 1975 (music by Mikis Theodorakis); *Ploughmen of the Glacier*, pr., pb. 1976; *Seven Hours to Sundown*, pr., pb. 1976; *Country and Western*, pb. 1976 (includes *A Portrait of Angelica*, *Ploughmen of the Glacier*, *Seven Hours to Sundown*); *Laddie Boy*, pb. 1978, pr. 1981; *Prometheus Bound*, pb. 1981 (adaptation of Aeschylus' play); *A Letter to My Son*, pr. 1981, pb. 1982.

Other literary forms

In addition to stage plays, plays for radio and television, poems, film scripts, and song lyrics, George Ryga wrote three novels and one fictionalized memoir of a journey through China. Ryga's first published novel, *Hungry Hills* (1963), is a story of a young man who returns to the cruel, barren prairie community that had exiled him three years earlier. Like many of Ryga's plays, *Hungry Hills* describes the suffering and isolation of the outcast whose social and spiritual alienation is further embittered by a "desperate climate which parch[es] both the soil and heart of man." Ryga's second novel, *Ballad of a Stone-Picker* (1966), tells of two brothers, one of whom stays to work on the family farm so that his younger brother can go to the university, where he becomes a Rhodes scholar; a revised edition was published in 1976. In *Night Desk* (1976), Ryga's third novel, the city (as always, in Ryga, a symbol of antilife) is given extended treatment. In a series of scenes narrated by a tough-talking Edmonton fight promoter, the city's grim and shabby underside is revealed. *Beyond the Crimson Morning: Reflections from a Journey Through Contemporary China* (1979) is based on Ryga's trip to China in 1976.

Achievements

In *The Ecstasy of Rita Joe*, Ryga wrote one of Canada's best-known and most widely produced plays. On July 9, 1969, less than two years after its premier performance in Vancouver during Canada's centennial, *The Ecstasy of Rita Joe* was performed at the festival opening of the National Arts Centre in Ottawa. The play was next produced by the Fondation Nationale de la Comédie Canadienne, Montreal, in a French version by Gratien Gélinas, Quebec's leading dramatist. Adapted as a ballet by Norbert Vesak and produced by the Royal Winnipeg Ballet, *The Ecstasy of Rita Joe* was performed on tour in 1971 throughout Canada, the United States, and Australia. Ryga received additional acclaim upon accepting the Edinburgh Festival Fringe Award for his play in 1974. Widely reprinted, *The Ecstasy of Rita Joe* has established itself as a classic of the Canadian dramatic repertoire.

As one of English Canada's major dramatists, Ryga received considerable recognition in a country where artists, even those of his stature, have had to struggle to have their work officially acknowledged. In 1972, he was awarded a Canada Council Senior Arts Grant to work on *Paracelsus and the Hero*; in 1979, he was nominated for an ACTRA Award for the *Newcomers* television series; in 1979 and 1980, he received the Frankfurt Academy of Performing Arts Award for *Ploughmen of the Glacier* (Ryga had a substantial foreign audience); and in 1980, he was invited to serve as writer-in-residence at the University of Ottawa.

Ryga's achievements were fueled by his fierce, often embattled commitment to a national theater in Canada. From his earliest days as a dramatist, Ryga resisted the imposition of British and American styles upon the Canadian theater and sought to establish a living theater fully responsive to his own country's heterogeneous culture. By his own admission, however, Ryga had equivocal success in establishing such a theater in Canada: "I have known electrifying national prominence, and I have known a decade of exclusion from the theatres of my country. . . ." Nevertheless, Ryga's plays, which transform Canadian myth and experience into a vivid dramatic language, have been of major significance in the struggle to establish a national theater.

Biography

George Ryga grew up in what he has referred to as "the internal third-world of Canada"—the rugged, depression-ridden prairieland of Northern Alberta. He was born in Deep Creek on July 27, 1932, the first child of George Ryga and Maria Kolodka, new immigrants from the Ukraine. Though formally educated in a one-room schoolhouse, and only up to the eighth grade, Ryga read widely as a child while nurturing himself on the songs, myths, and folktales of his heritage. Ryga's Ukrainian background, the severe poverty in which he was reared, and the dominating reality of the northern landscape were all of enduring significance to his development as an artist. Of the land and language with which he grew up, Ryga commented:

> The language took the form of the land—uncompromising, hard, defiant—for three seasons of the year the long months of winter isolation made the desire for human contact a constant ache.

Having grown up beside a Cree reservation, Ryga soon discovered another kind of poverty from the one that he knew: the social and spiritual degradation of the Indians, alongside of whom Ryga would work as a laborer on his father's farm.

Ryga drew heavily from this experience in writing his first play, *Indian*, a play that Ryga described as a "milestone" in his development as a playwright. (The play was broadcast as part of the Canadian Broadcasting Corporation's *Quest* television series in November, 1962.) In an interview, Ryga discussed his experience:

> You know I grew up on the outskirts of a Cree reservation. The demoralization and degradation was about as total as any society can experience anywhere in the world. These people had been worked over by the Church; they had been worked over by the Hudson's Bay Co.; there was nothing left. There was no language left anymore. Even their heroes they picked up on from the dominant culture, like a chocolate-bar wrapper dropped in the street that's picked up as a piece of art and taken home and nailed on the wall.

Ryga's keen awareness of social injustice continued to develop throughout his teens and early twenties, a period of casual labor, artistic exploration, and deepening political commitment. The early to mid-1950's in particular saw Ryga performing political gestures of various kinds: In 1952, he wrote a controversial antiwar script for the Edmonton radio show *Reverie*; in 1953, he demonstrated in response to the Julius and Ethel Rosenberg trial; in 1955, he represented the Canadian peace movement at the World Peace Assembly in Helsinki, meeting the Chilean poet Pablo Neruda, the Turkish poet Nazim Hikmet, the soviet writer Ilya Ehrenberg, and other Communist writers; in the same year, he traveled to Poland and Bulgaria. Though he left the Communist Party as a result of the Hungarian Revolution in 1956, Ryga claimed, in 1982, that "there has been no departure from the initial socialist commitment that I made a long time ago." In his plays, Ryga's "socialist commitment" emerges as a deep and abiding concern for the individual outcast, the person dispossessed economically, culturally, and spiritually who struggles to maintain dignity in the face of an impersonal system of domination, discrimination, and charity.

The early 1960's for Ryga marked the beginning of a great period of productivity and accomplishment. In 1960, he married Norma Lois Campbell, adopting her two daughters, Lesley and Tanya, and fathering, in 1961 and 1963, two sons, Campbell and Sergei. The early 1960's, moreover, saw Ryga coming to the theater via radio and television drama, where he had served his apprenticeship. Throughout the 1950's and into the early 1960's,

Ryga had written short plays and stories for radio broadcasts in Edmonton. After the television production of *Indian* in 1962, Ryga turned to the stage, again with *Indian*, in 1964. There followed a period of major accomplishment, Ryga writing in succession *Nothing but a Man*, *The Ecstasy of Rita Joe*, *Grass and Wild Strawberries*, *Captives of the Faceless Drummer*, and *Sunrise on Sarah*. During the year that *A Portrait of Angelica* and *A Feast of Thunder* were produced, Ryga spent six months in Mexico working on *Paracelsus and the Hero*, and then, in 1976, he wrote two more plays, *Ploughmen of the Glacier* and *Seven Hours to Sundown*, both of which were produced that year. Also in 1976, Ryga traveled to China and later wrote his memoir of the journey, *Beyond the Crimson Morning*. *A Letter to My Son* was published in the *Canadian Theatre Review* in 1982.

On his own development as an artist, Ryga spoke of Edward Albee and Robert Burns, the Scottish poet, as having been major influences. Of Albee, Ryga commented:

> I credit a large part of the fact that *Indian* was written at all, to seeing *The Zoo Story* on television, and watching how that particular play was constructed. It was the freedom that Albee was exercising in departing from the traditions as then practiced, and taking theatre into a kind of arid area, which I found fascinating and which to a great extent I have used ever since.

Ryga had gone to Dumfries in 1955 to study Burns's poetry, and while there, he discovered drafts of unpublished manuscripts, learning much from them about the interconnections of poetry and music. In Burns's rural origins and in his artistic resistance to English culture, Ryga also recognized much with which to identify:

> I began to see . . . that the English dominance of Scotland, and Burns' contribution in retaining a semblance of language, and around that language developing a rallying point for Scotland's national aspirations, were translatable indirectly to the Canadian experience.

Ryga was a guest professor at the University of British Columbia, at Banff School of Fine Arts, and at Simon Fraser University. As an active member in the Association of Canadian Television and Radio Artists, and an honorary member of the British Columbia Civil Liberties Association, he brought his liberal ideas to the political format. The travelogue, *Beyond the Crimson Morning*, published in 1979, was one of his last published works. He died in Summerland, British Columbia, November 18, 1987, of undisclosed causes, at the age of fifty-five.

Analysis

In George Ryga's first play, *Indian*, the dramatist compressed into one powerful act many basic materials of Canadian language, myth, and experience that he would develop in later plays. The play examines the poverty and despair of the variously named and ultimately anonymous "Indian," who elicits the intended guilt and sympathy from the members of the audience and who then rejects them violently in an outburst of rage, anguish, and guilt of his own. In the process, the play shatters the distorted and clichéd image of the Indian that has often been preserved in the Canadian consciousness.

Of the play's three characters, Indian, the boss Watson, and the Agent (a "comfortable civil servant" from the Department of Indian Affairs), it is the Agent who represents the "white man's" guilt over the Indians' degradation and who symbolizes the white man's attempts, primarily through impersonal charity and social welfare, to repair a tragic, structural flaw in Canadian society. Indian, however, is not interested in charity: "I want nothing from you—jus' to talk to me—to know who I am. . . . " In particular, Indian needs to tell of his brother, whom he was forced to kill in an act of mercy. The Agent, who is unable to conceive of Indian's essential humanity and who lacks, therefore, the emotional and moral strength to receive Indian's confession, is coerced, rather more violently than Samuel Taylor Coleridge's wedding guest in *The Rime of the Ancient Mariner* (1798), into hearing a story of great sin and suffering.

Against the Agent's cries of "No . . . no! This I don't understand at all," Indian describes how he killed his own brother (his brother had been trapped and left to die at the bottom of a well he was digging for a white "bossman," only to be finally rescued more dead than alive); how he "stole" his clothes; and how he allowed a half-breed to take the dead man's name so that he could collect the reservation subsidy on it ("All Indians same—nobody"). As he tells his story, the stereotyped image of the drunken and worthless Indian with which the play opened must be correlated with the profound humanity and existential integrity of the man who chose, at the cost of immense anguish, to save his own brother by murdering him:

> I . . . kill . . . my . . . brother! In my arms I hold him. He was so light, like small boy. I hold him . . . rock 'im back and forward like this . . . like mother rock us when we tiny kids. I rock 'im an' I cry . . . I get my hands tight on his neck, an' I squeeze an' I squeeze. I know he dead, and I still squeeze an' cry, for everything is gone, and I am old man now . . . only hunger an' hurt left now. . . .

Although the play is fundamentally realistic, its skillful compression of language, setting, and events produces powerful symbolic effects. The setting is a "flat, grey, stark non-country," a "vast empty expanse" which is at once the Northern Albertan landscape and a spiritual wasteland, reminiscent of the elemental settings in Samuel Beckett or T. S. Eliot. This simultaneous realism and symbolism in setting is matched on the levels of language and event, where the cadences of Indian dialect or the harsh hammer blows with which the play ends resonate with poetic force. The fusion of realism and symbolism at key points of *Indian* anticipates the more ambitious, sustained, and experimental techniques of *The Ecstasy of Rita Joe*, Ryga's more wide-ranging treatment of Indian experience.

The vibrant combination of dance, song, mime, recorded voices, and special lighting effects in *The Ecstasy of Rita Joe* signals Ryga's departure from the basic naturalism of *Indian*. Ryga dramatizes both the inner and the outer experience of Rita Joe by making use of a variety of impressionistic, expressionistic, and symbolic techniques. Thus, upon a forceful and realistic groundwork he builds a poetic structure in which Rita's subjective experience and inevitable doom emerge in flashbacks, shadow plays, and interludes of music, mime, or dance.

The groundwork of the play is the basic tragedy of Rita's life and death. Having left her father, the reserve, and her sexual innocence behind, Rita comes to the city, where she becomes trapped in a closing circle of poverty, theft, and prostitution—until she is raped and murdered by three white men. (The Three Murderers shadow Rita's presence throughout the play until they emerge, clearly illuminated, to murder Rita and her lover Jamie at the end.) The play's poetic structure, however, transforms this linear, deterministic plot into a mythical, often allegorical elaboration of Rita's fate, whereby the murder of the Indian woman becomes the ecstasy and apotheosis of the martyr. The fusion of realism and symbolism is pure and lacks sentimentality; appropriately, the play ends with the poignant words of Rita's sister Eileen, which focus upon the human being at the heart of the myth: "When Rita Joe first come to the city—she told me . . . The cement made her feet hurt."

The main action revolves around a recurring courtroom scene in which Rita stands accused—of vagrancy, prostitution, theft, and other crimes—before a sentimental and ineffectual Magistrate, symbol of white society's superficial understanding of Indian experience. By administering lectures and jail sentences, the Magistrate rests the blame for her degradation and despair on Rita herself, evading whatever responsibility he might have both as a man and as an official representative of white society. He tries unsuccessfully to harmonize the image of a tiny Indian girl he once saw in the Cariboo country with the woman Rita, whom he accuses of carrying a venereal disease, a symbol of her permanent condemnation.

The courtroom scenes are touchstones of a present reality which Rita strives to evade via memories and fantasies. In these imaginative interludes, the people of her past and the materials of her oppressed spirit emerge. In one scene of dramatic counterpoint, her old dead father, David Joe, speaks beautifully of a dragonfly emerging from its shell while her lover, Jamie Paul, rails against the white oppressors and advocates violence against them. Torn by this conflict of generations, trapped between impossible alternatives of urban despair and powerlessness and an extinct pastoral majesty, Rita stands paralyzed and doomed. When she recalls scenes of warmth and inspiration, as when she and her sister Eileen comforted each other after a storm, the Three Murderers loom menacingly in the background. Memory, then, is fraught with pain and contains the seeds of her inevitable doom.

Other significant characters who appear out of Rita's past are a Teacher, a Priest, a Policeman, and a welfare worker, Mr. Homer, all of whom, as representatives of white society, stand as accusers of Rita Joe. Throughout, Rita's essential isolation is dramatized as she is torn violently from her memories by a court policeman or as she stands alone in a shaft of light, separated by a barrier of memory from her surroundings. Often, the dialogue assumes a contrapuntal rhythm as the characters talk across one another's meanings, each alone in a fading world.

As the play progresses, it becomes more and more dominated by Rita's imagination, which strains against the tragic inevitability of events. Increasingly, as she emerges from her memories and imaginings, the present reality assumes a more hallucinatory quality, shaped as it has become by Rita's disorientation, fear, hunger, and exhaustion. At times the boundaries of time and space, of inner and outer reality, vanish completely. In a scene that approaches the nightmarish intensity of the Circe episode of James Joyce's *Ulysses* (1922), all the testimonies of white authority—of Priest, Policeman, Teacher, Magistrate—fuse into one "nightmare babble" of perpetual condemnation. Out of this babble comes the searing cry of the Magistrate, a cry which is also the voice of Rita's self-accusation, the bitter acknowledgment of her forced betrayal of sexual innocence and Indian heritage:

> MAGISTRATE: Have you any boils on your back? Any discharge? When did you bathe last?
> *The Three Murderers appear, and circle Rita.*
> MAGISTRATE: Answer me! Drunkenness! Shoplifting! Assault! Prostitution, prostitution, prostitution, prostitution!

In *Indian*, the Agent represents the audience's point of view and dramatizes its violent discovery of Indian's complex and painful reality. In *The Ecstasy of Rita Joe*, the audience almost exclusively shares Rita's point of view, which accounts for the play's nonsequential, associative order, its blending of Rita's spirit and memory with the nightmare-present from which she struggles in vain to escape. The play inhibits a complete identification with Rita, however, by insistently recalling the members of the audience to their own identity. Before the play begins, for example, the players make their entrances in a "workmanlike and untheatrical way" with the houselights up, thus enforcing a sense of common reality and frustrating the audience's desire to escape into the suspension of disbelief which a darkened theater encourages.

Even when the lights are lowered and the play is long under way, the audience continues to be reminded of its status, sometimes rudely so. At one stunning moment, for example, Ryga calls for Jamie Paul to cross downstage and confront a member of the audience: "You know me? . . . You think I'm a dirty Indian, eh? Get outa my way!" At another equally uncomfortable moment, David Joe, Rita's father, gestures angrily toward the audience exclaiming, "And tell her what? . . . Of the animals there . . . who sleep with sore stomachs because . . . they eat too much?"

Structural among the play's alienating devices, however, is Rita's alter ego, the Singer, "a white liberal folklorist" who weaves the scenes together with wistful songs that bespeak her "limited concern and understanding of an ethnic dilemma." If the audience wishes to identify with Rita, it must simultaneously come to terms with the Singer, who sits, appropriately, off to the side and "turned away from the focus of the play." The Singer, consequently, serves as an alter ego of the audience as well. Thus, between the poles of intimacy and alienation, between the life and final ecstasy of Rita Joe and the superficial and sentimental songs of the Singer, the audience must steer in this most demanding of Ryga's plays.

After *The Ecstasy of Rita Joe*, Ryga wrote several plays on subjects ranging from psychedelic culture to urban terrorism, small-town politics, and the Titan Prometheus. As might be expected, these plays use a wide variety of techniques, blending realism with myth, song, or dance while experimenting with both fluid and static settings. Among the plays Ryga has written since 1967, however, *Ploughmen of the Glacier*, an exploration of the myth of the Canadian West, is his most profound. In *Ploughmen of the Glacier*, Ryga is a virtuoso who masters continuously the development of his materials, creating a play which is rich in character, language, and symbolism.

In the stage directions, Ryga calls for a "possibly surrealistic" mountainside setting in which "all is staged and designed to highlight the elemental loneliness of the protagonists." Although the setting resembles that of *Indian* in its isolation and foreboding, the effect here is more dramatic as the Canadian Rockies loom unseen but felt in the background. The suggested mountainside functions in the play like the vast, mountainous range of the landscape painting: In both cases, the artist places human figures in the foreground of the vast scene to express human evanescence and isolation before nature's permanence and sublimity. At times, however, the lust and spirit of Ryga's characters succeed in dominating their surroundings.

The loneliness of the three protagonists is further reinforced by their distance from civilization. High on the mountain, the world below assumes a distant and obscure shape, formed only by the characters' infrequent allusion to the Gold Rush, the town, or the business "bandits" from Ontario. Thus isolated, the mountainside is free to open into abodes of myth, though its bearded, coughing men, moving about in clouds of real dust and speaking their raucous frontier language, suggest a particular history and region.

The action is structured upon the periodic meeting of Volcanic and Lowery—the natural, elemental man and the bookish man of culture—who disguise their suppressed affection for each other in zealous, occasionally violent, and often bitter arguments about the best way to live. Their spirited and voluble antagonism is interrupted, however, upon the entrance of Poor Boy, who wanders up and down the mountain with a pair of leaky water buckets in a futile attempt to hoard water against the coming Fire. (Wandering through the scene playing his harmonica, Poor Boy pauses to speak wistfully and discontinuously about a dimly remembered Western legend.) As the play's Sisyphus, Poor Boy brings with him a whiff of the abyss that stops Volcanic and Lowery cold. From this prospect of madness and futility, Volcanic and Lowery avert their faces, infected by a doubt that leaves them spiritually exhausted though somehow closer as men. When Poor Boy leaves, however, they resume their argument. According to this rhythm of spirited argument, despair, and brief communion, the play progresses.

The play's bleak existentialism is substantially countered throughout by its lusty language and humor. Responsible for the finest displays of both, Volcanic is also the Old West personified, a symbol of its tireless energy. As his name suggests, he is at once flowing lava and petrified rock—a living fossil from another time. Like the West itself, he combines the grandeur of the pioneering imagination with its ignorance and brutality (Volcanic once shot a man who trespassed unknowingly upon his land), and like most grand personifications, he is slightly absurd: For all Volcanic's dreams of wealth and talk of founding a city in his name, he, like Anse Bundren of William Faulkner's *As I Lay Dying* (1930), is dominated by the homely and pressing need for a set of false teeth. Nevertheless, Volcanic's vigorous speech achieves the force and resonance of poetry. When he rails against Lowery, he is at his best:

> You're worn out by poverty . . . you depress me! . . . You're like a preacher in a whorehouse. I want to dress up like a monkey to show the world I'm livin'. . . . I want to bleed myself . . . show God I can do without Him . . . that I can spill my life on the ground an' still have more left in me than men like you! . . . I want to smell out a claim an' go after it . . . all alone . . . just my body with a hammer an' chisel against the whole goddamned mountain! To eat what nobody's ever cooked for me . . . to stand on a cliff, pants aroun' my ankles . . . an' shake the sperm in me over the cliff into the valley . . . an' laugh to see a gull scoop down an' swallow it before it hits the ground . . . Hah! The seeds for children I could've had . . . eaten by a seagull!

An aged and failed editorialist and languid spokesman of civilization, Lowery is impelled periodically to climb the mountain to berate Volcanic and to assail him with issues from "down below"—from the society and culture of man which Lowery has increasingly come to doubt. Though he is attracted by Volcanic's tireless optimism and arrogant independence, he is also dumbfounded and deeply annoyed by it. Unable to live like Volcanic but no longer at home in civilization, Lowery is the most isolated and pathetic of the play's characters. Lacking the robust constitution of Volcanic or the single-minded purpose of Poor Boy, Lowery is alone between the frontier and society, living primarily with a painful memory of the beautiful woman with whom he declined to make love, so ashamed was he of his own nakedness.

The argument of Volcanic and Lowery continues until they die facing each other in their tracks. When they are finally still, Poor Boy comes on to deliver the eulogy for the dead whom he is already beginning to forget. As Poor Boy wanders off playing his harmonica, he will have yet another half-remembered tale to ponder as he carries his leaky water buckets up the mountain.

George Ryga was a major dramatist who, like *Ploughmen of the Glacier*'s prospector Volcanic, continued to dig into his Canadian material and reach through to some universal truths.

Other major works

NOVELS: *Hungry Hills*, 1963; *Ballad of a Stone-Picker*, 1966 (revised 1976); *Night Desk*, 1976.

NONFICTION: "Theatre in Canada: A Viewpoint on its Development," 1974; "Contemporary Theatre and Its Language," 1977; "The Need for a Mythology," 1977; *Beyond the Crimson Morning: Reflections from a Journey Through Contemporary China*, 1979; "The Artist in Resistance," 1982.

TELEPLAYS: *The Storm*, 1962; *Bitter Grass*, 1963; *For Want of Something Better to Do*, 1963; *The Tulip Garden*, 1963; *Two Soldiers*, 1963; *The Pear Tree*, 1963; *Man Alive*, 1965; *The Kamloops Incident*, 1965; *A Carpenter by Trade*, 1967 (documentary); *Ninth Summer*, 1972; *The Mountains*, 1973 (documentary); *The Ballad of Iwan Lepa*, 1976 (documentary).

RADIO PLAYS: *Reverie*, 1952; *A Touch of Cruelty*, 1961; *Half-Caste*, 1962; *Masks and Shadows*, 1963; *Bread Route*, 1963; *Departures*, 1963; *Ballad for Bill*, 1963; *The Stone Angel*, 1965; *Seasons of a Summer Day*, 1975; *One Sad Song for Henry Doyle Matkevitch*, 1981.

Bibliography

Boire, Gary. "Tribunalations: George Ryga's Postcolonial Trial 'Play.'" *Ariel* 22, no. 2 (April, 1991): 5-20. A "clumsily beautiful trial play," *The Ecstasy of Rita Joe* is compared with Margaret Atwood's novel *The*

Handmaid's Tale (1986) and other anticolonial literature as a paradigm for examining the "encoding of class violence under the guise of social contract . . . [a] crucial feature of anti-colonial literatures." Strong postmodern, semiotic deconstructionist look at "what postcolonial theorists call the reclamation of a world through irony."

Burgess, Patricia, ed. *Annual Obituary 1987.* Chicago: St. James Press, 1990. A good recapitulation of Ryga's themes, approaches to character, and patterns of composition during his career, along with an updated biography. "The lack of integration between land and people and between the individual and the group is the essential duality in Ryga's work," states the anonymous writer of this obituary. In his earlier life, before making a living as a writer, Ryga was concerned "with the degradation of human beings who are displaced and isolated, who lack a spiritual origin," a trait connected to Canadian life and society and one that informs Ryga's dramatic characterizations.

Carson, Neil. "George Ryga and the Lost Country." In *Dramatists in Canada: Selected Essays*, edited by William H. New. Vancouver: University of British Columbia Press, 1972. Discusses *The Ecstasy of Rita Joe*, commissioned by the Playhouse Theatre in Vancouver and performed there in 1967. Carson's opinion is that the play "establishes Ryga as the most exciting talent writing for the stage in Canada today." He believes that Ryga "rejects romantic and physical love, but does not preclude all meaningful human relationships."

Grace, Sherrill. "The Expressionist Legacy in the Canadian Theatre." *Canadian Literature*, no. 118 (Autumn, 1988): 47-58. This study of Ryga and Robert Gurik examines the nonnaturalistic aspects of both writers. Mentions the influences of Edward Albee, Fyodor Dostoevski, Eugene O'Neill, Franz Kafka, and Bertolt Brecht. Details *The Ecstasy of Rita Joe*, especially the characters identified by function, and the fragmented structure.

Saddlemyer, Ann. "Crime in Literature: Canadian Drama." In *Rough Justice: Essays on Crime in Literature*, edited by M. L. Friedland. Toronto: University of Toronto Press, 1991. Ryga's *Indian* is discussed as drama that "involves the process of judgment, assigning responsibility for action, distinguishing truth from fiction." In Ryga's one-act, originally written for television, the "deliberately Canadian, almost regional setting" ("a fence post, some telephone wires, a few tufts of scraggy growth in the distance, high fierce white light, the harsh sound of low wind") serves to explore social issues and uses "the historical situation as a metaphor for the present."

Michael Zeitlin
(Updated by *Thomas J. Taylor*)

HOWARD SACKLER

Born: New York, New York; December 19, 1929
Died: Ibiza, Spain; October 14, 1982

Principal drama

Uriel Acosta, pr. 1954; *A Few Enquiries*, wr. 1959, pr. 1965, pb. 1970 (4 one-acts: *Sarah, The Nine O'Clock Mail, Mr. Welk and Jersey Jim, Skippy*); *Mr. Welk and Jersey Jim*, pr. 1960, pb. 1970 (one act); *The Yellow Loves*, pr. 1960; *The Pastime of Monsieur Robert*, pr. 1966; *The Great White Hope*, pr. 1967, pb. 1968; *Semmelweiss*, pr. 1977; *Goodbye Fidel*, pr. 1980.

Other literary forms

In addition to his book of poetry, *Want My Shepherd* (1954), Howard Sackler wrote numerous screenplays, including *Desert Padre* (1950), *Fear and Desire* (1953), *A Midsummer Night's Dream* (1961), *The Great White Hope* (1970), *Bugsy* (1973), *Gray Lady Down* (1978; with James Whittacker and Frank P. Rosenberg), *Jaws II* (1978; with Carl Gottlieb and Dorothy Tristan), and *Saint Jack* (1979; with Paul Theroux and Peter Bogdanovich). *The Nine O'Clock Mail* was also televised, in 1965.

Achievements

While the triple prizes for *The Great White Hope* (the Pulitzer Prize, the New York Drama Critics Circle Award, and a Tony Award) were the highlight of Sackler's career, they were by no means his first achievements. He had earlier received the Maxwell Anderson Award for his verse play *Uriel Acosta*, as well as Rockefeller Foundation and Littauer Foundation grants for work in his early twenties. A prolific director, especially of classical and verse plays, Sackler founded and became director of Caedmon Records in 1953, where he worked with the great British and American actors and authors whose work is now preserved in the Caedmon series. Sackler was busily employed in directing projects and screenwriting when, with *The Great White Hope*, he found the mature epic verse form that worked better onstage than any verse form since Maxwell Anderson. His contribution to American drama lies in the size and scope of his vision, his meticulous research on historical subjects and personalities, and the grace and rhythms of his language. After *The Great White Hope*, Sackler succeeded in the form with *Semmelweiss*, a harrowing study of the nineteenth century physician who discovered that examining doctors were spreading infection among their patients and who was ostracized and broken for his trouble. Because of production problems outside the script itself, *Semmelweiss* was not produced on Broadway; nevertheless, it remains one of the finest plays in modern dramatic literature. In 1980, Sackler's last Broadway play, *Goodbye Fidel*, closed after poor reviews. At his death, Sackler was working on "Klondike," a Gold Rush comedy.

Biography

Born on December 19, 1929, in the Bronx, Howard Sackler attended Brooklyn College, earning the bachelor of arts degree in 1950. A natural writer, Sackler wrote in verse, publishing in respected poetry journals such as *Hudson Review* and *Poetry*; his early work was gathered in *Want My Shepherd* and published by Caedmon in 1954. Combining his interest in the theater with his verse writing, Sackler wrote *Uriel Acosta*, for which he received the Maxwell Anderson Award in 1954. His tendency was always to look to historical settings for his plays; after his success with *Uriel Acosta*, about a Portuguese Jew in the generation before Baruch Spinoza, Sackler looked at the life of the French poet Tristan Corbière; the play, his first in prose, won the Sergel Award in 1959 and marked the beginning of his interest in nineteenth century health practices, which was to find its best voice in *Semmelweiss*. While building his playwriting career, Sackler founded Caedmon Records, which provided his livelihood as he built a reputation for screenplay writing. Another career, in directing, took him to the New School for Social Research, where readings of several poetic plays augmented his growing number of recordings of William Shakespeare's plays at Caedmon, with such notable voices as those of Paul Scofield, Albert Finney, and Dame Edith Evans. Sackler's next venture into live theater came with *A Few Enquiries*, four one-act plays separate in setting and characters but joined in their thematic investigation of human contact and the need of the individual to find his place in a larger community; his mature work continued this investigation in more elaborate forms.

All Sackler's experiences came together in 1967, with *The Great White Hope*, the meticulously researched and carefully structured epic dramatization of the life of Jack Jefferson (based on the career of heavyweight champion Jack Johnson). The play earned for Sackler international recognition when it received the Pulitzer Prize, the New York Drama Critics Circle Award, and a Tony Award in 1969. By 1970, Sackler had turned his work into a highly successful screenplay, starring the actors who had appeared in the stage version: James Earl Jones as Jack Jefferson, and Jane Alexander, who had played Ellie Bachman, Jefferson's white mistress. Partly because of his busy screenwriting career and partly because of his insistence on very careful research into each of his historical plays, it was not until 1977 that Sackler offered his next stage work, *Semmelweiss*, which opened in Buffalo, New York, but did not reach Broadway. Sackler's last Broadway play, *Goodbye Fidel*, which opened in 1980, closed quickly after unfavorable reviews. *The New Yorker* praised it, however, saying, "So many roles and settings give the play a welcomely old-fashioned air of amplitude, even of extravagance; we sense that the playwright has shared the novelist's luxurious privilege of inventing an abundance of characters and then letting them wander wherever they will." At his death, from pulmonary thrombosis, in Ibiza, Spain, on October 14, 1982, Sackler was near the finish of yet another major historical play, "Klondike," about the Alaskan Gold Rush. Sackler's papers are in the archives of the Humanities Research Center, University of Texas, Austin.

Analysis

The quality that Howard Sackler brought to his historical subjects is not a simpleminded romanticism but rather an underlying universality of emotions that connects the past with his audience's immediate responses. These plays are more than well-researched panoramas of a time gone; the point of Sackler's portraits is that these times are never gone, that the anguish and the joys one feels have been present in every history.

No better example of everything Sackler tried to do in his work is available than the first play in the four-play collection, *A Few Enquiries*, entitled *Sarah*. A coroner, his assistant, some witnesses, and the mother of the victim of a tragic accident are gathered backstage in a ballet theater to re-enact the circumstances of the awful event: A promising young ballerina perished when her costume caught fire from the gaslights during a performance. The businesslike voice of the coroner, the subdued retelling of the witnesses, the monosyllabic responses of the mother—all make a music of their own, to which the understudy dances, acting out the tragic events, to the very moment of the stagehand's feeble attempts to extinguish the flaming dress with his hands (now bandaged), a slow pantomime observed clinically by some and with emotion by others. The final cries of anguish by the mother of Sarah, the victim, echoing in the bare theater, bring the incident out of the mid-Victorian past (it was based on a real incident) into the dramatic present. The effect is emblematic of Sackler's writing gifts, which came to maturity in his Pulitzer Prize-winning *The Great White Hope*.

The episodic treatment (nineteen scenes in three acts) of Jack Jefferson's career gives *The Great White Hope* the epic scope necessary to depict not only the character but also his era and his world. On one level, the play is a portrait of the times, when America was adolescent in its attitudes toward racial prejudice, civil rights, and the free enterprise system at work in the sports industry. The crowd scenes, effectively designed, focus the action where it belongs, not on the prizefights themselves (all occurring off-stage) but on those waiting for the results of their wagers. Jefferson is the kind of gladiator who is envied to destruction, not because of his strength but because of his penetration of the folly and hypocrisy of the games he is forced to dignify with his talent. In the scenes with Ellie, his lover, one sees Jefferson preparing for his real fight, against a society which will not let him be simply a man but which demands that he live out the symbolic function it has assigned to him. His eventual and inevitable defeat in Cuba is anticlimactic in relationship to his loss of Ellie, and by the time he emerges from the ring, bloody and dazed, he has already understood the fact that there is to be no refuge for him from mankind's indifference and exploitation.

The same pattern in a different setting is found in *Semmelweiss*. This time the fighter is the nineteenth century physician Ignaz Philipp Semmelweiss, and the indifferent and envious crowd is the closed-minded medical community, which refuses to treat seriously his hospital sanitation reforms. Without reducing the story to cheap symbolism, Sackler uses the diseases of the body, as revealed in the autopsy rooms of a government hospital for the poor, as external manifestations of the more insidious diseases of indifference, inhumanity, hypocrisy, and ambition which prevent the doctors and their student interns from experiencing and putting into practice the humanitarian principles of their profession. After risking his medical career by challenging the examination practices of his superiors in a maternity ward, Semmelweiss retreats to a safe marriage, not from cowardice but from helplessness. In the climactic scene, a lecture in which he purposely infects himself, the metaphor equating the infected patient with the corrupt medical profession is brought home in the most astounding image since the engine room scene from Eugene O'Neill's *The Hairy Ape* (pr. 1922). Driven mad by the self-inflicted infection, going blind among his plants, Semmelweiss agonizingly repeats the oath of medicine by which he tried to live and which has destroyed him. In the final, silent scene, a new group of interns begin their examination on a new anonymous cadaver, but it is the body of Semmelweiss they uncover, lying on the slab as though admonishing them from another world.

In Sackler's last Broadway play, *Goodbye Fidel*, the *mise en scène* is Cuba at the dawn of the Castro regime, and the characters are members of the privileged upper class, the jet set whose lives are disrupted by the new strength of the common people. Here the usually successful technique of embodying the ills of the world in the personal story of one man or woman falls short of Sackler's ambitions, primarily because, in an attempt to avoid oversimplification, he shows both sides of the economic and political struggle with equal strength and clarity. The central figure, Natalia, a beautiful woman forced by Fidel Castro to give up not only her life-style but also her clandestine affair with an attaché, is not a heroine in the easily recognizable mold. Her "tragedy" is more obscure; because it was difficult to sympathize with the idle rich being suddenly disenfranchised, first-night critics failed to see the love story and the private anguish lying inside the external political situation of the play. Natalia, too, however, has fought with considerable bravery against the danger of self-pity and nostalgia in which a lesser person would find refuge. She has lost her home, her friends, her lover, her child, her security, her sense of place. In the face of these losses, she dances a brave little dance, head held high.

Sackler's contributions to the American stage, modest in number but vast in significance, stand as challenges to playwrights to come. The easy little three-character, hyperreal playlet will always look timid and careful in the light of Howard Sackler's large canvases of the hero amid a world gone mad.

Other major works

POETRY: *Want My Shepherd*, 1954.

SCREENPLAYS: *Desert Padre*, 1950; *Fear and Desire*, 1953; *A Midsummer Night's Dream*, 1961; *The Great White Hope*, 1970; *Bugsy*, 1973; *Gray Lady Down*, 1978 (with James Whittacker and Frank P. Rosenberg); *Jaws II*, 1978 (with Carl Gottlieb and Dorothy Tristan); *Saint Jack*, 1979 (with Paul Theroux and Peter Bogdanovich).

Bibliography

Funke, Lewis. "Howard Sackler." In *Playwrights Talk About Writing: Twelve Interviews with Lewis Funke.* Chicago: Dramatic Publishing, 1975. Sackler's interview is prefaced with a summary of his professional accomplishments and a brief biography. He discusses his working habits, sources of inspiration, and the relationship between his work as a director and his work as a writer. He interprets *The Great White Hope* and *The Pastime of Monsieur Robert*, distinguishing these dramas from history, and offers opinions on drama in general.

Gill, Brendan. "Passing Losses On." Review of *Goodbye Fidel. The New Yorker* 46 (May 5, 1980): 109-110. *Goodbye Fidel*, a play about upper-class Cubans who deal with changes in their lives between 1958 and 1962, suggests the richness of a novel with its large cast and historical subject. Sackler's attempt, however, to parallel the quarrels between the lovers Natalia and James Sinclair with political events is not convincing. The play closed four days after it opened.

Gottfried, Martin. Introduction to *A Few Enquiries.* New York: Dial Press, 1970. Gottfried summarizes and interprets the four one-act plays that appear in this volume. *Sarah, The Nine O'Clock Mail, Mr. Welk and Jersey Jim*, and *Skippy* reflect Sackler's interest in history, poetry, and ritualism. Gottfried describes them as well structured, and classical and modern in their treatment of reality. Their common theme is that people seek contact with those they love but fail to achieve it.

Hewes, Henry. Review of *The Great White Hope. Saturday Review* 50 (December 30, 1967): 18. The capability of the Arena Stage to mount a work that is large in size and scope was demonstrated in its production of *The Great White Hope.* While the change of many scenes and movement of many actors were handled flawlessly, Hewes finds that the script itself needs revision. Sackler almost achieves a complex presentation of racial problems but fails to do so. Rather, the play disintegrates into an unsatisfactory delineation of Jack Jefferson's journey to the denouement, his throwing of the fight.

Kroll, Jack. "The Champ." Review of *The Great White Hope. Newsweek* December 25, 1967, 73. Both strengths and weaknesses were found in the epic quality of *The Great White Hope* performed at the Arena Stage in Washington, D.C. Although the play is too long, too ambitious, and somewhat unfocused, some episodes attained real power through Edwin Sherin's direction and James Earl Jones and Jane Alexander's performances. It is the most successful use of sports in drama since Clifford Odet's *Golden Boy* (pr., pb. 1937).

Novick, Julius. "Tragic Cakewalk." Review of *The Great White Hope. The Nation* 206 (January 15, 1968): 93-94. The choice of the Arena Stage to produce *The Great White Hope* fulfilled the conviction of the theater's founder, Zelda Fichandler, that drama must appeal to a broad spectrum of people through the presentation of plays that deal with current social problems. In this play, Sackler realizes the significance of his historical subject and presents it in powerful human terms.

Trousdale, Marion. "Ritual Theatre: *The Great White Hope. Western Humanities Review* 23 (1969): 295-303. The performances of *The Great White Hope* at the Arena Stage (Washington, D.C.) and in New York were profoundly different. Those at the Arena Stage were characterized by ritualistic and ludic qualities, achieving Aristotle's definition of drama—the imitation of an action by means of an action. By contrast, the New York·production reduced the play to a simple antiracist message.

Thomas J. Taylor
(Updated by *Frank Ardolino*)

WILLIAM SAROYAN

Born: Fresno, California; August 31, 1908
Died: Fresno, California; May 18, 1981

Principal drama

The Hungerers: A Short Play, pb. 1939, pr. 1945; *My Heart's in the Highlands*, pr., pb. 1939; *The Time of Your Life*, pr., pb. 1939; *Love's Old Sweet Song*, pr., pb. 1940; *Three Plays: My Heart's in the Highlands, The Time of Your Life, Love's Old Sweet Song*, pb. 1940; *Subway Circus*, pb. 1940; *The Ping-Pong Game*, pb. 1940 (one act); *The Beautiful People*, pr. 1940, pb. 1941; *The Great American Goof*, pr. 1940; pb. 1942; *Across the Board on Tomorrow Morning*, pr., pb. 1941; *Three Plays: The Beautiful People, Sweeney in the Trees, Across the Board on Tomorrow Morning*, pb. 1941; *Hello Out There*, pr. 1941, pb. 1942 (one act); *Jim Dandy*, pr., pb. 1941; *Razzle Dazzle*, pb. 1942 (collection); *Talking to You*, pr., pb. 1942; *Get Away Old Man*, pr. 1943, pb. 1944; *Sam Ego's House*, pr. 1947, pb. 1949; *A Decent Birth, a Happy Funeral*, pb. 1949; *Don't Go Away Mad*, pr., pb. 1949; *The Slaughter of the Innocents*, pb. 1952, pr. 1957; *The Cave Dwellers*, pr. 1957, pb. 1958; *One Around the Block*, pb. 1959; *Sam the Highest Jumper of Them All: Or, The London Comedy*, pr. 1960, pb. 1961; *Settled Out of Court*, pr. 1960, pb. 1962; *The Dogs: Or, The Paris Comedy and Two Other Plays*, pb. 1969.

Other literary forms

William Saroyan is perhaps even better known as the author of short stories, novels, and autobiographical prose than as a playwright. Early short-story collections include: *The Daring Young Man on the Flying Trapeze and Other Stories* (1934), *Inhale and Exhale* (1936), *Three Times Three* (1936), and *Love, Here Is My Hat and Other Short Romances* (1938). His best-known novel is *The Human Comedy* (1943).

Achievements

Saroyan's plays are vehicles for his vision of what one of his characters calls "the miracle of life." Like his prose, Saroyan's drama is predicated upon a largely optimistic perception of life as a joyous festival whose bounty is spiritual rather than materialistic. His critical and commercial success in the theater reached a zenith with the production of *The Time of Your Life*, for which he was awarded the Pulitzer Prize (he declined to accept). In this and many of his other plays, Saroyan drew heavily upon his own and his family's experience to dramatize the rhythms, opportunities, and joy of life, particularly in America. In the course of his playwriting career, Saroyan experimented with dramatic styles (such as surrealism and expressionism) and techniques (such as direct address to the audience), but never adopted a codified aesthetic theory. Although threatened by his proclivity toward sentimentality and naïveté, Saroyan's best plays still offer the sense of what he called "that quality of beauty as it is in the living, in the plainest of people."

Biography

William Saroyan was the fourth child of Armenian immigrants, Armenak and Takoohi Saroyan, who settled in Fresno, California. Three years after Saroyan's birth, his father died, and Saroyan, along with his brother and sisters, was sent to an orphanage in Oakland, California. His mother, while working in San Francisco, tried to maintain the family, and by 1915, they were reunited in Fresno. Saroyan's formal education ended before he completed high school, but by the age of twenty, he had committed himself to a career as a writer. In 1934, he won the O. Henry Award for his short story "The Daring Young Man on the Flying Trapeze." During the 1930's, Saroyan traveled widely, published five novels, and worked briefly as a screenwriter in Hollywood. Between 1939 and 1942, Saroyan enjoyed a meteoric career on Broadway. In the early 1940's, he produced and directed several of his own plays before entering the army in October, 1942. In 1943, he married Carol Marcus, whom he divorced in 1949, remarried in 1951, later divorced again, and by whom he had two children, Aram and Lucy. In the late 1940's, he published several plays that were not produced on Broadway. After 1943, Saroyan wrote only one important work for the theater, *The Cave Dwellers*, although he continued to write prolifically in other genres.

Analysis

William Saroyan's career as a playwright covered more than forty years, but his best and most acclaimed work in the theater was concentrated in the period between 1939 and 1942. A preliminary dramatic effort, *Subway Circus*, evocative of the *commedia dell'arte* tradition, is actually a series of sketches: the independent fantasies of ten riders of a subway car. Even this early work, however, demonstrates Saroyan's interest in the theater's potential to depict the inner, imaginary world of his characters and to create an atmosphere of carnival excitement and gaiety.

With *My Heart's in the Highlands*, which he later referred to as his first play, Saroyan displayed his ability to transform overtly autobiographical experience into drama and to work within a much more conventional (although hardly rigorous) structure. Set in Fresno in 1914 at the beginning of World War I and produced in 1939 at the beginning of World War II, *My Heart's in the Highlands* strikes a note of foreboding and anxiety, but more important is its resilient optimism. The plot revolves around the reception of an eccentric, itinerant Scots immigrant, Jasper MacGregor, who plays "My Heart's in the Highlands" on his bugle, in the home of a generous and equally eccentric California family. The play's movement is steeped in optimism: The homeless find homes; strangers recognize their common humanity; individuals are brought together, both in the pleasure of enjoying MacGregor's bugling and in the sorrow of mourning his death. In this play, Saroyan introduced what was to become a recurring structural feature of his plays, the performance of song, dance, dramatic reading, or musical composition. MacGregor has a number of qualities that reappear in Saroyan's later characters: Like Kit Carson in *The Time of Your Life*, he is a teller of tall tales; like the king in *The Cave Dwellers*, he has played King Lear; like the majority of Saroyan's characters, he is a searcher, displaced, uprooted, and homeless.

Saroyan's most celebrated play, *The Time of Your Life*, for which he received both the Pulitzer Prize and the New York Drama Critics Circle Award, opened on Broadway only six months after *My Heart's in the Highlands*. Saroyan said that he wrote the play in only six days while staying at the Great Northern Hotel in New York City. *The Time of Your Life* effectively captures the variety and vitality of American life that is the essence of Saroyan's vision. Here, he assembles a virtual cross-section of the American people: The rich and the poor, the young and the old, the powerful and the powerless all meet at Nick's Pacific Street Saloon, Restaurant, and Entertainment Palace in San Francisco. It is, as Saroyan proclaims in his stage directions, "an American place" alive with humor, energy, and imagination. The plot of the play is diffused among its twenty-six characters whose stories provide a panoramic view of American society. Much of the action is orchestrated by Nick, the saloon's owner, and Joe, a benevolent, eccentric, philosophical man who describes himself as a student of life. When Tom, a young man in love with a prostitute named Kitty, questions Joe's motive for helping strangers, Joe tells him that "when my study reveals something of beauty in a place or in a person where by all rights only ugliness or death should be revealed, then I know how full of goodness this life is." Joe is, in fact, the pivotal character in the play because he consciously tries to make every moment of his life the time of his life and seeks to ensure that others share in his enjoyment. Having worked hard to earn enough money to be comfortable, Joe now lives to be happy and to make others happy. Early in the play, he dispatches Tom to buy him some toys, simply because he knows they will bring him and others pleasure. His main accomplishment in the play is the reform of Kitty Duval, the prostitute whom Tom loves, and the uniting of Tom and Kitty. When Kitty first appears in the bar, she is abrasive, cold, and hard, but under Joe's questioning, her true nature and past are revealed. After hearing her story and seeing her response to Tom's love, Joe concludes that Kitty is "one of the few truly innocent people I have ever met." Finally, Tom and Kitty leave for San Diego to be married. Although their story serves as the focus of Joe's generosity, his amiability and robust vigor pervade the entire play.

The subplots of *The Time of Your Life* are nearly as numerous as its characters: There is the story of McCarthy, an idealistic longshoreman engaged in a strike; of Krupp, an honest cop who questions his profession after years on the force; of a wealthy couple slumming in search of adventure; of Kit Carson, a gadfly with an inexhaustible supply of outrageous stories; and of Blick, another policeman, who epitomizes the abuse of authority. Several other characters perform routines which give the play a remarkable ebullience: Harry (originally played by Gene Kelly) dances and tells jokes; Wesley plays the piano; the Newsboy sings "When Irish Eyes Are Smiling"; an Arab plays the harmonica. In an atmosphere that recalls vaudeville, each of them, like the characters in *The Time of Your Life*, reveals a special talent or gift which can only be fully realized when shared with others. The play's bustling activity, episodic structure, and occasional mayhem enable it to range from hope to despair, from sorrow to happiness, and from loneliness to love. *The Time of Your Life* is a rich panoply of life informed by Saroyan's strongest themes: the need for compassion, understanding, and love; the search for identity and intimacy; and the importance of imagination.

While *The Time of Your Life* was still running on Broadway, two other works by Saroyan appeared in New York: a ballet-play, *The Great American Goof*, and *Love's Old Sweet Song*. As Saroyan became successful in theater, he also became increasingly involved in the direction, production, and casting of his plays; he codirected *Love's Old Sweet Song* in 1940 and later directed and produced *The Beautiful People*, *Across the Board on Tomorrow Morning*, and *Talking to You*.

Love's Old Sweet Song tells of the courtship and marriage of Barnaby Gaul, a charming confidence man of the type familiar in American literature, and Ann Hamilton, a rather innocent, financially comfortable woman. Their story is juxtaposed with that of a family of Okies, Cabot and Lena Yearling and their fourteen children. The Yearling family camps on the front lawn of the Hamiltons' Bakersfield home, which the youngest Yearling child eventually burns to the ground. The play's conclusion, however, is a happy one: Ann and Barnaby will be married and plan to adopt the child who started the fire.

A large, friendly California house that welcomes both strangers and friends also serves as the setting for Saroyan's *The Beautiful People*. Jonah Webster, owner of the house and lay preacher to the beautiful people, clearly states the play's theme: "Every life in the world is a miracle." The action, characters, setting, and themes of this play are those that had by this time become typical of Saroyan's work. In *The Beautiful People*, however, the importance of the valiant human struggle against adversity has diminished because adversity amounts to little more than a pet mouse which has lost its home. In reviewing this play, Joseph Wood Krutch wrote of Saroyan's "genuine naïveté," which accounts for much of the freshness of *The Time of Your Life* but also, when coupled with Saroyan's proclivity toward sentimentality, produces the simplistic vision of *The Beautiful People.*

Three short plays conclude Saroyan's intensive dramatic productivity in the early 1940's. *Across the Board on Tomorrow Morning* and *Talking to You*, both directed by Saroyan, were produced as a double bill which ran for only eight performances at the Belasco Theatre. In 1961, however, these two plays were revived and successfully produced by Arthur Storch at the East End Theatre. *Talking to You* is especially interesting for its manipulation of the fourth wall. As in his treatment of vaudevillian material in *The Time of Your Life*, Saroyan effectively integrated direct address to the audience and extradramatic material in *Talking to You.*

Hello Out There, the last of Saroyan's Broadway successes in the 1940's, is an uncharacteristically grim depiction of human loneliness. Rather than chancing upon the generosity and hospitality found in *My Heart's in the Highlands* or *The Beautiful People*, the itinerant protagonist of *Hello Out There* finds himself in jail, unjustly accused of rape. Trapped, injured, and desperate, he uses a spoon to telegraph a message no one receives: "Hello out there." He briefly engages the sympathies of a young cook, but finally he is murdered by the husband of the woman he is accused of raping. *Hello Out There* is decidedly more realistic and less optimistic than any of Saroyan's earlier plays. It depicts evil not as aberrations or misunderstandings but as very real threats to human happiness.

Between 1943—a year after he entered the army—and 1957, when *The Cave Dwellers* opened, Saroyan wrote few conventional full-length plays. In 1943, *Get Away Old Man* appeared at the Cort Theatre for a dismal run of thirteen performances. Subsequently, Saroyan published several plays, most of which were not initially produced in New York: *Jim Dandy* (in 1947, its first substantial edition), *Don't Go Away Mad*, *Sam Ego's House*, *A Decent Birth, a Happy Funeral*, and *The Slaughter of the Innocents.*

In *The Cave Dwellers*, Saroyan's potential for drama crystallized once again. As its setting, *The Cave Dwellers* employs a condemned New York theater where an ensemble of the displaced, homeless, and vulnerable take refuge from the cruelty of the world. In this setting, characters with names such as King, Queen, Boy, and Mother play out what seem to be the final days of their way of life. Characters periodically venture outside the theater in search of food and provisions, but the world outside is brutal and pitiless. Much of their time in the theater is spent recalling past glories and happiness, particularly King's former stage triumphs. The element of hope in *The Cave Dwellers* is offered by the birth of a child and by the camaraderie shared by the play's characters.

In the early 1960's, Saroyan produced some drama that was performed in London, such as *Sam the Highest Jumper of Them All: Or, The London Comedy* and *Settled Out of Court*, or in American universities, and he also wrote for television. His dramatic reputation, however, rests on his plays of the late 1930's and early 1940's, most notably his much-acclaimed *The Time of Your Life.*

Other major works

NOVELS: *The Human Comedy*, 1943; *The Adventures of Wesley Jackson*, 1946; *Rock Wagram*, 1951; *Tracy's Tiger*, 1951; *The Laughing Matter*, 1953 (reprinted as *The Secret Story*, 1954); *Mama I Love You*, 1956; *Papa You're Crazy*, 1957; *Boys and Girls Together*, 1963; *One Day in the Afternoon of the World*, 1964.

SHORT FICTION: *The Daring Young Man on the Flying Trapeze and Other Stories*, 1934; *Inhale and Exhale*, 1936; *Three Times Three*, 1936; *A Gay and Melancholy Flux: Short Stories*, 1937; *Little Children*, 1937; *Love, Here Is My Hat and Other Short Romances*, 1938; *The Trouble with Tigers*, 1938; *Three Fragments and a Story*, 1939; *Peace, It's Wonderful*, 1939; *My Name Is Aram*, 1940; *Saroyan's Fables*, 1941; *The Insurance Salesman and Other Stories*, 1941; *Forty-eight Saroyan Stories*, 1942; *Thirty-one Selected Stories*, 1943; *Some Day I'll Be a Millionaire: Thirty-four More Great Stories*, 1944; *Dear Baby*, 1944; *The Saroyan Special: Selected Stories*, 1948; *The Fiscal Hoboes*, 1949; *The Assyrian and Other Stories*, 1950; *The Whole Voyage and Other Stories*, 1956; *William Saroyan Reader*, 1958; *Love*, 1959; *After Thirty Years: The Daring Young Man on the Flying Trapeze*, 1964; *Best Stories of William Saroyan*, 1964; *The Tooth and My Father*, 1974; *My Name Is Saroyan*, 1983; *The Man with His Heart in the Highlands and Other Early Stories*, 1989.

NONFICTION: *The Time of Your Life*, 1939; *Harlem as Seen by Hirschfield*, 1941; *Hilltop Russians in San Francisco*, 1941; *Why Abstract?*, 1945 (with Henry Miller and Hilaire Hiler); *The Twin Adventures: The Adventures of William Saroyan*, 1950; *The Bicycle Rider in Beverly Hills*, 1952; *Here Comes, There Goes, You Know Who*, 1961; *A Note on Hilaire Hiler*, 1962; *Not Dying*, 1963; *Short Drive, Sweet Chariot*, 1966; *Look at Us: Let's See: Here We Are*, 1967; *I Used to Believe I Had Forever: Now I'm Not So Sure*, 1968; *Letters from 74 Rue Taitbout*, 1969; *Days of Life and Death and Escape to the Moon*, 1970; *Places Where I've Done Time*, 1972; *Sons Come and Go, Mothers Hang in Forever*, 1976; *Chance Meetings*, 1978; *Obituaries*, 1979; *Births*, 1983; *The Armenian Trilogy*, 1986; *The Pheasant Hunter*, 1986; *Madness in the Family*, 1988 (edited by Leo Hamalian).

SCREENPLAYS: *The Good Job*, 1942; *The Human Comedy*, 1943.

RADIO PLAY: *A Special Announcement*, 1940.

CHILDREN'S LITERATURE: *Me*, 1963; *Horsey Gorsey and the Frog*, 1968; *The Circus*, 1986.

MISCELLANEOUS: *The New Saroyan Reader*, 1984 (edited by Brian Darwent).

Bibliography

Bedrosian, Margaret. "William Saroyan and the Family Matter." *MELUS* 9 (Winter, 1982): 13-24. With an interest in the Armenian American aspect of Saroyan's work, Bedrosian offers insightful analysis of *The Laughing Matter*, *Rock Wagram*, *My Heart's in the Highlands*, "The Assyrian," "The Daring Young Man on the Flying Trapeze," and "Seventy Thousand Assyrians." Her description of Saroyan's picaresque portrayals captures his ambivalence, the "darkly ironic" side that counters his general "refusal to deal with evil."

Calonne, David Stephen. *William Saroyan: My Real Work Is Being.* Chapel Hill: University of North Carolina Press, 1983. This volume offers a thematic analysis of Saroyan's work. Calonne compares Saroyan's life and work to those of Walt Whitman, Sherwood Anderson, Thomas Wolfe, George Bernard Shaw, Henry Miller, and Samuel Beckett. This critical analysis is well written, substantial in its detail, and important in establishing the literary tradition from which Saroyan's work derives, but Calonne may be overzealous in his praise of Saroyan as a major influence in his own right. Six pages of bibliography and an index provide ample background.

Fisher, William J. "What Ever Happened to Saroyan?" *College English* 24 (March, 1955): 336-340. Fisher describes and analyzes effectively how Saroyan's life represents a microcosmic "history of American optimism." Taking a sociological approach, Fisher points out the progress and popularity of Saroyan's work.

Floan, Howard. *William Saroyan.* Boston: Twayne, 1966. This critical analysis of Saroyan's work includes discussion of his struggles with poverty as a young writer, his encounters with such figures as Ben Schulberg in Hollywood, and his eventual descent in writing to "earn as much money as possible." This survey, while remaining one of the best sources on Saroyan, lacks highly personal information, focusing more on evaluation of Saroyan's forays into various genres, including drama, novel, short story, and even songwriting. Written in an accessible style, this work, with thirteen pages of bibliography and index, is useful for both scholars and general readers.

Shinn, Thelma J. "William Saroyan: Romantic Existentialist." *Modern Drama* 14 (September, 1972): 185-194. Shinn looks at how Saroyan writes in the romantic tradition, evaluating his work on a philosophical basis. She contends that, despite his resistance to the kind of existentialist darkness of Harold Pinter or Samuel Beckett, Saroyan is an artist of serious ideas and a "sensitive awareness to living." This essay focuses primarily on *The Time of Your Life*, *Hello Out There*, *Across the Board on Tomorrow Morning*, and *My Heart's in the Highlands*.

Joan F. Dean
(Updated by *Rebecca Bell-Metereau*)

MURRAY SCHISGAL

Born: Brooklyn, New York; November 25, 1926

Principal drama

A Simple Kind of Love Story, pr. 1960, pb. 1980; *The Postman*, pr. 1960 (one act); *The Typists*, pr. 1960, pb. 1963 (one act); *Ducks and Lovers*, pr. 1961, pb. 1972; *The Tiger*, pr., pb. 1963 (one act; originally as *The Postman*); *Knit One, Purl Two*, pr. 1963; *Luv*, pr. 1963, pb. 1965; *Windows*, pr., pb. 1965; *Reverberations*, pb. 1965, pr. 1967 (as *The Basement*); *The Old Jew*, pb. 1965, pr. 1967; *Fragments*, pb. 1965, pr. 1967; *Memorial Day*, pb. 1965, pr. 1968; *Fragments, Windows and Other Plays*, pb. 1965 (includes *Reverberations*, *The Old Jew*, *Memorial Day*); *Jimmy Shine*, pr. 1968, pb. 1969 (music by John Sebastian); *The Chinese*, pr. 1968, pb. 1970; *A Way of Life*, pr. 1969; *Dr. Fish*, pr., pb. 1970; *An American Millionaire*, pr., pb. 1974; *All over Town*, pr. 1974, pb. 1975; *Roseland*, pr. 1975; *Popkins*, pr. 1978, pb. 1984; *The Pushcart Peddlers*, pr. 1979, pb. 1980; *The Downstairs Boys*, pr. 1980 (revision of *Roseland*); *Walter, and The Flautist*, pr., pb. 1980 (2 plays); *Little Johnny*, pb. 1980; *The Pushcart Peddlers, The Flautist, and Other Plays*, pb. 1980 (includes *A Simple Kind of Love Story*, *Little Johnny*, *Walter*); *Twice Around the Park*, pr. 1982 (2 one-act comedies: *A Need for Brussels Sprouts* and *A Need for Less Expertise*); *Luv and Other Plays*, pb. 1983; *Closet Madness and Other Plays*, pb. 1984; *The Rabbi and the Toyota Dealer*, pb. 1984, pr. 1985; *Road Show*, pr., pb. 1987; *Songs of War*, pr. 1989; *Extensions*, pr., pb. 1991 (one act); *Theatrical Release*, pr. 1991.

Other literary forms

Murray Schisgal has published the novel *Days and Nights of a French Horn Player* (1980) and has written television plays, *The Love Song of Barney Kempenski* (1966) and *Natasha Kovolina Pipishinsky* (1976), and an expanded version of his one-act play *The Tiger*, which was produced as a screenplay, *The Tiger Makes Out* (1967), starring Eli Wallach. Schisgal's play *Luv* was also produced as a screenplay (1965). Schisgal and Larry Gelbart collaborated to produce the screenplay for the hit 1982 film *Tootsie*.

Achievements

Schisgal is known for his experimental plays (*The Typists*) and, even more so, for his farces, including *Luv* and *The Tiger*. He is prominent in the theater world and a friend of many on the New York theater scene, such as Eli Wallach, Anne Jackson, and Dustin Hoffman (to whom he dedicated a number of his scripts, including *Popkins*). His plays reflect some of the mainstream comic situations and themes of New York theater from the mid-twentieth century to the present day. His forte, light comedy and satire, manifests itself in witty, often topical plays that are written primarily to evoke quick laughter and that have been produced by some of the best professional theater troupes of modern times.

Biography

Murray Joseph Schisgal was born on November 25, 1926, to Abraham and Irene (née Sperling) Schisgal, in Brooklyn, New York. His father was a tailor in the East New York section of Brooklyn. Schisgal was in high school during World War II, but he quit to join the United States Navy in 1943, in which he served until 1946, earning the rank of radioman, third class. He returned to earn his high school diploma at night, and attended Long Island University. He gained a bachelor of laws degree in 1953 from Brooklyn Law School and a bachelor of arts from New York's New School for Social Research in 1959.

From the age of twenty-one, Schisgal knew that his main professional interest was in writing. His initial efforts in the world of letters were in prose fiction: more than sixty stories and three novels, none of which was immediately published. He supported himself through a variety of odd jobs, including setting pins in a bowling alley, pushing clothing racks in the garment district, and playing saxophone and clarinet in a small band. After receiving his law degree, Schisgal practiced law for two years on Delancey Street, near Greenwich Village, but he gave this up to devote more time to his writing. He then turned to teaching English while he continued to write on the side. From 1955 through 1960, he taught English at James Fenimore Cooper Junior High School in East Harlem, New York City. While teaching, he turned to writing plays.

Like his contemporary Edward Albee, Schisgal saw his first commercial production mounted in another country. While traveling to Europe to spend time writing, he succeeded in arranging for his first works, *The Typists* and *The Tiger*, to be produced by the British Drama League. After this breakthrough, Schisgal became a full-time playwright; since 1960, he has been able to practice his craft on a full-time basis.

Schisgal's best-known work is the comedy *Luv*, which premiered in London in 1963 and opened in the United States in November, 1964, at the Booth Theatre in New York. Directed by Mike Nichols—a television actor and comic who was to become famous as a film director with his work in *The Graduate*—*Luv*'s three-person cast consisted of Alan Arkin, recently moved over from Second City in Chicago, and Eli Wallach and Anne Jackson, two well-known personalities of the New York stage and the world of cinema. The recognition that Schisgal first gained with *The Typists* and *The*

Tiger turned into financial and commercial success with the long-running *Luv*, and he became a fixture of the Broadway scene.

In 1975, however, disillusioned by the failure of the ambitious *All over Town*, Schisgal stopped writing for Broadway. He turned his attention to film and television work and received an Academy Award nomination for his work on *Tootsie*; he also wrote his first novel. He continued to write plays for Off-Broadway production before returning to Broadway with *Twice Around the Park* in 1982. He has continued to write plays, largely for European production; *Popkins* was produced in Paris in 1990, and *Theatrical Release* was performed there in 1991.

Analysis

Murray Schisgal's forte is the light comedy, with genial satire and topical references often worked into the content of the play. Schisgal's plays have often enjoyed commercial success. *Luv* had a long run on Broadway in the mid-1960's, and *The Tiger* (which Schisgal revised as the screenplay *The Tiger Makes Out*) was a moderately successful movie in 1967. For several decades, Schisgal has been a commercially successful, full-time playwright and theater person—no mean accomplishment in the financially difficult medium of playwriting. He has earned the friendship of influential theater persons in New York and elsewhere.

In their zany, topical, and often absurd touches, Schisgal's light comedies are similar to those of his contemporaries Neil Simon and Saul Bellow and of the younger but similarly satiric filmmaker Woody Allen. His people are usually wealthy New Yorkers who remember a younger, poorer time in their lives and who are often comically bored with their marriages—sexual or psychological problems provide the motivation for the plots of most of Schisgal's works. Schisgal often writes to evoke laughter and spectacle; his dramas are characterized by humorous sexual references and by satiric references to current fads in contemporary culture in general (especially New York City culture) and to the theater world in particular. Schisgal's plays tend to refer to current trends in mainstream commercial New York or related milieus during the time of the particular play's production. Although he made his initial breakthrough Off-Off-Broadway, Schisgal has become a central figure of commercial Broadway. His dramatic voice is conservative, urbane, witty, slightly cynical, and lightly comic.

Typical of Schisgal's drama is the 1960's comedy *Luv*, which has two major comic targets: the nihilistic tradition of theater, often called Theater of the Absurd, and some of the insincere posturings that are often substituted for a deeper definition of "love." Like the Theater of the Absurd that Schisgal's play satirizes, *Luv* is not literally realistic or even psychologically plausible in its presentation of characters; rather, it is an idea play, a series of gags and satiric jabs at its targets. Two men, Harry Berlin and Milt

Manville, in effect pass a somewhat overbearing, bluestocking woman back and forth between them in the twists and turns of the plot. The action is rapid, basically lighthearted, played with gusto, and aimed at provoking laughter. Foibles and fads, not major cultural undercurrents, are the butt of Schisgal's comic critique.

Luv is set at the edge of a bridge on a dark, isolated night. Harry Berlin, an out-at-the-elbows Bohemian character (his nickname in high school, we learn, was "Dostoyevsky"), is about to leap off the bridge when his suicide is halted by an old friend, Milt Manville. Manville is as crass and philistine as Berlin is neurotic and typical of the counterculture. Manville has come to the bridge to pick valuables out of the garbage, thereby to add further wealth to his already considerable income. Berlin tells Manville that his (Berlin's) life is meaningless, that he has abandoned all of his projects and education. Milt attempts to cheer Harry and restore in him a sense of life's significance by reiterating the key word of the play, "love." Harry responds, saying that he feels suddenly, absurdly alive again simply when the word is mentioned. The audience soon learns that love has its meaning for Manville as well—sending him to walk by the bridge, for he is in love with a woman, Linda, who is not his wife. In short order, Milt arranges for Harry to meet his wife, Ellen. In comically fast fashion, Harry falls for Ellen. With the second act, Milt has returned to the bridge, now bored with his new marriage with Linda, and Ellen returns there, discontented with her marriage with the neurotic Harry. Milt and Ellen rapidly come back together, and the play ends with Harry being pursued by a zealous dog snapping at his pants leg as he vainly pursues the once-again-happy pair, Milt and Ellen.

The stock dramatic techniques and situations of a typical Schisgal comedy are apparent in the plot of *Luv*. There is the contrast between the commercially successful Milt Manville and the artistic, neurotic Bohemian Harry Berlin. There is a comic love triangle, some version of which is in each of Schisgal's plays. A current fashion is satirized—here, the nihilistic despair largely mouthed by Harry Berlin, especially in act 1. There are also many one-liners about adultery; the comical treatment of a potentially serious subject is typical of Schisgal's drama.

Luv can be seen as a kind of a farce-parody of a slightly older, also very successful play which eventually ran well in New York—Edward Albee's *The Zoo Story*. In Albee's play, a tragic, neurotic isolate meets a relatively conservative philistine and has the philistine assist him in his own suicide. *The Zoo Story*, however, is serious, downbeat, somber, whereas *Luv* is a lighthearted and satiric reversal of a similar situation. Even the attempted suicides off the bridge, complete with water splashing up on the stage, prove humorously unsuccessful. Each time, the character comes back wet but very much alive. The human condition is not nearly as bad as the nihilistic Absurdists would have us believe, Schisgal implies in *Luv*. Schisgal's is a conservative, mainstream comedy.

The Tiger illustrates another version of Schisgal's satiric comedy. The play's premise provoked some adverse commentary (a man carries a woman off to his apartment by force, and she proceeds to fall for him), yet the action of the play proves far less upsetting or radical than a bare summary of the plot would indicate. A one-act play, *The Tiger* is set in a secluded New York apartment owned by Ben, a pseudo-Nietzschean isolate. Ben carries Gloria into the apartment as the play opens; she is over his shoulder, kicking and fighting. He ties her up and they talk—which constitutes the main action of the play until its climax, their love scene. Ben calls himself a "tiger," and his posturing language is full of animal imagery. He threatens Gloria with references to how he will "finish her off" and "claw" her. One learns that Ben is forty-two, insecure about his middle-aged bachelordom, a college dropout who works as a postman. Gloria is a former social worker, now a bored Long Island suburban housewife. Soon, Ben and Gloria find common ground, agreeing that conformity and boredom permeate American culture of the day (around 1963), and, speaking French to each other, they grow romantic, the lights are cut, and a love scene takes place. When the lights come back up, Gloria is dressed again and they fix a date for another adulterous tryst.

Both the play and the subsequent screenplay, *The Tiger Makes Out*, can be seen as presenting the fantasies of the middle-aged American male: Gloria is submissive and sexually accessible in an almost dreamlike way. What is being satirized in this fantasy-comedy is conformity, but the play's patent wish fulfillment almost overwhelms its satire.

Jimmy Shine is one of Schisgal's most elaborate plays. Its two acts embrace large sweeps of space and time, and it is designed for a three-level stage somewhat reminiscent of the set of Arthur Miller's *Death of a Salesman*. One follows the title character through some significant steps in his life. Schisgal's triangle theme becomes evident when Jimmy's youthful romantic interest marries his best friend. The best friend talks Jimmy into dropping out of business society and living in Greenwich Village to pursue a life of painting and the arts. Then Jimmy's friend ironically reneges and becomes a wealthy businessman, while Jimmy stays artistically pure and first flees to San Francisco, then returns to New York, where he takes up with a prostitute and continues to work as a painter. The flashback technique is similar to that of Schisgal's novel, *Days and Nights of a French Horn Player*: Like the novel, *Jimmy Shine* charts the development of a wisecracking protagonist who happens to be an artist, someone who pursues his vision and who learns through experience, particularly through his love affairs.

Twice Around the Park, consisting of the one-act plays *A Need for*

Brussels Sprouts and *A Need for Less Expertise*, marked Schisgal's return to Broadway after a prolonged absence. *A Need for Brussels Sprouts* portrays the unorthodox courtship of Margaret, a policewoman, and Leon, an aging, unemployed actor. The play was Schisgal's first written for specific performers, and his characterizations of Margaret and Leon were strongly influenced by the performers (Anne Jackson and Eli Wallach) who inaugurated the roles. *A Need for Less Expertise* depicts the disastrous yet comic results of a marriage counselor's bizarre advice to a middle-aged couple. The playwright later observed, "I don't have more than a few themes that interest me: the 'accredited' expert telling others how to live is one of them."

Schisgal's best plays are distinguished by a flair for light comedy. There is in much of his work a nostalgia for a youthful, less financially comfortable past, a winking understanding of adultery (especially male adultery), a tendency to satirize fads, and a general assumption of familiarity with New York locations; a belief in the old verities is just below the surface of his satire. Things are not so bad, Schisgal seems to be saying: People are basically good if limited, sexual creatures given to little adventures that tend to right themselves.

Other major works

NOVEL: *Days and Nights of a French Horn Player*, 1980.

SCREENPLAYS: *Ducks and Lovers*, 1962 (co-adaptor; adaptation of his play); *Luv*, 1965 (adapted from his play); *The Tiger Makes Out*, 1967 (adaptation of his *The Tiger*); *Tootsie*, 1982 (with Larry Gelbart).

TELEPLAYS: *The Love Song of Barney Kempenski*, 1966; *Natasha Kovolina Pipishinsky*, 1976.

Bibliography

Herman, Jan. "Murray Schisgal Puts on a Show—So What Else Is New?" *Los Angeles Times*, July 11, 1989, p. F2. This preview of *Songs of War*, which includes a biographical profile, chronicles Schisgal's American and European reputation and recalls the fresh voice of *Luv* in 1965. *Songs of War*, with "refrains of family skirmishes," is reviewed by Don Shirley three days later.

Kerr, Walter. "Walter Kerr's *Luv* Review." Review of *Luv*. *New York Herald Tribune*, November 12, 1964. This long, positive review brings *The Typist* and *The Tiger* into the discussion. Kerr states that Schisgal "can make an entire play out of our insincerities" and that the playwright considers the play "the answer to a theatregoer's prayer." Comparisons are made to the Theater of the Absurd, farce, comedy of manners, vaudeville, and low comedy.

Klein, Alvin. "*Luv* Offers Vaudeville of Neuroses." Review of *Luv*. *The*

New York Times, February 9, 1992, p. 15. This review of the New Jersey Forum Theater Group's revival of *Luv* appeared in the New Jersey section of the newspaper. Klein includes a brief biography and a fairly long appreciation of Schisgal's sense of theater and his contribution to light comedy over several decades.

Lambert, Mike. "Awards Close Out Menu of Delicious One-Act Plays." *The Washington Post*, July 25, 1991, p. 5. The occasion, a one-act play festival at the Northern Virginia Theatre Alliance, included Schisgal's play *A Need for Brussels Sprouts*. The play went on in September to another production, directed by Stephen Rothman, at the West Hollywood Tiffany Theater.

Stein, Howard, and Glenn Young, eds. *The Best American Short Plays, 1991-1992.* New York: Applause, 1992. As a preface to *Extensions*, the editors sum up Schisgal's career and his success with *Luv*, discuss his promising future, and bring into focus his later work.

Raymond Miller, Jr.
(Updated by *Thomas J. Taylor*
and *Robert McClenaghan*)

THOMAS SHADWELL

Born: Norfolk, England; 1640(?)
Died: Chelsea, England; November 19, 1692

Principal drama

The Sullen Lovers: Or, The Impertinents, pr., pb. 1668; *The Royal Shepherdess*, pr., pb. 1669; *The Humorists*, pr. 1670, pb. 1671; *The Miser*, pr. c. 1671-1672, pb. 1672 (adaptation of Molière's play *L'Avare*); *Epsom-Wells*, pr. 1672, pb. 1673; *The Tempest: Or, The Enchanted Island*, pr., pb. 1674 (libretto); *Psyche*, pr., pb. 1675 (libretto); *The Libertine: A Tragedy*, pr. 1675, pb. 1676; *The Virtuoso*, pr., pb. 1676; *The History of Timon of Athens, the Man-Hater*, pr., pb. 1678; *A True Widow*, pr. 1678, pb. 1679; *The Woman-Captain*, pr. 1679. pb. 1680; *The Lancashire Witches, and Tegue o Divelly the Irish Priest*, pr. 1681, pb. 1682; *The Squire of Alsatia*, pr., pb. 1688; *The Amorous Bigot, with the Second Part of Tegue o Divelly*, pr. c. 1689, pb. 1690; *Bury Fair*, pr., pb. 1689; *The Scowrers*, pr. 1690, pb. 1691; *The Volunteers: Or, The Stock Jobbers*, pr. 1692, pb. 1693.

Other literary forms

Thomas Shadwell, a prolific writer of comic drama, was also an energetic theatrical critic and polemicist, and a writer of pastorals, operas, and adaptations. His poetic output is divided into four categories: prologues and largely satiric epilogues that are found included in the printed texts of his own or others' drama; songs from his plays; satires and lampoons; a translation of *The Tenth Satyr of Juvenal* (1687), to which is prefixed the translation of a short poem by Lucan. Shadwell was an active and fierce participant in the literary wars of his time and produced many pamphlets flaying the enemies of the Whig cause. *The Horrid Sin of Man-Catching, the Second Part* (1681) is dedicated to the Whig leader, the Earl of Shaftesbury. *Some Reflections upon the Pretended Parallel in the Play Called "The Duke of Guise"* (1683) provoked a savage attack from Thomas Otway in his play *The Atheist: Or, The Second Part of the Soldier's Fortune* (pr. 1683). A few of Shadwell's letters have survived, but the chief interest of his nondramatic work lies in the theatrical polemics found in the prose dedications to his plays. The ideas Shadwell presented in these dedications constitute a theory of dramatic method. His prologues are used as pleas for a reintroduction of Jonsonian classical values into dramatic structure as an alternative to prevailing Restoration comic misrule.

Achievements

Shadwell owes his immortality in large part to ridicule. John Dryden, his former friend, reserved some of his fiercest satiric lines for Shadwell. Dryden wrote in his mock paean of praise to fools, *MacFlecknoe* (1682): "Sh—alone, of all my sons, is he/ Who stands confirm'd in full stupidity./ The rest to some faint meaning make pretense,/ But Sh— never deviates into sense." It is a tribute of sorts to Shadwell that he generated such brilliant and lasting malice. In far less memorable lines, another contemporary poet and dramatist, John Wilmot, Earl of Rochester, in his "Allusion to the Tenth Satyr . . . of Horace" (1675), indicates some other elements in Shadwell's achievements: "Of all our Modern Wits, none seems to me/ Once to have toucht upon true Comedy,/ But hasty *Shadwell,* and slow *Wycherley./ Shadwell's* unfinish'd works do yet impart/ Great proofs of Nature, none of Art."

Shadwell's plays were performed on the London stage well into the eighteenth century. He has not been regarded as a great dramatist but as one of interest in theatrical history. Contemporaries saw him as a force to be reckoned with, as an advocate of once fashionable Jonsonian classicism. Sir Walter Scott, writing on Restoration drama long after Dryden and Shadwell and their quarrels had turned to dust, felt compelled to defend Shadwell. Scott pointed out that Shadwell's strengths lie in his comedies, which, although lacking "any brilliancy of wit, or ingenuity of intrigue," have "characters that are truly dramatic, original and well drawn, and the picture of manners which they exhibit gives us a lively idea of those of the author's age." Between 1887 and 1907, at least eight doctoral dissertations, largely concentrating on Shadwell's use of his source materials in his comedies, appeared in Germany and Switzerland. Praise for Shadwell's "uncompromising and at the same time felicitous realism" in George Saintsbury's introduction to the Mermaid edition of four of Shadwell's plays, which appeared in the early twentieth century, contributed to creating the climate for Montague Summers' sumptuous five-volume *The Complete Works of Thomas Shadwell,* which was published in 1927. Limited to 1,290 sets, privately printed in magnificent typography by the Fortune Press (which produced ninety five-volume sets on Kelmscott unbleached handmade paper, and the remainder on machine-made paper, with lavish illustrative portraits), the volumes are collectors' items. The bibliophilic elements in Summers' edition reflect the fact that Shadwell's reputation is largely confined to scholarly circles and to students of dramatic history. Summers concludes his introduction of more than two hundred pages by asserting that Shadwell's work is "incalculably important as a picture of his times." In his comedies, "we have the whole tribe of fops, virtuosos, debauches, cuckolds, coarse country clowns, crooked politicians, business men, minor poets, sportsmen, loose wives, whores, puritans, cavaliers, the whole kaleidoscope of Restoration life."

For a man who "never deviates into sense," Shadwell has spawned some intense twentieth century devotees. In 1928, Albert S. Borgman published a detailed study of Shadwell's life and comedies. In 1967, a Twayne English Authors Series monograph by Michael W. Alssid was devoted to a thorough examination of Shadwell's output, followed by the 1972 publication of Don R. Kunz's lengthy study, *The Drama of Thomas Shadwell*. There is a consensus that Shadwell's plays, whatever their artistic deficiencies, are of great value as a reservoir of information about their times. Shadwell's canvas is a wide one, and, in this respect, he differs from other late seventeenth century dramatists of comparable stature, who generally limited their attentions to narrow court circles. Shadwell has survived Dryden's mockery to become recognized as an adherent of Jonsonian traditions on the Restoration stage, as a superb recorder of contemporary life and manners, and, at his best, as a master of vibrant comedy.

Biography

The facts of Thomas Shadwell's life are unclear, and even the date of his birth is shrouded in uncertainty. He was born between 1640 and 1642, probably at Santon Hall in Norfolk, to John and Sarah Shadwell; his father was a Royalist lawyer. After receiving a liberal education, being tutored from an early age in music and the general arts, he attended the King Edward VI Grammar School at Bury St. Edmunds. The theme of the apposite education for a young man entering the world is especially prominent in Shadwell's later drama. His early years on the family estate provided the foundation for the pastoral and Horatian ideals that pervade his writings, where they are more than a mere literary convention.

Shadwell was admitted to Gonville and Caius College, Cambridge, which he left without taking a degree; on July 7, 1658, he enrolled in the Middle Temple, London, no doubt hoping to follow his father in a legal career. There is evidence that between 1664 and 1665, Shadwell was with his father, recorder of Galway and Attorney General of Connacht, in Ireland. In the years immediately preceding the 1668 production of his first comedy, *The Sullen Lovers*, Shadwell met the man who was to become his patron, the influential and well-connected William Cavendish, Duke of Newcastle. Dedications in printed texts of Shadwell's plays to Cavendish and members of his family attest Shadwell's indebtedness to a man who had known Ben Jonson and had patronized the arts for a long period. Sometime between 1663 and 1667, Shadwell married a leading lady in the Duke's Company, Anne Gibbs, who appeared in the prominent role of Emilia in his first produced drama. Subsequently, Shadwell's life followed the routine of the professional writer and dramatist heavily engaged in literary activity in post-Restoration London. In defense of his artistic beliefs, and as a paid propagandist for the Whig cause, Shadwell was constantly involved in literary feuds with rivals. In 1681, a year of particularly intense political activity, Shadwell was forced to leave the theater and to write under assumed names. In 1688, the year of the Glorious Revolution, and the start of the reign of William and Queen Mary, Shadwell's personal and theatrical fortunes were restored. He returned to the London stage with *The Squire of Alsatia*, became the poet laureate, and until his death enjoyed prestige and success.

Evidence suggests that physically, Shadwell was big and by character blustering, hardly noted for tact, but rather for crudity of expression. He died in 1692 from an overdose of opium, to which he was addicted (in common with many of his contemporaries, he suffered from severe gout), and is buried at St. Luke's Church, Chelsea, London. Shadwell had five children, one of whom, John, achieved eminence as Queen Anne's royal physician and was knighted by her.

Analysis

The 1680's were times of personal danger for Thomas Shadwell. He was lampooned, personally assaulted by Tory bullyboys, and his plays were hissed off the stage. Attacks on Catholicism in his *The Lancashire Witches, and Tegue o Divelly the Irish Priest*, and his known association with the Earl of Shaftesbury and his circle, made Shadwell particularly vulnerable after the failure of the 1678 Popish Plot. Shadwell's creative works are indissolubly intertwined with the attitudes of his age. He spiritedly defended himself against his enemies. Of particular relevance to analysis of his work is his philosophical, rather than political, battle with the Earl of Rochester. Conducted in poems, pamphlets, and plays, it was a conflict between two basically opposed attitudes toward life and ways of living: Rochester's hedonism and love of extremes had their foundations in the writings of Thomas Hobbes; Shadwell's love of the middle way and his adherence to altruism were rooted in the classics. These contrasting ideologies found their way in one form or another into Shadwell's eighteen known dramas, which move from adherence to Jonsonian principles, through the fierce satires of the late 1670's and early 1680's, to the mellow, less intemperate, late plays extolling the middle way of conduct.

The Sullen Lovers, Shadwell's first London comedy, created a stage sensation with its caricaturing of contemporary court personalities. Samuel Pepys went to see the play three times in three days, noting in his diary that "Sir Positive At-all . . . is . . . Sir Robert Howard": Both men were singularly competent in pronouncing opinions upon everything from warfare and domestic architecture to ball games and how they should be played. Pepys' enthusiasm also owed something to his fascination with the reaction of court figures to the play as they watched it being performed early in May, 1668. Pepys saw it again in April, 1669; Charles II chose *The Sullen Lovers* as one of the plays to be acted at Dover when his court, in May, 1670, went to meet his sister the Duchess of Orleans on her return from overseas; and there was a revival at Lincoln's Inn Fields on October 5, 1703, when it was announced that the play had not been acted for twenty-eight years. Shadwell's main source was Molière's *Les Fâcheux* (1661; *The Bores*). Shadwell utilizes Molière's method of exhibiting various fools, individually and in pairs or various combinations, before the audience. In Shadwell's play, the fools represent the humors of classical Jonsonian drama. *The Sullen Lovers* is interesting as a Jonsonian play of humors using neoclassic structural and characterization devices, as an attempt to produce a psychological drama, and as a satire on contemporary court figures. Each character represents an idea or controlling thesis, the idea being made concrete by the dramatist's skillful play of contemporary allusions juxtaposed to the specific gestures, mannerisms, and speech peculiarities of living persons.

In *The Sullen Lovers*, Shadwell considers various modes of living in a world of utter folly. Contrast is provided by the device of marrying three pairs of humors: a pair of social misfits, Emilia and Stanford; a couple, appositely named Sir Positive At-All and Lady Vaine, totally devoted to the pursuit of folly; and Lovel and Carolina, wry and detached. Lovel and Carolina best represent the Shadwellian middle course, in contrast to the total isolation of the first pair, Emilia and Stanford, and the uncritical participation of the second pair, Sir Positive At-All and Lady Vaine, in the vanities and follies of the world in which they live. The plot dynamics revolve around the two self-confessed misanthropes, Emilia and Stanford, who are given much of Shadwell's powerful satiric invective and who are persistently pursued by a gang of idiots. The misanthropes escape from London, which is identified, as in so many of Shadwell's dramas, with corruption and vice. Emilia, influenced by Robert Burton's *The Anatomy of Melancholy* (1621), cultivates privacy and thinks of taking vows and entering a nunnery. Stanford dreams of an escape to a deserted Caribbean island. Deliberately refusing the company of others, they attract some idiosyncratic characters. The attack upon Stanford's citadel is led by the self-obsessed dramatist, Sir Positive At-all, while Lady Vaine, a prostitute disguised as an aristocrat and the first of Shadwell's long line of theatrical hedonists, leads the attack upon Emilia. In the second act, the "sullen lovers" of the title, Stanford and Emilia, meet. Acts 3 and 4 trace the development of their relationship and their realization that dissembling is the sole way to deal with idiocy. In the final act, they marry. Shadwell's *The Sullen Lovers* is an interesting synthesis of Jonsonian and Restoration modes of drama. Its use of humors is decidedly Jonsonian, while its emphasis upon wit, sexual intrigue, and satire are typical of Restoration comedy.

In *Epsom-Wells*, in many ways his most representative Restoration drama, Shadwell brilliantly utilizes the indecent characters and libertines about whom he complained in the preface to *The Sullen Lovers*. *Epsom-Wells* has as its setting a fashionable spa not too far from London where a rich galaxy of bawds, pimps, courtesans, gamblers, fops, and other contemporary types gather. The plot structure is multidimensional. Lucia and Carolina, two honorable young girls on holiday, are pursued by two rakes, Rains and Bevil, who have deliberately gone to Epsom to seduce women and to drink. They are debauchees whom Shadwell uses as commentators upon the folly of their world. Lucia and Carolina are representatives of freedom. They prefer Rains's and Bevil's antics, without succumbing to them, to the hypocrisy of London. According to Shadwell's *dramatis personae*, usually a rich source of information about the humors of his characters or their dominating ideas, Lucia and Carolina are "Two young ladies, of Wit, Beauty and Fortune," not pressured, as are so many of their contemporaries, into finding a rich husband or forced into marriage by their father. They have the privilege of bestowing their virginity upon men of their own choosing. After having tantalized Rains and Bevil throughout the play, they marry them in the final act.

Other plot strands focus upon the Woodlys, a young married couple. Mr. Woodly romps with Rains and Bevil: Mrs. Woodly, driven by licentious passion, sleeps with them. The last act sees them divorcing and celebrating their freedom. In addition to the Woodlys, Shadwell's *Epsom-Wells* is inhabited by the Biskets, Fribbles, and Justice Clodpates of the world. Bisket and Fribble, both London merchants, are cuckolded in the liberating Epsom atmosphere. Bisket is a "Comfit-maker, a quiet, humble, civil Cuckold, governed by his Wife, whom he very much fears and loves at the same time, and is very proud of." Fribble, on the other hand, is "A Haberdasher, a surly Cuckold, very conceited and proud of his Wife, but pretends to govern and keep her under." Mrs. Bisket is "An impertinent, imperious Strumpet, Wife to Bisket." Dorothy Fribble is "an humble, submitting Wife, who Jilts her Husband that way, a very Whore." Bisket and Fribble transform everything, including their own wives, into objects for materialistic exploitation, and value their wives' sexual indiscretions for the business opportunities thereby created. Clodpate is "A Country Justice, a publick spirited, politick, discontented Fop, an immoderate Hater of London, and a Lover of the Country above measure, a hearty true English coxcomb." Clodpate is given some magnificent lines of raillery against London, a "Sodom" full of "Pride, Popery, Folly, Lust, Prodigality, Cheating Knaves, and Jilting Whores; Wine of half a crown a quart, and Ale of twelve pence." Clodpate pursues Lucia and Carolina; jilted by them, he turns to Mrs. Jilt, a London prostitute in search of a wealthy husband and pretending at Epsom to be a lady of virtue. Luckily for Clodpate, the marriage between them turns out to be invalid. He returns to the country having enjoyed Epsom. Mrs. Jilt returns considerably richer to London. She is more in accord with Kick and Cuff, "cheating, sharking, cowardly Bullies," gigolos who fill out Shadwell's rich galaxy of the various humors congealing in a world such as Epsom-Wells.

Underpinning the play are differing attitudes to life and how it should be lived. The play opens with its characters taking the waters of the wells, waters that liberate the self from the inhibitions and artificial disguises of London and its social world. In Epsom, the true, animalistic Hobbesian nature of people is allowed to run rife. Cuff and Kick are unabashed animals, visualizing the vacationing women as wild beasts. Cuff has "a great mind to run roaring in amongst 'em," although there is a danger that he will be torn "in pieces." Bevil and Rains are intellectual hedonists. The chief target of their invective is Clodpate, the failed hedonist forced to spend his existence in far away Sussex, railing at folly. In his epilogue, Shadwell urges "Gallants, leave your lewd whoring and take wives,/ Repent for shame your Covent-Garden lives," although this message ill accords a play in which marriage encourages whoring. *Epsom-Wells* is a fascinating mixture of sexual intrigue, philosophical debate, satire, allusion, and sheer entertainment. It is hardly a wonder that it was a contemporary hit, first performed December 2, 1672, and seen three times in a single month by Charles II, who included it among his Christmas revels. *Epsom-Wells* remained in the London repertory for many years; Henry Purcell wrote music for a 1693 revival, and there is a record of a 1724 performance. A play of such obvious theatrical vitality demands a good modern revival.

Shadwell's comedies have obscured his efforts in other dramatic modes. Like many other Restoration dramatists, he turned his talents to adaptation. *The Libertine: A Tragedy*, based largely upon Molière's *Dom Juan: Ou, Le Festin de Pierre* (pr. 1665, pb. 1682; *Don Juan*, 1755), is a variation upon the Don Juan theme. Written in prose, the play exhibits fantastic extremes, coincidences, masques, brutality, and farce. Shadwell revels in the Hobbesian hedonism epitomized in his presentation of the flouting of all religious and civil authority by Don Juan (named "Don John" by Shadwell). It is not surprising that Shadwell's next adaptation should be a rewriting of William Shakespeare's *Timon of Athens* (pr. c. 1607-1608). His major deviation from Shakespeare's text is to give Timon a faithful mistress named Evandra and an unfaithful one named Melissa; further, he allows Timon to die onstage with Evandra, who stays with him when all his seemingly faithful but false friends have deserted him. Shadwell makes his spectacle serve a purpose, uses cosmopolitan scenes and stage devices such as machines, and deals with Restoration social problems. The play is of interest both in the history of Shakespearean adaptations and as an illustration of Shadwell's recurring devices, particularly the use of paired characters.

Shadwell's experiments with pastoral and opera are not without interest. *The Royal Shepherdess* exhibits his use of dance, song, and exaggerated farce not in a comic mode but in a pastoral form, drawing upon his master Ben Jonson and using his masque forms. Didacticism creeps in with a contrast between Horatian genteel life and the squalor of low life presented against a backdrop of pastoral illusion. Shadwell's two operas, the first based on Dryden and Sir William Davenant's *The Tempest* (1667), the second, *Psyche,* on the Molière-Corneille-Quinault tragedy ballet, were considered "significant milestones in the evolution of English opera" by Michael W. Alssid. Both illustrate Shadwell's dexterity at stagecraft. In *The Tempest,* he shortens and rearranges between forty and fifty speeches, creating space and time for dancing, singing, and dramatic spectacle. In *Psyche,* he produces a moral allegory of the struggle within the heroine, Psyche, between the forces of ambition, power, plenty, and peace. Both operas and the pastoral are professional theatrical pieces written to make money. They reveal Shadwell's mastery of stagecraft, his didactic strain, and his sense of spectacle, providing as well an insight into the multiple forms of drama found on the Restoration stage.

For a number of reasons, *The Lancashire Witches, and Tegue o Divelly the Irish Priest* is among Shadwell's most interesting works. The genesis of this play was deeply political, reflecting Shadwell's role as a Whig propagandist. Shadwell's address to his readers gives an account of the delays and excisions in the text of the play demanded by his Tory political opponents before it could be performed in the autumn of 1681. Shadwell was forced to omit most of his political materials, and censorship transformed the play into an absurd but highly popular farce. Explicit political ideology was replaced by supernatural motifs which implicitly represent forces of disruption at work in society.

The play is set far away from the intrigues of London, on a country estate, an emblem for tranquillity and positive values. The action focuses on the master of the estate, Sir Edward Hartford, "a worthy Hospitable true English Gentleman, of good understanding, and honest Principles." Sir Edward detests "Foppery, slavish Principles, and Popish Religion." He is an empiricist who argues that witchcraft has natural causes. Often misled in personal matters and motivated by materialistic considerations, he tries to marry his daughter Isabella to Sir Timothy Shacklehead, "a very pert, confident, simple Fellow." Sir Edward's son Hartfort—"A Clownish, sordid Country Fool, that loves nothing but drinking Ale, and Country Sports"— is intended for the highly intelligent Theodosia Shacklehead. Witchcraft conspires to bring two reformed rakes, Bellfort and Doubty, to Sir Edward's estate. Much of the action of the play is concerned with the ways in which Isabella and Theodosia disrupt the estate, play elaborate games with Bellfort and Doubty, and disguise themselves as witches. Mistaken identity and disguise give Shadwell the opportunity to present highly amusing dramatic moments. In act 4, Lady Shacklehead, on the way to a nighttime assignation with Doubty, finds herself attacked by a lecherous priest named Tegue, who mistakenly has intercourse with a witch, Mother Dickenson, thinking that she is Lady Shacklehead. In act 5, Sir Edward's friend Sir Jeffery Shacklehead discovers his scarcely clothed wife wandering around in the dark. He is duped by her sleepwalking performance and quickly improvised nightmare, in which she exclaims "Oh! the Witch, the Witch, oh she pulls the cloaths off me. Hold me, Sir Jeffery, hold me."

Although there are many farcical elements in the play, ranging from rock throwing, chair pulling, disrobing on a darkened stage, and chases, the chaos has a serious side. The buffoons, witches, Smerk, Sir Edward's chaplain, and Tegue are representatives of the forces of disorder threatening the ordered Hartford estate and, by implication, Charles II and England itself. Shadwell, playing upon audience prejudice, depicts his arch villain Tegue as both Irish and Catholic, a dissembling troublemaker plotting insurrection. Lively theater is created by Tegue's lecherous drunken antics and by the highly energetic activities of the witches.

Shadwell even includes a witchhunt which degenerates "into a mad farce controlled by secular and religious professionals seeking to enhance their own reputations by finding and condemning great numbers," according to Kunz. Passages in the play expunged by the censor are printed in italics in the printed text, revealing that Sir Edward's estate is but a microcosm for the garden of England, which—if it is to survive—must be cultivated according to solid Whig principles. This political statement forced Shadwell as a dramatist and verse satirist into seven years of submerged existence while the country changed religions and rulers and then did an about-face.

George Saintsbury was right, in his introduction to *Thomas Shadwell* (1903), to draw attention to Shadwell's accuracy of observation, his keen eye for contemporary manners, and his dramatic energy and gusto. Attacked by some critics for a seeming lack of selectivity, Shadwell was in fact a dramatist whose techniques reveal careful selective principles at work: the pairing of characters into types and humors in order to present antithetical viewpoints; the reworking of source materials; the interesting use of metaphor and place to convey meaning. Shadwell is, in the words of John Loftis in *The Revels History of Drama in English, Volume V: 1660-1750* (1976), "Among the major dramatists" of the Restoration, the only one who "broadens the social range, providing engaging portraits of men outside fashionable society and venturing to criticize gentlemen not only for social affectation." Shadwell's dramatic rendering of the conflict between hedonism and altruism is universal. As the shrewd Sir Walter Scott observed, in his notes to *Peveril of the Peak* (1823), acknowledging his debt to Shadwell's *The Volunteers*, Shadwell was indeed "no mean observer of human nature."

Other major works

POETRY: *The Medal of John Bayes: A Satyr Against Folly and Knavery*, 1682; *A Congratulatory Poem on His Highness the Prince of Orange His Coming into England*, 1689; *Ode on the Anniversary of the King's Birth*, 1690; *Votum Perenne*, 1692.

NONFICTION: *Notes and Observations on the Empress of Morocco*, 1674; *The Horrid Sin of Man-Catching, the Second Part*, 1681; *Some Reflections upon the Pretended Parallel in the Play Called "The Duke of Guise,"* 1683.

TRANSLATION: *The Tenth Satyr of Juvenal*, 1687.

MISCELLANEOUS: *The Complete Works of Thomas Shadwell*, 1927 (5 volumes; Montague Summers, editor).

Bibliography

Alssid, Michael W. *Thomas Shadwell.* New York: Twayne, 1967. This volume, part of Twayne's English Authors series, gives a straightforward account of Shadwell's life and drama, attempting some critical evaluation. A useful introduction. Supplemented by a bibliography and an index.

Armistead, J. M., and Werner Bies. *Four Restoration Playwrights: A Reference Guide to Thomas Shadwell, Aphra Behn, Nathaniel Lee, and Thomas Otway.* Boston: G. K. Hall, 1984. One of the Reference Guides to Literature series, this volume carries basic information on dates, plays, editions, and includes a bibliography. It is invaluable for research papers.

Bruce, Donald. *Topics of Restoration Comedy.* London: Victor Gollancz, 1974. This survey of Restoration comedy concentrates on it as a "debating" comedy, with a moral pupose in this debate. Bruce refers to Shadwell's plays extensively and examines seven of his plays within the context of the moral topics enumerated. Notes, bibliography, chronology, and index.

Burns, Edward. *Restoration Comedy: Crises of Desire and Identity.* Basingstoke, England: Macmillan, 1987. Chapter 4 deals with Shadwell as a professional dramatist, as one of a group of dramatists whose plays are still underrated. Burns praises these writers for their energy and ferocity, opposing them to the suavity of the gentlemen playwrights. Chronology, notes, short bibliography, and index.

Hume, Robert D. *The Development of English Drama in the Late Seventeenth Century.* Oxford, England: Clarendon Press, 1976. Hume tries to correct earlier stereotypes of Restoration drama by examining a large number of plays and paying special attention to their chronological sequencing. Contains many references to Shadwell and a full analysis of his *The Squire of Alsatia.* Two indexes.

Loftis, John, Richard Southern, Marion Jones, and A. H. Scouten. *The Revels History of Drama in English, Volume V: 1660-1750.* London: Methuen, 1976. Contains a section on Shadwell in connection with the comedy of humors and includes other useful references to his plays throughout the volume. Complemented by a bibliography and an index.

Nicoll, Allardyce. *A History of Restoration Drama, 1660-1700.* 2d ed. Cambridge, England: Cambridge University Press, 1928. This volume is one of the finest surveys of the period. While there is no particular section on Shadwell, there are references to practically all of his plays in the volume. Includes particularly useful appendices on the history of the playhouses, a full list of all Restoration drama, additional notes, and an index.

William Baker
(Updated by *David Barratt*)

PETER SHAFFER

Born: Liverpool, England: May 15, 1926

Principal drama

Five Finger Exercise, pr., pb. 1958; *The Private Ear*, pr., pb. 1962 (one act); *The Public Eye*, pr., pb. 1962 (one act); *The Merry Roosters Panto*, pr. 1963 (music by Stanley Myers, lyrics by Lionel Bart); *The Royal Hunt of the Sun*, pr., pb. 1964; *Black Comedy*, pr. 1965, pb. 1967 (one act); *The White Liars*, pb. 1967, 1968 (one act; originally as *White Lies*, pr., pb. 1967); *Shrivings*, pb. 1973 (with *Equus*; originally as *The Battle of Shrivings*, pr. 1970); *Equus*, pr., pb. 1973; *Amadeus*, pr. 1979, pb. 1980; *The Collected Plays of Peter Shaffer*, pb. 1982; *Yonadab: The Watcher*, pr. 1985; Lettice and Lovage, pr., pb. 1987.

Other literary forms

Peter Shaffer began his writing career with a teleplay. *The Salt Land* (1955), and a radio play, *The Prodigal Father* (1955). Shaffer has also written several novels. With his twin brother, Anthony Shaffer, he wrote *Woman in the Wardrobe* (1951), published in England under the collective pen name Peter Antony. The two brothers also collaborated on two more novels: *How Doth the Little Crocodile?* (1952), likewise issued under the pen name Peter Antony, and *Withered Murder* (1955), published under both authors' real names. Macmillan published *Withered Murder* (1956) and *How Doth the Little Crocodile?* (1957) in the United States, using the authors' real names. Shaffer also wrote the screenplays for *The Public Eye* (1972), *Equus* (1977), and *Amadeus* (1984), the last of which won the 1985 Academy Award for Best Screenplay Adaptation.

Achievements

Once Shaffer settled on playwriting as a career, most of his plays succeeded on both sides of the Atlantic. *Five Finger Exercise*, his first work for the stage, earned the London *Evening Standard* Drama Award for 1958 and the New York Drama Critics Circle Award for Best Foreign Play of the season in 1960. The one-act comedies *The Private Ear* and *The Public Eye* sustained Shaffer's reputation as a skilled playwright, as did the exceptional pageantry of *The Royal Hunt of the Sun*. *Equus* won the Tony Award for Best Play of the 1974-1975 season, the New York Drama Critics Circle Award, the Outer Critics Circle Award, and the Los Angeles Drama Critics Award. With 1,207 performances on Broadway, *Equus* ranks among the top twenty-five longest-running plays in the history of New York theater. *Amadeus* again took the *Evening Standard* Drama Award, the Plays and Players Award, and the London Theatre Critics Award for Best Play. The

New York production won the New York Drama Critics Circle Award and the Outer Critics Circle Award for 1981. The film version of *Amadeus* won eight Oscars in 1984, including Best Film and Best Adapted Screenplay. In 1987, Shaffer was honored with the title of Commander of the British Empire.

Biography

Peter Levin Shaffer was born to Orthodox Jewish parents, Jack and Reka Shaffer, in Liverpool, England, on May 15, 1926, with a twin brother, Anthony. Another brother, Brian, was born in 1929. Anthony is also a writer, author of the prizewinning play *Sleuth* (pr. 1970). Brian is a biophysicist.

A middle-class British family, the Shaffers moved to London in 1936. World War II brought several relocations, in part because of safety concerns and in part because of the demands of Jack Shaffer's real estate business. In 1942, Shaffer was enrolled in St. Paul's School in London. In 1944, the twin brothers were conscripted for duty in the coal mines, working first in Kent, then in Yorkshire. Shaffer entered Trinity College, Cambridge University, on a scholarship in 1947.

At Cambridge, Shaffer discovered his talent and taste for writing while editing a college magazine. Taking his degree in history in 1950, he sought employment with various publishers in England, to no avail. He moved to New York in 1951. From a brief stint as a salesman in a Doubleday bookstore, he moved to a job in the acquisitions section of a branch of the New York Public Library. Shaffer returned to London in 1954 and worked for the music publisher Boosey and Hawkes for about a year. With the broadcast of his teleplay *The Salt Land* and his radio play *The Prodigal Father* in 1955, he decided to turn to writing as a full-time career.

The 1958 success of *Five Finger Exercise* at London's Comedy Theater in the West End brought Shaffer renown as a serious playwright. The play opened in New York in December, 1959, setting a pattern followed by most of his subsequent stage plays. His pair of one-act plays, *The Private Ear* and *The Public Eye*, opened in London in 1962 and in New York in 1963. The Christmas season of 1963 saw the production of *The Merry Roosters Panto* in London.

During 1964, Shaffer and Peter Brook worked on a film script of William Golding's *Lord of the Flies* (1954), but it was not used for the eventual film version of the novel. Shaffer's *The Royal Hunt of the Sun* opened at the National Theater in Chichester, England, in July, 1964; in London in December of that year; and in New York in October of 1965. At the behest of Sir Laurence Olivier, the director of the National Theatre, Shaffer wrote *Black Comedy*. It played at Chichester in July, 1965, then in London, and was presented in tandem with *White Lies* in 1967. This second pair of one-act plays was staged again in London in 1968, by which time Shaffer had rewritten *White Lies* and retitled it *The White Liars*.

For Shaffer, the 1970's began with a lull: *The Battle of Shrivings* opened in London in February, 1970, but did not run for long. July, 1973, however, saw the London premiere of *Equus*, which in October, 1974, opened in New York for its remarkably long run. When Atheneum issued its edition of *Equus* in 1973, Shaffer included in it the book *Shrivings*, his revised version of *The Battle of Shrivings*, which had not survived onstage. In this general time period, Shaffer also developed the screenplay for the film version of *Equus*, which was released in 1977.

Finishing the 1970's with the highly successful *Equus*, Shaffer moved into the 1980's with the equally noteworthy *Amadeus*, which opened at the National Theatre, Chichester, in November, 1979, and subsequently opened in London. Shaffer revised his already very successful script during a run of the production in Washington, D.C., prior to its December, 1980, opening at New York's Broadhurst Theater. A film version was released in 1984 under the direction of Miloš Forman.

After the unsuccessful *Yonadab*, based on biblical themes, Shaffer returned to comedy with a star vehicle written for Maggie Smith, *Lettice and Lovage*, which received favorable reviews. Shaffer calls New York City home, despite his British citizenship and frequent returns to England.

Analysis

Writing for *Theatre Arts* in February, 1960, Peter Shaffer made a declaration of independence: "Labels aren't for playwrights." His independence shows in both his life and his art. Shaffer admits in a 1963 article in *Transatlantic Review*, "All art is autobiographical inasmuch as it refers to personal experience," but the adolescent torment in *Five Finger Exercise* and the passions he stages in other works stem from his personal experience only in a general sense. Shaffer does tell of seeing, hearing, or reading of events which trigger ideas for his plays. Seeing, in 1968 and 1969, pro- and anti-Vietnam War demonstrations in New York and watching the American people agonize over the war led him to write *Shrivings*. Still, he maintains a degree of distance between his personal life and his plays. John Russell Taylor sees in *Five Finger Exercise* the sort of detachment other critics agree is characteristic of Shaffer's work: "The playwright does not seem to be personally involved in his play. . . . This balance of sympathy in a dramatist . . . makes for effective drama."

Within the mainstream of theatrical tradition, Shaffer maintains his artistic independence, varying conventional form or shifting his approach to a theme in almost every play. *Five Finger Exercise* is a middle-class domestic drama written at a time when numerous domestic dramas were in vogue, but Shaffer did not repeat himself. He moved on to romantic triangles in his one-act plays, then to epic drama with *The Royal Hunt of the Sun*, to psychological drama in *Equus*, and to a historical play, *Amadeus*.

Sets of the earlier plays are realistic. *The Royal Hunt of the Sun, Equus*, and *Amadeus*, however, use impressionistic sets, rely on varying amounts of flashback technique, and employ varying amounts of coordinate action. Besides varying set types and play genres, Shaffer varies emphasis in theatrical appeal. Sounds or music are important secondary factors in *Five Finger Exercise, The Royal Hunt of the Sun*, and *Equus* and are central to the plots of *The Private Ear* and *Amadeus*. Seeing in silence is the proposed cure for a troubled marriage in *The Public Eye*, visual display is lavish in *The Royal Hunt of the Sun*, and the sight of characters groping and stumbling through the action as though in pitch dark makes *Black Comedy* a vivid farce.

Given Shaffer's drive for fresh rendering of theatrical matter, various trends do appear in his plays. One such trait is cultural or ethnic variety. Possibly, being reared by Orthodox Jewish parents in nominally Protestant England sensitized him to the assets of ethnic identities and the liabilities of stereotypes. Whatever the reason, Shaffer commonly includes multicultural groupings of characters. *Five Finger Exercise* includes Louise, overly proud of her French ancestry, and Walter, the young German tutor who wants desperately to become a British subject. The protagonist of *The Public Eye*, Julian Christoforou, is Greek. *The Royal Hunt of the Sun* portrays the clash between the Spanish and Inca empires, and with Pizarro as Commander of Artillery is Pedro de Candia, a Venetian. *Black Comedy* includes both an electrician and a prospective buyer of a young sculptor's art who are German. *Shrivings* includes an American secretary and an English poet who spends most of his time on the island of Corfu. *Amadeus* features an Italian composer in the Austrian court at Vienna, and the dialogue occasionally includes Italian and French exchanges.

Generally, Shaffer's Northern European characters are identified with more rational or more placid behavior, while the Mediterranean characters are posed as more vivacious or romantic. Whatever the specific mix in a given play, each cultural alternative usually exposes a deficit in the *status quo* or brings a valuable influence to compensate for some perceived lack. The Greek private detective, Christoforou, is able to explain to the older, middle-class accountant that the young wife he suspects of infidelity really only needs some excitement in her life with her mate. Martin Dysart, the controlled, rational psychiatrist, tells of traveling each summer through Greece, yearning for the wild passion of the ancient festivals of Dionysus. Mozart, bored with writing opera according to the dominant Italian conventions, is glad for a commission from the Austrian King Joseph to write opera in German.

Despite the cosmopolitan flavor of Shaffer's work, his plays are consistently male-dominated. Significant conflicts tend to be between males. In *The Private Ear*, Tchaik loses Doreen to Ted. In *The Public Eye*, while following the wife is a major factor in the action, it is reported in dialogue between the two men. The wife does appear and interact with her husband and the detective, but she does not have equivalent exposure onstage. *The Royal Hunt of the Sun*, *Equus*, and *Amadeus* all feature conflicts between males. Only in *White Lies*, one of Shaffer's less notable efforts, is there a female protagonist. While she achieves a moral victory in that she sees and tells the truth in the end, she is forced to return her fortune-telling fee to the belligerent male antagonist and thereby faces an ethical defeat. In rewriting *Shrivings*, Shaffer strengthened the conflict by removing Sir Gideon Petrie's wife altogether, leaving the American secretary, Lois Neal, as the sole female party in a struggle primarily among men.

Significantly, Shaffer's strongest plays have usually included either more female characters or more active female characters than have the less successful plays. Even in their activity, however, the women may not be wholly ideal types. Louise in *Five Finger Exercise* is a domineering mother. Her daughter Pamela is aware of the family politics but is never permitted significant access to the actual struggles played out among the older members of the family, since she is only fourteen. *Black Comedy* features young Brindsley contending with Carol, his current and very superficial fiancée, on the night his former lover, Clea, returns. His upstairs neighbor, Miss Furnival, helps build the farce as a typical middle-aged spinster getting tipsy during the action, but she remains a convenient comic stereotype. All three women are actively involved in the plot, and all three have considerable dialogue. The protagonist, though, is a male.

Equus and *Amadeus*, Shaffer's strongest works, include women as supporting characters. Dysart turns several times to Hester Salomon for emotional support during the course of *Equus*. Wise and compassionate, she is the most wholesome of Shaffer's female characters. Constanze Mozart, too, is a support for her husband in *Amadeus* and is the only woman in the play who has a speaking role. The few others onstage are seen but not heard.

Since Shaffer is a twin, Jules Glenn suggests that his various pairs of male characters embody the conflicts and complementary satisfactions typical of twins. Although none of the character-pairs is portrayed as biological twins in the plays, their roles often have parallel aspects. Two men are involved with a single woman in *The Private Ear*, *The Public Eye*, and *White Lies*; two men in *Equus*, Martin Dysart and his patient, Alan Strang, are inadequate in their sexual relationships with women. In *Amadeus*, both Mozart and Salieri have affairs with Katherina Cavalieri. *The Royal Hunt of the Sun* features two men who claim the role of a god.

The key to an overview of Shaffer's work is his talent for revelation of character through self-disclosure. *Five Finger Exercise*, conventional in many respects, is outstanding for its characters' multiple levels of self-disclosure, from Stanley, who rants without understanding, to Walter, who understands both the Harringtons' needs and his own and attempts suicide when fulfillment of his needs seems impossible. Shaffer's other plays take their depth and texture from this technique, if not their basic purpose. Self-disclosure is the major structural pattern for *The Royal Hunt of the Sun*, *Equus*, and *Amadeus*, each of which is presented by a narrator recalling past events. Similarly, Shaffer's choice of themes as his craft matures leads to a progressive revelation of the human condition. Clive, Shaffer's first stage protagonist, searches for individual identity and independence. Protagonists in the one-act plays, both the serious and the comic, are generally reaching for satisfactory relationships with other individuals. Leading characters in the major serious plays probe the ambitions, ideals, and institutions of humankind in the world at large.

Shaffer's comments on *The Royal Hunt of the Sun* reveal a salient concern obvious in that play and others overtly dealing with worship: He is disturbed that "man constantly trivializes the immensity of his experience" and "settles for a Church or Shrine or Synagogue . . . and over and over again puts into the hands of other men the reins of oppression. . . ." Even his earliest play, though portraying domestic rather than political or religious struggles, shows that revelation of character, the self-disclosure essential to informed, mature relationships, makes the individual human being vulnerable to another's control.

Dennis A. Klein observes that "there is not one happy marriage in all of Shaffer's plays . . . and the prototype is the marriage between Louise and Stanley Harrington." Clive Harrington, the protagonist of *Five Finger Exercise*, is his mother's pet; he is also the target of his father's criticism because he lacks "practical" or "useful" interests. Struggling for identity and independence, Clive is never safe in the family bickering. Agreeing with Stanley that the new tutor is a needless expense draws reproach from Louise. Admitting that he is writing a review of a performance of the Greek play *Electra* triggers one more paternal lecture on the really useful pursuits in life. Clive shows contradictory responses to Walter Langer, the young German whom his mother has hired as the family tutor. Clive needs and wants the contact with an understanding, mature role model. At the same time, he is jealous of his mother's attraction to Walter, and therefore opposes Walter's efforts to become part of the Harrington family.

Home from Cambridge, Clive drinks to avoid parental control. Walter advises him to get out on his own but declines to travel with him during the coming holidays. Seeing Louise cradle Walter's head in her arms during a tender moment, Clive reports to Stanley that the two were engaged in love-making. Warmed by Walter's Continental graces—he is fluent in French, plays classical music on the piano and on his phonograph, and brings her wildflowers—Louise enjoys toying with the young man in somewhat the same fashion as she toys with Clive. When Walter makes it clear that he esteems her as a mother, though, Louise urges Stanley to fire Walter for being "a bad influence on Pamela."

Stanley, although he doubts that Clive's accusation is true, resents Walter's advice to Clive and uses the claim of an illicit relationship as a reason for dismissal. The lie is a very versatile weapon. It can help rid Stanley of the unwanted cost of the tutor and simultaneously serve vengeance on the young German for counseling Clive to leave home. It will punish Louise for her affectations. It will embarrass Clive—due vengeance for the boy's lack of filial piety—and weaken Clive's relationship with his mother, a bond Stanley could never match in his attempts at fathering and could never before attack so severely. Though he still understands his family no better than before, Stanley can dominate them all in one stroke.

Clive is shocked that the lie he told in private becomes his father's bludgeon in public. He realizes that his capacity to injure others is as great as that of his parents. Walter, who has opened himself to Clive and Louise in his bid for acceptance as a family member, cannot tolerate the betrayal, the victimization, resulting from his vulnerability. Walter's suicide attempt shows Clive the need for all the Harringtons to change: "The courage. For all of us. Oh God—give it."

Pairs of one-act plays bracket Shaffer's epic drama *The Royal Hunt of the Sun*, which turns squarely to the issue of worship in both institutional and individual dimensions. Old Martin, the narrator, tells of his youthful adventure as page boy to Pizarro, conqueror of Peru. To Young Martin, Pizarro is a hero to worship. To the priests Valverde and De Nizza, military conquest is a necessary evil which will bring the Incas the good of institutional Christianity. To Estete, the Royal Overseer, Pizarro's personal ambition and the blessings of the Church are the necessary tools for advancing the dominion of King Carlos and thus for increasing his personal status within the king's domain. Pizarro takes the noble justifications of Church and State and the outright greed of his soldiers as the means for attaining personal glory. A hard man, he warns Young Martin never to trust him: He will surely betray anyone and anything in his drive for fame.

Atahuallpa, god-king of the Incas, believes the approaching Pizarro must be the White God of ancient legend returning as foretold. Estete declares to the Inca general, Challcuchima, that the Spanish come in the names of King Carlos of Spain and of Jesus Christ, the Son of God. Challcuchima insists that it is he who comes to them in the name of the Son of God—Atahuallpa, Son of the Sun. The two leaders are fascinated with each other. When cautioned against blasphemy in this duel of rank, Pizarro exclaims, "He is a God: I am a God."

Young Martin's faith in his hero and their cause is challenged when the Spanish massacre three thousand unarmed Inca warriors and capture Atahuallpa. Hernando de Soto gives the boy the stock rationale for the "huntsmen of God": "There must always be dying to make new life." Young Martin replaces a treacherous native translator for Pizarro and Atahuallpa and witnesses their growing kinship. The thirty-three-year-old Inca ruler learns Spanish and swordsmanship from his sixty-year-old captor. In return, Atahuallpa teaches Pizarro Inca songs and dances as the subdued empire collects gold to ransom its god-king.

Once the ransom is paid, Pizarro demands that Atahuallpa pledge that the Spanish will have safe passage out of Peru. He refuses, and Pizarro's officers insist that Atahuallpa must die. Though he himself has found no special meaning in his mother Church, Pizarro persuades the Inca to accept Christian baptism. Without it, he would be burned to ashes. The god-king does not fear death; he believes his Father Sun will resurrect him. By accepting the rites of the Spanish Church, he earns death by strangulation and will leave a body to be restored.

There is no resurrection. Pizarro, however, weeps for his personal loss for the first time in his life and takes solace in the humanistic observation that at least Atahuallpa and he will be buried in the same earth under the same sun.

For Young Martin, Pizarro's betrayal of Atahuallpa is the end of faith: "Devotion never came again." Thus, Shaffer poses the high personal cost of trusting individuals and institutions further than they merit. The conquest was possible because Church and State accepted each other as justifications for destroying competing systems—and both fed on human greed and ambition. The Inca empire fell because its supreme ruler was convinced of his own divinity and was fascinated by the invader's claim of equal status. He never ordered a significant counterattack.

Shaffer gives a macrocosmic study of worship through the conflict of whole systems in *The Royal Hunt of the Sun*, with glimpses of the personal cost of faith in such systems in the lives of Atahuallpa, Pizarro, and Young Martin. *Equus*, by contrast, provides a detailed microcosmic study of the elements of worship. Seventeen-year-old Alan Strang has blinded six horses in the stable where he works. Hester Salomon, a magistrate and friend of psychiatrist Martin Dysart, brings the boy to Dysart for treatment. The psychoanalyst uncovers, little by little, the attitudes and symbols Alan has fashioned into a mysterious personal religion—worship of Equus, the horse-god.

Alan Strang is more than the average troubled adolescent of the usual domestic drama. He is the most isolated, most disturbed of all Shaffer's characters. The son of a printer and former schoolteacher, Alan is practically illiterate. His father forbids television in the home, so Alan sneaks off to watch Westerns at the neighbors' house. An avowed atheist, Frank Strang considers the religious instruction Dora gives to Alan just so much "bad sex." Dora, for her part, assures Alan that God sees him everywhere; she has read the Bible to him often. Alan especially enjoyed passages from Job and Revelation which refer to the strength and power of horses. Not wanting to interfere with her son, Dora allowed him to have a graphic poster of Christ being flogged by Roman centurions even though she believed it was a little "extreme." After an argument over religion, Frank once stormed into Alan's room and ripped the poster off the wall. Alan was devastated. A few weeks later, Frank gave Alan a picture of a horse, which Alan hung in the same spot at the foot of his bed. Frank once observed Alan chanting a genealogy, haltering himself with string, and beating himself with a coathanger before the horse picture. Frank never discussed sex with his son; Dora did so only in generalities which linked it with the love of God.

Shaffer opens both the first and second acts of *Equus* with Dysart pondering what the horse might want of Alan, and why, of all the things in the world "equal in their power to enslave . . . one suddenly strikes." When Dysart questions the propriety of "curing" Alan, whose exotic worship is "the core of his life," Hester Salomon assures the doctor that the boy must be relieved of his pain and helped to normal living. Expert in his profession, Dysart knows what he must do in order to lead the minds of troubled children into normal patterns, but he is himself led back to the borders of the rational, sensing something vital beyond: "that boy has known a passion more ferocious than I have felt in any second of my life. . . . I envy it."

The self-disclosure integral to Shaffer's drama, which built the dialogue and plot of *Five Finger Exercise* and which became a structural device as well via the narrator in *The Royal Hunt of the Sun*, rises to full force in *Equus*. Dysart is both narrator and protagonist. He relates the numerous episodes which present and then unravel the mystery of Alan's attack on the horses. Through his speeches to the audience about the plot and through his confidences shared with Hester Salomon as the protagonist within the action, Dysart exposes his own character, just as he exposes Alan's. Shaffer's use of games—which appears in the follow-the-leader ploy of *The Public Eye*, the pretended shock-treatment scene of *Shrivings*, and so on—is important in *Equus* as well. As Dysart elicits one disclosure after another from Alan, the boy extracts significant answers from Dysart in return. The methods of revelation become more intimate as the plot advances. Alan at first sings commercials when Dysart asks questions. He later divulges information via tape recordings. He finally responds in direct encounters, first with resistance, then relying on supposed hypnosis, and finally under the pretended use of a truth drug which allows him to reenact the events of the night he attacked the horses.

Alan had been out with Jill Mason, who suggested a tryst in the stable—the Holy of Holies for Equus. Alan's worship was so exclusive that his god blocked intimacy with any other. Caught between passion for another human being and passion for his horse-god—which, like his mother's God, could see him everywhere—Alan struck out to blind the god who thwarted his relationship with Jill Mason.

Martin Dysart concludes that he can lead Alan into a normal existence, but it will probably be a drab, routine life. He himself remains drawn to the nonrational source of human passion: "I need—more desperately than my children need me—a way of seeing in the dark." His need is marked with a remnant of the worship he is taking away from Alan; "There is now, in my mouth, this sharp chain. And it never comes out."

For Pizarro, the late attraction of a meaningful, dominating force appeared and died with Atahuallpa, a confident believer in an alien faith, but a faith with numerous parallels to the Christian tradition familiar to the conquistador. Pizarro had used his own religious heritage as a weapon for so long that he could only hope for meaning among a new set of symbols enlivened by a personal contact with the god-king the symbols supported. Martin Dysart's relationship with his patient also draws him into confrontation with passionate worship. The motion from Pizarro to Dysart, however, is an ideological step from a protagonist who concludes that human beings make their own gods to one who can destroy a god and still sense some force beyond human reason that endures regardless of whether the belief-system of a given worshiper is destroyed. Shaffer's next protagonist steps further into premises consistent with those of the Judeo-Christian tradition.

Antonio Salieri continues Shaffer's trend of self-disclosing characters by serving as both narrator and protagonist of *Amadeus*. Old Martin and Young Martin in *The Royal Hunt of the Sun* give the narrator's view and the more passionate view of Pizarro's page, respectively, and are cast as separate characters who both may be onstage at once. Dysart serves as narrator and protagonist in turn for *Equus*, not needing a distinction in age for the separate facets of the character, because the story Dysart tells took place in the recent past. His explanations and deliberations unify the flow of cinematic scenes, which include recent events retold from Dysart's viewpoint and flashbacks to some more distant events in Alan's past. Salieri, too, serves as both narrator and protagonist, but he must bridge a temporal gap of decades, as must Old Martin. Shaffer keeps Salieri a single character, similar to Dysart, but has Salieri change costume onstage and specify the shifts in time—covering two different eras in his life through changes in the character before the eyes of the audience. The transitions are yet one more method for effecting character revelation without simply repeating a narrative technique.

Salieri is Shaffer's first protagonist to operate so nearly within traditional premises of religious devotion. Salieri interacts with a God anthropomorphic enough to respond to his prayers—but a deity shaped by the Salieri family's mercantile values. In his youth, Salieri knelt "before the God of Bargains" and prayed to be a composer. In return, he would live virtuously, help other musicians, and "honor God with much music." Mozart's appearance in Vienna threatens the established Salieri's self-esteem. Mozart the man is rash, vulgar, and obnoxious. For all the faults of the man, however, Salieri hears the voice of God in some of Mozart's music. He prays for such inspiration in his own work, since "music is God's art," but to no avail.

Salieri's star voice pupil, Katherina Cavalieri, sings the lead in Mozart's opera *The Abduction from the Seraglio* and has an affair with him as well. A jealous Salieri considers seducing Mozart's fiancée, Constanze, in revenge. Mozart marries Constanze, despite his father's objections, and struggles to support himself and his wife. Constanze Mozart approaches Salieri for help in securing an appointment for her husband. Salieri nearly exacts her virtue as the price for any assistance, but in the musical scores she has brought to further her husband's cause, Salieri has seen Absolute Beauty. He recognizes his own mediocrity and rages at his God, "To my last breath, I shall block You on earth as far as I am able!"

Narrator Salieri introduces act 2 as his "battle with God" in which "Mozart was the battleground." Salieri soon breaks his vow of virtue. Although he turns away a resentful offer of an interlude with Constanze, he takes Katherina Cavalieri as his mistress. Breaking his vow to help fellow musicians, he hinders Mozart's career whenever possible. He recommends that Mozart not be appointed to tutor the Princess Elizabeth. He does suggest that Mozart be appointed chamber composer after the death of Christoph Gluck—but at one tenth the former salary. Salieri is determined to "starve out the God." As Mozart thinks through the plot of *The Magic Flute*, Salieri raises the notion of using the rites and ideals of the Masonic order in the opera. The two composers were among many notables in Vienna who belonged to the lodge. As all the rituals and doctrines are to be kept secret, Mozart's stage parallels of Masonic practices alienate the very lodge brothers who have helped him to find what work he can get.

Alone and ailing, Mozart begs God for time to complete his *Requiem Mass*. He asks Salieri to speak for God and to explain the continual suffering of his adult years. Salieri declares, "God does not love! He can only use!"

Salieri lives to see Mozart's music come into vogue after the composer's death. His own music dies before he does. He takes this as his punishment; "I must survive to see myself become extinct." His claim to be Mozart's murderer is his last attack on God. If his fame cannot last, perhaps his infamy can. Even so negative a grasping for glory proves vain: No one really believes him.

Salieri's actions are reminiscent of those of the ancient Hebrew heroes who were held to covenants with their God. Salieri's assertion that his virtue merits blessing while Mozart's vices deserve punishment echoes a plaint recurrent in the Psalms. The pattern of Israel's God favoring the unworthy or the unlikely candidate for leadership—the naïve Gideon, the young shepherd David, and so on—also has its reflex in *Amadeus* as the esteemed court composer finds the voice of God in the music of an immature, foulmouthed upstart. In a sense, Salieri also is a failed Cain. Jealous of God's favor to Mozart regardless of all of Salieri's musical and moral efforts, the aging narrator cannot even secure for himself the name of murderer. The biblical Cain bore a mark to signify his archetypal fratricide. Salieri cannot even invent the curse for himself. His God of Bargains wins the battle. Salieri gets no more and no less than he asked for when the bargain was struck, and he is punished for failing to keep his part of the covenant.

Thus, the trend of character revelation begun in the Harrington household persists. The issues of self-control versus domination by authority are broached from varying perspectives, institutional and individual, as Shaffer moves from a protagonist searching for self, through others searching for meaningful relationships with individuals, to characters exploring the human being's relationship to the structures and forces of the world at large. From *The Royal Hunt of the Sun* to *Shrivings* (which probes the limits of secular humanism as thoroughly as other plays challenge aspects of traditional religion) and on through *Equus* and *Amadeus*, Shaffer's protagonists become more overtly self-revealing and steadily more concerned with a focused search for meaning. Shaffer's mature use of a character's personal disclosures culminates in the award-winning cinematic narratives of *Equus* and *Amadeus*, in which there is a great passion to pursue, and in which the revelation of character shapes form, theme, and technique all at once.

Other major works

NOVELS: *Woman in the Wardrobe*, 1951 (with Anthony Shaffer, together as Peter Antony); *How Doth the Little Crocodile?*, 1952 (with Anthony Shaffer, together as Peter Antony); *Withered Murder*, 1955 (with Anthony Shaffer).

SCREENPLAYS: *The Public Eye*, 1972; *Equus*, 1977; *Amadeus*, 1984.

TELEPLAYS: *The Salt Land*, 1955; *Balance of Terror*, 1957.

RADIO PLAY: *The Prodigal Father*, 1955.

Bibliography

Beckerman, Bernard. "The Dynamics of Peter Shaffer's Drama." In *The Play and Its Critic: Essays for Eric Bentley*, edited by Michael Bertin.

Lanham, Md.: University Press of America, 1986. A structural study, especially of *Equus*, by one of the best dramatic critics of the twentieth century. Examines Shaffer's "binary form . . . the tendency of plays to be a sequence of scenes between two characters" in his work. This essay was originally given in 1983, in Shaffer's presence, at the Modern Language Association (MLA) convention in New York.

Cooke, Virginia, and Malcolm Page, comps. *File on Shaffer*. London: Methuen, 1987. An indispensable source of information in the Methuen series format. Contains brief comments, play by play (not including, however, *Lettice and Lovage*), and Shaffer's own comments on his methods of work, sedulous rewrites, film adaptations, and more. The production dates and publication information are more accessible here than in Eberle Thomas' work (below).

Plunka, Gene A. *Peter Shaffer: Roles, Rites, and Rituals in the Theatre*. Rutherford, N.J.: Fairleigh Dickinson University Press, 1988. Disappointing in the absence of coverage of later plays, but strong on *The Royal Hunt of the Sun*, *Equus*, and *Amadeus*. This work is part sociology and part mythology, and it is fed by an interview with the playwright in 1986. It contains occasional insights but is generally too scholarly to get at the essence of Shaffer's examination of the ways of God to humankind.

Taylor, John Russell. *Peter Shaffer*. London: Longman, 1974. A brief but provocative essay on Shaffer's contributions through *Equus*. Taylor sees detachment in this work and "a tendency to analyze emotions without too far engaging himself in them as a dramatist." He concludes, however, that "there is no guessing what he can do next, but it seems inevitable that it will be grand and glorious," a foresight of *Amadeus* and *Lettice and Lovage*. Select bibliography.

Thomas, Eberle. *Peter Shaffer: An Annotated Bibliography*. New York: Garland, 1991. A thorough checklist of work on Shaffer, from full-length studies (four) to dissertations and theses (six), to individual studies of plays through *Lettice and Lovage*. The introduction outlines the scope of the book and notes the paucity of biographical information on this private playwright, "the most widely produced and most popular of England's playwrights during the post-World War II era." A general chronology follows, but exact production information is found at each play's entry. Page-number index.

Ralph S. Carlson
(Updated by *Thomas J. Taylor*)

WILLIAM SHAKESPEARE

Born: Stratford-upon-Avon, England; April 23, 1564
Died: Stratford-upon-Avon, England; April 23, 1616

Principal drama

Henry VI, Part I, wr. 1589-1590, pr. 1592, pb. 1623; *Henry VI, Part II*, pr. c. 1590-1591, pb. 1594; *Henry VI, Part III*, pr. c. 1590-1591, pb. 1595; *Richard III*, pr. c. 1592-1593, pb. 1597 (revised 1623); *The Comedy of Errors*, pr. c. 1592-1594, pb. 1623; *The Taming of the Shrew*, pr. c. 1593-1594, pb. 1623; *Titus Andronicus*, pr., pb. 1594; *The Two Gentlemen of Verona*, pr. c. 1594-1595, pb. 1623; *Love's Labour's Lost*, pr. c. 1594-1595 (revised 1597 for court performance), pb. 1598; *Romeo and Juliet*, pr. c. 1595-1596, pb. 1597; *Richard II*, pr. c. 1595-1596, pb. 1600; *A Midsummer Night's Dream*, pr. c. 1595-1596, pb. 1600; *King John*, pr. c. 1596-1597, pb. 1623; *The Merchant of Venice*, pr. c. 1596-1597, pb. 1600; *Henry IV, Part I*, pr. c. 1597-1598, pb. 1598; *The Merry Wives of Windsor*, pr. 1597 (revised c. 1600-1601), pb. 1602; *Henry IV, Part II*, pr. 1598, pb. 1600; *Much Ado About Nothing*, pr. c. 1598-1599, pb. 1600; *Henry V*, pr. c. 1598-1599, pb. 1600; *Julius Caesar*, pr. c. 1599-1600, pb. 1623; *As You Like It*, pr. c. 1599-1600, pb. 1623; *Hamlet, Prince of Denmark*, pr. c. 1600-1601, pb. 1603; *Twelfth Night: Or, What You Will*, pr. c. 1600-1602, pb. 1623; *Troilus and Cressida*, pr. c. 1601-1602, pb. 1609; *All's Well That Ends Well*, pr. c. 1602-1603, pb. 1623; *Othello, the Moor of Venice*, pr. 1604, pb. 1622 (revised 1623); *Measure for Measure*, pr. 1604, pb. 1623; *King Lear*, pr. c. 1605-1606, pb. 1608; *Macbeth*, pr. 1606, pb. 1623; *Antony and Cleopatra*, pr. c. 1606-1607, pb. 1623; *Coriolanus*, pr. c. 1607-1608, pb. 1623; *Timon of Athens*, pr. c. 1607-1608, pb. 1623; *Pericles, Prince of Tyre*, pr. c. 1607-1608, pb. 1609; *Cymbeline*, pr. c. 1609-1610, pb. 1623; *The Winter's Tale*, pr. c. 1610-1611, pb. 1623; *The Tempest*, pr. 1611, pb. 1623; *The Two Noble Kinsmen*, pr. c. 1612-1613, pb. 1634 (with John Fletcher); *Henry VIII*, pr. 1613, pb. 1623 (with Fletcher).

Other literary forms

William Shakespeare's two long erotic poems, *The Rape of Lucrece* (1594) and *Venus and Adonis* (1593), are in the tradition established by Ovid (*Metamorphoses*, c. A.D. 8). He had been working on them for some time before deciding to publish them during a lull in stage production caused by the plague. The poems are carefully corrected and were probably taken to the printer by Shakespeare himself. They are prefaced by dedications to Henry Wriothesley, the Earl of Southampton, a man from whom Shakespeare hoped to receive patronage. No evidence exists that full support was forthcoming; Shakespeare was forced to return to acting and playwriting in order to earn a living. The *Sonnets* (1609) were no doubt composed at various times throughout Shakespeare's career between 1593 and 1599. Although not of uniform excellence, several of the 154 poems, each of which can stand alone but which together make up a sequence or rough story, are classic examples of Elizabethan love poetry. The first 126 sonnets are addressed to a young man (various contemporary figures have been proposed as contenders, most notably the Earl of Southampton), whom Shakespeare urges to marry and produce "copies" of his beauty. A dark-haired woman, the Dark Lady, is addressed in sonnets 127 through 152; her attractiveness and potential to deceive are central themes in this group. (The last two sonnets fall into neither group.) In both major groups of sonnets, Shakespeare dramatizes a triangular affair, with the "I" of the poems represented as one who is deceived first by his mistress and later by a friend. Although the sonnets have been minutely examined for evidence of Shakespeare's personal life, they provide no direct clues about the identity of his friend or of the Dark Lady. Three other poems, *The Phoenix and the Turtle* (1601), *A Lover's Complaint* (1609), and *The Passionate Pilgrim* (1599), are now attributed to Shakespeare; of these, *The Phoenix and the Turtle* reveals the skill in design and use of imagery that has come to be associated with the playwright.

Achievements

Few dramatists can lay claim to the universal reputation achieved by Shakespeare. His plays have been translated into many languages and performed on amateur and professional stages throughout the world. Radio, television, and film versions of the plays in English, German, Russian, French, and Japanese have been heard and seen by millions of people. The plays have been revived and reworked by many prominent producers and playwrights, and they have directly influenced the work of others. Novelists and dramatists such as Charles Dickens, Bertolt Brecht, William Faulkner, and Tom Stoppard, inspired by Shakespeare's plots, characters, and poetry, have composed works that attempt to re-create the spirit and style of the originals and to interpret the plays in the light of their own ages. A large and flourishing Shakespeare industry exists in England, America, Japan, and Germany, giving evidence of the playwright's popularity among scholars and laypersons alike.

Evidence of the widespread and deep effect of Shakespeare's plays on English and American culture can be found in the number of words and phrases from them that have become embedded in everyday usage: Expressions such as "yeoman's service" are used by speakers of English with no consciousness of their Shakespearean sources. It is difficult to imagine what the landscape of the English language would be like without the mountain of neologisms and aphorisms contributed by the playwright. Writing at a time when English was still pliable, Shakespeare's linguistic facility and poetic sense transformed English into a richly metaphoric tongue.

Working as a popular playwright, Shakespeare was also instrumental in fusing the materials of native and classical drama in his work. *Hamlet*, with its revenge theme, its ghost, and its bombastic set speeches, appears to be a tragedy based on the style of the Roman playwright Seneca (first century). Yet the hero's struggle with his conscience and his deep concern over the disposition of his soul reveal the play's roots in the native soil of English miracle and mystery dramas. The product of this fusion is a tragedy that compels spectators and readers to examine their own deepest emotions as they ponder the effects of treacherous murder on individuals and the state. Except for Christopher Marlowe, the predecessor to whom Shakespeare owes a considerable debt, no other Elizabethan playwright was so successful in combining native and classical strains.

Shakespearean characters, many of whom are hybrids, are so vividly realized that they seem to have achieved a life independent of the worlds they inhabit. Hamlet stands as the symbol of a man who, in Sir Laurence Olivier's words, "could not make up his mind." His name has likewise become synonymous with excessive rationalizing and idealism. Othello's jealousy, Lear's madness, Macbeth's ambition, Romeo and Juliet's star-crossed love, Shylock's flinty heart—all of these characters and the psychic states they represent have become familiar landmarks in Western culture. Their lifelikeness can be attributed to Shakespeare's talent for creating the illusion of reality in mannerisms and styles of speech. His use of the soliloquy is especially important in fashioning this illusion; the characters are made to seem fully rounded human beings in the representation of their inner as well as their outer natures. Shakespeare's keen ear for conversational rhythms and his ability to reproduce believable speech between figures of high and low social rank also contribute to the liveliness of action and characters.

In addition, Shakespeare excels in the art of grasping the essence of relationships between husbands and wives, lovers, parents and children, and friends. Innocence and youthful exuberance are aptly represented in the fatal love of Romeo and Juliet; the destructive spirit of mature and intensely emotional love is caught in the affair between Antony and Cleopatra. Other relationships reveal the psychic control of one person by another (of Macbeth by Lady Macbeth), the corrupt soul of a seducer (Angelo in *Measure for Measure*), the twisted mind of a vengeful officer (Iago), and the warm fellowship of simple men (Bottom and his followers in *A Midsummer Night's Dream*). The range of emotional states manifested in Shakespeare's characters has never been equaled by succeeding dramatists.

These memorable characters have also been given memorable poetry to speak. Indeed, one of the main strengths of Shakespearean drama is its synthesis of action and poetry. While Shakespeare's poetic style is marked by the bombast and hyperbole that characterize much of Elizabethan drama, it also has a richness and concreteness that make it memorable and quotable. One need think only of Hamlet's "sea of troubles" or Macbeth's daggers "unmannerly breech'd with gore" to substantiate the imagistic power of Shakespearean verse. Such images are also worked into compelling patterns in the major plays, giving them greater structural unity than the plots alone provide. Disease imagery in *Hamlet*, repeated references to blood in *Macbeth*, and allusions to myths of children devouring parents in *King Lear* represent only a few of the many instances of what has been called "reiterated imagery" in Shakespearean drama. Word play, puns, songs, and a variety of verse forms, from blank verse to tetrameter couplets—these features, too, contribute to the "movable feast" of Shakespeare's style.

In a more general sense, Shakespeare's achievement can be traced to the skill with which he used his medium—the stage. He created certain characters to fit the abilities of certain actors, as the role of Falstaff so vividly demonstrates. He made use of every facet of the physical stage—the trapdoor, the second level, the inner stage, the "heavens"—to create special effects or illusions. He kept always before him the purpose of entertaining his audience, staying one step ahead of changes in taste among theatergoers. That both kings and tinkers were able to find in a Shakespearean play something to delight and instruct them is testimony to the wide appeal of the playwright. No doubt the universality of his themes and his deep understanding of human nature combined to make his plays so popular. These same strengths generate the magnetic power that brings large audiences into theaters to see the plays today.

Biography

William Shakespeare was born in Stratford-upon-Avon, England, on April 23, 1564. His father was John Shakespeare, a glovemaker and later bailiff (or mayor) of the town; his mother was Mary Arden, the daughter of a well-to-do landowner in nearby Wilmcote. His parents had eight children; William was the oldest. Although no records exist to prove the fact, Shakespeare probably began attending a Stratford grammar school at six or seven years of age. There, he studied Latin grammar, literature, rhetoric, and logic for between eight and ten hours a day, six days a week. William Lily's largely Latin text, *A Short Introduction of Grammar* (1527), was the staple of the course, but Shakespeare also read Cicero, Plautus, Terence, Vergil, and Ovid. Many of these authors influenced the playwright's later work; Ovid in particular was a favorite source of material, used in such plays as *A Midsummer Night's Dream* and *Romeo and Juliet*. Shakespeare probably knew very little of other languages, although he does exhibit an understanding of French in such plays as *Henry V* and *All's Well That Ends Well.* (The sources for most, if not all, of the plays existed in English translations published during Shakespeare's lifetime.)

Shakespeare may have left school around 1577, the year in which his father fell on hard times. Legend says the young man worked as a butcher's apprentice, but there is no proof to support this notion. His marriage to Anne Hathaway of Shottery took place in 1582; she was eight years his senior and pregnant at the time of the wedding. Whether Shakespeare felt obliged to marry her or simply took pity on her unfortunate predicament is yet another matter for speculation. Their first child, Susanna, was born in May, 1583, and in 1585, twins named Hamnet and Judith were born to the young couple. (It is interesting to note that by 1670, the last of Susanna's descendants died, thereby ending the Shakespeare family line.)

There is no evidence concerning Shakespeare's activities between 1585 and 1592. Legend asserts that he was forced to leave Stratford in order to escape punishment for poaching deer on the estate of Sir Thomas Lucy, one of Stratford's leading citizens. Another popular story has Shakespeare taking a position as schoolmaster at the grammar school, where he supposedly improved his Latin. None of these accounts can be substantiated by fact, yet they continue to seduce modern readers and playgoers. One intriguing suggestion is that Shakespeare joined a troupe of professional actors that was passing through Stratford in 1587. This company, called the Queen's Men, may have been in need of a new performer, since one of their members, William Knell, had been murdered in a brawl with a fellow actor.

In 1592, Robert Greene, a playwright and pamphleteer, attested Shakespeare's presence in London in a sneering remark about the young upstart whose "tiger's heart [is] wrapped in a player's hide." This reference is a parody of a line from one of Shakespeare's earliest plays, *Henry VI, Part III.* Greene's "Shake-scene in a country" is clearly Shakespeare, who by this date was identifiable as both an actor and a playwright. Greene's remark also implies that the uneducated upstart had probably served an apprenticeship of a few years revising old plays, a practice that was common in this period. By 1594, Shakespeare had become a member of the Lord Chamberlain's Men, who were then performing at the Theatre in Shoreditch, to the north of the city. He continued as a member of this essentially stable company, which constructed the Globe Theatre in 1599 and, in 1603, became the King's Men, until he retired from the stage in 1611 or 1612. In part because of the popularity of Shakespeare's plays and in part because of the strong support of Elizabeth and James I, the company achieved considerable financial success. Shakespeare shared in that success by acquiring a one-tenth interest in the corporation. By 1596, he was able to purchase a coat of arms for his father, and in the next year, he acquired the second-best house in Stratford. This degree of prominence and success was unusual for someone in a profession that was not highly regarded in Renaissance England. Robert Greene, Shakespeare's harsh critic, died a pauper, a condition that was typical of many Elizabethan playwrights.

Actors and playwrights were in fact regarded as entertainers whose companions were bearbaiters, clowns, and jugglers. Confirmation of this fact comes from evidence that some public theaters were used both for plays and for bearbaiting and bullbaiting. After 1590, moreover, the playhouses had to be constructed in the Bankside district, across the Thames from London proper. City fathers afraid of plague and opposed to public entertainments felt that the Bankside, notorious for its boisterous inns and houses of prostitution, was the fitting locale for "playing" of all kinds. Indeed, theatrical productions were not regarded as high art; when plays were published, by the company or by individual actors, apparently no effort was made to correct or improve them. As has already been pointed out, Shakespeare himself never corrected or took to the printer any of the thirty-eight plays attributed to him. Poetry was valued as true literature, and there is considerable evidence that Shakespeare hoped to become a recognized and respected poet like Sir Philip Sidney or Edmund Spenser. His economic background and lack of formal education, however, combined to close that avenue of fame to him. He had instead to become a public entertainer, a role that he played with convincing brilliance.

The company to which this best of the entertainers belonged was relatively small—fifteen or twenty players at most. The actors were generally well-known to the audience, and their particular talents were exploited by the playwrights. Richard Burbage, the manager of Shakespeare's company for many years, was renowned for his skill in acting tragic parts, while William Kemp and Robert Armin were praised for their talents as comic actors. Shakespeare composed his plays with these actors in mind, a fact borne out by the many comedies featuring fat, drunken men such as Sir John Falstaff and Sir Toby Belch. Shakespeare could not compose his works for an ideal company; he suited his style to the available talent.

Since his company was underwritten to some degree by the government, Shakespeare and his fellows were often called upon to perform at court— thirty-two times during Elizabeth's reign, 177 times under James I. The king and queen did not venture to the Theatre or Globe to mingle with the lower classes, depending instead on the actors to bring their wares to them. Plays such as *A Midsummer Night's Dream*, *Twelfth Night*, and *Macbeth* were composed for court performance at a wedding, on a holiday, and during a state visit, respectively. *Macbeth* was written as a direct compliment to James I: Banquo, the brave general treacherously murdered by the villain-hero, was one of James's ancestors. Shakespeare had to change the facts of history to pay the compliment, but the aim of pleasing his and the company's benefactor justified the change.

There were no women actors on Shakespeare's stage; they made their appearance when Charles II returned to the throne in 1660. Young boys (eleven to fourteen years old) played the female parts, and Shakespeare manipulated this convention with considerable success in his comedies, where disguises created delightful complications and aided him in overcoming the problem of costuming. The lady-disguised-as-page device is worked with particular effect in such plays as *As You Like It, Twelfth Night,* and *Cymbeline.*

Since there were few actors and sometimes many parts, members of the company were required to double (and sometimes triple) their roles. The effect of this requirement becomes evident when one notes that certain principal characters do not appear in consecutive scenes. One should likewise remember that performance on the Elizabethan stage was continuous; there was no falling curtain or set change to interrupt the action. No scenery to speak of was employed, although signs may have been used to designate cities or countries, and branches may have been tied around pillars to signify trees. The absence of scenery allowed for a peculiar imaginative effect: A place on the stage that had been a throne room could within a few seconds become a hovel hiding its inhabitants from a fierce storm. Shakespeare and his contemporaries could thereby demonstrate the slippery course of Fortune, whose wheel, onstage and in real life, might turn at any moment to transform kings into beggars.

The apronlike stage jutted out into an area called "the pit," where the groundlings, or those who paid the lowest admission fee (a penny), could stand to watch heroes perform great deeds. The octagonal-shaped building had benches on the two levels above the pit for customers willing to pay for the privilege of sitting. Although estimates vary, it is now generally believed that the Globe could accommodate approximately twenty-five hundred people. The design of the stage probably evolved from the model of innyards, where the traveling companies of actors performed before they took up residence in London in the 1570's. On either side of the stage were two doors for entrances and exits, and at the back, some kind of inner stage behind which actors could hide and be discovered at the right moment. A trapdoor was located in the middle of the apron stage, while above it was a cupola-like structure that housed a pulley and chair. This chair could be lowered to the stage level when a *deus ex machina* was required to resolve the action. This small house also contained devices for making sound effects and may have been the place from which the musicians, so much a part of Elizabethan drama, sent forth their special harmonies. The little house was called "the heavens" (stars may have been painted on its underside), while the trapdoor was often referred to as "hell." For Shakespeare's Globe audience, then, the stage was a world in which the great figures of history and imagination were represented doing and speaking momentous things.

In 1608, the King's Men purchased an indoor theater, the Blackfriars, which meant that the company could perform the year-round. This theater was located within the city proper, which meant that a somewhat more sophisticated audience attended the plays. Seating capacity (there was no pit to stand in) was approximately seven hundred, and there is some evidence that the stage machinery was more elaborate than the equipment at the Globe. This fact has led some critics to argue that plays written after 1608—*Cymbeline, Pericles, Prince of Tyre, The Winter's Tale, The Tempest*—were composed especially for performance at the Blackfriars. These tragicomedies or romances teem with special effects and supernatural characters, and this emphasis on spectacle differentiates them from Shakespeare's earlier comedies. While such a theory is attractive, at least a few of these plays were also performed at the supposedly "primitive" Globe.

By 1608, Shakespeare had achieved the fame and recognition for which he had no doubt hoped. He was in a position to reduce his output to two plays a year, a schedule that probably allowed him to spend more time in Stratford with his family. In 1611, he left London for Stratford, returning from time to time to see plays performed at both theaters and possibly to engage in collaborative efforts with new playwrights such as John Fletcher. His last play, *Henry VIII*, was a collaboration with Fletcher; it was produced on June 29, 1613, a fateful day for the Globe. A spark from one of the cannon shot off during the performance set the thatched roof on fire and burned the building to the ground.

From 1613 until his death in 1616, Shakespeare led the life of a prosperous citizen in his native town. No doubt the happiest moment of this period came with the marriage of his daughter Judith in 1616. One of the persistent legends about the cause of the playwright's death is that he celebrated too vigorously at the reception with his friends Ben Jonson and Michael Drayton and contracted a fatal fever. Whatever the cause, Shakespeare died on April 23, 1616, and was buried in Holy Trinity Church. His epitaph gives no hint of the poetic strength that marked his plays, but it does express a concern common among men of his age:

> Good friend for Jesus sake forbear
> To dig the dust enclosed here.
> Blessed be the man that spares these stones
> And cursed be he that moves my bones.

Analysis

William Shakespeare began his career as a playwright by experimenting with plays in the three genres—comedy, history, and tragedy—that he would perfect as his career matured. The genre that dominated his attention throughout his early career, however, was history. Interest in the subject as proper stuff for drama was no doubt aroused by England's startling victory over Spain's vaunted Armada in 1588. This victory fed the growing popular desire to see depicted the critical intrigues and battles that had shaped the country's destiny as the foremost Protestant power in Europe. This position of power had been buttressed by the shrewd and ambitious Elizabeth, the virgin queen who, in the popular view, was the flower of the Tudor line. Many critics believe that Shakespeare composed the histories to trace the course of destiny that led to the emergence of the Tudors as England's greatest kings and queens. The strength of character and patriotic spirit exhibited by Elizabeth seem to be foreshadowed by the personality of Henry V, the Lancastrian monarch who was instrumental in building an English empire in France. Since the Tudors traced their line back to the Lancastrians, it was an easy step for Shakespeare to flatter his monarch and please his audiences with nationalistic spectacles that reinforced the belief that England was a promised land.

Whatever his reasons for composing the plays, Shakespeare certainly must be seen as an innovator of the form, for which there was no model in classical or medieval drama. Undoubtedly, he learned much from his immediate predecessors, however, most notably from Christopher Marlowe, whose *Edward II* (pr. c. 1592) treated the subject of a weak king nearly destroying the kingdom through his selfish and indulgent behavior. From Marlowe, Shakespeare also inherited the idea that the purpose of the history play was to vivify the moral dilemmas of power politics and to apply those lessons to contemporary government. That such lessons were heeded by contemporaries is amply illustrated by Elizabeth's remark upon reading about the life of one of her predecessors: "I am Richard II."

Shakespeare's contribution to the history-play genre is represented by two tetralogies (that is, two series of four plays), each covering a period of English history. He wrote two other plays dealing with English kings, *King John* and *Henry VIII*, but they are not specifically connected to the tetralogies in theme or structure. The first tetralogy concerns the period from the death of Henry V in 1422 to the death of Richard III in 1485 at the Battle of Bosworth Field in 1485. Although he probably began this ambitious project in 1588, Shakespeare apparently did not compose the plays according to a strict chronological schedule. *Henry VI, Part I* is generally considered to have been written after the second and third parts of Henry's story; it may also have been a revision of another play. Using details from Raphael Holinshed's *Chronicles of England, Scotland and Ireland* (1577) and Edward Hall's *The Union of the Two Noble and Illustre Families of Lancaster and York* (1548), his chief chronicle sources for the plays in both tetralogies, Shakespeare created in *Henry VI, Part I*, an episodic story of the adventures of Lord Talbot, the patriotic soldier who fought bravely to retain England's empire in France. Talbot fails and is defeated primarily because of a combination of intrigues by men such as the Bishop of Winchester and the indecisiveness of young King Henry VI. Here, as in the other history plays, England appears as the central victim of these human actions, betrayed and abandoned by men attempting to satisfy personal desires at the expense of the kingdom. The characters are generally two-dimensional, and their speeches reveal the excesses of Senecan bombast and hyperbole. Although a few of the scenes involving Talbot and Joan of Arc—as well as Talbot's death scene, in which his demise is made more painful by witnessing a procession bearing his son's corpse—aspire to the level of high drama, the play's characters lack psychological depth, and the plot fails to demonstrate the unity of design that would mark Shakespeare's later history plays. Joan's nature as a strumpet-witch signals the role of other women characters in this tetralogy; Margaret, who will become England's queen, helps to solidify the victory that Joan cleverly achieves at the close of *Henry VI, Part I*. Henry V's French empire is in ruins and England's very soul seems threatened.

Henry VI, Part II represents that threat in the form of what might be called "civil-war clouds." The play focuses on the further degeneration of rule under Henry, whose ill-considered marriage to French Margaret precipitates a power struggle involving the two houses of York and Lancaster. By eliminating wise Duke Humphrey as the chief protector of the king, Margaret in effect seizes control of the throne. In the meantime, however, a rebellion is broached by Jack Cade, the leader of a group of anarchist commoners. This rebellion lends occasion for action and spectacle of the kind that is lacking in *Henry VI, Part I*; it also teaches a favorite Shakespearean lesson: The kingdom's "children" cannot be expected to behave when their "parents" do not. Scenes involving witchcraft, a false miracle, and single combat seem to prove that the country is reverting to a primitive, chaotic state. Though the uprising is finally put down, it provides the excuse for Richard, Duke of York, and his ambitious sons to seize power. York precipitates a vengeful struggle with young Clifford by killing his father; in response, Clifford murders York's youngest son, the Earl of Rutland. These murders introduce the theme of familial destruction, of fathers killing sons, sons killing fathers, which culminates in the brutal assassination of Prince Edward. As *Henry VI, Part III* begins, England's hopes for a strong successor to weak King Henry are dashed on the rocks of ambition and civil war. When Henry himself is murdered, one witnesses the birth of one of Shakespeare's most fascinating villain-heroes, Richard, Duke of Gloucester. Although Richard's brother Edward becomes king and restores an uneasy peace, Shakespeare makes it clear that Richard will emerge as the political force of the future. Richard's driving ambition also appears to characterize the Yorkist cause, which, by contrast with the Lancastrian, can be described as self-destructive on the biblical model of the Cain and Abel story. While one is made to see Richard's wolfish disposition, however, Shakespeare also gives him a superior intellect and wit which help to attract one's attention and interest. Displaying touches of the irony and cruelty that will mark his behavior in *Richard III*, Richard declares at the close of *Henry VI, Part III*: "See how my sword weeps for the poor king's death."

In order to present Richard as an arch-villain, Shakespeare was obliged to follow a description of him that was based on a strongly prejudiced biographical portrait written by Sir Thomas More. More painted Richard as a hunchback with fangs, a beast so cruel that he did not flinch at the prospect of murdering the young princes. To More—and to Shakespeare—Richard must be viewed as another Herod; the imagery of the play also regularly compares him to a boar or hedgehog, beasts that know no restraint. Despite these repulsive features, Richard proves to be a consummate actor, outwitting and outperforming those whom he regards as victims. The most theatrical scene in the play is his wooing of the Lady Anne, who is drawn to him despite the knowledge that he has killed her husband (Prince Edward) and father-in-law, whose corpse she is in the process of accompanying to its grave. Many of the audacious wooing tricks used in this scene suggest that one of the sources for Richard's character is the Vice figure from medieval drama.

Richard III documents the breakneck pace and mounting viciousness of Richard's course to the throne. (Steeplechase imagery recurs throughout, culminating in the picture of Richard as an unseated rider trying desperately to find a mount.) He arranges for the murder of his brother Clarence, turns on former supporters such as Hastings and Buckingham, whom he seemed to be grooming for office, and eventually destroys the innocent princes standing in his path. This latter act of barbarism qualifies as a turning point, since Richard's victories, which have been numerous and easily won, now begin to evaporate at almost the same rate of speed. While Richard moves with freedom and abandon from one bloody deed to another, he is hounded by the former Queen Margaret, who delivers curses and prophecies against him in the hope of satisfying her vengeful desires. She plays the role of a Senecan Fury, even though her words prove feeble against her Machiavellian foe. Retribution finally comes, however, in the character of the Lancastrian Earl of Richmond, who defeats Richard at Bosworth Field. On the eve of the battle, Richard's victims visit his sleep to announce his fall, and for the first time in the play, he experiences a twinge of conscience. Unable to respond by confessing and asking forgiveness, Richard fights fiercely, dying like a wounded animal that is finally cornered. With Richmond's marriage to Elizabeth York, the Wars of the

Roses end, and England looks forward to a prosperous and peaceful future under Henry Richmond, founder of the Tudor line.

Whether Shakespeare wrote *King John* in the period between the first and second tetralogies is not known, but there is considerable support for the theory that he did. In the play, he depicts the career of a monarch who reigned into the twelfth century and who defied papal authority, behavior that made him into something of a Protestant hero for Elizabethans. Shakespeare's John, however, lacks both the dynamism and the charisma of Henry V; he is also guilty of usurping the throne and arranging for the death of the true heir, Arthur. This clouded picture complicates the action and transforms John into a man plagued by guilt. Despite his desire to strengthen England and challenge the supremacy of Rome, John does not achieve either the dimensions of a tragic hero or the sinister quality of a consummate villain; indeed, his death seems anticlimactic.

The strongest personality in the play belongs to Faulconbridge the Bastard, whose satiric commentary on the king's maneuvering gives way to patriotic speeches at the close. Faulconbridge speaks out for Anglo-Saxon pride in the face of foreign challenge, but he has also played the part of satirist-onstage throughout much of the action. Something of the same complexity of character will be seen in Prince Hal, the model fighter and king of the second tetralogy. In *King John*, Shakespeare managed only this one touch of brilliant characterization in an otherwise uninteresting and poorly constructed play. He may have been attempting an adaptation of an earlier chronicle drama.

Shakespeare began writing the second tetralogy, which covers the historical period from 1398 to 1422, in 1595. The first play in this group was *Richard II*, a drama which, like the *Henry VI* series, recounts the follies of a weak king and the consequences of these actions for England. Unlike Henry, however, Richard is a personage with tragic potential; he speaks the language of a poet and possesses a self-dramatizing talent. Richard invites his fall (the fall of princes being a favorite Elizabethan topic that was well represented in the popular *A Mirror for Magistrates*, first published in 1559) by seizing the land of the deceased John of Gaunt to pay for his war preparations against Ireland. This dubious act brings Henry Bolingbroke, Gaunt's son, rushing back from France, where he had been exiled by Richard, for a confrontation with the king. The result of their meeting is Richard's sudden deposition—he gives up the crown almost before he is asked for it—and eventual death, which is so movingly rendered that many critics have been led to describe this as a tragedy rather than a political play. Such a reading must overlook the self-pitying quality in Richard; his actions rarely correspond to the quality of his speech. Yet there has been little disagreement about Shakespeare's achievement in advancing the history-play form by forging a world in which two personalities, one vacillating, the other resourceful, oppose each other in open conflict. *Richard II* likewise qualifies as the first play in which Shakespeare realizes the theme of the fall by means of repeated images comparing England to a garden. Richard, the gardener-king, has failed to attend to pruning; rebels, like choking weeds, grow tall and threaten to blot out the sun. Because Bolingbroke usurps the crown and later arranges for Richard's death, however, he is guilty of watering the garden with the blood of England's rightful—if fool-ish—ruler. The result must inevitably be civil war, which is stirringly proph-esied by the Bishop of Carlisle as the play draws to a close: "The blood of English shall manure the ground,/ And future ages groan for this foul act."

The civil strife that Carlisle predicted escalates in *Henry IV, Part I.* Bolingbroke, now King Henry IV, is planning a crusade in the midst of a serious battle involving rebels in the north and west of Britain. This obliv-iousness to responsibility is clearly motivated by Henry's guilt over the seiz-ing of the crown and Richard's murder. It will take the courage and in-genuity of his son, Prince Hal, the future Henry V, to save England and to restore the order of succession that Shakespeare and his contemporaries saw as the only guarantee of peaceful rule. Thus, *Henry IV, Part I* is really a study of the rise of Hal, who in the opening of the play appears to be a carefree timewaster, content with drinking, gambling, and carousing with a motley group of thieves and braggarts led by the infamous coward Sir John Falstaff. Using a kind of Aristotelian mode of characterization, Shake-speare reveals Hal as a balanced hero who possesses the wit and humanity of Falstaff, without the debilitating drunkenness and ego, and the physical courage and ambition of Henry Hotspur, the son of the Earl of Northum-berland and chief rebel, without his destructive choler and impatience.

The plot of *Henry IV, Part I* advances by means of comparison and con-trast of the court, tavern, and rebel worlds, all of which are shown to be in states of disorder. Hal leaves the tavern world at the end of the second act with an explicit rejection of Falstaff's fleshly indulgence; he rejoins his true father and leads the army in battle against the rebels, who are unable to organize the English, Welsh, and Scottish factions of which they are formed. They seem to be leaderless—and "fatherless." Above all, Hal proves capable of surprising both his own family and the rebels, using his reputation as a madcap to fullest advantage until he is ready to throw off his disguise and defeat the bold but foolish Hotspur at Shrewsbury. This emergence is nicely depicted in imagery associated by Hal himself with the sun (punning on "son") breaking through the clouds when least suspected. Falstaff demonstrates consistency of character in the battle by feigning death; even though Hal allows his old friend to claim the prize of Hotspur's body, one can see the utter bankruptcy of the Falstaffian philosophy of self-preservation.

In *Henry IV, Part II*, the struggle against the rebels continues. Northum-

berland, who failed to appear for the Battle of Shrewsbury because of illness, proves unable to call up the spirit of courage demonstrated by his
dead son. Glendower, too, seems to fade quickly from the picture, like a
dying patient. The main portion of the drama concerns what appears to be
a replay of Prince Hal's reformation. Apparently Shakespeare meant to
depict Hal's acquisition of honor and valor at the close of *Henry IV, Part I*,
while *Part II* traces his education in the virtues of justice and rule. Falstaff
is again the humorous but negative example, although he lacks the
robustness in sin that marked his character in *Part I*. The positive example
or model is the Lord Chief Justice, whose sobriety and sense of responsibility eventually attract Hal to his side. As in *Part I*, Shakespeare adopts a
morality-play structure for depicting the rejection of the "bad" angel (or
false father) and the embracing of the "good" one (or spiritual father) by
the hero. The banishment of Falstaff and his corrupt code takes place during the coronation procession. It is a particularly poignant moment—to
which many critics object, since Hal's harshness seems so uncharacteristic
and overdone—but this scene is well prepared for by Hal's promise, at the
end of act 2 in *Part I*, that he would renounce the world and the flesh at
the proper time. The example of Hal's father, whose crown Hal rashly
takes from his pillow before his death, demonstrates that for the king there
can be no escape from care, no freedom to enjoy the fruits of life. With
the Lord Chief Justice at his side, Hal prepares to enter the almost
monklike role that the kingship requires him to play.

It is this strong and isolated figure that dominates *Henry V*, the play that
may have been written for the opening of the Globe Theatre. (Until 1599,
Shakespeare's company performed at a theater located north of the river in
Shoreditch.) Appropriately enough, the Chorus speaker who opens the
play asks if "this wooden O" can "hold the vasty fields of France," the
scene of much of the epic and episodic action. Hal shows himself to be an
astute politician—he outwits and traps the rebels Scroop, Cambridge, and
Grey—and a heroic leader of men in the battle scenes. His rejection of
Falstaff, whose death is recounted here in tragicomic fashion by Mistress
Quickly, has transformed Hal's character into something cold and unattractive. There is little or no humor in the play. Yet when Hal moves among
his troops on the eve of the Battle of Agincourt, he reveals a depth of
understanding and compassion that helps to humanize his character. His
speeches are masterpieces of political rhetoric, even though Pistol, the
braggart soldier, tries to parody them. "Once more into the breach, dear
friends, once more . . ." is probably one of the best-known prebattle scenes
in the language.

With the defeat of the French at Agincourt, Hal wins an empire for England, strengthening the kingdom that had been so sorely threatened by
the weakness of Richard II. Both tetralogies depict in sharp outline the

pattern of suffering and destruction that results from ineffective leadership. In Henry VII and Henry V, one sees the promise of peace and empire realized through the force of their strong, patriotic identities. At the close of *Henry V*, the hero's wooing of Katherine of France, with its comic touches resulting from her inability to speak English, promises a wedding that will take place in a new garden from which it is hoped man will not again fall. The lesson for the audience seems to be that under Elizabeth, the last Tudor monarch, England has achieved stability and glory, and that this role of European power was foreshadowed by the victories of these earlier heroes. Another clear lesson is that England cannot afford another civil war; some capable and clearly designated successor to Elizabeth must be chosen.

Shakespeare's last drama dealing with English history is *Henry VIII*, which is normally classed with romances such as *The Tempest* and *Cymbeline*. It features none of the military battles typical of earlier history plays, turning instead for its material to the intrigues of Henry's court. The play traces the falls of three famous personages, the Duke of Buckingham, Katharine of Aragon, and Cardinal Wolsey. Both Buckingham and Queen Katharine are innocent victims of fortune, while Wolsey proves to be an ambitious man whose scheming is justly punished. Henry seems blind and self-satisfied through much of the play, which is dominated by pageantry and spectacle, but in his judgment against Wolsey and his salvation of Cranmer, he emerges as something of a force for divine justice. The plot ends with the christening of Elizabeth and a prophecy about England's glorious future under her reign. Shakespeare's audience knew, however, that those atop Fortune's Wheel at the close—Cranmer and Anne Bullen, in particular—would soon be brought down like the others. This last of his English history plays, then, sounds a patriotic but also an ironic note.

Of the thirty-eight plays that are wholly or partly attributed to Shakespeare, seventeen are comedies. In addition, many scenes in plays such as *Henry IV, Part I* and *Romeo and Juliet* feature comic characters and situations. Even in the major tragedies, one finds scenes of comic relief: the Porter scene in *Macbeth*, the encounters between the Fool and Lear in *King Lear*, Hamlet's inventive punning and lugubrious satire. There can be little doubt that Shakespeare enjoyed creating comic situations and characters and that audiences came to expect such fare on a regular basis from the playwright.

In his first attempt in the form, *The Comedy of Errors*, Shakespeare turned to a source—Plautus, the Roman playwright—with which he would have become familiar at Stratford's grammar school. Based on Plautus' *Menaechmi* (second century B.C.), the comedy depicts the misadventures of twins who, after several incidents involving mistaken identity, finally meet and are reunited. The twin brothers are attended by twin servants, compounding the possibilities for humor growing out of mistaken identity. Considerable buffoonery and slapstick characterize the main action involving the twins—both named Antipholus—and their servants. In one hilarious scene, Antipholus of Ephesus is turned away from his own house by a wife who believes he is an impostor. This somewhat frivolous mood is tempered by the presence of the twins' father in the opening and closing scenes. At the play's opening, Egeon is sentenced to death by the Duke of Ephesus unless someone can pay a ransom set at a thousand marks. Egeon believes that his wife and sons are dead, which casts him deep into the pit of despair. By the play's close, Egeon has been saved from the duke's sentence and has been reunited with his wife, who has spent the many years of their separation as an abbess. This happy scene of reunion and regeneration strikes a note that will come to typify the resolutions of later Shakespearean comedy. Providence appears to smile on those who suffer yet remain true to the principle of family.

Shakespeare also unites the act of unmasking with the concept of winning a new life in the fifth act of *The Comedy of Errors*. Both Antipholus of Syracuse, who in marrying Luciana is transformed into a "new man," and Dromio of Ephesus, who is freed to find a new life, acquire new identities at the conclusion. The characters are, however, largely interchangeable and lacking in individualizing traits. Types rather than full-blown human beings people the world of the play, thus underscoring the theme of supposing or masking. Shakespeare offers a gallery of familiar figures—young lovers, a pedantic doctor, a kitchen maid, merchants, and a courtesan—all of whom are identified by external traits. They are comic because they behave in predictably mechanical ways: Dr. Pinch, the mountebank based on Plautus' *medicus* type, is a good example of this puppetlike caricaturing. The verse is designed to suit the speaker and occasion, but it also reveals Shakespeare's range of styles; blank verse, prose, rhymed stanzas, and alternating rhymed lines can be found throughout the play. This first effort in dramatic comedy was an experiment using numerous Plautine elements, but it also reveals, in the characters Egeon and Emilia, the playwright's talent for humanizing even the most typical of characters and for creating life and vigor in stock situations.

In *The Taming of the Shrew*, Shakespeare turned to another favorite source for the theme of transformation: Ovid's *Metamorphoses*. He had already used this collection for his erotic poems *Venus and Adonis* and *The Rape of Lucrece*; now he plundered it for stories about pairs of lovers and the changes effected in their natures by the power of love. In *The Taming of the Shrew*, he was also improving upon an earlier play which dealt with the theme of taming as a means of modifying human behavior. Petruchio changes Kate's conduct by regularly praising her "pleasant, gamesome" nature; by the end of the play, she has been tamed into behaving like a dutiful wife. (Her sister Bianca, on the other hand, has many suitors, but her father will not allow Bianca to marry until Kate has found a husband.) The process of taming sometimes involves rough and boisterous treatment—Petruchio withholds food from his pupil, for example—as well as feigned madness: Petruchio whisks his bride away from the wedding site as if she were a damsel in distress and he were playing the role of her rescuer. In the end, Kate turns out to be more pliant than her sister, suggesting that an ideal wife, like a bird trained for the hunt, must be instructed in the rules of the game.

Shakespeare reinforces the theme of transformation by fashioning a subplot featuring a drunken tinker named Christopher Sly, who believes he has been made into a lord during a ruse performed by a fun-loving noble and his fellows. The Sly episode is not resolved, since this interlude ends with the play's first scene, yet by employing this framing device, Shakespeare invites a comparison between Kate and Sly, both of whom are urged to be "better" than they thought they were.

The Two Gentlemen of Verona takes a comic tack that depends less on supposing than on actual disguise. Employing a device he would later perfect in *As You Like It* and *Twelfth Night*, Shakespeare put his heroine Julia in a page's outfit in order to woo her beloved Proteus. The main theme of the comedy is the rocky nature of love as revealed in male friendship and romantic contest. Valentine, Proteus' friend, finds him to be fickle and untrue to the courtly code when Proteus tries to force his affections on Silvia, Valentine's love. Although Proteus deserves worse punishment than he receives, he is allowed to find in Julia the true source of the romantic love which he has been seeking throughout the play. These pairs of lovers and their clownish servants, who engage in frequent bouts of punning and of horseplay, perform their rituals—anatomizing lovers, trusting false companions—in a forest world that seems to work its magic on them by bringing about a happy ending. As in the other festive comedies, *The Two Gentlemen of Verona* concludes with multiple marriages and a mood of inclusiveness that gives even the clowns their proper place in the celebration. The passion of love has led Proteus (whose name symbolizes fickleness) to break oaths and threaten friendships, but in the end, it has also forged a constant love.

After this experiment in romantic or festive, as opposed to bourgeois, comedy, Shakespeare next turned his hand to themes and characters that reflect the madness and magic of love. *Love's Labour's Lost* pokes fun at florid poetry, the "taffeta phrases [and] silken terms precise" that typified Elizabethan love verses. There is also a satiric strain in this play, which depicts the foiled attempt of male characters to create a Platonic Utopia, free of women. The King of Navarre and his court appear ludicrous as, one by one, they violate their vows of abstinence in conceits that gush with sentiment. Even Berowne, the skeptic-onstage, proves unable to resist the temptations of Cupid. As if to underscore the foolishness of their betters, the clowns and fops of this comic world produce an interlude featuring the Nine Worthies, all of whom overdo or distort their roles in the same way as the lover-courtiers have theirs. (This interlude was also the playwright's first attempt at the play-within-the-play.) When every Jack presumes to claim his Jill at the close, however, Shakespeare deputizes the princess to postpone the weddings for one year while the men do penance for breaking their vows. The women here are victorious over the men, but only for the purpose of forcing them to recognize the seriousness of their contracts. Presumably the marriages to come will prove constant and fulfilling, but at the end of this otherwise lighthearted piece, Shakespeare interjects a surprising note of qualification. Perhaps this note represents his commentary on the weight of words, which the courtiers have so carelessly—and sometimes badly—handled.

In *A Midsummer Night's Dream*, Shakespeare demonstrates consummate skill in the use of words to create illusion and dreams. Although he again gives us pairs of young lovers whose fickleness causes them to fall out, then back into, love, these characters display human dimensions that are missing in the types of the earlier comedies. The multiple plots concern not only the lovers' misadventures but also the marriage of Duke Theseus and Hippolyta, the quarrel between Oberon and Titania, king and queen of the fairy band, and the bumbling rehearsal and performance of "Pyramus and Thisbe" by Bottom and his workmen companions. All of these actions illustrate the themes of love's errant course and of the power of illusion to deceive the senses. The main action, as in *The Two Gentlemen of Verona*, takes place in a wood, this time outside Athens and at night. The fairy powers have free reign to deceive the mortals who chase one another there; Puck, Oberon's servant, effects deception of the lovers by mistakenly pouring a potion in the wrong Athenian's eyes. By the end of the play, however, the young lovers have found their proper partners, Oberon and Titania have patched up their quarrel, and Bottom, whose head was changed into that of an ass and who was wooed by the enchanted Titania while he was under this spell, rejoins his fellows to perform their tragic and comic interlude at the wedding reception. This afterpiece is a burlesque rendition of the story of Pyramus and Thisbe, whose tale of misfortune bears a striking resemblance to that of Romeo and Juliet. Through the device of the badly acted play-within-the-play, Shakespeare instructs his audience in the absurdity of lovers' Petrarchan vows and in the power of imagination to transform the bestial or the godlike into human form. In design and execution, *A Midsummer Night's Dream*, with its variety of plots and range of rhyme and blank verse, stands out as Shakespeare's most sophisticated early comedy.

The Merchant of Venice shares bourgeois features with *The Taming of the*

Shrew and *The Two Gentlemen of Verona*, but it has a much darker, near-tragic side, too. Shylock's attempt to carve a pound of flesh from the merchant Antonio's heart has all the ingredients of tragedy—deception, hate, ingenuity, and revenge. His scheme is frustrated only by the superior wit of the heroine Portia during a trial scene in which she is disguised as a young boy judge. Requiring Shylock to take nothing more than is specified in his bond, while at the same time lecturing him on the quality of mercy, Portia's speeches create the elements of tension and confrontation that will come to epitomize the playwright's mature tragedies. With the defeat and conversion of Shylock, the pairs of lovers can escape the threatening world of Venice and hope for uninterrupted happiness in Belmont, Portia's home. Venice, the scene of business, materialism, and religious hatred, is contrasted with Belmont (or "beautiful world"), the fairy-tale kingdom to which Bassanio, Antonio's friend, has come to win a fair bride and fortune by entering into a game of choice involving golden, silver, and leaden caskets. Though the settings are contrasted and the action of the play alternates between the two societies, Shakespeare makes his audience realize that Portia, like Antonio, is bound to a contract (set by her dead father) which threatens to destroy her happiness. When Bassanio chooses the leaden casket, she is freed to marry the man whom she would have chosen for her own. Thus "converted" (a metaphor that refers one back to Shylock's conversion), Portia then elects to help Antonio, placing herself in jeopardy once again. Portia emerges as Shakespeare's first major heroine-in-disguise, a character-type central to his most stageworthy and mature comedies, *Twelfth Night* and *As You Like It*.

Much Ado About Nothing likewise has a dark side. The main plot represents the love of Claudio and Hero; her reputation is sullied by the melodramatic villain Don Juan. Claudio confronts his supposedly unfaithful partner in the middle of their wedding ceremony, his tirade causing her to faint and apparently expire. The lovers are later reunited, however, after Claudio recognizes his error. This plot is paralleled by one involving Beatrice and Benedick, two witty characters who in the play's beginning are set against each other in verbal combat. Like Claudio and Hero, they are converted into lovers who overcome selfishness and pride to gain a degree of freedom in their new relationships. The comedy ends with the marriage of Claudio and Hero and the promise of union between Beatrice and Benedick.

A central comic figure in the play is Dogberry, the watchman whose blundering contributes to Don Juan's plot but is also the instrument by which his villainy is revealed. His behavior, especially his hilariously inept handling of legal language, is funny in itself, but it also illustrates a favorite Shakespearean theme: clownish errors often lead to happy consequences. Like Bottom in *A Midsummer Night's Dream*, Dogberry and his men are made an important part of the newly transformed society at the end of the play.

As You Like It and *Twelfth Night* are widely recognized as Shakespeare's wittiest and most stageworthy comedies; they also qualify as masterpieces of design and construction. In *As You Like It*, the action shifts from the court of Duke Frederick, a usurper, to the forest world of Arden, the new "court" of ousted Duke Senior. His daughter Rosalind enters the forest world in disguise, along with her friend Celia, to woo and win the young hero Orlando, forced to wander by his brother Oliver, another usurping figure. Although his florid verses expressing undying love for Rosalind are the object of considerable ridicule, Orlando earns the title of true lover, worthy of Rosalind's hand. She proves successful in winning the support of the audience by means of her clever manipulation of Orlando from behind her mask. His inept poetry and her witty commentary can be taken "as we like it," as can the improbable conversions of Oliver and Duke Frederick that allow for a happy ending. Two characters—Touchstone, the clown, and Jacques, the cynical courtier—represent extreme attitudes on the subjects of love and human nature. Touchstone serves as Rosalind's protector and as a sentimental observer, commenting wistfully and sometimes wittily on his own early days as a lover of milkmaids. Jacques, the trenchant commentator on the "Seven Ages of Man," sees all this foolery as further evidence, along with political corruption and ambition, of man's fallen state. He remains outside the circle of happy couples at the end of the play, a poignant, melancholy figure. His state of self-centeredness, it might be argued, is also "as we like it" when our moods do not identify so strongly with youthful exuberance.

Twelfth Night also deals with the themes of love and self-knowledge; like *As You Like It*, it features a disguised woman, Viola, as its central figure. Motifs from other earlier Shakespearean comedies are also evident in *Twelfth Night*. Viola and Sebastian are twins (see *The Comedy of Errors*) who have been separated in a shipwreck but, unknown to each other, have landed in the same country, Illyria. From *The Two Gentlemen of Verona*, Shakespeare took the motif of the disguised figure serving the man she loves (Duke Orsino) and even playing the wooer's role with the woman (Olivia) the duke wishes to marry. Complications arise when Olivia falls in love with Viola, and the dilemma is brought to a head when Orsino threatens to kill his page in a fit of revenge. Sebastian provides the ready solution to this dilemma, but Shakespeare holds off introducing the twins to each other until the last possible moment, creating effective comic tension. The play's subplot involves an ambitious and vain steward, Malvolio, who, by means of a counterfeited letter (the work of a clever servant named Maria), is made to believe that Olivia loves him. The scene in which Malvolio finds the letter and responds to its hints, while being observed not only by the theater audience but also by an audience onstage, is one of the funniest stretches of comic pantomime in drama. When Malvolio attempts to woo his mistress, he is thought mad and cast in prison. Although he is finally released (not before being tormented by Feste the clown in disguise), Malvolio does not join the circle of lovers in the close, vowing instead to be revenged on all those who deceived him. In fact, both Feste and Malvolio stand apart from the happy company, representing the dark, somewhat melancholy clouds that cannot be dispelled in actual human experience. By this stage in his career, Shakespeare had acquired a vision of comedy crowded by elements and characters that would be fully developed in the tragedies.

The Merry Wives of Windsor was probably composed before Shakespeare reached the level of maturity reflected in *As You Like It* and *Twelfth Night*. Legend suggests that he interrupted his work on the second history cycle to compose the play in two weeks for Queen Elizabeth, who wished to see Falstaff portrayed as a lover. What Shakespeare ended up writing was not a romantic but a bourgeois comedy that depicts Falstaff attempting to seduce Mistress Ford and Mistress Page, both wives of Windsor citizens. He fails, but in failing manages to entertain the audience with his bragging and his boldness. Shakespeare may have been reworking an old play based on a Plautine model; there is a subplot in which a clever young man (Fenton) and his beloved manage to deceive her parents in order to get married. This is the only strain of romance in the comedy, whose major event is the punishment of Falstaff: He is tossed into the river, then singed with candles and pinched by citizens disguised as fairies. That this punishment has symbolic weight is argued by critics who see Falstaff as the embodiment of Vice; his attempted seduction of honest citizens' wives makes him a threat to orderly society. Regardless of whether this act has a ritual purpose, the character of Falstaff, and those of Bardolph, Pistol, and Justice Shallow, bear little resemblance to the comic band of *Henry IV, Part I*. In fact, *The Merry Wives of Windsor* might be legitimately seen as an interlude rather than a fully developed comedy, and it is a long distance from the more serious, probing dramas Shakespeare would soon create.

All's Well That Ends Well and *Measure for Measure* were composed during a period when Shakespeare was also writing his major tragedies. Because they pose questions about sin and guilt that are not satisfactorily resolved, many critics have used the terms "dark comedies" or "problem plays" to describe them. *All's Well That Ends Well* features the familiar disguised heroine (Helena) who pursues the man she loves (Bertram) with skill and determination. The play differs from the earlier romantic comedies, however, because the hero rejects the heroine, preferring instead to win honor and fame in battle. Even though Helena is "awarded" the prize of Bertram by the King of France, whom she has cured of a near-fatal disease, she must don her disguise and pursue him while undergoing considerable suffering and hardship. In order to trap him, moreover, she must resort to a "bed trick," substituting her body for that of another woman whom Bertram plans to seduce. When Bertram finally assents to the union, he bears little resemblance to comic heroes such as Orlando or Sebastian; he could be seen in fact as more a villain (or perhaps a cad) than a deserving lover. The forced resolution makes the play a "problem" for many critics, but for Shakespeare and his audience, the ingenuity of Helena and the multiple marriages at the close probably satisfied the demands of romantic comedy.

Measure for Measure has at the center of its plot another bed trick, by which a patient and determined woman (Mariana) manages to capture the man she desires. That man, Angelo, is put in the position of deputy by Duke Vincentio at the opening of the action. He determines to punish a sinful Vienna by strictly enforcing its laws against fornication; his first act is to arrest Claudio for impregnating his betrothed Juliet. When Isabella, Claudio's sister, who is about to take vows as a nun, comes to plead for his life, Angelo attempts to seduce her. He asks for a measure of her body in return for a measure of mercy for her brother. Isabella strongly resists Angelo's advances, although her principled behavior most certainly means her brother will die. Aided by Vincentio, disguised as a holy father, Isabella arranges for Mariana to take her place, since this woman is in fact Angelo's promised partner. Thus, Angelo commits the deed that he would punish Claudio for performing. (Instead of freeing Claudio, moreover, he sends word to have him killed even after seducing his "sister.") Through another substitution, however, Claudio is saved. In an elaborate judgment scene, in which Vincentio plays both duke and holy father, Angelo is forgiven—Isabella being required by the duke to beg for Angelo's life—and marries Mariana. Here, as in *All's Well That Ends Well*, the hero proves to be an unpunished scoundrel who seems to be in fact rewarded for his sin, but the biblical "Judge not lest ye be judged" motivates much of the action, with characters finding themselves in the place of those who would judge them and being forced to display mercy. Some critics have argued that this interpretation transforms Duke Vincentio into a Christ figure, curing the sins of the people while disguised as one of them. Whether or not this interpretation is valid, *Measure for Measure* compels one to explore serious questions concerning moral conduct; practically no touches of humor in the play are untainted by satire and irony.

For about four years following the writing of *Measure for Measure*, Shakespeare was busy producing his major tragedies. It is probably accurate to say that the problem comedies were, to a degree, testing grounds for the situations and characters he would perfect in the tragedies, but in the later years of his career, Shakespeare returned to writing comedy of a special kind: tragicomedy or romance. The four plays usually referred to as "the romances" are *Pericles*, *Cymbeline*, *The Winter's Tale*, and *The Tempest*. Three of these portray situations in which fathers are separated from daughters, then are rejoined through some miraculous turn of fortune. Except for *The Tempest*, the events cover many years and involve travel to exotic locales by the heroes and heroines. Sharp contrasts between the court and pastoral settings vivify the theme of nature as the ideal teacher of moral values. In *Pericles, Prince of Tyre*, *Cymbeline*, and *The Winter's Tale*, the plots move inexorably toward tragedy, but through some form of intervention by Providence—or in some cases, by the gods themselves—happiness is restored and characters are reunited. All the plays witness the power of faith as instrumental in the process of regeneration; the loyal counselor or servant is a regular character-type in the plays. The general outlook of the romances is optimistic, suggesting that man is indeed capable of recovering from the Fall and of creating a new Paradise.

Pericles recounts the adventures of a good king who seems hounded by fortune and forced to wander through the Mediterranean. The plot is faintly reminiscent of that of *The Comedy of Errors*, suggesting that Shakespeare was returning to tested materials from his earliest comedies. During a storm at sea, Pericles' wife, Thaisa, apparently dies in childbirth and is set ashore in a coffin. He then leaves his daughter Marina in the care of a scheming queen, who tries to have her murdered. Instead, Marina is captured by pirates and eventually sold to a brothel owner. After many years of lonely sojourning, Pericles is finally reunited with his daughter; later, through the offices of a doctor figure named Cerimon, they find Thaisa in the temple of Diana at Ephesus, where she has been resting for years. Throughout, the sea represents both a threatening and a peaceful force; Marina's name points to the theme of the sea as a great restorative power. She "cures" her father aboard a ship.

Cymbeline, set in ancient Britain, recounts the misfortunes of its characters against the background of the Roman invasion of England. The tragicomedy has strong patriotic overtones, but it does not qualify as a history play such as those in the two tetralogies. The play depicts the moral education of Posthumus, the hero, whose desire to marry Imogen, Cymbeline's daughter, is frustrated by his low birth. While in exile in Italy, Posthumus brags to an Italian acquaintance, Iachimo, that his beloved would never consider deceiving him. Thus challenged, Iachimo visits Imogen's room while she sleeps and, through a clever ruse involving a ring and a birthmark, convinces Posthumus that he has slept with her. As a result of numerous plot turns, one of which calls for Imogen to disguise herself as a page, the two lovers are finally reunited when Iachimo confesses his sin. Comingled with this strain of plot is another involving two sons of Cymbeline who have been reared in the rugged world of caves and mountains by an old counselor banished by the king. (He originally kidnaped the boys to seek revenge against Cymbeline.) In a climactic scene brought about by the Roman invasion, the mountain-men heroes are reunited with their father and sister, whom all believed was dead. So complex is the plot that many readers and audiences have found the play confusing and sometimes unintentionally humorous. The characters are not fully developed, and it is difficult to determine just what is the central story. Here, too, spectacle overpowers dialogue and characterization, with little or no attention paid to plausibility. Shakespeare seems preoccupied with demonstrating the healthfulness of pastoral life, the patriotic spirit of Englishmen, and the melodramatic quality of evil. Clearly, this agenda of themes and values places one in a comic world that is distinct from the one that typifies the mature comedies.

In *The Winter's Tale*, Shakespeare again explores the motif of the daughter separated from her father, but in this play, the father, King Leontes, must be seen as a potentially tragic figure. His jealousy leads him to accuse his wife, Hermione, of unfaithfulness with his friend and fellow-king Polixenes. When Leontes confronts her, even after consultation of the oracle indicates her honesty, she faints and apparently expires. Leontes banishes the child Perdita, who is his daughter but whom he refuses to acknowledge because of his suspicions, and the third act ends with a loyal servant depositing the baby on the shore of Bohemia to be favored or destroyed by Fortune. (A bear pursues and kills the servant, thus destroying any link between Leontes' court and the baby.) Perdita, "the lost one," is found and reared by a shepherd; as sixteen years pass, she grows into a kind of pastoral queen, revealing those traits of goodness and innocence that Shakespeare associates with the Golden Age. When Polixenes repeats Leontes' sin by banishing his son Florizel for falling in love with a lowly shepherdess, the couple, with the help of a rejected servant still loyal to Leontes, returns to Sicilia to seek the aid of the now repentant king. Through a series of revelations and with the help of the old shepherd, Perdita's identity is discovered, she and Florizel are married, and the two kings are reunited in friendship. As a final tour de force, Hermione, who has been hidden away for the whole time by another loyal servant, comes to life as a statue supposedly sculpted by a famous artist. As in the other romances, some divine force has obviously been operating in the affairs of men to bring about this happy reunion of families, friends, and countries. *The Winter's Tale* comes closer than the others to a realistic treatment of emotion, with all of its destructive possibilities, and to a more nearly honest vision of the pastoral world. Autolycus the clown, for example, pretends to be nothing other than a successful thief, "a snapper-up of unconsidered trifles."

The Tempest is the only romance in which father and daughter are together from the beginning. It also possesses the only plot that observes the classical unities of time and place. Many commentators believe that the play represents Shakespeare's greatest dramatic achievement, blending together beautiful verse, richly realized characters, and the moving wonders of the imagination. There can be no question that *The Tempest* is a refined and elevating statement of the themes of Providence and of order and degree. Prospero, the Duke of Milan, exiled by his usurping brother Antonio, vows to punish both Antonio and his chief supporter, King Alonso; the two are aboard a ship sailing near the island on which Prospero and his daughter Miranda reside. Using magical power and the aid of a spirit named Ariel, Prospero apparently wrecks the ship, saving all the voyagers but supposedly drowning Ferdinand, Alonso's son. Once on the island, the party is tormented by disorienting music and distracting sights, especially when Prospero's brother Antonio attempts to convince Alonso's brother Sebastian to kill him and seize the crown. Another rebellion is attempted by Caliban (his name an anagram for "cannibal"), the half-human, half-bestial servant of Prospero. Both rebellions fail, but instead of punishing his victims further, Prospero, moved by the compassion displayed by Ariel, decides to give up his magic and return to civilization. The decision proves crucial, since Prospero was on the verge of becoming a kind of Faust, forgetting his identity as a man. When he acknowledges Caliban, "this thing of darkness," as his own, one realizes that this gesture betokens an internal acceptance of the passions as a legitimate part of his nature. Instead of revenging himself on Alonso, Prospero allows Ferdinand to woo Miranda in a mood and manner that recall Eden before the Fall. It should also be noted that Prospero creates a marriage masque featuring Iris, Ceres, and Juno, at the close of which he delivers the famous "Our revels now are ended" speech. Some critics claim that Prospero's words constitute Shakespeare's farewell to the stage, but there is considerable evidence that he continued to write plays for at least another year.

The Two Noble Kinsmen was probably one of the plays composed during that period. It is not included in the First Folio (published 1623), appearing in print in 1634 and bearing a title page ascribing the comedy to John Fletcher and William Shakespeare. Although collaboration was common among Elizabethan and Jacobean playwrights, it was not a form of composition in which Shakespeare regularly engaged. Since *Henry VIII* was also most likely a collaborative effort, there seems to be compelling evidence that Shakespeare was enjoying a state of semiretirement during this period. Based on Geoffrey Chaucer's "The Knight's Tale," *The Two Noble Kinsmen* depicts the love of Palamon and Arcite for Emilia in a polite and mannered style that can be easily identified with Fletcher's other work. The play is similar to the other romances in its emphasis on spectacle: It opens with a magnificent wedding ceremony before the Temple of Hymen, and there are other excursions to the shrines of Mars and Diana as well. There are, however, no scenes of regeneration involving fathers and daughters, no emphasis on the forgiveness of sin. If this was Shakespeare's last play, it shows him returning to old sources for oft-told tales; his interest in developing new comic forms had obviously waned. On the whole, the romances represent a more sophisticated but less playful and inventive style than that of the character-oriented comedies, such as *Twelfth Night* and *Much Ado About Nothing*.

Titus Andronicus was the earliest—and clumsiest—of Shakespeare's attempts at tragedy. The plot no doubt came from Ovid, a school subject and one of the playwright's favorite Roman authors. From Seneca, the Roman playwright whose ten plays had been translated into English in 1559, Shakespeare took the theme of revenge: the inflexible, honor-bound hero seeks satisfaction against a queen who has murdered or maimed his children. She was acting in retaliation, however, because Titus had killed her son. Titus' rage, which is exacerbated by the rape and mutilation of his daughter Lavinia, helps to classify him as a typical Senecan tragic hero. He and the wicked queen Tamora are oversimplified characters who declaim set speeches rather than engaging in realistic dialogue. Tamora's lover and accomplice, the Moor Aaron, is the prototype of the Machiavellian practicer that Shakespeare would perfect in such villains as Iago and Edmund. While this caricature proves intriguing, and while the play's structure is more balanced and coherent than those of the early history plays, Titus' character lacks the kind of agonizing introspection shown by the heroes of the major tragedies. He never comes to terms with the destructive code of honor that convulses his personal life and that of Rome.

With *Romeo and Juliet*, Shakespeare reached a level of success in characterization and design far above the bombastic and chaotic world of *Titus Andronicus*. Based on a long narrative and heavily moralized poem by Arthur Brooke, this tragedy of "star-crossed lovers" excites the imagination by depicting the fatal consequences of a feud between the Veronese families of Montague and Capulet. Distinguished by some of Shakespeare's most beautiful poetry, the style bears a strong resemblance to that of the *Sonnets*: elaborate conceits, classical allusions, witty paradoxes, and observations on the sad consequences of sudden changes of fortune. Some critics have in fact faulted the tragedy because its plot lacks the integrity of its poetry; Romeo and Juliet come to their fates by a series of accidents and coincidences that strain credulity. The play also features abundant comic touches provided by the remarks of Romeo's bawdy, quick-witted friend Mercutio and the sage but humorous observations of Juliet's nurse. Both of these humor characters (that is, character-types whose personalities are determined by one trait, or "humor," to use the Renaissance term) remark frequently, and often bawdily, on the innocent lovers' dreamy pronouncements about their passion for each other. With the accidental murder of Mercutio, whose last words are "A plague on both houses!" the plot accelerates rapidly toward the catastrophe, showing no further touches of humor or satire. The tireless Friar Lawrence attempts, through the use of a potion, to save Juliet from marrying Paris, but he proves powerless against the force of fate that seems to be working against the lovers. Although it lacks the compelling power of the mature tragedies, whose heroes are clearly responsible for their fate, *Romeo and Juliet* remains a very popular play on the subject of youthful love. The success of Franco Zeffirelli's 1968 film version, with its teenage hero and heroine and its romantically moving score, proved that the play has a timeless appeal.

At least three years passed before Shakespeare again turned his attention to the tragic form. Instead of treating the subject of fatal love, however, he explored Roman history for a political story centering on the tragic dilemma of one man. In *Julius Caesar*, he could have dealt with the tale of the assassination of Caesar, taken from Plutarch's *Parallel Lives* (105-115, translated 1579), as he did with material from English history in the chronicle dramas he had been writing in the 1590's. That is, he might have presented the issue of the republic versus the monarchy as a purely political question, portraying Caesar, Brutus, Cassius, and Antony as pawns in a predestined game. Instead, Shakespeare chose to explore the character of Brutus in detail, revealing the workings of his conscience through moving and incisive soliloquies. By depicting his hero as a man who believes his terrible act is in the best interest of the country, Shakespeare establishes the precedent for later tragic heroes who likewise justify their destructive deeds as having righteous purposes.

The tragic plot is developed by means of irony and contrast. Cassius, jealous of Caesar's achievements, seduces Brutus into taking part in the conspiracy by appealing to his idealism. It is this political naïveté that stands in sharp contrast to Antony's Machiavellianism, which is so brilliantly demonstrated in his crowd-swaying funeral oration. Antony's transformation from playboy to power broker displays Shakespeare's belief that the historical moment shapes the natures of great men. Caesar appears to be a superstitious, somewhat petty figure, but in typical fashion, Shakespeare makes one see that, just as the conspirators are not free of personal motives such as jealousy, so Caesar is not the cold and uncompromising tyrant they claim he is. With the visit by Caesar's ghost to Brutus' tent on the eve of the final battle at Philippi, Shakespeare foreshadows the ultimate revenge of Caesar in the character of his grandson, Octavius, who emerges as a strong personality at the close of the play. Brutus and Cassius quarrel before the end, but they nevertheless achieve a kind of nobility by committing suicide in the Roman tradition. For Brutus, the events following the assassination demonstrate the flaw in his idealism; he could not destroy the spirit of Caesar, nor could he build a republic on the shifting sand of the populace. In *Julius Caesar*, one witnesses a tragedy that is both politically compelling and morally complex.

While the revenge theme is an important part of *Julius Caesar*, it dominates the action of *Hamlet*. Learning from his father's ghost that Claudius, the new king, is a brother-murderer and a usurper, the hero sets out passionately to fulfill his personal duty by destroying the villain-king. Like Brutus, however, Hamlet is also a reflective man, given to "saucy doubts" about the veracity of the ghost, about the effect on his soul of committing regicide, and about the final disposition of Claudius' soul. The resultant delay in acting has preoccupied audiences, readers, and critics for centuries, and numerous reasons have been proposed for the delay: Hamlet is melancholic; his morality does not condone murder; he is a coward; he is secretly envious of Claudius for murdering his "rival" for his mother's affections. These explanations, while appealing, tend to shift attention away from other, equally significant elements in the play. Hamlet's soliloquies illustrate the range of Shakespearean blank verse and provide the means for exploring character in detail. The trap motif can be seen to represent effectively the doomed, claustrophobic atmosphere of the play. Indeed, those who deliberatively set traps in the play—Polonius, Claudius, Laertes, Hamlet— find that those traps snap back to catch the "inventor." Hamlet's relationships with Ophelia and with Gertrude amply reveal his self-destructive belief that his mother's marriage to Claudius has tainted his own flesh and transformed all women into strumpets. Throughout the action as well, one becomes aware that Shakespeare is using the theatrical metaphor "All the world's a stage" to illustrate the way in which deceit and corruption can be masked. In another sense, Hamlet's behavior is that of a bad actor, one who either misses his cues (as in the accidental murder of Polonius) or fails to perform when the audience expects action (as in his behavior following the play-within-the-play). There is a good deal of reflection on death and disease in *Hamlet* as well; the hero's preoccupation with these images seems to mirror the sickness of the state and of his own enterprise. When Hamlet finally acts, however, he does so in the role of an avenger and scourge. He murders Claudius after the king has arranged for Laertes to slay him in a duel and after the queen has fallen dead from a poisoned drink intended for Hamlet. With Hamlet's death, the kingdom reverts to the control of young Fortinbras, whose father Hamlet's father had killed in another duel. Though Fortinbras stands as a heroic figure, one cannot help but observe the irony of a situation in which the son, without a struggle, inherits what his father was denied.

In *Troilus and Cressida*, one encounters another kind of irony—satire. This strange play, which may have been composed for a select audience, possibly of lawyers, was placed between the histories and tragedies in the

First Folio. The dual plot concerns the political machinations among the Greeks during their siege of Troy and the tortured love affair between Troilus and the unfaithful Cressida. There are no epic battles in the play; indeed, the murder of Hector by a band of Achilles' followers might easily be viewed as cowardly or ignominious at best. Much of the political action consists of debates: Hector argues eloquently that Helen should be sent back to Menelaus; Ulysses produces many pithy arguments urging the reluctant Achilles to fight. Many of these scenes, moreover, end in anticlimax, and action is often frustrated. Throughout, Thersites, the satirist-onstage, bitterly attacks the warring and lecherous instincts of men; even the love affair between Troilus and Cressida seems tainted by the general atmosphere of disillusion. Although the two lovers share genuine affection for each other, one cannot ignore the truth that they are brought together by Pandarus and that their passion has a distinctly physical quality. When Cressida proves unable to resist the advances of Diomedes, Troilus becomes a cuckold like Menelaus; his bitterness and misogyny push one toward Thersites' assessment that the "argument" of the war "is a whore and a cuckold." Still it is possible to see tragic dimensions in the characters of both Hector and Troilus, one the victim of treachery in war, the other the victim of treachery in love.

Although probably written after the other major tragedies, *Timon of Athens* shares a number of similarities with *Troilus and Cressida.* Here again is an ironic vision of man, this time in a social rather than martial setting; that vision is expanded by the trenchant comments, usually in the form of references to sexual disease, of Apemantus, another cynical choric commentator. In addition, Timon appears to be a tragic rather than misanthropic figure only if one sees him as the victim of his idealistic reading of humankind. When those on whom he has lavishly bestowed gifts and money consistently refuse to return the favor, Timon then becomes a bitter cynic and outspoken satirist. This exploding of a naïve philosophy or political idea, with its attendant destructive effect on the believer, would seem to be the basis for tragedy in a character like Brutus or Hamlet, but even Hamlet fails to achieve the degree of misanthropy that typifies Timon's outlook. Although he is loyally followed to the end by his servant Flavius, moreover, he dies alone and not as a result of someone else's direct attack. One cannot say that the hero acquires a larger view of humanity or of himself as the result of his experience; he simply seems to swing from one extreme view to its opposite. A comparison of Timon with more sympathetic "railers" such as Hamlet and Lear shows how narrow and shallow are his character and the dimensions of the play. The fragmented nature of the text has led some critics to question Shakespeare's authorship, but it is probably closer to the truth to say that this was an experiment that failed.

An experiment that clearly succeeded is *Othello*, an intense and powerful domestic tragedy. Based on an Italian tale by Giraldi Cintio, the story concerns a Moor who is made to believe by a treacherous, vengeful ensign that his new Venetian bride has cuckolded him. In a rage, the Moor suffocates his bride, only to discover too late that his jealousy was unfounded; rather than face the torture of a trial and his own conscience, he commits suicide as he bitterly accuses himself of blindness. In its simple outline, this story has the appearance of a crude melodrama, but Shakespeare brilliantly complicates the play's texture through skillful manipulation of scenes, characters, and language. He also creates a world with two distinct symbolic settings: Venice and Cyprus. In Venice, Othello shows himself to be a cool, rational captain, deserving of the respect he receives from the senators who send him to Cyprus to defend it from the Turks. Once Othello is on the island, however, Iago begins to chip away at the hero's veneer of self-control until he transforms him into a terrifyingly destructive force. Iago's success depends not only on his close contact with Othello on the island but also on the generally held opinion that he is an honest man. He is thus able to manipulate all the central characters as if he were a puppeteer. These characters share information with Iago that he later uses in ensnaring them in his web, as when Desdemona begs him to find some way to reinstate Cassio in his lord's favor. Iago is especially adept at using the handkerchief Othello gave to Desdemona but which she dropped while trying to ease her husband's headache. When Iago's wife Emilia dutifully hands her husband this handkerchief, he easily makes Othello believe that Desdemona gave it to Cassio as a love token. Although some critics have ridiculed Shakespeare for depending so heavily on one prop to resolve the plot, they fail to note the degree of psychological insight Shakespeare has displayed in using it. The handkerchief represents Othello's wife's honor and his own; she has given both away, in Othello's mind, as if they were trifles.

This play features a hero whose reason is overwhelmed by the passion of jealousy—"the green-eyed monster," in Iago's words. This theme is realized through numerous sea images, by which Shakespeare likens the hero's violent reaction to a storm or tidal wave that drowns everything in its path. Like Shakespeare's other great villains, Iago is a supreme individualist, acknowledging no authority or power beyond himself. That this attitude was a copy of Satan's would not have escaped the attention of Shakespeare's audience, which no doubt interpreted the plot as a replay of the Fall of Man. It may be especially important to perceive Iago as another Satan, since commentators have suspected the sufficiency of his motive (he says he wants revenge because Othello passed over him in appointing Cassio as his lieutenant). The extreme evilness of Iago's nature and the extreme purity of Desdemona's have led others to claim that Shakespeare was simply intent on fashioning a contemporary morality play for his audience. Such a reading tends to simplify what is in fact a thoroughgoing study of the emotions that both elevate and destroy man. As Othello discovers before his suicide, he was one "who loved not wisely but too well"; one might observe ironically that it was Iago and not Desdemona whom he loved "too well."

If Othello's tragedy results from the corrosive disease of jealousy, the hero of *King Lear* suffers from the debilitating effects of pride and self-pity. When the play opens he is in the process of retiring from the kingship by dividing his kingdom into three parts, basing his assignment of land on the degree of affection mouthed by each of the three daughters to whom he plans to assign a part. Cordelia, his youngest and favorite, refuses to enter into this hollow ceremony, and Lear responds by suddenly and violently banishing her. Left in the hands of his evil and ambitious daughters Goneril and Regan, Lear quickly discovers that they plan to pare away any remaining symbols of his power and bring him entirely under their rule. This theme of children controlling, even destroying, their parents is echoed in a fully developed subplot involving old Gloucester and his two sons, Edmund and Edgar. With Cordelia and Edgar cast out, the former to live in France, the latter in disguise as Poor Tom, Lear and Gloucester suffer the punishing consequences of their sins. Lear runs mad into a terrible storm, accompanied by the Fool, a witty and poignant commentator on the unnaturalness of his master's decision; there, Lear goes through a "dark night of the soul" in which he sees for the first time the suffering of others whom he has never regarded. Gloucester, who is also lacking insight into the true natures of his sons, is cruelly blinded by Regan and her husband and cast out from his own house to journey to Dover. On the way, he is joined by his disguised son, who helps Gloucester to undergo a regeneration of faith before he expires. Cordelia performs a similar task for Lear, whose recovery can only be partial, because of his madness. After Cordelia is captured and killed by the forces of Edmund, whose brother conquers him in single combat, Lear, too, expires while holding the dead Cordelia in his arms.

This wrenching ending, with its nihilistic overtones, is only one of the elements that places this play among the richest and most complex tragedies in English. Lear's blindness, which is expertly represented in image clusters dealing with sight and insight, leads to cataclysmic suffering for his family and the state. More than any other Shakespearean tragedy, *King Lear* also succeeds in dramatizing the relationship between the microcosm, or little world of man, and the macrocosm, or larger world. One sees how the breakdown of the king's reason and control leads to the breakdown of control in the state and in nature. At the moment when Lear bursts into tears, a frightening storm breaks out, and civil war soon follows. Images of human suffering and torture likewise crowd the action, the most compelling of which is the representation of the hero tied to a "wheel of fire" and scalded by his own tears as the wheel turns. The Wheel of Fortune emblem is clearly evoked by this image, revealing Shakespeare's purpose of depicting the king as another fallen prince brought low by his own mistakes and by the caprice of the goddess. That Lear has created the circumstances of his own fall is underscored by the antic remarks of his companion the Fool, the choric speaker who early in the play tries to keep Lear's mind from cracking as he comes to realize how wrong was the banishment of Cordelia. The Fool speaks in riddles and uses barnyard analogies to make the point that Lear has placed the whip in the child's hand and lowered his own breeches. Gloucester must learn a similar lesson, although his dilemma involves a crisis of faith. Lear must strip away the coverings of civilization to discover "unaccommodated man," a discovery he begins to make too late; just as he realizes that Cordelia represents those qualities of truth and compassion that he has been lacking, she is suddenly and violently taken from him.

Macbeth treats the theme of the fall of princes, but from a different perspective. Unlike Lear, Macbeth is a usurper who is driven to kill King Duncan by the witches' prophecy, by his own ambition, and by his wife's prompting. Once that deed is done, Macbeth finds himself unable to sleep, a victim of conscience and guilt. Although Lady Macbeth tries to control his fears, she proves unsuccessful, and her influence wanes rapidly. Evidence of this loss of power is Macbeth's plot to kill Banquo, his fellow general, to whom the witches announced that he would be the father of kings. During the climactic banquet scene, Duncan's ghost enters, invisible to the other guests, to take Macbeth's place at the table; when the host reacts by raging and throwing his cup at the specter, the celebration is broken up and the guests scatter. Immediately, Macbeth rushes to the witches to seek proof that he is invincible. They tell him that he will not be conquered until Birnam Wood comes to Dunsinane and that no man born of woman can kill him. They also show him a procession of eight child-kings, all of whom represent Banquo's descendants, including the last king, who is meant to be James I. (This procession has helped many critics to conclude that *Macbeth* was written as an occasional play to honor James, who became the company's protector in 1603.)

Seeking to tighten his control of Scotland and to quiet his conscience, Macbeth launches a reign of terror during which his henchmen kill Lady Macduff and her children. Macduff, exiled in England with Duncan's son Malcolm, learns of this vicious deed and spearheads an army that returns to Scotland to destroy the tyrant. In the final battle, which commences with the attacking army tearing down branches from trees in Birnam Wood to camouflage its advance, Macbeth discovers that his nemesis, Macduff, "was from his mother's womb/ Untimely ripped." Thus standing alone (Lady Macbeth commits suicide) and defeated, Macbeth represents himself as a "poor player" who has had his moment onstage and is quickly gone. This use of the theatrical metaphor looks back to the world of *Hamlet* at the same time that it underscores the villain-hero's role as an impostor king. Macbeth is also depicted as a Herod figure (recalling Richard III) when he murders the innocent children of Macduff in an obsessive fit brought on by the realization that he is childless and heirless. Two strains of imagery reinforce this perception, featuring recurring references to blood and to children. When Macbeth kills Duncan, he describes his blood as "gilding" his flesh, suggesting that the king is God's anointed representative on earth. Shakespeare also depicts Macbeth's nemesis as a bloody child; this image hints at the strength-in-innocence theme that dominates the latter part of the play. That is, as Macbeth grows into the "man" that Lady Macbeth claimed he should be, he becomes more destructive and less humane, the caricature of a man. Macduff, on the other hand, in tears over the brutal murder of his wife and children, emerges as a stronger and more compassionate man because he has shown himself capable of deep feeling. The bloody-babe image might also be defined as a Christ emblem, with the attendant suggestion that Macduff comes to free the land from a tyrant's grasp by spreading a philosophy of goodness and mercy. If the play was written to honor James I, it might also be argued that the comparison between his reign and that of Christ was intended. Whatever the intention of these image patterns, they help one to trace the transformation in Macbeth's character from battlefield hero to usurping tyrant, a transformation brought about by the powerful motive of ambition.

Written soon after *Macbeth*, *Antony and Cleopatra* again traces the complex psychological patterns of a male-female relationship. Like Lady Macbeth, Cleopatra appears to control and direct the behavior of her man, Antony, but as the play progresses, she, too, begins to lose power. Unlike Lady Macbeth, Cleopatra outlasts her love, gaining from his death the spirit and stature of rule that was not evident throughout much of the play. Indeed, most of the action involves quarrels between these two mature but jealous and petulant lovers as they struggle to escape the harsh political world created by Octavius Caesar, Antony's rival. Angered by Antony's reveling in Egypt and later by his desertion of Caesar's sister Octavia, whom Antony married only to buy time and an unsteady truce, Octavius begins to move against Antony with a powerful army and navy. During a first encounter between the two forces, in which Antony foolishly decides to fight at sea and also depends on Cleopatra's untested ships, Antony leaves the field in pursuit of the retiring Cleopatra. Angered by her withdrawal and his own alacrity in following her, Antony rages against his "serpent of old Nile" and vows to have nothing further to do with her, but Cleopatra's pull is magnetic, and Antony joins forces with her for a second battle with Caesar. When a similar retreat occurs and Antony finds Cleopatra apparently arranging a separate peace with one of Caesar's representatives, he has the messenger beaten and sent back to Octavius with a challenge to single combat. These wild and desperate moves are commented on by Enobarbus, associate of Antony and choric voice; after the threat of single combat, Enobarbus leaves his master to join forces with Octavius. (Overcome by remorse, however, Enobarbus dies on the eve of battle.)

Believing that Cleopatra has killed herself, Antony decides to commit suicide and calls upon his servant Eros to hold his sword so that he can run himself on it. Instead, Eros kills himself, and Antony must strike the blow himself. Still alive, he is carried to the monument where Cleopatra has decided to take up residence. There, Antony expires, "a Roman, by a Roman/ Valiantly vanquished." Almost immediately, Cleopatra's character seems to change into that of a noble partner; her elegant speeches on Antony's heroic proportions are some of the most powerful blank verse in the play. It is also clear that she intends to escape Octavius' grasp, knowing that he intends to parade her and her children before a jeering Roman crowd. Putting on her royal robes and applying the poison asps to her breast, Cleopatra hurries off to join her lover in eternity.

This complicated story is brilliantly organized by means of placing in balance the two worlds of Rome and Egypt. While Rome is presented as a cold, calculating place, reflective of the character of Octavius, Egypt stands out as a lush paradise in which the pursuit of pleasure is the main business of the inhabitants. This contrast is particularly telling because Antony's status as a tragic hero depends on one's seeing him as caught between the two worlds, at home in neither, master of neither. Water and serpent imagery dominate the play, creating a picture of Cleopatra as a Circe figure or a spontaneously generated creature that has seduced the once heroic Antony. Although this is the Roman view of the "gypsy" queen, Shakespeare requires one to appreciate her infinite variety: She is beautiful and playful, demanding and witty, cool and explosive. On the other hand, the assessment of Octavius as a puritanical, unfeeling man of destiny is also oversimplified; his reaction to Antony's death reveals genuine emotion. At the close of the play, one realizes that Antony and Cleopatra's vast empire has been reduced to the size of her monument—Caesar must attend a while longer to make this discovery himself. Antony and Cleopatra, however, have found a world of love that Octavius could never enter, and the tragedy is as much concerned with tracing the boundaries of that empire as it is with marking the triumphs of Octavius.

While reading the story of Antony and Cleopatra in Plutarch's *Parallel Lives*, to which the play reveals a number of similarities, Shakespeare found another Roman figure whose career he saw as appropriate matter for tragedy: Coriolanus. Composed in the period between 1607 and 1608, *Coriolanus* dramatizes the career of a general in the age of Republican

Rome. He proves to be a superhuman figure in battle, earning his name by single-handedly subduing the town of Corioles and emerging from its gates covered in blood. (This birth image has a mixed meaning, since the blood is that of his victims.) Unfortunately, Coriolanus refuses to humble himself before the Roman plebeians, whom he despises, as a requirement for holding the office of consul. Indeed, many of his bitter comments about the fickleness and cowardice of the populace remind one of characters such as Thersites and Apemantus. Such contempt and condescension make it hard to identify with Coriolanus, even though one is made aware that the Roman crowd is set against him by the jealous and ambitious tribunes, Brutus and Sicinius. Driven by his pride and anger, Coriolanus challenges the citizens' rights and is subsequently banished. He then joins forces with his former enemy Aufidius, and the two of them lead an army to the very gates of Rome. Coriolanus' mother comes out to plead with her son to spare Rome—and his family—in the most emotional scene of the play. Deeply moved by his mother's arguments, Coriolanus relents and urges his companion to make peace with their enemy. Aufidius agrees but awaits his opportunity to ambush his partner, whom he regards as a lifelong enemy. In a masterstroke of irony, Coriolanus is brought down by the citizens of the very town—Corioles—that he conquered in acquiring his name. Because the play is so heavily laden with swatches of Coriolanus' vitriol and instances of irony such as the final one, it is difficult to classify this tragedy with those in which the heroes present richly complex characters. If Hamlet, Othello, Macbeth, and Lear possess tragic flaws, those flaws are only a part of their complicated makeup. Coriolanus, on the other hand, can be understood only in terms of his flaw, and the character and play are therefore one-dimensional.

There is little argument, however, that Shakespeare's tragedies constitute the major achievement of his career. These dramas continue to appeal to audiences because their stories are intriguing; because their characters are fully realized human beings, if somewhat larger than life; and because their poetic language is metaphorically rich. Shakespeare possessed a profound insight into human nature and an ability to reveal what he found there in language unequaled in its power and beauty.

Other major works

POETRY: *Venus and Adonis*, 1593; *The Rape of Lucrece*, 1594; *The Passionate Pilgrim*, 1599 (miscellany with poems by Shakespeare and others); *The Phoenix and the Turtle*, 1601; *A Lover's Complaint*, 1609; *Sonnets*, 1609.

Bibliography

Bloom, Harold, ed. *Shakespeare: The Tragedies.* New York: Chelsea House,

1985. A collection of influential scholarly articles by various Shakespeare authorities, originally published between 1930 and 1983, this book covers a variety of themes and approaches to Shakespeare's major tragedies. Bloom's introduction glosses major trends in Shakespeare criticism in the twentieth century. Includes a select bibliography.

Bradley, A. C. *Shakespearean Tragedy.* London: Macmillan, 1904. A seminal work that has influenced virtually all subsequent discussion of Shakespearean tragedy. Reproduces Bradley's college lectures at the University of Oxford and other British universities, beginning with "The Substance of Shakespearean Tragedy" and continuing with a lecture on tragic construction and two lectures each on *Hamlet, Othello, King Lear,* and *Macbeth.*

French, Marilyn. *Shakespeare's Division of Experience.* New York: Summit, 1981. A groundbreaking feminist analysis of Shakespeare's entire canon, this book takes gender-based discussion of Shakespeare beyond character roles to an analysis of the way Shakespeare, as a representative of his time, saw the world in male-female polarities. French also suggests ways in which Shakespeare transcended those poles.

Granville-Barker, Harley. *Prefaces to Shakespeare's Plays.* 4 vols. Princeton, N.J.: Princeton University Press, 1947. This four-volume work is really the equivalent of a small book on each of Shakespeare's plays. It is a "preface" in the original sense of an essay giving readers what they need to know or think about in order to understand or interpret a particular work.

Harbage, Alfred. *William Shakespeare: A Reader's Guide.* New York: Farrar, Straus, 1963. Written on the most basic level, this book is designed as a first resort for Shakespeare students. Each play is introduced with a few pages of interpretive suggestions, summarized scene by scene, and interwoven with further interpretations. The introductory chapters on Shakespeare's words and verse techniques are valuable to the beginner.

Spurgeon, Caroline F. E. *Shakespeare's Imagery and What It Tells Us.* Cambridge, England: Cambridge University Press, 1935. This pioneer work on Shakespeare's imagery is still the ideal starting point for anyone interested in that aspect of his art. In addition to a demonstration of the patterns of imagery in each of Shakespeare's plays, Spurgeon offers appendices of color-coded charts demonstrating the patterns in Shakespeare and his contemporaries.

Robert F. Willson, Jr.
(Updated by *John R. Holmes*)

NTOZAKE SHANGE
Paulette Williams

Born: Trenton, New Jersey; October 18, 1948

Principal drama

For colored girls who have considered suicide/ when the rainbow is enuf, pr., pb. 1976; *A Photograph: Still Life with Shadows; A Photograph: A Study in Cruelty*, pr. 1977 (revised as *A Photograph: Lovers in Motion*, pr. 1979, pb. 1981); *Where the Mississippi Meets the Amazon*, pr. 1977; *From Okra to Greens: A Different Kinda Love Story*, pr. 1978, pb. 1985; *Spell No. 7*, pr. 1979, pb. 1981; *Boogie Woogie Landscapes*, pr. 1979, pb. 1981; *Mother Courage and Her Children*, pr. 1980 (adaptation of Bertolt Brecht's play); *Three Pieces*, pb. 1981; *Betsey Brown*, pr. 1991 (based on her novel); *The Love Space Demands: A Continuing Saga*, pb. 1991, pr. 1992.

Other literary forms

Ntozake Shange's three genres—plays, poems, and novels—so overlap that one might say she has invented a new genre, the "choreopoem." She has published several volumes of poetry, including *Nappy Edges* (1978), parts of which were included in her 1976 play *for colored girls who have considered suicide/ when the rainbow is enuf*; *Natural Disasters and Other Festive Occasions* (1979); *A Daughter's Geography* (1983); and *Ridin' the Moon in Texas: Word Paintings* (1987). Among her novels are *Sassafrass, Cypress, and Indigo* (1982) and *Betsey Brown* (1985). She has gathered writings about her work from 1976 to 1984 into *See No Evil: Prefaces, Essays, and Accounts, 1976-1983* (1984), essential for study of her art.

Achievements

Shange's work embodies a rich confusion of genres and all the contradictions inherent in a world where violence and oppression polarize life and art. These polarizations in Shange's work both contribute to her artistry and complicate it. She has been criticized and praised for her unconventional language and structure, for her almost religious feminism, and for her stand on black/white and male/female issues. Her first play, *for colored girls who have considered suicide/ when the rainbow is enuf*, produced in 1976 by Joseph Papp's New York Shakespeare Festival, was honored in that year by the Outer Critics Circle, comprising those who write about the New York theater for out-of-town newspapers. Shange's 1980 adaptation of Bertolt Brecht's *Mother Courage and Her Children* won one of the *Village Voice's* Obie awards.

Biography

Ntozake Shange (pronounced "En-to-zaki Shong-gay") was born Paulette

Williams in Trenton, New Jersey, on October 18, 1948, daughter of a surgeon and a psychiatric social worker. She grew up surrounded by music, literature, art, and her parents' prominent friends, among them Dizzy Gillespie, Chuck Berry, and W.E.B. Du Bois, as well as Third World writers and musicians. Her ties with her family were strong; she also was close to her family's live-in black maids. She was graduated from Barnard College with honors in 1970, then received a graduate degree at the University of Southern California in Los Angeles. While in California, she began studying dance, writing poetry, and participating in improvisational works (composed of poems, music, dance, and mime) at bars, cabarets, and schools. These gradually grew into *for colored girls who have considered suicide/ when the rainbow is enuf*, which she carried across the country to perform in workshops in New York, then at the Public Theatre, and eventually on Broadway. The contrasts between her privileged home and education and the realities of the lives of black women led her, in 1971, to change her name legally from what she called the "slave name" of Paulette Williams to Ntozake Shange, meaning "she who comes with her own things" and "she who walks like a lion" in Xhosa (Zulu). Her two failed marriages, her suicide attempts, and her contact with city violence resulted in an anger which found its outlet in her poems. During the late 1970's, she lived in New York City, but she later moved to Houston, Texas, with her daughter, Savannah. She has taught and lectured at many colleges and universities, including Mills College in Oakland California; The State University in Rutgers, New Jersey; the University of California, Berkeley; and the University of Houston.

Her work with Emily Mann on the script version of *Betsey Brown* brought her into prominence among feminists and experimental theaters. Working under the auspices of the New York Shakespeare Festival, the two women brought the play into its production form through a series of staged readings, workshops, and tryouts, and their collaboration techniques were the subject of forums among dramaturges in 1990.

Shange's poetic "reading/performance" piece, *The Love Space Demands*, in which she reads her own work (accompanied by guitarist Billie Patterson), was performed in New Jersey at the Crossroads Theatre and in San Francisco at the Hansberry Theatre in 1992.

Analysis

Ntozake Shange's plays have evoked a range of critical responses commensurate with their unconventional nature. Should her work be characterized as poetry or drama, prose or poetry, essay or autobiography? All these forms can be found in her plays, which are unified by a militant feminism in which some critics have seen a one-sided attack on black men. Others, however, point out the youthful spirit, flair with language, and lyricism that carry her plays to startling and radical conclusions. Her style and its contradictions (embracing black English and the erudite vocabulary of the educated) are at the heart of her drama. Influenced by their method of development—public poetry reading in bars, cafés, schools, Off-Off-Broadway theaters—the plays are generally somewhere between a poetry reading and a staged play.

First among the contrasts is her blending of genres: Her poems shade into drama, her dramas are essentially verse monologues, her novels incorporate poetic passages. Second, her language varies radically—on a single page and even in a single phrase—from black dialect ("cuz," "wanna," "awready," "chirren") to the language of her middle-class upbringing and education ("i cant count the number of times i have viscerally wanted to attack deform n maim the language that i waz taught to hate myself in/"). In the published texts of her poetry, plays, and essays, in addition to simplified phonetic spellings, she employs the slash instead of the period and omits capitalization. Many recordings of her work are available, and these will provide the reader with a much fuller sense of the dynamic quality of her language in performance.

Shange's first dramatic success, *for colored girls who have considered suicide/ when the rainbow is enuf*, she called a "choreopoem"—the recital, individually and in chorus, of the lives and growth of seven different black women, named according to their dress colors: "lady in red," "lady in blue," "lady in orange," "lady in brown," "lady in yellow," "lady in purple," and "lady in green." The term "colored girls" in the title evokes a stereotype of black women yet also contains a germ of hope for the future (the "rainbow," both of color and of eventual salvation).

These seven stylized figures are representative voices of black women, and they express their fury at their oppression both as women and as blacks. The first segment shows high school graduation and the social and sexual rite of passage for "colored girls" in the working-class suburbs. Some of the women who have been cruelly disappointed in relationships with men discuss their spiritual quest. A black woman pretends to be Puerto Rican so that she can dance the merengue in Spanish Harlem. A woman breaks up with her lover by returning to him his plant to water. The scenes become more somber, portraying rape, abuse, city dangers, and abortion. Ties with a more heroic black past appear in "Toussaint," while the glamorized prostitute evicts her lover from her bed. The women begin to analyze their predicament and to assert their independence in segments entitled "somebody almost walked off wid alla my stuff" and "pyramid," in which three women console one another for the actions of the faithless lover whom they share. In the brutal culminating scene, a crazed Vietnam veteran, Beau Willie Brown, abuses his woman Crystal and kills their infant children, dropping them from a window.

Ultimately, the theme of the play is the thwarting of dreams and aspirations for a decent life by forces beyond one's control: war, poverty, and ignorance. There is, however, a saving grace. Toward the end of the play, the seven women fall into a tighter circle of mutual support, much like a religious "laying on of hands" ceremony, in which they say,

> i found god in myself
> & i loved her/ i loved her fiercely

Their bitter pain, shown throughout the dramatic episodes, turns into a possibility of regeneration. Thus, the play is a drama of salvation for women who do not receive their full value in society.

Though it was a landmark in the emergence of new black women playwrights, *for colored girls who have considered suicide/ when the rainbow is enuf* has been criticized for its lack of discussion of black traditions in religion, family, and ordinary work, and for its omissions of both black literary and political history and the influence of whites. Its style, considered as an attack on language, part of blacks' "enslavement," has also been criticized. Later plays, however, include these elements in a constantly enriching network of allusions.

Shange's second major work, *A Photograph: A Still Life with Shadows; A Photograph: A Study in Cruelty*, was produced in 1977; its title was changed in a later version to *A Photograph: Lovers in Motion* (which is the source of the text analyzed here). *A Photograph* is a set of meditations and sketches involving an ideal black woman named Michael and her lover Sean, a failed photographer. Sean, trying to objectify the world about him in his photographs, provides both the play's title and the technological representation of the play as a picture or mirror of the world. Rich allusions such as these, as in most of Shange's plays, are thickly sown throughout the characters' speeches and typically not explained. Sean and Michael's world is not that of *for colored girls who have considered suicide/ when the rainbow is enuf* (New York slums, ridden with violence) but that of San Francisco's arty world, peopled with dancers, lawyers, and intellectuals. The problems addressed are not those of Shange's previous play but those of middle-class, professional, and artistic blacks in a complicated urban society. In this play, Shange expands her black world's boundaries.

Sean tells Michael that she must share him, just as all sorts of women shared Alexandre Dumas in nineteenth century France. Michael dreams of an idealized lover who is not "all-American," while Sean boasts that "lil sean david who never got over on nothing but bitches/ is building a world in his image/" when one of his women, Nevada, an attorney, tears up his photographs. Michael expresses the world of her grandmother as "alla the blood & the fields & the satchels dragging in the dust. all the boogies & stairways late at night oozing the scent of love & cornbread/ the woods smelling of burnt flesh & hunger."

In addition, the idea of art as either survival (Sean's view) or love (Michael's) emerges. All the characters show insecurity and find no solution for their dilemmas, sexual or political. In manipulating one another, they realize how much they have been manipulated in the way they were reared and by the environment in which they live. They cannot love one another enough.

After examining the identity of isolated young black women in *for colored girls who have considered suicide/ when the rainbow is enuf* and of couples in *A Photograph*, Shange concentrates in her next play on one woman's visions, dreams, and memories. *Boogie Woogie Landscapes* was first produced as a one-woman poetry piece in 1978 and then cast as a play in 1979, with music and dance. Layla, a young black woman, entertains in her dreams a series of nightlife companions who exemplify her perceptions of herself and her memories. "Layla" means "night" in Arabic, and the whole play exists in Layla's subconscious, in her dreams. Layla's memories of Fidel Castro's Cuba, of primitive cruelties to African women, and of rock and roll and blues interweave with her feelings about growing up, family, brothers and sisters, parents, maids (some of which appear later in Shange's semiautobiographical novel *Betsey Brown*).

Shange's 1979 play *Spell No. 7*, like her first play, is structured like a highly electric poetry reading, but this time the cast is mixed male and female. A huge blackface mask forms the backdrop for actors and actresses of an imitation old-time minstrel show, where actors did skits, recited, and joked, all under the direction of a Mr. Interlocutor. The actors come offstage, relax at an actors' bar, and gradually remove their masks, revealing their true selves. One magician says that he gave up the trade when a colored child asked for a spell to make her white. The new spell the actors discover is a pride in their blackness. They arrive at this through telling classic "tall stories"; one of these concerns a child who thought blacks were immune to dread diseases such as polio since television pictures show polio victims as all white. She is disillusioned when she finds that blacks can hurt one another, so she buys South African gold to remind her of that pain. Another woman loves her baby while it is in the womb but kills it after it is born. Still another girl vows to brush her "nappy" hair constantly so that she can toss it like white girls. By these contrasts and by wry lists and surprising parallels, Shange shows the pain and difficulty, as well as the hopefulness, of being black. She concludes, "we gonna be colored & love it." As in her play *for colored girls who have considered suicide/ when the rainbow is enuf*, the power of love and self-realization becomes their salvation.

Shange has also done distinguished work as a director, of both her own work and that of others, notably Richard Wesley's *The Mighty Gents* in

1979. In 1980, Shange adapted Bertolt Brecht's _Mutter Courage und ihre Kinder_ (1941; _Mother Courage and Her Children_, 1941), changing the scene from mid-seventeenth century Europe to post-Civil War America, making the protagonist an emancipated slave doing business with the army oppressing the Western Indians, and changing the language to black English.

In 1991, Shange adapted her own novel _Betsey Brown_ into a play. The semiautobiographical work tells the story of a thirteen-year-old African American girl growing up in a middle-class household in 1950's St. Louis. _The Love Space Demands_, a loosely connected series of poems and monologues Shange herself performs with musical accompaniment, revolves around sexual relations in the age of acquired immune deficiency syndrome (AIDS).

Though she has not always succeeded, Shange's bold and daring use of language, her respect for people formerly given little value, and her exploration of the roles of black men and women have opened a new dimension in theater. Her blendings of poetry, music, and dance bring theater back to its origins and simultaneously blaze a trail toward the drama of the future.

Other major works

NOVELS: _Sassafras: A Novella_, 1976; _Sassafras, Cypress, and Indigo_, 1982; _Betsey Brown_, 1985.

POETRY: _Nappy Edges_, 1978; _Natural Disasters and Other Festive Occasions_, 1979; _A Daughter's Geography_, 1983; _From Okra to Greens: A Different Love Story_, 1984; _Ridin' the Moon in Texas: Word Paintings_, 1987.

NONFICTION: _See No Evil: Prefaces, Essays, and Accounts, 1976-1983_, 1984.

Bibliography

Brown-Guillory, Elizabeth. _Their Place on the Stage: Black Women Playwrights in America._ New York: Greenwood Press, 1988. A good study of Shange, along with Alice Childress and Lorraine Hansberry. Analyzes _for colored girls who have considered suicide/ when the rainbow is enuf_ at considerable length, as well as the 1979 trilogy, _Spell No. 7_, _Boogie Woogie Landscapes_, and _A Photograph: Lovers in Motion._ Disappointing regarding Shange's later works.

Russell, Sandi. _Render Me My Song: African-American Women Writers from Slavery to the Present._ New York: St. Martin's Press, 1990. Supplies a list of Shange's work up to _Betsey Brown_, whose stage version was written with Emily Mann. Good biography and comments on the "choreopoem" format. Discusses the trilogy of plays ending with _A Photograph: Lovers in Motion_ and compares Shange's work with Bertolt Brecht's _Mutter Courage und ihre Kinder_ (pr. 1941, pb. 1949; _Mother Courage and Her Children_, 1941). Puts Shange in context with Alexis DeVeaux, Rita

Dove, and Toni Cade Bambara, women trying blues styles fed by oral traditions, of which *for colored girls who have considered suicide/ when the rainbow is enuf* is exemplary.

Shange, Ntozake, and Emily Mann. "The Birth of an R&B Musical." Interview by Douglas J. Keating. *Inquirer* (Philadelphia), March 26, 1989. Follows the story of how Emily Mann and Shange took Shange's *Betsey Brown* from book to stage, in a long interview with both playwrights to mark the opening of the play at the Forum Theater in Philadelphia, as part of the American Music Theater Festival. Shange says of Mann, "Emily is one of the few American playwrights who understands the drama of the blending of voices."

Sommers, Michael. "Rays of Hope in a Sky of Blues." Review of *The Love Space Demands. Star-Ledger* (Newark, N.J.), March 12, 1992. This appreciative review of *The Love Space Demands* provides an insightful overview of how Shange takes her poetry to the stage. Sommers finds the work "[a] very accessible, dramatically gripping and altogether handsomely-done theater piece." He describes the staging, costumes, and the ensemble style of the piece, and suggests that the show "needs a fuller conclusion."

"*Spell No. 7* Takes Us on Magical Trip." Review of *Spell No. 7. Times* (Washington, D.C.), May 9, 1991. This unsigned descriptive review of the "choreopoem" that begins the 1979 trilogy of such works places the piece in the context of a continuing struggle of black women for a dignified place in society: "After all the tribulations and outpourings of feeling, the lingering message is one of racial pride."

Anne Mills King
(Updated by *Thomas J. Taylor*)

GEORGE BERNARD SHAW

Born: Dublin, Ireland; July 26, 1856
Died: Ayot St. Lawrence, England; November 2, 1950

Principal drama

Widowers' Houses, wr. 1885-1892, pr. 1892, pb. 1893; *Mrs. Warren's Profession*, wr. 1893, pb. 1898, pr. 1902; *The Philanderer*, wr. 1893, pb. 1898, pr. 1905; *Arms and the Man*, pr. 1894, pb. 1898; *Candida: A Mystery*, pr. 1897, pb. 1898; *The Devil's Disciple*, pr. 1897, pb. 1901; *The Man of Destiny*, pr. 1897, pb. 1898; *You Never Can Tell*, pb. 1898, pr. 1899; *Captain Brassbound's Conversion*, pr. 1900, pb. 1901; *Caesar and Cleopatra*, pb. 1901, pr. 1906; *The Admirable Bashville*, pr. 1903, pb. 1909 (based on Shaw's novel *Cashel Byron's Profession*); *Man and Superman*, pb. 1903, pr. 1905; *How He Lied to Her Husband*, pr. 1904, pb. 1907; *John Bull's Other Island*, pr. 1904, pb. 1907; *Major Barbara*, pr. 1905, pb. 1907; *Passion, Poison, and Petrifaction*, pr., pb. 1905; *The Doctor's Dilemma*, pr. 1906, pb. 1911; *The Interlude at the Playhouse*, pr., pb. 1907 (playlet); *Getting Married*, pr. 1908, pb. 1911; *Press Cuttings*, pr., pb. 1909; *The Shewing Up of Blanco Posnet*, pr. 1909, pb. 1911; *The Fascinating Foundling*, wr. 1909, pb. 1926, pr. 1928; *The Glimpse of Reality*, wr. 1909, pb. 1926, pr. 1927; *The Dark Lady of the Sonnets*, pr. 1910, pb. 1914; *Misalliance*, pr. 1910, pb. 1914; *Fanny's First Play*, pr. 1911, pb. 1914; *Androcles and the Lion*, pr. 1912 (in German), pr. 1913 (in English), pb. 1916; *Overruled*, pr. 1912, pb. 1916; *Pygmalion*, pb. 1912, pr. 1914 (in English), pr. 1913 (in German); *Beauty's Duty*, wr. 1913, pb. 1932 (playlet); *Great Catherine*, pr. 1913, pb. 1919; *Heartbreak House*, wr. 1913-1919, pb. 1919, pr. 1920; *The Music Cure*, pr. 1914, pb. 1926; *The Inca of Perusalem*, pr. 1916, pb. 1919; *O'Flaherty, V.C.*, pr. 1917, pb. 1919; *Augustus Does His Bit*, pr. 1917, pb. 1919; *Annajanska, the Bolshevik Empress*, pr. 1918, pb. 1919; *Back to Methuselah*, pb. 1921, pr. 1922; *Jitta's Atonement*, pr. 1923, pb. 1926; *Saint Joan*, pr. 1923, pb. 1924; *The Apple Cart*, pr. 1929, pb. 1930; *Too True to Be Good*, pr. 1932, pb. 1934; *How These Doctors Love One Another!*, pb. 1932 (playlet); *On the Rocks*, pr. 1933, pb. 1934; *Village Wooing*, pr., pb. 1934; *The Six Men of Calais*, pr. 1934, pb. 1936; *The Simpleton of the Unexpected Isles*, pr., pb. 1935; *Arthur and Acetone*, pb. 1936; *The Millionairess*, pr., pb. 1936; *Cymbeline Refinished*, pr. 1937, pb. 1938 (adaptation of William Shakespeare's *Cymbeline*, act 5); *Geneva*, pr. 1938, pb. 1939; *In Good King Charles's Golden Days*, pr., pb. 1939; "The British Party System," wr. 1944 (playlet); *Buoyant Billions*, pb. 1947, pr. 1948 (in German), pr. 1949 (in English); *Shakes Versus Shaw*, pr. 1949, pb. 1950; *Far-Fetched Fables*, pr., pb. 1950; *The Bodley Head Bernard Shaw: Collected Plays with Their Prefaces*, pb. 1970-1974 (7 volumes).

Other literary forms

Although George Bernard Shaw is generally thought of as a dramatist, he wrote a considerable amount of nondramatic prose. He completed, for example, several novels before turning to the stage and, even though none of them is likely to be remembered for its own sake, all show Shaw's gift for witty dialogue. His *The Intelligent Woman's Guide to Socialism and Capitalism* (1928), written for his sister-in-law, is one of the clearest expositions of socialism or Communism ever written. *The Quintessence of Ibsenism* (1891), *The Perfect Wagnerite* (1898), and *The Sanity of Art* (1908) are representative of his criticism in drama, music, and art, respectively. The prefaces to his plays—some of which are longer than the plays they preface and which often explain little about the plays themselves—are brilliantly written criticisms of everything from the four Gospels to the contemporary prison system.

Other notable Shaw works include *Fabian Essays in Socialism* (1889), *The Common Sense of Municipal Trading* (1904), *Dramatic Opinions and Essays* (1907), *The Adventures of the Black Girl in Her Search for God* (1932), and several collections of letters: *Letters to Miss Alma Murray* (1927), *Ellen Terry and Shaw* (1931), *Correspondence Between George Bernard Shaw and Mrs. Patrick Campbell* (1952), *Collected Letters* (1965-   , 3 volumes; Dan H. Laurence, editor), and *The Nondramatic Literary Criticism of Bernard Shaw* (1972; Stanley Weintraub, editor).

Achievements

Shaw came to an English theater settled into the well-made play, a theater that had not known a first-rate dramatist for more than a century. The pap upon which its audiences had been fed, not very different from television fare today, provided a soothing escape from the realities of the working world. Instead of fitting himself to this unreal mold, Shaw offered reality in all its forms: social, political, economic, religious. He was a didact, a preacher who readily acknowledged that the stage was his pulpit. In startling contrast to his contemporary Oscar Wilde and Wilde's fellow aesthetes, Shaw asserted that he would not commit a single sentence to paper for art's sake alone; yet he beat the aesthetes at their own artistic game. Though he preached socialism, creative evolution, the abolition of prisons, real equality for women, and railed against the insincerity of motives for war, he did so as a jester in some of the finest comedy ever written. He had no desire to be a martyr and insisted that, though his contemporaries might merely laugh at his plays, "a joke is an earnest in the womb of time." The next generation would get his point, even if the current generation were only entertained.

Many of the next generations have gotten his point, and Shaw's argument—that he who writes for all time will discover that he writes for no time—seems to have been borne out. Only by saying something to the age can one say something to posterity. Today, evolution and creationism and Shaw's ideas on creative evolution and the Life Force remain timely issues. In Shaw's own day, as Dan Laurence points out, Henri Bergson changed the dramatist's Life Force into the élan vital four years after Shaw wrote of it in *Man and Superman*, and Pierre Teilhard de Chardin's evolutionary ideas, so appealing to moderns, about the movement of the "noosphere" toward an omega man, show the timeliness of Shaw's evolutionary theory that humankind is in the process of creating a God. Shaw's condemnation of the prison system as a vindictive, not a rehabilitative force, matches the widespread concern with the ineffectiveness of that system today. His struggle for the genuine equality of women with men before the law also gives his work a surprisingly contemporary thrust.

Shaw brought serious themes back to the trivialized English stage, creating a body of drama that left him second to none among twentieth century dramatists.

Biography

George Bernard Shaw was born in Dublin, Ireland, at No. 3 Upper Synge Street on July 26, 1856. The house still stands, though the address became 33 Synge Street, and the residence is marked by the surprisingly understated plaque, "Bernard Shaw, author of many plays, was born in this house." Shaw's father was a cheerful drunk, and the son's loss of faith in the father might have affected his faith in general. In any event, though he was baptized into the Church of Ireland, he became a lifelong scoffer at organized religion while always remaining a profoundly religious thinker.

Shaw's mother and sister were fine singers and eventually left Shaw's father to move in with the eccentric music teacher, George Vandeleur Lee. From Lee, Shaw himself learned the voice control that would later stand him in good stead as a public debater. He also learned a great deal from respected uncles: From one, a curate at St. Bride's in Dublin, he learned Latin; another, a ship's surgeon, taught him that the Bible was the greatest pack of lies ever invented.

Shaw left secondary school because of boredom. The Latin he had learned early put him too far ahead of his classmates to make the instruction profitable, and by the time the others caught up, his interest had been lost and poor study habits had been formed. He worked for a firm of land agents before finally leaving Ireland when he was nineteen years old, joining his mother and Vandeleur Lee in London.

For a time after arriving in London, Shaw wrote music criticism which Lee had been commissioned to write but which he turned over to Shaw. Shaw was later to write music criticism (under the pen name "Corno di Bassetto") that qualified him, in the judgment of W. H. Auden and other observers, as the finest music critic ever. By the time he was twenty-three years old, Shaw was convinced that he could not return to office work, and he began a career as a novelist. He wrote five novels, none of which was immediately published, although later, all but the first novel would find publishers.

Around 1884, Shaw made the acquaintance of William Archer at the British Museum. The meeting launched Shaw on his career as a critic, first as an art critic, then as a music critic (as mentioned above), and finally as a drama critic for more than three years for the *Saturday Review*.

While Shaw was a struggling novelist and critic, he became a vegetarian and a Socialist; both of these causes were to color his writing for the rest of his life. The conversion to vegetarianism came when he was twenty-five years old and under the influence of Percy Bysshe Shelley's Idealism. His conversion to socialism came somewhat later, probably through the influence of a lecture by Henry George and subsequent reading of Karl Marx. In 1884, Shaw helped Beatrice and Sidney Webb found the Fabian Society, a Socialist organization later joined by H. G. Wells. When Shaw's nervousness made him stumble badly during a lecture on John Stuart Mill for the society, he determined to make a public speaker of himself by promptly planting his soapbox for socialism in Hyde Park. Considering the extraordinary public speaker and debater Shaw became, it is hard to believe that he began as a young man who was so shy he could not visit a friend without pacing up and down the street trying to gain courage to ring the door bell.

In 1892, the Independent Theatre was about to open and needed plays. Shaw quickly finished *Widowers' Houses*, which he had begun seven years earlier with William Archer. The noted drama critic, however, decided Shaw was no playwright and was never to change his mind. Although Shaw had accepted Archer's opinion at first, he gave the play a second try and began a career that was to continue until 1950.

When Shaw was awarded the Nobel Prize in Literature in 1925, he refused it at first, but, upon learning he could donate the money to a fund for popularizing Scandinavian literature, he accepted the award and gave the money away. This award marked the high point of his career, though he was still to write seventeen plays. In September, 1950, Shaw, who seemed on the way to becoming the ageless superman he proclaimed, fell from an apple tree he was pruning. He died in November of that year, of complications stemming from that injury. His ashes were mingled with his wife's and spread on his garden.

Analysis

A religious thinker, George Bernard Shaw saw the stage as his pulpit. His major interest was to advance the Life Force, a kind of immanent Holy

Spirit that would help to improve and eventually perfect the world. Shaw believed that to help in this conscious purpose, human beings must live longer in order to use their intellectual maturity. They must be healthier, without the debilitating force of poverty, and—most important—they must be interested in purpose, not simply pleasure. As the giraffe could develop its long neck over aeons because of a need to eat from the tops of trees, so can human beings, with a sense of purpose, work toward the creation of healthier, longer-lived, more intelligent individuals.

According to Shaw, evolution is not merely haphazard; it is tied to will. Human beings can know what they want and will what they know. Certainly, individuals cannot simply will that they live longer and expect to do so. Such desire might help, but it is the race, not the individual, that will eventually profit from such a common purpose. Ultimately, Shaw believed, this drive toward a more intelligent and spiritual species would result after aeons in human beings' shucking off matter, which had been taken on by spirit in the world's beginning so that evolution could work toward intelligence. When that intelligence achieves its full potential, matter will no longer be necessary. Humankind is working toward the creation of an infinite God.

Shaw's plays are not restricted to such metaphysics. They treat political, social, and economic concerns: the false notion that people help criminals by putting them in jail or help themselves by atonement (*Major Barbara, Captain Brassbound's Conversion, The Simpleton of the Unexpected Isles*), the need for tolerance (*On the Rocks, Androcles and the Lion*), the superstitious worship of medicine and science (*The Philanderer, The Doctor's Dilemma*), the superiority of socialism to capitalism (*Widowers' Houses, The Apple Cart, The Inca of Perusalem*), the evils of patriotism (*O'Flaherty, V.C., Arms and the Man*), the need for a supranational state (*Geneva*), the necessity for recognizing women's equality with men (*In Good King Charles's Golden Days, Press Cuttings*), and so on. Nevertheless, all of Shaw's efforts to question social and political mores were subsumed by his religious purpose. All were meant to help free the human spirit in its striving toward the creation of a better and more intelligent person, the creation of a superman, the creation, finally, of a God.

In 1894, two years after completing his first play, Shaw wrote *Arms and the Man*. Although lighter and less complex than later plays, it is typical of the later plays in that Shaw uses comedy as a corrective—a corrective, as Louis Crompton effectively puts it, that is intended to shame the audience *out* of conformity, in contrast to Molière's, which is intended to shame the audience *into* conformity.

The year is 1885. Bulgaria and Serbia are at war, the Serbs have just been routed, and the play opens with one of the Serbs' officers, Captain Bluntschli, climbing through the window of a Bulgarian house. The house belongs to Major Petkoff, and Raina Petkoff lies dreaming of her lover, a dashing Byronic hero, Sergius Saranoff, who has led the cavalry charge that routed the Serbs. Bluntschli comes into her room, gun in hand, but convinces her not to give him away, more because a fight will ensue while she is not properly dressed than for any fear she has of being shot.

Bluntschli turns out to be Saranoff's opposite. He is a practical Swiss who joined the Serbs merely because they were the first to enlist his services, not because he believed either side to be in the right. When the Bulgarian soldiers enter the house and demand to search Raina's room, she hides Bluntschli on impulse. After the soldiers' departure, he describes for Raina the recent battle in which some quixotic fool led a cavalry charge of frightened men against a battery of machine guns. All were trying to rein in their horses lest they get there first and be killed. The Serbs, however, happened not to have the right ammunition, and what should have been a slaughter of the Bulgarians turned out to be a rout of the Serbs. Yet for his irresponsible foolishness, this "Don Quixote" is sure to be rewarded by the Bulgarians. When Raina shows Bluntschli the picture of her lover, and Saranoff turns out to be "Quixote," Bluntschli is duly embarrassed, tries to cover by suggesting that Saranoff might have known in advance of the Serbs' ammunition problem, but only makes it worse by suggesting to this romantic girl that her lover would have been such a crass pretender and coward as to attack under such conditions.

This is Shaw's first ridicule of chivalric notions of war. The viewpoint is corroborated in the next act by Saranoff when he returns disillusioned because he has not been promoted. He did not follow the scientific rules of war and was thus undeserving. Saranoff has discovered that soldiering is the cowardly art of attacking mercilessly when one is strong and keeping out of harm's way when weak.

In this second act, which takes place at the war's end only four months later, the audience is treated to some satire of Victorian "higher love," which Saranoff carries on with Raina before more realistically flirting with her maid, Louka. Later, in a momentary slip from his chivalric treatment of Raina, Saranoff jokes about a practical Swiss who helped them with arrangements for prisoner exchange and who bragged about having been saved by infatuating a Bulgarian woman and her mother after visiting the young woman in her bedroom. Recognizing herself, Raina chides Saranoff for telling such a crass story in front of her, and he immediately apologizes and reverts to his gallant pose.

Finally in act 3, after Bluntschli has returned for an overcoat and Saranoff discovers that Raina and her mother were the women who saved the Swiss, Saranoff challenges Bluntschli to a duel. Bluntschli, however, will not return the romantic pose and calls Saranoff a blockhead for not realizing that Raina had no other choice at gunpoint. When Saranoff realizes that there is no romance in fighting this prosaic shopkeeper, he backs off. Bluntschli wins Raina's hand, Saranoff wins Louka's, and all ends happily. Yet at the very point at which the audience might expect the play to use its romantic, well-made plot to criticize romanticism, Shaw again changes direction by showing his antihero Bluntschli to be a romantic. To everyone's consternation, Saranoff's in particular, Bluntschli points out that most of his problems have been the result of an incurably romantic disposition: He ran away from home twice as a boy, joined the army rather than his father's business, climbed the balcony of the Petkoff house instead of sensibly diving into the nearest cellar, and came back to this young girl, Raina, to get his coat when any man his age would have sent for it. Thus, Shaw uses *Arms and the Man* not only to attack romanticism about war or love but also to assert the importance of knowing and being true to oneself, to one's life force. It matters little whether Bluntschli is a romantic. He knows and is true to himself. He does not pose and does not deceive himself, as do Saranoff and Raina.

Only one who is true to himself and does not deny himself can attune himself to the Life Force and help advance the evolutionary process. Although Saranoff changes his career when he renounces soldiering, he does so because he was not justly rewarded for his dashing cavalry charge. He does not abandon his habitual self-deception. Even his marriage to the servant girl, Louka, has something of the romantic pose about it; it is rebellious. Raina's marriage to Bluntschli has more potential; at least she has come to see her own posing.

Although the play seems light when set beside the later, more complex triumphs, Shaw's "religious" purpose can be seen here at the beginning of his career. It will be better argued in *Man and Superman* and more fully argued in *Back to Methuselah*, but the failure of the latter, more Utopian work shows that Shaw's religious ideas most engaged his audience when they were rooted in the social, political, or economic criticism of his times, as they were in *Arms and the Man*.

A year after *Arms and the Man*, Shaw wrote *Candida*, his version of Henrik Ibsen's 1879 play, *A Doll's House*. *Candida* showed that, while Shaw was as much a proponent of equality as was his early mentor, he saw women's usual familial role from an opposite perspective. As Ibsen saw it, women suffer in marriage from being treated like children; a wife is denied the larger responsibilities which are the province of her husband. As a consequence, the wife's personal maturity is arrested. She becomes, in a word, a doll. Shaw did not think this the usual marital paradigm; his view of marriage included a husband who does tend to see himself as the dominant force in the family, but the wife is seldom the petted child that Ibsen's Nora is. Much more frequently, she is like Candida, the real strength of the family, who, like her husband's mother before her, allows her husband to live in a "castle of comfort and indulgence" over which she stands sentinel. She makes him master, though he does not know it. Men, in other words, are more often the petted, indulged children, and women more often the sustaining force in the family.

Candida is set entirely in St. Dominic's Parsonage, and the action is ostensibly a very unoriginal love triangle involving the parson, James Morell, his wife, Candida, and a young poet, Eugene Marchbanks. The originality comes from the unique twist given this stock situation. Morell is a liberal, aggressive preacher, worshiped by women and by his curate. Marchbanks is a shy, effeminate eighteen-year-old, in manner somewhat reminiscent of a young Percy Bysshe Shelley, and he is possessed too of Shelley's inner strength, though this is not immediately apparent. The young poet declares to Morell his love for Candida, Morell's beautiful thirty-three-year-old wife. The self-assured Morell indulges the young man and assures him that the whole world loves Candida; his is another version of puppy love that he will outgrow. The ethereal Marchbanks cannot believe that Morell thinks Candida capable of inspiring such trivial love in him. He is able, as no one else is, to see that Morell's brilliant sermons and his equally brilliant conversation are nothing but the gift of gab; Morell is an inflated windbag. Marchbanks forces Morell to see himself in this way, and Morell shows that the poet has hit home when he almost throttles him.

Morell broaches the subject of Marchbanks' love to Candida, at the young man's insistence, and Candida assures her husband that she already knows Eugene is in love with her. She is surprised, however, to find Morell upset by it. Nevertheless, the two foolish men force a crisis by making Candida choose between them. When she plays their game and asks what each has to offer, Morell offers his strength for her defense, his honesty for her surety, his industry for her livelihood, and his authority and position for her dignity. Eugene offers his weakness and desolation.

Candida, bemused that neither offers love and that each wishes to own her, acknowledges that the poet has made a good offer. She informs them that she will give herself, because of his need, to the weaker of the two. Morell is desolate, but Eugene is, too, since he realizes that Candida means Morell. Eugene leaves with the now famous "secret in his heart." The secret the poet knows is that he can live without happiness, that there is another love than that of woman—the love of purpose.

The twist Shaw gives the standard triangle, then, is not merely that the effeminate young poet is stronger than the commanding figure of Morell, but also that Candida is stronger than both. Morell is clearly the doll in this house. Even so, to identify Shaw with Marchbanks, as his fine biographer Archibald Henderson does, makes little sense. Marchbanks is an aesthete like Wilde or the young William Butler Yeats, and the poetic sentiments he expresses to Candida sound very like Shelley's *Epipsychidion*.

Shaw, who did not share Shelley's rapture about romantic love and who liked aestheticism so little that he swore he would not face the toil of writing a single sentence for art's sake alone, clearly cannot be confused with Marchbanks. He has more in common with Morell, who is socialistic and industrious. It is Morell who voices Shaw's sentiments when he tells Marchbanks that people have no more right to consume happiness without producing it than they have to consume wealth without producing it. The character in this play who comes closest to Shaw, however, is Candida herself. Much stronger than Ibsen's Nora, she is the only character who does not deceive herself. Morell does not realize that he needs to be coddled in order to play his role as a dynamic, liberal clergyman. Only at the play's end and with Candida's help, does Marchbanks discover the truth she has known all along.

Candida is subtitled *A Mystery*, and, though Shaw is treating a dramatic convention with humor, there is perhaps a more serious sense in which he uses the subtitle: There is some mystery involved in the ties that bind people together in marriage. In the climactic scene, in which Candida is made to choose between the two men, a traditional dramatist might have demonstrated the lover to be a cad and have thrown him out. A more romantic dramatist would have shown the husband to be a tyrant and had the wife and lover elope. Shaw chooses neither solution. He has the wife remain with the husband, but not because the lover is a cad or because she owes it to her husband contractually or for any of the standard reasons Morell offers, but because he needs her and she loves him. In this mystery about what binds partners in marriage, Shaw seems to suggest that it is not the contract, still less any ideal of purity, but simply mutual love and need.

Finally, what connects *Candida* with *Arms and the Man*, as well as with the later plays, is the demand that persons be true to themselves. Morell taught Candida to think for herself, she tells him, but it upsets him when that intellectual independence leads to conclusions different from his own. Candida will not submit to Christian moralism any more than she will to poetic romanticism. If there is any salvation for Marchbanks, it is that he has learned from Candida the secret that lies hidden in his heart: He is not dependent upon happiness or upon the love of a woman. In becoming aware of this, he has the potential to be a true artist, one attuned to purpose and not to self-indulgence. Thus, the play leads to the more lengthy dramatization of the struggle between the philosopher-artist and the woman-mother that is evident in *Man and Superman*.

Man and Superman promotes Shaw's philosophy of the Life Force more explicitly than do any of his previous plays. Indeed, much of the play is given to discussion, particularly during the long dream sequence in act 3; Shaw never thought that a play's action need be physical. The dynamics of argument, of intellectual and verbal exchange, were for Shaw much more exciting than conventional action.

The drama originated in a suggestion by Arthur Bingham Walkley that Shaw write a Don Juan play. After all, did not Shaw suffer as a playwright from an excess of cerebration and a lack of physicality? Surely, Walkley reasoned, the subject of the amours of Don Juan would force him off his soapbox and into the boudoir. In response to this challenge, Shaw wrote a much more cerebral play than he had ever written before. In his lengthy "Epistle Dedicatory" to Walkley, Shaw explains why. The essence of the Don Juan legend is not, like Casanova's, that its hero is an "oversexed tomcat." Rather, its essence lies in Juan's following his own instincts rather than law or convention.

The play is as diffuse and difficult to stage as *Candida* is concise and delightful to produce. Most of the difficulty has to do with the lengthy Don Juan in Hell dream sequence during act 3, which causes the play to run more than four hours. More often than not, the sequence has been separated from the play. Not until 1964, in fact, when the Association of Producing Artists staged the play at New York City's Phoenix Theatre was the entire play produced in the United States.

As the delightful first act opens, Ann Whitefield has lost her father, and everyone is waiting to learn from the will who her guardian will be. Roebuck Ramsden, close friend of her father and self-styled liberal, is the leading candidate and is at the moment lecturing Ann's young suitor, Octavius, on his friend, Jack Tanner, who is not fit to be seen with Octavius, much less with Ann. Tanner has scandalized this Victorian liberal by his newly published "The Revolutionist's Handbook," whose entire text Shaw appends to the play. "The Revolutionist's Handbook" is a didact's device for getting across some of the ideas that would have been unpalatable in the play, as when Tanner argues (here without opposition) that the Life Force would be served better if people were given more freedom in mating. That is to say, people who might not be compatible as marriage partners might nevertheless produce the finest offspring.

When Tanner appears, the audience is delighted by his wit. He good-humoredly but repeatedly scandalizes Ramsden, particularly when he announces that he and Ramsden have been named joint guardians of Ann. Tanner is not eager to undertake his role; he knows how manipulative Ann can be, but he does not yet recognize what even his chauffeur could have told him: Ann has designs upon him and not upon his friend, Octavius. Ann is in the grip of the Life Force, which drives all women in their capacity as mothers to want to reproduce, and she implicitly knows that Tanner would be the proper father for her offspring, not the romantic but spiritually flabby young Octavius. Tanner, however, is Shaw's philosopher-artist and, as such, Tanner knows that he must flee the stifling bliss of marriage and domesticity to pursue his own purpose—something that Marchbanks learned at the end of *Candida*.

When Tanner learns of Ann's designs, he flees to Spain. Here, he and his chauffeur are captured by a group of brigands led by an Englishman named Mendoza. While captive, Tanner dreams the lengthy dream that constitutes the Don Juan in Hell scene. The scene is a brilliant debate involving Don Juan (looking like John Tanner), the Devil (looking like Mendoza), Doña Ana (looking remarkably like Ann Whitefield), and Ana's father, Don Gonzalo (looking like Roebuck Ramsden). The debate centers on the relative merits of Heaven and Hell. Doña Ana, "a good Catholic," is astonished to find herself a newcomer to Hell and has to have it explained to her that some of the best company are here. One can go to Heaven if he or she wishes, but one must remember that the gulf between the two is really a matter of natural inclination or temperament. Hell is a place for those in whom enjoyment predominates over purpose, desires over reason, the heart over the head, the aesthetic over the ideological, and romance over realism. Don Juan is about to depart for Heaven because he is sick of the Devil's cant about the aesthetic values, the enjoyment of music, the pleasures of the heart. An eternity of enjoyment is an intolerable bore. He wishes not to enjoy life but to help it in its struggle upward. The reason Juan went to Hell to begin with was that he thought he was a pleasure-seeker, but he has discovered, as Shaw indicates in the dedicatory epistle, that his amours were more a form of rebellion than of pleasure-seeking. Realizing that he is temperamentally a philosophical man, who seeks to learn in contemplation the inner will of the world, to discover in invention the means of achieving that will, and to follow in action those means, he prefers Heaven.

The dream sequence is also concerned with woman's maternal role in advancing the Life Force. If it seems, at first glance, that the ardent feminist who authored *Candida* has here turned his coat and relegated women to a merely sexual role, it must be remembered that for the moment Shaw is speaking only of one side of woman. When Ana corrects Don Juan's view of woman's mind, he points out to her that he speaks not of woman's whole mind but only of her view of man as a separate sex. Only sexually is woman's nature a contrivance for perpetuating its highest achievement. She too can be the philosopher-artist attuned to the work of advancing the Life Force. Thus, two ways of achieving the inner will of the world are open to her.

In the fourth and final act, having awakened from his dreams, Tanner shows that he is not yet as forceful as his ancestor, Don Juan, when he gives in to Ann's superior force and agrees to marry her. Ironically, the romantic Octavius is the one who resigns himself to bachelorhood.

The play, then, is a philosophical comedy whose theme is that the Life Force is dependent upon man and woman if it is to move creation upward.

A man or woman possessed of a sense of purpose must attune himself or herself to the Life Force, since the only true joy lies in being used for its purposes, in being willing to burn oneself out and heap oneself on the scrap pile at the end without any promise of a personal reward. Although a number of critics see Tanner as the epitome of Shavian man, Tanner does capitulate to Ann. He lacks the fiber of Don Juan, who realizes the boredom of a life of pleasure. Indeed, Marchbanks of *Candida* is more truly Shavian than Tanner.

Notwithstanding Shaw's overt didacticism in this play, he is true to his belief that, like the Ancient Mariner, he must tell his tale entertainingly if he is to hold the attention of the wedding guest. Consequently, he claims full responsibility for the opinions of Don Juan but claims equal responsibility for those of the other characters. For the dramatic moment, each character's viewpoint is also Shaw's. Those who believe there is an absolutely right point of view, he says in the "Epistle Dedicatory," usually believe it is their own and cannot, in consequence, be true dramatists.

In *Major Barbara*, published not long after *Man and Superman*, Shaw's dramatic means of advancing his theory of the Life Force was to assert that poverty was the world's greatest evil. What critics, even astute ones such as G. K. Chesterton, thought materialistic in Shaw, the author would insist was spiritual. Only with money could one save one's soul.

Major Barbara opens in the home of Lady Britomart Undershaft, whose estranged millionaire husband has been invited to the house for the first time since the children, now adults, were toddlers. Her purpose in inviting this scandalous old atheist to her house is to get more money for her daughters, Barbara and Sarah, who are about to marry. Moreover, she would like Andrew Undershaft to break the ridiculous custom of having the Undershaft munitions business go to an orphan and instead give it to his own son, Stephen. When Undershaft meets his family, he is favorably impressed by Barbara, who is a major in the Salvation Army, and by Adolphus Cusins, her suitor, who is a professor of Greek. He recognizes that Stephen is hopelessly inept and that Charles Lomax, Sarah's young man, is less pompous than Stephen but no less foolish. Barbara invites her father to West Ham so that he might see the constructive work of the Salvation Army, and he agrees, provided that she come to see his munitions plant at Perivale St. Andrews. Thus, the play's structure is neatly determined, with a second act at West Ham and a third at Perivale St. Andrews.

In act 2, Barbara shows her father the Salvation Army's good work, only to learn from her father and the Army's Commissioner, Mrs. Baines, the painful fact that the Army—like all religious organizations—depends upon contributions from whiskey distillers and munitions owners such as her father. When Barbara is told that the Army could not subsist without this "tainted" money, she realizes that she is not changing the essential condition of the poor but simply keeping them alive with a bowl of soup; she is helping the capitalists justify themselves with conscience money. She thus serves capital rather than God.

When in act 3 the family visits the munitions factory, Undershaft surprisingly reveals the existence of a model Socialist community at Perivale St. Andrews. Though Undershaft lives off the need of people to conduct war, he accepts that need and uses it to destroy society's greatest evil, poverty. In his community, all men work, earn a decent wage, and can thus turn to matters of the soul, such as religion, without being bribed to do so. Since Barbara has come to realize that religious organizations exist by selling themselves to the rich, she decides to get Peter Shirley a job rather than feed him and ask him to pray in thanksgiving at West Ham. She herself joins her father's model village, especially since Cusins is conveniently discovered to be an orphan and the ideal person to inherit the munitions factory.

Shaw's lengthy preface to the play sets out a good deal of his ethical philosophy: Poverty is the worst evil against which man struggles; religious people should work for the betterment of the one world they have and not turn from it for a vision of private bliss in the hereafter; the world will never be bettered by people who believe that they can atone for their sins and who do not understand that their misdeeds are irrevocable; while society should divide wealth equally, no adult should receive his allowance unless he or she produces by personal exertion more than he or she consumes; society should not punish those guilty of crime, especially by putting them in prisons that render them worse, but neither should it hesitate to put to death anyone whose misconduct is incorrigible, just as people would not hesitate to destroy a mad dog.

Though these ideas are familiar to Shavians, and though most of them are fleshed out in the play itself, *Major Barbara* may first take a reader by surprise. Can the pacifist and Socialist Shaw be making a hero of a capitalist who makes his living on the profits of warfare? It is not enough to answer that the capitalist uses his capital to create an ideal Socialist community; for this, Shaw could have chosen a banker. On the contrary, he deliberately chooses a munitions manufacturer because the irony helps make his point. However horrid warfare is, it is not so horrid as poverty. Undershaft tells Barbara and Cusins in the final act that poverty is the worst of crimes, for it blights whole cities, spreads pestilence, and strikes dead any souls within its compass. Barbara cannot save souls in West Ham by words and dreams, but if she gives a West Ham ruffian thirty-eight shillings a week, with a sound house in a handsome street and a permanent job, she will save his soul.

When Barbara turns from the Salvation Army to Undershaft's community at Perivale St. Andrews, she is not giving up religion. She is turning, Shaw would have it, from a phony religion dependent upon a bribe to the poor and upon the maintenance of inequitable present conditions, to a genuine religion which will bring significant social change. Her conversion is completely consistent with her character. When her father asks her to tell Cusins what power is, she answers that before joining the Salvation Army, she was in her own power and, as a consequence, did not know what to do with herself. Once she joined the Army, she thought herself in the power of God and did not have enough time for all that needed to be done. Undershaft helps her to transfer this commitment to a more realistic cause, which will genuinely improve the lot of the poor, but a cause which is still essentially spiritual.

Since Undershaft sees his work in the same light as Barbara sees hers, he can insist that he is not a secularist but a confirmed mystic. Perivale St. Andrews is driven by a will of which he is a part. Thus, once again, Shaw's hero is chosen because he is attuned to the Life Force. It matters little that he is a munitions maker. In *Saint Joan*, the heroine is a saint, yet she is chosen not as a representative of Christian orthodoxy but because she was mystic enough to see that she served a will greater than her own.

In *Major Barbara*, Shaw also makes use of a host of lesser characters to dramatize his political, moral, and ethical theories. When Stephen Undershaft is asked by his father what he is able to do in life, so that Undershaft can give him a fair start, he makes it evident that he is capable of nothing, except—he asserts defensively—of knowing the difference between good and evil, something he implies his father does not know. With this, Undershaft has great fun. Stephen knows nothing of law, of business, of art, or of philosophy, yet he claims to know the secret that has baffled philosophers for ages. Since Stephen knows nothing but claims to know everything, Undershaft declares him fit for politics. To this remark, Stephen takes exception; he will not hear his father insult his country's government. Undershaft once again, however, reflects Shaw's conviction that big business rules government when he sputters, "The government of your country! I am the government of your country."

Peter Shirley, rather than Barbara, provides the real contrast with Undershaft. Barbara shares her father's "heavenly" temper, his sense of purpose. The Army shares with him the recognition that it needs money. Peter Shirley, the unemployed visitor at West Ham, plays Lazarus to Undershaft's Dives, as Shaw puts it. Because the majority of the world believes that an "honest" poor man such as Shirley is morally superior to a "wicked" rich one such as Undershaft, the misery of the world continues. It is significant that when Undershaft gives Shirley a job, the man is unhappy.

Bill Walker, who beats up an old woman visiting the West Ham shelter and then a young woman member of the Army itself, tries to atone by having himself beaten up in turn by a professional boxer, Todger Fermile. Such a grotesque instance of atonement is no more grotesque than any other attempt at atonement, Shaw believes, and both Barbara and Cusins agree with Undershaft that one cannot atone for evil; one does good only by changing evil ways. It can be argued, as in the case of many other Shavian criticisms of Christianity, that Shaw did not understand the Christian doctrine. Perhaps, however, he understood *de facto* Christianity all too well.

Adolphus Cusins also plays a significant role in the drama, certainly the most significant after those of Undershaft and Barbara, and he eventually takes over the munitions factory. A man of greater intelligence and more humane sympathies than Undershaft, he may be the hope for the Life Force taking a significant step forward. Undershaft repeatedly refers to this professor of Greek as "Dionysius," which suggests in Cusins a capacity to stand outside himself to achieve union with the Life Force. Clearly, Undershaft invites him to make war on war when he turns over the munitions works to him.

Major Barbara is perhaps freighted with too much paradox to do its job convincingly. Certainly, act 1 is sparkling comedy as Undershaft meets his family without knowing who is who. Moreover, the contrast between Undershaft's "gospel" and Barbara's is convincingly set forth. Act 2 is occasionally excellent comedy, and comedy fused with meaning, as when Barbara deals with the bully Bill Walker, but Walker's part becomes a bit too obtrusive a vehicle for attacking atonement and Undershaft's demonstration of how all religious organizations exist by selling themselves to the rich is somewhat more asserted than dramatized. Perhaps the concluding act is the least successful, since Barbara's and Cusins' conversion is necessarily hurried to preserve the unities, and Shaw has difficulty making his Utopia convincing, a difficulty he later experienced more keenly in *Back to Methuselah*. To do Shaw justice, he acknowledged that, while one can know that the Life Force is driving upward, one cannot know precisely how. Thus, attempts to dramatize future points of progress in creative evolution present insuperable obstacles.

More than in *Major Barbara* and perhaps more than in *Man and Superman*, Shaw found in *Saint Joan* a fit medium to dramatize his major religious ideas. He had intended to write a play about Christ, but he was not permitted to portray divinity on the English stage. Yet no play by Shaw succeeds more unobtrusively in carrying his ideas about the Life Force. As captivating a play as *Major Barbara* is, Undershaft has straw men with whom to do battle, and, though such was not the case in *Man and Superman*, Shaw needed for his purposes the lengthy dream sequence that has made the play so difficult to stage. *Candida* might be a more perfectly structured play, but it does not carry so much of Shaw's mature philosophy.

Among Shaw's major dramas, then, *Saint Joan* is perhaps the finest blend of matter and form.

Saint Joan is divided into six scenes and an epilogue. In the first scene, Joan appeals to Robert de Baudricourt for horse and armor to aid in the siege of Orleans and to see to the coronation of the Dauphin. Although he at first scoffs at this request, made through his servant, when faced with Joan, he is persuaded by the strength of her person, as everyone else is. In scene 2, the courtiers try to dupe her and pretend that Gilles de Rais is the Dauphin. Not taken in, she carries the Dauphin, too, by her force of persuasion and convinces this weakling that he, too, has a divine mission which he must be strong enough to accept. In scene 3, Joan joins Dunois, the leader of the French forces, and under their combined leadership, France enjoys a series of victories. In scene 4, the Earl of Warwick and the Bishop of Beauvais plan Joan's eventual execution. The Englishman wants her dead for obvious military reasons; the Frenchman, because she is a dangerous heretic. In scene 5, she is told to give up fighting, that there is no need for more victories. She is told to let the English have Paris. Her sense of destiny, however, convinces her that the English must be driven from French soil. In scene 6, Joan has been arrested; she is given by the Inquisition what Shaw considers a fairer trial than is available to defendants today; she finally recants what the clergymen consider her heresy, but when told that she must remain forever in prison as punishment for her spiritual offenses, she tears up her recantation and goes to the stake under Warwick's authority. The epilogue gets the play back into the comic frame and allows Joan and the rest of the cast of characters to appear twenty-five years later before Charles, now King, and discuss the Church's recent reversal in favor of Joan. There is even a time-shift of several centuries, to the year 1920, so that Joan's canonization can be mentioned. Yet the epilogue ultimately suggests that, were she to return to France in the twentieth century, Joan would again be put to death by the very people who now praise her.

The greatness of *Saint Joan* lies in its scrupulous dramatization of a universal problem. The problem of how one reconciles the dictates of the individual conscience with the demands of authority is one without easy solutions, whether the individual stands against ecclesiastical, civil, military, or familial authority. The sympathy Shaw extends to Joan in declaring her one of the first "Protestant" saints he extends also to the Inquisitors, who, he asserts, tried Joan more fairly than they themselves were later tried when the judgment on Joan was reversed.

Shaw's fairness is evident in scene 4, for example, when Peter Cauchon makes clear to the Earl of Warwick that, even though both men want Joan captured, they differ in every other respect. Cauchon, Bishop of Beauvais, does not believe that Joan is a witch and will not allow Warwick to get rid of her on this trumped-up charge. Joan is a heretic, much more dangerous than a witch, but he would prefer to save her soul. She is a pious and honest girl who, through pride, is caught up in the Devil's mighty purpose: to wrack the Church with discord and dissension—the same purpose for which the Devil used John Huss and John Wycliffe. If a reformer will not finally effect reform within the pale of Church authority, every crackpot who sees visions will be followed by the naïve populace, and the Church will be wrecked beyond repair.

These arguments are completely familiar to the present age, in which soldiers are told they must obey commanding officers who order the extinction of noncombatants. Can one obey such orders? Yet there surely must be obedience to authority, despite doubts about its wisdom, or there will be anarchy. Humankind has come no closer to finding a solution to the tensions between individual conscience and authority than it had in Joan's day, and it is that insoluble problem that forces audiences to move beyond easy condemnation of the Inquisition and equally easy sanctification of Joan.

Critics have often objected to Shaw's epilogue on the ground that Joan's tragedy is trivialized by it, yet the epilogue is necessary for Shaw's theme: that from the same elements, the same tragedy would come again. The trial at which Joan's judges were judged and she was exonerated was a much more unscrupulous affair than was Joan's trial. Ladvenu, who had been the most sympathetic of those who tried Joan, tells King Charles that the old trial was faultless in every respect except in its unjust verdict, while the new trial is filled with perjury and corruption yet results in a just verdict. Charles, who is concerned only about his having been crowned by a woman who was considered a witch and a heretic, and who is relieved now by having his reign validated, asserts that no matter what the verdict, were Joan brought back to life, her present admirers would burn her within six months.

In his preface, Shaw argues that there was no inconsistency in the Church's reversal on Joan. Although the Catholic Church does not defer to private judgment, it recognizes that the highest wisdom may come to an individual through private revelation and that, on sufficient evidence, the Church will eventually declare such an individual a saint. Thus, many saints have been at odds with the Church before their canonization. In fact, Shaw contends, had Francis of Assisi lived longer, he might have gone to the stake, while Galileo might yet be declared a saint. Thus, the epilogue helps dramatize the complexity inherent in Joan's struggle with the Church.

In none of the plays discussed—perhaps nowhere else in his canon, with the possible exception of *Caesar and Cleopatra*—does Shaw present an example of a character in the grip of the Life Force so convincingly as he does in the character of Joan. Bluntschli is an amusing soldier-adventurer;

Marchbanks, a callow poet; Tanner, a failed revolutionary; and Undershaft, a munitions maker who has built a Socialist community. Joan is both a Christian and a Shavian saint. She is caught up in a sense of purpose to a degree none of Shaw's other characters is. *Saint Joan*, then, is the culmination of Shaw's art. Although other plays might embrace more of his standard literary and philosophical obsessions, none takes his most central obsessions, those relating to the Life Force and creative evolution, and fleshes them out with such dramatic integrity.

Other major works

NOVELS: *Cashel Byron's Profession*, 1886; *An Unsocial Socialist*, 1887; *Love Among the Artists*, 1900; *The Irrational Knot*, 1905; *Immaturity*, 1930.

SHORT FICTION: *The Adventures of the Black Girl in Her Search for God*, 1932.

NONFICTION: *Fabian Essays in Socialism*, 1889 (editor); *The Quintessence of Ibsenism*, 1891; *The Perfect Wagnerite*, 1898; *The Common Sense of Municipal Trading*, 1904; *Dramatic Opinions and Essays*, 1907; *The Sanity of Art*, 1908 (revised from 1895 serial publication); *Letters to Miss Alma Murray*, 1927; *The Intelligent Woman's Guide to Socialism and Capitalism*, 1928; *Ellen Terry and Shaw*, 1931; *Everybody's Political What's What*, 1944; *Sixteen Self Sketches*, 1949; *Correspondence Between George Bernard Shaw and Mrs. Patrick Campbell*, 1952; *The Matter with Ireland*, 1961; *Platform and Pulpit*, 1961 (Dan H. Laurence, editor); *Collected Letters*, 1965- (3 volumes; Dan H. Laurence, editor); *An Autobiography: 1856-1898*, 1969; *An Autobiography: 1898-1950*, 1970; *The Nondramatic Literary Criticism of Bernard Shaw*, 1972 (Stanley Weintraub, editor); *Shaw: Interviews and Recollections*, 1990 (A. M. Gibbs, editor); *Bernard Shaw's Book Reviews*, 1991 (Brian Tyson, editor).

MISCELLANEOUS: *Works*, 1930-1938 (33 volumes); *Short Stories, Scraps, and Shavings*, 1932; *Works*, 1947-1952 (36 volumes).

Bibliography

Adams, Elsie B. *Bernard Shaw and the Aesthetes*. Columbus: Ohio State University Press, 1971. An argumentative but insightful source study of Shaw's theories of art, despite his contemptuous attitude toward "art for art's sake." After examining *Candida* as a Pre-Raphaelite drama influenced by John Ruskin and others, Adams analyzes Shaw's career from his theory of moral art to his practice of prophetic/didactic art. Includes notes, a bibliography, and an index.

Costello, Donald P. *The Serpent's Eye: Shaw and the Cinema*. Notre Dame, Ind.: University of Notre Dame Press, 1965. Analyzes Shaw's interest in films, from his fascination with photography to cinema theories and screenwriting. Reviews the cinematic influence on Shavian drama, as well as Shaw's dramatic influence on films. Focuses on film versions of *Pygmalion*, *Major Barbara*, and *Caesar and Cleopatra.* Contains a foreword by film director Cecil Lewis, illustrations, appendices, a bibliography of sources, and an index.

Holroyd, Michael. *The Search for Love: 1856-1898.* Vol. 1 in *Bernard Shaw.* New York: Random House, 1988. In this superb beginning to his authoritative biography, Holroyd describes Shaw's Irish origins and trials of following his mother to London. His journalistic and musical career is interwoven with various love affairs, culminating in marriage in 1898. Sensitive analyses of political and aesthetic ideas are balanced with insights into early drama. Includes illustrations, a bibliographic note, and an index.

_____. *The Pursuit of Power: 1898-1918.* Vol. 2 in *Bernard Shaw.* New York: Random House, 1989. Describes the complicated interrelationships of Shaw's middle plays (from *Caesar and Cleopatra* to *Heartbreak House*) with ethics, politics, economics, medicine, religion, and war. The popularity of his drama is explained and analyzed, while the sophistication of his personality is narrated through his friendships with such persons as G. K. Chesterton, H. G. Wells, and Mrs. Patrick Campbell. Illustrations, index.

_____. *The Lure of Fantasy: 1918-1950.* Vol. 3 in *Bernard Shaw.* New York: Random House, 1991. The final volume covers Shaw's drama from *Saint Joan*, with late plays such as *Geneva* and *In Good King Charles's Golden Days* receiving balanced attention. Also surveys Shaw's films from his plays, including *Pygmalion* and *Major Barbara.* Shaw's interest in Communism and the Soviet Union receives attention, as does his criticism of American culture. Illustrations, bibliographic note, and index.

Wall, Vincent. *Bernard Shaw: Pygmalion to Many Players.* Ann Arbor: University of Michigan Press, 1973. Studies Shaw's relationships with actresses in his plays and those whom he taught to improve their performances. Provides a brief history of his successes and failures as drama coach and director, from his earliest years in London playhouses to his later years at the Malvern Festival in 1929. Illustrations, notes, bibliography, and index.

Henry J. Donaghy
(Updated by *Richard D. McGhee*)

12573